r

U

York Medieval Texts, second series

General Editors †Elizabeth Salter and Derek Pearsall
University of York

The York Plays

Edited by Richard Beadle

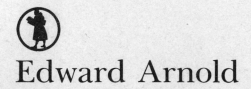

Edward Arnold

© 1982 Richard Beadle

First published 1982 by
Edward Arnold (Publishers) Ltd
41 Bedford Square, London WC1B 3DQ

British Library Cataloguing in Publication Data

The York plays. – (York medieval texts. Second
  series)
  1. Mysteries and miracle-plays, English
  2. English drama – To 1500
  I. Beadle, Richard   II. Series
  822'.0516   PR1260

  ISBN 0-7131-6326-7

Text set in 10/10½ pt. Baskerville Linotron 202
by Huron Valley Graphics, Ann Arbor, USA.
Printed and bound in Great Britain by
R Clay (The Chaucer Press) Ltd, Bungay, Suffolk.

Contents

Contents

Preface

The purpose of this volume is to present a freshly edited text of the York Plays, based on a thorough examination of the unique manuscript preserved in the British Library. It is the first critical edition of the entire cycle to be published since the appearance of Lucy Toulmin Smith's *editio princeps* in 1885. In the intervening period, much new information has come to light concerning the history of the cycle and the social and economic circumstances of the drama in York, some of which may be brought to bear on the task of editing the text. The plays themselves have been the object of ample historical, textual and interpretative investigation, whilst (in a modernized form) they have attracted widespread public interest through enterprising revivals at York and elsewhere – an afterlife their authors and early performers could scarcely have envisaged.

No single edition can hope to serve, in the same degree, all the various interests which the original publication of the cycle engendered. Work on the present one began with the assumption that the time was ripe for an annotated edition resembling earlier volumes in 'York Medieval Texts: Second Series', an assumption partly fostered by the high esteem in which the *editio princeps* was generally held. Close examination of the manuscript, together with consideration of relevant documentary evidence, revealed, however, unexpected and rather numerous problems of a textual and bibliographical nature; and it rapidly became clear that any satisfactory presentation of the text would have to be accompanied by solutions – or attempts at solutions – to these problems. It is to this important, if more limited, objective of an accurate text that the present edition is primarily addressed, and if all the difficulties in establishing it have not been overcome, it is to be hoped that scholarly investigation of the cycle may at least go forward in a fuller knowledge of where many of them lie.

The plan of the edition is as follows. The Introduction is intended to convey necessary information about the manuscript, and the local and historical setting of the cycle. The treatment of the Text is explained in detail in a section entitled 'Editorial Procedures'. Some indication has been given in the Introduction of developments in the study of the language of the plays, their sources, the versification, and the relation of the York and Towneley cycles, but there has been no attempt to venture into the field of criticism and interpretation: significant studies in this area are listed in the Select Bibliography, alongside all the works cited in the Introduction and Notes. The Text is accompanied by Textual Notes at the foot of the page giving running details of the construction of the manuscript, noting the numerous alterations and additions by later hands, and reporting a selection of modern criticism of the text; relevant readings from corresponding plays or passages in the Towneley

1

manuscript are also included. Following the Text are supplementary
Notes on the plays discussing the varied editorial problems met with,
drawing where appropriate on documentary evidence as an aid to
explaining what appears in the manuscript. The Glossary, whilst not an
index verborum, is designed to be rather fuller than those of earlier
volumes in this series, in view of the absence here of explanatory
annotation.

The six songs of play XLV have been transcribed in an Appendix,
with introduction and annotation, by Professor John Stevens.

Readers familiar with Miss Toulmin Smith's edition will quickly
perceive that the work now in their hands differs from hers in major
ways, as well as in the expected minutiae underlying the development
towards a received text. Her plays XVI and XVII have been amalgamated to form a single piece, here no. XVI, in response to the present
editor's interpretation of the bibliographical and documentary evidence.
The place of no. XVII is now rightfully occupied by the episode of the
Purification, whereas Miss Toulmin Smith had followed the *ad hoc*
arrangement of the manuscript in placing it after play XL. As a result,
Miss Toulmin Smith's plays XLII to XLVIII have here been re-numbered XLI to XLVII. From play XXVI onwards the typography of Miss
Toulmin Smith's edition followed the scribal practice in the manuscript,
of setting down the long alliterative line in two halves, the second pair of
staves beneath the first. Here, the single lines have been reconstituted in
an attempt to represent more clearly the stanzaic patterns in the minds
of the dramatists. In a number of plays the lineation, and therefore the
numbering of the lines has been revised. These and other less noticeable
changes in the outward aspect of the cycle are dealt with in more detail
as they arise.

I am indebted to the Trustees of the British Library for permission to
base this edition on the manuscript in their care, and I am grateful to the
staff of the Students' Room for their courtesy and assistance. The work
of others to whom I owe thanks appears in several places in the book:
Appendix 1, dealing the music of play XLV, is by Professor John
Stevens, and the map of medieval York in the Introduction was drawn
by Mrs Meg Twycross. Throughout the Introduction and in the Notes I
have made constant reference to the York civic documents relating to
the drama so admirably edited by Professor Alexandra Johnston and Dr
Margaret Rogerson in the series *Records of Early English Drama*. Their
York appeared whilst this edition was in progress, and Professor
Johnston kindly answered various enquiries beforehand. In examining
the manuscript I was fortunate enough to work in collaboration with Mr
Peter Meredith. He noted a good many points which I had missed or
misinterpreted, and has been a constant source of advice and information about York and its drama in general. I have also benefited from
discussions with Dr Richard Axton, Professor Alan Nelson and Mr
Malcolm Parkes, and for practical help I must thank Mr Seán Magee and
Mr Ian Pattinson. The Master and Fellows of my College kindly
approved a grant towards the cost of having part of the book typed.

I owe a particular debt of gratitude to Professor Derek Pearsall, who as
General Editor of the series in which this book appears was more than

generous with his time, patience and good humour throughout its protracted gestation. The possibility that I should undertake a new edition of the York Plays was first suggested to me by the late Elizabeth Salter. Its completion, and indeed such use and merit as it may have, are due in large part to her inspiration.

St John's College, Cambridge   Richard Beadle

The author and publishers wish to thank the University of Toronto Press and Manchester University Press for permission to quote extracts from *Records of Early English Drama: York* by A.F. Johnston and M. Rogerson.

Abbreviations

AnM	*Annuale Mediævale*
Archiv	*Archiv für das Studium der Neueren Sprachen*
EconHR	*Economic History Review*
EETS	Early English Text Society
	OS Original Series
	ES Extra Series
	SS Supplementary Series
ELN	*English Language Notes*
JEGP	*Journal of English and Germanic Philology*
LSE	*Leeds Studies in English*
MED	*Middle English Dictionary*, ed. H Kurath *et al.*, (Ann Arbor, 1952–) in progress.
MLN	*Modern Language Notes*
MP	*Modern Philology*
MS	*Mediaeval Studies*
NM	*Neuphilologische Mitteilungen*
OED	*Oxford English Dictionary*
PMLA	*Publications of the Modern Language Association of America*
PQ	*Philological Quarterly*
REED	*Records of Early English Drama*
REED: York	*Records of Early English Drama: York*, ed. A.F. Johnston and M. Rogerson (2 vols, Toronto, 1979).
SP	*Studies in Philology*
UTQ	*University of Toronto Quarterly*
VCH	*Victoria County History*
YES	*Yearbook of English Studies*
YWES	*The Year's Work in English Studies*

Quotations from the Vulgate are given in the Douai–Reims translation (NT, 1582). For the abbreviations used in the Textual Notes, see the section 'Editorial Procedures' in the Introduction.

Select Bibliography

Bartlett, J.N., 'The Expansion and Decline of York in the Later Middle Ages', *EconHR*, 2nd Ser., xii (1959), pp. 17–33.

Baumann, I., *Die Sprache der Urkunden aus Yorkshire im 15. Jahrhundert*, Anglistische Forschungen, xi (1902).

Beadle, R., and Meredith, P., 'Further External Evidence for Dating the York Register (BL Additional MS 35290)', *LSE*, NS, xi (1980), pp. 51–8.

——— 'An Unnoticed Lacuna in the York Chandlers' Pageant', *So Meny People, Longages and Tonges: Philological Essays in Scots and Medieval English presented to Angus McIntosh*, ed. M. Benskin and M.L. Samuels (Edinburgh, 1981), pp. 229–35.

——— 'The Origins of Abraham's Preamble in the York Play of *Abraham and Isaac*', *YES*, xi (1981), pp. 178–87.

——— and Meredith, P., *The York Play*, Leeds Texts and Monographs: Medieval Drama Facsimiles (forthcoming).

Brawer, R.A., 'The Characterization of Pilate in the York Cycle Play', *SP*, lxix (1972), pp. 289–303.

Bridbury, A.R., *Economic Growth: England in the Later Middle Ages* (London, 1962).

Brown, A., 'Some Notes on Medieval Drama in York', *Early English and Norse Studies presented to A.H. Smith*, ed. A. Brown and P. Foote (London, 1963), pp. 1–5.

Butterworth, P., 'The York Mercers' Pageant Vehicle, 1433–1467: Wheels, Steering and Control', *Medieval English Theatre*, i (1979), pp. 72–81.

Cady, F.W., 'Towneley, York, and True-Coventry', *SP*, xxvi (1929), pp. 386–400.

Catalogue of the Additions to the Manuscripts in the British Museum 1894–1899 (London, 1901).

Cawley, A.C., 'The Sykes Manuscript of the York Scriveners' Play', *LSE* vii–viii (1952), pp. 45–80.

——— 'Middle English Metrical Versions of the Decalogue with Reference to the English Corpus Christi Cycles', *LSE*, NS, viii (1975), pp. 129–45.

——— 'Thoresby and Later Owners of the Manuscript of the York Plays (BL Additional 35290)', *LSE*, NS, xi (1980), pp. 74–85.

Chambers, A.F., 'The Vicars Choral of York Minster and the Tile-makers' Corpus Christi Pageant', *REED Newsletter*, 1977:1, pp. 2–9.

Chambers, E.K., *English Literature at the Close of the Middle Ages* (Oxford, 1945).

Coffman, G. R., 'A Plea for the Study of the Corpus Christi Plays as Drama', *SP*, xxvii (1929), pp. 411–24.

Collier, R. J., *Poetry and Drama in the York Corpus Christi Play* (Hamden, Conn., 1978).

Collins, F., *Register of the Freemen of the City of York*, Surtees Society, xcvi and cii (1897–9).

Cowling, D., 'The Liturgical Celebration of Corpus Christi in Medieval York', *REED Newsletter*, 1976:2, pp. 5–9.

Cozart, W.R., *The Northern Middle English Harrowing of Hell Plays of the York and Towneley Cycles. An Edition and Commentary* (unpubl. diss., Harvard University, 1963).

Craig, H., *English Religious Drama of the Middle Ages* (Oxford, 1955).

Craigie, W.A., 'The Gospels of Nicodemus and the York Mystery Plays', *An English Miscellany Presented to Dr Furnivall* (Oxford, 1901).

Davidson, Charles, *Studies in the English Mystery Plays* (New Haven, 1892).

Davidson, Clifford, 'Civic Concern and Iconography in the York Passion', *AnM*, xv (1974), pp. 125–49.

—— 'After the Fall: Design in the Old Testament Plays in the York Cycle', *Medievalia*, i (1975), pp. 1–23.

—— 'The Realism of the York Realist and the York Passion', *Speculum*, l (1975), pp. 270–83.

—— 'From *Tristia* to *Gaudium:* Iconography and the York–Towneley *Harrowing of Hell*', *American Benedictine Review*, xxviii (1977), pp. 260–75.

—— and Mason, N., 'Staging the York *Creation, and Fall of Lucifer*', *Theatre Survey*, xvii (1976), pp. 162–78.

Davis, N., *Non-Cycle Plays and Fragments*, EETS, SS, 1 (1970).

Dorrell (Rogerson), M., 'The Mayor of York and the Coronation Pageant', *LSE*, NS, v (1971), pp. 35–45.

—— 'Two Studies of the York Corpus Christi Play', *LSE*, NS, vi (1972), pp. 63–111.

—— 'The Butchers', Saddlers', and Carpenters' Pageants: Misreadings of the York *Ordo*', *ELN*, xiii (1975), pp. 3–4.

Dobson, R.B., 'Admissions to the Freedom of the City of York in the Later Middle Ages', *EconHR*, 2nd Ser., xxvi (1973), pp. 1–22.

Dustoor, P.E., 'The York "Creation of Adam and Eve" ', *Allahabad University Studies*, xiii (1937), pp. 23–8.

Foster, F.A., *The Northern Passion*, vol. II, EETS, OS, 147 (1916).

Frampton, M.G., 'The Date of the "Wakefield Master": Bibliographical Evidence', *PMLA*, liii (1938), pp. 86–117.

—— 'The York Play of Christ Led Up to Calvary (Play XXXIV)', *PQ*, xx (1941), pp. 198–204.

Frank, G., 'St Martial of Limoges in the York Plays', *MLN*, xliv (1929), pp. 233–5.

Freeman, E., 'A Note on Play XXX of the York Cycle', *MLN*, xlv (1930), pp. 392–4.

Gayley, C.M., *Plays of Our Forefathers* (New York, 1907).

Greg, W.W., *Bibliographical and Textual Problems of the English Miracle Cycles* (London, 1914).

—— ' "Christ and the Doctors" and the York Play', *The Trial and*

Flagellation with Other Studies in the Chester Cycle, Malone Soc. Studies (Oxford, 1935).

Grove, T.N., 'Light in Darkness: The Comedy of the York *Harrowing of Hell* as seen against the Chester *Harrowing of Hell*', *NM*, lxxv (1974), pp. 115–25.

Hagen, S., *The Norse Loan-Words in the York Mystery Plays* (unpubl. diss., The Johns Hopkins Univ., Baltimore, 1900).

Hanks, D.T., 'New Sources for York Play XLV [XLIV], "The Death of Mary": *Legenda Aurea* and Vincent's *Speculum Historiale*', *ELN*, xiv (1976–7), pp. 5–7.

Hemingway, S.B., *English Nativity Plays* (New York, 1909).

Herttrich, O., *Studien zu den York Plays* (Breslau, 1886).

Hoffman, C.F., 'The Source of the Words to the Music in York 46 [XLV]', *MLN*, lxv (1950), pp. 236–9.

Hohlfeld, A., 'Die Altenenglischen Kollektivmisterien, Unter besonderer Berücksichtigung des Verhältnisses der York- und Towneley-Spiele', *Anglia*, xi (1899), pp. 219–310.

Holthausen, F., 'Beiträge zur Erklärung und Textkritik der York Plays', *Archiv*, lxxxv (1890), pp. 411–28.

———— 'Nachtrag zu den Quellen der York Plays', *Archiv*, lxxxvi (1891), pp. 280–2.

Hulme, W.H., *The Middle English Harrowing of Hell and the Gospel of Nicodemus*, EETS, ES, C (1907).

Johnston, A.F., 'The Procession and Play of Corpus Christi in York after 1426', *LSE*, NS, vii (1973–4), pp. 55–62.

———— 'The Plays of the Religious Guilds of York: The Creed Play and the Paternoster Play', *Speculum*, l (1975), pp. 55–90.

———— review of A. Nelson, *The Medieval English Stage*, *UTQ*, xliv (1975), pp. 238–48.

———— 'The Guild of Corpus Christi and the Procession of Corpus Christi in York', *MS*, xxxviii (1976), pp. 372–84.

———— and Dorrell (Rogerson), M., 'The Doomsday Pageant of the York Mercers, 1433', *LSE*, NS, v (1971), pp. 29–34.

———— and Dorrell (Rogerson), M., 'The York Mercers and their Pageant of Doomsday 1433–1526', *LSE*, NS, vi (1972), pp. 10–35.

———— and Rogerson, M., *Records of Early English Drama: York* (2 vols, Toronto, 1979).

Justice, A.D., 'Trade Symbolism in the York Cycle', *Theatre Journal*, xxxi (1979), pp. 47–58.

Kamann, P., *Über Quellen und Sprache der York Plays* (Halle, 1887).

Kalén, H., *A Middle English Metrical Paraphrase of the Old Testament* (Gothenburg, 1923).

Kolve, V.A., *The Play Called Corpus Christi* (Stanford, 1966).

Leiter, L.H., 'Typology, Paradigm, Metaphor and Image in the York *Creation of Adam and Eve*', *Drama Survey*, vii (1969), pp. 113–32.

Luick, K. 'Zur Textkritik der Spiele von York', *Anglia*, xxii (1899), pp. 384–91.

Lyle, M.C., *The Original Identity of the York and Towneley Cycles* (Minneapolis, 1919).

MacKinnon, E., 'Notes on the Dramatic Structure of the York Cycle', *SP*, xxviii (1931), pp. 443–9.

McNeir, W.F., 'The Corpus Christi Passion Plays as Dramatic Art', *SP*, xlviii (1951), pp. 601–28.

Mill, A.J., 'The York Bakers' Play of the Last Supper', *MLR*, xxx (1935), pp. 145–58.

———— 'The York Plays of the Dying, Assumption, and Coronation of Our Lady', *PMLA*, lxv (1950), pp. 866–76.

———— 'The Stations of the York Corpus Christi Play', *Yorkshire Archaeological Journal*, xxxvii (1951), pp. 492–502.

Miller, E., 'Medieval York', *VCH: City of York*, pp. 25–116; see under Tillott, P.M.

Miller, F.H., 'Metrical Affinities of the Shrewsbury *Officium Pastorum* and its York Correspondent', *MLN*, xxxiii (1918), pp. 91–5.

———— 'The Northern Passion and the Mysteries', *MLN*, xxxiv (1919), pp. 88–92.

———— 'Stanzaic Division in York Play XXXIX', *MLN*, xxxv (1920), pp. 379–80.

Mills, D., 'Approaches to Medieval Drama', *LSE*, NS, iii (1969), pp. 47–61.

Meredith, P., 'The Development of the York Mercers' Pageant Waggon', *Medieval English Theatre*, i (1979), pp. 5–18.

———— ' "Item for a grone – iijd" – Records and Performance', *REED: Proceedings of the First Colloquium*, ed. J. Dutka (Toronto, 1979), pp. 46–50.

———— 'The *Ordo Paginarum* and the Development of the York Tilemakers' Pageant', *LSE*, NS, xi (1980), pp. 59–73.

———— 'John Clerke's Hand in the York Register', *LSE*, NS, xii (1981), pp. 245–271.

———— 'The York Cycle and the Beginning of Vernacular Religious Drama in England', *Le Laudi Drammatiche umbre delle Origini*, Atti del V Convegno di Studio, Centro di Studi sul Teatro Medioevale e Rinascimentale di Viterbo (Viterbo, 1981), pp. 311–33.

———— see also under Beadle, R.

Oakden, J.P., *Alliterative Poetry in Middle English* (2 vols, Manchester, 1930–5).

Page, W., *The Victoria History of the County of York*, 3 vols (London 1907–13).

Parkes, M.B., *English Cursive Book Hands 1250–1500* (repr. London, 1979).

Palliser, D.M., 'The Trade Gilds of Tudor York', *Crisis and Order in English Towns 1500–1700*, ed. P. Clark and P. Slack (London, 1972).

———— 'The Medieval Street-names of York', *York Historian*, ii (1978), pp. 2–16.

———— *Tudor York* (Oxford, 1979).

Percy, J.W., *York Memorandum Book*, Part III, Surtees Society, clxxxvi (1973).

Prosser, E., *Drama and Religion in the English Mystery Plays: A Re-evaluation* (Stanford, 1961).

Purvis, J.S., *From Minster to Market Place* (York, n.d. [1969]).

Raine, A., *York Civic Records*, 8 vols, Yorkshire Archaeological Society ✕
Record Series, xcviii (1939), ciii (1941), cvi (1942), cviii (1945), cx
(1946), cxii (1948), cxv (1950), cxix (1953).
—— *Medieval York* (London, 1955).
Reese, J.B., 'Alliterative Verse in the York Cycle', *SP*, xlviii (1951), pp.
639–68.
Robinson, J.W., 'The Art of the York Realist', *MP*, lx (1962–3), pp. 241–
51.
—— *'Ad Majorem Dei Gloriam', Medieval Drama: A Collection of Festival
Papers*, ed. W. Selz (Vermillion, 1968), pp. 31–7.
—— 'A Commentary on the York Play of the Birth of Jesus', *JEGP*, lxx ✶
(1971), pp. 241–54.
Rogerson, M., 'The York Corpus Christi Play: Some Practical Details',
LSE, NS, x (1978), pp. 97–106.
—— see also under Dorrell, M., and Johnston, A.F.
Scroggs, J.H., *A Phonological Study of the Riming Words of the York Plays* ✶
(unpubl. diss., Univ. of N. Carolina, Chapel Hill, 1959).
Sellers, M., *York Memorandum Book*, Parts I and II, Surtees Society, cxx
(1912) and cxxv (1915).
Sisam, K., *Fourteenth Century Verse and Prose* (Oxford, 1921).
Stevens, M., and Dorrell (Rogerson), M., 'The *Ordo Paginarium* [*sic*]
Gathering of the York *A/Y Memorandum Book*', *MP*, lxxii (1974), pp.
45–59.
Sundén, K.F., 'The Etymology of the ME verbs *roþe, roþele* and *ruþe*', *A
Grammatical Miscellany Offered to Otto Jespersen on his Seventieth Birthday*,
ed. A. Bøgholm *et al.* (Copenhagen and London, 1930), pp. 109–11.
Tillott, P.M., *The Victoria History of the County of York: The City of York*
(Oxford, 1961).
Trusler, M., 'The Language of the Wakefield Playwright', *SP*, xxxiii ✶
(1936), pp. 15–39.
Twycross, M., ' "Places to Hear the Play": Pageants Stations at York,
1398–1572', *REED Newsletter*, 1978:2, pp. 10–33.
—— 'Playing "The Resurrection" ', *Medieval Studies for J.A.W. Bennett
Aetatis Suae LXX*, ed. P.L. Heyworth (Oxford, 1981), pp. 273–96.
Wall, C., 'The Apocryphal and Historical Backgrounds of "The
Appearance of Our Lady to Thomas" (Play XLVI [XLV] of the York
Cycle)', *MS*, xxxii (1970), pp. 172–92.
Wells, H.W., 'Style in the English Mystery Plays', *JEGP*, xxxviii (1939),
pp. 360–81.
Whitehall, H., 'The Etymology of Middle English *Myse*', *PQ*, xviii (1939),
pp. 314–6.
Wolff, E., 'Proculas Traum: Der Yorker Misterienzyklus und die
Epische Tradition', *Chaucer und seine Zeit: Symposion für Walter F.
Schirmer*, ed. A. Esch (Tübingen, 1968), pp. 419–50.
Woolf, R., *The English Mystery Plays* (London, 1972).
Zippel, O., 'Zwei Angebliche Mittelenglische Interjektionen', *Archiv*,
cxxxiv (1916), pp. 131–2.

Introduction

The manuscript

The manuscript volume containing the York Plays is London, British Library, MS Additional 35290. It was acquired by the then British Museum in 1899[1] from the collection of the fifth Earl of Ashburnham, who some years previously had permitted Lucy Toulmin Smith to publish her *editio princeps* of the cycle: *York Plays: The Plays. Performed by the Crafts or Mysteries of York on the Day of Corpus Christi in the 14th, 15th and 16th Centuries. Now First Printed from the Unique Manuscript in the Library of Lord Ashburnham* (Oxford, Clarendon Press, 1885). Since then, no other complete edition of the cycle has been published, though the manuscript, or photographic reproductions of it, have been used in the preparation of editions of single plays or selections from the cycle.[2] A second copy of one of the plays, no. XLI, the Scriveners' play of the *Incredulity of Thomas*, exists in the York, Yorkshire Museum, Sykes MS.[3]

Date of the manuscript

The date at which the bulk of the original manuscript was copied by its main scribe may be determined by reference to external evidence, namely the histories of certain individual plays in the cycle.[4] Play XLVI, the *Coronation of the Virgin*, is attributed in the manuscript to the Hostelers' gild. Documents exist which record that a play on this subject was once performed at the expense of the governing body of the city, but it is also recorded that by 1468, and perhaps as early as 1463, it had handed over responsibility for the performance to the Hostelers. The manuscript's attribution of the play to the Hostelers makes it likely that the compilation dates from after 1463.[5] The other *terminus* is fixed by reference to the history of play XVII, the *Purification of the Virgin*. As is explained at more length in the Note on no. XVII, the main scribe of the manuscript did not include this play in his plan of compilation, and there is some doubt as to whether it was a functioning component of the

1 *Catalogue of the Additions to the Manuscripts in the British Museum 1894–1899* (London, 1901), pp. 236–8.
2 For example, A. Brandl and O. Zippel, *Mittelenglische Sprache und Literaturproben* (2nd edn, Berlin, 1927), and D.M. Bevington, *Medieval Drama* (Boston, 1975). See below, 'Editorial Procedures'.
3 A.C. Cawley, 'The Sykes Manuscript of the York Scriveners' Play', *LSE*, NS, vii–viii (1952), pp. 45–80.
4 This section is based on the more extended discussion by R. Beadle and P. Meredith, 'Further External Evidence for Dating the York Register (BL Additional MS 35290)', *LSE*, NS, xi (1980), pp. 51–8.
5 M. Dorrell, 'The Mayor of York and the Coronation Pageant', *LSE*, NS, v (1971), pp. 35–45.

cycle during the time he was at work. The documents, however, record that the gild of Masons was given responsibility to bring forth the *Purification* play in 1477. The manuscript, on the other hand, attributes the Herod episodes of no. XVI to them, a responsibility they are known to have had from 1432–3. It therefore appears that the manuscript was copied whilst the Masons were still involved with no. XVI, and before they took over no. XVII in 1477.

Given these considerations, it is likely that the main scribe's work on the manuscript took place at some time between 1463 and 1477. Rather than being a relatively short and continuous stint, the process of copying was probably an extended and (to the scribe) an unusual task, involving the collection of a large number of scattered exemplars in different handwritings, and different states of preservation.[6]

Purpose and early history of the manuscript

The manuscript was intended to be the official record of the text of the York Corpus Christi play, and was the property of the corporation. No relevant documentary evidence is known to survive from the time when it was commissioned and executed, but its purpose may be safely inferred from the nature of the volume itself, and from later references to it. Why the civic authorities should have chosen to call for an official record of the text of the cycle in the third quarter of the fifteenth century is open to speculation. A Corpus Christi play is first heard of in York near the end of the fourteenth century, and the form it is known to have taken in 1415 resembles in many particulars what was set down in the manuscript at some time between 1463 and 1477. Judging by a number of bibliographical details set out below, the extant manuscript was unlikely to have been copied from, or even modelled upon another large volume of similar character and appearance. It was compiled from the various 'originals', prompt copies in the form of small booklets, held by each of the gilds having responsibility for a play in the cycle.[7] No documentary evidence exists as to whether the British Library manuscript had any predecessor as a complete record of the cycle, but variations in the work of the main scribe, especially near the beginning of the manuscript, suggest that the undertaking was to him new and unusual, and that he had no model from which to proceed.

In later documentary references the manuscript is sometimes called the 'Register', (though other large civic volumes were similarly styled) and it was natural to refer to the 'registering' of plays, or to plays being 'registered' in it.[8] Such references are not numerous, but several which

6 It is of interest to note that the period when the Register was compiled probably coincided with the time when the Corpus Christi procession in York was displaced from the day of the feast to the day after. See below, 'The Corpus Christi procession'.

7 W.W. Greg held that in York the gild copies were known as 'originals', and that the large volume containing the whole cycle was called the 'Register', a view borne out by the documentary references in the following footnote. It appears, however, that both terms were used with the opposite senses elsewhere: *Bibliographical and Textual Problems of the English Miracle Cycles* (London, 1914), pp. 23–5.

8 A.F. Johnston and M. Rogerson, *Records of Early English Drama: York* (2 vols, Toronto, 1979) (hereafter *REED: York*), pp. 324, 330, 351.

occur towards the middle of the sixteenth century contain a statement of one of the uses to which the manuscript was put. The first 'station' at which each play in the cycle was in turn performed (see below, 'Mode of performance') was before the gates of Holy Trinity Priory, Micklegate. From 1501 the Common Clerk of the city or his deputy are referred to in a number of years as being present at this place on the occasion of the annual performance, and several times between 1527 and 1554 it is specified that this is where they 'keep the Register'.[9] The expression is generally taken to mean that the surviving manuscript was used to check what was taking place in performance, and many of the numerous annotations in it by later hands, such as those alluding to stage business or to plays having been revised or rewritten, are likely to have derived from this activity.

Though the Register was intended to be a full record of the text of the cycle, it was never completed. When the copy for a given play was not forthcoming, the scribe left blank pages in the appropriate place, heading them with the name of the gild which had not produced its 'original'. Provision was made for plays IV, XXIIA and XXIIIA in this way. Plays XVII and XLIVA the main scribe probably never expected to receive, as he left no blank leaves in their respective positions in the sequence. The civic authorities made at least two attempts to complete the compilation during the sixteenth century. In 1557 a general order was issued for the registration of 'suche pageauntz as be not registred in the Cite book', which resulted in the appearance of play IV by 1559. A further order ten years later specified, amongst other things, that plays XXIIA, XXIIIA and XVII should be copied into the book.[10] In the event only no. XVII was forthcoming, and the spaces for XXIIA and XXIIIA remain blank. Play XLIVA was by this time no longer part of the cycle.

Further evidence of the Register's official status is found towards the end of the cycle's career, during the religious controversies of the sixteenth century. In 1568 a request that a performance of the cycle should take place was met by a decision on the part of the city authorities that 'the book thereof should be perused and otherwaise amendyd before it were playd'.[11] The manuscript is last heard of in its official capacity in 1579, when it was agreed that 'Corpus Christi play shalbe played this yere and that first the booke shalbe caried to my Lord

9 The references have been conveniently collected by A.F. Johnston, *UTQ*, xliv (1975), pp. 245–7 (review article). See also P. Meredith, 'John Clerke's Hand in the York Register', *LSE*, NS, xii (1981), pp. 245–71, esp. pp. 255–60.

10 *REED: York*, pp. 324, 330, 351.

11 *REED: York*, p. 354. In 1575, several of the city's 'play bookes' were described as being in the custody of the archbishop, the civic authorities at that time requesting that 'his grace will apoynt twoe or thre sufficiently learned to correcte the same wherein by the Lawe of this Realme they ar to be reformed' (*ibid*, p. 378). It is not known whether the Register was amongst the books mentioned. The widespread belief that some of the marginal annotations by later hands in the Register were the work of ecclesiastical censors (it originated in the Introduction to Miss Toulmin Smith's edition, pp. xv–xvi) is erroneous: see Meredith, 'John Clerke's Hand in the York Register', pp. 247–9.

Archebisshop and Mr Deane to correcte, if that my Lord Archebisshop doo well like theron'.[12] There is no evidence that either of these decisions was ever implemented, and apart from another abortive attempt at a revival in the following year, no more is heard of performances of the cycle, or of the Register.

Later history of the manuscript[13]

The earliest known post-Tudor owner of the manuscript was Henry Fairfax, second son of Henry, fourth Baron Fairfax. He wrote on one of the flyleaves at the front of the volume 'H: Fairfax's Book 1695'. It is not known how or where Fairfax acquired it, though the prominence of the Fairfax family in York and Yorkshire affairs, and their interest in local antiquarian matters, are well attested.[14] At some time between 1695 and his death in 1708, Fairfax gave the manuscript to Ralph Thoresby, the noted antiquarian and historian of Leeds, who recorded his acquisition on the back of the flyleaf already inscribed by Fairfax: 'Donum Hon:[mi] Hen: Fairfax Arm: Rad.° Thoresby'. Thoresby included the volume in a catalogue of his manuscripts in *Ducatus Leodiensis* (quoting the first eight lines of play XXXV), but without any apparent awareness of its original provenance. From Fairfax and Thoresby to the present day the pedigree of the manuscript is on the whole sound, as it passed through the hands of a series of mostly well-known antiquarians and bibliophiles. When Thoresby's library was sold at auction in 1764 the volume moved to the library of Horace Walpole at Strawberry Hill, where it remained until bought by the bookseller Thomas Rodd for Benjamin Heywood Bright in 1842. Bright died in the subsequent year, and in 1844 the manuscript – then for the first time identified as being that of the York Plays – apparently passed to the Revd Thomas Russell, from whom Lord Ashburnham acquired it in 1847. Its final move to the British Museum in 1899 has been noted above. Credit for identifying the manuscript as containing the York cycle is due to Sir Frederic Madden, who mentioned the discovery in an entry in his journal in April 1844.[15]

Description of the manuscript

Construction

The text occupies 268 leaves of parchment disposed in 35 quires. There are nine flyleaves of various dates at both the beginning and the end of

---

12 *REED: York*, p. 390.

13 This section is largely based on A.C. Cawley's article 'Thoresby and Later Owners of the Manuscript of the York Plays (BL Additional MS 35290)', *LSE*, NS, xi (1980), pp. 74–85. There is slight doubt as to who owned the volume between 1844 and 1847 (see Cawley, pp. 77–9). To Professor Cawley's information about the later history of the Register may be added the description of it in a notebook of the Revd Joseph Hunter (1783–1861), Assistant Keeper of the Public Records and a Yorkshire antiquary: London, British Library, Additional MS 24480, ff.159–61ᵛ. Hunter saw the manuscript at some time between 1842 and 1848.

14 Toulmin Smith, *York Plays*, pp. xii–xiii.

15 Quoted by Cawley, 'Thoresby and Later Owners. . .', p. 82.

the original manuscript.[16] It is still in an early and perhaps the original binding of leather-covered oak boards, the leather being in a poor state of preservation.[17] The backing is modern, and the lettering on the spine reads YORK/MYSTERY PLAYS/BRIT. MUS./ADDITIONAL/35,290.

The leaves are of medium quality parchment, varying in thickness from place to place in the manuscript, and measuring approximately 11 inches by 8 inches. Two modern pencil foliations appear in the top right hand corners of most, but not all of the rectos: (i) the foliation quoted in Miss Toulmin Smith's edition of 1885, now deleted; and (ii) the current British Library foliation. Both modern foliations omit leaves which do not carry any writing, though all were pricked and ruled by the main scribe. The foliation used in this edition numbers all the extant leaves in a series from 1 to 268.[18]

All the quires were originally eights, except the last, which is a four. Quire and leaf signatures are visible in the bottom right-hand corners of the rectos of nearly all leaves occupying the first halves of quires, except in the first quire, which was unsigned.[19] The quire signatures from the second to the thirty-fifth quires run as follows: an alphabetical sequence [A] to 3 (or Z) (omitting J, U and W); a Tironian nota (here denoted by &); an elaborated form of the Latin abbreviation for the syllable 'con'; and a numerical sequence xxvj^{ti} to xxxiiij^{ti}. The first (unsigned) quire is hereafter denoted by [A*]. The leaf signatures run j to iiij. With a few exceptions, a catchword appears at the foot of the verso of the last leaf in each quire.[20]

The collation of the manuscript may be summarized as follows: [A*]– [A]^8, B^8(wants 4,5), C–D^8, E^8+one (f.47, inserted after 8), F^8, G^8(wants 4,5)+one (inserted after 6, now wanting), H–N^8, O^8(wants 3,6), P–Q^8, R^8(wants 2,7), S–3^8, &^{8}(wants 2,7), con–xxvj$^{ti\,8}$, xxvij$^{ti\,8}$(1 cancelled)+one (f.208, inserted before 2), xxviij^{ti}–xxix$^{ti\,8}$, xxx$^{ti\,8}$(1 cancelled)+two (ff.232, 233, inserted before 2), xxxj^{ti}–xxxiiij$^{ti\,8}$, xxxiiij$^{ti\,4}$.

It will be perceived that five pairs of conjugate leaves and one singleton are now missing from the manuscript. The loss of the inner bifolium of quire G presumably did not involve loss of text, as the preceding leaves are a series of blanks following play XIV (ff.56^v–58^v), with play XV beginning on the leaf immediately following (f.59). The

16 At the beginning, i is a modern paper insert, ii is parchment, originally the pastedown, iii is a modern paper insert and iv–ix are parchment. At the end, i–vii are parchment, viii is parchment, originally a pastedown, and ix is a modern paper insert.

17 When Joseph Hunter wrote a description of the manuscript at some time between 1842 and 1848 he noted that it once had clasps, and that 'Two brass rings still exist in the side of the back board' (London, British Library, Additional MS 24480, f.159). The rings have now disappeared.

18 This foliation was devised for the forthcoming facsimile edition of the manuscript, *The York Play*, edited by R. Beadle and P. Meredith, 'Leeds Texts and Monographs: Medieval Drama Facsimiles'.

19 A few of the signatures have been cropped away, mainly in the early quires, and none are visible in the quire immediately preceding B: it is here denominated [A].

20 There are the following exceptions: [A*] and N (ff.8^v and 109^v) have no catchwords; in G and xxix^{ti} (ff.58^v and 231^v) the catchwords have been erased; E has a catchword in the usual place on the eighth leaf (f.46^v) but so also has a singleton added to the quire by the main scribe (f.47^v). Leaf xxx^{ti} j (f.218) is a singleton with which the main scribe replaced a cancel, and it too carries a catchword on the verso.

losses in quires B, O, R and & all carried away parts of the text, and are dealt with as they arise: see plays VII, XXIV, XXVII, XXVIII, XXXIII and XXXIV. In B the inner bifolium is missing, but this is not the case in O, R and &, where the losses may therefore not have been accidental. It is not possible to say when the missing leaves disappeared, but it is worth noting that there are no annotations by later hands alluding to defects in the texts at the places where the losses occur – though the annotators sometimes draw attention to less drastic shortcomings in surrounding areas of the text.[21]

Layout and presentation of the text[22]

Each page of the manuscript was pricked and ruled in such a way as to provide a frame approximately seven inches by four inches, within which the text was generally but by no means invariably confined. Each play was begun on a fresh page, and in most cases one, two or three blank pages were left between plays.[23] There is no visible line ruling. The disposition of the text on the page varies from place to place in the manuscript. Near the beginning, the task being new, the scribe tended to experiment with the layout.[24] When he later settled on a suitable pattern, it was sometimes necessary to vary it in order to accommodate specialities in the metre or in the dialogue. Wherever possible the scribe preferred to write in a single column, giving each verse a line to itself, but many of the metres used in the plays contained 'bob' lines, which appear to the right of the main column. Two lines are sometimes found written as one. In a number of places a single verse was divided between two and sometimes three speakers, and on such occasions the scribe often began each new speech on a fresh line. With no. XXVI, the first of several plays in the long alliterative line, the scribe changed the layout in a number of ways. Though he continued to write in a single column, he divided the long lines between the second and third stressed words, copying the second half of the line beneath the first, and beginning it with a capital letter.

Punctuation marks were used sparingly by the main scribe, if it at all. A virgule or double virgule added at the rubrication stage served to separate two lines of verse written as one. The character-designations, which are almost all in Latin, were inserted to the right of the column of verse, and were added at the rubrication stage. They were written in a more formal variety of script than the dialogue. Each new speech was separated from its predecessor by a horizontal red line, and, until the change of format occurring with play XXVI, rhymes were bracketed to

21 The loss of the singleton in quire G is a special case: see the Note on play XV, and R. Beadle, 'An Unnoticed Lacuna in the York Chandlers' Pageant', *Philological Essays in Scots and Medieval English presented to Angus McIntosh*, ed. M. Benskin and M.L. Samuels (Edinburgh, 1981), pp. 229–35.

22 The following remarks refer to the work of the main scribe only. For the practices of the other scribes see the section on Handwriting, below.

23 Exceptions to this pattern, some of which are of importance, are discussed in detail in the Notes on the plays.

24 See especially the Notes on plays V and VI.

the right, also in red. The original stage-directions (i.e. those not added by later hands) were usually written in red, in an ornamental script. All are in Latin. Most of them were copied within the column of the text, but occasionally they appear to the left or right.[25] Five of the plays have titles, in Latin, and throughout the manuscript the name of the gild or gilds responsible for a play appears at the head of each of its pages, as a running-title. The running-titles are all in English.[26] At the end of one play, no. XX, the scribe copied a list of the *dramatis personae*. The initial letter of the first line of most plays was intended by the scribe to be a *littera notabilior*, to be finished in red, but the spaces left remained unfilled until crude capitals were supplied by later hands.[27]

Handwriting

Two fifteenth-century scribes (A and B) were involved in the compilation of the original manuscript, and two others (C and D) made substantial contributions to it during the sixteenth century.

Scribes A and B were responsible for greatly differing proportions of the original manuscript. The hand of the minor contributor, A, appears in the first (unsigned) quire and nowhere else in the manuscript. He copied plays I and II, and the first or 'A' copy of play III. The hand of scribe B, the main scribe of the manuscript, also appears in this quire, contributing the running-titles to play I. Scribe B copied the rest of the original manuscript, that is, quires [A] to xxxiiij[ti], including all the plays from the second or 'B' copy of play III to play XLVII, excepting nos. IV, XVII and XLVIA.

Scribe C is identifiable as John Clerke (1510–1580), servant of the Common Clerk of York. He is first heard of in this post in 1538–9, and he appears to have occupied it until the end of his life.[28] As well as contributing very numerous marginal observations and alterations, he registered play IV at some time between 1557 and 1559, and play XVII in or soon after 1567.[29] At an unknown date he also supplied a passage to compensate for material lacking through the loss or removal of leaves from quire B, where play VII appears. Scribe D copied no. XLVIA on a blank leaf at the end of the manuscript, possibly in or soon after 1559.[30] His hand appears nowhere else in the manuscript.

The main scribe, B, was a competent professional copyist. The bulk of the text, that is, the dialogue, he copied in a hand modelled on the

25 The treatment of the stage-directions is recorded in the Textual Notes. Plays V, XII, XV, XXI, XXIII, XXX, XXXIII, XXXVIII, XLIII, XLIV, XLVI and XLVII have stage-directions by the main scribe.
26 The running-titles and the titles are discussed in the Notes on the plays.
27 For further details of the presentation of individual plays in the manuscript, see the Notes.
28 See Meredith, 'John Clerke's Hand in the York Register' (cited in n.9 above) for biographical details of Clerke.
29 See above 'Purpose and early history of the manuscript'. In 1557 the city authorities attempted to secure copies of plays which were not in the Register, and Clerke was paid by them for registering no. IV in 1559. No. XVII was amongst several plays listed as still lacking from the manuscript in 1567: see *REED: York*, pp. 324, 330, 351.
30 Regarding the presence of no. XLVIA in the Register, see the Note on no. XLVI.

variety of script known as Bastard Secretary, varying somewhat in size and duct from place to place in the manuscript.[31] The written parts of the rubrication – the character-designations and the stage-directions – were copied in one of two varieties of ornamental script, usually Bastard Anglicana, occasionally Textura. All the scripts employed by the main scribe were based on models of the more formal varieties available at the time. Whatever his exemplars were like,[32] and they doubtless varied widely in appearance, it is clear that the main scribe chose and executed his scripts with the intention of producing a dignified volume of homogeneous appearance, perhaps as befitted the importance of the Corpus Christi cycle in civic eyes. It appears that he worked unsupervised. There are no contemporary marginal indications of the type found in manuscripts produced in a 'commercial' manner, where the work might be checked by a supervisor and returned to the scribe for amendment. The scribe did, however, use the process of rubrication as an opportunity to 'proofread' what he had copied, a fact suggested by the number of corrections which he made in red. The insertion of the character-designations must have entailed close attention to the sense of what had already been copied, and the process naturally threw up errors.[33]

Scribe A wrote a hand which is based primarily on a Bastard Secretary model, but with an admixture of Anglicana letter-forms, and some tendency towards currency. Palaeographically speaking, there is no need to date it later than the main scribe's hand. As is shown in the Note on play I, the first (unsigned) quire was originally prepared by the main scribe, who inserted running-titles for the first play and then either left the quire otherwise blank, or handed it over to Scribe A. Scribe A used it to copy plays I, II and the first or 'A' copy of play III. Plays I and IIIA were set out in a manner similar to that generally used by the main scribe, but in play II, two verses are written on one line throughout, separated by a punctuation mark.

Marginalia and alterations to the text by later hands

Later users of the manuscript have left evidence of their activities in the form of numerous marginal annotations and alterations to the text. All are recorded in the Textual Notes as they appear, and many of them are the object of further discussion in the Notes on the individual plays. The marginalia[34] may be classed under several headings. Many take the form of simple comment or *aide-mémoire*, frequently 'hic', 'caret' and 'hic caret', sometimes 'hic deficit', 'nota' and 'memorandum'. More lengthy and

31 For the palaeographical terms used in this section, see M.B. Parkes, *English Cursive Book Hands 1250–1500* (repr. London, 1979), pp. xiii–xxv. Plays XI and XXXIII were copied in a smaller and more calligraphic variety of the main scribe's usual hand, and must have been part of the same stint.
32 The Sykes MS of play XLI is very informal in appearance. See Cawley, 'The Sykes Manuscript. . .' (cited in n.3 above), p. 46, and the plate facing p. 45.
33 See the Notes on the plays for evidence of the main scribe's methods of correction.
34 A list of the marginalia will appear in the forthcoming facsimile of the Register (see n.18 above).

explicit observations also occur, such as 'caret nova loquela' and 'de nouo facto'. All the comments of this type were evidently intended to record shortcomings in the registered text. There are also a number of added stage-directions, or, perhaps more accurately, marginal observations about what happened in performance expressed like stage-directions. Many refer to music (such as 'tunc cantant', sometimes with the piece specified), some to action (e.g. 'tunc bibit rex', 'tunc lauat manus'), and occasionally there are references to more complicated pieces of stage-business, such as 'Nota: The Harrode passeth, and the iij kynges commyth agayn to make there offerynges' in no. XVI.[35] In several plays, dialogue originally left unregistered, or perhaps newly composed, was added in the margin, and the gild-names which constituted the running-titles were also occasionally altered.[36] Almost all the plays have some sort of alteration to the text as originally set down by the main scribe. Character-designations were often corrected or supplied, lines left blank were filled and anything from a single letter to a whole phrase altered by erasure and substitution, or deletion and interlineation.

The hand responsible for the majority of the marginalia and alterations was that of John Clerke, servant of the Common Clerk of York in the mid-sixteenth century (see above, 'Handwriting'). His name is first connected for certain with the Register in 1554, when the following entry was made in a City Chamberlains' Book: 'Item payd to John Clerke for kepyng of the Register of Corpuscrysty play at the furst place accustomyd xxd.'[37] From this it appears that Clerke, on at least one occasion, had the responsibility referred to above, of checking the registered text against what occurred in performance at the first station (see 'Purpose and early history of the manuscript'). Judging by the frequency with which his handwriting appears in the Register, it must often have been in his hands during performances and perhaps at other times in the 1550s and 1560s.[38] Perusal of the Textual Notes and Notes will show that Clerke contributed marginalia and alterations of every kind noted above, particulary 'stage-directions' and allusions to the fact that certain texts were 'defective', 'wanting' or obsolete.[39] At the ends of most of the plays he wrote 'finis', and he sometimes altered running-titles to bring the Register up to date with changes in ownership amongst the plays.[40] Clerke's hand is in general confidently identifiable. In addition to the inscriptions firmly attributed to him in the Textual Notes, he was also probably responsible for a good number of those necessarily attributed only to 'a later hand' because of their brevity or

35 The following plays have 'stage-directions' by later hands: IX, XII, XVI, XXII, XXV, XXVII, XXIX, XXXI, XXXIII, XXXVII, XLII and XLIII.
36 Plays IIIA and B, X, XII, XXIX, XXXV, XXXVII, XXXVIII, XLIII and XLVII have dialogue added in the margin by later hands. For alterations to running-titles see the Notes on the plays.
37 *REED: York*, p. 317.
38 Clerke occasionally made later additions to his own marginalia. See, for example, the Textual Notes at III 44 and XLVII 229, and the discussion by Meredith, 'John Clerke's Hand. . .' (cited in n.9 above), pp. 255–7.
39 For examples of plays which had probably been partially or wholly rewritten by Clerke's time, see the Notes on nos. XII, XIX and XXI.
40 See the Notes on nos. XXXIII, XXXIX and XL.

informality or script. Many of Clerke's annotations were likely to have been the result of comparing the written text with what was going on in performance, but it is possible that some were not. For reasons unknown he gave the text of play VIII particularly minute attention, making numerous small alterations aimed at improving the metre or modernizing the dialect and orthography (see the Note on no. VIII). In spite of repeated injunctions by the city authorities (1557 and 1567, see above, 'Purpose and early history of the manuscript'), the 'originals' of plays XXIIA and XXIIIA were never produced for registration, a point to which Clerke also gave attention in the manuscript itself. On one of the pages left blank by the main scribe in order to receive no. XXIIA he wrote the *incipit* of the missing play. In the space left for no. XXIIIA he wrote 'This matter lakkes videlicet. . .' and went on to give a description of the missing play which derives from the *Ordo Paginarum* of 1415, in the city's A/Y Memorandum Book (see the Notes on nos. XXIIA and XXIIIA. For the *Ordo Paginarum,* see below, 'Development of the cycle'). It is clear that Clerke was conscientiously concerned with the state of the text recorded in the Register, and the great majority of his marginalia and alterations were evidently intelligent and well-informed. He is an important witness to the state of the cycle in the mid-sixteenth century.

Several names appear on the flyleaves of the manuscript. On the first blank leaf after the end of the text (f.268) are the following: 'Corpus Cristi playe' (twice), 'Thomas Cutler', 'Richard Nandicke'. These names also appear on the flyleaves at the beginning and end of the manuscript, and other inscriptions in the same handwriting (including the initials of the two men, ff.94 and 97) appears occasionally within the manuscript. It is not at present known who these persons were, or precisely when the manuscript was in their hands. The handwriting used is *c.* 1600.[41] Other early names on the flyleaves are: 'Killingbe(c)k', 'William Pennell' and 'John Willson'.

Development of the cycle

Origins and early history of the cycle

The Register of the York Corpus Christi cycle described above is for the most part a record of the text in use during the third quarter of the fifteenth century. A Corpus Christi cycle is first heard of in York towards the end of the fourteenth century, and its last recorded performance took place in 1569.[42] Various changes in the structure of the cycle and in the organization underlying it took place both before and after the Register was compiled, and some of them are reflected in the manuscript itself.

41 The unusual name Nandick twice appears in connection with the Mercers' play (no. XLVII) in the records. In 1461 a Thomas Nandyke was a pageant-master of the Mercers' gild, and 1547 a Cuthbert Nendyke held the same office: *REED: York*, pp. 91, 653.
42 See the documents printed in *REED: York*, pp. 3–12 and 355–7.

The Corpus Christi play was usually an annual event,[43] the performance always taking place on Corpus Christi day,[44] a moveable feast falling on the first Thursday after Trinity Sunday.[45] The manner in which the cycle was presented was most extraordinary, and a fuller account will be found below in the section 'Mode of performance'. It is generally thought that each of the individual plays which go to make up the cycle was staged on a wagon. The wagons are believed to have processed in the appropriate order along a traditional route round the streets of the city, pausing at a number of 'stations' where audiences were gathered, a performance of each play being given at each station. The number of stations could vary, but twelve tended to be the figure which was often favoured. The performance is known to have begun at 4.30 a.m. and an approximate reconstruction based on the number of plays in the Register performed at each of twelve stations suggests that the cycle as a whole would not have been completed until shortly after midnight.

There is at present no known documentary evidence as to precisely how or when the Corpus Christi cycle originated in York.[46] The casual mention of a place where three Corpus Christi pageant-wagons were stored in 1376 is the first possible indication that some sort of dramatic presentation may have been taking place, but whether this should be taken to imply the existence of a cycle of the kind found more fully documented in the fifteenth century is a matter for dispute. According to a contemporary chronicler, the feast of Corpus Christi was first widely observed in England in 1318, and it was proclaimed in York in 1325. An outdoor procession in which the clergy and laity followed a vessel containing the sacred host around the thoroughfares of the community was a notable requirement of the new feast.[47] How a processional play arose on the same annual occasion at York is open to speculation.

The fact that craft-gilds were involved in some kind of presentation at York first emerges in a document dated 1386–7, where the Tailors (later connected with play XLII) are mentioned as having a 'pagyn de Corpore christi'. Similar information about the Skinners, Bakers and Litsters (later, plays XXV, XXVII and XXXI respectively) may be inferred from a document dated 1387, and the same fact emerges about the Fletchers in 1388 and the Plasterers in 1390 (later, plays XXIX and II respectively).[48] References such as these have been widely accepted to imply the existence, from at least the late 1370s, of a cycle similar in

---

43 It was sometimes cancelled because of external circumstances (such as war and plague in 1558, see *REED: York*, p. 327), and occasionally the authorities chose to substitute either the Creed Play or the Paternoster Play, which were also large-scale civic productions: see A.F. Johnston, 'The Plays of the Religious Guilds of York: The Creed Play and the Pater Noster Play', *Speculum*, l (1975), pp. 55–90, esp. pp. 64 and 72.
44 The only known exception occurred in 1569, the last recorded performance of the cycle, which took place on the Tuesday in Whitsun week: *REED: York*, p. 355.
45 Corpus Christi may fall on any date between May 23 and June 24.
46 For an up-to-date account of the early history of the cycle see P. Meredith, 'The York Cycle and the Beginning of Vernacular Religious Drama in England', in *Le Laudi Drammatiche umbre delle Origini* (Viterbo, 1981), pp. 331–33.
47 See H. Craig, *English Religious Drama of the Middle Ages* (Oxford, 1955), pp. 127–9, and references there.
48 *REED: York*, pp. 4–7.

scope and organization to the one fully documented from 1415, and later recorded in the Register. The origins of this cycle have been assumed to lie much earlier in the fourteenth century, but the evidence for such an assumption is decidedly slender.

Responsibility for financing the plays fell on the craft-gilds of the city. Persons who wished to practise a trade were obliged to take out the franchise of the city, which was generally conferred after a period of satisfactory apprenticeship, though it could also be inherited. The expenses of each play in the cycle were defrayed by an annual levy on the members of the gild which had responsibility for it. The names of York gildsmen, usually with their crafts, were in general recorded on the Freemen's Roll of the city, an important document which amongst other things gives some idea of the size and composition of the gilds, and yields an index of their varying fortunes – and of the city's degree of prosperity – during the fourteenth, fifteenth and sixteenth centuries.[49] One of its oft-noted features is the spectacular contrast in the number of freemen admitted before and after the Black Death of 1349. In spite of the great mortality of that year 212 freemen were admitted in 1350, a surprisingly high figure in view of the fact that the average number admitted annually between 1345 and 1349 had been 59. Figures of this kind are echoed in more general statistics for the periods immediately before and after the Black Death. For instance, in the decade from 1331 to 1341, 659 freemen were admitted, whilst between 1361 and 1371 the number was 1049; in the final decade of the century almost 1200 freemen were admitted.[50] Whether figures of this kind reflect a rise in the population of York through immigration, or whether they indicate new and advantageous economic circumstances brought about by a temporarily *less* populous city are matters for debate amongst historians.[51] What is not in doubt is that not long after the Black Death York began to look forward to its 'halcyon years' (as Professor Dobson has it) towards the end of the fourteenth century. It was at this time that York stood second only to London as the most prosperous city in the kingdom,[52] and it is the documents of this period which begin to yield possible references to the existence of its Corpus Christi cycle.[53] Various

49 York, City Archives, MS D 1 (*olim* C/Y), Freemen's Roll, 1272–1671; transcribed by F. Collins, *Register of the Freemen of the City of York*, Surtees Soc., xcvi and cii (1897–9). For comments on Collins's transcription, and important observations on the kinds of statistical information which may be derived from the document see R.B. Dobson, 'Admissions to the Freedom of the City of York in the Later Middle Ages', *EconHR*, 2nd Ser., xxvi (1973), pp. 1–22.

50 Dobson, 'Admissions to the Freedom. . .', p. 17 (and see the graph on p.22, showing the number of admissions to the freedom by decades in this period); J.N. Bartlett, 'The Expansion and Decline of York in the Later Middle Ages', *EconHR*, 2nd Ser., xii (1959), pp. 24, 26.

51 Dobson, 'Admissions to the Freedom. . .', p. 18; Bartlett, 'Expansion and Decline. . .', p. 24; E. Miller, 'Medieval York', *VCH: City of York*, ed. P. Tillott (Oxford, 1963), p. 85; A.R. Bridbury, *Economic Growth: England in the Later Middle Ages* (London, 1962), pp. 62ff., 74, 106.

52 Bartlett, 'Expansion and Decline. . .', pp. 25–7.

53 York's intense division of labour, which enabled over 50 gilds to participate in the production of the cycle during the fifteenth century, seems to have become fully developed in the latter half of the fourteenth. Some of the gilds which later had

dates in the first half of the fourteenth century have been canvassed as the likely period of origin for the cycle,[54] all of them entirely speculative. It is possible that further research into the social and economic organization of York in the mid to late fourteenth century – particularly the development of the craft-gilds – will produce evidence relevant to the issue.

Certain general statements can, however, be made with some confidence regarding the likely size of the cycle, and the underlying financial arrangements towards the end of the last decade of the fourteenth century. In 1399 the commons of the city presented a petition in the form of a proposed ordinance for the cycle. The document, which was recorded in the city's official Memorandum Book (A/Y), may be allowed to speak for itself:

> To the honourable men, the mayor and aldermen of the city of York, the commons of the same city beg that, inasmuch as they incur great expense and costs in connection with the pageants and plays of Corpus Christi day, the which cannot be played or performed on the same day as they ought to be, because the aforesaid pageants are played in so many places at considerable hardship and deprivation to the said commons and strangers who have travelled to the said city on the same day for the same purpose, that it please you to consider that the said pageants are maintained and supported by the commons and the craftsmen of the same city in honour and reverence of our Lord Jesus Christ and for the glory and benefit of the same city, that you decree that the aforesaid pageants be played in the places to which they were limited and assigned by you and by the aforesaid commons previously, the which places are annexed to this bill in a schedule, or in other places from year to year according to the disposition and will of the mayor and the council of the Chamber, and that anyone who acts in contravention of the aforesaid ordinances and regulations shall incur a fine of 40s to be paid to the Council Chamber of the said city, and that if any of the aforesaid pageants be delayed or held back through fault or negligence on the part of the players, that they shall incur a penalty of 6s 8d to the same Chamber. And they (the commons) beg that these aforesaid matters be performed, or otherwise the said play shall not be played by the aforesaid commons. And they (the commons) ask these things for the sake of God and as a work of charity for the benefit of the said commons and of the strangers who have travelled to the said city for the honour of God and the promotion of charity among the same commons.
>
> Places where the play of Corpus Christi will have been played: first at the gates of Holy Trinity in Micklegate; second at Robert Harpham's door; third at John de Gyseburne's door; fourth at Skeldergate and North Street; fifth at

---

responsibility for plays were evidently very small, or in some cases apparently non-existent before 1349, judging by the tables of admissions which Professor Miller has derived from the Freemen's Roll. See *VCH: City of York*, pp. 114–16, showing very small or nil entries in the half-century prior to 1349 for the following gilds, which later had plays in the cycle: Plasterers (play II), Cardmakers (III), Shipwrights (VIII), Pewterers and Founders (XIII), Vintners (XXIIA), Ironmongers XXIIIA), Tapiters and Couchers (XXX), Woolpackers (XL) and Scriveners (XLI). All show substantial rises in the numbers admitted between 1350 and 1399.

54 Miss Toulmin Smith suggested 1340–50 (*York Plays*, p. xlv) and Hardin Craig *c.* 1328 (*English Religious Drama*, p. 205). Greg, who saw the development of the cycle in terms of successive periods of literary activity, dated the first period around 1350 (*Bibliographical and Textual Problems*, cited in n.7 above, p. 79).

the end of Coney Street opposite the Castlegate; sixth at the end of Jubbergate; seventh at Henry Wyman's door in Coney Street; eighth at the end of Coney Street next to the Common Hall; ninth at Adam del Brigg's door; tenth at the gates of the Minster of blessed Peter; eleventh at the end of Girdlergate in Petergate; twelfth on the Pavement.

And it has been ordained that the banners of the play with the arms of the city be delivered by the mayor on the eve of Corpus Christi, to be set in the places where the play of the pageants will be, and that each year on the day after Corpus Christi, the banners be returned to the Chamber to the hands of the mayor and chamberlains of the city and kept there for the entire year following, under penalty of 6s 8d to be paid to the needs of the commons by anyone who shall have kept the banners beyond the next day and shall not have given them up in the manner which is stated.[55]

Allowing for the florid language of the petition, it seems safe to say that by 1399 some kind of performance was taking place which was sufficiently long to overrun its allotted day. It was also spoken of as a considerable burden on the gilds, and the route through the city indicated by the list of stations proves to be the one used throughout the lifetime of the cycle. Nothing however is said of the content of the performance, a matter to which the civic authorities gave detailed attention sixteen years later.

The Ordo Paginarum of 1415

The single most informative document concerning the scope and later development of the cycle was begun in 1415. This is the *Ordo Paginarum* in the city's principle volume of medieval records, the A/Y Memorandum Book,[56] a large composite manuscript containing materials dated between 1327 and 1547. Though the *Ordo* is habitually spoken of as 'of 1415', and the bulk of the entries do indeed date from that time, it must be borne in mind that the document was heavily annotated and amended throughout the fifteenth century. Recent publications have done a good deal to encourage the notion of the *Ordo* as a document which began life with the idea of recording the cycle as a fixed entity, but which evolved in such a way as to reflect many features of the cycle's later development.[57]

The *Ordo Paginarum* was compiled by Roger Burton, Common Clerk

---

55 After the translation in *REED: York*, pp. 697–8. For the original document, which is in Anglo-Norman, see pp.11–12.

56 See M. Sellers, *York Memorandum Book*, Parts I and II, Surtees Soc., cxx (1912) and cxxv (1915). The A/Y Memorandum Book was principally a record of offical administrative decisions made by the governing body of the city. As well as the *Ordo Paginarum*, it contains many civic and gild ordinances, and other documents which shed light on the development of the cycle. It was supplemented by a second volume of similar character, now known as the B/Y Memorandum Book: see J.W. Percy, *York Memorandum Book*, Part III, Surtees Soc., clxxxvi (1973). For further details see *REED: York*, pp. xx and 868.

57 M. Stevens and M. Dorrell, 'The *Ordo Paginarium* [*sic*] Gathering in the York A/Y *Memorandum Book*', *MP*, lxxii (1974), pp. 45–59; *REED: York*, pp. 16–24. Though the Johnston and (Dorrell) Rogerson *REED* transcription is the best that has yet appeared, 'a number of important alterations remain un-noted there' according to P. Meredith, *LSE*, NS, xi (1980), p. 71, n.1.

of York from 1415 to 1433. It consists of a list of the gilds which performed plays in the Corpus Christi cycle, together with a brief description of each play. This was entered, along with other material bearing on the performance of the cycle, at the end of what is now the first section of the A/Y Memorandum Book, known in its time as the *maior registrum*. It has been plausibly suggested that the list occupied this position because it was the object of constant reference, and needed to be found easily.[58]

The *Ordo* was undoubtedly intended at its inception to be the city's official record of the content of the cycle and the 'order' of its performance. This assumes, as is likely, that the Register had no predecessor as a complete record of the text. Most of the alterations later made to the *Ordo* seem to date from the fifteenth century, and it may be that with the appearance of the Register between 1463 and 1477 one of the *Ordo*'s original functions was superseded. The precise use to which the *Ordo* was put in relation to the annual performance of the cycle is described in more detail below, under 'Mode of performance'. The civic authorities, it appears, caused the Common Clerk to copy out each play-description or 'schedule' in the form of a 'billet', which was then delivered to the relevant gild early in Lent. This process gave authorization for the performance, and incidentally reminded the gild of what it was obliged to bring forth. If this indeed was one of the *Ordo*'s primary functions, then it is not surprising that efforts were made to keep it up-to-date by altering the entries when the content of plays changed, or when changes of ownership took place. It is these alterations, taken together with discrepancies between the *Ordo* descriptions and the texts as registered in the third quarter of the fifteenth century, which give important clues to the development of the cycle.

It is not possible to give here much more than a sketch of the main developments which took place between the compilation of the *Ordo* and the appearance of the Register, partly because of continuing uncertainty as to the reading and interpretation of a number of *Ordo* entries. It is however safe to say that the broad scope and structure of the cycle was the same in the third quarter of the fifteenth century as it had been in 1415: a series of Old Testament plays; a series of plays on the life, passion and resurrection of Christ; plays on the later life of the Virgin, and a play of the Last Judgement. In the majority of cases there is considerable similarity between what was described in 1415 and what is found in the Register sixty or so years later. It would however be unwise simply to assume that the surviving plays were for this reason extant in 1415. Because of the traditional and standardized treatment of many of the episodes in medieval art and literature, the revision or rewriting of a play need not have called for any change in a brief description of its outward aspect, of the kind found in the *Ordo*.

Following closely upon the *Ordo* in the A/Y Memorandum Book is a second list of the gilds accompanied by succinct one-line descriptions of

58 See P. Meredith, ' "Item for a grone—iijd" – Records and Performance', *REED: Proceedings of the First Colloquium*, ed. J. Dutka (Toronto, 1979), pp. 42–3. I am most grateful to Peter Meredith for allowing me to see and to discuss with him the results of his examination of the *Ordo*.

their plays. Though its exact date and purpose are still uncertain, it is not much later, if at all, than the *Ordo* itself. What is more, the second list survives practically unaltered to give a picture of the cycle at a relatively early stage in its career.[59] The following translation of the second list is based on the transcription in *Records of Early English Drama: York*, pp. 25–6, omitting the few interlineations by later hands. Correspondences with the numbering of the plays in the Register used in this edition are given to the right.

1	Barkers	Creation of heaven and earth	I
2	Plasterers	Work of the five days	II
3	Cardmakers	Creation of Adam and Eve	III
4	Fullers[60]	Prohibition of the Tree of Knowledge	IV
5	Coopers	Deception of the Devil in a serpent	V
6	Armourers	Assignment of work to Adam	VI
7	Glovers	Cain killing Abel	VII
8	Shipwrights	Building of Noah's ark	VIII
9	Fishmongers } Mariners	Noah's ark in the Flood	IX
10	Parchmentmakers	Sacrifice of Isaac by Abraham	X
11	Hosiers	Pharaoh with Moses and the Children of Israel	XI
12	Spicers	Annunciation to Mary by Gabriel	XII
13	Founders	Joseph wanting to put her away secretly	XIII
14	Tilers	Bethlehem with the new-born boy	XIV
15	Chandlers	Offering of the shepherds	XV
16	Goldsmiths	Offering of the three Kings	XVI
17	St Leonard's	Presentation of Christ in the Temple	XVII
18	Marshals	How Christ escaped into Egypt	XVIII
19	Girdlers	Slaughter of the Innocents instead of Christ	XIX
20	Spurriers	Finding of Christ in the temple among the doctors	XX
21	Barbers	Baptism of Christ by John	XXI

59 A dating often quoted for the second list is *c.* 1420; see M.G. Frampton, 'The Date of the Wakefield Master: Bibliographical Evidence', *PMLA*, liii (1938), p. 103. If the list is in Roger Burton's hand, then it is not the more formal variety of it which he used for copying the *Ordo*. It may be of importance that the second list gives in each case only the main gild responsible for a play, and mentions none of the contributory gilds often listed or inserted later in the *Ordo*. Peter Meredith has recently observed that the second list enables one to see the entire ordering of the gilds and their plays on one page of the A/Y Memorandum Book: '. . .it may be that the second list provided a convenient check-list for anyone needing to see quickly the order in which the pageants should appear, perhaps even on the spot as the pageants moved out to perform "fast folowyng ilkon after other" on Corpus Christi day itself'; see 'The York Cycle and the Beginning of Vernacular Religious Drama. . .', cited in n.46 above, p. 326.
60 MS 'Walkers', an alternative name for the Fullers. No. 6, 'Armourers', is 'Fourbours' in the MS, no. 22 'Vintners' is 'Taverners', and no. 46, 'Carpenters' is 'Wrights'.

22 Vintners	Marriage at Cana in Galilee	XXIIA
23 Smiths	Temptation of Christ in the desert	XXII
24 Curriers	Transfiguration of Christ	XXIII
25 Ironmongers	Feast in the house of Simon	XXIIIA
26 Plumbers	Woman taken in adultery ⎱	XXIV
27 Hartshorners	The Raising of Lazarus ⎰	
28 Skinners	Jerusalem with citizens and boys	XXV
29 Cutlers	Selling of Christ by Judas	XXVI
30 Bakers	Supper of Christ with the disciples ⎱	XXVII
31 Waterleaders	Washing of the feet of the apostles ⎰	
32 Cordwainers	Capture of Christ praying on the mountain	XXVIII
33 Bowyers	Appearance of Christ before Caiaphas	XXIX
34 Tapiters	Accusation of Christ before Pilate	XXX
35 Litsters	Presentation of Christ before Herod	XXXI
36 Cooks	Penitence of Judas before the Jews	XXXII
37 Saucemakers	Hanging of Judas	
38 Tilemakers	Condemnation of Christ by Pilate ⎱	XXXIII
39 Turners ⎱ Bowlmakers ⎰	Scourging and crowning with thorns ⎰	
40 Shearmen	Leading of Christ and the showing to Veronica.	XXXIV
41 Millers	Division of the garments of Christ	XXXIII
42 Painters	Stretching and nailing of Christ ⎱	XXXV
43 Latteners	Raising of Christ on the mountain ⎰	
44 Butchers	Death of Christ on Calvary	XXXVI
45 Saddlers	Harrowing of Hell	XXXVII
46 Carpenters	Resurrection of Christ	XXXVIII
47 Winedrawers	Appearance of Christ to Mary Magdalene	XXXIX
48 Woolpackers	Appearance of Christ to the pilgrims	XL
49 Scriveners	Appearance of Christ to Thomas and others	XLI
50 Tailors	Ascension of Christ into heaven	XLII
51 Potters	Descent of the Holy Ghost	XLIII
52 Drapers	Death of the blessed Mary	XLIV
53 Masons	Carrying of the body of Mary	XLIVA
54 Weavers	Assumption of the blessed Mary	XLV
55 Mayor etc.	Coronation of the same	XLVI
56 Mercers	Last Judgement	XLVII

The 56 plays into which the cycle was subdivided when the second list was compiled reflected the 'extreme division of labour' which arose in the city during the fourteenth century.[61] By the time the Register was

61 See Miller, *VCH: City of York,* cited in n.51 above, p. 91

compiled the cycle may be said to have consisted of 50 plays, though it should be added that nos. XVII and XLIVA were probably not being performed at that time, and the main scribe did not plan to include them in the volume. Both were revived shortly after the Register was completed, no. XLIVA only temporarily, no. XVII for a longer period.[62] The main scribe recorded 45 plays. Nos. IV and XVII were added by John Clerke in the mid-sixteenth century, but nos. XXIIA, XXIIIA and XLIVA were never registered.

Documents exist which help to explain a number of the changes in gild organization and in the structure of the cycle between the time of the second list and the appearance of the Register. The progressive amalgamation of four earlier units to comprise the single episode later covered by play XXXIII began in 1422–3 and was probably completed in 1436.[63] The uniting of the two plays attributed respectively to the Painters and Latteners also took place in 1422.[64] The Register has a single play, no. XXXV, dealing with the same episodes, and attributed to the Pinners. There is however nothing to show how or when the events earlier covered in the Plumbers' 'Raising of Lazarus' and the Harts-horners' 'Woman taken in Adultery' later became the Cappers' play, no. XXIV, in the Register.[65] Nor is there any indication of how the earlier Waterleaders' 'Washing of the Apostles' Feet' came to be assimilated into the version of the Bakers' play found in the Register (no. XXVII). In 1432, no. XVI, previously produced by the Goldsmiths alone, was divided between the Goldsmiths and the Masons, who chose to relinquish control of no. XLIVA at that time. After the Register was compiled (1477) the Masons left no. XVI in favour of no. XVII, though it is not known at what date St Leonard's Hospital ceased to perform the latter. At the same time no. XLIVA underwent a temporary revival, until 1485.[66] The episode of the *Coronation of the Virgin*, attributed to the 'Mayor etc.' in the list, came under the control of the Hostlers at some time between 1463 and 1468.[67]

Later history of the cycle

Changes continued throughout the period from the compilation of the Register to the suppression of the cycle towards the end of the third quarter of the sixteenth century. Amongst those reflected in the manuscript were the amalgamation of plays III and IV in 1529, the taking over of no. XL by the Sledmen at an unknown date prior to 1535, and the suspension from the cycle of the Marian plays, XLIV, XLV and XLVI, between 1548 and 1554. It appears that these three plays temporarily reappeared with the return of Catholicism under Mary, but

---

62 See the Notes on nos. XVII and XLIVA.
63 P. Meredith, 'The *Ordo Paginarum* and the Development of the York Tilemakers' Pageant', *LSE*, NS, xi (1980), pp. 59–73.
64 See the document printed in *REED: York*, pp. 37–8.
65 In the *Ordo* of 1415, 'Lazarus' was attributed to the Pouchmakers, Bottlemakers and Cappers, with no mention of the Hartshorners, whose presence in the second list remains to be explained.
66 Beadle and Meredith, 'Further External Evidence. . .', as cited in n.4 above.
67 Dorrell, 'The Mayor of York and the Coronation Pageant', as cited in n.5 above.

were once again prohibited in 1561.[68] It is clear that changes also took place in the texts used by the gilds in performance. Annotations in the Register by later hands often draw attention to partial revisions or complete rewritings of plays, for instance nos. XII, XIX and XXI.

In spite of these and other changes in its external organization and internal composition, the basic scope and structure of the cycle remained largely stable. It should not, however, necessarily be assumed that the entire 'repertoire' was actually produced on every occasion upon which the cycle was given, though no doubt the prestige of the city and the artistic logic of the enterprise made as complete a performance as possible something that was to be desired. Evidence exists in a document of 1535 which may perhaps indicate the number of plays that would have been performed if the production had not been cancelled. In that year the governing body of the city rescinded its decision to have the Corpus Christi cycle, and substituted the Creed play instead.[69] It nevertheless called in the money collected by those gilds which were apparently preparing to put on their plays, and diverted it to another purpose. The sums surrendered were listed in an account, and vary widely in magnitude. If the gilds listed as contributors in the Chamberlains' Book in 1535 were indeed the only ones proposing to put forth their plays, the cycle, had it been performed, would have had a rather chequered appearance. Not only would about a dozen plays presumably have been absent, but the lavishness of those which did appear (a maximum of perhaps 35) would have varied a great deal.[70]

The Corpus Christi procession

The fact that the Corpus Christi cycle at York originally shared its occasion in the calendar with a procession of Corpus Christi has been mentioned above. At York as elsewhere the procession was an ecclesiastical matter, and in this it contrasted with the plays, whose organization lay in the hands of civic bodies, the corporation and the officers of the craft-gilds. It is clear that the procession and the cycle were entirely separate events from the time that they are both first described, at the very end of the fourteenth century. At this period both occurred on Corpus Christi day, but their separateness was futher emphasized in the third quarter of the fifteenth century, when the procession was displaced to the day following, leaving the cycle of plays as the principal celebration of the feast proper. The documents concerning the development of the relationship between the cycle and the procession have been collected and discussed by Dr Rogerson (as Margaret Dorrell) and Professor Johnston.[71] It has been shown that

68 See the Notes on nos XLIV, XLV and XLVI for further discussion and references to the documents.
69 See n.43, above.
70 See the transcription of the document in *REED: York*, pp. 256–61. The following gilds were evidently not contributors: Plasterers (play II), Shipwrights (VIII), Fishers and Mariners (IX), Tilethatchers (XIV), Chandlers (XV), Masons (XVII), Vintners (XXIIA), Ironmongers (XXIIIA), Cooks and Waterleaders (XXXII), Shearmen (XXXIV), Winedrawers (XXXIX), Scriveners (XLI) and Hostelers (XLVI).
71 M. Dorrell, 'Two Studies of the York Corpus Christi Play', *LSE*, NS, vi (1972), pp. 63–74 (from 1399 to 1426), and A.F. Johnston, 'The Procession and Play of Corpus Christi in

during the period whilst the two events occurred on Corpus Christi day, the procession preceded the plays along the city's ceremonial route from Holy Trinity Priory, Micklegate, as far as the end of Stonegate, but there, instead of turning into Petergate, it crossed into the Minster precincts and ended eventually at St Leonard's Hospital.[72] The procession was led by the clergy, who carried a sacred host in a monstrance, so that it should be visible to bystanders. They were followed by the mayor, other civic dignitaries and members of the craft-gilds, who supplied torches for the procession. A report of a riot in the procession in 1419, which delayed the plays, indicates that the dramatic performance (known to have begun at 4.30 a.m.) must have followed immediately upon the procession.[73] In 1426 a Minorite friar named William Melton urged that the plays be performed on the day after Corpus Christi, as the proper observance of the feast was marred by the eating, drinking and merrymaking of the civic event. Though it is recorded that the citizens at the time agreed with his proposal, any change that was made must have been short-lived, as the next time that a performance of the cycle is mentioned in the documents, in 1432, Corpus Christi day was the occasion.[74] Evidence that the procession had been displaced to the day after Corpus Christi begins to accumulate in 1468 and may be said to be firm from 1476. The situation whereby the cycle of plays became the principal celebration of Corpus Christi in York appears to have prevailed into the sixteenth century.[75]

Ownership of plays

Little can be said of a final point bearing on the development of the cycle, because of the paucity of evidence from the earliest period of its career. This is the issue of how the gilds came to have responsibility for their particular plays. In a number of cases there is an obvious resemblance between the occupation of the craft and the matter of their play. Well-known examples are the Shipwrights' play of Noah building the Ark (no. VIII), the Fishers' and Mariners' play of the Flood (no. IX), the Vintners' *Marriage at Cana* (no. XXIIA), and the Bakers' *Last Supper* (no. XXVII).[76] It has been suggested that appropriate assignments of

York after 1426'. *LSE*, NS, vii (1973–4), pp. 55–62. For further details of the social organization behind the procession and the local liturgical observances see A.F. Johnston, 'The Guild of Corpus Christi and the Procession of Corpus Christi in York', *MS*, xxxviii (1976), pp. 372–84, and D. Cowling, 'The Liturgical Celebration of Corpus Christi in Medieval York', *REED Newsletter,* 1976:2, pp. 5–9.

72 For the contrasting route of the play-procession after Stonegate, see below, the section on Stations under 'Mode of performance'.

73 Dorrell, 'Two Studies. . .', p. 70.

74 Dorrell, 'Two Studies. . .', pp. 70–3, Johnston, 'The Procession and Play of Corpus Christi. . .', pp. 55–6.

75 Johnston, 'The Procession and Play of Corpus Christi. . .', pp. 58–9.

76 Such 'appropriate' assignments were not necessarily permanent. For instance the second list of gilds and their plays quoted above aptly has the Waterleaders performing a play of the washing of the disciples' feet. By the time of the Register, this episode was part of the Bakers' play, and the Waterleaders had joined the Cooks in putting on *The Remorse of Judas* (no. XXXII).

this kind were sought out with the intention of pointing to the sanctity of the craft's daily labour, an explanation which has more appeal than the modern notion of the 'advertising' of products or workmanship in the plays.[77] In the majority of cases, however, no obvious correspondence is to be seen between the activity of the gild and the subject matter of its play, and the reason for the assignment – if indeed it was not arbitrary – must be sought elsewhere. That the Carpenters performed the *Resurrection* (no. XXXVIII) may be connected with the fact that the gild was also known as the Holy Fraternity of the Resurrection.[78] The Cordwainers' play of the *Agony in the Garden* (no. XXVIII) includes the episode of the Vigil of the Apostles, and the ordinances of the gild reveal that the Cordwainers held the feast of that name in special reverence.[79] Further research into the histories of the gilds may reveal other possible connections between their activities and their plays.[80]

Mode of performance

Preparations for performance; financial arrangements

The annual arrangements for the performance of the Corpus Christi cycle in York occupied a period from early Lent to the day of Corpus Christi, some fourteen or fifteen weeks. A meeting of the civic authorities was held early in Lent to initiate the process. When authorization for the performance had been given, the fact was notified to those gilds having primary responsibility for a play by the sending out of 'billets'. This practice is referred to in a note added at the head of the *Ordo Paginarum* of 1415: 'The billets [*sedule*] of pageants must be delivered in succession in the subscribed form to the craftsmen by six sergeants-at-arms of the mayor in the first or second week of Lent, yearly, (and) are to be written by the common clerk'.[81] The 'billets' or 'schedules' referred to here have generally been taken to contain the descriptions of the plays set down in the *Ordo Paginarum*. Upon receipt of the billets the gilds held meetings to begin the detailed arrangements for their plays.[82]

Each gild was responsible for the costs of its play, or for instituting a levy where formal ordinances provided that other gilds or craftsmen (usually those engaged in related activities) should be contributory. When the costs could not for some reason be met, gilds occasionally

---

77 See J.W. Robinson, *'Ad Majorem Dei Gloriam'*, *Medieval Drama: A Collection of Festival Papers*, ed. W. Selz (Vermillion, 1968), pp. 31–7; J.W. Robinson, 'A Commentary on the York Play of the Birth of Jesus', *JEGP*, lxx (1971), pp. 250–1; E. Freeman, 'A Note on Play XXX of the York Cycle', *MLN*, xlv (1930), pp. 392–4.
78 Percy, *York Memorandum Book*, Part III, cited in n.56 above, p. 254.
79 Sellers, *York Memorandum Book*, Part I, cited in n.56 above, p. 188.
80 For a recent investigation see A.D. Justice, 'Trade Symbolism in the York Cycle', *Theatre Journal*, xxxi (1979), pp. 47–58.
81 *REED: York*, pp. 17 (original document) and 703 (translation quoted).
82 The Shearmen enshrined this meeting in their ordinances of 1405, including a heavy fine for anyone 'qest troue rebell': *REED: York*, pp. 14–15, 700–1.

appealed to the corporation for relief.[83] The money paid by the craftsmen towards their play was often known as 'pageant silver'. It was collected from them by elected officers, the 'pageant-masters', who might be accompanied on their rounds by sergeants-at-mace provided by the mayor. The pageant-masters were in effect the producers of the plays, and were responsible for the financial and administrative organization behind them. Money used towards financing the plays was also raised by other means, some of the contributions being on a regular basis, others being incidental, mainly fines. They have recently been classified and discussed by Dr Rogerson: yearly contributions from non-members of gilds who gained income from practising the skills of a play-owning craft; special payments made on becoming a master in a craft, or upon becoming a member of a gild; a percentage of fines levied for infringement of craft ordinances; and contributions from crafts which did not have plays in the cycle.[84] The A/Y and B/Y Memorandum Books of the city record numerous gild ordinances of the fifteenth and sixteenth centuries, and many of them give details of fines to be levied on craftsmen for such things as the infringement of the strict demarcations between trades, the infringement of technical regulations (especially those concerning apprenticeships), or poor workmanship. 'Foreigners', craftsmen from elsewhere temporarily in the city, or seeking to settle permanently, could also be subject to financial exactions connected with the plays.[85] There were financial penalties for those who declined to pay pageant-money, and an extreme case could lead to threat of suspension of the right to trade.[86]

The uses to which the pageant-money was put included the maintenance of the pageant-wagon, rent for its storage, properties and costumes, refreshment for actors and others concerned with the performance at rehearsals and on Corpus Christi day, payment to the 'director' and the actors, and finally a supper shortly after the performance at which the officers of the gild made a reckoning of their financial position. Accounts of the Bakers (play XXVII) and the Mercers (play XLVII) survive to show in some detail exactly how the money was laid out. They also give some impression of how the quality and lavishness of the productions could vary from year to year, and at different periods in the life of the cycle.[87] In 1535 the Corpus Christi play was not performed, the Creed play being preferred instead.

83 For instance, the Armourers in 1444 and the Painters in 1561: *REED: York*, pp. 62–3, 332.

84 M. Rogerson, 'The York Corpus Christi Play: Some Practical Details', *LSE*, NS, x (1978), pp. 97–101.

85 Amongst early examples are regulations of the Shearmen relating to bad workmanship (1405), of the Plasterers concerning apprenticeship (1411–12), of the Tapiters in connection with foreigners (1419–20), and of the Masons, Tilethatchers and Plasterers over demarcation: *REED: York*, pp. 14, 700; 16, 702; 32, 717; 33, 718–19 (original documents and translations). For sixteenth-century examples see J.S. Purvis, *From Minster to Market Place* (York, n.d. [1969]), pp. 45–6.

86 *REED: York*, p. 313.

87 See A.J. Mill, 'The York Bakers' Play of the Last Supper', *MLR*. xxx (1935), pp. 145–58; A.F. Johnston and M. Dorrell, 'The York Mercers and their Pageant of Doomsday, 1433–1526', *LSE*, NS, vi (1972), pp. 10–35.

Pageant-money was nevertheless collected and diverted to the city treasury to defray the expenses of some civic business in London. From lists in the City Chamberlains' accounts it appears that about 35 of the plays were being prepared for performance, the sums collected by the gilds ranging from a minimum of two shillings and fourpence to a maximum of twenty shillings.[88]

In 1476 the following ordinance was minuted by the civic authorities, providing for an official check on the plays and the pageant-wagons, together with auditions for actors, all to take place during Lent when the gilds were engaged in preparing for the performance:

> Ordinacio pro Ludi Corporis christi. Also it is ordeined and stablished by þe ful consent and auctoritie of þe Counsaile aforesaide, þe day and yere within writen from þis day furth perpetually to be obserued and keped: That is to saie þat yerely in þe tyme of Lentyn there shall be called afore the Maire for þe tyme beyng iiij of þe moste connyng, discrete and able playeres within þis Citie to serche, here and examen all þe plaiers and plaies and pagentes thurghoute all þe artificeres belonging to Corpus Christi plaie; And all suche as þay shall fynde sufficiant in personne and connyng to þe honour of þe Citie and worship of þe saide craftes for to admitte and able, and all oþer insufficiant personnes either in connyng, voice or personne to discharge, ammove and avoide.
>
> And þat no plaier þat shall plaie in þe saide Corpus Christi plaie be conducte and reteyned to plaie but twise on þe day of þe saide playe. And þat he or thay so plaing, plaie not ouere twise þe saide day vpon payne of xl s. to forfet vnto þe Chaumbre as often tymes as he or þay shall be founden defautie in þe same.[89]

Stations

Final preparations for the performance included the assigning of 'stations' on a regular and traditional route through the streets of the city. The stations were officially designated positions provided with scaffolds for the accommodations of the audience, the bulk of whom paid for their places. Each play in the cycle was given at each station, where refreshment was doubtless available to the audience through the long performance. A considerable quantity of information concerning the stations has survived, partly because they came to be a means whereby profit accrued to the city treasury from the performance, and official records were kept. The earliest reference to stations in the documents occurs in 1394, when they were termed 'antiquitus assignatis', but there is no information as to where they were then situated.[90] A

88 *REED: York*, pp. 256–61. See also 'Later History of the Cycle' and nn. 69 and 70, above.
89 After the transcription in *REED: York*, p. 109 (punctuation added). Judging by the wording of the ordinance, this may have been an entirely new institution, though the possibility that it replaced some earlier unrecorded or less official vetting of the plays should not be overlooked. It is worth noting that this ordinance dates from about the time when the Register was compiled, and also from the time when the Corpus Christi procession was displaced from the day of the feast to the day following. See above, 'Date of the manuscript' and 'The Corpus Christi procession'.
90 *REED: York*, pp. 8 (original document) and 694 (translation). Much significance has been attached to the fact that the stations where the plays were performed were described as

list of the stations was however included in the proposed ordinance for the cycle of 1399, printed above in translation (see 'Origins and early history of the cycle'). Twelve stations are noted and the document speaks of them in terms which suggest that they were intended if possible to be permanent. The route along which they lay was the one used throughout the life of the cycle.

Official control over the stations was signified by banners, bearing the coat-of-arms of the city, which the mayor caused to be set up in the appropriate places on the vigil of Corpus Christi. The route along which the stations were distributed began just within Micklegate, proceeded over the river by Ouse Bridge, turned left along Coney Street, right along Stonegate, right again at the Minster Gates, down Petergate and Colliergate, and finally arrived at the Pavement, the commercial centre of the city.[91]

The financial arrangements regarding the stations changed in 1417. Prior to this date it appears that any profits from the sale of seats at the stations went directly to those fortunate enough to own property in the officially sanctioned places. After some discussion it was decided in 1417 that the city would lease the stations to the highest bidders, thereby giving the corporation a source of revenue from the performance.[92] This system prevailed throughout the rest of the cycle's career, and the Chamberlains' accounts from 1454–5 onwards often given the names of the lessees and other details of the positions and functions of the stations.[93]

The minimum number of stations recorded was ten and the maximum sixteen, and the positions of a number of them varied as leases changed hands. The sites of certain stations appear however to have remained permanent: the first, at the gates of Holy Trinity Priory, Micklegate, where the Common Clerk or his deputy 'kept the Register' in the sixteenth century (see above, 'Purpose and early history of the manuscript'); the last, on the Pavement; the Common Hall, where the governing body of the city saw the plays free; the Minster Gates. The accompanying map, kindly supplied by Mrs Meg Twycross, shows the approximate positions of the stations when the cycle was performed in 1468, about the time when the Register was being compiled.[94]

'antiquitus assignatis' in 1394–Craig, for instance, in *English Religious Drama* (cited in n.47 above), p. 205, took the expression to mean thirty to fifty years. That a long period of time was not necessarily being invoked is suggested by another document of 1493, where the expression 'of Auncien tyme' can be shown to refer to a period of not more than eight years: Beadle and Meredith, 'Further External Evidence. . .', cited in n.4 above, p. 57, n.11.
91 This was, or became, the city's traditional route for processions. It was also used for other civic plays and royal entries: Dorrell, 'Two Studies. . .', cited in n.71 above, p. 86.
92 *REED: York*, pp. 28–30 (original document) and 713–15 (translation); for discussion, see Dorrell, 'Two Studies. . .', pp. 86–90.
93 A.J. Mill, 'The Stations of the York Corpus Christi Play', *Yorks. Archaeological Journal*, xxxvii (1951), pp. 492–502; M. Twycross, ' "Places to Hear the Play": Pageant Stations at York, 1398–1572', *REED Newsletter*, 1978:2, pp. 10–33.
94 For notes on the positions indicted by the numbers on the map, see the table on pp. 28–33 in ' "Places to Hear the Play". . .'. Mrs Twycross's identifications of the lessees' properties point to the tentative conclusion that the stations (i.e. the places where the audiences were accommodated) were all on the left-hand side of the processional route: see pp. 18–20 of her article.

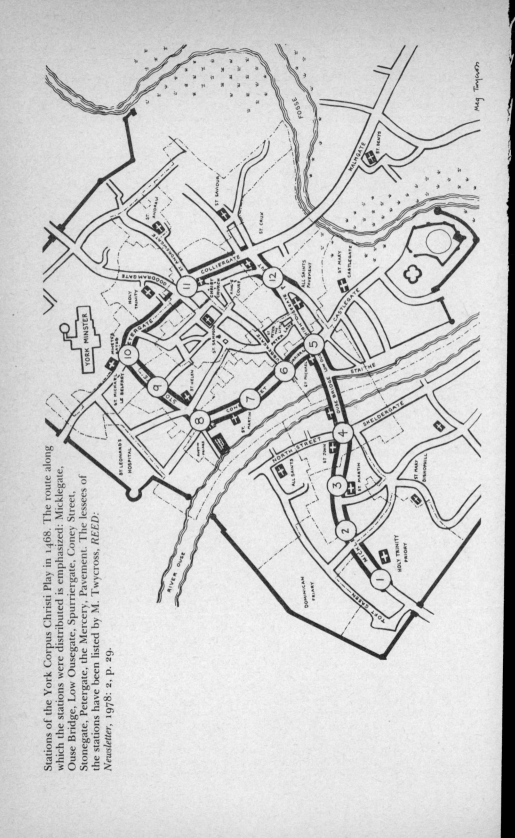

Stations of the York Corpus Christi Play in 1468. The route along which the stations were distributed is emphasized: Micklegate, Ouse Bridge, Low Ousegate, Spurriergate, Coney Street, Stonegate, Petergate, the Mercery, Pavement. The lessees of the stations have been listed by M. Twycross, *REED: Newsletter*, 1978: 2, p. 29.

The records of the rents brought in to the city by the stations show that, as a commercial proposition, the cycle was at its strongest in the fifteenth century. Receipts declined dramatically in the sixteenth century, the period when York's economy in general went into a depression.[95]

Proclamation

The stations for the performance were decided upon annually by the civic authorities about a week before Corpus Christi. On the same day as the official banners were set up in the designated positions, the following proclamation – 'Proclamacio ludi Corporis Christi facienda in vigilia Corporis Christi' – was made:

> Oiez &c. We comand of þe kynges behalue and þe mair & þe shirefs of þis Citee þat no man go armed in þis Citee with swerdes, ne with carlill axes, ne none othir defences in distourbaunce of þe kynges pees & þe play, or hynderyng of þe processioun of Corpore Christi; and þat þai leue þare hernas in þare ines, saufand knyghtes and squwyers of wirship þat awe haue swerdes borne eftir þame, of payne of forfaiture of þaire wapen & inprisonment of þaire bodys. And þat men þat brynges furth pacentes, þat þai play at the places þat is assigned þerfore, and nowere elles, of þe payne of forfaiture to be raysed þat is ordayned þerfore, þat is to say xl s . . . And þat all maner of craftmen þat bringeth furthe ther pageantez in order & course by good players, well arayed & openly spekyng, vpon payn of lesyng of c s., to be paid to the chambre withoute any pardon. And that euery player that shall play be redy in his pagiaunt at convenyant tyme, that is to say at the mydhowre betwix iiij[th] & v[th] of the cloke in the mornyng, & then all oþer pageantes fast folowyng ilkon after oþer as þer course is, without tarieng, sub pena facienda camere vj s. viij d.[96]

The proclamation speaks for itself as to the expected conduct of the performance. The initial mustering of the pageant-wagons and the players took place in the open area called Toft Green (also known as Pageant Green), close to the first station. The very early start was necessary if all the plays were to be seen within a reasonable span of time. It has been calculated, on the basis of all the plays in the Register being performed at twelve stations, that a performance starting at 4.30 a.m. would end about half an hour after midnight with the close of the *Last Judgement* at the twelfth station.[97] The great length of the cycle was of periodic concern to the authorities, and some of the amalgamations of episodes which took place in the 1420s seem to have been aimed at expediting the performance.[98] The final clause in the Proclamation,

95 Mill, 'Stations of the York Corpus Christi Play', p. 498. On York's decline in the sixteenth century see Bartlett, 'Expansion and Decline of York. . .', cited in n.50 above, pp. 31–3.

96 After the transcription in *REED: York*, pp. 24–5, with puntuation added, and minor orthographical alterations. The Proclamation appears in the A/Y Memorandum Book, after the *Ordo Paginarum* of 1415, and preceding the second list of gilds and plays.

97 Dorrell, 'Two Studies. . .', cited in n.71 above, p. 96.

98 See above, 'The *Ordo Paginarum* of 1415'. In 1422, the proposal that the two episodes then played by the Pinners and Painters respectively should amalgamated was explicitly commended by the corporation. It is possible that similar thinking lay behind the

mentioning a penalty for delaying the procession of plays, was evidently no idle threat. In 1554 the Girdlers (no. XIX) were fined because they did not '. . . . folowe with their pageant in dewe course accordyng to thordynaunce of proclamacion thereof made, but taried an wholle hower & more in hyndrans & stoppyng of the rest of the pageantz folowyng, and to the disorderyng of the same. . . .'.[99] Recognition of the force of the Proclamation in this respect is perhaps embodied in the closing lines of play XL, where a character addresses the following remark to the audience:

> Here may we notte melle more at þis tyde
> For prossesse of plaies þat precis in plight.

Pageant-wagons

It is generally agreed that each play in the cycle was staged on, and in some cases partially around, a vehicle known at the time as a 'pageant', and here termed a pageant-wagon. The exact structure and the appearance of these vehicles are currently matters for debate. It seems that they were manhandled from station to station along the processional route. The sixteenth-century Bakers' accounts mentioned above (see 'Financial arrangements') yield a few details about the pageant-wagon used in connection with play XXVII, but most information is to be found in a series of documents relating to the vehicle (and later, the vehicles) used by the Mercers for play XLVII.[100]

An indenture of 1433 records that the Mercers had at that time a vehicle later described as their 'great pageant'. It consisted basically of a wooden platform supported on four wheels, which is likely to have borne a superstructure in the form of a box-frame, also mostly wooden. It appears that three sides of this frame were hung with painted cloth backdrops, leaving the front of the structure open to the audience. It probably resembled a small proscenium stage. Other cloths hung from stage-level to the ground, concealing the wheels from sight. The superstructure also supported machinery used to create special effects specific to the *Last Judgement*. These included some carved angels designed to 'run about in the heaven' when drawn on a cord, and a hoist for raising and lowering the actor who played God the Father. The document also mentions a hell-mouth, which may have been a feature of the wagon, or a separate piece of scenery carried along with it. In 1463 a second and probably much smaller 'pageant' is mentioned as a new addition to the Mercers' equipment for their play, but nothing is known

amalgamation of several short plays into what later became the Tilemakers' play, at much the same time; see Meredith, 'The *Ordo Paginarum* and the Development of the York Tilemakers' Pageant', cited in n.63 above, p. 69.
99 *REED: York*, p. 312.
100 For documentary references to the Mercers' pageant-wagon see *REED: York*, pp. 55–6, 95–6, 99–100, 188–9, 200, 205, 241–2. For discussions (some illustrated) see: A.F. Johnston and M. Dorrell, 'The York Mercers and their Pageant of Doomsday. . .', cited in n.87 above, and their 'The Doomsday Pageant of the York Mercers, 1433', *LSE*, NS, v (1971), pp. 29–34; P. Meredith, ' "Item for a grone – iiij d". . .', cited in n.58 above, and his 'The Development of the York Mercers' Pageant Waggon', *Medieval English Theatre*, i (1979), pp. 5–18; P. Butterworth, 'The York Mercers' Pageant Vehicle, 1433–1467: Wheels, Steering and Control', *idem*, pp. 72–81.

for certain of its appearance or its precise purpose. In 1501 it was decided to scrap the old 'great pageant', and a replacement for it was commissioned from a distinguished carver. The new vehicle was probably ready by 1507, and some scanty and obscure descriptive details of it survive from 1526.

The documentary evidence concerning the Mercers' pageant-wagons serves as a general guide to the kind of vehicles which the other gilds might have used – though the relative wealth of the gilds and the varied needs of their plays should be borne in mind. The Mercers' documents also serve as a warning that such vehicles were liable to adaptation or replacement over the years, in ways which parallel the revision or rewriting of the plays they were intended to stage.

The pageant-wagons were valuable and prestigious objects to the gilds, and care was taken to store them properly between performances of the cycle. There are a number of documents which record the existence of buildings known as 'pageant-houses', in which the wagons were laid up from year to year. Many of these buildings were in the vicinity of Toft Green (or Pageant Green), where the actors and their vehicles were required to assemble early on the morning of Corpus Christi day before proceeding in turn to the first station. Many of the places where pageant-wagons were stored were rented from the city on an annual basis.[101]

Responsibility for marshalling the pageant-wagons at Toft Green on time and for ensuring their expeditious progress from station to station rested with the master-craftsmen of the gilds.[102] The ordinances of a number of play-performing gilds contain a clause requiring the masters, or a body of them appointed for the purpose, to attend upon their pageant-wagon along the processional route. For instance, as late as 1572, the Plasterers, Tilers and Bricklayers (plays II and XIV) entered revised ordinances including the requirement 'that the Artificers of the said Craft shall goo with their pageantes throughe the Citie as other occupacions and artificers doeth'.[103] Masters who declined to perform this duty, or who failed to attend, could be liable to fines. It is difficult to say whether mere attendance on the occasion was sufficient, adding to the ceremoniousness of the performance, or whether actual work was involved, such as marshalling the crowds along the route, or help with manhandling the wagon.

Actors, 'directors', properties and costumes

What the audiences saw being performed upon the pageant-wagons, and the properties and costumes which were used, are largely matters of

101 The city officials responsible for collecting the rents were the Ouse Bridgemasters: see the extracts from their accounts from 1424–5 onwards in *REED: York*, pp. 40 *et seq*. There is also evidence for gilds sub-letting space in pageant-houses to one another. For a summary of the information on these buildings see Rogerson, 'York Corpus Christi Play: Some Practical Details', cited in n.84 above, pp. 101–3.
102 In 1484 the city chamberlains made a payment to four men for 'labouring about the settyng forward and ordoring of the Pageantes vpon Corpus christi day' (*REED: York*, p. 135), but it is not known whether people were regularly employed to attend to this matter.
103 *REED: York*, p. 370; for other examples see pp. 30, 104 and 176.

inference from the texts of the plays. The Proclamation of 1415 and the ordinance of 1476 printed above both call for actors and acting of good quality, and it appears that it was the responsibility of the pageant-masters to secure the services of competent individuals in this sphere. Such evidence as survives from the fifteenth century, and it is scanty, suggests that the 'directors' of the plays could be clerics in the hire of the pageant-masters. In 1461, the Mercers paid eighteen shillings 'to þe Klarke for playeng', and a payment of ten pence was made by the same gild 'to Wylliam Clark & his players for rehersyng' in 1467.[104] In 1449, whilst play XLVI was still the responsibility of the mayor and his bretheren, the city chamberlains paid a Robert Clerk eight shillings 'pro ludo Coronacionis beate marie virginis ex parte Maioris'.[105] In the mid-sixteenth century the Bakers' accounts often contain record of payments to an individual referred to as 'the player' (twice named as John Huntington) who evidently had responsibility for the direction of their play.[106] The sums paid to these 'clerks' and 'players' were often a quite considerable proportion of the pageant-masters' budget for the performance as a whole, and it is possible that the 'directors' were therefore paid a lump sum for their part in the production, which apparently included the hiring and payment of actors. With so little evidence available, however, it is not properly possible to estimate the degree of 'professionalism' in the direction and acting of the plays in general, but it may be significant that both the Mercers' and the Bakers' accounts, chance survivals, contain payments to non-gildsmen for such services.[107]

Documentary references to the properties and costumes used in the plays are, with one exception, also scanty. In 1446 the Girdlers received a bequest for their play (no. XIX, *The Slaughter of the Innocents*) consisting of a 'gilded brazen crown' and a 'girdle with gilded and enamelled bosses', perhaps for the use of Herod. The Bakers' accounts of a century or so later occasionally refer to properties such as certain 'diadems', and the actual Paschal Lamb mentioned in the text (XXVII 8).[108] The gilds also rented out and borrowed properties and costumes. In the 1460s the Mercers borrowed some angels' wings, and in 1561 the Goldsmiths entered an ordinance relating to the lending out of their crowns and gowns—presumably those of the Three Kings.[109]

The fullest picture of the kinds of properties and costumes which the gilds might own in relation to their plays appears in an inventory forming part of an indenture concerning the Mercers, dated 1433.[110]

---

104 *REED: York,* pp. 92, 99, and cf. pp. 96, 97.
105 Dorrell, 'The Mayor of York and the Coronation Pageant', cited in n.5 above, pp. 37–8, discusses the evidence for payments to named individuals in connection with this play. See also *REED: York,* p. 75.
106 The references have been collected by Mill, 'York Bakers' Play of the Last Supper', cited in n.87 above, pp. 148–9.
107 David Mills has observed that the York cycle has about 320 speaking parts: see his article 'Approaches to Medieval Drama', *LSE,* NS, iii (1969), p. 59.
108 *REED: York,* pp. 68, 746; Mill, 'York Bakers' Play of the Last Supper', p. 152.
109 *REED: York,* pp. 92, 95–6; 334.
110 This is the document which also includes the information about the Mercers' 'great pageant' mentioned above: see the articles by Johnston and Dorrell cited in nn. 87 and 100 above, and *REED: York,* pp. 55–6.

Included are a tunic bearing the marks of the Passion, a gilded mask and a diadem, costumes and two-faced masks for devils, costumes for good and bad souls, costumes for apostles, and trumpets and wings for angels. The Mercers' accounts from the 1460s give references to the repair and replacement of some of these items.[111] Like the pageant-wagons, the properties and costumes of the plays were carefully looked after and accounted for from year to year by the pageant-masters.

Studies of the York Plays

The following pages are intended as a brief bibliographical guide to the main developments in the study of the York Plays since the publication of Miss Toulmin Smith's edition. Full references to all the books and articles mentioned will be found in the Select Bibliography.

For bibliographies of the cycle see C. Stratman, *Bibliography of Medieval Drama*, 2 vols (2nd edn., New York, 1972), entries 4857–5184, and A.J. Mill, 'York Plays', in *A Manual of the Writings in Middle English*, ed. A. E. Hartung, vol. v (New Haven, 1975), pp. 1330–4 and 1576–80.

Language

A detailed study of the language of the York Plays remains to be made. The account given by Miss Toulmin Smith in her edition (pp. lxix–lxxiii, based on remarks supplied by Richard Morris) was supplemented by Herttrich in *Studien zu den York Plays* (1886), pp. 1–2, and by Kamann's description of the inflections in *Über Quellen und Sprache der York Plays* (1887), pp. 39–75. The language of the plays was compared with that of Yorkshire documentary souces of the period by Baumann in *Die Sprache der Urkunden aus Yorkshire im 15. Jahrhundert* (1902). See also Oakden, *Alliterative Poetry in Middle English*, i (Manchester, 1930), pp. 12–39, Trusler, *SP*, xxxiii (1936), pp. 15–39 and Cawley, *LSE*, vii–viii (1952), pp. 52–6. An unpublished dissertation containing material of value is Scroggs's *A Phonological Study of the Riming Words in the York Plays* (1959).

The dialect of the plays is Northern, with considerable Midland modifications, for which the main scribe was at least partly responsible. Variations in spelling in the main scribe's work from place to place in the manuscript show the influence of varied orthography in the underlying exemplars, the gilds' 'originals' from which the Register was compiled. The case of play III, where copies were made from the same original by both Scribe A and the main scribe, has been investigated by Dustoor, *Allahabad University Studies*, xiii (1937), pp. 23–4, showing that Scribe A preserved the Northern complexion of the language to a greater degree than the main scribe.

There are brief discussions of lexical points in the following places: Zippel, *Archiv*, cxxxiv (1916), pp. 131–2, Sundén, *Grammatical Miscellany offered to O. Jespersen*, pp. 109–11, and Whitehall, *PQ*, xviii (1939), pp. 314–16. It has not proved possible to see a copy of Hagen's unpublished dissertation *The Norse Loan-Words in the York Mystery Plays* (1900).

111 Johnston and Dorrell, 'York Mercers and their Pageant of Doomsday. . .', cited in n.87 above, pp. 20–1.

Versification

The great metrical variety of the York cycle has long been recognized as one of its most conspicuous and interesting formal characteristics. Miss Toulmin Smith gave a 'Sketch-Analysis of the Metres' in her edition (pp. li–lii), the arrangement of which has been followed here, in the table in Appendix 2. Observations on the versification in individual plays will be found in the Notes.

Study of the versification in the York Plays for many years served the purposes of distinguishing different 'levels of composition' in the cycle, and of identifying the workmanship of the various dramatists: see Hohlfeld, *Anglia*, xi (1889), p. 248, Charles Davidson, *Studies in the English Mystery Plays* (1892), chapter XII, and Gayley, *Plays of Our Forefathers* (1907), pp. 154–8. In a theory first developed by Greg in *Bibliographical and Textual Problems of the English Miracle Cycles* (1914), pp. 78–80, and later modified and elaborated by Chambers in *English Literature at the Close of the Middle Ages* (1945), pp. 29–33, three periods of literary activity were isolated on metrical grounds: a simple and dull didactic cycle dated *c.* 1350; the introduction of the work of a 'great metrist' early in the fifteenth century; and the rewriting of a number of plays in the Passion section of the cycle later in the fifteenth century by a very able dramatist, also notable as a 'realist'. It remains to be seen how far this theory will stand up to scrutiny in the light of documentary evidence about the development of the cycle, and it has already been challenged on metrical grounds by Reese in an important article, 'Alliterative Verse in the York Cycle', *SP*, xlviii (1951), pp. 639–68.

For studies of the stylistic and poetic qualities of the York verse see Wells, *JEGP*, xxxviii (1939), pp. 360–81, and Collier, *Poetry and Drama in the York Corpus Christi Play* (1978).

Early textual critics of the plays, especially Holthausen and Kölbing, offered numerous emendations on purely metrical grounds (see below, 'Editorial Procedures'). The bases upon which many of their proposals may be challenged were set out in an illuminating article by Luick, discussing the limits of normal variation in the metres: 'Zur Textkritik der Spiele von York', *Anglia*, xxii (1899), pp. 384–91.

Sources

Many of the ultimate biblical, apocryphal and legendary sources of the plays were indicated by Miss Toulmin Smith in marginal notes to her text, and in a summary in her introduction (pp. xlvii–1). Her work was immediately supplemented by Kamann's *Über Quellen und Sprache der York Plays* (1887; the section on sources also appears in *Anglia*, x (1888), pp. 189–226), and by Holthausen in *Archiv*, lxxxv (1890), pp. 425–8 and lxxxvi (1891), pp. 280–2. Remarks on the sources of individual plays will be found in the following places: play III, Dustoor, *Allahabad University Studies*, xiii (1937), pp. 29–39; plays XII–XV, Hemingway, *English Nativity Plays* (1909), pp. 262–73, Robinson, *JEGP*, lxx (1971), pp. 241–54 (play XIV); play XXXVII, Sisam, *Fourteenth Century Verse and Prose* (1921), pp. 259–61; play XLIV, Hanks, *ELN*, xiv (1976–7), pp. 5–7; play XLV, Hoffman, *MLN*, lxv (1950), pp. 236–9, Wall, *MS*, xxxii

(1970), pp. 172–92. There is also valuable information on sources of various York plays in Woolf, *The English Mystery Plays* (1972) chapters VI–XII, *passim*.

In the cases of a number of plays it is possible to show that the dramatists were familiar with earlier Middle English treatments of their source material. Use of these vernacular sources sometimes determined their selection and ordering of events, and gave rise to verbal reminiscences of the narrative texts in the plays. Plays II, X, XI: see Kalén, *A Middle English Metrical Paraphrase of the Old Testament* (1923), pp. clxxxviii–cxci, and Beadle, *YES*, xi (1981), pp. 178–87. Plays XXVII–XXXVIII: see (i) Hulme, *The Middle English Harrowing of Hell and the Gospel of Nicodemus* (1907), pp. xviii–xxi and lxvi–lxvii, and Craigie, *Furnivall Miscellany* (1901), pp. 52–61. (The issue of the indebtedness of the York Plays to the Gospel of Nicodemus became connected with the complicated debate concerning the relation between the York and Towneley cycles: see below). See (ii), Foster, *The Northern Passion* (1916), pp. 81–6, Miller, *MLN*, xxiv (1919), pp. 88–92, and Frank, *MLN*, xliv (1929), pp. 233–5.

Relation of the York and Towneley cycles

The publication of Miss Toulmin Smith's edition was followed almost immediately by a prolonged and complicated debate concerning the relationship between the York and Towneley cycles. Amongst the theories put forward were that both were descended from a lost 'parent' cycle (Davidson, *Studies in the English Mystery Plays* (1892)); that the Towneley manuscript, containing the Wakefield cycle, reflected the borrowing of the complete York cycle *c.* 1390, modified by alterations and additions in the fifteenth century (Lyle, *The Original Identity of the York and Towneley Cycles* (1919)); or that the cycles descended from a liturgical source (Cady, *SP*, xxvi (1929), pp. 386–400). The debate continued into the 1940s, and included a number of less sweeping proposals based on studies of plays or groups of plays in the two cycles, sometimes emphasizing the importance of common narrative sources. For summaries, see Everett, *YWES*, ix (1928), pp. 106–7, x (1929), pp. 134–7, and for a list of the main contributions, Mill, in *A Manual of the Writings in Middle English*, vol. v (1975), pp. 1336–7, 1579 and 1584. Summing up in 1955, Craig was inclined to return to Lyle's theory as the only satisfactory explanation of all the facts, though Chambers had firmly rejected it ten years earlier (Craig, *English Religious Drama of the Middle Ages*, pp. 214–18, Chambers, *English Literature at the Close of the Middle Ages*, p. 36). The attribution of the Towneley manuscript to Wakefield is now widely accepted. Perhaps the most straightforward explanation of its contents is the establishment of a cycle there under the influence of York during the fifteenth century, when changing economic circumstances transformed Wakefield from a relatively small settlement into a thriving wool-town. The process would appear to have involved the borrowing of several complete York plays, together wtih the composition of others by someone well acquainted with the York cycle: but insufficient evidence exists to show precisely when and how such a process might have taken place.

Editorial procedures

The spelling of the manuscript has been retained. The main scribe wrote
ȝ for both ȝ and z, and where z was intended it is so printed. Long *i* has
been printed as *j* or *J* when consonantal and *i* or *I* when vocalic. The
character used by the main scribe to represent both þ and *y* varies
considerably in the way it was formed, and may approximate to either þ
or *y* proper, irrespective of function. Usage has been regularized, and a
few doubtful cases (such as whether *þou* or *you* was intended) are
mentioned in the apparatus. Final *e* standing for earlier *i* or French *é* is
printed with an acute accent. Abbreviations have been silently ex-
panded, conventional flourishes being ignored, and any doubtful cases
referred to the apparatus. The few numerals which appear have been
left as they are, except where confusion might arise, e.g. between *I* as
numeral or pronoun. Word-division has in general been regularized
without notice, and a number of hyphenated forms have been
introduced for collocations where no modern equivalent exists, e.g.
ay-lastande (I 24), *ouer-past* (XI 306), *lang-are* (XIII 300). Punctuation and
capital letters have been introduced according to modern usage.

The Textual Notes, supplemented by the Notes on individual plays
printed after the text, have two functions. In the first place they are
intended to provide a running account of the way in which the
manuscript was compiled, as a number of facts bearing on the history
and development of the cycle are bound up with the bibliographical and
textual problems which arise. For the same reason, the Textual Notes
are also intended to provide a record of the corrections, alterations and
marginalia inserted by users of the manuscript in the medieval and
immediately post-medieval periods. As has been explained in the
Introduction (see 'Marginalia and alterations to the text by later hands'),
many of these inscriptions were added by John Clerke in the mid-sixteenth century, and where his hand is undoubtedly identifiable this is
stated. Where insufficient writing exists to form a confident judgement,
or where the script is very informal, or in most places where an erased
inscription has been recovered with the aid of ultra-violet light, the
formula 'by (a) later hand' is employed, though it should be borne in
mind that Clerke was probably responsible in a good number of these
cases as well.

The second function of the Textual Notes is to show how the text has
been established and to furnish some account of the textual criticism
which has accumulated since the publication of the *editio princeps*. All
intended departures from the readings of the manuscript are noticed in
the critical apparatus. The layout of the apparatus is on the whole
conventional, with the lemma separated from the collations and other
kinds of information by a square bracket. Unless otherwise stated in the
information which follows the square bracket, the reading shown in the
lemma is intended to be that of the manuscript. Where the present
editor disputes a reading with Miss Toulmin Smith (or another previous
editor) the lemma is followed by 'This ed', and the contrasting reading,
e.g. thoghte] *This ed; TS* + thoghts (I 19), where the + indicates that later
editors have followed or accepted the reading of the *editio princeps*.
Where a reading of Miss Toulmin Smith's has already been disputed,

and the proposed alternative reading is accepted in the present edition, the lemma is followed by an abbreviated form of the proposer's name, and the contrasting reading given by Miss Toulmin Smith and any other editors, e.g. es] *P; TS, Ca* so (I 9). Where an emendation has been printed in the text instead of a manuscript reading, the lemma shows the emendation, followed by an abbreviated form of the name of its proposer, the manuscript reading, Miss Toulmin Smith's reading, and any other proposals which seem to merit consideration, e.g. mene] *TS; MS* meve (XXVI 216), þer þe bowe] *D²; MS, TS* þer bowe þer (VIII 110), bringe thiding] *Ho¹, Ca; MS, TS* bringe thidings, *M* tidingis bringe (XXXVIII 29). Emendations proposed by the present editor are signified by 'This ed', followed by the manuscript reading and its treatment by previous editors, e.g. bedward] *This ed; MS, TS* bodword (XXXI 34). *Conj* signifies 'conjectured by' and *(conj)* 'conjecturally'. *Conj* is used where Miss Toulmin Smith or another editor proposed an emendation in a footnote or elsewhere but did not incorporate it in the text, e.g. neȝe] *Conj TS; MS* nere (XXV 415). Where she or another editor incorporated an emendation in the text, removing the manuscript reading to a footnote, and that manuscript reading is restored in the present edition, *(conj)* is used, e.g. For] *This ed; TS* Fro *(conj)* (II 142). *Om* and *suppl* signify 'omitted by' or 'omits' and 'supplied by' or 'supplies' respectively, according to context. *SD* stands for 'stage-direction'; and *u-v* for 'ultra-violet light'. A + after a line-number in the apparatus is used to indicate a feature in the manuscript (often a stage-direction) occurring between that line and the next. When the number of the last line of a play is followed by a +, the features referred to appear between the end of that play and the beginning of the next. A minus-sign after a line-number (usually a first line) indicates that a special feature of the manuscript precedes that line. Many of the character-designations in the manuscript involve the use of numerals, which were usually given in roman form (j^{us}, ij^{us}) or occasionally written out (Primus, Secundus). In the text printed below, all are rendered in upper-case roman numerals (I, II) irrespective of how they appear in the manuscript.

The following abbreviations are used in the Textual Notes:

Manuscripts

MS   London, British Library, MS Additional 35290. (In the apparatus to play III, *A* signifies the copy made by Scribe A, and *B* the copy in the hand of Scribe B; see the Note on play III).

Sy   York, Yorkshire Museum, Sykes MS, as printed by A.C. Cawley, 'The Sykes Manuscript of the York Scriveners' Play', *LSE*, vii–viii (1952), pp. 45–80 (text, pp. 74–80) (play XLI).

T   San Marino, USA, Huntington Library HM 1, as printed by G. England and A.W. Pollard, *The Towneley Plays*, EETS, ES, LXXI (1897) (Towneley texts related to plays XI, XX, XXXVII, XXXVIII, XLVII; see the Notes).

Textual criticism

Co   H.E. Coblentz, 'Some Suggested Rhyme Emendations to the York Plays', *MLN*, x (1895), pp. 77–81.

D^1 P. E. Dustoor, 'Some Textual Notes on the English Mystery Plays', *MLR*, xxi (1926), pp. 427–8.

D^2 P.E. Dustoor, 'Textual Notes on the York Old Testament Plays', *Anglia*, lii (1928), pp. 26–36.

Gr^1 W.W. Greg, *Bibliographical and Textual Problems of the English Miracle Cycles* (London, 1914), pp. 93–100 (discussion of play XX).

Ha   J. Hall, review of *TS*, *EStn*, ix (1886), pp. 448–53.

He   O. Herttrich, *Studien zu den York Plays* (Breslau, 1886), pp. 20–31.

Ho^1 F. Holthausen, 'Beiträge zur Erklärung und Textkritik der York Plays', *Archiv*, lxxxv (1890), pp. 411–28.

Ho^2 F. Holthausen, 'Zur Textkritik der York Plays', *Philologische Studien: Festgabe für E. Sievers* (Halle, 1896), pp. 30–7.

Ho^3 F. Holthausen, 'Zu Alt- und Mittelenglischen Dichtungen: No. 57, York Plays', *Anglia*, xxi (1899), pp. 433–52.

Ho^4 F. Holthausen, 'Zur Erklärung und Textkritik der York Plays', *EStn*, xli (1909–10), pp. 380–4.

K   E. Kölbing, 'Beiträge zur Erklärung und Textkritik der York Plays', *EStn*, xx (1895), pp. 179–220.

Zu   J. Zupitza, review of *TS*, *Deutsche Literaturzeitung*, xxxvii (1885), pp. 1304–6.

The apparatus embodies a selection only, not a full display of all the very numerous proposals put forward by the foregoing commentators. Many of the emendations proposed by Holthausen and Kölbing, in particular, were made on purely metrical grounds, and are generally unacceptable; see K. Luick, 'Zur Textkritik der Spiele von York', *Anglia*, xxii (1899), pp. 384–91.

Editions

Of the editions consulted, the following have contributed to the establishment of the text, either through independent authority derived from the manuscript (*TS, P, BrZi, Si, G^2, D^3, Be*) or by virtue of embodying textual criticism (*Ma, Hm, Ca*):

Be   D.M. Bevington, *Medieval Drama* (Boston, 1975) (plays V, XV, XVIII, XXXV, XXXVI).

BrZi   A. Brandl and O. Zippel, *Mittelenglische Sprach und Literaturproben* (2nd edn, Berlin, 1927) (plays XIV, XV).

Ca   A.C. Cawley, *Everyman and Medieval Miracle Plays* (revised edn, London, 1974) (plays I, III, V, XXXV, XXXVIII, XLVII).

D^3 P.E. Dustoor, 'The York "Creation of Adam and Eve" ', *Allahabad University Studies*, xiii (1937), pp. 23–39 (play IIIA).

Gr^2 W.W. Greg, ' "Christ and the Doctors" and the York Play', *The Trial and Flagellation with Other Studies in the Chester Cycle* (Malone Society Studies, Oxford, 1935) (parts of play XX).

Hm   S.B. Hemingway, *English Nativity Plays* (New York, 1909) (plays XII–XV).

Ma   J.M. Manly, *Specimens of Pre-Shakespearean Drama* (New York, 1897–8) (plays XXXVIII, XLVII)

P   A.W. Pollard, *English Miracle Plays, Moralities and Interludes* (8th edn, Oxford, 1927) (play I).

Si Sisam, *Fourteenth Century Verse and Prose* (Oxford, 1921) (play XXXVII).

TS L. Toulmin Smith, *York Plays: The Plays Performed by the Crafts or Mysteries of York on the Day of Corpus Christi* etc. (Oxford, 1885).

The York Plays

I The Barkers

The Fall of the Angels

Deus
Ego sum Alpha et O: vita, via, veritas, primus et nouissimus.   f.1

I am gracyus and grete, God withoutyn begynnyng,
  I am maker vnmade, all mighte es in me;
I am lyfe and way vnto welth-wynnyng,
  I am formaste and fyrste, als I byd sall it be.
    My blyssyng o ble sall be blendyng,   5
      And heldand, fro harme to be hydande,
      My body in blys ay abydande,
    Vnendande, withoutyn any endyng.

Sen I am maker vnmade and most es of mighte,
  And ay sall be endeles and noghte es but I,   10
Vnto my dygnyté dere sall diewly be dyghte
  A place full of plenté to my plesyng at ply;
    And therewith als wyll I haue wroght
      Many dyuers doynges bedene,
      Whilke warke sall mekely contene,   15
    And all sall be made euen of noghte.

But onely þe worthely warke of my wyll
  In my sprete sall enspyre þe mighte of me;
And in þe fyrste, faythely, my thoughte to fullfyll,
  Baynely in my blyssyng I byd at here be   20
    A blys al-beledande abowte me,
      In þe whilke blys I byde at be here
      Nyen ordres of aungels full clere,
    In louyng ay-lastande at lowte me.

Tunc cantant angeli, 'Te deum laudamus, te dominum confitemur'.

Here vndernethe me nowe a nexile I neuen,   25
  Whilke ile sall be erthe. Now all be at ones

1 – *First quire (unsigned) begins*
    Deus] *Suppl* TS+
5. My blyssyng o ble] *Ha, Ca* O blyssyng my ble
6. hydande] *TS+; MS* hyndande
8. Vnendande] *TS+; MS* Vne dande
9. es] *P; TS, Ca* so
19. thoghte] *This ed;* TS+ thoghts
24+ *SD (in red) partially illegible;* -eli . . . laudamus te domin- *suppl* TS+

49

Erthe haly, and helle, þis hegheste be heuen,   f.1ᵛ
  And that welth sall welde sall won in þis wones.
    This graunte I ȝowe, mynysters myne,
      To-whils ȝhe ar stabill in thoghte —   30
      And also to þaime þat ar noghte
    Be put to my presone at pyne.

Of all þe mightes I haue made, moste nexte after me
  I make þe als master and merour of my mighte;
I beelde þe here baynely in blys for to be,   35
  I name þe for Lucifer, als berar of lyghte.
    Nothyng here sall þe be derand;
      In þis blis sall be ȝhour beeldyng,
      And haue all welth in ȝoure weledyng,
    Ay-whils ȝhe ar buxumly berande.   40

Tunc cantant angeli, 'Sanctus, sanctus, sanctus, dominus deus sabaoth'.

I Angelus, Seraphyn
A, mercyfull maker, full mekill es þi mighte,
  Þat all this warke at a worde worthely has wroghte.
Ay loued be þat lufly lorde of his lighte,
  That vs thus mighty has made þat nowe was righte noghte,
    In blys for to byde in his blyssyng.   45
      Ay-lastande in luf lat vs lowte hym,
      At beelde vs thus baynely abowete hym,
    Of myrthe neuermore to haue myssyng.

I Angelus Deficiens, Lucifer
All the myrth þat es made es markide in me!
  Þe bemes of my brighthode ar byrnande so bryghte,   50
And I so semely in syghte myselfe now I se,
  For lyke a lorde am I lefte to lende in þis lighte.   f.2
    More fayrear be far þan my feres,
      In me is no poynte þat may payre;
      I fele me fetys and fayre,   55
    My powar es passande my peres.

Angelus Cherabyn
Lorde, with a lastande luf we loue þe allone,
  Þou mightefull maker þat markid vs and made vs,
And wroghte us thus worthely to wone in this wone,
  Ther neuer felyng of fylth may full vs nor fade vs.   60
    All blys es here beeldande aboute vs;

   28. welth] *TS+; MS* wethth
   34. merour] *TS+; MS* morour
   39. welth] l *interlined*
   40+ *SD in red*
   42. a] *interlined*
   59. wone²]*TS+; MS* won+us *contraction*

To-whyls we are stabyll in thoughte
In þe worschipp of hym þat us wroght,
Of dere neuer thar vs more dowte vs.

II Angelus Deficiens
O, what I am fetys and fayre and fygured full fytt!   65
Þe forme of all fayrehede apon me es feste,
All welth in my weelde es, I wote be my wytte;
Þe bemes of my brighthede are bygged with þe beste.
My schewyng es schemerande and schynande,
So bygly to blys am I broghte;   70
Me nedes for to noy me righte noghte,
Here sall neuer payne me be pynande.

Angelus Seraphyn
With all þe wytt at we welde we woyrschip þi wyll,
Þou gloryus God þat es grunde of all grace;
Ay with stedefaste steuen lat vs stande styll,   75
Lorde, to be fede with þe fode of thi fayre face.
In lyfe that es lely ay-lastande,
Thi dale, lorde, es ay daynetethly delande,   f.2ᵛ
And whoso þat fode may be felande –
To se thi fayre face – es noght fastande.   80

I Angelus Deficiens, Lucifer
Owe, certes, what I am worthely wroghte with wyrschip, iwys!
For in a glorius gle my gleteryng it glemes;
I am so mightyly made my mirth may noghte mys –
Ay sall I byde in this blys thorowe brightnes of bemes.
Me nedes noghte of noy for to neuen,   85
All welth in my welde haue I weledande;
Abowne ʒhit sall I be beeldand,
On heghte in þe hyeste of hewuen.

Ther sall I set myselfe full semely to seyghte,
To ressayue my reuerence thorowe righte o renowne;   90
I sall be lyke vnto hym þat es hyeste on heghte.
Owe, what I am derworth and defte – Owe! Dewes! All goes downe!
My mighte and my mayne es all marrande –
Helpe, felawes! In faythe I am fallande.
II Angelus Deficiens
Fra heuen are we heledande on all hande,   95
To wo are we weendande, I warande.

65.   *II Angelus Deficiens*] *So MS; TS + I Angelus . . . Lucifer*
67.   es, I] *MS* w *between*
92.   *Lineation TS;* Owe! Dewes! . . . downe *separate line in MS*

Lucifer, Deiabolus in inferno
Owte! Owte! Harrowe! Helples, slyke hote at es here;
  This es a dongon of dole þat I am to dyghte.
Whare es my kynde become, so cumly and clere?
  Nowe am I laytheste, allas, þat are was lighte.   100
     My bryghtnes es blakkeste and blo nowe,
      My bale es ay betande and brynande –
     That gares ane go gowlande and gyrnande.
    Owte! Ay walaway! I well euen in wo nowe.

II Diabilus
Owte! Owte! I go wode for wo, my wytte es all wente nowe,   f.3
  All oure fode es but filth we fynde vs beforn.   106
We þat ware beelded in blys, in bale are we brent nowe –
    Owte on þe Lucifer, lurdan, oure lyghte has þou lorne.
     Þi dedes to þis dole nowe has dyghte us,
      To spill vs þou was oure spedar,   110
      For thow was oure lyghte and oure ledar,
     Þe hegheste of heuen hade þou hyght vs.

Lucifer in inferno
Walaway! Wa es me now, nowe es it war thane it was.
  Vnthryuandely threpe ȝhe – I sayde but a thoghte.
II Diabolus
We, lurdane, þou lost vs.
Lucifer in inferno
                 ȝhe ly! Owte, allas!   115
  I wyste noghte þis wo sculde be wroghte.
    Owte on ȝhow, lurdans, ȝhe smore me in smoke.
II Diabolus
    This wo has þou wroghte vs.
Lucifer in inferno
                   ȝhe ly, ȝhe ly!
II Diabolus
    Thou lyes, and þat sall þou by:
    We, lurdane, haue at ȝowe, lat loke!   120

Angelus Cherubyn
A, lorde, louid be thi name þat vs þis lyghte lente,
  Sen Lucifer oure ledar es lighted so lawe,
For hys vnbuxumnes in bale to be brente –
    Thi rightewysnes to rewarde on rowe
     Ilke warke eftyr is wroghte –   125
      Thorowe grace of þi mercyfull myghte
      The cause I se itt in syghte,
     Wharefore to bale he es broghte.   f.3ᵛ

---

  104.   euen] *This ed; TS* enew; *P* even
  115–16.   *Lineation TS+;* ȝhe . . . wroghte *one line in MS*
  120.   lurdane] *D², Ca; MS, TS, P* lurdans

Deus

Those foles for þaire fayrehede in fantasyes fell,
  And hade mayne of mi mighte þat marked þam and made þam.   130
Forthi efter þaire warkes were, in wo sall þai well,
  For sum ar fallen into fylthe þat euermore sall fade þam,
    And neuer sall haue grace for to gyrth þam.
      So passande of power tham thoght þam,
      Thai wolde noght me worschip þat wroghte þam;   135
    Forþi sall my wreth euer go with þam.

Ande all that me wyrschippe sall wone here, iwys;
  Forthi more forthe of my warke, wyrke nowe I will.
Syn than þer mighte es for-marryde þat mente all omys,
  Euen to myne awne fygure þis blys to fulfyll,   140
    Mankynde of moulde will I make.
      But fyrste wille I fourme hym before
      All thyng that sall hym restore,
    To whilke þat his talente will take.

Ande in my fyrste makyng, to mustyr my mighte,   145
  Sen erthe es vayne and voyde and myrknes emel,
I byd in my blyssyng ȝhe aungels gyf lyghte
  To þe erthe, for it faded when þe fendes fell.
    In hell sall neuer myrknes by myssande,
      Þe myrknes thus name I for nighte;   150
      The day, þat call I this lyghte –
    My after-warkes sall þai by wyssande.

Ande nowe in my blyssyng I twyne tham in two,
  The nighte euen fro þe day, so þat thai mete neuer,
But ather in a kynde courese þaire gates for to go.   155
  Bothe þe nighte and þe day, does dewly ȝhour deyuer,   f.4
    To all I sall wirke be ȝhe wysshyng.
      This day warke es done ilke a dele,
      And all þis warke lykes me ryght wele,
    And baynely I gyf it my blyssyng.   160

Explicit.

129. *Deus] Added by a later hand; MS has also* ihc *in another later hand*
130. mi mighte] *This ed; MS* migh mighte, *TS+* mighte
144. talente] *This ed; TS+* talents
145. *Ruled off from 144 in error;* Deus *repeated to right in a later hand*
160+ *After* Explicit, *rest of f.4 blank except for offsets from f.3ᵛ and 1583 in a later hand*

II The Plasterers

The Creation

Deus   *In altissimis habito,*   f.4^v
      In the heghest heuyn my hame haue I;
     Eterne mentis et ego,
      Withoutyn ende ay-lastandly.

     Sen I haue wroght þire worldys wyde,   5
      Heuyn and ayre and erthe also,
     My hegh Godhede I will noght hyde
      All-yf sume foles be fallyn me fro.
     When þai assent with syn of pride
      Vp for to trine my trone vnto,   10
     In heuyn þai myght no lengger byde
      But wyghtly went to wone in wo;
       And sen þai wrange haue wroght
     My lyk ys to lat þam go,
       To suffir sorowe onsoght,   15
     Syne þai haue seruid so.

     Þare mys may neuer be amende
      Sen þai asent me to forsake,
     For all þere force non sall þame fende
      For to be fendys foule and blake.   20
     And þo þat lykys with me to lende,
      And trewly tent to me will take,
     Sall wonne in welth withoutyn ende
      And allway wynly with me wake;
       Þai sall haue for þare sele   25
     Solace þat neuer sall sclake.
       Þis warke me thynkys full wele
     And more now will I make.

     Syne þat þis world es ordand euyn,
      Furth well I publysch my power: 30
     Noght by my strenkyth, but by my steuyn
      A firmament I byd apere,
     Emange þe waterris, lyght so leuyn,
      Þere cursis lely for to lere,

---

   1. *Deus*] *Added to right of 4 and left of 5 by J. Clerke*
       altissimis] *i²* interlined
  11. lengger] *TS; MS* legger
  14. lyk ys] *This ed; MS* lykys, *TS* likes
  17. amende] *Co, D²; MS, TS* amendid

And þat same sall be namyd hewuyn, 35
   With planitys and with clowdis clere.
     Þe water I will be sent
   To flowe bothe fare and nere,
     And þan þe firmament
   In mydis to set þame sere. 40

Þe firmament sal nough moue,
   But be a mene, þus will I mene,
Ouir all þe worlde to halde and houe,
   And be þo tow wateris betwyne.
Vndir þe heuyn and als aboue 45
   Þe wateris serly sall be sene,
And so I wille my post proue
   By creaturis of kyndis clene.
     Þis warke his to my pay
   Righit will, withoutyn wyne; 50
     Þus sese þe secunde day
   Of my doyingys bydene.

Moo sutyll werkys assesay I sall,
   For to be set in seruice sere:
All þe wateris grete and smalle 55
   Þat vndir heuyne er ordande here, f.5
Gose togedir and holde yow all,
   And be a flode festynde in fere,
So þat the erthe, both downe and dale,
   In drynesch playnly may apere. 60
     Þe drynes 'lande' sall be
   Namyd bothe ferre and nere,
     And þen I name þe 'se',
   Geddryng of wateris clere.

Þe erthe sall fostyr and furthe bryng 65
   Buxsumly, as I wyle byde,
Erbys and also othyr thyng,
   Well for to wax and worthe to wede;
Treys also þaron sall spryng
   With braunchis and with bowis on brede, 70
With flouris fayr on heght to hyng
   And fruth also to fylle and fede.
     And þane I will þat þay
   Of þemselfe haue þe sede

---

37. sent] *He, Co; MS, TS* set
41. nough] *This ed; TS* nough[t]
44. þo] *This ed; MS* þ *or* y +°, *TS* you
49. his] *This ed; TS* is *(conj)*
50. will] *This ed; TS* well *(conj)*
69. þaron sall] also, *deleted, between*
71. hyng] y *superimposed on another letter*

And mater, þat þay may   75
Be lastande furth in lede.

And all þer materis es in mynde
For to be made of mekyl might,
And to be kest in dyueris kynde
So for to bere sere burgvns bright.   80
And when þer frutys is fully fynde
And fayrest semande vnto syght,
Þane þe wedris wete and wynde
Oway I will it wende full wyght;
And of þere sede full sone   85
New rotys sall ryse vpright.
Þe third day þus is done,
Þire dedis er dewly dyght.

Now sene þe erthe þus ordand es,
Mesurid and made by myn assent —   90
Grathely for to growe with gres
And wedis þat sone away bese went —
Of my gudnes now will I ges,
So þat my werkis no harmes hent,
Two lyghtis, one more and one lesse,   95
To be fest in þe firmament.
The more light to the day
Fully suthely sall be sent,
Þe lesse lyght allway
To þe nyght sall take entent.   100

Þir figuris fayre þat furth er fun
Þus on sere sydys serue þai sall:
The more lyght sall be namid þe son,
Dymnes to wast be downe and be dale.
Erbis and treys þat er bygune   105
All sall he gouerne, gret and smale;
With cald yf þai be closid or bun
Thurgh hete of þe sun þai sal be hale.
Als þei haue honours   f.5ᵛ
In alkyn welth to wale,   110
So sall my creaturis
Euir byde withoutyn bale.

Þe son and þe mone on fayre manere
Now grathly gange in ȝour degré,

 77.   materis] wateris *written first, deleted*
 95.   Two] *TS; MS* Towo
101.   furth er fun] *Ho', D²; MS* further f *or* s + um; *TS* further sun
103.   son] *TS; MS* som
109.   þei] *This ed; MS, TS* ye I

Als ye haue tane ʒoure curses clere   115
  To serue furth loke ye be fre,
For ye sall set þe sesons sere,
  Kyndely to knowe in ilke cuntré,
Day fro day and yere fro yere
  By sertayne signes suthly to se. *truly*   120
    Þe heuyn sall be ouerhyld
  With sternys to stand plenté.
    Þe furth day his fulfillid,
  Þis werke well lykys me.

Now sen þir werkis er wroght with wyne   125
  And fundyn furth be firth and fell,
Þe see now will I set within
  Whallis whikly for to dewell,
And othir fysch to flet with fyne —
  Sum with skale and sum with skell,   130
Of diueris materis more and myn —
  In sere maner to make and mell;
    Sum sall be milde and meke,
  And sum both fers and fell.
    Þis world þus wil I eke,   135
  Syn I am witt of well.

Also vp in þe ayre on hyght
  I byd now þat þore be ordande
For to be foulis fayre and bright,
  Dewly in þare degré dewlland,   140
With fedrys fayre to frast þer flight
  For stede to stede where þai will stande,
And also leythly for to lyght
  Whoreso þam lykis in ilke a londe.
    Þane fysch and foulis sere,   145
  Kyndely I ʒow commande
    To meng on ʒoure manere,
  Both be se and sande.

Þis materis more ʒitt will I mende,
  So for to fulfill my forþoght,   150
With diueris bestis in lande to lende
  To brede and be with balé furth brught.
And with bestis I wille be blende
  Serpentis to be sene vnsoght,

---

117. sall set] *TS; MS* sall ye set
133. milde and meke] *TS; MS* meke and milde
136. ? *read* Syn I of witt am well
140. dewlland] *This ed; TS* dwelland *(conj)*
142. For] *This ed; TS* Fro *(conj)*
147. manere] *This ed; MS* manen*er*, *TS* mannere *(conj)*
150. forþoght] *This ed; MS* for þoght, thoght *interlined by J. Clerke. TS* for-thoght

And wormis vpon þaire wombis sall wende   155
   To won in erth and worth to noght.
     And so it sall be kende
   How all þat eme is ought,
     Begynnyng, mydes and ende
I with my worde hase wrothe.   160

For als I byde bus all thyng be
   And dewly done als I will dresse,
Now bestys ar sett in sere degré
   On molde to moue, both more and lesse;
Þane foulis in ayre and fische in see   f.6
   And bestis on erthe of bone and flesch,   166
I byde ȝe wax furth fayre plenté
   And grathly growes, als I ȝow gesse.
     So multiply ȝe sall
Ay furth in fayre processe,   170
   My blyssyng haue ȝe all;
The fift day endyd es.

III The Cardmakers

The Creation of Adam and Eve

Deus   In heuyn and erthe duly bedene   f.6ᵛ
   Of v days werke, euyn onto ende,
I haue complete by curssis clene;
   Methynke þe space of þame well spende.

In heuyn er angels fayre and brighte,   5
   Sternes and planetis þer curssis to ga,
Þe mone seruis onto þe nyght
   The son to lyghte þe day alswa.

In erthe is treys and gres to springe,
   Bestis and foulys, bothe gret and smalle,   10

---

156. won] *Zu; MS, TS* wo
171. ȝe] *Interlined*
172+ finis *added by J. Clerke. Rest of f.6 blank*

  2. onto ende] *B* vnto þe ende
  6. þer] *B* þe

Fyschis in flode, all othyr thyng
  Thryffe and haue my blyssyng all.

Thys werke is wroght now at my will,
  But ȝet can I here no best see
Þat acordys be kynde and skyll,   15
  And for my werke myght worschippe me.

For perfytt werke ne ware it nane
  But ought ware made þat myght it ȝeme,
For loue mad I þis warlde alane,
  Þerfor my loffe sall in it seme.   20

To kepe þis warlde, bothe mare and lesse,
  A skylfull best þane will I make
Eftyr my schape and my lyknes,
  The wilke sall worschipe to me take.

Off þe symplest part of erthe þat is here   25
  I sall make man, and for þis skylle:
For to abate hys hauttande chere,
  Bothe his gret pride and oþer ille;

And also for to haue in mynde   f.7
  How simpyll he is at hys makyng,   30
For als febyll I sall hym fynde
  Qwen he is dede at his endyng.

For þis reson and skyll alane
  I sall make man lyke onto me.
Ryse vp, þou erthe, in blode and bane,   35
  In schape of man, I commaunde þe.

A female sall þou haue to fere,
  Her sall I make of þi lyft rybe,
Alane so sall þou nough be here
  Withoutyn faythcfull frende and sybe.   40

Takys now here þe gast of lyffe
  And ressayue both ȝoure saules of me;

14. here] *B, so D³; A om*
15. kynde and skyll] *B* kyndly skylle
21. mare] *o interlined over a by a later hand*
22. best] wyght *interlined by J. Clerke*
24. me] *B, so D³; A* my
27. hauttande] *B* haunttande
31. hym fynde] *B, so D³; A* fynde hym
39. nough] *B* nought, *so D³*

    Þis femall take þou to þi wyffe,
      Adam and Eue ȝour names sall be.

Adam   A, lorde, full mekyll is þi mighte   45
      And þat is sene in ilke a syde,
    For now his here a ioyful syght
      To se þis worlde so lange and wyde.

    Mony diueris thyngis now here es,
      Off bestis and foulis bathe wylde and tame;   50
    Ȝet is nan made to þi liknes
      But we alone – A, louyd by þi name.

Eue   To swylke a lorde in all degré
      Be euirmore lastande louynge,
    Þat tyll vs swylke a dyngnité   55
      Has gyffyne before all othyr thynge;

    And selcouth thyngis may we se here
      Of þis ilke warld so lange and brade,
    With bestis and fowlis so many and sere;   f.7ᵛ
      Blessid be he þat hase us made.   60

Adam   A, blyssid lorde, now at þi wille
      Syne we er wroght, wochesaff to telle
    And also say vs two vntyll
      Qwate we sall do and whare to dewell?

Deus   For þis skyl made I ȝow þis day,   65
      My name to worschip ay-whare;
    Louys me, forþi, and louys me ay
      For my makyng, I axke no mare.

    Bothe wys and witty sall þou be,
      Als man þat I haue made of noght;   70
    Lordschipe in erthe þan graunt I þe,
      All thynge to serue þe þat I haue wroght.

---

43. þis] *B so D³; A* The
44. *Marginal additions to right by J. Clerke, at different times:* Caret And leyd your lyves
    in good degree etc *(2nd addition)* / Adam here name I the etc and Eve etc *(1st*
    addition) / her name shall be and be / thy subgett right *(2nd addition). To left of*
    B44ff. (f.9ᵛ), also Clerke's hand: And leyd your lyves in good degré / Adam here
    make I the a man / of mykyll myght / This same shall thy subget be / And Eve
    her name shall hight
47. his] *B* is, *so D³*
51. þi] *B, so D³; A* þe
52. by] *B* be, *so D³*
53. all degré] *B, so D³; A* all þe degré
60. hase] *B, so D³; om A*
72. I haue] *B* is

In paradyse sall ʒe same wone,
    Of erthely thyng get ʒe no nede,
Ille and gude both sall ʒe kone,   75
    I sall ʒou lerne ʒoure lyue to lede.

Adam   A, lorde, sene we sall do no thyng
    But louffe þe for þi gret gudnesse,
We sall ay bay to þi biddyng
    And fulfyll it, both more and less.   80

Eue   His syng sene he has on vs sett
    Beforne all othir thyng certayne,
Hym for to loue we sall noght lett
    And worschip hym with myght and and mayne.

Deus   At heuyne and erth first I begane   85
    And vj days wroght or I walde ryst;
My warke is endyde now at mane,   f.8
    All lykes me will, but þis is best.

My blyssyng haue þai euer and ay.
    The seueynt day sall my restyng be,   90
Þus wille I sese, sothely to say,
    Of my doying in þis degré.

To blys I sall ʒow bryng,
    Comys forth, ʒe tow, with me;
Ʒe sall lyffe in lykyng—   95
    My blyssyng with ʒow be. Amen.

75. ʒe kone] *Unidentifiable character between*
79. ay bay] *B* a bey, *D³* ay bey
    biddyng] *B* gudnesse to þi biddyng
81. sene] *D³; A* sone; *B* sone, *TS*+ sen
82. othir] *B, so D³; A* oþithir
83. Hym] *B, so D³; A* Hem
85. Deus] *Added by a later hand in A; by main scribe in B*
86. ryst] *B* reste, *so D³*
88. will] *B* wele, *D³* well
    is] *B* þe
96. Amen] *In red in both A and B*
96+ *In A, faint and partially erased, in a later hand:* nota caret Adam and Eve this
    is . . . /that I haue grant you of my grace/to haue your . . . ; *rest of f.8 and f.8ᵛ*
    blank. In B (f.10), Clerke's hand: The Fullers pagyant / Adam and Eve this is the
    place—Deus

IV The Fullers

Adam and Eve in Eden

Deus   Adam and Eve, this is the place   f.10ᵛ
        That I haue graunte you of my grace
           To haue your wonnyng in.
        Erbes, spyce, frute on tree,
        Beastes, fewles, all that ye see   5
           Shall bowe to you, more and myn.
             This place hight paradyce,
           Here shall your joys begynne;
             And yf that ye be wyse,
        Frome thys tharr ye never twyn.   10

        All your wyll here shall ye haue,
        Lykyng for to eate or sayff
           Fyshe, fewle or fee;
        And for to take at your owen wyll
        All other creatours also theretyll,   15
           Your suggettes shall they bee.
             Adam, of more and lesse,
           Lordeship in erthe here graunte I the;
             Thys place that worthy is,
           Kepe it in honestye.   20

        Looke that ye ʒem ytt wetterly;
        All other creatours shall multeply,
           Ylke one in tender hower.
  ✠   Looke that ye bothe saue and sett
        Erbes and treys; for nothyng lett,   25
           So that ye may endower
             To susteyn beast and man,
            And fewll of ylke stature.
             Dwell here yf that ye cann,
         This shall be your endowre.   30

Adam   O lorde, lovyd be thy name,
        For nowe is this a joyfull hame
           That thowe hais brought vs to,
        Full of myrthe and solys faughe,
        Erbes and trees, frute on haugh,   35

---

12. Lykyng] *This ed; TS* Lyvyng
34. faughe] *MS long* s *or* f + aughe; *TS* saughe
35. on haugh] *This ed; MS, TS* on to haugh

Wyth spysys many one hoo.
 Loo, Eve, nowe ar we brought   f.11
Bothe vnto rest and rowe,
 We neyd to tayke no thought,
But loke ay well to doo.   40

Eve   Lovyng be ay to suche a lord,
To vs hais geven so great reward
 To governe bothe great and small,
And mayd vs after his owen read,
[. . .   . . .]
 Emonges these myrthes all.   45
 Here is a joyfull sight
Where that wee wonn in shall;
 We love the, mooste of myght,
Great God, that we on call.

Deus   Love my name with good entent   50
And harken to my comaundement,
 And do my byddyng buxomly:
Of all the frute in parradyce,
Tayke ye therof of your best wyse
 And mayke you right merry.   55
 The tree of good and yll,
What tyme you eates of thys
 Thowe speydes thyself to spyll,
And we brought owte of blysse.

All thynges is mayd, man, for thy prowe,   60
All creatours shall to the bowe
 That here is mayd erthly;
In erthe I mayke the lord of all,
And beast vnto the shall be thrall,
 Thy kynd shall multeply.   65
 Therefore this tree alone,
Adam, this owte-take I;
 Thc frutc of it negh none,
For an ye do, then shall ye dye.

Adam   Alas lorde, that we shuld do so yll,   f.11ᵛ
Thy blyssed byddyng we shall fulfyll   71
 Bothe in thought and deyd;
We shall no negh thys tre nor the bugh,
Nor yit the fruyte that thereon groweth
 Therewith oure fleshe to feyd.   75

40.   ay] *Conj TS; MS* a
44 +   *Line missing; no gap in MS*
73.   bugh] *He* bowes
74.   groweth] *He* growes

Eve	We shall do thy byddyng,
	We haue none other neyd;
	Thys frute full styll shall hyng,
	Lorde, that thowe hays forbyd.

Deus	Looke that ye doe as ye haue sayd,	80
	Of all that there is hold you apayd,	
	For here is welthe at wyll.	
	Thys tre that beres the fruyte of lyfe,	
	Luke nother thowe nor Eve thy wyf	
	Lay ye no handes theretyll.	85
	For-why it is knowyng	
	Bothe of good and yll,	
	This frute but ye lett hyng	
	Ye speyd yourself to spyll.	

Forthy this tree that I owt-tayke,	90
Nowe kepe it grathly for my sayke,	
That nothyng negh it neyre;	
All other at your wyll shall be,	
I owte-take nothyng but this tree,	
To feyd you with in feare.	95
Here shall ye leyd your lyffe	
With dayntys that is deare;	
Adam, and Eve thy wyfe,	
My blyssyng haue ye here.	

V The Coopers
The Fall of Man

Satanas incipit dicens: f.13ᵛ

For woo my witte es in a were
   That moffes me mykill in my mynde;
The Godhede þat I sawe so cleere,

86.   *Lineation Ho'; For-why to right of 84–5*, it is knowying *preceding 87 in MS. TS conj*
For-why [do my byddyng,] / It is knowen . . .
knowyng] *Ho'; MS, TS* knowen
90.   *Lineation TS;* Forthy *to right of 88–9 in MS*
99+   Fynys *in red; f.12 blank except for* The Fullers, *main scribe; ff.12ᵛ, 13 blank*

   1 –   *SD in same script and inking as dialogue; and so at* 79+, 82+, 105+
   1.   Diabolus *to left in hand of J. Clerke*

And parsayued þat he shuld take kynde
 Of a degree   5
That he had wrought, and I dedyned
 Þat aungell kynde shuld it noȝt be;
  And we wer faire and bright,
 Þerfore me thoght þat he
  The kynde of vs tane myght,   10
 And þerat dedyned me.

The kynde of man he thoght to take
 And theratt hadde I grete envye,
But he has made to hym a make,
 And harde to her I wol me hye   15
  That redy way,
 That purposc proue to putte it by,
  And fande to pike fro hym þat pray.
   My trauayle were wele sette
  Myght Y hym so betraye,   20
   His likyng for to lette,
  And sone I schalle assaye.

In a worme liknes wille Y wende,
 And founde to feyne a lowde lesynge.
Eue, Eue.

Eue   Wha es þare?
Satanas   I, a frende.   25
 And for thy gude es þe comynge
 I hydir sought.
 Of all þe fruyt that ye se hynge
  In paradise, why ete ye noght?
Eua   We may of tham ilkane   30
 Take al þat vs goode þought,
  Save a tree outt is tane,
 Wolde do harme to neyghe it ought.

Satanas And why þat tree, þat wold I witte,
 Any more þan all othir by?   35
Eua For oure lord God forbeedis vs itt,
 The frute þerof, Adam nor I
  To neghe it nere;
 And yf we dide we both shuld dye,
 He saide, and sese our solace sere. 40
Satanas Yha, Eue, to me take tente; f.14
 Take hede and þou shalte here

---

6. dedyned] *D¹, Ca; MS, TS, Be* denyed
6–7. *Lineation D¹; one line in MS; TS + divide after* kynde
16. *Added by a later hand in gap left by main scribe*
25. *Satanas*] Diabolus *added to right by J. Clerke*

What þat the matere mente
He moved on þat manere.

To ete þerof he you defende   45
  I knawe it wele, þis was his skylle:
Bycause he wolde non othir kende
  Thes grete vertues þat longes þertill.
    For will þou see,
  Who etis the frute of good and ille   50
    Shalle haue knowyng as wele as hee.

Eua   Why, what-kynne thyng art þou
    Þat telles þis tale to me?

Satanas   A worme, þat wotith wele how
    Þat yhe may wirshipped be.   55

Eue What wirshippe shulde we wynne therby?
  To ete þerof vs nedith it nought,
We have lordshippe to make maistrie
  Of alle þynge þat in erthe is wrought.

Satanas   Woman, do way!   60
  To gretter state ye may be broughte
  And ye will do as I schall saye.

Eue   To do is vs full lothe
    Þat shuld oure God myspaye.

Satanas   Nay, certis it is no wathe,   65
  Ete it saffley ye maye.

For perille ryght þer none in lyes,
  Bot worshippe and a grete wynnynge,
For right als God yhe shalle be wyse
  And pere to hym in all-kyn thynge.   70
    Ay, goddis shalle ye be,
  Of ille and gode to haue knawyng,
    For to be als wise as he.

Eue   Is þis soth þat þou sais?

Satanas   Yhe, why trowes þou noȝt me?   f.14ᵛ
    I wolde be no-kynnes wayes   76
    Telle noȝt but trouthe to þe.

Eua Than wille I to thy techyng traste
    And fange þis frute vnto oure foode.

Et tunc debet accipere pomum.

Satanas Byte on bodly, be nought abasshed,   80
    And bere Adam to amende his mode
    And eke his blisse.

Tunc Satanas recedet.

---

43. matere] *TS +; MS* materere
67. þer none in] *Ca, Be* none therein

Eua	Adam, have here of frute full goode.
Adam	Alas woman, why toke þou þis?

        Owre lorde comaunded vs bothe   85
To tente þe tree of his.
        Thy werke wille make hym wrothe –
Allas, þou hast done amys.

Eue   Nay Adam, greve þe nought at it,
        And I shal saie þe reasonne why.   90
A worme has done me for to witte
We shalle be as goddis, þou and I,
        Yf þat we ete
Here of this tree; Adam, forthy
        Lette noght þat worshippe for to gete.   95
        For we shalle be als wise
Als God þat is so grete,
        And als mekill of prise;
        Forthy ete of þis mete.

Adam   To ete it wolde Y nought eschewe   100
        Myght I me sure in thy saying.
Eue   Byte on boldely, for it is trewe,
        We shalle be goddis and knawe al thyng.
Adam   To wynne þat name
        I schalle it taste at thy techyng.   105

Et accipit et comedit.

        Allas, what haue I done, for shame!
          Ille counsaille, woo worthe the!
        A, Eue, þou art to blame,
          To þis entysed þou me –
        Me shames with my lyghame,   110

For I am naked as methynke.
Eue   Allas Adam, right so am I.   f.15
Adam   And for sorowe sere why ne myght we synke,
        For wc hauc grcvcd God almyghty
        Þat made me man –   115
Brokyn his bidyng bittirly.
        Allas þat euer we it began.
          Þis werke, Eue, hast þou wrought,
        And made þis bad bargayne.
Eue   Nay Adam, wite me nought.   120
Adam   Do wey, lefe Eue, whame þan?

Eue   The worme to wite wele worthy were,
        With tales vntrewe he me betrayed.
Adam   Allas, þat I lete at thy lare
        Or trowed þe trufuls þat þou me saide.   125

87.   wrothe] *TS +; MS* wrorthe

So may I byde,
For I may banne þat bittir brayde
And drery dede, þat I it dyde.
Oure shappe for doole me defes,
Wherewith þay shalle be hydde.   130

Eue   Late vs take there fygge-leves,
Sythen it is þus betydde.

Adam   Ryght as þou sais so shalle it bee,
For we are naked and all bare;
Full wondyr fayne I wolde hyde me   135
Fro my lordis sight, and I wiste whare,
Where I ne roght.

Dominus   Adam, Adam.
Adam   Lorde.
Dominus   Where art thou, yhare?
Adam   I here þe lorde and seys the noȝt.
Dominus   Say, wheron is it longe,   140
Þis werke why hast þou wrought?
Adam   Lorde, Eue garte me do wronge
And to þat bryg me brought.

Dominus   Say, Eue, why hast þou garte thy make   f.15ᵛ
Ete frute I bad þe shuld hynge stille,   145
And comaunded none of it to take?
Eua   A worme, lord, entysed me thertill;
So welaway,
That euer I did þat dede so dill.
Dominus   A, wikkid worme, woo worthe þe ay   150
For þou on þis maner
Hast made þam swilke affraye;
My malysoune haue þou here
With all þe myght Y may.

And on thy wombe þan shall þou glyde,   155
And be ay full of enmyté
To al mankynde on ilke a side,
And erthe it shalle thy sustynaunce be
To ete and drynke.
Adam and Eue alsoo, yhe   160
In erthe þan shalle ye swete and swynke,
And trauayle for youre foode.
Adam   Allas, whanne myght we synke,
We that haues alle worldis goode
Ful derfly may vs thynke.   165

130.   þay shalle] *K* shalle þay . . . ?
145.   þe] *D², Ca, Be; MS, TS* þei
147.   thertill] *TS+; MS* therto
158.   be] *Originally* by, e *superimposed*
159.   *Added to right in red, and in ornamental script (main scribe)*
163.   whanne] *Zu, Ho¹, Ca* why ne; *Be* wha ne
165.   derfly] *Ca, Be; MS, TS* defly

Dominus	Now Cherubyn, myn aungell bryght,
	To middilerth tyte go dryve these twoo.
Angelus	Alle redy lorde, as it is right,
	Syn thy wille is þat it be soo,
	And thy lykyng.
	Adam and Eue, do you to goo,
	For here may ʒe make no dwellyng;
	Goo yhe forthe faste to fare,
	Of sorowe may yhe synge.
Adam	Allas, for sorowe and care
	Oure handis may we wryng.

170

175

VI The Armourers

The Expulsion

Angelus	Alle creatures to me take tent,
	Fro God of heuen now am I sent
	Vnto þe wrecchis þat wronge has went
	Thaymself to woo;
	Þe joie of heuen þat thaym was lent
	Is lost thaym froo.

f.16ᵛ

5

Fro thaym is loste boþe game and glee;
He badde þat þei schuld maistirs be
Ouer alle-kynne thyng, oute-tane a tree
    He taught þem tille;
And þerto wente bothe she and he,
    Agayne his wille.

10

Agaynst his wille þus haue they wrought,
To greeffe grete God gaffe they right noght,
    Þat wele wytt ye;
And therfore syte is to þaym sought,
    As ye shalle see.

15

The fooles þat faithe is fallen fra
Take tente to me nowe, or ye ga;

170.   *Added by J. Clerke in gap left by main scribe*
176+   Et sic finis *added by J. Clerke; f.16 blank*

Fro God of heuen vnto yow twa   20
    Sente am I nowe,
For to warne you what-kynne wa
    Is wrought for you.

Adam   For vs is wrought, so welaway,
            Doole endurand nyghte and day;   25
            The welthe we wende haue wonnyd in ay
                Is loste vs fra.
            For this myscheffe full wele we may
                Euer mornyng ma.

Angelus   Adam, thyselffe made al þis syte,   30
            For to the tree þou wente full tyte
            And boldely on the frute gan byte
                My lord forbed.
Adam   Yaa, allas, my wiffe þat may I wite,
                For scho me red.   35

Angelus   Adam, for þou trowyd hir tale,
            He sendis þe worde and sais þou shale
                Lyffe ay in sorowe,
            Abide and be in bittir bale
                Tille he þe borowe.   40

Adam   Allas, wrecchis, what haue we wrought?
            To byggly blys we bothe wer brought;
                Whillis we wer þare
            We hadde inowe, nowe haue we noghte –
                Allas, for care.   45

Eua   Oure cares ar comen bothe kyne and colde,   f.17
            With fele fandyngis manyfolde;
            Allas, þat tyraunte to me tolde,
                Thurghoute his gyle,
            That we shulde haue alle welthis in walde,   50
                Wa worthe þe whyle.

Angelus   That while yee wrought vnwittely,
            Soo for to greue God almyghty,
            And þat mon ye full dere abye
                Or þat ye go;   55
            And to lyffe, as is worthy,
                In were and wo.

            Adam, haue þis, luke howe ye thynke,
            And tille withalle þi meete and drynke
                For euermore.   60

45+ *Catchword* Oure cares
46. *Quire B begins*

Adam   Allas, for syte why ne myght Y synke,
        So shames me sore.

Eue   Soore may we shame with sorowes seere,
    And felly fare we bothe in feere;
    Allas, þat euyr we neghed it nere,   65
        Þat tree vntill.
    With dole now mon we bye full dere
        Oure dedis ille.

Angelus   Giffe for þou beswyked hym swa,
    Trauell herto shalle þou ta,
    Thy barnes to bere with mekill wa –   70
        Þis warne I þe.
    Buxom shalle þou and othir ma
        To man ay be.

Eue   Allas for doole, what shall Y doo,   75
    Now mon I neuer haue rest ne roo.
Adam   Nay, lo, swilke a tale is taken me too
        To trauaylle tyte;
    Nowe is shente both I and shoo,
        Allas, for syte.   80

    Allas, for syte and sorowe sadde,
    Mournynge makis me mased and madde,
    To thynke in herte what helpe Y hadde
        And nowe has none.
    On grounde mon I neuyr goo gladde,   85
        My gamys ere gane.

    Gone ar my games withowten glee;   f.17ᵛ
    Allas, in blisse kouthe we noȝt bee,
    For putte we were to grete plenté
        At prime of þe day;
    Be tyme of none alle lost had wee,   90
        Sa welawaye.

    Sa welaway, for harde peyne,
    Alle bestis were to my biddyng bayne,
    Fisshe and fowle, they were fulle fayne   95
        With me to founde.
    And nowe is alle thynge me agayne
        Þat gois on grounde.

    On grounde ongaynely may Y gange,
    To suffre syte and peynes strange,   100

---

61.   ne] *Suppl Ho'*
69.   Eve for þat þou begylyd hym so *interlined by J. Clerke*
77.   tale] *?read* tole '*tool*' (*Adam's spade; cf. 58, 105, 113, 165*)

Alle is for dede I haue done wrange
  Thurgh wykkid wyle.
On lyve methynkith I lyffe to lange,
  Allas þe whille.

A, lord, I thynke what thynge is þis   105
That me is ordayned for my mysse;
Gyffe I wirke wronge, who shulde me wys
  Be any waye?
How beste will be, so haue Y blisse,
  I shalle assaye.   110

Allas, for bale, what may þis bee?
In worlde vnwisely wrought haue wee,
This erthe it trembelys for this tree
  And dyns ilke dele!
Alle þis worlde is wrothe with mee,   115
  Þis wote I wele.

Full wele Y wote my welthe is gone,
Erthe, elementis, euerilkane
For my synne has sorowe tane,
  Þis wele I see.   120
Was neuere wrecchis so wylle of wane
  As nowe ar wee.

Eue   We are fulle wele worthy iwis
To haue þis myscheffe for oure mys,
For broght we were to byggely blys,   125
  Euer in to be.
Now my sadde sorowe certis is þis
  Mysilfe to see.

Adam   To see it is a sytful syghte,
We bothe þat were in blis so brighte,   130
We mon go nakid euery ilke a nyghte
  And dayes bydene.
Allas, what womans witte was light!
  Þat was wele sene.

Eue   Sethyn it was so me knyth it sore,   135
Bot sethyn that woman witteles ware   f.18
Mans maistrie shulde haue bene more
  Agayns þe gilte.
Adam   Nay, at my speche wolde þou never spare,
  Þat has vs spilte.   140

136. sethyn] *MS* señ, *TS* sythen

Eue	Iff I hadde spoken youe oughte to spill
	Ye shulde haue taken gode tent þeretyll,
	And turnyd my þought.
Adam	Do way, woman, and neme it noght,

For at my biddyng wolde þou not be   145
And therfore my woo wyte Y thee;
Thurgh ille counsaille þus casten ar we
   In bittir bale.
Nowe God late never man aftir me
   Triste woman tale.   150

For certis me rewes fulle sare
That euere I shulde lerne at þi lare,
Thy counsaille has casten me in care,
   Þat þou me kende.

Eue   Be stille Adam, and nemen it na mare,   155
   It may not mende.

For wele I wate I haue done wrange,
And therfore euere I morne emange,
Allas the whille I leue so lange,
   Dede wolde I be.   160

Adam On grounde mon I never gladde gange,
   Withowten glee.

Withowten glee I ga,
This sorowe wille me sla,
This tree vnto me wille I ta   165
   Þat me is sende.
He þat vs wrought wisse vs fro wa,
   Whare-som we wende.

158. *Original rubric, Adam, deleted by a later hand*
161. *Adam] Added to right by a later hand, ? J. Clerke*
168+ *finis added by Clerke; f.18ᵛ blank*

VII The Glovers

Cain and Abel

Sacrificium Cayme et Abell

Angelus   That lord of lyffe lele ay-lastand
    Whos myght vnmesured is to meyne,
He shoppe þe sonne, bothe see and sande,
    And wroughte þis worlde with worde, I wene.
    His aungell cleere as cristall clene,   5
      Here vnto you þus am I sente
        Þis tide.
      Abell and Cayme, yei, both bydeyne
        To me enteerly takis entent;
        To meve my message haue I ment   10
        If þat ye bide.

Allemyghty God of myghtes moste,
    When he had wrought þis world so wide,
No thynge hym þoughte was wroughte in waste,
    But in his blissyng boune to bide   15
    Neyne ordurs for to telle, þat tyde,
      Of aungeles bryght he bad þer be.
        For pride
      And sone þe tente part it was tried,
        And wente awaye as was worthye;   20
        They heild to helle alle þat meyné
        Þerin to bide.

Þanne made he manne to his liknes
    That place of price for to restore,
And sithen he kyd hym such kyndnes   25
    Somwhat wille he wirke þerfore:
The tente to tyne he askis, no more,
      Of alle þe goodes he haues you sent.
        Full trew
      To offyr loke þat ye be yore,   30
        And to my tale yhe take entent,
        For ilke a lede þat liffe has lente
        So shalle you sewe.

7. Þat tyde *to right in red, main scribe*
8. yei] *This ed; MS* y– *or* þ–, *TS* þei, *K* ye
10. *Written twice, first instance deleted in red*
13. world] *TS: MS* wolrd
33. *Altered to* So shalle you ensewe *by J. Clerke*

Abell   Gramercy God, of thy goodnes
        That me on molde has marked þi man,   35
    I worshippe þe with worthynes,   f.19ᵛ
        With alle þe comforte þat I can.
    Me for to were fro warkes wanne,
        For to fulfille thy comaundement,
         Þe teynd   40
    Of alle þe gode sen I beganne
        Thow shalle it haue, sen þou it sent.
        Come, brothir Cayme, I wolde we wente
        With hert ful hende.

Caym   We! Whythir now, in wilde waneand?   45
        Trowes þou I thynke to trusse of towne?
    Goo, jape þe, robard jangillande,
        Me liste noȝt nowe to rouk nor rowne.
Abell   A, dere brothir, late vs be bowne
        Goddis biddyng blithe to fulfille,   50
        I tell þe.
Cayme   Ya, daunce in þe devil way, dresse þe downe,
        For I wille wyrke euen as I will.
        What mystris þe, in gode or ille,
        Of me to melle þe?   55

Abell   To melle of þe myldely I may.
        Bot goode brothir, go we in haste,
    Gyffe God oure teynde dulye þis day —
        He byddis vs þus, be nouȝt abassed.
Cayme   Ya, deuell, methynkeþ þat werke were waste,   60
        That he vs gaffe geffe hym agayne
        To se.
    Nowe fekyll frenshippe for to fraste
        Methynkith þer is in hym sarteyne.
        If he be moste in myghte and mayne   65
        What nede has he?

Abell   He has non nede vnto þi goode,
        But it will please hym principall
    If þou, myldly in mayne and moode,
        Grouche noȝt geue hym tente parte of all.   70
    [. . .   . . .
        . . .
        . . . . . .
    . . .   . . .
        . . .   . . .
        . . .
    . . .   . . .]

34-7. *Originally omitted, but added by main scribe at or immediately after rubrication.* Caret
    to left of 38 in red, an earlier Abell *to right in script and inking of dialogue*
62. se] *D²* fe

[At this point, two leaves, the inner bifolium of quire B, have been lost or removed from the MS as originally prepared by the main scribe. These leaves would have contained about 140–150 lines (including seven required to complete the stanza which breaks off at line 70) which no doubt depicted the following incidents: the offerings of Abel (a lamb) and Cain (sheaves); God's acceptance of Abel's offering and the rejection of Cain's; the murder of Abel by Cain (Genesis iv. 4–8); the sending of an angel by God to curse Cain. The reason for the loss or removal of these leaves is open to conjecture, but it is certain to have taken place before or at the time when the MS was in the hands of John Clerke, as additions by him occur on the following leaf (f.20^{r-v}) in what now appears as a partial attempt to provide either rectification (for a loss), or substitution (for material deliberately removed). Because the central and essential episode of the play is still missing, it is to be suspected that Clerke copied out a new pair of leaves, containing the murder of Abel, and that these, too, have disappeared. What survives in Clerke's hand are two lines at the top of f.20^r and 27 lines on f.20^v, lines 71–2 and 73–99 in this edition, a farcical interlude involving Cain's servant and the arrival of the angel to remonstrate with Cain. Lines 71–2 seem to be the fragmentary ending of a stanza in which the angel gives assent to God's command to visit Cain, and this increases the likelihood that lost material in Clerke's hand once preceded them. If Clerke did indeed provide a replacement or substitute inner bifolium, then it appears that he had more copy than could conveniently be fitted into such a space, and accordingly had to append the surviving passage in his hand on a convenient blank leaf at the end of the play. Miss Toulmin Smith followed Clerke's indications (see textual notes to lines 71–2 and 73–99) for the order in which the lines should come, and they are again followed here.]

[*Angelus*]	It shall be done evyn as ye bydd,	f.20
	And that anone.	

Brewbarret	Lo, maister Cayme, what shaves bryng I,	f.20^v
	Evyn of the best for to bere seyd,	
	And to the feylde I wyll me hye	75
	To fetch you moo, if ye haue neyd.	
Cayme	Come vp, sir knave, the devyll the speyd,	
	Ye will not come but ye be prayd.	
Brewbarret	O, maister Caym, I haue broken my to!	
Cayme	Come vp syr, for by my thryst,	80
	Ye shall drynke or ye goo.	

71–2. *Hand of J. Clerke, over erasure of two lines by main scribe. Reference mark to left and* Caret inde Lo maister Cayme what shaves bryng I *to right; see line 73 and next textual note*

73–99. *On f.20^v, in Clerke's hand, with reference mark as to left of 72 against first line. Below 99,* What hais thowe done beholde *and here; see line 100 and textual note*

73. shaves] *This ed; TS* shares

Angelus	Thowe cursyd Came, where is Abell?
	Where hais thowe done thy broder dere?
Cayme	What askes thowe me that taill to tell,
	For yit his keper was I never?

85

Angelus	God hais sent the his curse downe,
	Fro hevyn to hell, *maladictio dei.*
Cayme	Take that thyself, evyn on thy crowne,
	Quia non sum custos fratris mei,
	To tyne.

90

Angelus	God hais sent the his malyson,
	And inwardly I geve the myne.

Cayme	The same curse light on thy crowne,
	And right so myght it worth and be
	For he that sent that gretyng downe,

95

The devyll myght speyd both hym and the.
Fowll myght thowe fall!
Here is a cankerd company,
Therefore Goddes curse light on you all.

. . . .

Angelus	What hast þou done? Beholde and heere,	f.20
	Þe voice of his bloode cryeth vengeaunce	101

Fro erthe to heuen, with voice entere
Þis tyde.
That God is greved with thy greuaunce
Take hede, I schalle telle þe tydandis,   105
Þerfore abide.

Þou shall be curssed vppon þe grounde,
God has geffyn þe his malisonne;
Yff þou wolde tyll þe erthe so rounde
No frute to þe þer shalle be fonne.   110
Of wikkidnesse sen þou arte sonne,
Thou shalle be waferyng here and þere
Þis day.
In bittir bale nowe art þou boune,
Out-castyn shal þou be for care;   115
No man shal rewe of thy misfare
For þis affraie.

Cayme	Allas for syte, so may I saye,	
	My synne it passis al mercie,	
	For ask it þe lord I ne maye,	120

87.	maladictio] *This ed; TS* maldictio *(conj)*
100.	*Resumption of main scribe's work*
110.	fonne] *He; MS, TS* founde
120.	ask it] *TS; MS* askid

To haue it am I nouȝt worthy.
Fro þe shalle I be hidde in hye,
Þou castis me, lorde, oute of my kyth
In lande.
Both here and there oute-caste am I,   125
For ilke a man þat metis me with
They wille slee me, be fenne or frith,
With dynte of hande.

Angelus   Nay Cayme, nouȝt soo, haue þou no drede;
Who þat þe slees shalle ponnyshed be   130
Sevene sithis for doyng of þat dede.
Forthy a token shal þou see,
It shalle be prentyd so in þe
That ilke a man shalle þe knowe full wele.
Caym   Thanne wolle I fardir flee   f.20ᵛ
For shame.   136
Sethen I am sette þus out of seill,
That curse that I haue for to feill,
I giffe you þe same.

VIII The Shipwrights

The Building of the Ark

Deus   Fyrst qwen I wrought þis world so wyde,   f.21ᵛ
Wode and wynde and watters wane,
Heuyn and helle was noght to hyde,
Wyth herbys and gyrse þus I begane.
In endles blysse to be and byde.
And to my likenes made I man,   5
Lorde and syre on ilke a side
Of all medillerthe I made hym þan.

A woman also with hym wroght I,
Alle in lawe to lede þer lyffe,   10

135.   fardir] r *interlined*
139+   *Rest of f.20ᵛ, originally blank, now contains Clerke's addition (see textual note to 73–*
99); f.21 blank

I badde þame waxe and multiplye,
  To fulfille þis worlde, withowtyn striffe.
Syþn hays men wroght so wofully
  And synne is nowe reynand so ryffe,
Þat me repentys and rewys forþi   15
  Þat ever I made outhir man or wiffe.

Bot sen they make me to repente
  My werke I wroght so wele and trewe,
Wythowtyn seys will noght assente,
  Bot euer is bowne more bale to brewe.   20
Bot for ther synnes þai shall be shente
  And fordone hoyly, hyde and hewe;
Of þam shal no more be mente,
  Bot wirke þis werke I wille al newe.

Al newe I will þis worlde be wroght   25
  And waste away þat wonnys þerin,
A flowyd above þame shall be broght
  To stroye medilerthe, both more and myn.
Bot Noe alon, lefe shal it noght
  To all be sownkyn for ther synne;   30
He and his sones, þus is my thoght,
  And with þere wyffes away sall wynne.

Nooe, my seruand sad an cleyn,   f.22
  For þou art stabill in stede and stalle,
I wyll þou wyrke withowten weyn   35
  A warke to saffe þiselfe wythall.
Noe   O, mercy lorde, qwat may þis meyne?
Deus   I am þi Gode of grete and small
Is comyn to telle þe of thy teyn,
  And qwat ferly sall eftir fall.   40

Noe   A, lorde, I lowe þe lowde and still
  Þat vnto me – wretche vnworthye –
Þus with thy wordc, as is þi will,
  Lykis to appere þus propyrly.
Deus   Nooe, as I byd þe, doo fulfill: 45
  A shippe I will haue wroght in hye;
All-yf þou can litill skyll,
  Take it in hande, for helpe sall I.

Noe   A, worthy lorde, wolde þou take heede,
  I am full olde and oute of qwarte,   50

20. euer] *A final* e *erased*
27. above] –ve *by later hand, over erasure*
28. both] –th *by later hand, over erasure*
29. noght] not *interlined by later hand*
45. doo] *By later hand, over erasure*

   þat me liste do no daies dede
    Bot yf gret mystir me garte.
Deus Begynne my werke behoves þe nede
    And þou wyll passe from peynes smerte,
   I sall þe sokoure and the spede   55
    And giffe þe hele in hede and hert.

   I se suche ire emonge mankynde
    þat of þare werkis I will take wreke;
   þay shall be sownkyn for þare synne,
    þerfore a shippe I wille þou make.   60
   þou and þi sonnes shall be þerein,
    They sall be sauyd for thy sake.
   Therfore go bowdly and begynne   f.22ᵛ
    Thy mesures and thy markis to take.

Noe A, lorde, þi wille sall euer be wroght   65
    Os counsill gyfys of ilka clerk,
   Bot first, of shippe-craft can I right noght;
    Of þer makyng haue I no merke.
Deus Noe, I byd þe hartely haue no þought,
    I sall þe wysshe in all þi werke,   70
   And even to itt till ende be wroght;
    Therfore to me take hede and herke.

   Take high trees and hewe þame cleyne,
    All be sware and noght of skwyn,
   Make of þame burdes and wandes betwene   75
    þus thrivandly, and noght ouer-thyn.
   Luke þat þi semes be suttilly seyn
    And naylid wele þat þei noght twyne;
   þus I deuyse ilk dele bedeyne,
    þerfore do furthe, and leue thy dyne.   80

   iij C cubyttis it sall be lang,
    And fyfty brode, all for thy blys;
   þe highte, of thyrty cubittis strang,
    Lok lely þat þou thynke on þis.
   þus gyffe I þe grathly or I gang   85
    þi mesures, þat þou do not mysse.

57. suche] −che *by later hand, over erasure*
   ire] *First letter altered to capital by later hand*
59. sownkyn] o *inserted by later hand*
65. euer] *A final* e *erased*
66. counsill] i *altered to* e *by later hand*
74. skwyn] −kwyn *by later hand, over erasure*
75. of þame] *Ho'; MS, TS* þame of
81. lang] a *altered to* o *by later hand*
83. strang] a *altered to* o *by later hand*
86. do] *By later hand, over erasure*

Luk nowe þat þou wirke noght wrang
  Þus wittely sen I þe wyshe.

Noe A, blistfull lord, þat al may beylde,
    I thanke þe hartely both euer and ay;   90
  Fyfe hundreth wyntres I am of elde —
    Methynk þer ȝeris as yestirday.
  Ful wayke I was and all vnwelde,
    My werynes is wente away,
  To wyrk þis werke here in þis feylde   95
    Al be myselfe I will assaye.   f.23

  To hewe þis burde I wyll begynne,
    But firste I wille lygge on my lyne;
  Now bud it be alle inlike thynne,
    So þat it nowthyr twynne nor twyne.   100
  Þus sall I june it with a gynn
    And sadly sett it with symonde fyne:
  Þus schall I wyrke it both more and mynne
    Thurgh techyng of God, maistir myne.

  [. . .   . . .]
    More suttelly kan no man sewe;   105
  It sall be cleyngked euerilka dele
    With nayles þat are both noble and newe,
  Þus sall I feste it fast to feele.
    Take here a revette, and þere a rewe,
  With þer þe bowe nowe wyrke I wele;   110
    Þis werke I warand both gud and trewe.

  Full trewe it is who will take tente,
    Bot faste my force begynnes to fawlde.
  A hundercth wyntres away is wente
    Sen I began þis werk, full grathely talde,   115
  And in slyke trauayle for to be bente
    Is harde to hym þat is þus olde.

95+ *Catchword* All be my self
96. *Quire C begins*
99. bud] must *interlined by later hand*
100. þat] *This ed; TS* put
     twynne nor twyne] *TS; MS* twyne nor twynne
101. gynn] n^2 *added by later hand*
102–3. *Originally written in error between 110 and 111, and there deleted (in red). Rewritten to right of 101 and 104 (main scribe) with caret marks*
103. mynne] *TS; MS* myne
104+ *Line missing (D²; after 111 in TS)*
106. euer] *A final* e *erased*
110. þer þe bowe] *D²; MS, TS* þer bowe þer
113. force] e *by later hand, over erasure*

But he þat to me þis messages sent
   He wille be my beylde, þus am I bowde.

Deus Nooe, þis werke is nere an ende   120
   And wrought right as I warned þe.
Bot yit in maner it must be mende,
   Þerfore þis lessoun lerne at me:
For dyuerse beestis þerin must lende,
   And fewles also in þere degree,   125
And for þat þay sall not sam blende
   Dyuerse stages must þer be.

And qwen þat it is ordand soo
   With dyuerse stawllys and stagis seere,   f.23ᵛ
Of ilka kynde þou sall take twoo,   130
   Bothe male and femalle fare in fere.
Thy wyffe, thy sonnes, with þe sall goo
   And thare thre wyffes, withowten were;
Þere viij bodies withowten moo
   Sall þus be saued on þis manere.   135

Therfore to my biddyng be bayne,
   Tille all be herberd haste þe faste;
Eftir þe vij day sall it rayne
   Tille fowrty dayes be fully paste.
Take with þe geere sclyk os may gayne   140
   To man and beeste þare lyffes to laste.
I sall þe socoure for certeyne
   Tille alle þi care awey be kaste.

Noe A, lorde, þat ilka mys may mende,
   I lowe þi lare both lowde and stille,   145
I thanke þe both with herte and hende,
   That me wille helpe fro angrys hill.
Abowte þis werke now bus me wende
   With beestys and fewlys my shippe to fill.
He þat to me þis Crafte has kende,   150
   He wysshe vs with his worthy wille.

---

119. bowde] w *altered to* ll *by later hand*
120. nere an] −e an *by later hand, over erasure*
122. yit] *Interlined by later hand*
      must] *By later hand, over erasure; and so at 124, 127*
126. þat] *Interlined by later hand*
      sam] *A final* e *erased*
131. fere] *Botched, but given correctly in red to right (main scribe)*
143. away be, *partially deleted, between* be *and* kaste
147. w, *deleted, between* helpe *and* fro
151+ finis *added by J. Clerke. Bottom half of f.23ᵛ blank; ff.24, 24ᵛ blank*

IX The Fishers and Mariners
The Flood

Noye That lord þat leves ay-lastand lyff,
    I loue þe euer with hart and hande,
  That me wolde rewle be reasoune ryffe,
    Sex hundereth yere to lyffe in lande.
  Thre semely sonnes and a worthy wiffe   5
    I haue euer at my steven to stande;
  Bot nowe my cares aren keene as knyffe,
    Bycause I kenne what is commannde.
    Thare comes to ilke contré,
      3a, cares bothe kene and calde.   10
    For God has warned me
    Þis worlde wastyd shalle be,
    And certis þe sothe I see,
      As forme-fadres has tald.

  My fadir Lamech who, likes to neven,   15
    Heere in þis worlde þus lange gon lende,
  Seucne hundereth yere seuenty and seuene,
    In swilke a space his tyme he spende.
  He prayed to God with stabill steuene
    Þat he to hym a sone shuld sende,   20
  And at þe laste þer come from heuen
    Slyke hettyng þat hym mekill amende,
    And made hym grubbe and graue
      As ordand faste beforne,
    For he sone shulde haue,   25
    As he gon aftir crave;
    And as God vouchydsaue
      In worlde þan was I bornc.

  When I was borne Noye named he me,
    And saide þees wordes with mekill wynne: 30
  'Loo', he saide, 'þis ilke is he
    That shalle be comforte to mankynne'.
  Syrs, by þis wele witte may ye,
    My fadir knewe both more and mynne
  By sarteyne signes he couthe wele see,   35
    That al þis worlde shuld synke for synne;

1. *Noye] Centred, above first line*
14. forme-] *TS; MS* formed
24. As] *This ed; MS, TS* And
30. for ethe *written to right by a later hand*

Howe God shulde vengeaunce take,
    As nowe is sene sertayne,
And hende of mankynde make
    That synne wold nouȝt forsake;   40
And howe þat it shuld slake,
    And a worlde waxe agayne.

I wolde God itt wasted were,   f.25ᵛ
    Sa þat I shuld nott tente þertille.
My semely sonnes and doughteres dere,   45
    Takis ȝe entent vnto my skylle.

I Filius Fader we are all redy heere,
    Youre biddyng baynly to fulfille.

Noe Goos calle youre modir, and comes nere,
    And spede vs faste þat we nouȝt spille.   50

I Filius Fadir, we shal nouȝt fyne
    To youre biddyng be done.

Noe Alle þat leues vndir lyne
    Sall, sone, soner passe to pyne.

I Filius Where are ye, modir myne?   55
    Come to my fadir sone.

Vxor What sais þou sone?
I Filius   Moder, certeyne
    My fadir thynkis to flitte full ferre.
He biddis you haste with al youre mayne
    Vnto hym, þat no thyng you marre.   60

Vxor Ȝa, goode sone, hy þe faste agayne
    And telle hym I wol come no narre.

I Filius Dame, I wolde do youre biddyng fayne,
    But yow bus wende, els bese it warre.

Vxor Werre? Þat wolde I witte.   65
    We bowrde al wrange, I wene.

I Filius Modir, I saie you yitte,
    My fadir is bowne to flitte.

Vxor Now certis, I sall nouȝt sitte
    Or I se what he mene.   70

I Filius Fadir, I haue done nowe as ye comaunde,   f.26
    My modir comes to you this daye.

Noe Scho is welcome, I wele warrande;
    This worlde sall sone be waste awaye.

Vxor Wher arte þou Noye?
Noe   Loo, here at hande,   75
    Come hedir faste dame, I þe praye.

Vxor Trowes þou þat I wol leue þe harde lande
    And tourne vp here on toure deraye?

54. soner] *This ed; TS* son *(conj)*
71. *I Filius*] I *suppl* TS

        Nay Noye, I am nouȝt bowne
          To fonde nowe ouer þere fellis.   80
        Doo barnes, goo we and trusse to towne.

Noe   Nay, certis, sothly þan mon ye drowne.

Vxor   In faythe þou were als goode come downe
        And go do somwhat ellis.

Noe   Dame, fowrty dayes are nerhand past   85
        And gone sen it began to rayne,
    On lyffe sall no man lenger laste
        Bot we allane, is nought to layne.

Vxor   Now Noye, in faythe þe fonnes full faste,
        This fare wille I no lenger frayne;   90
    Þou arte nere woode, I am agaste,
        Farewele, I wille go home agayne.

Noe   O woman, arte þou woode?
          Of my werkis þou not wotte;
        All þat has ban or bloode   95
        Sall be ouere flowed with þe floode.

Vxor   In faithe, þe were als goode
        To late me go my gatte.

        We! Owte! Herrowe!

Noe   What now, what cheere?   f.26ᵛ

Vxor   I will no nare for no-kynnes nede.   100

Noe   Helpe, my sonnes, to holde her here,
        For tille hir harmes she takes no heede.

II Filius   Beis mery modir, and mende youre chere;
        This worlde beis drowned, withouten drede.

Vxor   Allas, þat I þis lare shuld lere.   105

Noe   Þou spilles vs alle, ill myght þou speede.

III Filius Dere modir, wonne with vs,
          Þer shal no þyng you greve.

Vxor   Nay, nedlyngis home me bus,
        For I haue tolis to trusse.   110

Noe   Woman, why dois þou þus?
        To make vs more myscheue?

Vxor   Noye, þou myght haue leteyn me wete;
        Erly and late þou wente þeroutte,
    And ay at home þou lete me sytte   115
        To loke þat nowhere were wele aboutte.

Noe   Dame, þou holde me excused of itt,
         It was Goddis wille withowten doutte.

80. fellis] *Added in dialogue by a later hand;* fellys *already written to right by main scribe, in*
     red

100. nare] *This ed;* TS nar[r]e

106. *Not ruled off from 105 and not assigned by main scribe;* Noe *added by a later hand*

Vxor	What, wenys þou so for to go qwitte?
	Nay, be my trouthe, þou getis a clowte.　　120
Noe	I pray þe dame, be stille.
	Thus God wolde haue it wrought.
Vxor	Thow shulde haue witte my wille,
	Yf I wolde sente þertille,
	And Noye, for þat same skylle,　　125
	Þis bargan sall be bought.

Nowe at firste I fynde and feele　　f.27
　Wher þou hast to þe forest soght,
Þou shuld haue tolde me for oure seele
　Whan we were to slyke bargane broght.　　130

Noe	Now dame, þe thar noȝt drede a dele,
	For till accounte it cost þe noght.

A hundereth wyntyr, I watte wele,
　Is wente sen I þis werke had wrought.
　　And when I made endyng,　　135
　　　God gaffe me mesore fayre
　　Of euery ilke a thyng;
　　He bad þat I shuld bryng
　　Of beestis and foules ȝynge,
　　　Of ilke a kynde a peyre.　　140

Vxor	Nowe certis, and we shulde skape fro skathe
	And so be saffyd as ye saye here,
	My commodrys and my cosynes bathe,
	Þam wolde I wente with vs in feere.
Noe	To wende in þe watir it were wathe,　　145
	Loke in and loke withouten were.
Vxor	Allas, my lyff me is full lath,
	I lyffe ouere-lange þis lare to lere.
I Filia	Dere modir, mende youre moode,
	For we sall wende you with.　　150
Vxor	My frendis þat I fra yoode
	Are ouere flowen with floode.
II Filia	Nowe thanke we God al goode
	That vs has grauntid grith.

III Filia	Modir, of þis werke nowe wolde ye noȝt wene,　　155
	That alle shuld worthe to watres wan.
II Filius	Fadir, what may þis meruaylle mene?　　f.27ᵛ
	Wherto made God medilerth and man?
I Filia	So selcouthe sight was never non seene,
	Sen firste þat God þis worlde began.　　160
Noe	Wendes and spers youre dores bedene,

134.　had] *Interlined by a later hand*
154.　vs] *This ed; TS* he
157.　*Filius*] *This ed; TS Filia*

    For bettyr counsell none I can.
     Þis sorowe is sente for synne,
      Therfore to God we pray
     Þat he oure bale wolde blynne.   165
III Filius   The kyng of al mankynne
     Owte of þis woo vs wynne,
      Als þou arte lorde, þat maye.

I Filius   Ȝa, lorde, as þou late vs be borne
    In þis grete bale, som bote vs bede.   170
Noe   My sonnes, se ȝe mydday and morne
    To thes catelles takes goode heede;
    Keppes þam wele with haye and corne;
     And women, fanges þes foules and feede,
    So þat þey be noȝt lightly lorne   175
     Als longe as we þis liffe sall lede.
II Filius   Fadir, we ar full fayne
     Youre biddyng to fulfille.
     ix monethes paste er playne
     Sen we wer putte to peyne.   180
III Filius   He þat is most of mayne
     May mende it qwen he wyll.

Noe   O barnes, itt waxes clere aboute,
    Þat may ȝe see ther wher ȝe sitte.
I Filius   I, leffe fadir, ye loke þareowte,   185
    Yf þat þe water wane ought ȝitt.
Noe   That sall I do withowten dowte,   f.28
    Þorbe the wanyng may we witte.
    A, lorde, to þe I love and lowte.
     The catteraks I trowe be knytte.   190
     Beholde, my sonnes al three
      Þe clowdes are waxen clere.
II Filius   A, lorde of mercy free,
     Ay louyd myght þou be.
Noe   I sall assaye þe see,   195
     How depe þat it is here.

Vxor   Loved be þat lord þat giffes all grace,
    Þat kyndly þus oure care wolde kele.
Noe   I sall caste leede and loke þe space,
    Howe depe þe watir is ilke a dele.   200
    Fyftene cobittis of highte itt hase
     Ouere ilke a hille fully to feylle;
    Butte beese wel comforte in þis casse,
     It is wanand, þis wate I wele.

188. Þorbe] *D²; MS, TS* For be
204. wate] *TS; MS* watir

Therfore a fowle of flight   205
  Full sone sall I forthe sende
To seke if he haue sight,
Som lande vppon to light;
Þanne may we witte full right
  When oure mornyng sall mende.   210

Of al þe fowles þat men may fynde
  The raven is wighte, and wyse is hee.
Þou arte full crabbed and al thy kynde,
  Wende forthe þi course I comaunde þe,
And werly watte, and yther þe wynd   215
  Yf þou fynde awdir lande or tree.
ix monethes here haue we bene pyned,
  But when God wyll, better mon bee.

I Filia   Þat lorde þat lennes vs lyffe
            To lere his lawes in lande,   220
          He mayd bothe man and wyffe,
          He helpe to stynte oure striffe.
III Filia   Oure cares are kene as knyffe,
            God graunte vs goode tydand.

I Filius   Fadir, þis foule is forthe full lange;   f.28ᵛ
            Vppon sum lande I trowe he lende,   226
          His foode þer fore to fynde and fange —
            That makis hym be a fayland frende.
Noe   Nowe sonne, and yf he so forthe gange,
            Sen he for all oure welthe gon wende,   230
          Then be he for his werkis wrange
            Euermore weried withowten ende.
              And sertis for to see
                Whan oure sorowe sall sesse,
              Anodyr foule full free   235
              Owre messenger sall be;
              Þou doufe, I comaunde þe
                Owre comforte to encresse.

A faithfull fewle to sende art þow
  Of alle within þere wanys wyde;   240
Wende forthe I pray þe, for owre prowe,
  And sadly seke on ilke a side
Yf þe floodes be falland nowe,
  Þat þou on þe erthe may belde and byde;
Bryng vs som tokenyng þat we may trowe   245
  What tydandes sall of vs betyde.

---

215. wynd] *TS; MS* wy + *three minims* + d
221. mayd] d *interlined by a later hand*
227. þer fore] *D²; MS, TS* þerfore *(MS* –er– *abbrev)*
240. wanys] *This ed; MS* wa + n *or* u + ys, *TS* wauys
245. þat] *This ed; TS* þar

II Filia	Goode lorde, on vs þou luke,
	And sesse oure sorowe seere,
	Sen we al synne forsoke
	And to thy lare vs toke. 250
III Filia	A twelmothe bott xij weke
	Have we be houerand here.

Noe	Now barnes, we may be blithe and gladde
	And lowe oure lord of heuenes kyng;
	My birde has done as I hym badde, 255
	An olyue braunche I se hym brynge.
	Blyste be þou fewle þat neuere was fayd,
	That in thy force makis no faylyng;
	Mare joie in herte never are I hadde,
	We mone be saued, now may we synge. f.29
	Come hedir my sonnes in hye, 261
	Oure woo away is wente,
	I se here certaynely
	Þe hillis of Hermonye.
I Filius	Lovyd be þat lord forthy 265
	That vs oure lyffes hase lente.

Tunc cantent Noe et filii sui &c.

Vxor	For wrekis nowe þat we may wynne
	Oute of þis woo þat we in wore;
	But Noye, wher are nowe all oure kynne
	And companye we knwe before? 270
Noe	Dame, all ar drowned, late be thy dyne,
	And sone þei boughte þer synnes sore.
	Gud lewyn latte vs begynne,
	So þat we greue oure God no more;
	He was greved in degré 275
	And gretely moved in mynde
	For synne, as men may see:
	Dum dixit 'Penitet me'.
	Full sore forthynkyng was he
	That euere he made mankynde. 280

	That makis vs nowe to tole and trusse;
	But sonnes, he saide— I watte wele when—
	'Arcum ponam in nubibus',
	He sette his bowe clerly to kenne
	As a tokenyng bytwene hym and vs, 285
	In knawlage tille all cristen men
	That fro þis worlde were fynyd þus,

263–4. *Lineation TS; one line in MS*
266+   *SD added to right by a later hand*
270.   knwe] *This ed; TS* kn[e]we

With wattir wolde he neuere wast yt þen.
Þus has God most of myght
  Sette his senge full clere   290
Vppe in þe ayre of heght;
The raynebowe it is right,
  As men may se in sight
    In seasons of þe yere.

II Filius   Sir, nowe sen God oure souerand syre   295
  Has sette his syne þus in certayne,
Than may we wytte þis worldis empire   f.29ᵛ
  Shall euermore laste, is noȝt to layne.
Noe   Nay sonne, þat sall we nouȝt desire,
  For and we do we wirke in wane;   300
For it sall ones be waste with fyre,
  And never worþe to worlde agayne.
Vxor   A, syre, owre hertis are soore
    For þes sawes that ȝe saye here,
  That myscheffe mon be more.   305
Noe   Beis noȝt aferde þerfore,
  ȝe sall noght lyffe þan yore
    Be many hundereth yhere.

I Filius   Fadir, howe sall þis lyffe be ledde
  Sen non are in þis worlde but we?   310
Noe   Sones, with youre wiffes ȝe sall be stedde,
  And multyplye youre seede sall ȝe.
ȝoure barnes sall ilkon othir wedde
  And worshippe God in gud degré;
Beestes and foules sall forthe be bredde,   315
  And so a worlde begynne to bee.
  Nowe travaylle sall ȝe taste
    To wynne you brede and wyne,
  For alle þis worlde is waste;
  Thez beestes muste be vnbraste,   320
  And wende we hense in haste,
    In Goddis blissyng and myne.

288. wast yt] *Zu, Ha; MS, TS* wastyd
294. *Begun* In ses *by main scribe, out of place; entered in correct position by a later hand*
303. soore] *Hoᵗ; MS* s *or* f + eere, *TS* feere
303–4. *Lineation Hoᵗ; written on one line in MS, red virgule between* sawes *and* that; *so divided by TS*
322+ finis *added by J. Clerke; f. 30 blank, f. 30ᵛ blank except for catchword* Grete God

X The Parchmentmakers and Bookbinders
Abraham and Isaac

Abraham	Grett God þat alle þis world has wrought,	f.31
	And wisely wote both gud and ille,	
	I thanke hym thraly in my thoght	
	Of alle his laue he lens me tille,	
	That þus fro barenhede has me broghte	5
	A hundereth wynter to fulfille,	
	Thou graunte me myght so þat I mowght	
	Ordan my werkis aftir þi wille.	
	For in þis erthely lyffe	
	Ar non to God more boune	10
	Then is I and my wyffe,	
	For frenshippe we haue foune.	

Vnto me tolde God on a tyde,
    Wher I was telde vnder a tree,
He saide my seede shulde be multyplyed   15
    Lyke to þe gravell of þe see,
And als þe sternes wer strewed wyde,
    So saide he þat my seede schuld be;
And bad I shulde be circumcicyd
    To fulfille þe lawe – þus lernynde he me.   20
        In worlde wherso we wonne
        He sendes vs richeys ryve;
        Als ferre as schynes þe sonne,
        He is stynter of stryve.

Abram first named was I,   25
    And sythen he sette a sylypp ma;
And my wiffe hyght Sarae
    And sythen was scho named Sara.

But Sara was vncertan thanne
    That euere oure seede shulde sagates ʒelde,   30
Because hirselfe sho was barrane
    And we wer bothe gone in grete eelde.
But scho wroght as a wyse woman:
    To haue a barne vs for to beelde,
Hir seruand prevely sho wan   35
    Vnto my bede my wille to welde.

1.   *Quire D begins*
15. be] *Suppl Co, K*
     multyplyed] d *added by later hand*
25. Abram] *TS; MS* Abraham

Sone aftir þan befelle
   When God oure dede wolde dight,   f.31ᵛ
Sho broght forthe Esmaell,
   A sone semely to sight.   40

Than aftirward when we waxed alde,
   My wyffe scho felle in feere for same;
Oure God nedes tythynges tyll vs talde
   Wher we wer in oure house at hame,
Tille haue a sone we shulde be balde,   45
   And Isaak shulde be his name,
And his seede shulde springe manyfalde.
   Gyff I were blythe, who wolde me blame?
     And for I trowed þis tythynge,
      That God talde to me þanne,   50
     The grounde and þe begynnyng
      Of trowthe þat tyme beganne.

Nowe awe I gretely God to yeelde,
   That so walde telle me his entente,
And noght gaynestandyng oure grete eelde   55
   A semely sone he has vs sente.
Now he is wight hymselfe to welde
   And fra me is all wightnes wente,
Therfore sall he be my beelde.
   I lowe hym þat þis lane has lente,   60
     For he may stynte oure stryve
      And fende vs fro alle ill;
     I love hym as my liff,
      With all myn herte and will.

Angelus   Abraham, Abraham.
Abraham   Loo, I am here.   65
Angelus   Nowe bodeword vnto þe I brynge:
God wille assaye þi wille and cheere,
   Giffe þou wille bowe tylle his byddyng;
Isaak þi sone þat is the dere,
   Whom þou loues our alle thyng,   f.32
To þe lande of vyssyon wende in feere   71
   And there of hym þou make offering.
     I sall þe shewe full sone
      The stede of sacrifice.
     God wille þis dede be done,   75
      And þerfore þe avise.

Abraham   Lord God þat lens ay-lastand light,
   This is a ferly fare to feele.
Tille haue a sone semely to sight,

70.   our] *This ed;* TS ouer *(conj)*

Isaak, þat I loue full wele —   80
He is of eelde to reken right
   Thyrty ȝere and more sumdele —
And vnto dede hym buse be dight.
   God has saide me so for my seele,
     And biddis me wende on all wise   85
       To þe lande of vysioune,
     Ther to make sacryfice
       Of Isaak þat is my sone.

And þat is hythyn thre daies jornay
   The ganeste gate þat I cane go;   90
And sertis, I sall noght say hym nay
   If God commaunde myself to sloo.
Bot to my sone I will noght saye,
   Bot take hym and my seruantis twoo,
And with our asse wende forthe our waye;   95
   As God has saide, it sall be soo.
     Isaak, sone, I vndirstande
       To wildirnesse now wende will we,
     Thare fore to make oure offerand,
       For so has God comaunded me.   100

Isaac   Fadir, I am euere at youre wille,
   As worthy is withowten trayne;
Goddis comaundement to fulfille
   Awe all folke for to be fayne.
Abraham   Sone, þou sais me full gode skille,   105
   Bott alle þe soth is noȝt to sayne.   f.32ᵛ
Go we sen we sall þertille —
   I praye God sand vs wele agayne.
Isaac   Childir, lede forthe oure asse
     With wode þat we sall bryne.   110
     Euen as God ordand has,
       To wyrke we will begynne.

I Famulus   Att youre biddyng we wille be bowne
   What way in worlde þat ȝe wille wende.
II Famulus   Why, sall we trusse ought forthe a towne   115
   In any vncouthe lande to lende?
I Famulus   I hope tha haue in þis sessoune
   Fro God of heuyn sum solayce sende.
II Famulus   To fulfille yt is goode reasoune,
   And kyndely kepe þat he has kende.   120

---

90.   I] *Interlined*
     cane] *Zu; MS, TS* gane
95.   asse] *This ed; MS, TS* Assee
108.   sand] a *altered to* e *by later hand*
     agayne] *Added by main scribe after rubrication (over rhyme-bracket)*

I Famulus	Bott what þei mene certayne
	Haue I na knowlage clere.
II Famulus	It may noght gretely gayne
	To move of swilke matere.

Abraham	No, noye you noght in no degré	125
	So for to deme here of oure dede,	
	For als God comaunded so wirke will we,	
	Vntill his tales vs bus take hede.	
I Famulus	All þos þat wille his seruandis be	
	Ful specially he wille thaym spede.	130
Isaac	Childir, with all þe myght in me	
	I lowe that lorde of ilke a lede,	
	And wirshippe hym certayne	
	My will is euere vnto.	
II Famulus	God giffe you myght and mayne	f.33
	Right here so for to doo.	136

Abraham	Sone, yf oure lord God almyghty	
	Of myselfe walde haue his offerande,	
	I wolde be glade for hym to dye,	
	For all oure heele hyngis in his hande.	140
Isaac	Fadir, forsuth, ryght so walde I,	
	Leuer þan lange to leue in lande.	
Abraham	A, sone, thu sais full wele, forthy	
	God geue þe grace gratthely to stande.	
	Childir, bide ȝe here still,	145
	No ferther sall ȝe goo,	
	For ȝondir I se þe hill	
	That we sall wende vntoo.	

Isaac	Kepe wele oure asse and all oure gere	
	To tyme we come agayne you till.	150
Abraham	My sone, þis wode behoues þe bere	
	Till þou come high vppon yone hill.	
Isaac	Fadir, þat may do no dere,	
	Goddis comaundement to fullfyll,	
	For fra all wathes he will vs were	155
	Wharso we wende to wirke his wille.	
Abraham	A, sone, þat was wele saide.	
	Lay doune þat woode euen here	
	Tille oure auter be grathide –	
	And, my sone, make goode cheere.	160

Isaac	Fadir, I see here woode and fyre,
	Bot wherof sall oure offerand be?

---

145. *Ruled off from 144, in red (error); Abram added to right by J. Clerke*

Abraham	Sertis son, gude God oure suffraynd syr
	Sall ordayne it in goode degré.
	For sone, and we do his dessyre,
	Full gud rewarde tharfore gette wee.
	In heuyn ther mon we haue oure hyre,
	For vnto vs so hight has hee.
	Therfore sone, lete vs praye
	To God, bothe þou and I,
	That we may make þis daye
	Oure offerand here dewly.

Grete God þat all þis worldé has wrought
  And grathely gouernes goode and ill,
Thu graunte me myght so þat I mowght   175
  Thy comaundementis to fullfill.
And gyffe my flessche groche or greue oght,
  Or sertis my saule assentte þertill,
To byrne all that I hydir broght
  I sall noght spare yf I shulde spille.   180

Isaac   Lorde God of grete pousté
      To wham all pepull prayes,
    Graunte bothe my fadir and me
      To wirke þi wille allweyes.

But fadir, nowe wolde I frayne full fayne   185
  Wharof oure offerand shulde be grathid?

Abraham Sertis sone, I may no lengar layne:
  Thyselfe shulde bide þat bittir brayde.
Isaac Why fadir, will God þat I be slayne?
Abraham Ȝa, suthly sone, so has he saide.   190
Isaac And I sall noght grouche þeragayne,
  To wirke his wille I am wele payed;
    Sen it is his desire,
      I sall be bayne to be
    Brittynd and brent in fyre,   f.34
      And þerfore morne noght for me.   196

Abraham Nay sone, this gatis most nedis be gone,
  My lord God will I noght gaynesaye,
Nor neuer make mornys nor mone
  To make offerand of þe this day.   200
Isaac Fadir, sen God oure lorde allane
  Vowchesaffe to sende when ȝe gon praye
A sone to you, whan ye had nane,
  And nowe will that he wende his waye,
    Therfore faynde me to fell   205
      Tille offerand in þis place;

164–5. *To right by J. Clerke* father wold God / I shuld be slayne, *deleted; small crosses to left and right of dialogue (? error; cf. 189)*
202. Vowchesaffe] *Ho¹* Vowchedsaffe

   But firste I sall you telle
    My counsaille in þis case.

  I knaw myselfe be cours of kynde,
   My flessche for dede will be dredande.   210
  I am ferde þat ȝe sall fynde
   My force youre forward to withstande,
  Therfore is beste þat ye me bynde
   In bandis faste, boothe fute and hande.
  Nowe whillis I am in myght and mynde   215
   So sall ȝe saffely make offerrande,
    For fadir, when I am boune
     My myght may noght avayle.
    Here sall no fawte be foune
     To make youre forward faylle,   220

  For ȝe are alde and alle vnwelde,
   And I am wighte and wilde of thoght.
Abraham To bynde hym þat shuld be my beelde!
   Outtane Goddis will, þat wolde I noght.
  Bot loo, her sall no force be felde,   225
   So sall God haue that he has soght.
  Farewele my sone, I sall þe ȝelde
   Tylle hym þat all this world has wroght.   f.34ᵛ

  Nowe kysse me hartely I þe pray.
  Isaak, I take my leue for ay—   230
   Me bus þe mys.
  My blissyng haue þou enterly,
  And I beseke God allmyghty
   He giffe þe his.

  Thus aren we samyn assent   235
   Eftir thy wordis wise.
  Lorde God, to þis take tente,
   Ressayue thy sacrifice.

  This is to me a perles pyne,
   To se myn nawe dere childe þus boune.   240
  Me had wele leuer my lyf to tyne
   Than see þis sight þus of my sone.
  It is Goddis will, it sall be myne,
   Agaynste his saande sall I neuer schone,
  To Goddis cummaundement I sall enclyne,   245
   That in me fawte non be foune.

231. *Lineation this ed; TS places between 232 and 233*
235–8. *Bracketed, with* hic *to right of bracket, by later hand. Some words in a previous later
  hand to right of 235, erased and illegible*

                    Therfore my sone so dere,
                        If þou will anythyng saye,
                    Thy dede it drawes nere,
                        Farewele, for anes and ay.   250

Isaac   Now my dere fadir, I wolde you praye,
                    Here me thre wordes, graunte me my bone
                Sen I fro this sall passe for ay;
                    I see myn houre is comen full sone.
                In worde, in werke, or any waye   255
                    That I haue trespassed or oght mysdone,
                Forgiffe me fadir or I dye þis daye,
                    For his luffe þat made boþe sonne and mone.
                        Here sen we two sall twynne
                            Firste God I aske mercy,   260
                        And you in more and myne,
                        This day or euere I dy.

Abraham   Now my grete God Adonay
                    That all þis worlde has worthely wroght,   f.35
                Forgyffe the sone for his mercye,   265
                    In worde, in worke, in dede and thoght.
                    Nowe sone, as we are leryd
                        Our tyme may noȝt myscarie.
Isaac   Nowe farewele all medilerth,
                    My flesshe waxis faynte for ferde;   270
                    Nowe fadir, take youre swerde,
                        Methynke full lange ȝe tarie.

Abraham   Nay, nay sone, nay, I the behete,
                    That do I noght, withouten were.
                Thy wordis makis me my wangges to wete   275
                    And chaunges, childe, ful often my cheere.
                Therfore lye downe, hande and feete,
                    Nowe may þou witte thyn oure is nere.
Isaac   A, dere fadir, lyff is full swete,
                    The drede of dede dose all my dere.   280
                        As I am here youre sone
                        To God I take me till,
                        Nowe am I laide here bone,
                        Do with me what ȝe will.

                    For fadir, I aske no more respete,   285
                    Bot here a worde what I wolde mene:

266–8.   *To right of 266 caret hic by later hand. To right of 266–8, additions by J. Clerke at
            different times: (i) Nowe haue I chose / whether I had lever etc / ; (ii) My nowne
            swete son / to slo or greve my / God for ever*
267–8.   *Lineation TS; one line in MS*
271.   Caret *to right by later hand, deleted;* hic caret *to right of this, probably Clerke's hand*
272.   Me–] *TS; MS* ȝe
282–4.   Hic caret *to right by later hand*

        I beseke ȝou or þat ȝe smyte
          Lay doune þis kyrcheffe on myn eghne,
        Than may ȝoure offerand be parfite
          If ȝe wille wirke thus as I wene.   290
        And here to God my saule I wite
        And all my body to brenne bydene.
            Now fadir be noght myssyng,
              But smyte fast as ȝe may.

Abraham   Farewele, in Goddis dere blissyng   295
              And myn, for euer and ay.

        That pereles prince I praye
          Myn offerand heretill haue it,
        My sacryfice þis day
          I praye þe lorde ressayue it.   300

Angelus   Abraham, Abraham.
Abraham   Loo, here iwys.   f.35ᵛ
Angelus   Abraham, abide, and halde þe stille.
        Sla noght thy sone, do hym no mysse,
          Take here a schepe thy offerrand tyll,
         Is sente the fro the kyng of blisse   305
           That faythfull ay to þe is fone;
        He biddis þe make offerand of þis
           Here at this tyme, and saffe thy sone.

Abraham   I lowe þat lord with herte entier
          That of his luffe þis lane me lente,   310
        To saffe my sone, my darlyng dere,
          And sente þis schepe to þis entente,
         That we sall offir it to the here –
          So sall it be as þou has mente.
        My sone, be gladde and make goode cheere, 315
          God has till vs goode comforte sente.
            He will noght þou be dede,
             But tille his lawes take kepe;
           And se son, in thy stede
             God has sente vs a schepe.   320

Isaac   To make oure offerand at his wille
          All for oure sake he has it sente.
         To lowe þat lorde I halde grete skyll
          That tylle his menȝe þus has mente.
         This dede I wolde haue tane me till   325
          Full gladly lorde, to thyn entent.
Abraham   A, sone, thy bloode wolde he noght spill,
          Forthy this shepe thus has he sente;

297–300. Hic *to right by later hand*
327. he] *Interlined in red*

And sone, I am full fayne
  Of oure spede in þis place – 330
Bot go we home agayne
  And lowe God of his grace.

Angelus   Abraham, Abraham.
Abraham   Loo, here indede.
  Harke sone, sum saluyng of our sare.
Angelus   God sais þou sall haue mekill mede f.36
  For thys goode will þat þou in ware. 336
Sen þou for hym wolde do þis dede –
  To spille thy sone and noght to spare –
He menes to multiplie youre seede
  On sides seere, as he saide are; 340
    And yit he hight you this,
      That of youre seede sall ryse,
    Thurgh helpe of hym and his,
      Ouere-hande of all enmys.

Luk ȝe hym loue, þis is his liste, 345
  And lelly lyff eftir his laye,
For in youre seede all mon be bliste
  That ther bese borne be nyght or day.
If ȝe will in hym trowe or triste
  He will be with ȝou euere and aye. 350
Abraham   Full wele wer vs and we it wiste,
  Howe we shulde wirke his will alwaye.
Isaac   Fadir, þat sall we frayne
      At wyser men þan wee,
    And fulfille it ful fayne 355
      Indede eftir oure degree.

Abraham   Nowe sone, sen we þus wele hase spede,
  That God has graunted me thy liffe,
It is my wille þat þou be weddc
  And welde a woman to thy wyffe; 360
So sall thy sede springe and be spredde
  In the lawez of God be reasoune ryffe.
I wate in what steede sho is stede
  That þou sall wedde, withowten stryffe:
    Rabek þat damysell, 365
      Hir fayrer is none fone,
    The doughter of Batwell
      Þat was my brothir sone.

Isaac   Fadir, as you likes my lyffe to spende f.36ᵛ
  I sall assente vnto the same. 370

362. lawez] z *(MS* ȝ*) apparently added*
369. *Isaac] Repeated by later hand*
    you] *This ed; TS* þou

Abraham One of my seruandis sone sall I sende
    Vnto þat birde to brynge hir hame.
    The gaynest gates now will we wende.
     My barnes, yee ar noght to blame
    ȝeff ȝe thynke lang þat we her lende;   375
     Gedir same oure gere, in Goddis name,
     And go we hame agayne
      Euyn vnto Barsabé.
     God þat is most of mayne
      Vs wisse and with ȝou be.   380

XI The Hosiers

Moses and Pharaoh

Rex Pharao O pees, I bidde þat no man passe,   f.38
     But kepe þe cours þat I comaunde,
    And takes gud heede to hym þat hasse
     Youre liff all haly in his hande.
    Kyng Pharo my fadir was,   5
     And led þe lordshippe of this lande,
    I am his hayre as elde will asse,
     Euere in his steede to styrre and stande.
     All Egippe is myne awne
      To lede aftir my lawe,   10
     I will my myght be knawen
      And honnoured as it awe.

    Therfore als kyng I commaunde pees
     To all þe pepill of þis empire,
    That no man putte hym fourthe in prees   15
     But þat will do als we desire.
    And of youre sawes I rede you sees,
     And sesse to me, youre sufferayne sire,
    That most youre comforte may encrese
     And at my liste lose liffe and lyre.   20

380+ finis *added by J. Clerke; bottom half of f. 36ᵛ blank, ff. 37, 37ᵛ blank*

 1. *Rex Pharao*] *This ed; TS Rex*
   O pees] *A deleted capital between*
 2. comaunde] *Five minims between* a *and* d
 12. as it] *This ed; MS* as it als it, *TS* als it

I Consolator	My lorde, yf any were	
	Þat walde not wirke youre will,	
	And we wist whilke thay were	
	Ful sone we suld þaym spill.	

Rex	Thurghoute my kyngdome wolde I kenn,	25
	And konne tham thanke þat couthe me telle,	
	If any wer so weryd þen	
	That wolde aught fande owre forse to fell.	
II Consolator	My lorde, þar are a maner of men	
	That mustirs grete maistris þam emell,	30
	The Jewes þat wonnes here in Jessen	
	And er named the childir of Israell.	
	They multyplye so faste	
	Þat suthly we suppose	
	Thay are like, and they laste,	35
	Yowre lordshippe for to lose.	

Rex	Why, devill, what gawdes haue they begonne?	
	Er þai of myght to make afrayse?	
I Consolator	Tho felons folke, sir, first was fonn	
	In kyng Pharo 3oure fadyr dayse.	40
	Thay come of Joseph, Jacob sonn,	
	That was a prince worthy to prayse,	
	And sithen in ryste furthe are they run,	
	Now ar they like to lose our layse.	
	Thay sall confounde vs clene	45
	Bot if þai sonner sese.	
Rex	What devill ever may it mene	
	Þat they so fast encrese?	

II Consolator	Howe they encrese full wele we kenn,	f.38ᵛ
	Als oure elders before vs fande,	50
	Thay were talde but sexty and ten	
	Whan þei enterd into þis lande.	
	Sithen haue they soionerd here in Jessen	
	Foure houndereth 3ere, þis we warande,	
	Now are they noumbered of myghty men	55
	Wele more þan thre hundereth thowsande,	
	Withowten wiffe and childe	
	And herdes þat kepes ther fee.	
Rex	So myght we be bygillid;	
	Bot certis þat sall noght be,	60

---

24. suld] *D²*, *after T* shuld*; MS, TS* sall
32. Israell] Is—*inserted by later hand (probably J. Clerke) over beginning of main scribe's* iraell
38. afrayse] *This ed; MS, TS* a frayse
41. of] *MS* of of, of' *deleted*
42. a] *Interlined*

For with qwantise we sall þam qwelle,
  Þat þei sall no farrar sprede.
I Consolator Lorde, we have herde oure fadres telle
  Howe clerkis, þat ful wele couthe rede,
Saide a man shulde wax þam emell   65
  That suld fordo vs and owre dede.
Rex Fy on þam, to þe devell of helle!
  Swilke destanye sall we noght drede.
  We sall make mydwayes to spille þam,
    Whenne oure Ebrewes are borne,   70
  All þat are mankynde to kille þam,
    So sall they sone by lorne.

For of the other haue I non awe.
  Swilke bondage sall we to þam bede:
To dyke and delfe, beere and drawe,   75
  And do all swilke vnhonest dede.
Þus sall þe laddis beholden lawe,
  Als losellis ever thaire lyff to leede.
II Consolator Certis lorde, þis is a sotell sawe,
  So sall þe folke no farrar sprede.   80
Rex Yaa, helþ es to halde þam doune,
  Þat we no fantyse fynde.
I Consolator Lorde, we sall ever be bowne
  In bondage þam to bynde.

Moyses Grete God þat all þis grounde began   85
  And governes euere in gud degree,
That made me Moyses vnto man   f.39
  And saued me sythen out of þe see –
Kyng Pharo he comaundjed þan
  So þat no sonnes shulde saued be,   90
Agayns his wille away I wan –
  Thus has God shewed his myght in me.
    Nowe am I here to kepe,
    Sett vndir Synay syde,
    The bisshoppe Jetro schepe,   95
    So bettir bute to bide.

A, mercy God, mekill is thy myght,
  What man may of thy meruayles mene!
I se ȝondyr a ful selcouth syght
  Wherof befor no synge was seene.   100
A busk I se yondir brennand bright
  And þe leues last ay inlike grene;

61. qwantise] *TS; MS* qwantile, *T* quantyse
72. by] *This ed; TS* be *(conj)*
82. fantyse] *This ed; MS* fantynse, *TS* fantnyse *(conj)*, *T* fayntnes
86+ *Catchword* That made me Moyses
87. *Quire E begins*
102. inlike] *D²; MS, TS* in like

	If it be werke of worldly wight	
	I will go witte withowten wene.	
Deus	Moyses, come noght to nere	105
	Bot stille in þat stede dwelle,	
	And take hede to me here,	
	And tente what I þe telle.	

I am thy lorde, withoutyn lak,
   To lengh þi liffe euen as me list, 110
And the same God þat somtyme spak
   Vnto thyne elders als þei wiste;
Both Abraham and Ysaac
   And Jacob, saide I, suld be bliste
And multyplyeand, þam to mak, 115
   So þat þer seede shulde noght be myste.
    And nowe kyng Pharo
     Fuls þare childir ful faste.
    If I suffir hym soo
     Þare seede shulde sone be past. 120

To make þe message haue I mende
   To hym þat þam so harmed hase,
To warne hym with wordes hende
   So þat he lette my pepull passe,
That they to wildirnesse may wende 125
   And wirshippe me als whilom was.
And yf he lenger gar them lende
   His sange ful sone sall be 'allas'.

Moyses   A, lord, syth, with thy leue,
     Þat lynage loves me noght, 130
    Gladly they walde me greve
     And I slyke boodword brought.

Therfore lord, late sum othir fraste
   Þat hase more forse þam for to feere.

Deus   Moyses, be noght abaste 135
    My bidding baldely to here.
If thai with wrang ought walde þe wrayste,
   Owte of all wothis I sall þe were.

Moyses   We, lord, þai wil noght to me trayste
   For al the othes þat I may swere. 140
    To neven slyke note of newe
     To folke of wykkyd will,
    Withouten taken trewe,
     They will noght take tente þertill.

---

113. Both] *D²; MS, TS* But
115. multyplyeand] *Zu; MS, TS* multyplye and
121. To] *This ed; TS* Go
123. To] *This ed; TS* Go

Deus	And if they will noght vndirstande	f.39ᵛ
	Ne take heede how I haue þe sente,	146
	Before the kyng cast downe thy wande	
	And it sall seme as a serpent.	
	Sithen take the tayle in thy hande	
	And hardely vppe þou itt hente,	150
	In the firste state als þou it fande —	
	So sall it turne by myn entent.	
	Hyde thy hande in thy barme	
	And as a lepre it sall be like,	
	Sithen hale withouten harme;	155
	Þi syngnes sall be slyke.	

And if he wil not suffre than
  My pepull for to passe in pees,
I sall send vengeaunce ix or x
  To sewe hym sararre, or I sesse.   160
Bot þe Jewes þat wonnes in Jessen
  Sall noȝt be merked with þat messe,
Als lange als þai my lawes will kenne
  Þer comfort sal I euere encresse.

Moyses	A, lorde, lovyd be thy wille	165
	Þat makes thy folke so free,	
	I sall tell þam vntill	
	Als þou telles vnto me.	

But to the kyng, lorde, whan I come
  And he ask me what is thy name,   170
And I stande stille þan, defe and dum,
  How sal I be withouten blame?

Deus	I saie þus: *ego sum qui sum*,	
	I am he þat I am the same,	
	And if þou myght not meve ne mum	175
	I sall þe saffe fro synne and shame.	
Moyses	I vndirstande þis thyng	
	With all þe myght in me.	
Deus	Be bolde in my blissyng,	
	Thy belde ay sall I be.	180

Moyses	A, lorde of lyffe, lere me my layre	
	Þat I þere tales may trewly tell.	
	Vnto my frendis nowe will I fare,	
	Þe chosen childre of Israell,	
	To telle þam comforte of ther care,	185
	And of þere daunger þat þei in dwell.	

154. as a lepre] *This ed, after T* as a lepre; *MS, TS* serpent
159. send] *Interlined by J. Clerke*
175. meve] *TS; MS* meke, *T* muf
181. my] *T* thy
183. will I fare] *Interlined by Clerke over main scribe's* fayne, *which is deleted*

God mayntayne you and me euermare,
And mekill myrthe be you emell.

I Puer   A, Moyses, maistir dere,
              Oure myrthe is al mornyng,   190
        We are harde halden here
          Als carls vndir þe kyng.

II Puer   Moyses, we may mourne and myne,
        Þer is no man vs myrþes mase;
        And sen we come al of a kynne,   195
         Ken vs som comforte in þis case.
Moyses   Beith of youre mornyng blyne,
        God wil defende you of your fays.
        Oute of þis woo he will you wynne
         To plese hym in more plener place.   200
           I sall carpe to þe kyng
          And fande to make you free.
III Puer   God sende vs gud tythynge,   f.40
          And allway with you be.

Moyses   Kyng Pharo, to me take tent.   205
Rex   Why, what tydyngis can þou tell?
Moyses   Fro God of heuen þus am I sente
        To fecche his folke of Israell;
        To wildirnesse he walde thei wente.
Rex   Ȝaa, wende þou to þe devell of hell.   210
        I make no force howe þou has mente,
         For in my daunger sall þei dwelle.
         And faytour, for thy sake,
          Þei sall be putte to pyne.
Moyses   Þanne will God vengeaunce take   215
         On þe and on al þyne.

Rex   Fy on the ladde, oute of my lande!
        Wenes þou with wiles to lose oure laye?
        When is þis warlowe with his wande
         Þat wolde þus wynne oure folke away?   220
II Consolator It is Moyses, we wele warrand,
        Agayne al Egipte is he ay.
        Youre fadir grete faute in hym fande,
        Nowe will he marre you if he may.
Rex   Nay, nay, þat daunce is done,   225
         Þat lordan leryd ouere-late.

---

197. Beith] *Altered to (?)* Beeth *by later hand; TS* Beeths, *T* Brethere
203. tythynge] *He, Co; MS, TS* tythyngis
204. allway] *This ed; TS* all may
208. Israell] *TS; MS* Israll
219. When] *This ed; TS* Where *(conj)*
219–20. *Misassignment to* I Consolator *(here written out, exceptionally, in full) deleted*

Moyses	God biddis þe graunte my bone.
	And late me go my gate.

Rex	Biddis God me? Fals lurdayne, þou lyes!	
	What takyn talde he, toke þou tent?	230
Moyses	ꝫaa sir, he saide þou suld despise	
	Botht me and all his comaundement.	
	In thy presence kast on this wise	
	My wande he bad by his assent,	
	And þat þou shulde þe wele avise	235
	Howe it shulde turne to a serpent.	
	And in his haly name	
	Here sal I ley it downe:	
	Loo ser, se her þe same.	
Rex	A! Dogg! Þe deuyll þe drowne!	240

Moyses	He saide þat I shulde take þe tayle	
	So for to proue his poure playne,	
	And sone he saide it shuld not fayle	
	For to turne a wande agayne.	
	Loo sir, behalde.	
Rex	Hopp illa hayle!	245
	Now certis þis is a sotill swayne,	
	But þis boyes sall byde here in oure bayle,	
	For all þair gaudis sall noght þam gayne;	
	Bot warse, both morne and none,	
	Sall þei fare for thy sake.	250
Moyses	God sende sum vengeaunce sone,	f.40ᵛ
	And on þi werke take wrake.	

I Egiptius	Allas, allas, þis lande is lorne,	
	On lif we may no lenger lende.	
II Egiptius	So grete myscheffe is made sen morne	255
	Þer may no medycyne vs amende.	
I Consolator	Sir kyng, we banne þat we wer borne,	
	Oure blisse is all with bales blende.	
Rex	Why crys you swa, laddis? Liste you scorne?	
I Egiptius	Sir kyng, slyk care was neuere kende.	260
	Oure watir þat was ordand	
	To men and beestis fudde,	
	Thurghoute al Egipte lande	
	Is turned to rede blude.	

	Full vgly and ful ill is it	265
	Þat was ful faire and fresshe before.	
Rex	This is grete wondir for to witt	
	Of all þe werkis þat ever wore.	

240. A] *TS; MS* Al
255–6. *Originally assigned to II Consolator, but corrected (main scribe)*
257. *I Consolator] I suppl this ed*

II Egiptius	Nay lorde, þer is anothir ȝitt
	That sodenly sewes vs ful sore, 270
	For tadys and frosshis we may not flitte,
	Thare venym loses lesse and more.
I Egiptius	Lorde, grete myses bothe morn and none
	Bytis vs full bittirlye,
	And we hope al by done 275
	By Moyses, oure enemye.

I Consolator	Lorde, whills ve with þis menyhe meve
	Mon never myrthe be vs emange.
Rex	Go saie we sall no lenger greve –
	But þai sall neuere þe tytar gang. 280
II Egiptius	Moyses, my lord has grauntyd leve f.41
	At lede thy folke to likyng lande,
	So þat we mende of oure myscheue.
Moyses	I wate ful wele þar wordes er wrange;
	That sall ful sone be sene, 285
	For hardely I hym heete,
	And he of malice mene
	Mo mervaylles mon he mett.

I Egiptius	Lorde, allas, for dule we dye,
	We dar not loke oute at no dore. 290
Rex	What deuyll ayles yow so to crye?
II Egiptius	We fare nowe werre þan euere we fure.
	Grete loppis ouere all þis lande þei flye,
	That with bytyng makis mekill blure.
I Egiptius	Lorde, oure beestis lyes dede and dry 295
	Als wele on myddyng als on more –
	Both oxe, horse and asse
	Fallis dede doune sodanly.
Rex	Therof no man harme has
	Halfe so mekill as I. 300

II Consolator	Ȝis lorde, poure men has mekill woo
	To see þer catell be out cast.
	The Jewes in Jessen faren noȝt soo,
	They haue al likyng in to last.
Rex	Go saie we giffe þam leue to goo 305
	To tyme there parellis be ouer-past –

---

277.   ve] *This ed; TS* we *(conj)*
282.   lande] *He, Co* lang, *after T* lang
284.   *Moyses] Inserted by J. Clerke over erasure of main scribe's original character-designation*
289.   *I Egiptius] In Clerke's hand, to right of main scribe's misassignment to Moyses, which is deleted*
291.   *Rex],* **292.** *II Egiptius] Originally misassigned in reverse, but corrected (main scribe)*
292.   fure] *TS; MS* fare
299.   *Rex] Originally misassigned I Egiptius, but corrected (main scribe)*

But or thay flitte over-farre vs froo
We sall garre feste þam foure so fast.

II Egiptius   Moyses, my lord giffis leue
Thy men for to remewe.   310
Moyses   He mon haue more mischeff   f.41ᵛ
But if his tales be trewe.

I Egiptius   We, lorde, we may not lede this liffe.
Rex   Why, is ther greuaunce growen agayne?
II Egiptius   Swilke poudre, lord, apon vs dryffe   315
That whare it bettis it makis a blayne.
I Egiptius   Like mesellis makis it man and wyffe.
Sythen ar they hurte with hayle and rayne;
Oure wynes in mountaynes may noȝt thryve,
So ar they threst and thondour-slayne.   320
Rex   How do thay in Jessen,
Þe Jewes, can ȝe aught say?
II Egiptius   Þis care nothyng they ken,
Þay fele no such affray.

Rex   No? Devill! And sitte they so in pees   325
And we ilke day in doute and drede?
I Egiptius   My lorde, þis care will euere encrese
Tille Moyses have leve þam to lede.
I Consolator   Lorde, war thay wente þan walde it sese,
So shuld we save vs and oure seede,   330
Ellis be we lorne— þis is no lese.
Rex   Late hym do fourth, þe devill hym spede!
For his folke sall no ferre
Yf he go welland woode.
II Consolator   Þan will itt sone be warre,   335
Ȝit war bettir þai ȝoode.

II Egiptius   We, lorde, new harme is comon to hande.
Rex   No! Devill! Will itt no bettir be?
I Egiptius   Wilde wormes is laide ouere al this lande,
Þai leve no frute ne floure on tree;   340
Agayne þat storme may nothyng stande.
II Egiptius   Lord, ther is more myscheff thynke me,   f.42
And thre daies hase itt bene durand,
So myrke þat non myght othir see.
I Egiptius   My lorde, grete pestelence   345
Is like ful lange to last.
Rex   Owe, come þat in oure presence?
Than is oure pride al past.

315.   poudre] *This ed*; MS poure, TS pou[d]re, T powder
331.   Ellis] TS; MS Eellis
342.   myscheff]–ff *added by a later hand*
345.   pestelence] *Interlined by a later hand (? J. Clerke)*
345–6.   *Lineation TS; one line in MS*

II Egiptius	My lorde, þis vengeaunce lastis lange,
	And mon till Moyses haue his bone. 350
I Consolator	Lorde, late þam wende, els wirke we wrang,
	It may not helpe to hover na hone.
Rex	Go saie we graunte þam leue to gange
	In the devill way, sen itt bus be done –
	For so may fall we sall þam fang 355
	And marre þam or tomorne at none.
I Egiptius	Moyses, my lorde has saide
	Þou sall haue passage playne.
Moyses	And to passe am I paied.
	My frendes, bees nowe fayne, 360

For at oure will now sall we wende,
  In lande of lykyng for to lende.

I Puer	Kyng Pharo, that felowns fende,
	Will haue grete care fro this be kende,
	Than will he schappe hym vs to shende 365
	And sone his ooste aftir vs sende.
Moyses	Beis noght aferde, God is youre frende,
	Fro alle oure fooes he will vs fende.
	Þarfore comes furthe with me,
	Haves done and drede yow noght. 370
II Puer	My lorde, loved mott þou bee,
	Þat us fro bale has brought.

III Puer	Swilke frenshippe never before we fande,	f.42ᵛ
	But in þis faire defautys may fall.	
	Þe Rede See is ryght nere at hande,	375
	Þer bus vs bide to we be thrall.	
Moyses	I sall make vs way with my wande,	
	For God hase sayde he saue vs sall;	
	On aythir syde þe see sall stande,	
	Tille we be wente, right as a wall.	380
	Therfore have ȝe no drede,	
	But faynde ay God to plese.	
I Puer	Þat lorde to lande vs lede,	
	Now wende we all at esse.	

I Egiptius	Kyng Pharro, ther folke er gane. 385
Rex	Howe nowe, es ther any noyes of newe?
II Egiptius	The Ebrowes er wente ilkone.
Rex	How sais þou þat?
I Egiptius	Þer talis er trewe.
Rex	Horse harneys tyte, þat þei be tane,
	Þis ryott radly sall þam rewe. 390

351. we] *Interlined by a later hand*
372. us] *Ha, after T* us; *MS, TS* þus
388. How] *This ed; TS* Now

We sall not sese or they be slone,
  For to þe se we sall þam sew.
    Do charge oure charyottis swithe
    And frekly folowes me.

II Egiptius   My lorde we are full blithe   395
    At youre biddyng to be.

II Consolator Lorde, to youre biddyng we er boune
    Owre bodies baldely for to bede,
  We sall noght byde, but dyng þam doune
    Tylle all be dede, withouten drede.   400
Rex   Hefe vppe youre hartis ay to Mahownde,
    He will be nere vs in oure nede.
  Owte! Ay herrowe! Devill, I drowne!
I Egiptius   Allas, we dye for alle our dede.
I Puer   Nowe ar we wonne fra waa   f.43
    And saued oute of þe see,   406
  Cantemus domino,
    To God a sange synge wee.

XII The Spicers

The Annunciation and the Visitation

Doctour Lord God, grete meruell es to mene   f.44
    Howe man was made withouten mysse,
  And sette whare he sulde euer haue bene
    Withouten bale, bidand in blisse;
  And howe he lost þat comforth clene   5
    And was putte oute fro paradys,
  And sithen what sorouse sor warr sene
    Sente vnto hym and to al his;

392. þe se] *Ha; MS, TS* þese
405–8. *Lineation* D²; *two lines in MS, TS*
408+ finis *added by J. Clerke; rest of f. 43 blank, f. 43ᵛ blank*

  1. *Doctour] Suppl by J. Clerke (as character-designation). Later, he added to the right of 1–3* this matter is / newly mayde wherof / we haue no coppy
  7. sor] *TS +; MS* ?for

And howe they lay lange space
   In helle, lokyn fro lyght,   10
Tille God graunted þam grace
   Of helpe, als he hadde hyght.

Þan is it nedfull for to neven
   How prophettis all Goddis counsailes kende,
Als prophet Amos in his steuen   15
   Lered whils he in his liffe gun lende:
Deus pater disposuit salutem fieri in medio terre, etc.
He sais þus: God þe fadir in heuen
   Ordand in erthe mankynde to mende;
And to grayth it with Godhede euen,
   His sone he saide þat he suld sende   20
      To take kynde of mankyn,
         In a mayden full mylde;
      So was many saued of syn
         And the foule fende begyled.

And for the feende sulde so be fedd   25
   Be tyne, and to no treuth take tentt,
God made þat mayden to be wedde
   Or he his sone vnto hir sentte.
So was the Godhede closed and cledde
   In wede of weddyng whare thy wente;   30
And þat oure blisse sulde so be bredde
   Ful many materes may be mente:
Quoniam in semine tuo benedicentur omnes gentes, etc.
      God hymself sayde this thynge   f.44ᵛ
         To Abraham als hym liste:
      Of thy sede sall vppe sprynge   35
         Wharein folke sall be bliste.

To proue thes prophette ordande er,
   Als Isay, vnto olde and yenge,
He moued oure myscheues for to merr,
   For thus he prayed God for this thynge: 40
Rorate, celi, desuper—
   Lord, late þou doune at thy likyng
Þe dewe to fall fro heuen so ferre,
   For than the erthe sall sprede and sprynge

16+   *disposuit*] *TS+; MS* dispsuit
27.   wedde] *TS+; MS* wedded
30.   thy] *K, Hm* th[e]y
32+   *Quoniam*] *TS+; MS* Qnia
37–8.   *Lineation Zu, Hm; MS* ordande / Er, *TS* ordande [wer] / Er
38.   Isay] *Zu; MS, TS+* I say
      vnto] vn–*interlined*
41.   *Rorate] This ed; TS* Orate. *Lineation 41–2 TS; one line in MS*

A seede þat vs sall saue,   45
  Þat nowe in blisse are bente.
Of clerkis whoso will craue
  Þus may þer gatis be mente:

Þe dewe to þe gode haly gaste
  May be remened in mannes mynde,   50
The erthe vnto þe mayden chaste,
  Bycause sho comes of erthely kynde.
Þir wise wordis ware noght wroght in waste,
  To waffe and wende away als wynde,
For this same prophett sone in haste   55
  Saide forthermore, als folkes may fynde:
Propter hoc dabit dominus ipse vobis signum, etc.
    Loo, he sais þus: God sall gyffe
      Hereof a syngne to see
    Tille all þat lely lyffe,
      And þis þare sygne sal be,   60
Ecce uirgo concipiett, et pariet filium, etc.

Loo, he sais a mayden mon
  Here on this molde mankynde omell,
Ful clere consayue and bere a sonne,
  And neven his name Emanuell.
His kyngdom þat euere is begonne   65
  Sall never sese, but dure and dwell;
On Dauid sege þore sall he wonne,
  His domes to deme and trueth to telle.
Zelus domini faciet hoc, etc.   f.45
    He says, luffe of oure lorde
      All þis sall ordan þanne;   70
    That mennes pees and accorde
      To make with erthely manne.

More of þis maiden meves me;
  This prophett sais for oure socoure
Egredietur virga de Jesse —   75
  A wande sall brede of Jesse boure,
And of þis same also sais hee:
  Vpponne þat wande sall springe a floure
Wheron þe haly gast sall be,
  To governe it with grete honnoure.   80
    That wande meynes vntill vs
      Þis mayden, even and morne,
    And þe floure is Jesus,
      Þat of þat blyst bees borne.

46.   bente] *Ho'* blente
50.   remened] *This ed; TS* remeued
73.   meves me] *This ed; MS* me meves, *TS +* me meves [he]
83.   Jesus] *MS* Jhc *altered to* Jhs

Þe prophet Johell, a gentill Jewe,   85
  Somtyme has saide of þe same thyng,
He likenes Criste euen als he knewe
  Like to þe dewe in doune-commyng:
Ero quasi ros; et virgo Israell germinabit sicut lilium.
Þe maiden of Israell al newe,
  He sais, sall bere one and forthe brynge   90
Als þe lelly floure, full faire of hewe.
   Þis meynes sa to olde and ȝenge,
     Þat þe hegh haly gaste
      Come oure myscheffe to mende
    In Marie, mayden chaste,   95
     When God his sone walde sende.

Þis lady is to þe lilly lyke–
  Þat is bycause of hir clene liffe,
For in þis worlde was neuer slyke
  One to be mayden, modir, and wyffe.   100
And hir sonne, kyng in heuen-ryke,   f.45ᵛ
  Als oft es red be reasoune ryfe,
And hir husband, bath maistir and meke,
  In charité to stynte all striffe–
   Þis passed all worldly witte,   105
    How God had ordand þaim þanne
    In hir one to be knytte,
     Godhed, maydenhed, and manne.

Bot of þis werke grete witnes was
  With forme-faders, all folke may tell.   110
Whan Jacob blyst his sone Judas
  He tolde þe tale þaim two emell:
Non auferetur septrum de Juda,
donec ueniat qui mittendus est.
He sais þe septer sall noght passe
  Fra Juda lande of Israell,
Or he comme þat God ordand has   115
  To be sente fccndis force to fell.
Et ipse erit expectacio gencium.
    Hym sall alle folke abyde,
     And stande vnto his steuen.
    Ther sawes wer signified
     To Crist, Goddis sone in heuen.   120

For howe he was sente, se we more,
  And howe God wolde his place puruay;
He saide, sonne, I sall sende byfore
  Myne aungell to rede þe thy way–

88+   *Ero] TS+; MS Ego*
112+ *donec] Suppl K, Hm (after Gen. xlix. 10)*

> *Ecce mitto aungelum meum ante faciem tuam,*
> *qui preparabit viam tuam ante te.*
> Of John Baptist he menyd þore,   125
>   For in erthe he was ordand ay
> To warne þe folke þat wilsom wore
>   Of Cristis comyng, and þus gon say:
> *Ego quidem baptizo in aqua vos, autem*
> *baptizabimini spiritu sancto.*
>   Eftir me sall come nowe   f.46
>   A man of myghtis mast,   130
>   And sall baptis ȝowe
>   In the high haly gast.
>
> Þus of Cristis commyng may we see
>   How sainte Luke spekis in his gospell:
> Fro God in heuen es sent, sais he,   135
>   An aungell is named Gabriell,
> To Nazareth in Galalé,
>   Where þan mayden mylde gon dwell,
> Þat with Joseph suld wedded be;
>   Hir name is Marie— þus gan he telle.   140
>   How God his grace þan grayd
>   To man in þis manere,
>   And how þe aungell saide,
>   Takes hede, all þat will here.
>
> *Tunc cantat angelus.*

Angelus
> Hayle Marie, full of grace and blysse,   145
>   Oure lord God is with þe
> And has chosen þe for his,
>   Of all women blist mot þou be.

Maria
> What manner of halsyng is þis
>   Þus preuely comes to me?   150
> For in myn herte a thoght it is,
>   Þe tokenyng þat I here see.
>
> *Tunc cantat angelus, 'Ne timeas Maria'.*

Angelus
> Ne drede þe noght mylde Marie,
>   For nothyng þat may befalle,
> For þou has fun soueranly   155
>   At God a grace ouer othir all.
> In chastité of thy bodye
>   Consayue and bere a childe þou sall;

---

130. myghtis] *Ha, Hm; MS, TS* myghtist
141. How] *Ha, Zu; MS, TS, Hm* To
144+ *SD added to right by J. Clerke*
152+ *SD added to right by Clerke*
156. ouer othir] *MS* all, *erased, between*

This bodword brynge I þe, forthy
   His name Jesu sall þou calle.   160

Mekill of myght þan sall he bee,
   He sall be God and called God sonn.
Dauid sege, his fadir free,   f.46ᵛ
   Sall God hym giffe to sytte vppon;
Als kyng for euer regne sall hee,   165
   In Jacob house ay for to wonne,
Of his kyngdome and dignité
   Shall noo man erthly knaw ne con.

Maria   Þou Goddis aungell meke and mylde,
   Howe sulde it be, I the praye,   170
That I sulde consayve a childe
   Of any man by nyght or daye?
I knawe no man þat shulde haue fyled
   My maydenhode, the sothe to saye;
Withouten will of werkis wilde   175
   In chastité I haue ben ay.

Angelus   Þe haly gast in þe sall lighte,
   Hegh vertuc sall to þe holde,
The holy birthe of the so bright
   God sonne he sall be calde.   180
Loo, Elyzabeth þi cosyne ne myght
   In elde consayue a childe for alde;
Þis is þe sexte moneth full ryght,
   To hir þat baran has ben talde.

Maria   Thou aungell, blissid messanger,   185
   Of Goddis will I holde me payde;
I love my lorde with herte clere,
   Þe grace þat he has for me layde.
Goddis handmayden, lo me here
   To his wille all redy grayd;   190
Be done to me of all manere
   Thurgh thy worde als þou hast saide.

Now God þat all oure hope is in,   f.47
   Thur the myght of þe haly gaste,
Saue þe, dame, fro sak of synne,   195
   And wisse þe fro all werkis wast.
Elyzabeth myn awne cosyne,
   Methoght I coveyte alway mast

168. *Added to right by a later hand*
177. Þe] Th—*superimposed by a later hand*
187. clere] *This ed; TS+* dere
192+ *Catchword* Now God þat all oure. *The next leaf, f. 47, is a singleton*
193–6. *Assigned [Angelus] in TS; Hm follows MS, as here*

To speke with þe of all my kynne,
Therfore I comme þus in þis hast.   200

Elizabeth A, welcome mylde Marie,
Myne aughen cosyne so dere,
Joifull woman am I
Þat I nowe see þe here.
Blissid be þou anely   205
Of all women in feere,
And the frute of thy body
Be blissid ferre and nere.

Þis is joyfull tydyng
Þat I may nowe here see,   210
Þe modyr of my lord kyng
Thus-gate come to me.
Sone als þe voyce of þine haylsing
Moght myn neres entreand be,
Þe childe in my wombe so yenge   215
Makes grete myrthe vnto þe.

Maria Nowe lorde, blist be þou ay
For þe grace þou has me lente;
Lorde, I lofe þe, God verray,
Þe sande þou hast me sente.   220
I þanke þe nyght and day,
And prayes with goode entente
Þou make me to thy paye,
To þe my wille is wentte.

Elizabeth Blissed be þou grathely grayed   f.47ᵛ
To God thurgh chastité,   226
Þou trowed and helde þe payed
Atte his wille for to bee.
All þat to þe is saide
Fro my lorde so free,   230
Swilke grace is for the layde
Sall be fulfilled in þe.

Maria To his grace I will me ta,
With chastité to dele,
Þat made me þus to ga   235
Omange his maidens feele.
My saule sall louying ma
Vnto þat lorde so lele,

201. A] *This ed; om TS +*
214. entreand] *Zu; MS* entre &, *TS +* entre and
216. vnto þe] *MS originally* alway to þe; alway *deleted*, vnto *interlined by J. Clerke*
218. grace] *TS +; MS* grrace
236. feele] *This ed; TS +* fele *(conj)*

And my gast make ioye alswa
   In God þat es my hele. 240

Tunc cantat Magnificat.

XIII The Pewterers and Founders
Joseph's Trouble about Mary

Joseph   Of grete mornyng may I me mene   f.48
          And walke full werily be þis way,
    For nowe þan wende I best hafe bene
          Att ease and reste by reasoune ay.
             For I am of grete elde,   5
             Wayke and al vnwelde,
          Als ilke man se it maye;
             I may nowder buske ne belde
             But owther in frith or felde;
          For shame what sall I saie,   10

    That þus-gates nowe on myne alde dase
          Has wedded a yonge wenche to my wiff,
    And may noȝt wele tryne over two strase?
          Nowe lorde, how lange sall I lede þis liff?
             My bancs er heuy als lede   15
             And may noȝt stande in stede,
          Als kende it is full ryfe.
             Now lorde, þou me wisse and rede
             Or sone me dryue to dede,
          Þou may best stynte þis striffe.   20

    For bittirly þan may I banne
          The way I in þe temple wente,

240+   *SD: Magnificat by main scribe, in red; Tunc cantat added above by J. Clerke. Finis added by J. Clerke. Rest of f. 47ᵛ blank except for catchword* Of grete mornyng

  1. *Quire F begins*
      Joseph] Suppl by a later hand
  3. hafe] *This ed; TS +* hase
11. dase] *Main scribe* tase, t *altered to* d *by a later hand*
14. lange sall] *This ed; TS +* langes all
18. me] *TS +; MS* we

Itt was to me a bad barganne,
　For reuthe I may it ay repente.
　　For þarein was ordande　　　　　　　　25
　　Vnwedded men sulde stande,
　Al sembled at asent,
　　And ilke ane a drye wande
　　On heght helde in his hand,
　And I ne wist what it ment.　　　　　　30

In-mange al othir ane bare I;
　Itt florisshed faire, and floures on sprede,
And thay saide to me forthy
　þat with a wiffe I sulde be wedde.
　　þe bargayne I made þare,　　　　　　35
　　þat rewes me nowe full sare,
　So am I straytely sted.
　　Now castes itt me in care,　　　　　f.48ᵛ
　　For wele I myght eueremare
　Anlepy life haue led.　　　　　　　　40

Hir werkis me wyrkis my wonges to wete;
　I am begiled – how, wate I noȝt.
My ȝonge wiffe is with childe full grete,
　þat makes me nowe sorowe vnsoght.
　　þat reproffe nere has slayne me,　　45
　　Forthy giff any man frayne me
　How þis þing miȝt be wroght,
　　To gabbe yf I wolde payne me,
　　þe lawe standis harde agayne me:
　To dede I mon be broght.　　　　　　50

And lathe methinkeþ, on þe todir syde,
　My wiff with any man to defame,
And whethir of there twa þat I bide
　I mon noȝt scape withouten schame.
　　þe childe certis is noght myne;　　55
　　þat reproffe dose me pyne
　And gars me fle fra hame.
　　My liff gif I shuld tyne,
　　Sho is a clene virgine
　For me, withouten blame.　　　　　　60

But wele I wate thurgh prophicie
　A maiden clene suld bere a childe,
But it is nought sho, sekirly,
　Forthy I wate I am begiled.

31.　I] *Added by a later hand*
47.　miȝt] *This ed; MS three minims* + ȝt, *TS* + may
49.　agayne] *TS* +; *MS* agayns

	And why ne walde som yonge man ta her?	65
	For certis I thynke ouer-ga hir	
	Into som wodes wilde,	
	Thus thynke I to stele fra hir.	
	God childe ther wilde bestes sla hir,	
	She is so meke and mylde.	70

Of my wendyng wil I non warne,
Neuere þe lees it is myne entente
To aske hir who gate hir þat barne,
Ʒitt wolde I witte fayne or I wente.

	All hayle, God be hereinne.	75
I Puella	Welcome, by Goddis dere myght.	
Joseph	Whare is þat ʒonge virgine	f.49
	Marie, my berde so bright?	

I Puella	Certis Joseph, ʒe sall vndirstande	
	Þat sho is not full farre you fra,	80
	Sho sittis at hir boke full faste prayand	
	For ʒou and vs, and for all þa	
	Þat oght has nede.	
	But for to telle hir will I ga	
	Of youre comyng, withouten drede.	85
	Haue done and rise vppe, dame,	
	And to me take gud hede –	
	Joseph, he is comen hame.	
Maria	Welcome, als God me spede.	

	Dredles to me he is full dere;	90
	Joseph my spouse, welcome er yhe.	
Joseph	Gramercy Marie, saie what chere,	
	Telle me þe soth, how est with þe?	
	Wha has ben there?	
	Thy wombe is waxen grete, thynke me,	95
	Þou arte with barne, allas for care.	
	A, maidens, wa worthe ʒou,	
	Þat lete hir lere swilke larc.	
II Puella	Joseph, ʒe sall noʒt trowe	
	In hir no febill fare.	100

Joseph	Trowe it noght arme? Lefe wenche, do way!	
	Hir sidis shewes she is with childe.	
	Whose ist Marie?	
Maria	Sir, Goddis and youres.	
Joseph	Nay, nay,	

---

65. ta] *TS +; MS* take
80–4. fra, þa, ga] a *altered to* o *by a later hand*
91. yhe] *Altered to* ye *by a later hand*
103. *Lineation K, Hm; MS, TS* Nay nay *at beginning of 104*

Now wate I wele I am begiled,
And reasoune why?   105
With me flesshely was þou neuere fylid,
And I forsake it here forthy.
    Say maidens, how es þis?
Tels me þe soþe, rede I;
    And but ȝe do, iwisse,   110
Þe bargayne sall ȝe aby.

II Puella   If ȝe threte als faste as yhe can
Þare is noght to saie þeretill,
For trulye her come neuer no man
    To waite þe body with non ill   115
    Of this swete wight,
For we haue dwelt ay with hir still   f.49ᵛ
And was neuere fro hir day nor nyght.
    Hir kepars haue we bene
    And sho ay in oure sight,   120
    Come here no man bytwene
To touche þat berde so bright.

I Puella   Na, here come no man in þere wanes
And þat euere witnesse will we,
Saue an aungell ilke a day anes   125
    With bodily foode hir fedde has he,
    Othir come nane.
Wharfore we ne wate how it shulde be
    But thurgh þe haly gaste allane.
    For trewly we trowe þis,   130
    Is grace with hir is gane,
    For sho wroght neuere no mys,
We witnesse euere ilkane.

Joseph   Þanne se I wele youre menyng is
Þe aungell has made hir with childe.   135
Nay, som man in aungellis liknesse
    With somkyn gawde has hir begiled,
    And þat trow I.
Forthy nedes noght swilke wordis wilde
    At carpe to me dissayuandly.   140
    We, why gab ye me swa
    And feynes swilk fantassy?
    Allas, me is full wa,
For dule why ne myght I dy.

---

107.   it] *Zu, Hm* the
115.   þe] *K; MS, TS+* her
116.   *Suppl to right by J. Clerke.* hic caret *in the same place deleted*
117.   *An otiose* & *follows*
129, 131.   allane, gane] a *altered to* o *by a later hand*

To me þis is a carefull cas;   145
 Rekkeles I raffe, refte is my rede.
I dare loke no man in þe face,
 Derfely for dole why ne were I dede;
  Me lathis my liff.
  In temple and in othir stede   150
   Ilke man till hethyng will me dryff.
    Was neuer wight sa wa,
   For ruthe I all to-ryff;
    Allas, why wroght þou swa
  Marie, my weddid wiffe?   155

Maria To my witnesse grete God I call,
   Þat in mynde wroght neuere na mysse.
Joseph Whose is þe childe þou arte withall?
Maria   Youres sir, and þe kyngis of blisse.
Joseph   Ye, and hoo þan?   f.50
   Na, selcouthe tythandis than is þis,   161
    Excuse þam wele there women can.
    But Marie, all þat sese þe
   May witte þi werkis ere wan,
    Thy wombe allway it wreyes þe   165
   Þat þou has mette with man.

  Whose is it, als faire mot þe befall?
Maria   Sir, it is youres and Goddis will.
Joseph Nay, I ne haue noght ado withall –
   Neme it na more to me, be still!   170
    Þou wate als wele as I,
    Þat we two same flesshly
   Wroght neuer swilk werkis with ill.
    Loke þou dide no folye
    Before me preuely   175
   Thy faire maydenhede to spill.

  But who is þe fader? Telle me his name.
Maria None but youresclfc.
Joseph   Late be, for shame.
  I did it neuere; þou dotist dame, by bukes and belles!
  Full sakles shulde I bere þis blame aftir þou telles,   180
  For I wroght neuere in worde nor dede
  Thyng þat shulde marre thy maydenhede,
   To touche me till.
  For of slyk note war litill nede,
  Yhitt for myn awne I wolde it fede,   185
   Might all be still;

146. refte] *This ed; TS +* reste; *MS long* s *or* f
157. na] a *altered to* o *by a later hand*
167. þe] *This ed; TS +* ye

	Þarfore þe fadir tell me, Marie.	
Maria	But God and yhow, I knawe right nane.	
Joseph	A, slike sawes mase me full sarye,	
	With grete mornyng to make my mane.	190
	Therfore be noȝt so balde,	
	Þat no slike tales be talde,	
	But halde þe stille als stane.	
	Þou art yonge and I am alde,	
	Slike werkis yf I do walde,	195
	Þase games fra me are gane.	

	Therfore, telle me in priuité,	f.50ᵛ
	Whos is þe childe þou is with nowe?	
	Sertis, þer sall non witte but we,	
	I drede þe law als wele as þou.	200
Maria	Nowe grete God of hys myght	
	Þat all may dresse and dight,	
	Mekely to þe I bowe.	
	Rewe on þis wery wight,	
	Þat in his herte myght light	205
	Þe soth to ken and trowe.	

Joseph	Who had thy maydenhede Marie? Has þou oght mynde?	
Maria	Forsuth, I am a mayden clene.	
Joseph	Nay, þou spekis now agayne kynde,	
	Slike þing myght neuere na man of mene.	210
	A maiden to be with childe?	
	Þase werkis fra þe ar wilde,	
	Sho is not borne I wene.	
Maria	Joseph, yhe ar begiled,	
	With synne was I neuer filid,	215
	Goddis sande is on me sene.	

Joseph	Goddis sande? Yha Marie, God helpe!	
	Bot certis þat childe was neuere oures twa.	
	But woman-kynde gif þam list yhelpe,	
	Yhitt walde þei na man wiste þer wa.	220
Maria	Sertis it is Goddis sande	
	[. . . . . .]	
	Þat sall I neuer ga fra.	
Joseph	Yha, Marie, drawe thyn hande,	
	For forther ȝitt will I fande,	
	I trowe not it be swa.	225

188. knawe . . . nane] a *altered to* o *by a later hand*
190–6. mane, stane, gane] a *altered to* o *by a later hand*
218–25. twa, wa, fra, swa] a *altered to* o *by a later hand*
219. þam] *Ha; MS, TS +* þat
221+ *Line missing. Lineation 221–2 TS +; MS one line*
224. I] *Interlined by a later hand*
       fande] *Ha, Zu; MS, TS* frande *(MS* r *perhaps added)*

        Þe soth fra me gif þat þou layne,
        Þe childe-bering may þou noȝt hyde;
      But sitte stille here tille I come agayne,
        Me bus an erand here beside.

Maria   Now grete God he you wisse,   230
          And mende you of your mysse
        Of me, what so betyde.
          Als he is kyng of blisse,   f.51
          Sende yhou som seand of þis,
        In truth þat ye might bide.   235

Joseph   Nowe lord God þat all þing may
        At thyne awne will bothe do and dresse,
      Wisse me now som redy way
        To walke here in þis wildirnesse.
          Bot or I passe þis hill,   240
          Do with me what God will,
      Owther more or lesse,
          Here bus me bide full stille
          Till I haue slepid my fille,
        Myn hert so heuy it is.   245

Angelus   Waken, Joseph, and take bettir kepe
        To Marie, þat is þi felawe fest.
Joseph   A, I am full werie, lefe, late me slepe,
        Forwandered and walked in þis forest.
Angelus   Rise vppe, and slepe na mare,   250
        Þou makist her herte full sare
      Þat loues þe alther best.
Joseph   We, now es þis a farly fare
        For to be cached bathe here and þare,
      And nowhere may haue rest.   255

      Say, what arte þou? Telle me this thyng.
Angelus   I, Gabriell, Goddis aungell full euen
      Þat has tane Marie to my kepyng,
        And sente es þe to say with steuen
        In lele wedlak þou lede þe.   260
        Leffe hir noȝt, I forbid þe,
      Na syn of hir þou neuen,
          But tille hir fast þou spede þe
          And of hir noght þou drede þe,
      It is Goddis sande of heuen.   265

      The childe þat sall be borne of her,
      Itt is consayued of þe haly gast.

---

230. he] *This ed;* TS be
235. *Suppl to right by a later hand*
246. Hic deficit *written to right by a later hand, deleted*

Alle joie and blisse þan sall be aftir,   f.51ᵛ
And to al mankynde nowe althir mast.
　Jesus his name þou calle,   270
　For slike happe sall hym fall
Als þou sall se in haste.
　His pepull saffe he sall
　Of euyllis and angris all,
Þat þei ar nowe enbraste.   275

Joseph　　And is this soth, aungell, þou saise?
Angelus　　Yha, and þis to taken right:
Wende forthe to Marie thy wiffe alwayse,
　Brynge hir to Bedlem þis ilke nyght.
　Ther sall a childe borne be,   280
　Goddis sone of heuen is hee
And man ay mast of myght.
Joseph　　　Nowe lorde God full wele is me
　That euyr þat I þis sight suld see,
I was neuer ar so light.   285

For for I walde haue hir þus refused,
　And sakles blame þat ay was clere,
Me bus pray hir halde me excused,
　Als som men dose with full gud chere.
　Saie Marie, wiffe, how fares þou?   290
Maria　　　Þe bettir sir, for yhou.
　Why stande yhe þare? Come nere.
Joseph　　　My bakke fayne wolde I bowe
　And aske forgifnesse nowe,
Wiste I þou wolde me here.   295

Maria　　Forgiffnesse sir? Late be, for shame,
　Slike wordis suld all gud women lakke.
Joseph　　Yha, Marie, I am to blame
　For wordis lang-are I to þe spak.   f.52
　But gadir same nowe all oure gere,   300
　Slike poure wede as we were,
And prike þam in a pak.
　Till Bedlem bus me it bere,
　For litill thyng will women dere;
Helpe vp nowe on my bak.   305

286.　haue] *Suppl Hoᵗ*
294.　forgifnesse] *TS+; MS* fogifnesse
305+　finis *added by J. Clerke. Rest of f. 52 blank; ff. 52ᵛ, 53, 53ᵛ blank*

XIV The Tilethatchers
The Nativity

Joseph All-weldand God in trinité,
    I praye þe lord, for thy grete myght,
Vnto thy symple seruand sec,
    Here in þis place wher we are pight,
      Oureself allone.   5
    Lord, graunte vs gode herberow þis nyght
      Within þis wone.

For we haue sought bothe vppe and doune
    Thurgh diuerse stretis in þis cité.
So mekill pepull is comen to towne   10
    Þat we can nowhare herbered be,
      Þer is slike prees;
    Forsuthe I can no socoure see,
      But belde vs with þere bestes.

And yf we here all nyght abide   15
    We schall be stormed in þis steede,
Þe walles are doune on ilke a side,
    Þe ruffe is rayued aboven oure hede,
      Als haue I roo;
    Say Marie, doughtir, what is thy rede,   20
      How sall we doo?

For in grete nede nowe are we stedde
    As þou thyselffe the soth may see,
For here is nowthir cloth ne bedde,
    And we are weyke and all werie   25
      And fayne wolde rest.
    Now gracious God, for thy mercie,
      Wisse vs þe best.

Maria God will vs wisse, full wele witt ȝe,
    Þerfore Joseph be of gud chere,   30
For in þis place borne will he be
    Þat sall vs saue fro sorowes sere,
      Boþe even and morne.
    Sir, witte ȝe wele þe tyme is nere
      He will be borne.   35

   1. *Joseph] Centred, written at same time as dialogue*
   4. *Faint addition by a later hand, including* self alone, *to right*
  18. rayued] *Ha; TS* + rayned

Joseph	Þan behoves vs bide here stille,	
	Here in þis same place all þis nyght.	
Maria	ȝa sir, forsuth it is Goddis will.	
Joseph	Þan wolde I fayne we had sum light,	
	What so befall.	40
	It waxis right myrke vnto my sight,	f.54ᵛ
	And colde withall.	

I will go gete vs light forthy,
    And fewell fande with me to bryng.

Maria   All-weldand God yow gouerne and gy,   45
    As he is sufferayne of all thyng
        For his grete myght,
    And lende me grace to his louyng
        Þat I me dight.

Nowe in my sawle grete joie haue I,   50
    I am all cladde in comforte clere,
Now will be borne of my body
    Both God and man togedir in feere,
        Blist mott he be.
    Jesu my sone þat is so dere,   55
        Nowe borne is he.

Hayle my lord God, hayle prince of pees,
    Hayle my fadir, and hayle my sone;
Hayle souereyne sege all synnes to sesse,
    Hayle God and man in erth to wonne.   60
        Hayle, thurgh whos myht
    All þis worlde was first begonne,
        Merknes and light.

Sone, as I am sympill sugett of thyne,
    Vowchesaffe, swete sone I pray þe,   65
That I myght þe take in þe armys of myne
    And in þis poure wede to arraie þe.
        Graunte me þi blisse,
    As I am thy modir chosen to be
        In sothfastnesse.   70

Joseph   A, lorde God what þe wedir is colde,
    Þe fellest freese þat euere I felyd.
I pray God helpe þam þat is alde
    And namely þam þat is vnwelde,
        So may I saie.   75
    Now gud God þou be my bilde
        As þou best may.

47.   For] *TS, Hm, BrZi (conj); MS* Fo, *Be* Of *(conj)*
66.   þe] *Hm; TS, BrZi* þe[r], *Be* the[se]
71.   God] *Be; om TS+*
        what] *MS* what what, *what² deleted*

A, lord God, what light is þis
  Þat comes shynyng þus sodenly?
I can not saie als haue I blisse.   80
  When I come home vnto Marie
    Þan sall I spirre.
  A, here be God, for nowe come I.

Maria   3e ar welcum sirre.

Joseph Say Marie, doghtir, what chere with þe?   85
Maria   Right goode Joseph, as has ben ay.   f.55
Joseph O Marie, what swete thyng is þat on thy kne?
Maria   It is my sone, þe soth to saye,
    Þat is so gud.
Joseph   Wele is me I bade þis day   90
    To se þis foode.

Me merueles mekill of þis light
  Þat þus-gates shynes in þis place,
Forsuth it is a selcouth sight.
Maria   Þis hase he ordand of his grace,   95
    My sone so 3ing,
  A starne to be schynyng a space
    At his bering.

For Balam tolde ful longe beforne
  How þat a sterne shulde rise full hye,   100
And of a maiden shulde be borne
  A sonne þat sall oure saffyng be
    Fro caris kene.
  Forsuth it is my sone so free
    Be whame Balam gon meene.   105

Joseph Nowe welcome, floure fairest of hewe,
  I shall þe menske with mayne and myght.
Hayle my maker, hayle Crist Jesu,
  Hayle riall kyng, roote of all right,
    Hayle saueour.   110
  Hayle my lorde, lemer of light,
    Hayle blessid floure.

Maria Nowe lord þat all þis worlde schall wynne,
  To þe my sone is þat I saye,
Here is no bedde to laye the inne,   115
  Þerfore my dere sone I þe praye,
    Sen it is soo,
  Here in þis cribbe I myght þe lay
    Betwene þer bestis two.

83. here] *K, Hm* here[d]

And I sall happe þe, myn owne dere childe,   120
With such clothes as we haue here.

Joseph   O Marie, beholde þes beestis mylde,   f.55ᵛ
They make louyng in ther manere
    As þei wer men.
Forsothe it semes wele be ther chere   125
    Þare lord þei ken.

Maria   Ther lorde þai kenne, þat wate I wele,
They worshippe hym with myght and mayne;
The wedir is colde as ye may feele,
    To halde hym warme þei are full fayne   130
    With þare warme breth,
And oondis on hym, is noght to layne,
    To warme hym with.

O, nowe slepis my sone, blist mot he be,
    And lyes full warme þer bestis bytwene.   135
Joseph   O, nowe is fulfillid, forsuth I see,
Þat Abacuc in mynde gon mene
    And prechid by prophicie.
He saide oure sauyoure shall be sene
    Betwene bestis lye,   140

And nowe I see þe same in sight.
Maria   Ȝa sir, forsuth þe same is he.
Joseph   Honnoure and worshippe both day and nyght,
    Ay-lastand lorde, be done to þe
    Allway, as is worthy;   145
And lord, to thy seruice I oblissh me
    With all myn herte, holy.

Maria   Þou mercyfull maker, most myghty,
My God, my lorde, my sone so free,
Thy handemayden forsoth am I,   150
And to thi seruice I oblissh me,
    With all myn herte entere.   f.56
Thy blissing, beseke I thee,
    Þou graunte vs all in feere.

151+   *Catchword* With all myn herte
152.   *Quire G begins*
154+   *Additions by 3 later hands: (i)* Br.th.r with haste *(to right of 154, erased, but visible under u-v); (ii)* hic caret pastoribus *(to right of (i)); (iii)* sequitur postea *(beneath (ii)). Rest of f. 56 blank; ff. 56ᵛ–58 blank. Two leaves, the inner bifolium of quire G, missing between ff. 58ᵛ and 59*

XV The Chandlers
The Shepherds

I Pastor	Bredir, in haste takis heede and here	f.59
	What I wille speke and specifie;	
	Sen we walke þus, withouten were,	
	What mengis my moode nowe meve yt will I.	
	Oure forme-fadres faythfull in fere,	5
	Bothe Osye and Isaye,	
	Preued þat a prins withouten pere	
	Shulde descende doune in a lady,	
	And to make mankynde clerly,	
	To leche þam þat are lorne.	10
	And in Bedlem hereby	
	Sall þat same barne by borne.	

II Pastor	Or he be borne in burgh hereby,	
	Balaham, brothir, me haue herde say,	
	A sterne shulde schyne and signifie	15
	With lightfull lemes like any day.	
	And als the texte it tellis clerly	
	By witty lerned men of oure lay,	
	With his blissid bloode he shulde vs by,	
	He shulde take here al of a maye.	20
	I herde my syre saye,	
	When he of hir was borne,	
	She shulde be als clene maye	
	As euer she was byforne.	

III Pastor	A, mercifull maker, mekill is thy myght,	25
	That þus will to þi seruauntes see,	
	Might we ones loke vppon þat light	
	Gladder bretheren myght no men be.	
	I haue herde say, by þat same light	
	The childre of Israell shulde be made free,	30
	The force of the feende to felle in fighte,	
	And all his pouer excluded shulde be.	

1. *I Pastor*] *Added by J. Clerke*
4. meve yt] *TS (conj), BrZi; MS, Be* mevyd
7. a] *TS +; MS* I
12. by] *BrZi; TS, Be* be *(conj)*
13. *II Pastor*] *Added by J. Clerke*
20. al] *Interlined*
25. *III Pastor*] *Added by J. Clerke*
31. fighte] *This ed; TS +* sighte, *MS long s— or* f—

Wherfore, brether, I rede þat wee   f.59ᵛ
   Flitte faste ouere thees felles,
To frayste to fynde oure fee,   35
   And talke of sumwhat ellis.

I Pastor	We, Hudde!
II Pastor	We, howe?
I Pastor	Herkyn to me.
II Pastor	We, man, þou maddes all out of myght.
I Pastor	We, Colle!
III Pastor	What care is comen to þe?
I Pastor	Steppe furth and stande by me right, 40
	And tell me þan
	Yf þou sawe euere swilke a sight.
III Pastor	I? Nay, certis, nor neuere no man.

II Pastor	Say felowes, what, fynde yhe any feest,
	Me falles for to haue parte, pardé! 45
I Pastor	Whe, Hudde, behalde into the heste,
	A selcouthe sight þan sall þou see
	Vppon þe skye.
II Pastor	We, telle me men, emang vs thre,
	Whatt garres yow stare þus sturdely? 50

III Pastor	Als lange as we haue herde-men bene
	And kepid þis catell in þis cloghe,
	So selcouth a sight was neuere non sene.
I Pastor	We, no Colle. Nowe comes it newe inowe,
	Þat mon we fynde 55
	[. . . . . .
	. . . . . .]

[A leaf is missing from the MS at this point. It must have contained the appearance of the Angel to sing 'Gloria in excelsis deo' etc., a spoken message from the Angel to the shepherds, and the first part of their response; see the Note. Two lines making up the stanza beginning at line 51 and five belonging with a stanza ending with 56–7 have been carried away. Lines 56–7 must be assigned to II or III Pastor, probably III, as the shepherds often speak in numerical order.]

        [. . .   . . .
          . . .   . . .
        . . .   . . .
         . . .   . . .
          . . .   . . .]

37. *Main scribe's character-designations (which begin here) assign speeches only as I, II, III; Pastor suppl TS +*
41–2. *Original designation III deleted by a later hand. Lineation TS +; one line in MS*
43. *III*] *TS +; MS II*
52. kepid] *BrZi, Be; TS* kepis

[*III Pastor*]	Itt menes some meruayle vs emang,	f.60
	Full hardely I you behete.	

I Pastor	What it shulde mene þat wate not ȝee,	
	For all þat ȝe can gape and gone.	
	I can synge itt alls wele as hee,	60
	And on asaie itt sall be sone	
	Proued or we passe.	
	Yf ȝe will helpe, late see, halde on,	
	For þus it was:	

Et tunc cantant.

II Pastor	Ha! ha! þis was a mery note,	65
	Be the dede þat I sall dye,	
	I haue so crakid in my throte	
	Þat my lippis are nere drye.	
III Pastor	I trowe þou royse,	
	For what it was fayne witte walde I	70
	That tille vs made þis noble noyse.	

I Pastor	An aungell brought vs tythandes newe	
	A babe in Bedlem shulde be borne,	
	Of whom þan spake oure prophicie trewe –	
	And bad us mete hym þare þis morne –	75
	Þat mylde of mode.	
	I walde giffe hym bothe hatte and horne	
	And I myght fynde þat frely foode.	

III Pastor	Hym for to fynde has we no drede,	
	I sall you telle achesoune why:	80
	Ȝone sterne to þat lorde sall vs lede.	
II Pastor	Ȝa, þou sais soth. Go we forthy	
	Hym to honnour,	
	And make myrthe and melody,	
	With sange to seke oure savyour.	85

Et tunc cantant. .

I Pastor	Breder, bees all blythe and glad,	f.60ᵛ
	Here is the burgh þer we shulde be.	

63. late see, halde on] *Ho'; MS, TS +* halde on, late see
64. *Two additions to right by J. Clerke, apparently at different times: (i)* caret nova loquela; *(ii, beneath)* de pastores
64 + *SD (main scribe) in red*
69. þou] *This ed; TS +* you
78. I] *Interlined by a later hand*
83, 85. *Written to right of 82, 84, respectively. Lineation TS +; with (85) at end of 83 in MS*
85. savyour] *Originally om by main scribe, but added later by him to right, in red. Inserted correctly in text by J. Clerke*
85 + *SD (main scribe) in red*
87. burgh] *Ho'; MS, TS +* burght

II Pastor	In þat same steede now are we stadde,
	Tharefore I will go seke and see.
	Slike happe of heele neuere herde-men hadde; 90
	Loo, here is the house, and here is hee.
III Pastor	3a forsothe, þis is the same,
	Loo whare þat lorde is layde
	Betwyxe two bestis tame,
	Right als þe aungell saide. 95

I Pastor	The aungell saide þat he shulde saue
	This worlde and all þat wonnes þerin,
	Therfore yf I shulde oght aftir crave
	To wirshippe hym I will begynne:
	Sen I am but a symple knave, 100
	Þof all I come of curtayse kynne,
	Loo here slyke harnays as I haue –
	A baren-broche by a belle of tynne
	At youre bosom to be;
	And whenne 3e shall welde all 105
	Gud sonne, forgete no3t me
	Yf any fordele falle.

II Pastor	Þou sonne þat shall saue boþe see and sande,
	Se to me sen I haue þe soght;
	I am ovir poure to make presande 110
	Als myn harte wolde, and had I ought.
	Two cobill notis vppon a bande,
	Loo, litill babe, what I haue broght,
	And whan 3e sall be lorde in lande
	Dose goode agayne, forgete me noght, f.61
	For I haue herde declared 116
	Of connyng clerkis and clene,
	That bountith askis rewarde;
	Nowe watte 3e what I mene.

III Pastor	Nowe loke on me, my lorde dere, 120
	Þof all I putte me noght in pres,
	Ye are a prince withouten pere,
	I haue no presentte þat you may plees.
	But lo, an horne spone þat haue I here –
	And it will herbar fourty pese – 125
	Þis will I giffe you with gud chere,
	Slike novelté may noght disease.
	Farewele þou swete swayne,

99.   *Additions to right by later hand or hands: (i)* hic caret; *(ii, by J. Clerke)* nova loquela

106–7.   *Lineation TS +; written in reverse order in MS*

108.   Hic caret *added to right by a later hand*

118.   askis] *Conj TS, BrZi; MS,* Be aftir

120.   Hic caret *added to left by a later hand*

128.   Farewele]–wele *suppl TS +; Shrewsbury Fragment (ed. Davis) A47* Farewele

> God graunte vs levyng lange,
> And go we hame agayne 130
> And make mirthe as we gange.

131+ *Beneath last line, in Clerke's hand, partially erased (visible under u-v):* Here wantes the conclusyon of this matter; *to the right of this, a thoroughly erased inscription by a later hand. Bottom half of f. 61 blank; f. 61ᵛ now blank, but at foot, erased catchword* The clowdes clapped; *f. 62 (beginning of quire H) blank*

XVI The Masons
Herod

The Goldsmiths
The Magi

[The Masons]

Herodes The clowdes clapped in clerenes þat þer clematis inclosis –
       Jubiter and Jouis, Martis and Mercurij emyde –
       Raykand ouere my rialté on rawe me reioyses,
          Blonderande þer blastis to blaw when I bidde.
          Saturne my subgett, þat sotilly is hidde,   5
            Listes at my likyng and laies hym full lowe.
       The rakke of þe rede skye full rappely I ridde,
          Thondres full thrallye by thousandes I thrawe
            When me likis.
          Venus his voice to me awe,   10
            Þat princes to play in hym pikis.

       Þe prince of planetis þat proudely is pight
          Sall brace furth his bemes þat oure belde blithes,
       Þe mone at my myght he mosteres his myght,
          And kayssaris in castellis grete kyndynes me kythes.   15
       Lordis and ladis, loo, luffely me lithes,
          For I am fairer of face and fressher on folde –
       Þe soth yf I saie sall – seuene and sexti sithis
          Þan glorius gulles þat gayer is þan golde
            In price.   20
       How thynke ȝe þer tales þat I talde?
       I am worthy, witty, and wyse.

1. Herodes] *Suppl to left by a later hand*
2. Mercurij] *This ed;* TS Mercury
6. Listes] *Ha;* MS, TS I list
14. myght'] *Ha* mynt
19. is] *Interlined by a later hand*

134

I Miles	All kynges to youre croune may clerly comende
	Youre lawe and youre lordshippe as lodsterne on hight;
	What traytoure vntrewe þat will not attende, 25
	ȝe sall lay þaim full lowe, fro leeme and fro light.
II Miles	What faitoure, in faithe, þat dose ȝou offende,
	We sall sette hym full sore, þat sotte, in youre sight.
Herodes	In welthe sall I wisse ȝou to wonne or I wende, f.63
	For ȝe are wightis ful worthy, both witty and wighte. 30

	But ȝe knawe wele, ser knyghtis in counsaill full conande,
	Þat my regioun so riall is ruled her be rest,
	For I wate of no wighte in þis worlde þat is wonnande
	Þat in forges any felouné, with force sall be fest.
	Arest ȝe þo rebaldes þat vnrewly are rownand, 35
	Be they kyngis or knyghtis, in care ȝe thaim cast,
	ȝaa, and welde þam in woo to wonne, in þe wanyand;
	What browle þat is brawlyng his brayne loke ȝe brest,
	And dynge ȝe hym doune.
I Miles	Sir, what foode in faith will ȝou feese, 40
	Þat sott full sone myselfe sall hym sesse.
II Miles	We sall noght here doute to do hym disesse,
	But with countenance full cruell we sall crake her his
	croune.

Herodes	My sone þat is semely, howe semes þe ther sawes?
	Howe comely þer knyghtis þei carpe in þis case. 45
Filius	Fadir, if þai like noght to listyn youre lawes,
	As traytoures ontrewe ye sall teche þem a trace,
	For fadir, vnkyndnes ȝe kythe þem no cause.
Herodes	Faire falle þe my faire sone, so fettis of face.
	And knyghtis, I comaunde, who to dule drawes, 50
	Þas churles as cheueleres ye chastise and chase,
	And drede ȝe no doute.
Filius	Fadir, I sall fell þam in fight,
	What renke þat reves you youre right.
I Miles	With dyntes to dede bes he dight f.63ᵛ
	Þat liste not youre lawes for to lowte. 56

42. *Miles] Suppl TS*
43. *Lineation Ho'; two lines in MS, TS*
47. *ye] This ed; TS* þe
48. *vnkyndnes] Ha, Ho' of vnkyndnes*
56. *Several words, apparently including* hic caret, *and a Maltese cross added to right by J. Clerke, now erased (visible under u-v). Offset of cross visible between first two words on opposite page (f. 64). See the Note.*

[The Goldsmiths]

I Rex	A, lorde that levis, euerelastande light,	f.68
	I loue þe evir with harte and hande,	
	That me has made to se this sight	
	Whilke my kynrede was coveytande.	60
	Thay saide a sterne with lemys bright	
	Owte of the eest shulde stabely stande,	
	And þat it shulde meffe mekill myght	
	Of one þat shulde be lorde in lande,	
	That men of synne shulde saff.	65
	And certis I sall saye,	
	God graunte me happe to haue	
	Wissyng of redy waye.	

II Rex All-weldand God þat all has wroght,
I worshippe þe als is worthye,   70
That with thy brightnes has me broght
Owte of my reame, riche Arabie.
I shall noght seys tille I haue sought
What selcouth thyng it sall syngnyfie,
God graunte me happe so þat I myght   75
Haue grace to gete goode companye,
And my comforte encrese
With thy sterne schynyng shene;
For certis, I sall noght cesse
Tille I witte what it mene.   80

III Rex Lorde God þat all goode has bygonne
And all may ende, both goode and euyll,
That made for man both mone and sonne,
And stedde yone sterne to stande stone stille,
Tille I þe cause may clerly conne,   85
God wisse me with his worthy wille.
I hope I haue her felaws fonne
My yarnyng faþfully to fullfille.
Sirs, God yowe saffe ande see,   f.68ᵛ
And were ȝow euere fro woo.   90

I Rex   Amen, so myght it bee,
And saffe yow sir, also.

---

57.   *Preceded by a Maltese cross in a later hand.*
A] *This ed; om TS*
light] *He, Co; MS, TS* lyff
63–4. *Lineation TS; Of at end of 63 in MS*
64.   one] *Ho'; MS, TS* I
65.   saff] *TS; MS* saff be
73.   noght] *Suppl TS*
85.   conne] *He, Co; MS, TS* knowe
87.   fonne] *He, Co; MS, TS* fonde
88.   faþfully] *This ed; TS* fayfully

III Rex	Sirs, with youre wille, I wolde yow praye
	To telle me some of youre entent,
	Whedir ye wende forthe in this way, 95
	And fro what contré ȝe are wente?
II Rex	Full gladly sir I shall ȝou say.
	A sodayne sight was till vs sente,
	A royall sterne þat rose or day
	Before vs on the firmament, 100
	Þat garte vs fare fro home
	Som poynte therof to preffe.
III Rex	Sertis syrs, I sawc þc same
	Þat makis vs þus to moyfe;
	For sirs, I haue herde saye sertayne 105
	Itt shulde be seyne of selcowthe seere,
	And ferther therof I wolde freyne;
	That makis me moffe in this manere.
I Rex	Sir, of felashippe are we fayne,
	Now sall we wende forth all in feere, 110
	God graunte vs or we come agayne
	Som gode hartyng þerof to here.
	Sir, here is Jerusalem
	To wisse vs als we goo,
	And beyonde is Bedleem, 115
	Þer schall we seke alsoo.
III Rex	Sirs, ȝe schall wele vndirstande,
	For to be wise nowe were it nede; f.69
	Sir Herowde is kyng of this lande
	And has his lawes her for to leede. 120
I Rex	Sir, sen we neghe now þus nerhand,
	Vntill his helpe vs muste take heede,
	For haue we his wille and his warande
	Þan may we wende withouten drede.
II Rex	To haue leve of the lorde, 125
	Þat is resoune and skyll.
III Rex	And therto we all accorde,
	Wende we and witte his wille.

102. preffe] *This ed; TS* presse

his wille   [f.63ᵛ]

[The Masons]

Nuncius	My lorde ser Herowde, kyng with croune!	
Herodes	Pees dastarde, in þe deueles dispite.	130
Nuncius	My lorde, now note is nere þis towne.	
Herodes	What, false harlott, liste þe flight?	
	Go betis yone boy and dyngis hym downe.	
II Miles	Lorde, messengeres shulde no man wyte,	
	It may be for youre awne renoune.	135
Herodes	Þat wolde I here, do telle on tyte.	
Nuncius	My lorde, I mette at morne	
	Thre kyngis carpand togedir	
	Of a barne þat is borne,	
	And þei hight to come hiddir.	140

Herodes	Thre kyngis, forsoth?	
Nuncius	Sir, so I say,	
	For I saw þaim myselffe all fere.	
I Consolator	My lorde, appose hym I you pray.	
Herodes	Say felowe, are they ferre or nere?	
Nuncius	Mi lorde, þei will be here þis day,	145
	Þat wote I wele, withouten were.	
Herodes	Do rewle vs þan in riche array,	f.64
	And ilke man make þam mery chere,	
	Þat no sembelant be sene	
	But frendshippe faire and still,	150
	Till we witte what þei mene,	
	Whedir it be gud or ill.	

I Rex	The lord þat lenes ay-lastand light	
	Whilke has vs ledde owte of oure lande,	
	Kepe þe, ser kynge and comely knyght	155
	And all thy folke þat we her fynde.	
Herodes	Mahounde, my god and most of myght,	
	Þat has myn hele all in his hande,	
	He saffe you sirs, semely in sight;	
	And telle vs nowe som new tithand.	160
II Rex	Some sall we saie ʒou sir—	
	A sterne stode vs beforne,	
	That makis vs speke and spir	
	Of one þat is new-borne.	

Herodes	New-borne? Þat burden hald I bad;	165
	And certis, vnwitty men ye wore	

Two copies of 129–272 in MS here printed in parallel; see the Note.

129– *See line 128, and the Note. To left of 129 sequitur postea in a later hand, now erased (visible under u-v)*

141–2. *Latter half of 141 and 142 one line in MS*

151. *we] Interlined*

153. *Handwriting markedly smaller and more closely spaced from here to 272*

[The Goldsmiths] [f.69]

Nuncius	Mi lorde ser Herowde, kyng with croune!
Herodes	Pees dastard, in þe deueles dispite. 130
Nuncius	Sir, new nott is full nere þis towne.
Herodes	What, false losell, liste þe flighte?
	Go bette boþ and dyng þam downe.
II Miles	Lorde, messengers shulde no man wyte,
	It may be for youre awne rennowne. 135
Herodes	That wolde I here, telle on tyte.
Nuncius	Mi lorde, I mette at morne
	Iij kyngis carpand togedir
	Of one þat is nowe borne,
	And þai hight to come hedir. 140

Herodes	Thre kyngis, forsothe? f.69ᵛ
Nuncius	Sir, so I saie,
	For I saughe þem myself all feere.
I Consolator	My lorde, appose hym we yow praye.
Herodes	Say felowe, ar they ferre or nere?
Nuncius	Mi lorde, þei will be here þis day, 145
	Þat wotte I wele, withouten were.
Herodes	Haue done. Dresse vs in riche array,
	And ilke man make tham mery chere,
	That no sembland be seenc
	But frenshippe faire and stille, 150
	Tille we wete what þei meene,
	Whedir it be gud or ill.

I Rex	The lorde þat lenys þis lastand light
	Whilke has vs ledde oute of oure lande,
	Kepe þe, sir kyng and comly knyght, 155
	And all þi folke þat we here fande.
Herodes	Mahounde, my god and most of myght,
	Þat has myn hele all in his hande,
	He saffe you sirs, semely in sight;
	And telle vs nowe som new tythande. 160
II Rex	Sum shall we saie sir –
	A sterne stud vs byforne,
	That makis vs speke and spir
	Of ane þat is nowe-borne.

Herodes	Nowe-borne? Þat birthe halde I badde; 165
	And certis, vnwitty men ȝe werre

133. boþ] *or* boy
135–6. *Lineation and character-designation as M; lines reversed in MS and attributed to* Nuncius
137–40. *Lineation as M; two lines in MS*
153. The] *M; MS, TS* A
166+ *Catchword* To lepe ouere land

To leppe ouere lande to laite a ladde.
　　Say, whan loste ȝe hym? Ought lange before?
All wise men will wene ȝe madde
　　And þerfore moves þis neuer more.　　　　　　170

III Rex　　　ȝis certis, swilke hertyng haue we hadde
　　We will not cesse or we come þore.

Herodes　　　This were a wondir-thyng.
　　　　Saie, what barne shulde þat be?

I Rex　　　Forsoth, he sall be kynge　　　　　　f.64ᵛ
　　Of Jewes and of Judé.　　　　　　176

Herodes　　Kyng? In þe deueles name, dogges, fye!
　　Nowe se I wele ȝe roye and raue.
Be any skemeryng of þe skye
　　When shulde ye knawe outhir kyng or knave?　180

Filius　　Naye, he is kyng and non but he,
　　Þat sall ȝe kenne if þat ȝe craue,
And he is jugge of all Jurie,
　　To speke or spille, to saie or saffe.

Herodes　　　Swilke gawdes may gretely greue,　　　185
　　　To witnesse þat nere was.

II Rex　　Nowe lorde, we axe but leve
　　Be youre poure to passe.

Herodes　　Whedirward, in þe deuelis name?
　　To layte a ladde here in my lande?　　　　　190
Fals harlottis, bot yhe hye ȝou hame
　　ȝe sall be bette and bune in bande.

II Consolator　Mi lorde, to fell þis foule defame,
　　Late alle þere hye wordis falle on hande,
And spere þaim sadly of þe same,　　　　　195
　　So sall ȝe stabely vndirstande
　　　Þaire mynde and ther menyng,
　　　And takes gud tente therto.

Herodes　　　I thanke þe of thys þing,　　　　　200
　　　And certis so sall I doo.

Nowe kyngis, to cache all care awaye
　　Sen ȝe are comen oute of youre kyth,
Loke noght ye legge agaynste oure laye,　　f.65
　　Vppon payne to lose both lymme and lith.　205

177.　Kyng] *G; MS* Kyngis
178.　ȝe] *G; MS* þe
　　　raue] *G; MS* rase
180.　shulde ye] *This ed; MS* ye shulde
187.　*II Rex] Numeral suppl this ed*
199–200.　*Lineation as G; two lines in MS*
200.　thys] *After G* þis; *MS* thy
　　　þing] *Interlined over deletion of* counsaille

To lepe ouere lande to late a ladde.   f.70
  Say, when lost ʒe hym? Ought lange before?
All wyse men will wene ʒe madde
  And therfore moffis it neuere more.   170

III Rex   ʒis certis, such hartyng haue we hadde
  We schall noʒt seys or we come thore.

Herodes   This were a wondir-thyng.
    Say, what barne shulle þat be?

I Rex   Sir, he shall be kyng   175
    Of Jewes and of Judé.

Herodes Kyng? In þe deuyl way, dogges, fy!
  Now I se wele ʒe roþe and raue.
Be ony skymeryng of the skye
  When shulde ʒe knawe owthir kyng or knave?   180
Nay, I am kyng and non but I,
  That shall ʒe kenne yff þat ʒe craue,
And I am juge of all Jury,
  To speke or spille, to saie or saffe.
    Swilke gawdes may gretely greue,   185
    To wittenesse þat neuere was.

II Rex   Lorde, we aske noght but leue
    Be youre poure to passe.

Herodes Whedir, in þe deuyls name?
  To late a ladde here in my lande?   190
Fals harlottis, but ʒe hye you hame
  ʒe shall be bette and boune in bande.

II Consolator My lorde, to felle þis foule deffame,
  Lattis all such wondir falle on hande,
And speres þaim sadly of þe same,   f.70ᵛ
  So shall ʒe stabely vndirstande   196
    Þer mynde and þer menyng,
    And takis gud tente þam too.

Herodes I thanke þe of þis thyng,
    And certis so will I doo.   200

Nowe kyngis, to cache all care away
  Sen ʒe ar comen oute of youre kytht,
Loke noght ye legge agayne oure lay,
  Uppon peyne to lose both lyme and litht.

167. *Quire I begins*
168. *Lineation as M; two lines in MS*
176. Judé] *Deleted, and* all Jury *written to right by J. Clerke*
180. shulde ʒe] *This ed; MS, TS* ʒe shulde
181. Filius *written twice to right by J. Clerke, first instance deleted*
184. orʲ] *M; MS* of
187. II Rex] *Numeral suppl this ed*
201. care] *Suppl from M*

And so þat ȝe þe soth will saye
To come and go I graunte you grith,
And yf youre poyntes be to my paye
May fall myselfe sall wende ȝou with.

I Rex   Sir kyng, we all accorde,
                    And sais a barne is borne   210
Þat sall be kyng and lorde,
                    And leche þam þat ar lorne.

II Rex   Sir, ye thar meruaylle nothynge
Of this ilke noote þat þusgattes newes,
For Balaham saide a starne shulde sprynge   215
Of Jacob kynde, and þat is Jewes.

III Rex   Isaie sais a maiden yonge
Sall bere a barne emange Ebrewes,
Þat of all contrees sal be kynge
And gouerne all þat on erthe grewes;   220
Emanuell beiths his name,
                    To say, 'Goddis sone of heuene',
And certis þis is þe same
Þat we her to you neuen.

I Rex   Sir, þe proued prophete Ossee   225
Full trewly tolde in towne and toure,
A maiden of Israell, forsoth saide he,
Sall bere oone like to lilly floure.
He menes a childe consayued sall be
                    Withouten seede of mannys socoure,   230
And his modir a mayden free,   f.65ᵛ
                    And he both sonne and saueour.

II Rex   That fadres talde me beforne
                    Has no man myght to marre.

Herodes   Allas, þan am I lorne,   235
                    Þis wax ay werre and werre.

I Consolator My lorde, be ȝe nothyng abast,
                    Þis brigge tille ende sall wele be broght.
Byde þam go furth and frendly frayste
                    Þe soth of þis þat þei haue soght,   240
And telle it ȝou – soo sall ȝe traste
                    Whedir þer tales be trewe or noght.

209.   *I Rex] Numeral suppl this ed, after G*
213.   *II Rex] Numeral suppl this ed, after G*
214.   newes] *G; MS* newe
217.   *III Rex] Numeral suppl this ed, after G*
219.   contrees] *Deleted, and* the world *interlined by Clerke*
225.   *I Rex] This ed, after addition by later hand in G; MS III Rex*
233.   *II Rex] Numeral suppl this ed, after G*

	And so þat ʒe þe soth will saye	205
	To come and goo I graunte yow grith,	
	And yf youre poynte be to my pay	
	May falle myselfe shall wende you with.	
I Rex	Sir kyng, we all accorde,	
	And says a barne is borne	210
	Þat shall be kyng and lorde,	
	And leche þam þat ar lorne.	

II Rex	Sir, the thar meruayle nothyng	
	Of þis ilke nott þat þus-gate newes,	
	For Balaham saide a starne shulde spring	215
	Of Jacobe kynde, and þat is Jewes.	
III Rex	Sir, Isaie sais a mayden ʒenge	
	Shall bere a sone amonge Ebrewes,	
	Þat of all contrees shall be kyng	
	And gouerne all þat on erthe grewes;	220
	Emanuell shal be his name,	
	To saie, 'God sone of heuen',	
	And certis þis is þe same	f.71
	Þat we now to you neuen.	

I Rex	Sirs, þe proved prophete Osee	225
	Full trulye talde in towne and toure,	
	Þat a mayden of Israell, sais he,	
	Shall bere one like to þe lely floure.	
	He menys a barne consayued shulde be	
	Withouten seede of man socour,	230
	And is modir a mayden free,	
	And he both sone and saueour.	
II Rex	Þat fadirs has talde beforne	
	Has no man myght to marre.	
Herodes	Allas, þan am I lorne,	235
	Þis waxith ay werre and werre.	

I Consolator	My lorde, be ʒe nothyng abast,	
	Þis bryge shall well to ende be broght.	
	Bidde þam go furthe and frendly frast	
	Þe soth of þis þat þei haue soght,	240
	And telle it ʒou – so shall ʒe trast	
	Whedir þer tales be trew or noght.	

---

209. *I Rex] Numeral suppl by a later hand (same hand at 213, 217, 225, 233)*
213. *II Rex] Numeral suppl by a later hand*
the thar] *of this interlined above by J. Clerke*
217. *III Rex] Numeral suppl by a later hand*
225. *I Rex] Numeral by later hand; main scribe III Rex*
231. a] *M; MS and*
233. *II Rex] Numeral suppl by a later hand*
238. bryge] *an a interlined over* y

Þan sall ȝe waite þaim with a wraste
And make all waste þat þei haue wroght.

Herodes   Nowe certis, þis is wele saide,   245
This matere makes me fayne.
Sir kyngis, I halde me paied
Of all youre purpose playne.

Wende furth youre forward to fulfill,
To Bedlem is but here at hande;   250
And speris grathely both gud and ille
Of hym þat shulde be lorde in lande;
And comes agayne þan me vntill
And telle me trulye youre tithande —
To worshippe hym þan were my will,   255
Þis sall ye stabely vndirstande.

II Rex   Certis ser, we sall you say
Þe soth of þat same childe,
In all þe haste we may.

II Consolator   Fares wele — ye be bygilyd.   f.66

Herodes   Now certis, þis is a sotell trayne.   261
Nowe sall þai trulye take þere trace,
And telle me of þat swytteron swayne,
And all þare counsaille in þis case.
Giffe itt be soth þai shall be slayne,   265
No golde shall gete them bettir grace;
Bot go we tille they come agayne
And playe vs in som othir place.
This holde I gude counsaill,
Yitt wolde I na man wiste;   270
For certis, we shall noght faile
To lose þam as vs liste.

272   *Beneath and to right:* Hic caret / I Rex / Alake fosoth what shall I say / We lake þat
syne þat we haue sought; *and written at a different time* sequitur postea; *all erased
(visible under u-v light) and all except possibly the last two words by J. Clerke. Rest of f.
66 blank; ff. 66ᵛ–67ᵛ blank.*

	Than shall we wayte þam with a wrest	
	And make all wast þat þei haue wroght.	
Herodes	Nowe certis, þis was wele saide,	245
	Þis matere makes me fayne.	
	Sir kyngis, I halde me paide	
	Of all youre purpose playne.	

Wendis furth youre forward to fulfill,
   To Bedlem, it is but here at hande;   250
And speris grathe bothe goode and ill
   Of hym þat shulde be lorde in lande;
And comes agayne þan me vntill   f.71ᵛ
   And telle me trulye youre tythande —
To worshippe hym, þat is my will,   255
   Þus shall ȝe stabely vndirstande.

II Rex   Sertis syr, we sall you say
          Alle þe soth of þat childe,
      In alle þe hast þat we may.
II Consolator   Fares wele — ȝe be bygilid.   260

Herodes   Nowe certis, þis is a sotille trayne.
         Nowe shall þei trewly take þer trace,
      And telle me of þat littil swayne,
         And þer counsaill in þis case.
      If it be soth þei shall be slayne,   265
         No golde shall gete þam bettir grace.
      Go we nowe till þei come agayne
         To playe vs in som othir place.
         This halde I gud counsaill,
           Yitt wolde I no man wist;   270
      For sertis, we shall not faill
         To loyse þam as vs list.

Nota: The Harrode passeth, and the iij kynges
commyth agayn to make there offerynges.

[The Goldsmiths]

I Rex   A, sirs, for sight what shall I say?
         Whare is oure syne? I se it noth.
II Rex   No more do I. Nowe dar I lay   275
         In oure wendyng som wrange is wroght.
III Rex   Vnto þat prince I rede we praye,
         That till vs sente his syngne vnsoght,
      Þat he wysse vs in redy way
         So frendly þat we fynde hym moght. 280
I Rex   A, siris, I se it stande
         Aboven where he is borne,

---

261. *Herodes] Suppl by a later hand*
272 + *Nota: The Harrode . . . etc] Written to the left by J. Clerke, the first word at some time*
     before the remainder

Lo, here is þe house at hande,
We haue noȝt myste þis morne.

Ancilla	Whame seke ȝe syrs, be wayes wilde,	f.72
	With talkyng, trauelyng to and froo?	286
	Her wonnes a woman with hir childe	
	And hir husband, her ar no moo.	
II Rex	We seke a barne þat all shall bylde,	
	His sartayne syngne hath saide vs soo,	290
	And his modir, a mayden mylde,	
	Her hope we to fynde þam twoo.	
Ancilla	Come nere gud syirs and see,	
	Youre way to ende is broght.	
III Rex	Behalde here syirs, her and se	295
	Þe same þat ȝe haue soght.	

I Rex   Loved be þat lorde þat lastis aye,
           Þat vs has kydde þus curtaysely
           To wende by many a wilsom way,
           And come to þis clene companye.   300
II Rex   Late vs make nowe no more delay,
           But tyte take furth oure tresurry
           And ordand giftis of gud aray,
           To worshippe hym als is worthy.
III Rex   He is worthy to welde   305
           All worshippe, welthe, and wynne;
           And for honnoure and elde
           Brother, ȝe shall begynne.

I Rex   Hayle, þe fairest of felde, folke for to fynde,
           Fro the fende and his feeres faithefully vs fende; 310
           Hayll, þe best þat shall be borne to vnbynde   f.72ᵛ
           All þe barnes þat are borne and in bale bende.
           Hayll, þou marc us þi men and make vs in mynde,
           Sen þi myght is on molde misseis to amende.
           Hayll, clene þat is comen of a kynges kynde,   315
           And shall be kyng of þis kyth, all clergy has kende.
           And sith it shall worþe on þis wise,
           Thyselffe haue I soght sone, I say þe,
           With golde þat is grettest of price;
           Be paied of þis present I pray þe.   320

295–6. *Lineation TS; and se at beginning of 296 in MS*
309–10. *Lineation TS; both written as two lines in MS*
312. bende] *Conj TS; MS* boune
316. all] *Hoᵗ* als
318. I'] *Suppl Hoᵗ*

II Rex	Hayll, foode þat thy folke fully may fede,
	Hayll floure fairest, þat neuer shall fade,
	Hayll, sone þat is sente of þis same sede
	Þat shall saue vs of synne þat oure syris had.

II Rex   Hayll, foode þat thy folke fully may fede,
           Hayll floure fairest, þat neuer shall fade,
           Hayll, sone þat is sente of þis same sede
           Þat shall saue vs of synne þat oure syris had.
           Hayll mylde, for þou mett to marke vs to mede,   325
             Off a may makeles þi modir þou made;
           In þat gude thurgh grace of thy Godhede
             Als þe gleme in þe glasse gladly þou glade.
             And sythyn þow shall sitte to be demand,
               To helle or to heuen for to haue vs,   330
             Insens to þi seruis is semand.
               Sone, se to þi suggettis and saue vs.

III Rex   Hayll barne þat is best oure balys to bete,
             For our boote shall þou be bounden and bett;
           Hayll frende faithtfull, we fall to thy feete,   335
             Thy fadiris folke fro þe fende to þe fette.
           Hayll, man þat is made to þi men mette,
             Sen þou and thy modir with mirthis ar mette;
           Hayll duke þat dryues dede vndir fete,
             But whan thy dedys ar done to dye is þi dette.   340
             And sen thy body beryed shal be,
               This mirre will I giffe to þi grauyng.
             The gifte is not grete of degree,   f.73
               Ressayue it, and se to oure sauyng.

Maria   Sir kyngis, ȝe trauel not in vayne.   345
             Als ȝe haue ment, hyr may ȝe fynde,
           For I consayued my sone sartayne
             Withouten misse of man in mynde,
           And bare hym here withouten payne,
             Where women are wonte to be pynyd.   350
           Goddis aungell in his gretyng playne
             Saide he shulde comforte al mankynde,
               Tharfore doute yow no dele
                 Here for to haue youre bone,
               I shall witnesse full wele   355
                 All þat is saide and done.

I Rex   For solas ser now may we synge,
             All is parformed þat we for prayde;
           But gud barne, giffe vs thy blissing,
             For faire happe is before þe laide.   360
II Rex   Wende we nowe to Herowde þe kyng
             For of þis poynte he will be paied,

---

329. þow] *This ed;* TS yow
336. *Ho'; MS* Thy fadiris folke free þu fende fals þe (*interlined*) to thy (*deleted*) fette;
          TS Thy fadirs fro þe fende fals þe to fette (*conj*)
337. mette] TS meete (*conj*)

And come hymselffe and make offeryng
Vnto þis same, for so he saide.

III Rex   I rede we reste a thrawe,   365
For to maynteyne our myght,
And than do as we awe,
Both vnto kyng and knyght.

Angelus   Nowe curtayse kynges, to me take tent
And turne betyme or ȝe be tenyd,   370
Fro God hymselfe þus am I sent
To warne yow als youre faithfull frende.   f.73ᵛ
Herowde the kyng has malise ment
And shappis with shame yow for to shende,
And for þat ȝe non harmes shulde hente,   375
Be othir waies God will ye wende
Euen to youre awne contré.
And yf ȝe aske hym bone,
Youre beelde ay will he be
For þis þat ȝe haue done.   380

I Rex   A, lorde, I loue þe inwardly.
Sirs, God has gudly warned vs thre,
His aungell her now herde haue I,
And how he saide.
II Rex   Sir, so did we.
He saide Herowde is oure enmye,   385
And makis hym bowne oure bale to be
With feyned falsed, and forthy
Farre fro his force I rede we flee.
III Rex   Syrs, faste I rede we flitte,
Ilkone till oure contré,   390
He þat is welle of witte
Vs wisse, and yow be.

371. God hymselfe] of *between, deleted*
392 + *Rest of f. 73ᵛ blank; for f. 74, see Note on play XVII; f. 74ᵛ blank*

XVII The Hatmakers, Masons and Labourers

The Purification

Prisbeter   Almyghty God in heven so hy,   f.227ᵛ
                 The makcr of all heven and erth,
            He ordenyd here all thynges evenly,
                 For man he ment to mend his myrth.

            In nomber, weight, and mesure fyne   5
                 God creat here al thyng, I say,
            His lawes he bad men shulde not tyne,
                 But kepe his commandmentes allway.

            In the mount of Syney full fayre,
                 And in two tabyls to you to tell,   10
            His lawes to Moyses tuke God there
                 To geve to the chylder of Isracll,

            That Moyses shuld theme gyde alway,
                 And lerne theme lely to knowe Goddes wyll,
            And that he shulde not it denay,   15
                 But kepe his lawes stable and styll.

            For payn that he hadd putt therefore,
                 To stone all theme that kepis it nott
            Vtterly to death, both lesse and moore;
                 There shulde no marcy for them be soght.   20

            Therefore kepe well Goddes commandement,
                 And leyd your lyf after his lawes,
            Or ells surely ye mon be shent
                 Bothe lesse and moore, ylkonc on rawes.

            This is his wyll after Moyses lawe: 25
                 That ye shulde bryng your beistes good
           And offer theme here your God to knawe,
                 And frome your synns to turne your moode.

            Suche beestes as God hais marked here,   f.228
                 Vnto Moyses he spake as I yow tell,   30

13.   shuld] *He; MS, TS* shull
15.   he] *Interlined*
30.   Vnto] Vn- *apparently deleted*
         as . . . tell] *Originally* full yell (*so TS*), *the later reading interlined*

And bad hyme boldly with good chere,
    To say to the chylder of Israell

That after dyvers seknes seer
    And after dyvers synes alsoo,
Go bryng your beestes to the preest even here   35
    To offer theme vp in Goddes sight, loo.

The woman that hais borne her chylde,
    She shall comme hether at the forty day
To be puryfied where she was fylde,
    And bryng with her a lame, I say,   40

And two dove-byrdes for her offerand,
    And take them to the preest of lay
To offer theme vp with his holy hand;
    There shulde no man to this say nay.

The lame is offeryd for Goddes honour   45
    In sacrefyes all onely dight,
And the preistes prayer purchace secure
    For the woman that was fylyd in God sight.

And yf so be that she be power
    And haue no lame to offer, than   50
Two tyrtle-doves to Godes honoure
    To bryng with her for her offrand.

Loo, here am I, preest present alway,
    To resave all offerandes that hydder is broght,
And for the people to God to pray   55
    That helth and lyfe to theme be wroght.

Anna
Prophetissa Here in this holy playce I say
    Is my full purpose to abyde,
To serve my God bothe nyght and day
    With prayer and fastyng in ever-ylk a tyde.   60

For I haue beyn a wyddo this threscore yere
    And foure yere to, the truthe to tell,
And here I haue terryed with full good chere
    For the redempcyon of Israell.

And so for my holy conversacion   65
    Grete grace to me hais nowe God sent,

33.   after dyvers] *K; MS, TS* after that dyvers
34.   after dyvers] *K; MS, TS* after that dyvers

To tell by profecy for mans redempcion
　　What shall befall by Goddes intent.

I tell you all here in this place　　　　　　　　　　f.228ᵛ
　　By Godes vertue in prophecy,　　　　　　　　　70
That one is borne to oure solace,
　　Here to be present securely
　　　　Within short space,
　　　　　Of his owen mother, a madyn free,
　　　　　Of all vyrgens moost chaist suthly,　　　75
　　　　　The well of mekenes, blyssed myght she be,
　　　Moost full of grace.

And Symeon, that senyour
　　That is so semely in Godes sight,
He shall hyme se and do honour　　　　　　　　　80
　　And in his armes he shall hym plight,
　　　That worthy leyd.
　　　　Of the holy goost he shall suthly
　　　　Take strength, and answere when he shall hy
　　　　Furth to this temple and place holy　　　85
　　　To do þat deyd.

Symeon　　A, blyssed God, thowe be my beylde
　　　And beat my baill bothe nyght and day,
In hevynes my hart is hylde,
　　Vnto myself, loo thus I say.　　　　　　　　　90
For I ame wayke and all vnwelde,
　　My welth ay wayns and passeth away,
Whereso I fayre in fyrth or feylde
　　I fall ay downe for febyll, in fay.

In fay I fall whereso I fayre,　　　　　　　　　95
　　In hayre and hewe and hyde I say.
Owte of this worlde I wolde I were,
　　Thus wax I warr and warr alway
　　And my myscheyf growes in all that may.
Bot thowe myghty lorde my mornyng mar;　　　100
　　Mar ye, for it shulde me well pay,
So happy to se hyme yf I warr.

Nowe certys then shulde my gamme begynne
　　And I myght se hyme, of hyme to tell,
That one is borne withouten synne　　　　　　　105
　　And for mankynde mans myrth to mell.
　　　Borne of a woman and madyn fre,
　　　As wytnesse Davyt and Danyell,

106. mankynde] *This ed; MS, TS* mans kynde

Withouten synne or velanye,
As said also Isacheell.   110

And Melachiell that proffett snell
Hais tolde vs of that babb so bright,
That he shulde comme with vs to dwell
In our temple as leme of light.
And other proffettes prophesieth   115
And of this blyssed babb dyd mell,
And of his mother, a madyn bright,
In prophecy the truth gan tell,

That he shulde comme and harro hell   f.229
As a gyant grathly to glyde,   120
And fersly the feyndes malles to fell
And putt there poors all on syde.
The worthyest wight in this worlde so wyde
His vertues seer no tong can tell,
He sendes all soccour in ylke tyde   125
As redemption of Israell.
Thus say they all,
There patryarkes and ther prophettes clere:
'A babb is borne to be oure fere,
Knytt in oure kynde for all our chere   130
To grete and small'.

Ay, well were me for ever and ay
If I myght se that babb so bright
Or I were buryed here in clay,
Then wolde my cors here mend in myght   135
Right faithfully.
Nowe lorde, thowe grant to me thy grace
To lyf here in this worlde a space,
That I myght se that babb in his face
Here or I dy.   140

A, lorde God, I thynke may I endure,
Trowe we that babb shall fynde me here;
Nowe certys with aige I ame so power
That ever it abaites my chere.

Yet yf kynde fale for aige in me,   145
God yett may length my lyfe suthly,
Tyll I that babb and foode so free
Haue seyn in sight.
For trewly, yf I wyst relesse
Thare shulde nothyng my hart dyseas;   150

---

149.   relesse] *He; MS, TS* reverce

Lorde, len me grace yf that thowe pleas
   And make me light.

When wyll thowe comme babb? Let se, haue done;
   Nay, comme on tyte and tarry nott,
For certys my lyf-days are nere done,   155
   For aige to me grete wo hais wroght.

Great wo is wroght vnto mans harte
   Whan he muste want that he wolde haue;
I kepe no longar to haue quarte
   For I haue seen that I for crave.   160

A, trowes thowe these ij eyes shall see
   That blyssed babb or they be owte?
Ye, I pray God so myght it be –
   Then were I putt all owte of dowte.

Angelus   Olde Symeon, Gods seruaunt right,   165
   Bodworde to the I bryng I say,
For the holy goost moost of myght,
   He says thowe shall not dye away
      To thowe haue seen
         Jesu the babb that Mary bare,   170
         For all mankynde to slake there care.
         He shall do comforth to lesse and mayr,
      Both morne and even.

Symeon   A, lorde, gramarcy nowe I say   f.229ᵛ
   That thowe this grace hais to me hight,   175
Or I be buryed here in clay
   To see that semely beam so bright.

No man of molde may haue more happ
   To my solace and myrth allway,
Than for to se that Mary lapp   180
   Jesu my joy and savyour ay,
      Blyssyd be his name.
         Loo, nowe mon I se, the truth to tell,
         The redempcion of Israell,
         Jesu my lorde Emanuell,   185
      Withouten blame.

Mary   Joseph my husbonde and my feer,
   Ye take to me grathely entent,
I wyll you showe in this manere
   What I wyll do, thus haue I ment: 190

166.   Bodworde] *Ha; MS, TS* Bolde worde
180.   that] *K* in

Full xl days is comme and went
  Sens that my babb Jesu was borne,
Therefore I wolde he were present
  As Moyses lawes sais hus beforne,

Here in this temple before Goddes sight   195
  As other women doith in feer,
So methynke good skyll and right
  The same to do nowe with good chere,
    After Goddes sawe.

Joseph   Mary my spowse and madyn clene,   200
  This matter that thowe moves to me
Is for all these women bedene
  That hais conceyved with syn fleshely
    To bere a chylde.
        The lawe is ledgyd for theme right playn,   205
        That they muste be puryfied agayne,
        For in mans pleasoure for certayn
    Before were they fylyd.

But Mary, byrde, thowe neyd not soo
For this cause to bee puryfiede, loo,   210
  In Goddes temple.
For certys thowe arte a clene vyrgyn
For any thoght thy harte within,
Nor never wroght no flesly synne
  Nor never yll.   215

Mary   That I my madenheade hais kept styll
It is onely throgh Godds wyll,
  That be ye bold.
Yett to fulfyll the lawe ewysse,
That God almyghty gon expresse,   220
And for a sample of mekenesse
  Offer I wolde.

Joseph   A, Mary, blyssed be thowe ay,
  Thowe thynkes to do after Goddes wyll,
As thowe haist said Mary, I say,   225
  I will hartely consent theretyll
    Withouten dowte.
        Wherefore we dresse vs furth oure way   f.230
        And make offerand to God this day,
        Even lykwyse as thyself gon say   230
    With hartes devowte.

Maria   Therto am I full redy dight,
  But one thyng Joseph I wolde you meyve.

---

205. ledgyd] *This ed; TS* hedgyd

Joseph	Mary my spouse and madyn bright,	
	Tell on hartely, what is your greyf?	235
Maria	Both beest and fewll hus muste neydes haue,	
	As a lambe and ij dove-byrdes also.	
	Lame haue we none nor none we crave,	
	Therefore Joseph what shall we do,	
	What is your read?	240
	And we do not as custome is,	
	We are worth to be blamyd iwysse,	
	I wolde we dyd nothyng amys	
	As God me speyd.	
Joseph	A, good Mary, the lawe is this:	245
	To riche to offer bothe the lame and the byrd,	
	And the poore ij tyrtles iwys.	
	Or two doyf-byrdes shall not be fyrd	
	For our offerand;	
	And Mary, we haue doyf-byrdes two	250
	As falls for hus, therefore we goo —	
	They ar here in a panyer, loo,	
	Reddy at hand.	
	And yf we haue not both in feer,	
	The lame, the burd, as ryche men haue,	255
	Thynke that vs muste present here	
	Oure babb Jesus, as we voutsaue	
	Before Godes sight.	
	He is our lame Mary, kare the not,	
	For riche and power none better soght;	260
	Full well thowe hais hym hither broght,	
	This our offerand right.	
	He is the lame of God I say,	
	That all our syns shall take away	
	Of this worlde here.	265
	He is the lame of God verray	
	That muste hus fend frome all our fray,	
	Borne of thy wombe, all for our pay	
	And for our chere.	
Maria	Joseph my spowse, ye say full trewe,	270
	Than lett vs dresse hus furth our way.	
Joseph	Go we than Mary, and do oure dewe,	
	And make meekly offerand this day.	

237.   *Two minims, deleted, follow*
247.   poore] *Suppl K*
261.   hais] *This ed; TS* have
262.   right] *This ed; TS* dight
268.   pay] *TS; MS* pray

Lo, here is the tempyll on this hyll
And also preest ordand by skyll,   275
  Power havand.
And Mary, go we thyther forthy,
And lett vs both knele devowtly,
And offre we vp to God meekly
  Our dewe offrand.   280

Maria   Vnto my God highest in heven   f.230ᵛ
  And to this preest ordand by skyll,
Jesu my babb I offer hyme
  Here with my harte and my good wyll
    Right hartely.   285
      Thowe pray for hus to God on hyght
      Thowe preest, present here in his myght,
      At this deyd may be in his sight
    Accept goodly.

Joseph   Loo sir, and two doyf-byrddes ar here,   290
  Receyve them with your holy handes,
We ar no better of power,
  For we haue neyther rentes ne landes
    Trewely.
      Bott good sir, pray to God of myght   295
      To accepte this at we haue dight,
      That we haue offeryd as we arr hight
    Here hartely.

Presbiter   O God and graunter of all grace,
  Blyst be thy name both nyght and day,   300
Accepte there offerand in this place
  That be here present to the alway.
  A, blyssed lorde, say never nay,
    But lett thys offerand be boot and beylde
  Tyll all such folke lyvand in clay,   305
    That thus to the mekly wyll heyld;

That this babb lord, present in thy sight,
  Borne of a madyns wombe vnfylde,
Accepte for there specyall gyft
  Gevyn to mankynde, both man and chylde,   310
    So specyally.
      And this babb borne and here present
      May beylde vs, that we be not shent,
      But ever reddy his grace to hent
    Here verely.   315

283.   *He suppl* even *after* hyme
304.   thys] *K; MS, TS* thy
309.   Accepte for] *TS* Accepte [lord] for

A, blyssyd babb, welcome thowe be,
Borne of a madyn in chaistety,
Thowe art our beylde, babb, our gamme and our glee
    Ever sothly.
Welcome oure wytt and our wysdome,   320
Welcome, our joy all and somme,
Welcomme *redemptour omnium*
    Tyll hus hartely.

**Anna
Prophetissa**   Welcome blyssed Mary and madyn ay,
Welcome, mooste meke in thyne array;   325
Welcome bright starne that shyneth bright as day,
    All for our blys.
Welcome, the blyssed beam so bryght,
Welcome the leym of all oure light,
Welcome that all pleasour hais plight   330
    To man and wyfe.

Welcome thowe blyssed babb so free,   f.231
Welcome oure welfayre wyelly
And welcome all our seall, suthly,
    To grete and small.   335
Babb, welcome to thy beyldly boure,
Babb, welcome nowe for our soccoure,
And babb, welcomme with all honour
    Here in this hall.

Angelus   Olde Symeon, I say to the   340
    Dresse the furth in thyne array,
Come to the temple, there shall þu see
    Jesus that babb that Mary barre,
       That be thowe bolde.
Symeon   A, lorde, I thanke þe ever and ay,   345
    Nowe am I light as leyf on tree,
My age is went, I feyll no fray,
    Methynke for this that is tolde me
       I ame not olde.

Nowe wyll I to yon temple goo   350
    To se the babb that Mary bare,
He is my helth in well and woo,
    And helps me ever frome great care.
Haill blyssed babb that Mary bare,
    And blyssed be thy mother, Mary mylde,   355
Whose wombe that yeildyd fresh and fayr
    And she a clean vyrgen ay vnfyld.

331. and wyfe] *He* iwisse
341. thyne array] *He* thy gare; *Ho'* (retaining MS reading) suppl full yare
356. that] *He* the

Haill babb, the father of heven own chylde
  Chosen to chere vs for our myschance;
No erthly tong can tell vnfylyd   360
  What thy myght is in every chance.
  Haill, the moost worthy to enhance,
    Boldly thowe beylde frome all yll,
  Withoute thy beylde we gytt grevance
    And for our deydes here shulde we spyll.   365

Haill floscampy and flower vyrgynall,
The odour of thy goodnes reflars to vs all.
Haill, moost happy to great and to small
  For our weyll.
Haill ryall roose, moost ruddy of hewe,   370
Haill flour vnfadyng, both freshe ay and newe,
Haill the kyndest in comforth that ever man knewe
  For grete heyll.

And mekly I beseke the here where I kneyll
  To suffre thy servant to take the in hand,   375
And in my narmes for to heue the here for my weyll,
  And where I bound am in bayll to bait all my bandes.

Nowe come to me, lorde of all landes,   f.231ᵛ
Comme myghtyest by see and by sandes,
Come myrth by strete and by strandes   380
  On moolde.
· Come halse me, the babb that is best born,
Come halse me, the myrth of our morne,
Come halse me, for ells I ame lorne
  For olde.   385

I thanke the lord God of thy greet grace
That thus haith sparyd me a space,
This babb in my narmes for to inbrace
  As the prophecy telles.
I thanke the that me my lyfe lent,   390
I thanke the that me thus seyll sent,
That this sweyt babb, that I in armes hent
  With myrth my myndes alwais melles.

Mellyd are my myndes ay with myrth,
  Full fresh nowe I feyll is my force,   395
Of thy grace thowe gave me this gyrth

---

360. vnfylyd] *Ho¹; MS, TS* fylyd
363. beylde frome] *TS* beylde [us] frome
389. telles] *TS; MS* tell
393. myndes] *Ho¹; MS, TS* myght

Thus comly to catch here thy corse
  Moost semely in sight.
    Of helpe thus thy freynd never faills,
    Thy marcy as every man avaylls,   400
    Both by downes and by daylls,
  Thus mervelous and muche is thy myght.

A, babb, be thowe blyssed for ay,
For thowe art my savyour I say
And thowe here rewles me in fay,   405
  In all my lyfe.
Nowe blist be þi name,
For thowe saves hus fro shame,
And here thou beyld vs fro blame
  And frome all stryfe.   410

Nowe care I no moore for my lyfe
Sen I haue seen here this ryall so ryfe,
My strength and my stynter of stryfe
  I you say.
In peace lorde nowe leyf thy servand   415
For myne eys haith seyn that is ordand,
The helth for all men that be levand
  Here for ay.

'That helth lorde hais thowe ordand I say
  Here before the face of thy people,   420
And thy light hais thowe shynyd this day
  To be knowe of thy folke that was febyll
    For evermore.
      And thy glory for the chylder of Israell,
      That with the in thy kyngdome shall dwell   425
      Whan the damnyd shall be drevyn to hell
    Than with great care.

Joseph   Mary, my spowse and madyn mylde,
      In hart I marvell here greatly
    Howe these folke spekes of our chylde.   430
      They say and tells of great maistry
        That he shall doo.
Maria   Yea certes, Joseph, I marvell also,   f.232
      But I shall bere it full styll in mynde.

---

407. *Added later to left*
422–3. *Lineation He; reversed in MS, TS*
432+ *Main scribe's catchword erased*
433. *Quire xxx^li begins. The rest of the text is on a singleton added by Clerke to the MS (f. 232).*
     It is pasted on to the stub of a leaf cancelled by the main scribe, originally the first of quire
     xxx^li; see the textual note to play XLI, line 1–

Joseph   God geve hyme grace here well to do,   435
    For he is comme of gentyll kynde.
Symeon   Harke Mary, I shall tell the þe truth or I goo.

This was putt here to welde vs fro wo,
In redemtion of many and recover also,
    I the say.   440
And the sworde of sorro thy hart shal thyrll
Whan thowe shall se sothly thy son soffer yll
For the well of all wrytches, þat shall be his wyll
    Here in fay.

But to be comforth agayn right well thowe may,   445
And in harte to be fayne, the suth I the say,
For his myght is so muche thare can no tong say nay
    Here to his wyll.
For this babb as a gyant full graythly shall glyde
And the myghtiest mayster shall meve on ylke syde,   450
To all the wightes that wons in this worlde wyde,
    For good or for yll.

Tharefore babb, beylde vs that we here not spyll,
And fayrwell the former of all at thy wyll,
Fayrwell starne stabylyst by lowde and be styll,   455
    In suthfastnes.
Fayrwell the ryolest roose that is renyng,
Fayrwell the babb best in thy beryng,
Fayrwell God son, thowe grant vs blyssyng
    To fyne our dystresse.   460

438.   wo] *Suppl Ha*
449.   gyant] *TS; MS* gyane
460.   fyne] *He; MS, TS* fynd
460+   Explicit Liber *in red, in a red scroll. Bottom half of f.232 blank, f.232ᵛ blank*

XVIII The Marshals
The Flight into Egypt

Joseph	Thow maker þat is most of myght,	f.75
	To thy mercy I make my mone;	
	Lord, se vnto þis symple wight	
	Þat hase non helpe but þe allone.	
	For all þis worlde I haue forsaken,	5
	And to thy seruice I haue me taken	
	With witte and will	
	For to fulfill	
	Þi commaundement.	
	Þeron myn herte is sette	10
	With grace þou has me lente,	
	Þare schall no lede me lette.	
	For all my tristc lordc is in þe	
	That made me man, to thy liknes.	
	Thow myghtfull maker, haue mynde on me	15
	And se vnto my sympplenes.	
	I waxe as wayke as any wande,	
	For febill me faylles both foote and hande;	
	Whateuere it mene,	
	Methynke myne eyne	20
	Hevye as leede.	
	Þerfore I halde it best	
	A whille her in þis stede	
	To slepe and take my reste.	
Maria	Thow luffely lord þat last schall ay,	25
	My God, my lorde, my sone so dere,	
	To thy Godhede hartely I pray	
	With all myn harte holy entere.	
	As þou me to thy modir chaas,	
	I beseke þe of thy grace	30
	For all mankynde	
	Þat has in mynde	
	To wirshippe þe.	
	Þou se thy saules to saue,	f.75ᵛ

1. *Joseph] Centred, above first line*

1–2. This matter is mayd of newe after anoþer forme *to right in hand of J. Clerke, deleted*

3. þis] *Third letter doubtful; TS +* þin

12. *To right in a later hand (? J. Clerke)* Caret, deleted

33. *To right in a later hand* Maria ad huc

161

Jesu my sone so free,   35
    Þis bone of þe I crave.

Angelus   Wakyn Joseph, and take entent,
    My sawes schall seece thy sorowe sare.
    Be noght heuy, þi happe is hentte,
    Þarefore I bidde þe slepe no mare.   40
Joseph   A, myghtfull lorde, whateuere þat mente?
    So swete a voyce herde I neuere ayre.
        But what arte þou with steuen so shylle
        Þus in my slepe þat spekis me till?
        To me appere   45
        And late me here
            What þat þou was.
Angelus   Joseph, haue þou no drede,
        Þou shalte witte or I passe,
        Therfore to me take hede.   50

For I am sente to þe,
    Gabriell, Goddis aungell bright,
Is comen to bidde þe flee
    With Marie and hir worthy wight.
        For Herowde þe kyng gars doo to dede   55
        All knave-childer in ilke a stede,
        Þat he may ta
        With ʒeris twa
            Þat are of olde.
                Tille he be dede, away   60
        In Egipte shall ʒe beelde
                Tille I witte þe for to saie.

Joseph   Aye-lastand lord, loved mott þou be   f.76
    That thy swete sande wolde to me sende.
But lorde, what ayles þe kyng at me,   65
    For vnto hym I neuere offende?
        Allas, what ayles hym for to spille
        Smale ʒonge barnes þat neuere did ille
        In worde ne dede,
        Vnto no lede   70
            Be nyght nor day?
                And sen he wille vs schende,
        Dere lorde, I þe praye,
                Þou wolde be oure frende,

For be he neuere so wode or wrothe   75
    For all his force þou may vs fende.

---

47. What þat] *TS +; MS* What at þat
55. Herowde] *This ed; MS, TS +* Horowde
66. neuere offende] *MS* didde *between, deleted*

I praye þe lorde, kepe us fro skathe,
  Thy socoure sone to vs þou sende;
    For vnto Egipte wende we will
    Thy biddyng baynly to fulfill,   80
    As worthy is
    Þou kyng of blisse,
      Þi will be wroght.
      Marie my doughtir dere,
      On þe is all my þought.   85

Maria   A, leue Joseph, what chere?

Joseph Þe chere of me is done for ay.
Maria   Allas, what tythandis herde haue ȝe?
Joseph Now certis, full ille to þe at saye,
    Ther is noght ellis but us most flee   90
      Owte of oure kyth where we are knowyn,
      Full wightely bus vs be withdrawen,
      Both þou and I.
Maria   Leue Joseph, why?   f.76ᵛ
      Layne it noght,   95
        To doole who has vs demed,
      Or what wronge haue we wroght
        Wherfore we shulde be flemyd?

Joseph Wroght we harme? Nay, nay, all wrange,
    Wytte þou wele it is noght soo.   100
  Þat yonge page liffe þou mon forgange
    But yf þou fast flee fro his foo.
Maria   His foo? Allas, what is youre reede,
    Wha wolde my dere barne do to dede?
    I durk, I dare,   105
    Whoo may my care
      Of balis blynne?
      To flee I wolde full fayne,
    For all þis worlde to wynne
      Wolde I not se hym slayne.   110

Joseph I warne þe he is thraly thrette
    With Herowde kyng, harde harmes to haue.
  With þat mytyng yf þat we be mette
    Þer is no salue þat hym may saue.
    I warne þe wele, he sleeis all   115
    Knave-childir, grete and small,
    In towne and felde
    Within þe elde
      Of two ȝere,
      And for thy sones sake.   120
      He will fordo þat dere,
      May þat traytoure hym take.

Maria	Leue Joseph, who tolde yow þis?	f.77
	How hadde ȝe wittering of þis dede?	
Joseph	An aungell bright þat come fro blisse	125
	This tythandis tolde withowten drede,	
	And wakynd me oute of my slepe	
	Þat comely childe fro cares to kepe,	
	And bad me flee	
	With hym and þe	130
	Onto Egipte.	
	And sertis I dred me sore	
	To make any smale trippe,	
	Or tyme þat I come þare.	

Maria	What ayles þei at my barne	135
	Slike harmes hym for to hete?	
	Allas, why schulde I tharne	
	My sone his liffe so swete?	
	His harte aught to be ful sare,	
	On slike a foode hym to forfare	140
	Þat nevir did ill,	
	Hym for to spill,	
	And he ne wate why.	
	I ware full wille of wane	
	My sone and he shulde dye,	145
	And I haue but hym allone.	

Joseph	We, leue Marie, do way, late be!	
	I pray þe, leue of thy dynne,	
	And fande þe furthe faste for to flee,	
	Away with hym for to wynne,	150
	That no myscheue on hym betyde,	
	Nor none vnhappe in no-kyn side	
	Be way nor strete,	
	Þat we non mete	
	To slee hym.	155
Maria	Allas Joseph, for care,	f.77ᵛ
	Why shuld I forgo hym,	
	My dere barne þat I bare?	

Joseph	Þat swete swayne yf þou saue	
	Do tyte pakke same oure gere,	160
	And such smale harnes as we haue.	
Maria	A, leue Joseph, I may not bere.	
Joseph	Bere arme? No, I trowe but small.	
	But God it wote I muste care for all,	
	For bed and bak	165
	And alle þe pakke	

---

133. any] *Be; TS* my
137. tharne] *TS +; MS* thrane

Þat nedis vnto vs.
  It fortheres to fene me;
Þis þakald bere me þus,
  Off of all I plege and pleyne me.   170

But God graunte grace I noght forgete
  No tulles þat we schulde with vs take.
Maria   Allas Joseph, for greuance grete,
    Whan shall my sorowe slake,
      For I wote noght whedir to fare?   175
Joseph   To Egipte—talde I þe lang are.
Maria   Whare standith itt?
        Fayne wolde I witt.
Joseph   What wate I?
          I wote not where it stande.   180
Maria   Joseph, I aske mersy,
          Helpe me oute of þis lande.

Joseph Nowe certis Marie, I wolde full fayne   f.78
    Helpe þe al þat I may,
And at my poure me peyne   185
    To wynne with hym and þe away.
Maria   Allas, what ayles þat feende
      Þus wilsom wayes make vs to wende?
      He dois grete synne,
        Fro kyth and kynne   190
          He gares vs flee.
Joseph   Leue Marie, leue thy grete.
Maria   Joseph, full wo is me
          For my dere sone so swete.

Joseph I pray þe Marie, happe hym warme   195
    And sette hym softe þat he noght syle,
And yf þou will ought ese thyn arme
    Gyff me hym, late me bere hym awhile.
Maria   I thanke you of youre grete goode dede;
      Nowe gud Joseph tille hym take hede,   200
      Þat fode so free,
      Tille hym ȝe see
        Now in this tyde.
Joseph   Late me and hym allone,
        And yf þou can ille ride   205
          Haue and halde þe faste by þe mane.

168. fortheres to] *He, Be* fortheres no(gh)t to
170. Off of all] *TS +* Of all
180. stande] *He; MS, TS +* standis
182+ *Catchword* Now certis Marie
183. *Quire K begins*

Maria	Allas Joseph, for woo,	
	Was neuer wight in worde so will.	
Joesph	Do way Marie, and say nought soo,	
	For þou schall haue no cause thertill.	210
	For witte þou wele, God is oure frende,	
	He will be with vs wherso we lende.	f.78ᵛ
	In all oure nede	
	He will vs spede,	
	Þis wote I wele.	215
	I loue my lorde of all;	
	Such forse methynke I fele,	
	I may go where I schall.	
	Are was I wayke, nowe am I wight,	
	My lymes to welde ay at my wille.	220
	I loue my maker most of myght	
	That such grace has graunte me tille.	
	Nowe schall no hatyll do vs harme,	
	I haue oure helpe here in myn arme.	
	He wille vs fende	225
	Wherso we lende	
	Fro tene and tray.	
	Late vs goo with goode chere –	
	Farewele and haue gud day –	
	God blisse vs all in fere.	230
Maria	Amen as he beste may.	

XIX The Girdlers and Nailers

The Slaughter of the Innocents

Herod	Powre bewsheris aboute,	f.80
	Peyne of lyme and lande,	
	Stente of youre steuenes stoute	
	And stille as stone ȝe stande,	
	And my carping recorde.	5

231+ *Bottom half of f.78ᵛ blank; f.79 originally a blank,* Mylners *added at head of page by J. Clerke, later deleted. For f.79ᵛ, see first textual note to play XIX*

1– *The preceding page, f.79ᵛ, was originally a blank. At the head, in the hand of J. Clerke,* This matter of the gyrdlers agreyth not with the Coucher (TS Coucheȝ) in no poynt, it begynnyth, Lysten lordes vnto my lawe

1. *Herod] Suppl by Clerke, centred*

1–4. *Lineation TS; two lines in MS*

3e aught to dare and doute,
And lere you lowe to lowte
 To me youre louely lord.

3e awe in felde and towne
 To bowe at my bidding,   10
With reuerence and renoune,
 As fallis for swilk a kyng,
  Þe lordlyest on lyue.
Who herto is noght bowne,
Be allmyghty Mahounde,   15
 To dede I schall hym dryue.

So bolde loke no man be
 For to aske helpe ne helde
But of Mahounde and me,
 Þat hase þis worlde in welde, 20
  To mayntayne vs emell.
For welle of welthe are we
And my cheffe helpe is he;
 Herto what can 3e tell?

I Consolator Lord, what you likis to do   25
 All folke will be full fayne
To take entente þerto,
 And none grucche þeragayne.
  Þat full wele witte shall 3e,
And yf þai wolde no3t soo   30
We shulde sone wirke þam woo.
Herodes 3a, faire sirs, so shulde it bee.

II Consolator Lorde, þe soth to saie,   f.80ᵛ
 Fulle wele we vndirstande
Mahounde is God werraye,   35
 And 3e ar lorde of ilke a lande.
  Therfore, so haue I seell,
In rede we wayte allway
What myrthe most mende 3ou may.
Herodes Sertis, 3e saie right well. 40

But I am noyed of newe,
 Þat blithe may I no3t be,
For thre kyngis as 3e knowe
 That come thurgh þis contré,
  And saide þei sought a swayne. 45
I Consolator Þat rewlle I hope þam rewe,
For hadde þer tales ben trewe
 They hadde comen þis waye agayne.

18. helde] *TS; MS* holde

II Consolator	We harde how þei ȝou hight,	
	Yf they myght fynde þat childe	50
	For to haue tolde ȝou right,	
	But certis þei are begilyd.	
	Swilke tales ar noght to trowe,	
	Full wele wotte ilke a wight,	
	Þer schalle neuere man haue myght	55
	Ne maystrie unto ȝou.	

I Consolator	Þam schamys so, for certayne,	
	That they dar mete ȝou no more.	
Herodes	Wherfore shulde þei be fayne	
	To make swilke fare before,	60
	To saie a boy was borne	
	That schulde be moste of mayne?	
	This gadlyng schall agayne	
	Yf þat þe deuyll had sworne.	

	For be well neuer þei wotte	f.81
	Whedir þei wirke wele or wrang,	66
	To frayne garte þam þus-gate	
	To seke that gedlyng gang,	
	And swilke carping to kith.	
II Consolator	Nay lorde, they lered ouere-latte	70
	Youre blisse schal neuere abatte,	
	And therfore lorde, be blithe.	

Nuncius	Mahounde withouten pere,	
	My lorde, ȝou saue and see.	
Herodes	Messenger, come nere,	75
	And bewcher, wele þe be.	
	What tydyngis? Telles þou any?	
Nuncius	Ȝa lorde. Sen I was here	
	I haue sought sidis seere,	
	And sene merueyllis full many.	80

Herodes	And of meruayles to mene	
	That wer most myrthe to me.	
Nuncius	Lorde, euen as I haue seene	
	The soth sone schall ȝe see,	
	Yf ȝe wille, here in hye.	85
	I mette tow townes betwene	
	Thre kyngis with crounes clene,	
	Rydand full ryally.	

Herodes	A, my blys, boy, þou burdis to brode.	
Nuncius	Sir, þer may no botment be.	90

68.   gang] *He; MS, TS* gane
76.   þe] *This ed; TS* ye
81.   mene] *Ha; MS, TS* move
90.   *Nuncius] Suppl TS*

Herodes	Owe, by sonne and mone,
	Þan tydis vs talis tonyght.
	Hopes þou þei will come sone
	Hedir, as þei haue hight,
	For to telle me tythande?
Nuncius	Nay lorde, þat daunce is done.
Herodes	Why, whedir are þei gone?
Nuncius	Ilkone into ther owne lande.

95
f.81ᵛ

Herodes	How sais þou ladde? Late be.
Nuncius	I saie, for they are past.
Herodes	What, forthe away fro me?
Nuncius	3a lord, in faitht ful faste,
	For I herde and toke hede
	How þat þei wente all thre
	Into ther awne contré.
Herodes	A, dogges, þe deuell 3ou spede.

100

105

Nuncius	Sir, more of þer menyng
	3itt well I vndirstode,
	How þei hadde made offering
	Vnto þat frely foode
	Þat nowe of newe is borne.
	Þai saie he schulde be kyng
	And welde all erthely thyng.
Herodes	Allas, þan am I lorne.

110

	Fy on thaym, faytours, fy!
	Wille þei begylle me þus?
Nuncius	Lorde, by ther prophicy
	Þei named his name Jesus.
Herodes	Fy on þe ladde, þou lyes.
II Consolator	Hense tyte but þou þe hye,
	With doulle her schall þou dye,
	That wreyes hym on this wise.

115

120

Nuncius	3e wyte me all with wrang,
	Itt is þus and wele warre.
Herodes	Thou lyes, false traytoure strange,
	Loke neuere þou negh me nere.
	Vppon liffe and lymme
	May I þat faitour fange,
	Full high I schall gar hym hange,
	Both þe, harlott, and hym.

f.82
126

130

Nuncius	I am nott worthy to wyte,
	Bot fareswele all þe heppe.

91. *Herodes] Suppl TS*
107–10. *Lineation TS; two lines in MS*

I Consolator	Go, in þe deueles dispite,	
	Or I schall gar the leppe	
	And dere aby this bro.	135
Herodes	Als for sorowe and sighte	
	My woo no wighte may wryte;	
	What deuell is best to do?	

II Consolator	Lorde, amende youre chere	
	And takis no nedles noy,	140
	We schall ʒou lely lere	
	Þat ladde for to distroye,	
	Be counsaille if we cane.	
Herodes	Þat may ʒe noght come nere,	
	For it is past two ʒere	145
	Sen þat þis bale begane.	

I Consolator	Lorde, þerfore haue no doute,	
	Yf it were foure or fyve.	
	Gars gadir in grete rowte	
	Youre knyghtis kene belyue,	150
	And biddis þam dynge to dede	
	Alle knave childir kepte in clowte,	
	In Bedlem and all aboute,	
	To layte in ilke a stede.	

II Consolator	Lorde, saue none, for youre seell,	f.82ᵛ
	Þat are of ij ʒere age withinne,	156
	Þan schall þat fandelyng felle	
	Belyue his blisse schall blynne,	
	With bale when he schall blede.	
Herodes	Sertis, ʒe saie right wele,	160
	And as ʒe deme ilke dele	
	Shall I garre do indede.	

	Sir knyghtis, curtayse and hende,	
	Þow the nott bees nowe all newe,	
	ʒe schall fynde me youre frende	165
	And ʒe þis tyme be trewe.	
I Miles	What saie ʒe lorde? Lette see.	
Herodes	To Bedlehem bus ʒe wende,	
	That schorwe with schame to schende	
	Þat menes to maistir me.	170

And abowte Bedlehem bathe	
Bus yowe wele spere and spye,	

136. Als] *This ed;* TS Alas *(conj)*
152. clowte] *This ed;* TS dowte
153. and] TS; MS and and
164. the] Zu; MS, TS ne
167. I Miles] *This ed;* MS, TS I Consolator
169. schorwe] *This ed;* TS schrewe *(conj)*
171. bathe] Zu, Ha; MS, TS boght he

	For ellis it will be wathe	
	Þat he losis þis Jury,	
	And certis þat were grete schame.	175
II Miles	My lorde, þat wer vs lathe,	
	And he escapid it wer skathe	
	And we welle worthy blame.	

I Miles	Full sone he schall be soughte,	
	That make I myne avowe.	180
I Consolator	I bide for him ȝow loghte,	
	And latte me telle yowe howe	
	To werke when ȝe come there:	f.83
	Bycause ȝe kenne hym noght,	
	To dede they muste be brought,	185
	Knave-childre, lesse and more.	

Herodes	Ȝaa, all withinne two ȝere,	
	That none for speche be spared.	
II Miles	Lord, howe ȝe vs lere	
	Full wele we take rewarde,	190
	And certis we schall not rest.	
I Miles	Comes furth felowes in feere,	
	Loo, fondelyngis fynde we here	
	[. . . . . .]	

I Mulier	Owte on ȝow theves, I crye,	
	Ȝe slee my semely sone.	195
II Miles	Ther browls schall dere abye	
	This bale þat is begonne,	
	Þerfore lay fro þe faste.	
II Mulier	Allas for doule, I dye,	
	To saue my son schall I,	200
	Aye-whils my liff may last.	

I Miles	A, dame, þe deuyll þe spede	
	And me, but itt be quytte.	
I Mulier	To dye I haue no drede	
	I do þe wele to witte,	205
	To saue my sone so dere.	
I Miles	Asarmes, for nowe is nede;	
	But yf we do yone dede	
	Ther quenys will quelle vs here.	

II Mulier	Allas, þis lothly striffe,	f.83ᵛ
	No blisse may be my bette,	211

173. wathe] *Zu, Ha; MS, TS* waghe
176. *II Miles] This ed; MS, TS* II Consolator
183. To] *This ed; TS* Go
193+ *Line missing; no gap in MS*

	Þe knyght vppon his knyffe	
	Hath slayne my sone so swette,	
	And I hadde but hym allone.	
I Mulier	Allas, I lose my liffe,	215
	Was neuere so wofull a wyffe	
	Ne halffe so wille of wone;	

	And certis, me were full lotht	
	Þat þei þus harmeles ʒede.	
I Miles	Þe deuell myght spede you bothe,	220
	False wicchis, ar ʒe woode?	
II Mulier	Nay, false lurdayns, ʒe lye.	
I Miles	Yf ʒe be woode or wrothe	
	Ye schall noʒt skape fro skathe;	
	Wende we vs hense in hye.	225

I Mulier	Allas þat we wer wroughte	
	In worlde women to be,	
	Þe barne þat wee dere bought	
	Þus in oure sighte to see	
	Disputuously spill.	230
II Mulier	And certis, þer nott is noght,	
	The same þat þei haue soughte	
	Schall þei neuere come till.	

I Miles	Go we to þe kyng.	
	Of all þis contek kene	235
	I schall nott lette for nothyng	
	To saie as we haue sene.	
II Miles	And certis, no more shall I;	
	We haue done his bidding	f.84
	How so they wraste or wryng,	240
	We schall saie sothfastly.	

I Miles	Mahounde oure god of myght,	
	Saue þe, sir Herowde þe kyng.	
I Consolator	Lorde, take kepe to youre knyght,	
	He wille telle ʒou nowe tyding	
	Of bordis wher they haue bene.	245
Herodes	Ʒaa, and þei haue gone right	
	And holde þat þei vs hight,	
	Þan shall solace be sene.	

| *II Miles* | Lorde, as ʒe demed vs to done | 250 |
| | In contrees wher we come— | |

---

223. *I Miles] Suppl TS*
240–1. *Lineation this ed; reversed in MS, TS*
245. tyding] *Zu, He; MS, TS* thydingis, i' *interlined*

Herodes	Sir, by sonne and mone,
	3e are welcome home
	And worthy to haue rewarde.
	Haue 3e geten vs þis gome? 255
I Miles	Wher we fande felle or fone
	Wittenesse we will þat þer was none.
II Miles	Lorde, they are dede ilkone,
	What wolde 3e we ded more?
Herodes	I aske but aftir oone 260
	Þe kyngis tolde of before,
	Þat schulde make grete maistrie;
	Telle vs if he be tane.
I Miles	Lorde, tokenyng hadde we none
	To knawe þat brothell by. 265
II Miles	In bale we haue þam brought f.84ᵛ
	Aboute all Bedleham towne.
Herodes	3e lye, 3oure note is nought,
	Þe deueles of helle 3ou droune.
	So may þat boy be fledde, 270
	For in waste haue 3e wroght
	Or þat same ladde be sought
	Schalle I neuere byde in bedde.
I Consolator	We will wende with you than,
	To dynge þat dastard doune. 275
Herodes	Asarme euere-ilke man
	That holdis of Mahounde.
	Wer they a thousand skore
	This bargayne schall þai banne.
	Comes aftir as yhe canne, 280
	For we will wende before.

257. *See Ha, Ho¹ for conjectures*
274–5. *Ruled off as distinct speech, but not assigned; I Consolator suppl TS. Lineation TS;*
than *at beginning of 275 in MS*
276–81. *Ruled off as distinct speech, but not assigned; Herodes suppl this ed; TS suppl II*
Consolator
279. banne] *TS; MS* bande
281+ *Bottom half of f.84ᵛ blank, f.85 blank; f.85ᵛ blank except for catchword* Marie of
mirthis

XX The Spurriers and Lorimers

Christ and the Doctors

Joseph	Marie, of mirthis we may vs mene,	f.86
	And trewly telle betwixte vs twoo	
	Of solempne sightis þat we haue sene	
	In þat cité where we come froo.	
Maria	Sertis Joseph, ȝe will noȝt wene	5
	What myrthis within my harte I maie,	
	Sen þat oure sone with vs has bene	
	And sene ther solempne sightis alswae.	
Joseph	Hamward I rede we hye	
	In all þe myght we maye,	10
	Because of company	
	Þat will wende in oure waye,	

For gode felawshippe haue we fone
   And ay so forward schall we fynde.

Maria	A, sir, where is oure semely sone?	15
	I trowe oure wittis be waste as wynde.	
	Allas, in bale þus am I boone,	
	What ayleth vs both to be so blynde?	
	To go ouere-fast we haue begonne	
	And late þat louely leue behynde.	20
Joseph	Marie, mende thy chere,	
	For certis whan all is done	
	He comes with folke in feere,	
	And will oueretake vs sone.	

Maria	Oueretake vs sone sir? Certis nay,	25
	Such gabbyngis may me noȝt begyle,	
	For we haue trauelde all þis day	
	Fro Jerusalem many a myle.	
Joseph	I wende he hadde bene with vs aye,	f.86ᵛ
	Awaye fro vs how schulde he wyle?	30
Maria	Hit helpis nought such sawes to saie,	
	My barne is lost, allas þe whille,	
	Þat euere we wente þeroute	
	With hym in companye.	
	We lokid ouere-late aboute,	35
	Full wooe is me forthy,	

1. *Quire L begins*
4. where] *Gr²; TS* were
13. fone] *Co; MS, TS* founde
20. Hic caret *added to right by a later hand*

174

	For he is wente som wayes wrang,	
	And non is worthy to wyte but wee.	
Joseph	Agaynewarde rede I þat we gang	
	The right way to þat same citee,	40
	To spire and spie all men emang,	
	For hardely homward gone is he.	
Maria	Of sorowes sere schal be my sang,	
	My semely sone tille I hym see,	
	He is but xij ȝere alde.	45
Joseph	What way someuere he wendis	
	Woman, we may be balde	
	To fynde hym with oure frendis.	

I Magister	Maistirs, takes to me intente,	
	And rede youre resouns right on rawe,	50
	And all þe pepull in þis present,	
	Euere-ilke man late see his sawe.	
	But witte I wolde, or we hens wente,	
	Be clargy clere if we couthe knawe	
	Yf any lede þat liffe has lente	55
	Wolde aught allegge agaynste oure lawe,	
	Owthir in more or lesse.	
	Yf we defaute myght feele,	f.87
	Dewly we schall gar dresse	
	Be dome euery-ilk a dele.	60

II Magister	Þat was wele saide, so mot I the,	
	Swilke notis to neven methynke wer nede,	
	For maistirs in this lande ar we	
	And has þe lawes lelly to lede,	
	And doctoures also in oure degree	65
	Þat demyng has of ilka dede.	
	Laye fourthe oure bokes belyue, late see,	
	What mater moste were for oure mede.	
III Magister	We schall ordayne so wele,	
	Sen we all clergy knawe,	70
	Defaute shall no man fele	
	Nowdir in dede ne sawe.	

Jesus	Lordingis, loue be with ȝou lentte	
	And mirthis be vnto þis mené.	
I Magister	Sone, hense away I wolde þou wente,	75
	For othir haftis in hande haue we.	

42. gone] *Suppl Ha*
46. Joseph] *K; 46–8 originally unassigned in MS. 47–8 ruled off from 46 and assigned to Joseph by a later hand; so TS*
49. I Magister] *TS; MS Magister I*
50. rawe] *He, Co; MS, TS* rawes
52. sawe] *He, Co; MS, TS* sawes
56. aught] *This ed; TS* might

II Magister   Sone, whoso þe hedir sente,
        They were nouȝt wise, þat warne I þe,
    For we haue othir tales to tente
        Þan now with barnes bordand to be.   80
III Magister   Sone, yf þe list ought to lere
          To lyve by Moyses laye,
      Come hedir and þou shalle here
          Þe sawes þat we shall saye,

      For in som mynde itt may þe brynge,   f.87ᵛ
          To here our reasouns redde by rawes.   86
Jesus   To lerne of you nedis me nothing,
          For I knawe both youre dedys and sawes.
I Magister   Nowe herken ȝone barne with his bowrdyng,
        He wenes he kens more þan we knawes.   90
    We, nay, certis sone, þou arte ouere-ȝonge
        By clergy ȝitt to knowe oure lawes.
Jesus   I wote als wele as yhe
             Howe þat youre lawes wer wrought.
II Magister   Cum sitte, sone schall we see,   95
          For certis so semys it noght.

    Itt wer wondir þat any wight
    · Vntill oure reasouns right schulde reche.
    And þou sais þou hast insight
        Oure lawes truly to telle and teche?   100
Jesus   The holy gost has on me light
    And has anoynted me as a leche,
    And geven me pleyne poure and myght
        The kyngdom of heuene for to preche.
I Magister   Whens-euere this barne may be   105
          That shewes þer novellis nowe?
Jesus   Certis, I was or ȝe,
          And schall be aftir ȝou.

I Magister   Sone, of thy sawes, als haue I cele,
        And of thy witte is wondir thyng,   110
    But neuere the lesse fully I feele
        Itt may falle wele in wirkyng.
    For Dauid demys of ilka dele,   f.88
        And sais þus of childir ȝing:
    Of ther mouthes, he wate full wele,   115
        Oure lord has parformed loving.
        But ȝitt sone, schulde þou lette
          Here for to speke ouere-large,

82.   lyve] v *superimposed on* k
89.   bowrdyng] *Gr¹, after T* bowrdyng; *MS, TS* brandyng, *Gr²* braudyng
90.   we] *T, Chester* he *(see Gr¹)*
115.   Of] *Ho³, after T* Of; *MS, TS* And of

For where maistirs are mette
   Childre wordis are noȝt to charge,   120

And if þou wolde neuere so fayne,
  Yf all þe liste to lere þe lawe,
Þou arte nowthir of myght ne mayne
  To kenne it as a clerke may knawe.

Jesus   Sirs, I saie ȝou for sartayne   125
  That suthfast schal be all my sawe,
And poure haue playnere and playne
  To say and aunswer as me awe.

I Doctor   Maistirs, what may þis mene?
     Meruayle methynke haue I,   130
  Whens-euere þis barne haue bene
    That carpis þus connandly?

II Doctor   Als wyde in worlde als we haue wente
    Ȝitt fand we neuere swilke ferly fare,
For certis I trowe þis barne be sente   135
  Full souerandly to salue oure sare.

Jesus   Sirs, I schall proue in youre present
  Alle þe sawes þat I saide are.

III Doctor Why, whilke callest þou þe firste comaundement,
  And þe moste in Moyses lare?   140

Jesus   Sirs, sen ȝe are sette on rowes
    And has youre bokes on brede,
  Late se sirs, in youre sawes,   f.88ᵛ
    Howe right þat ȝe can rede.

I Doctor   I rede þis is þe firste bidding   145
  Þat Moyses taught vs here vntill:
To honnoure God ouere all thing
  With all thy witte and all þi will,
And all thyn harte in hym schall hyng,
  Erlye and late, both lowde and still.   150

Jesus   Ȝe nedis non othir bokes to bring,
  But fandis þis for to fulfill.
    The secounde may men preve
    And clerly knawe, wherby
    Ȝoure neghbours shall ȝe loue   155
    Als youreselffe, sekirly.

This comaunded Moyses to all men
  In his x comaundementis clere,
In þer ij biddingis, schall we kene,
  Hyngis all þe lawe þat we shall lere.   160

127. playnere] *T* plene
128. *Lineation Ha, Co, after T; MS, TS place* To say *at end of 127*
132. That] *K, after T* That; *MS, TS* And
134. Ȝitt] *Gr²; TS* Itt

Whoso ther two fulfilles then
  With mayne and myght in goode manere,
He trulye fulfillis all þe ten
  Þat aftir folowes in feere.
    Þan schulde we God honnoure   165
      With all oure myght and mayne,
    And loue wele ilke a neghboure
    Right as oureselfe, certayne.

I Doctor   Nowe sone, sen þou haste tolde vs two,
        Whilke ar þe viij, can þou ought saye?   170
Jesus   The iij biddis whareso ȝe goo
        Þat ȝe schall halowe þe halyday;
Than is þe fourthe for frende or foo
    That fadir and modir honnoure ay.   f.89
The v^{te} you biddis noght for to sloo   175
  No man nor woman by any way.
    The vj^{te}, suthly to see,
      Comaundis both more and myne
    That thei schalle fande to flee
    All filthes of flesshely synne.   180

The vij^{te} forbedis you to stele
  Ȝoure neghboures goodes, more or lesse,
Whilke fautez nowe are founden fele
  Emang þer folke, þat ferly is.
The viij^{te} lernes ȝou for to be lele,   185
  Here for to bere no false witnesse.
Ȝoure neghbours house, whillis ȝe haue hele,
    The ix^{te} biddis take noȝt be stresse.
    His wiffe nor his women
      The x^{te} biddis noȝt coveyte.   190
    Thez are þe biddingis x,
    Whoso will lelly layte.

II Doctor   Behalde howe he alleggis oure layse,
        And lered neuere on boke to rede;
        Full subtill sawes methinkeþ he saies,   195
        And also trewe, yf we take hede.
III Doctor Ȝa, late hym wende fourth on his wayes,
        For and he dwelle, withouten drede,

161. *Lineation TS, after T; then at beginning of 162 in MS*
164. aftir folowes] *Ho'* aftir thaym folowes, *after T* after thaym folows
166. oure] *Zu, after T* our; *MS, TS* youre
168. oure] *Zu, after T* oure; *MS, TS* youre
174. modir honnoure] *K* modir ȝe honnoure
181. forbedis] *TS; MS* fobedis
187. whillis] *This ed; TS* whilkis
191. Thez] *This ed; MS* Theȝ, *TS* They
193. layse] *Co; MS, TS* lawe; *Gr² conj* lays

	The pepull schall full sone hym prayse	
	Wele more þan vs for all oure dede.	200
I Doctor	Nay, nay, þan wer we wrang,	
	Such speking wille we spare.	
	Als he come late hym gang,	
	And move vs nowe no more.	

Maria A, dere Joseph, what is youre rede? 205
Of oure grete bale no bote may be, f.89ᵛ
Myne harte is heuy as any lede
My semely sone tille hym I see.
Nowe haue we sought in ilke a stede
Boþe vppe and doune ther dayes thre, 210
And whedir þat he be quyk or dede
Ʒitt wote we noght, so wo is me.

Joseph Mysese had neuere man more,
But mournyng may not mende;
I rede forther we fare 215
Till God some socoure sende.

Aboute ʒone tempill if he be ought
I wolde we wiste þis ilke nyght.
Maria A, sir, I see þat we haue sought,
In worlde was neuere so semely a sight. 220
Lo where he sittis, se ʒe hym noght
Emong ʒone maistiris mekill of myght?
Joseph Now blist be he vs hedir brought,
For in lande was neuere non so light.

Maria A, dere Joseph, als we haue cele, 225
Go furthe and fette youre sone and myne.
This day is done nere ilke a dele
And we haue nede for to gang hyne.
Joseph With men of myght can I not mell,
Than all my trauayle mon I tyne; 230
I can noʒt with þem, þis wate þou wele,
They are so gay in furres fyne.

Maria To þam youre herand for to say
Suthly ʒe thar noʒt drede no dele,
They will take rewarde to you allway 235
Because of elde, þis wate ʒe wele.
Joseph When I come there what schall I saye? f.90
I wate neuere, als haue I cele.
Sertis Marie, þou will haue me schamed for ay,
For I can nowthir croke nor knele. 240

---

209. we] *Suppl TS*
210. ther] *TS; MS* thre
221. se ʒe] *K, Gr¹, after T* se ye; *MS* ʒ se, *TS, Gr²* ʒ[e] se
227. done] *This ed; MS* d *superimposed on* g; *TS, Gr²* gone, *T* goyn

Maria	Go we togedir, I halde it beste,	
	Vnto ȝone worthy wysse in wede;	
	And yf I see – als haue I reste –	
	Þat ȝe will noȝt, þan bus me nede.	
Joseph	Gange on Marie, and telle thy tale firste,	245
	Thy sone to þe will take goode heede.	
	Wende fourth Marie, and do thy beste,	
	I come behynde, als God me spede.	
Maria	A, dere sone Jesus,	
	Sen we loue þe allone,	250
	Why dosse þou þus till vs	
	And gares vs make swilke mone?	
	Thy fadir and I betwyxte vs twa,	
	Son, for thy loue has likid ill.	
	We haue þe sought both to and froo,	255
	Wepand full sore as wightis will.	
Jesus	Wherto shulde ȝe seke me soo?	
	Ofte tymes it hase ben tolde you till,	
	My fadir werkis, for wele or woo,	
	Thus am I sente for to fulfyll.	260
Maria	There sawes, als haue I cele,	
	Can I noȝt vndirstande.	
	I schall thynke on þam wele	
	To fonde what is folowand.	
Joseph	Now sothely sone, þe sight of þe	265
	Hath salued vs of all oure sore.	
	Come furth sone, with þi modir and me,	f.90ᵛ
	Att Nazareth I wolde we wore.	
Jesus	Beleves wele, lordis free,	
	For with my frendis nowe will I fare.	270
I Doctor	Nowe sone, wher þou schall bide or be,	
	Gode make þe gode man euermore.	
	No wondir if ȝone wiffe	
	Of his fynding be full fayne,	
	He schall, and he haue liff,	275
	Proue till a praty swayne.	
	But sone, loke þat þou layne for gud or ill	
	Þe note þat we haue nemed her nowe,	
	And if it like þe to lende her stille	
	And wonne with vs, welcome art þowe.	280

249. *Maria] Jhc written first, deleted*
253. twa] *MS* twa son, son *deleted by a later hand*
254. Son] *Added to left by a later hand*
255. and] *(MS &) interlined*
271. *Lineation TS;* or be *at beginning of 272 in MS*
275. and he] *One or two words erased between*

Jesus	Graunte mercy sirs, of youre gode will,
	No lenger liste me lende with 30u,
	My frendis thoughtis I wol fulfille
	And to þer bidding baynely bowe.
Maria	Full wele is vs þis tyde,	285
	Nowe maye we make goode chere.
Joseph	No lenger will we bide,
	Fares wele all folke in feere.

Jesus Maria Joseph Primus doctor secundus doctor et tercius doctor

XXI The Barbers
The Baptism

Johannes	Almyghty God and lord verray,	f.92
	Full woundyrfull is mannys lesyng,	
	For yf I preche tham day be day	
	And telle tham, lorde, of thy comyng,	
	Þat all has wrought,	5
	Men are so dull þat my preching	
	Serues of noght.	
	When I haue, lord, in the name of the	
	Baptiste þe folke in watir clere,	
	Þan haue I saide þat aftir me	10
	Shall he come þat has more powere	
	Þan I to taste;	
	He schall giffe baptyme more entire	
	In fire and gaste.	
	Þus am I comen in message right	15
	And be fore-reyner in certayne,	
	In wittnesse-bering of þat light,	
	Þe wiche schall light in ilka man	
	Þat is comand	

288+ *List of characters by main scribe; ff.91, 91ᵛ blank*

2. De nouo facto *added to right by a later hand (? J. Clerke)*
18. ilka man] *This ed; MS, TS* ilka a man

Into this worlde; nowe whoso can   20
   May vndirstande.

Thez folke had farly of my fare
   And what I was full faste þei spied;
They askid yf I a prophette ware
   And I saide nay, but sone I wreyede –   25
      High aperte
   I saide I was a voyce that cryede
      Here in deserte.

Loke þou make þe redy – ay saide I –
   Vnto oure lord God most of myght,   30
Þat is þat þou be clene haly
   In worde, in werke ay redy dight
      Agayns oure lord,
   With parfite liffe þat ilke a wight
      Be well restored.   35

For if we be clene in levyng,
   Oure bodis are Goddis tempyll þan,
In the whilke he will make his dwellyng.
   Therfore be clene, bothe wiffe and man,
      Þis is my reed;   40
   God will make in yowe haly þan
      His wonnyng-steed.

And if ȝe sette all youre delyte
   In luste and lykyng of þis liff,
Than will he turne fro yow als tyte   f.92^v
   Bycause of synne, boyth of man and wiffe,   46
      And fro ȝou flee,
   For with whome þat synne is riffe
      Will God noght be.

I Angelus   Þou John, take tente what I schall saye,   50
   I brynge þe tythandis wondir gode:
My lorde Jesus schall come þys day
   Fro Galylee vnto þis flode
      Ȝe Jourdane call,
   Baptyme to take myldely with mode   55
      Þis day he schall.

---

26. High aperte] *Ha, K* High in aperte
48. with] *TS; MS* wth
49. *Cross in later hand to left, and at foot of page in hand of J. Clerke* Her wantes a pece newely mayd for saynt John Baptiste
50. *I Angelus] I suppl this ed*
52. þys] *Originally written* þus *at beginning of 53, but there deleted;* þus *added to 52 in red (main scribe),* u *altered to* y *by a later hand*
     day] *Added by a later hand (probably J. Clerke)*
55. myldely with] *K* with myldely

John, of his sande therfore be gladde
And thanke hym hartely, both lowde and still.

Johannes I thanke hym euere, but I am radde
I am noȝt abill to fullfill   60
Þis dede certayne.

II Angelus John, þe aught with harte and will
To be full bayne

To do his bidding, all bydene.
Bot in his baptyme John, take tente, 65
Þe heuenes schalle be oppen sene,
The holy gost schalle doune be sente
To se in sight,
The fadirs voyce with grete talent
Be herde full riȝt,   70

Þat schall saie þus to hym forthy

. . . .

Johannes . . . . . . with wordes fewne
I will be subgett nyght and day
As me well awe,
To serue my lord Jesus to paye 75
In dede and sawe.

Bot wele I wote, baptyme is tane
To wasshe and clense man of synne,
And wele I wotte þat synne is none
In hym, withoute ne withinne. 80
What nedis hym þan
For to be baptiste more or myne
Als synfull man?

Jesus John, kynde of man is freele f.93
. . . .
To þe whilke þat I haue me knytte, 85
But I shall shewe þe skyllis twa
Þat þou schallt knawe by kyndly witte
Þe cause why I haue ordand swa,
And ane is þis:
Mankynde may noȝt vnbaptymde go 90
Te endles blys.

---

59. *Originally unassigned. Joseph first inserted by a later hand, but deleted, and Johannes substituted; apparently the work of Clerke*
63–4. *Separated by a red line (otiose)*
71. Hic caret *added to right by a later hand*
72–3. *Lineation TS; one line in MS*
84. De nouo facto *added to right by a later hand (? J. Clerke)*
88. Þe] *K; MS, TS* By
91. te] *This ed; TS* to *(conj)*

And sithen myselffe haue taken mankynde,
For men schall me þer myrroure make
And haue my doyng in ther mynde,
Also I do þe baptyme take.   95
I will forthy
Myselfe be baptiste for ther sake
Full oppynly.

Anodir skill I schall þe tell:
My will is þis, þat fro þis day   100
Þe vertue of my baptyme dwelle
In baptyme-watir euere and ay,
Mankynde to taste,
Thurgh my grace þerto to take alway
Þe haly gaste.   105

Johannes   All-myghtfull lorde, grete is þi grace,
I thanke þe of þi grete fordede.
Jesus   Cum, baptise me John, in þis place.
Johannes   Lorde, saue thy grace þat I forbede
Þat itt soo be,   110
For lorde, methynketh it wer more nede
Þou baptised me.

Þat place þat I yarne moste of all,
Fro thens come þou lorde, as I gesse.
How schulde I þan, þat is a thrall,   115
Giffe þe baptyme, þat rightwis is
And has ben euere?
For thow arte roote of rightwissenesse,
Þat forfette neuere.

What riche man gose from dore to dore   120
To begge at hym þat has right noght?
Lorde, þou arte riche and I am full poure,
Þou may blisse all, sen þou all wrought.
Fro heuen come all
Þat helpes in erthe, yf soth be sought,   125
Fro erthe but small.

Jesus   Thou sais full wele John, certaynly,   f.93ᵛ
But suffre nowe for heuenly mede

<hr>

94. And] *Ho'; MS, TS* I
95. Also] *This ed; MS, TS* And also
101. vertue] *Interlined by J. Clerke over deletion of main scribe's* wittnesse
107. Hic caret *to right in a later hand, deleted*
114. lorde] *TS; MS* lorede
118. thow] *This ed; TS* þou
125. erthe] *TS; MS* erther

Þat rightwisnesse be noȝt oonlye
   Fullfillid in worde but also in dede,   130
     Thrughe baptyme clere.
   Cum, baptise me in my manhed
     Appertly here.

Fyrst schall I take, sen schall I preche,
   For so behovis mankynde fulfille   135
All rightwissenesse, als werray leche.

Johannes   Lord, I am redy at þi will,
     And will be ay
   Thy subgett lord, both lowde and still,
     In þat I may.   140

A, lorde, I trymble þer I stande,
   So am I arow to do þat dede.
But saue me, lord þat all ordand,
   For the to touche haue I grete drede
     For doyngs dark.   145
   Now helpe me lorde, thurgh þi Godhede,
     To do þis werk.

Jesus, my lord of myghtis most,
   I baptise þe here in þe name
Of the fadir and of the sone and holy gost;   150
   But in þis dede lorde, right no blame
     Þis day by me,
   And bryngis all thase to thy home
     Þat trowes in þe.

Tunc cantabunt duo angeli, 'Veni creator spiritus'.

Jesus   John, for mannys prophyte – wit þou wele –   155
   Take I þis baptyme certaynely.
The dragons poure ilk a dele
   Thurgh my baptyme distroyed haue I,
     Þis is certayne,
   And saued mankynde, saule and body,   160
     Fro endles payne.

What man þat trowis and baptised bes
Schall saued be and come to blisse.

---

131.   *Added in red, in ornamental script (main scribe)*
141–4. *Originally written 141, 144, 141(again), 142, 143, 144 (again). Duplicates of 141*
     and 144 deleted and correct order of lines indicated by letters a — d in red to left (main
     scribe)
151.   right] *Ha* wite
153.   bryngis] *Ho'* bryng
154+ *SD (main scribe) in red.* cantabunt] *This ed; TS* cantabant *(MS could be either)*
162.   bes] *He; MS, TS* be
163+ *Catchword* Whoso trowes

f.94

Whoso trowes noȝt, to payne endles
   He schal be dampned sone, trowe wele þis.   165
      But wende we nowe
      Wher most is nede þe folke to wisse,
         Both I and þou.

Johannes   I loue þe, lorde, as souereyne leche
      That come to salue men of þare sore,   170
   As þou comaundis I schall gar preche
   And lere to euery man þat lare,
      That are was thrall.
   Now sirs, þat barne þat Marie bare
      Be with ȝou all.   175

XXII The Smiths

The Temptation

Diabolus   Make rome belyve, and late me gang!   f.95
      Who makis here all þis þrang?
      High you hense, high myght ȝou hang
         Right with a roppe.
      I drede me þat I dwelle to lang   5
         To do a jape.

      For sithen the firste tyme þat I fell
      For my pride fro heuen to hell,
      Euere haue I mustered me emell
         Emonge mannekynde,   10
      How I in dole myght gar tham dwell
         Þer to be pynde.

      And certis, all þat hath ben sithen borne
      Has comen to me, mydday and morne,

164.   *Quire M begins*
168.   þou] *This ed; MS, TS* ȝou
175+   *To left of last line, in hand of J. Clerke* Hic caret finem. *Beneath last line, in Clerke's hand* This matter is newly mayd and devysed, wherof we haue no coppy regystred. *Beneath this (? in hand of Thomas Cutler)* The Shavors, *and the letters* T C *separated by penwork. Bottom half of f.94 blank; f.94ᵛ blank*

And I haue ordayned so þam forne 15
  None may þame fende,
Þat fro all likyng ar they lorne
  Withowten ende.

And nowe sum men spekis of a swayne,
Howe he schall come and suffre payne 20
And with his dede to blisse agayne
  Þei schulde be bought.
But certis þis tale is but a trayne,
  I trowe it noȝt.

For I wotte ilke a dele bydene 25
Of þe mytyng þat men of mene,
How he has in grete barett bene
  Sithen he was borne,
And suffered mekill traye and tene
  Boþe even and morne. 30

And nowe it is brought so aboute
Þat lurdayne þat þei loue and lowte
To wildirnesse he is wente owte,
  Withowtyne moo;
To dere hym nowe haue I no doute, 35
  Betwyxte vs two.

Before þis tyme he has bene tent
Þat I myght gete hym with no glent,
But now sen he allone is wente
  I schall assay, 40
And garre hym to sum synne assente
  If þat I may.

He has fastid – þat marris his mode – f.95ᵛ
Ther fourty dayes withowten foode.
If he be man in bone and bloode 45
  Hym hungris ill;
In glotonye þan halde I gude
  To witt his will.

For so it schall be knowen and kidde
If Godhed be in hym hidde, 50
If he will do as I hym bidde
  Whanne I come nare.
Þer was neuere dede þat euere he dide
  Þat greued hym warre.

Þou witty man and wise of rede, 55
If þou can ought of Godhede

22. Þei] *TS; MS* Þⁱ

Byd nowe þat þer stones be brede,
  Betwyxte vs two;
Þan may þei stande thyselfe in stede,
  And othir moo.   60

For þou hast fastid longe I wene,
I wolde now som mete wer sene
For olde acqueyntaunce vs bytwene,
  Thyselue wote howe.
Ther sall no man witte what I mene   65
  But I and þou.

Jesus   My fadir, þat all cytte may slake,
Honnoure eueremore to þe I make
And gladly suffir I for thy sake
  Swilk velany,   70
And þus temptacions for to take
  Of myn enemy.

Þou weried wight, þi wittis are wode,
For wrytyn it is, whoso vndirstode,
A man lyvis noght in mayne and mode   75
  With brede allone,
But Goddis wordis are gostly fode
  To men ilkone.

Iff I haue fastid oute of skill,
Wytte þou me hungris not so ill   80
Þat I ne will wirke my fadirs will
  In all degré;
Þi biddyng will I noȝt fullfill,
  Þat warne I þe.

Diabolus   A, slyke carping neuere I kende,   f.96
Hym hungres noȝt, as I wende.   86
Nowe sen thy fadir may þe fende
  Be sotell sleghte,
Late se yf þou allone may lende
  Þer vppon heghte,   90

Vppon þe pynakill parfitely.

Tunc cantant angeli, 'Veni creator'.

Aha, nowe go we wele therby;
I schall assaye in vayne-glorie
  To garre hym falle,

---

74. vndirstode] *Zu; MS, TS* vndirstande
91+ *SD added to right by J. Clerke*
92. *Ruled off from 91 and Diabolus added to right by a later hand*

And if he be Goddis sone myghty,   95
   Witt I schall.

Nowe liste to me a litill space:
If þou be Goddis sone, full of grace,
Shew som poynte here in þis place
   To proue þi myght.   100
Late se, falle doune vppon þi face
   Here in my sight.

For it is wretyn, as wele is kende,
How God schall aungellis to þe sende,
And they schall kepe þe in þer hende   105
   Wherso þou gose,
Þat þou schall on no stones descende
   To hurte þi tose.

And sen þou may withouten wathe
Fall and do thyselffe no skathe,
Tumbill downe to ease vs bathe   110
   Here to my fete;
And but þou do I will be wrothe,
   Þat I þe hette.

Jesus   Late be, warlowe, thy wordis kene,   115
For wryten it is, withouten wene,
Thy God þou schall not tempte with tene
   Nor with discorde,
Ne quarell schall þou none mayntene
   Agaynste þi lorde.   120

And þerfore trowe þou, withouten trayne,
Þat all þi gaudes schall nothyng gayne;
Be subgette to þi souereyne
   Arely and late.
Diabolus   What, þis trauayle is in vayne   125
   Be ought I watte.

He proues þat he is mekill of price,
Þerfore it is goode I me avise,
And sen I may noȝt on þis wise
   Make hym my thrall,   130
I will assaye in couetise
   To garre hym fall,

For certis I schall noȝt leue hym ȝitt.   f.96ᵛ
Who is my souereyne, þis wolde I witte?

---

105. hende] *K; MS, TS* hande
108. tose] s *superimposed on* c

Myselffe ordande þe þore to sitte,   135
  Þis wote þou wele,
And right euen as I ordande itt
  Is done ilke dele.

Þan may þou se sen itt is soo
Þat I am souerayne of vs two,   140
And ȝitt I graunte þe or I goo
  Withouten fayle,
Þat if þou woll assente me too
  It schall avayle.

For I haue all þis worlde to welde,   145
Toure and toune, forest and felde;
If þou thyn herte will to me helde
  With wordis hende,
ȝitt will I baynly be thy belde
  And faithfull frende.   150

Behalde now ser, and þou schalt see
Sere kyngdomes and sere contré;
Alle þis wile I giffe to þe
  For euermore,
And þou fall and honour me   155
  As I saide are.

Jesus Sees of thy sawes, þou Sathanas,
I graunte nothyng þat þou me asse,
To pyne of helle I bide þe passe
  And wightely wende,   160
And wonne in woo, as þou are was,
  Withouten ende.

Non othyr myght schal be thy mede,
For wretyn it is, who right can rede,
Thy lord God þe aught to drede   165
  And honoure ay,
And serue hym in worde and dede
  Both nyȝt and day.

And sen þou dose not as I þe tell
No lenger liste me late þe dwell,   170
I comaunde þe þou hy to hell
  And holde þe þar,
With felawschip of fendis fell
  For euermar.

154. *First written in main column, there deleted, and rewritten to right in red (main scribe)*
155. me] *A half-formed letter follows*
158. asse] *He; MS, TS* askis
173. fendis] *This ed; TS* frendis

Diabolus	Owte! I dar noȝt loke, allas,	f.97
	Itt is warre þan euere it was.	176
	He musteres what myght he has,	
	Hye mote he hang.	
	Folowes fast, for me bus pas	
	To paynes strang.	180

I Angelus	A, mercy lorde, what may þis mene?	
	Me merueyles þat ȝe thole þis tene	
	Of this foule fende cant and kene	
	Carpand ȝou till,	
	And ȝe his wickidnesse, I wene,	185
	May waste at will.	

	Methynke þat ȝe ware straytely stedde	
	Lorde, with þis fende þat nowe is fledde.	
Jesus	Myn aungell dere, be noȝt adred,	
	He may not greue;	190
	The haly goste me has ledde,	
	Þus schal þow leue.	

	For whan þe fende schall folke see	
	And salus þam in sere degré,	
	Þare myrroure may þei make of me	195
	For to stande still,	
	For ouerecome schall þei noȝt be	
	Bot yf þay will.	

II Angelus	A, lorde, þis is a grete mekenesse	
	In yow in whome al mercy is,	200
	And at youre wille may deme or dresse	
	Als is worthy;	
	And thre temptacions takes expres,	
	Þus suffirrantly.	

Jesus	My blissing haue þei with my hande	205
	Þat with swilke greffe is noȝt grucchand,	
	And also þat will stiffely stande	
	Agaynste þe fende.	
	I knawe my tyme is faste comand,	
	Now will I wende.	210

---

181.   *I Angelus*] *I this ed; om TS*
192.   þou leve *originally written in main column, there deleted; the complete line added to right in red (main scribe)*
193.   see] *K* ne ('nigh', *v.*)
210+   *Beneath the last line (? in hand of Richard Nandicke)* The Smythes *and the letters* R N *separated by penwork. Beneath this in the same or a very similar hand* Ille ego qui quondam . . . *and other words, only partially legible (?* michi modulatus)

XXIIA The Vintners

The Marriage at Cana

Archedeclyne	Loo this is a yoyfull day	f.97ᵛ
	For me and . . .	

Play never registered. Opening lines quoted by J. Clerke as above; f.98 blank, ff.98ᵛ, 99 headed The Vinters *by the main scribe; ff.99ᵛ–101 blank; f.101ᵛ blank except for catchword* Petyr myn awne discipill. *See the Note*

XXIII The Curriers

The Transfiguration

Jesus	Petir myne awne discipill dere,	f.102
	And James and John my cosyns two,	
	Takis hartely hede, for ȝe schall here	
	Þat I wille telle vnto no moo.	
	And als ȝe schall see sightis seere	5
	Whilke none schall see bot ȝe alsoo,	
	Therfore comes forth with me in fere,	
	For to ȝone mountayne will I goo.	
	Ther schall ȝe see a sight	
	Whilk ȝe haue ȝerned lange.	10
Petrus	My lorde, we are full light	
	And glad with þe to gange.	
Jesus	Longe haue ȝe coveyte for to kenne	
	My fadir, for I sette hym before,	
	And wele ȝe wote whilke tyme and when	15
	In Galylé gangand we were.	

1. *Quire N begins*
5. sightis] *TS; MS* sighitis
9–12. *Lineation TS; two lines in MS*
13. *Jesus*] *cum Moysez et Elias added by a later hand*

'Shewe vs thy fadir'—þus saide ʒe then—
'Þat suffice us withouten more'.
I saide to ʒou and to all men
'Who seis me seis my fadyr þore'.   20
    Such wordis to ʒou I spakke
        In trewthe to make ʒou bolde;
    ʒe cowde noght vndyrtake
        The talez þat I ʒou tolde.

Anodir tyme, for to encresse   25
    ʒoure trouthe and worldly ʒou to wys,
I saide '*Quem dicunt homines*
    Esse filium hominis?'
I askid ʒow wham þe pepill chase
    To be mannys sone, withouten mys.   30
ʒe aunswered and saide 'Sum Moyses,'
    And sum saide þan 'Hely it is',
        And sum saide 'John Baptist'.   f.102ᵛ
        Þan more I enquered you ʒitt,
            I askid ʒiff ʒe ought wiste   35
            Who I was, by youre witte.

Þou aunswered, Petir, for thy prowe,
    And saide þat I was Crist, God sonne,
Bot of thyselffe þat had noght þowe,
    My fadir hadde þat grace begonne.   40
Þerfore bese bolde and biddis now
    To tyme ʒe haue my fadir fonne.
Jacobus Lord, to thy byddyng will we bowe
    Full buxumly, as we are bonne.
Johannes   Lorde, we will wirke thy will   45
        Allway with trewe entent,
        We love God lowde and stille
        Þat vs þis layne has lente.

Petrus Full glad and blithe awe vs to be,
    And thanke oure maistir mekill of mayne   50
Þat sais we schall þe sightis see,
    The whiche non othir schall see certayne.
Jacobus He talde vs of his fadir free,
    Of þat fare wolde we be full fayne.
Johannes All þat he hyghte vs holde will hee,   55
    Therfore we will no forther frayne,

27–8 *Lineation TS; one line in MS*
31. Sum] TS; MS Sam
37. Þou] *This ed;* TS You
41. *Lineation TS; first three words written to right of main column, second three written as first part of 42*
42. fonne] *This ed;* TS sonne

But as he fouchesaffe
So sall we vndirstande.
Beholde, her we nowe haue
In hast som new tythande.   60

Helyas   Lord God, I loue þe lastandly   f.103
And highly, botht with harte and hande,
Þat me, thy poure prophett Hely,
Has steuened in þis stede to stande.
In Paradise wonnand am I   65
Ay sen I lefte þis erthely lande;
I come Cristis name to clarifie
As God his fadir me has ordand,
And for to bere witnesse
In worde to man and wyffe,   70
Þat þis his owne sone is
And lord of lastand liff.

Moyses   Lord God þat of all welth is wele,
With wille and witte we wirschippe þe,
Þat vnto me, Moyses, wolde tell   75
Þis grete poynte of thy pryuyté,
And hendly hente me oute of hell
Þis solempne syght for I schuld see,
Whan thy dere darlynges þat þore dwell
Hase noght thy grace in swilk degree.   80
Oure forme-fadyrs full fayne
Wolde se this solempne sight,
Þat in þis place þus pleyne
Is mustered thurgh þi myght.

Petrus   Brethir, whateuere ȝone brightnes be?   85
Swilk burdis beforne was neuere sene.
It marres my myght, I may not see,
So selcouth thyng was neuere sene.

Jacobus   What it will worthe þat wote noȝt wee;
How wayke I waxe ȝe will not wene.   90
Are was þer one, now is ther thre,
Methynke oure maistir is betwene.

Johannes   That oure maistir is thare   f.103ᵛ
Þat may we trewly trowe,

---

59. nowe haue] *He; MS, TS* haue nowe
60. *Lineation He;* In hast *at end of 59 in MS, TS*
         tythande] *Zu, He, Co; MS, TS* tythandys
64. Has steuened] *Zu; MS, TS* Haue steuened me
68. As] *This ed; TS* And
69–72. *Lineation TS; two lines in MS*
73. of] *Suppl Ho'*
         welth is wele] *Ho', K; MS, TS* welthis wele
83. Þat] *TS; MS* Þan
92. Me-] *This ed; TS* We

He was full fayre before   95
But neuere als he is nowe.

Petrus His clothyng is as white as snowe,
His face schynes as þe sonne;
To speke with hym I haue grete awe,
Swilk faire before was neuere fune.   100

Jacobus Þe tothir two fayne wolde I knawe
And witte what werke þam hedir has wonne.

Johannes I rede we aske þam all on rowe
And grope þam how þis game is begonne.

Petrus My bredir, if þat ȝe come be   105
To make clere Cristis name,
Telles here till vs thre,
For we seke to þe same.

Elias Itt is Goddis will þat we ȝou wys
Of his werkis, as is worthy.   110
I haue my place in Paradise,
Ennok my brodyr me by.
Als messenger withouten mys
Am I called to this company,
To witnesse þat Goddis sone is þis,   115
Euyn with hym mette and allmyghty.
To dede we wer noght dight,
But quyk schall we come
With Antecrist for to fyght,
Beffore þe day of dome.   120

Moyses Frendis, if þat ȝe frayne my name,
Moyses þan may ȝe rede by rawe.   f.104
Two thousand ȝere aftir Adam
Þan gaffe God vnto me his lawe,
And sythen in helle has bene oure hame,   125
Allas, Adams kynne, þis schall ȝe knawe.
Vnto Crist come, þis is þe same
Þat vs schall fro þat dongeoun drawe.
He schall brynge þam to blys
Þat nowe in bale are bonne.   130
This myrthe we may not mys,
For this same is Goddis sonne.

Jesus My dere discipils, drede ȝou noȝt,
I am ȝoure souerayne certenly.
This wondir-werke þat here is wrought   135
Is of my fadir almyghty.

97.   as'] *This ed; om* TS
105. come be] *He; MS, TS* be come
112. brodyr me] *Ho'* brodyr is me
133. discipils] *K; MS, TS* discipill

    Þire both are hydir brought –
    Þe tone Moyses, þe todir Ely –
    And for youre sake þus are þei sought
      To saie ȝou, his sone am I.   140
        So schall bothe heuen and helle
        Be demers of þis dede,
        And ȝe in erth schall tell
        My name wher itt is nede.

Petrus   A, loued be þou euere my lord Jesus   145
    Þat all þis solempne sight has sent,
    Þat fouchest saffe to schew þe þus
    So þat þi myghtis may be kende.
    Here is full faire dwellyng for vs,
      A lykand place in for to lende.   150
    A, lord, late vs no forther trus,
      For we will make with herte and hende
        A taburnakill vnto þe   f.104ᵛ
        Belyue, and þou will bide;
        One schall to Moyses be   155
        And to Ely the thirde.

Jacobus   Ȝa, wittirly, þat were wele done,
    But vs awe noght swilk case to craue.
    Þam thare but saie and haue it sone,
      Such seruice and he fouchesaffe.   160
    He hetis his men both morne and none
    Þare herber high in heuen to haue,
    Therfore is beste we bide hys bone;
      Who othir reedis, rudely þei raue.
Johannes   Such sonde as he will sende   165
        May mende all oure mischeue,
        And where hym lykis to lende,
        We will lende, with his leue.

    Hic descendunt nubes.

Pater in nube Ȝe febill of faithe, folke affraied,
      Beis noȝt aferde for vs in feere.   170
    I am ȝoure God þat gudly grayde
      Both erthe and eyre with clowdes clere.
    Þis is my sone, as ȝe haue saide,
      As he has schewed by sygnes sere.
    Of all his werkis I am wele paied,   175
      Therfore till hym takis hede and here.

145. *Ruled off from 144 by main scribe but not assigned; Petrus added by a later hand*
168+ *SD written in red to right (main scribe)*
169. *Pater] Repeated by a later hand, deleted. This extended character-designation taken as part of preceding SD in TS*
171. *grayde] Ha; MS, TS grayth*

> Where he is, þare am I,
> He is myne and I am his,
> Who trowis þis stedfastly
> Shall byde in endles blisse.   180

Jesus   Petir, pees be vnto þe,   f.105
> And to ȝou also James and John.
> Rise vppe and tellis me what ȝe see,
> And beis no more so wille of wone.

Petrus   A, lorde, what may þis meruayle be,   185
> Whedir is þis glorious gleme al gone?
> We saugh here pleynly persones thre
> And nowe is oure lorde lefte allone.
> Þis meruayle movis my mynde
> And makis my flessh affrayed.   190

Jacobus   Þis brightnes made me blynde,
> I bode neuere swilke a brayde.

Johannes   Lorde God oure maker almyghty,
> Þis mater euermore be ment,
> We saw two bodis stande hym by   195
> And saide his fadir had þame sent.

Petrus   There come a clowde of þe skye
> Lyght als þe lemys on þame lent,
> And now fares all as fantasye
> For wote noȝt we how þai are wente.   200

Jacobus   Þat clowde cloumsed vs clene
> Þat come schynand so clere,
> Such syght was never sene,
> To seke all sydis seere.

Johannes   Nay, nay, þat noys noyed vs more   205
> Þat here was herde so hydously.

Jesus   Frendis, be noght afferde þerfore,
> I schall ȝou saye encheson why: f.105ᵛ
> My fadir wiste how þat ȝe were
> In ȝoure faith fayland, and forthy   210
> He come to witnesse ay-where,
> And saide þat his sone am I.
> And also in þis stede
> To witnesse þe same,
> A quyk man and a dede   215
> Come to make clere my name.

Petrus   A, lord, why latest þou vs noȝt see
> Thy fadirs face in his fayrenes?

---

180. Hic caret *to right in a later hand, deleted*
185. may] *TS; MS three minims*
200. we] *Suppl TS*
207. þerfore] *This ed; TS* afore

Jesus	Petir, þou askis over-grete degree,	
	That grace may noȝt be graunted þe, I gesse.	220
	In his Godhed so high is he	
	As all ȝoure prophetis names expresse,	
	Þat langar of lyffe schall he noght be	
	Þat seys his Godhede as it is.	
	Here haue ȝe sene in sight	225
	Poyntes of his priuité,	
	Als mekill als erthely wighte	
	May suffre in erthe to see.	
	And therfore wende we nowe agayne	
	To oure meyné, and mende þer chere.	230
Jacobus	Oure felaws ful faste wil vs frayne	
	How we haue faren, al in feere.	
Jesus	Þis visioun lely loke ȝe layne,	
	Vnto no leffand lede itt lere	
	Tille tyme mannys sone haue suffered payne	235
	And resen fro dede; kens it þan clere.	
	For all þat trowis þat thyng	
	Of my fadir and me,	
	Thay schall haue his blessing	f.106
	And myne, so motte it be.	240

XXIIIA The Ironmongers

Jesus in the House of Simon the Leper

Play never registered; f.106ᵛ headed The Ironmongers *by a later hand in ornamental script; f.107 headed* The Ironmongers *by the main scribe; beneath this in the hand of J. Clerke, but since erased,* This matter lakkes, videlicet: Jesus, et Symon leprosus rogans eum vt manducaret cum eo, duo discipuli, Maria Magdelena lauans pedes Jesu lacrimis et capillis suis tergens *(visible under u-v); ff.107ᵛ–110ᵛ blank. No catchword at the end of quire N, f.109ᵛ. See the Note*

238.   me] m *four minims*
240+   finis *added by J. Clerke; rest of f.106 blank*

XXIV The Cappers

The Woman Taken in Adultery/
The Raising of Lazarus

I Judeus	Steppe fourth, late vs no lenger stande,	f.111
	But smertely þat oure gere wer grayde;	
	Þis felowe þat we with folye fande,	
	Late haste vs fast þat she wer flayed.	
II Judeus	We will bere witnesse and warande	5
	How we hir raysed all vnarayed,	
	Agaynste þe lawes here of oure lande	
	Wher sche was with hir leman laide.	
I Judeus	3aa, and he a wedded man,	
	Þat was a wikkid synne.	10
II Judeus	Þat bargayne schall sche banne	
	With bale nowe or we blynne.	
I Judeus	A, false stodmere and stynkand stroye,	
	How durste þou stele so stille away	
	To do so vilaunce avowtry	15
	Þat is so grete agaynste oure lay?	
II Judeus	Hir bawdery schall sche dere abye,	
	For as we sawe so schall we saye,	
	And also hir wirkyng is worthy	
	Sho schall be demed to ded þis day.	20
I Judeus	The maistirs of þe lawe	
	Are here even at oure hande.	
II Judeus	Go we reherse by rawe	
	Hir fawtes as we þam fande.	
I Judeus	God saue 3ou maistirs, mekill of mayne,	25
	Þat grete clergy and counsaille can.	
III Judeus	Welcome frendis, but I wolde frayne	f.111ᵛ
	How fare 3e with þat faire woman?	
II Judeus	A, sirs, we schall 3ou saie certayne	
	Of mekill sorowe sen sche began.	30
	We haue hir tane with putry playne,	
	Hirselff may no3t gaynesaie it þan.	

1. Steppe] *This ed;* TS Leppe
29. certayne] *TS;* MS certaye

IV Judeus	What hath sche done, folye
	In fornicacioun and synne?
I Judeus	Nay, nay, in avowtery 35
	Full bolde, and will noȝt blynne.

III Judeus	Avowtery? Nemyn it noght for schame!
	It is so foule opynly I it fye.
	Is it sothe þat þei saie þe dame?
II Judeus	What sir, scho may it noȝt denye. 40
	We wer þan worthy for to blame
	To greve hir but sche wer gilty.
IV Judeus	Now certis, þis is a foule defame
	And mekill bale muste be þarby.
III Judeus	Ȝa sir, ȝe saie wele þore 45
	By lawe and rightwise rede,
	Ther falles noght ellis þerfore
	But to be stoned to dede.

I Judeus	Sirs, sen ȝe telle þe lawe this tyde
	And knawes þe course in þis contré, 50
	Demes hir on heght, no lenger hyde,
	And aftir ȝoure wordis wirke schall we.
IV Judeus	Beis noght so bryme, bewsheris, abide,
	A new mater nowe moues me
	[. . . . . .
	. . . . . .
	. . . . . .
	. . . . . .
	. . . . . .
	. . . . . .]

[A leaf is missing from the MS at this point. It probably contained 58
lines: four complete stanzas, together with the six lines required after
line 54 and the four wanting before 55. IV Judeus is about to suggest
that the woman be taken before Jesus, and the incident which follows is
related in John viii.3–9: And the Scribes and Pharisees bring a woman
taken in aduoutrie: and they did set her in the mids, And said to him,
this woman was euen now taken in aduoutrie. And in the law Moyses
commanded vs to stone such. What sayest thou therfore? And this they
said tempting him, that they might accuse him. But Jesus bowing himself
downe, with his finger wrote in the earth. When they therfore continued
asking him, he lifte vp himselfe, and said to them, He that is without
sinne of you, let him first throw the stone at her. And again bowing
himselfe, he wrote in the earth. And they hearing went out one by one,
beginning at the seniours . . .]

[. . .   . . .
   . . .   . . .

50. Hic deficit *added to right by J. Clerke*
51. hyde] *? read* byde

	. . .	. . .
	. . .	. . .]

III Judeus	He shewes my mysdedis more and myne,	f.112
	I leue ȝou here, late hym allone.	56
IV Judeus	Owe, here will new gaudes begynne –	
	Ȝa, grete all wele, saie þat I am gone.	
I Judeus	And sen ȝe are noght bolde,	
	No lengar bide will I.	60
II Judeus	Pees, late no tales be tolde,	
	But passe fourth preuylye.	

Jesus	Woman, wher are þo wighte men went	
	That kenely here accused þe?	
	Who hase þe dampned, toke þou entent?	65
Mulier	Lord, no man has dampned me.	
Jesus	And for me schall þou noȝt be schent.	
	Of all thy mys I make þe free,	
	Loke þou no more to synne assentte.	
Mulier	A, lord, ay loued mott þou bee.	70
	All erthely folke in feere	
	Loves hym and his high name,	
	Þat me on þis manere	
	Hath saued fro synne and schame.	

I Apostolus	A, lorde, we loue þe inwardly	75
	And all þi lore, both lowde and still,	
	That grauntes thy grace to þe gilty	
	And spares þam þat the folke wolde spill.	
Jesus	I schall ȝou saie encheson why:	
	I wote it is my fadirs will,	80
	And for to make þam ware þerby	f.112ᵛ
	To knawe þamselffe haue done more ill.	
	And euermore of þis same	
	Ensample schall be sene,	
	Whoso schall othir blame	85
	Loke firste þamself be clene.	

II Apostolus	A, maistir, here may men se also	
	How mekenes may full mekill amende,	
	To forgeue gladly where we goo	
	All folke þat hath vs oght offende.	90
Jesus	He þat will noȝt forgiffe his foo	
	And vse mekenesse with herte and hende,	
	The kyngdom may he noght come too	
	Þat ordande is withouten ende.	
	And more sone schall we see	95
	Here or ȝe forther fare,	

---

78. the] *K; MS, TS* thy
80+ *At this point (head of f.112ᵛ)* Lazare mortus *in red (main scribe); cf.* 98+

How þat my fadir free
Will mustir myghtis more.

Lazare Mortus

Nuncius	Jesu þat es prophett veray,	
	My ladys Martha and Marie,	
	If þou fouchesaffe þai wolde þe pray	100
	For to come vnto Bethany.	
	He whom þou loues full wele alway	
	Es seke, and like, lord, for to dye.	
	Yf þou wolde come, amende hym þou may	105
	And comforte all þat cumpany.	
Jesus	I saie 3ou þat sekeness	
	Is no3t onto þe dede,	
	But joie of Goddis gudnesse	
	Schal be schewed in þat stede.	110

And Goddis sone schall be glorified
By þat sekenesse and signes seere,
Therfore brethir no lenger bide,   f.113
Two daies fully haue we ben here.
We will go soiourne here beside   115
In þe Jurie with frendis in feere.

I Apostolus	A, lorde, þou wote wele ilke a tyde	
	Þe Jewes þei layte þe ferre and nere,	
	To stone þe vnto dede	
	Or putte to pereles payne,	120
	And þou to þat same stede	
	Covaites to gange agayne?	

Jesus	3e wote by cours wele for to kast,	
	Þe daie is now of xij oures lange,	
	And whilis light of þe day may last	125
	It is gode þat we grathely gange.	

For whan daylight is pleynly past
Full sone þan may 3e wende all wrang,
Therfore takes hede and trauayle fast
Whills light of liffe is 3ou emang.   130
And to 3ou saie I more,
How þat Lazar oure frende
Slepes nowe, and I therfore
With 3ou to hym will wende.

II Apostolus	We will be ruled aftir þi rede,	135
	But and he slepe he schall be saue.	

98+   *Title: see textual note to 80+*
107–10.   *Lineation TS; two lines in MS*
108.   onto þe] *This ed; MS, TS* onlye to
112.   seere] *This ed; TS* feere
124.   lange] a *altered to* o *by later hand*

Jesus	I saie to ʒou, Lazare is dede,	
	And for ʒou all grete joie I haue	
	ʒe wote I was noght in þat stede	
	What tyme þat he was graued in graue.	140
	His sisteres praye with bowsom beede	
	And for comforte þei call and craue,	
	Therfore go we togedir	f.113ᵛ
	To make þere myrthis more.	
I Apostolus	Sen he will nedes wende þedir,	145
	Go we and dye with hym þore.	
Maria	Allas, owtane Goddis will allone,	
	Þat I schulld sitte to see þis sight,	
	For I may morne and make my mone,	
	So wo in worlde was neuere wight.	150
	Þat I loued most is fro me gone,	
	My dere brothir þat Lazar hight,	
	And I durst saye I wolde be slone	
	For nowe me fayles both mynde and myght.	
	My welthe is wente for euere,	155
	No medycyne mende me may.	
	A, dede, þou do thy deuer	
	And haue me hense away.	
Martha	Allas, for ruthe now may I raue	
	And febilly fare by frith and felde,	160
	Wolde God þat I wer grathed in graue,	
	Þat dede hadde tane me vndir telde.	
	For hele in harte mon I neuere haue	
	But if he helpe þat all may welde,	
	Of Crist I will som comforte craue	165
	For he may be my bote and belde.	
	To seke I schal noʒt cesse	
	Tille I my souereyne see.	
	Hayle, pereles prince of pesse,	
	Jesu my maistir so free.	170
Jesus	Martha, what menes þou to make such chere?	
	[.	
	. . . . . .	
	. . . . . .	
	. . . . . .	
	. . . . . .	
	. . . . . .	
	. . . . . .	
	. . . . . .	
	. . . . . .	
	. . . . . .]	

164. he] *Suppl TS*

[A second leaf, conjugate with the one missing between lines 54 and 55, is wanting at this point. It is likely to have contained 57 lines: three complete stanzas, together with 11 lines missing after 171 and 10 missing before 172. The events lost are those of John xi.17–41: the arrival of Christ at Bethany, the meetings with Martha and Mary, and the scene before the tomb of Lazarus. Lines 172–3 evidently belong to a person involved in opening the tomb.]

[...   ...
    ...   ...
 ...   ...
    ...   ...
 ...   ...
    ...   ...
 ...   ...
    ...   ...
       ...   ...
    ...   ...]

        This stone we schall full sone   f.114
          Remove and sette on syde.

Jesus   Fadir, þat is in heuyn on highte,
          I þanke þe euere ouere all thyng   175
        That hendely heres me day and nyght,
          And takis hede vnto myn askyng.
        Wherfore fouchesaffe of thy grete myght
          So þat þis pepull, olde and ʒyng,
        That standis and bidis to se þat sight   180
          May trulye trowe and haue knowyng,
            This tyme here or I pas
            How þat þou has me sent.
          Lazar, veni foras,
            Come fro thy monument.   185

Lazarus   A, pereles prince, full of pitee,
          Worshipped be þou in worlde alway
        That þus hast schewed þi myght in me,
          Both dede and doluen, þis is þe fourþe day.
        By certayne singnes here may men see   190
          How þat þou art Goddis sone verray.
        All þo þat trulye trastis in þe
          Schall neuere dye, þis dar I saye.
          Therfore ʒe folke in fere,
            Menske hym with mayne and myght,   195
          His lawes luke þat ʒe lere,
            Þan will he lede ʒou to his light.

186. *Additions to right at different times by J. Clerke:* (i) Nota quia non concordat; (ii) novo addicio facto
189. Memorandum *and another word (? graiars, gravers) added to right by a later hand*

Maria	Here may men fynde a faythfull frende	
	Þat þus has couered vs of oure care.	
Martha	Jesu my lord and maistir hende,	200
	Of þis we thanke þe euermore.	
Jesus	Sisteres, I may no lenger lende,	f.114ᵛ
	To othir folke nowe bus me fare,	
	And to Jerusalem will I wende	
	For thyngis þat muste be fulfilled þere.	205
	Therfore rede I you right,	
	My men, to wende with me.	
	3e þat haue sene þis sight	
	My blissyng with 30 be.	

XXV The Skinners

The Entry into Jerusalem

Jesus	To me takis tent and giffis gud hede	f.115ᵛ
	My dere discipulis þat ben here,	
	I schall 3ou telle þat shal be indede:	
	My tyme to passe hense it drawith nere,	
	And by þis skill,	5
	Mannys sowle to saue fro sorowes serc	
	Þat loste was ill.	
	From heuen to erth whan I dyssende	
	Rawnsom to make I made promys,	
	The prophicie nowe drawes to ende,	10
	My fadirs wille forsoth it is	
	Þat sente me hedyr.	
	Petir, Phelippe, I schall 3ou blisse,	
	And go togedir	
	Vnto 3one castell þat is 3ou agayne,	15
	Gois with gud harte and tarie no3t,	
	My comaundement to do be 3e bayne.	

209+ finis *added by J. Clerke; rest of f.114ᵛ blank, f.115 blank*

11. is] *Followed by* I, *deleted*

Also I ʒou charge loke it be wrought
  Þat schal ʒe fynde
An asse þis feste als ʒe had soght.   20
  ʒe hir vnbynde

With hir foole, and to me hem bring,
  Þat I on hir may sitte a space,
So þe prophicy clere menyng
  May be fulfillid here in þis place: 25
    'Doghtyr Syon,
  Loo, þi lorde comys rydand an asse
  Þe to opon'.

Yf any man will ʒou gaynesaye,
  Say þat youre lorde has nede of þam   30
And schall restore þame þis same day
  Vnto what man will þam clayme;
    Do þus þis thyng.
  Go furthe ʒe both and be ay bayne
  In my blissyng.   35

Petrus   Jesu, maistir, evyn at þy wille
  And at þi liste vs likis to doo.
Yone beste whilke þou desires þe tille
  Euen at þi will schall come þe too,
    Vnto þin esse.   40
  Sertis lord, we will þedyre all go
  Þe for to plese.

Philippus Lord, þe to plese we are full bayne   f.116
  Boþe nyght and day to do þi will.
Go we broþere, with all oure mayne   45
  My lordis desire for to fulfill,
    For prophycye
  Vs bus it do to hym by skyll
  Þarto dewly.

Petrus   ʒa, brodir Phelipp, behalde grathely,   50
  For als he saide we schulde sone fynde,
Methinke ʒone bestis before myn eye
  Þai are þe same we schulde vnbynde.
    Þerfore frely

19. Þat] *Ho¹* Þar
24. prophicy] *K* prophetis
27. rydand an] *K; MS, TS* rydand on an
33. thyng] ki *(apparently) superimposed on* t *by a later hand*
41. go] *Suppl He*
42+ *Catchword* Lorde þe to plese
43. *Quire P begins*
49. Þarto] *Ho¹; MS, TS* To do

	Go we to hym þat þame gan bynde,	55
	And aske mekely.	
Philippus	The beestis are comen, wele I knawe,	
	Therfore vs nedis to aske lesse leue;	
	And oure maistir kepis þe lawe	
	We may þame take tyter, I preue.	60
	For noght we lett,	
	For wele I watte oure tyme is breue,	
	Go we þam fett.	
Janitor	Saie, what are ӡe þat makis here maistrie,	
	To loose þes bestis withoute leverie?	65
	Yow semes to bolde, sen noght þat ӡe	
	Hase here to do; þerfore rede I	
	Such þingis to sesse,	
	Or ellis ӡe may falle in folye	
	And grette diseasse.	70
Petrus	Sir, with þi leue, hartely we praye	
	Þis beste þat we myght haue.	
Janitor	To what intente firste shall ӡe saye,	
	And þan I graunte what ӡe will crave	
	Be gode resoune.	75
Philippus	Oure maistir sir, þat all may saue,	
	Aske by chesoune.	
Janitor	What man is þat ӡe maistir call	
	Swilke priuelege dare to hym clayme?	
Petrus	Jesus, of Jewes kyng and ay be schall,	80
	Of Nazareth prophete þe same.	
	Þis same is he,	
	Both God and man withouten blame,	
	Þis trist wele we.	
Janitor	Sirs, of þat prophette herde I haue,	f.116ᵛ
	But telle me firste playnly, wher is hee?	86
Philippus	He comes at hande so God me saue,	
	Þat lorde we lefte at Bephagé,	
	He bidis vs þere.	
Janitor	Sir, take þis beste with herte full free,	90
	And forthe ӡe fare.	
	And if ӡou thynke it be to don,	
	I schall declare playnly his comyng	

---

71. hartely] t *interlined by a later hand*
81. þe same] *K* by name
85. *Janitor*] *Suppl by J. Clerke*

To the chiffe of þe Jewes, þat þei may sone
 Assemble same to his metyng;   95
  What is your rede?

Petrus   Þou sais full wele in thy menyng.
  Do forthe þi dede,

And sone þis beste we schall þe bring
 And it restore as resoune will.   100

Janitor   This tydyngis schall haue no laynyng,
 But be þe citezens declared till
  Of þis cyté.
 I suppose fully þat þei wolle
  Come mete þat free.   105

And sen I will þei warned be,
 Both ȝonge and olde in ilke a state,
For his comyng I will þam mete
 To late þam witte, withoute debate.
  Lo, wher þei stande,   110
 The citezens cheff withoute debate
  Of all þis lande.

He þat is rewler of all right
 And freely schoppe both sande and see,
He saue ȝou, lordyngis gayly dight,   115
 And kepe ȝou in ȝoure semelyté
  And all honoure.

I Burgensis   Welcome porter, what novelté?
  Telle vs þis owre.

Janitor   Sirs, novelté I can ȝou telle   120
 And triste þame fully as for trewe:
Her comes of kynde of Israell
 Att hande þe prophette called Jesu,
  Lo, þis same day,
 Rydand on an asse. Þis tydandis newe 125
  Consayue ȝe may.

II Burgensis And is þat prophette Jesu nere?
 Off hym I haue herde grete ferlis tolde. f.117
He dois grete wounderes in contrees seere,
 He helys þe seke, both ȝonge and olde, 130
  And þe blynde giffis þam þer sight.

102. be] *This ed; MS, TS* to
   declared] *Ho¹; MS, TS* declare it
108. þam] *Ho¹; MS, TS* hym
   mete] *He* see
111. The] *This ed; MS, TS* That
   withoute debate] *Ho¹* within þe gate
114. sande and see] *TS; MS* see and sande

Both dome and deffe, as hymselffe wolde,
   He cures þame right.

III Burgensis   3a, v thowsand men with loves fyue
     He fedde, and ilkone hadde inowe.   135
   Watir to wyne he turned ryue,
     He garte corne growe withouten plogh
       Wher are was none.
     To dede men als he gaffe liffe,
       Lazar was one.   140

IV Burgensis   In oure tempill if he prechid
     Agaynste þe pepull þat leued wrong,
   And also new lawes if he teched
     Agaynste oure lawis we vsed so lang,
       And saide pleynlye   145
     The olde schall waste, þe new schall gang,
       Þat we schall see.

V Burgensis   3a, Moyses lawe he cowde ilke dele
     And all þe prophettis on a rowe,
   He telles þam so þat ilke a man may tele   150
     And what þei say interly knowe
       Yf þei were dyme.
     What þe prophettis saide in þer sawe,
       All longis to hym.

VI Burgensis   Emanuell also by right   155
     Þai calle þat prophette by þis skill,
   He is þe same þat are was hyght
     Be Ysaye before vs till,
       Þus saide full clere:
     Loo, a maydyn þat knew neuere ille   160
       A childe schuld bere.

VII Burgensis   Dauid spake of hym I wene
     And lefte witnesse 3e knowe ilkone,
   He saide þe frute of his corse clene
     Shulde royally regne vpon his trone,   165
       And þerfore he
     Of Dauid kyn and oþir none
       Oure kyng schal be.

VIII Burgensis   Sirs, methynketh 3e saie right wele   f.117ᵛ
     And gud ensampelys furth 3e bryng,   170

151. say] *Ho¹; MS, TS* may
159. Þus] *K* Þat
162. *VII Burgensis] Reassigned Zu; against 160 in MS, TS*
168+ david rex *in a post-medieval hand at foot of page*

And sen we þus þis mater fele
  Go we hym meete as oure owne kyng,
    And kyng hym call.
  What is youre counsaill in þis thyng?
    Now say ȝe all.   175

I Burgensis   Agaynste resoune I will noȝt plete
  For wele I wote oure kyng he is.
Whoso agaynst his kyng liste threte
  He is noȝt wise, he dose amys.
    Porter, come nere.   180
  What knowlage hast þou of his comyng?
    Tels vs all here,

And þan we will go mete þat free,
  And hym honnoure as we wele awe
Worthely tyll oure citee,   185
  And for oure souerayne lord hym knawe,
    In whome we triste.
Janitor   Sirs, I schall telle ȝou all on rowe
  And ȝe will lyste.

Of his discipillis, ij þis day   190
  Where that I stode þei faire me grette,
And on ther maistir halfe gan praye
  Oure comon asse þat þei myght gete
    Bot for a while,
  Wheron þer maistir softe myght sitte   195
    Space of a mile.

And all þis mater þai me tolde
  Right haly as I saie to ȝou,
And þe asse þei haue right as þei wolde
  And sone will bringe agayne I trowe,   200
    So þai beheste.
  What ȝe will doo avise ȝou nowe,
    Þus thinke me beste.

II Burgensis   Trewlye as for me I say
  I rede we make vs redy bowne,   205
Hym to mete gudly þis day
  And hym ressayue with grete rennowne
    As worthy is.
  And þerfore sirs, in felde and towne
    Ȝe fulfille þis.   210

181. *Ho'* What kanst þou of his comyng wiss?
204. say] *Followed by* I, *deleted*

Janitor	3a, and 3oure childer with 3ou take,
	Þoff all in age þat þei be 3onge,
	3e may fare þe bettir for þer sake f.118
	Thurgh þe blissing of so goode a kyng,
	Þis is no dowte. 215
III Burgensis	I kan þe thanke for thy saying,
	We will hym lowte.
	And hym to mete I am right bayne
	On þe beste maner þat I cane,
	For I desire to se hym fayne 220
	And hym honnoure as his awne man,
	Sen þe soth I see.
	Kyng of Juuys we call hym þan,
	Oure kyng is he.
IV Burgensis	Oure kyng is he – þat is no lesse – 225
	Oure awne lawe to it cordis will,
	Þe prophettis all bare full witnesse
	Qwilke of hym secrete gone telle,
	And þus wolde say:
	'Emang youreselff schall come grete seele 230
	Thurgh God verray'.
V Burgensis	Þis same is he, þer is non othir,
	Was vs beheest full lange before,
	For Moyses saide als oure owne brothir
	A newe prophette God schulde restore. 235
	Þerfore loke 3e
	What 3e will do, withouten more,
	Oure kyng is he.
VI Burgensis	Of Juda come owre kyng so gent,
	Of Jesse, Dauid, Salamon; 240
	Also by his modir kynne take tente,
	Þe genolagye beres witnesse on,
	This is right playne.
	Hym to honnoure right as I can
	I am full bayne. 245
VII Burgensis	Of youre clene witte and youre consayte
	I am full gladde in harte and þought,
	And hym to mete withouten latt
	I am redy, and feyne will noght,
	Bot with 3ou same 250

211. childer] *Suppl TS*
228. Qwilke of] *K; MS, TS* Qwilke full of
     telle] *Ha; MS, TS* felle
247. þought] th *interlined over* þ *by J. Clerke*
248. latt] *Interlined by Clerke over main scribe's* consayte

              Go hym agayne vs blisse hath brought,
                With myrthe and game.

VIII Burgensis   ȝoure argumentis þai are so clere
                I can noȝt saie but graunte you till,
              For whanne I of þat counsaille here   f.118ᵛ
                I coveyte hym with feruent wille   256
                  Onys for to see,
                I trowe fro þens I schall
                  Bettir man be.

I Burgensis   Go we þan with processioun   260
                To mete þat comely as vs awe,
              With braunches, floures and vnysoune.
                  With myghtfull songes her on a rawe
                  Our childir schall
                Go synge before, þat men may knawe.   265
II Burgensis   To þis graunte we all.

Petrus   Jesu, lord and maistir free,
                Als þou comaunde so haue we done.
              Þis asse here we haue brought to þe,
                  What is þi wille þou schewe vs sone   270
                  And tarie noȝt,
                And þan schall we withouten hune
                  Fulfill þi þouȝt.

Jesus   I þanke ȝou breþere mylde of mode.
                Do on þis asse youre cloþis ȝe laye,   275
              And lifte me vppe with hertis gud
                  Þat I on hir may sitte þis daye
                  In my blissing.
Philippus   Lord, þi will to do allway
                  We graunte þis þing.   280

Jesus   Now my breþere with gud chere
                Gyues gode entente, for ryde I will
              Vnto ȝone cyté ȝe se so nere.
                  Ȝe shall me folowe sam and still
                  Als I are sayde.   285
Philippus   Lord, as þe lyst we graunte þe till,
                  And halde vs payde.

---

251. Go] *Ha; MS, TS* To
254. you] *This ed; TS* þou
258. schall] *Ho¹ suppl with skill*
260. *I Burgensis*] *Reassigned TS; Against 261 in MS*
266. *II Burgensis*] *Reassigned this ed; against 265 in MS, om TS*
280. þis] *Suppl Ho¹*
286. lyst] *Ha; MS, TS* lyfe
287+ *SD added to left by a later hand; cantant could also be cantat or cantent*

Tunc cantant

Cecus	A, lorde, þat all þis world has made,
	Boþe sonne and mone, nyght and day,
	What noyse is þis þat makis me gladde? 290
	Fro whens it schulde come I can noȝt saye,
	Or what it mene.
	Yf any man walke in þis way
	Telle hym me bedene.
Pauper	Man, what ayles þe to crye? 295
	Where wolde þou be? Þou say me here. f.119
Cecus	A, sir, a blynde man am I
	And ay has bene of tendyr ȝere
	Sen I was borne.
	I harde a voyce with nobill chere 300
	Here me beforne.
Pauper	Man, will þou oght þat I can do?
Cecus	Ȝa sir, gladly wolde I witte
	Yf þou couþe oght declare me to
	This myrþe I herde, what mene may it 305
	Or vndirstande?
Pauper	Jesu þe prophite full of grace
	Comys here at hande,
	And all þe cetezens þay are bowne
	Gose hym to mete with melodye, 310
	With þe fayrest processioun
	That euere was sene in þis Jury;
	He is right nere.
Cecus	Sir, helpe me to þe strete hastely,
	Þat I may here 315
	Þat noyse, and also þat I myght thurgh grace
	My syght of hym to craue I wolde.
Pauper	Loo, he is here at þis same place.
	Crye faste on hym, loke þou be bolde,
	With voyce right high. 320
Cecus	Jesu þe sone of Dauid calde,
	Þou haue mercy.

296–337. *Lineation confused on f.119, rhyme brackets omitted. Lineation here follows TS*
298. bene of tendyr ȝere] *TS; MS* of tendyr ȝere bene
303. I] *Suppl TS*
307. *Ha* ... of grace full þe prophite
309. þay] *K* þat
319. *Lineation TS;* loke ... bolde *written to right of 318 and* Crye ... hym *together with 320 written as one line in MS*
320. right] *TS; MS* righ

	Allas, I crye, he heris me noȝt,	
	He has no ruthe of my mysfare.	
	He turnes his herre, where is his þought?	325
Pauper	Cry somwhat lowdar, loke þou noȝt spare,	
	So may þou spye.	
Cecus	Jesu þe saluer of all sare,	
	To me giffis gode hye.	

Phelippus	Cesse man and crye noȝt soo,	330
	The voyce of þe pepill gose þe by.	
	Þe aghe sette still and tente giffe to,	
	Here passez þe prophite of mercye–	
	Þou doys amys.	
Cecus	A, Dauid sone, to þe I crye,	335
	Þe kyng of blisse.	

Petrus	Lorde, haue mercy and late hym goo,	
	He can noȝt cesse of his crying.	f.119ᵛ
	He folows vs both to and froo,	
	Graunte hym his boone and his askyng	340
	And late hym wende.	
	We gette no reste or þat þis thyng	
	Be broȝt to ende.	

Jesus	What wolde þou man I to þe dede	
	In þis present? Telle oppynly.	345
Cecus	Lorde, my syght is fro me hydde,	
	Þou graunte me it, I crye mercy,	
	Þis wolde I haue.	
Jesus	Loke vppe nowe with chere blythely,	
	Þi faith shall þe saue.	350

Cecus	Wirschippe and honnoure ay to þe	
	With all þe seruice þat can be done,	
	The kyng of blisse loued mote he be	
	Þat þus my sight hath sente so sone,	
	And by grete skill.	355
	I was are blynde as any stone:	
	I se at wille.	

Claudus	A, wele wer þam þat euere had liffe,	
	Olde or yonge whedir it were,	
	Might welde þer lymmes withouten striffe,	360
	Go with þis mirthe þat I see here	
	And contynewe;	

---

327. *Lineation TS; to right of 325 in MS*
332. aghe] *TS; MS* age
346. syght] *TS; MS* syight
359. Hic caret *to right in a later hand*

For I am sette in sorowes sere
Þat ay ar newe.

Þou lord þat schope both nyght and day,   365
For thy mercy haue mynde on me
And helpe me lorde, as þou wele may
[. . .   . . .]
I may noȝt gang.
For I am lame as men may se
And has ben lang.   370

For wele I wote, as knowyn is ryffe,
Boþe dome and deffe þou grauntist þam grace,
And also þe dede þat þou hauyst geuen liff;
Therfore graunte me lord in þis place
My lymbis to welde.   375

Jesus   My man, ryse and caste þe crucchys gode space
Her in þe felde,

And loke in trouthe þou stedfast be,
And folow me furth with gode menyng.

Claudus   Lorde, lo my crouchis wharc þei flee   380
Als ferre as I may late þam flenge   f.120
With bothe my hende.
Þat euere we haue metyng
Now I defende,

For I was halte of lyme and lame   385
And I suffered tene and sorowes inowe.
Ay-lastand lord, loued be þi name,
I am als light as birde on bowe.
Ay be þou blist,
Such grace hast þou schewed to me   390
Lorde, as þe list.

Zaché   Sen firste þis worlde was made of noȝt
And all thyng sette in equité,
Such ferly thyng was neuere non wroght
As men þis tyme may see with eye.   395
What it may mene—
I can noȝt saye what it may be,
Comforte or tene.

367+   *Line missing; no gap in MS*
382.   *Originally written to right of 379 (foot of f.119ᵛ), there deleted. Recopied to right of 381 by J. Clerke*
385.   of] *This ed; MS, TS* both
390.   to me] *Ho'* me nowe
396.   it may] *Ho'* may it . . . ?

And cheffely of a prophete new
  Þat mekill is profite, and þat of latte   400
Both day and nyght þai hym assewe,
  Oure pepill same thurgh strete and gatte
    [. . .   . . .]
  Oure olde lawes as nowe þei hatte
    And his kepis ȝare.

Men fro deth to liffe he rayse,   405
  The blynde and dome geve speche and sight,
Gretely þerfor oure folke hym prayse
  And folowis hym both day and nyght
    Fro towne to towne.
  Thay calle hym prophite be right   410
    As of renowne.

And ȝit I meruayle of þat thyng,
  Of puplicans sen prince am I
Of hym I cowthe haue no knowyng,
  Yf all I wolde haue comen hym neȝe,   415
    Arly and late.
  For I am lawe, and of men high
    Full is þe gate.

Bot sen no bettir may befalle
  I thynke what beste is for to doo,   420
I am schorte ȝe knawe wele all,
  Þerfore ȝone tre I will go too
    And in it clyme.
  Whedir he come or passe me fro
    I schall se hym.   425

A, nobill tree þou secomoure,
  I blisse hym þat þe on þe erþe broght.
Now may I see both here and þore   f.120ᵛ
  That vndir me hid may be noȝt.
  Þerfore in þe   430
  Wille I bidde in herte and þought
    Till I hym se.

Vnto þe prophete come to towne
  Her will I bide what so befalle.

Jesus   Do Zaché, do faste come downe.   435
Zaché   Lorde, even at þi wille hastely I schall,
    And tarie noght.

402+ *Line missing, no gap in MS. TS conj* New lawes to lere, *Hoʹ* Both min and mare
415. neȝe] *Conj TS; MS* nere
417. men high] *Ha; MS, TS* myne hight
429. hid] *Ha; MS, TS* it
431. Wille] *TS; MS* Whiche

To þe on knes lord here I fall
For synne I wroght;

| | And welcome, prophete trast and trewe,
With all þe pepull þat to þe lange. | 440 |

Jesus Zaché, þi seruice new
Schall make þe clene of all þe wrong
Þat þou haste done.

Zaché Lorde, I lette noʒt for þis thrang   445
Her to say sone

Me schamys with synne but ouʒt to mende.
Mi synne forsake þerfore I will,
Halue my gud I haue vnspende
Poure folke to geue it till,   450
Þis will I fayne.
Whom I begylyd to hym I will
Make asith agayne.

Jesus Thy clere confessioun schall þe clense,
Þou may be sure of lastand lyffe.   455
Vnto þi house withouten offense
Is graunted pees withouten striffe.
Farewele Zaché.

Zaché Lord, þe lowte ay man and wiffe,
Blist myght þou be.   460

Jesus My dere discipulis, beholde and see,
Vnto Jerusalem we schall assende,
Man sone schall þer betrayed be
And gevyn into his enmys hende
With grete dispitte.   465
Ther spitting on hym þer schall þei spende
And smertly smyte.

Petir, take þis asse me fro
And lede it where þou are it toke.
I murne, I sigh, I wepe also   470
Jerusalem on þe to loke.
And so may þou rewe
Þat euere þou þi kyng forsuke
And was vntrewe.

438. fall] *He;* MS, TS shall
441. lange] *He;* MS, TS langis
442–4. *Lineation TS; two lines in MS*
447. ouʒt] *K;* MS, TS noʒt
448. Mi] M *added by a later hand; TS* I (*K conj* My)
449. Halue] *(Zu), K;* MS, TS Haue
vnspende] *K;* MS, TS vnspendid
452. I will] *TS;* MS will I
464. hende] *K;* MS, TS hande
472. rewe] *Suppl Ha*

	For stone on stone schall none be lefte	f.121
	But doune to þe grounde all schal be caste,	476
	Thy game, þi gle, al fro þe refte	
	And all for synne þat þou done hast.	
	Þou arte vnkynde;	
	Agayne þi kyng þou hast trespast,	480
	Haue þis in mynde.	

Petrus   Porter, take here þyn asse agayne,
                At hande my lorde comys on his fette.

Janitor   Behalde where all þe burgeis bayne
                Comes with wirschippe hym to mete.   485
                  Þerfore I will
                Late hym abide here in þis strete
                And lowte hym till.

I Burgensis Hayll prophette preued withouten pere,
                Hayll prince of pees schall euere endure,   490
                Hayll kyng comely, curteyse and clere,
                Hayll souerayne semely, to synfull sure;
                  To þe all bowes.
                Hayll lord louely oure cares may cure,
                Hayll kyng of Jewes.   495

II Burgensis Hayll florisshand floure þat neuere shall fade,
                Hayll vyolett vernand with swete odoure,
                Hayll marke of myrthe oure medecyne made,
                Hayll blossome bright, hayll oure socoure,
                  Hayll kyng comely.   500
                Hayll menskfull man, we þe honnoure
                With herte frely.

III Burgensis Hayll Dauid sone, doughty in dede,
                Hayll rose ruddy, hayll birrall clere,
                Hayll, welle of welthe may make vs mede,   505
                Hayll saluer of oure sores sere,
                  We wirschippe þe.
                Hayll hendfull, with solas sere
                Welcome þou be

IV Burgensis Hayll blisfull babe, in Bedleme borne,   510
                Hayll boote of all oure bittir balis,
                Hayll, sege þat schoppe boþe even and morne,
                Hayll talker trystefull of trew tales,
                Hayll comely knyght,

482. agayne] at hande, *deleted, follows*
484. þe] *Zu; MS, TS* þi
495. Hayll] *TS; MS* Hall, H *added by a later hand*
499. bright] *TS; MS* brigh
501. we] *Zu, Ha; MS, TS* with

Hayll of mode þat moste preuayles 515
To saue þe tyght.

V Burgensis Hayll dyamaunde with drewry dight,
Hayll jasper gentill of Jury,
Hayll lylly lufsome lemyd with lyght, f.121ᵛ
Hayll balme of boote, moyste and drye 520
To all has nede.
Hayll barne most blist of mylde Marie,
Hayll all oure mede.

VI Burgensis Hayll conquerour, hayll most of myght,
Hayll rawnsoner of synfull all, 525
Hayll pytefull, hayll louely light,
Hayll to vs welcome be schall,
Hayll kyng of Jues.
Hayll comely corse þat we þe call
With mirþe þat newes. 530

VII Burgensis Hayll sonne ay schynand with bright bemes,
Hayll lampe of liff schall neuere waste,
Hayll lykand lanterne, luffely lemys,
Hayll texte of trewþe þe trew to taste.
Hayll kyng and sire, 535
Hayll maydens chylde þat menskid hir most,
We þe desire.

VIII Burgensis Hayll domysman dredful, þat all schall deme,
Hayll þat all quyk and dede schall lowte,
Hayll whom worschippe moste will seme, 540
Hayll whom all thyng schall drede and dowte.
We welcome þe,
Hayll and welcome of all abowte
To owre ceté.

Tunc cantant.

518. Jury] *This ed; TS* Jewry
533. lanterne luffely] *K* lanterne þat luffely
539. þat . . . dede] *Hoᵗ* quyk and dede þat all
540+ *SD added (to left of 540) by a later hand; cantant could also be cantat or cantent. Beneath last line,* finis *added by J. Clerke. Bottom half of f.121ᵛ blank, ff.122, 122ᵛ blank*

XXVI The Cutlers

The Conspiracy

Pilatus	Vndir þe ryallest roye of rente and renowne	f.123
	Now am I regent of rewle þis region in reste,	
	Obeye vnto bidding bud busshoppis me bowne	
	And bolde men þat in batayll makis brestis to breste.	
	To me betaught is þe tent þis towre-begon towne,	5
	For traytoures tyte will I taynte þe trewþe for to triste.	
	The dubbyng of my dingnité may noȝt be done downe,	
	Nowdir with duke nor dugeperes, my dedis are so dreste.	
	My desire muste dayly be done	
	With þame þat are grettest of game,	10
	And þeragayne fynde I but fone,	
	Wherfore I schall bettir þer bone –	
	But he þat me greues for a grone,	
	Beware, for wyscus I am.	

	Pounce Pilatt of thre partis þan is my propir name,	15
	I am a perelous prince to proue wher I peere.	
	Emange þe philosofers firste ther fanged I my fame,	
	Wherfore I fell to affecte I fynde noȝt my feere.	
	He schall full bittirly banne þat bide schall my blame,	
	If all my blee be as bright as blossome on brere,	20
	For sone his liffe shall he lose or left be for lame	
	Þat lowtes noȝt to me lowly nor liste noȝt to leere.	
	And þus sen we stande in oure state	
	Als lordis with all lykyng in lande,	
	Do and late vs wete if ȝe wate	25
	Owthir, sirs, of bayle or debate	
	Þat nedis for to be handeled full hate,	
	Sen all youre helpe hanges in my hande.	

Caiphas	Sir, and for to certefie þe soth in youre sight,	f.123ᵛ
	As to ȝou for oure souerayne semely we seke.	30
Pilatus	Why, is þer any myscheue þat musteres his myȝt	
	Or malice thurgh meene menn vs musters to meke?	

1. *Pilatus] Suppl by a later hand*
3. me] *Ho¹* be
13. grone] *Ho¹; MS, TS* grume
14. wyscus] *This ed; TS* wystus
22. Þat] *This ed; TS* Þar
25. Do and late] *He* Do late

Anna	ʒa sir, þer is a ranke swayne whos rule is noʒt right,
	For thurgh his romour in þis reme hath raysede mekill
	reke.
Pilatus	I here wele ʒe hate hym; youre hartis are on heght, 35
	And ellis if I helpe wolde his harmes for to eke.
	But why are ʒe barely þus brathe?
	Bees rewly and ray fourth youre reasoune.
Caiphas	Tille vs sir his lore is full lothe.
Pilatus	Beware þat we wax noʒt to wrothe. 40
Anna	Why sir, to skyfte fro his skath
	We seke for youre socoure þis sesoune.
Pilatus	And if þat wrecche in oure warde haue wrought any wrong,
	Sen we are warned we walde witte, and wille or we wende.
	But and his sawe be lawfull, legge noʒt to lange, 45
	For we schall leue hym if us list with luffe here to lende.
I Doctor	And yf þat false faytor youre fortheraunce may fang,
	Þan fele I wele þat oure folke mon fayle of a frende.
	Sir, þe strenghe of his steuen ay still is so strange f.124
	That but he schortely be schent he schappe vs to schende,
	For he kennes folke hym for to call 51
	Grete God son — þus greues vs þat gome —
	And sais þat he sittande be schall
	In high heuen, for þere is his hall.
Pilatus	And frendis, if þat force to hym fall 55
	It semes noʒt ʒe schall hym consume.
	But þat hymselfe is þe same ʒe saide schulde descende
	ʒoure seede and ʒou þen all for to socoure.
Cayphas	A, softe sir, and sese,
	For of Criste whan he comes no kynne schall be kenned,
	But of þis caytiffe kynreden we knawe þe encrese. 60
	He lykens hym to be lyke God, ay-lastand to lende,
	To lifte vppe þe laby, to lose or relesse.
Pilatus	His maistreys schulde moue ʒou youre mode for to amende.
Anna	Nay, for swilke mys fro malice we may noʒt vs meese,
	For he sais he schall deme vs, þat dote, 65
	And þat tille vs is dayne or dispite.

34. thurgh] *TS; MS* thurgh thurgh
36. ellis] *Ho'* hedis
40. we] *Ho'* ye
41. skyfte] *This ed; TS* skyste
44. wille] *Ho'* wisse
48+ *Catchword* Sir þe strengh
49. *Quire Q begins*

Pilatus	To noye hym nowe is youre noote,
	But ȝitt þe lawe lyes in my lotte.
I Doctor	And yf ȝe will witt sir, ȝe wotte
	Þat he is wele worthy to wyte.

70

f.124

For in oure temple has he taught by tymes moo þan tenne
   Where tabillis full of tresoure lay to telle and to trye,
Of oure cheffe mony-changers – butte, curstely to kenne,
   He caste þam ouere, þat caystiffe, and counted noȝt þerby.

Cayphas	Loo sir, þis is a periurye to prente vndir penne, 75
	Wherfore make ȝe þat *appostita*, we praye ȝou, to plye.
Pilatus	Howe mene ȝe?
Cayphas	Sir, to mort hym for mouyng of men.
Pilatus	Þan schulde we make hym to morne but thurgh ȝoure
	maistrie.
	Latte be sirs, and move þat no more;
	But what in youre temple betyde? 80
I Miles	We, þare sir he skelpte oute of score
	Þat stately stode selland þer store.
Pilatus	Þan felte he þam fawté before
	And made þe cause wele to be kydde.

But what taught he þat tyme, swilk tales as þou telles?   85

I Miles	Sir, þat oure tempill is þe toure of his troned sire,
	And þus to prayse in þat place oure prophettis compellis,
	Tille hym þat has posté of prince and of empire; f.125
	And þei make *domus domini* þat deland þare dwellis
	Þe denn of þe derfenes and ofte þat þei desire. 90
Pilatus	Loo, is he noght a mad man þat for youre mede melles,
	Sen ȝe ymagyn amys þat makeles to myre?
	Ȝoure rankoure is raykand full rawe.
Cayphas	Nay nay sir, we rewle vs but right.
Pilatus	Forsothe, ȝe ar ouer-cruell to knawe. 95
Cayphas	Why sir? For he wolde lose oure lawe
	Hartely we hym hate as we awe,
	And þerto schulde ȝe mayntayne oure myght.

For why, vppon oure Sabbott day þe seke makes he saffe
    And will noȝt sesse for oure sawes to synke so in synne.

II Miles	Sir, he coueres all þat comes recoueraunce to craue 101
	But in a schorte contynuaunce, þat kennes all oure kynne.

85.   taies] *TS; MS* tales tales
87.   prayse] *K* praye
89.   deland] *This ed; MS, TS* derand
90.   and] *Ho'* als

But he haldis noght oure haly dayes, harde happe myght
              hym haue,
  And therfore hanged be he and þat by þe halse.

Pilatus   A, hoo sir nowe, and holde in.
  For þoff ȝe gange þus gedy hym gilteles to graue,   105
    Withouten grounde ȝow gaynes noght swilke greffe to
              begynne;
      And loke youre leggyng be lele,   f.125^v
      Withowtyn any tryfils to telle.

Anna   For certayne owre sawes dare we seele.
Pilatus   And þan may we prophite oure pele.   110
Cayphas   Sir, bot his fawtes were fele
      We mente noȝt of hym for to melle.

  For he pervertis oure pepull þat proues his prechyng,
    And for þat poynte ȝe schulde prese his poosté to paire.
II Doctor ȝa sir, and also þat caytiff he callis hym oure kyng,   115
    And for þat cause our comons are casten in care.
Pilatus   And if so be, þat borde to bayll will hym bryng
    And make hym boldely to banne þe bones þat hym bare.
  For-why þat wrecche fro oure wretthe schal not wryng
    Or þer be wrought on hym wrake.
I Doctor   So wolde we it ware, 120
    For so schulde ȝe susteyne youre seele
      And myldely haue mynde for to meke ȝou.
Pilatus   Wele witte ȝe, þis werke schall be wele,
    For kende schall þat knave be to knele.
II Doctor And so þat oure force he may feele   125
    All samme for þe same we beseke ȝou.

Judas   *Ingenti pro inuria* – hym Jesus, þat Jewe
  Vnjust vnto me, Judas, I juge to be lathe.
  For at oure soper as we satte, þe soþe to pursewe,   129
    With Symond luprus, full sone my skiffte come to scathe.
  Tille hym þer brought one a boyste my bale for to brewe
    That baynly to his bare feete to bowe was full   f.126
              braythe,
  Sho anoynte þam with an oynement that nobill was and newe,
    But for þat werke þat sche wrought I wexe woundir
              wrothe.
    And þis – to discouer – was my skill: 135
      For of his penys purser was I,
    And what þat me taught was vntill
    The tente parte þat stale I ay still.
    But nowe for me wantis of my will
      Þat bargayne with bale schall he by.   140

117–120a. *Originally unassigned. Cayphas suppl by J. Clerke, but deleted; Pilatus substituted by (?) another later hand*
128. Vnjust] *TS; MS* Vncust
133. That] *TS; MS* Tat

Þat same oynement, I saide, might same haue bene solde
  For siluer penys in a sowme thre hundereth, and fyne
Haue ben departid to poure men as playne pité wolde;
  But for þe poore, ne þare parte priked me no peyne—
But me tened for þe tente parte, þe trewthe to beholde,   145
  That thirty pens of iij hundereth so tyte I schulde tyne.
And for I mysse þis mony I morne on þis molde,
  Wherfore for to mischeue þis maistir of myne
    And þerfore faste forþe will I flitte
      The princes of prestis vntill,   150
    And selle hym full sone or þat I sitte
    For therty pens in a knotte knytte.
      Þus-gatis full wele schall he witte
      Þat of my wretthe wreke me I will.

Do open, porter, þe porte of þis prowde place   155
  That I may passe to youre princes to proue for   f.126ᵛ
                                              youre prowe.

| Janitor | Go hense þou glorand gedlyng, God geue þe ille grace, |

Go hense þou glorand gedlyng, God geue þe ille grace,
  Thy glyfftyng is so grymly þou gars my harte growe.

Judas   Goode sir, be toward þis tyme and tarie noght my trace,
  For I haue tythandis to telle.

Janitor   Ʒa, som tresoune I trowe,   160
For I fele by a figure in youre fals face
  It is but foly to feste affeccioun in ʒou.
    For Mars he hath morteysed his mark,
      Eftir all lynes of my lore,
    And sais ʒe are wikkid of werk   165
    And bothe a strange theffe and a stark.

Judas   Sir, þus at my berde and ʒe berk
    It semes it schall sitte yow full sore.

Janitor   Say bittilbrowed bribour, why blowes þou such boste?
  Full false in thy face in faith can I fynde.   170
Þou arte combered in curstnesse and caris to þis coste,
  To marre men of myght haste þou marked in thy mynde.

Judas   Sir, I mene of no malice but mirthe meve I moste.

Janitor   Say, on-hanged harlott, I holde þe vnhende,
  Thou lokist like a lurdayne his liffelod hadde loste.   f.127
  Woo schall I wirke þe away but þou wende.   176

Judas   A, goode sir, take tente to my talkyng þis tyde,
    For tythandis full trew can I telle.

Janitor   Say brethell, I bidde þe abide,
    Þou chaterist like a churle þat can chyde.   180

Judas   Ʒa sir, but and þe truthe schulde be tryed
    Of myrthe are þer materes I mell,

---

141.   might same haue] *He* might haue
149.   And þerfore] *K* Þerfore
173.   moste] *Hoᶦ; MS, TS* muste

	For thurgh my dedis youre dugeperes fro dere may be	
	drawen.	
Janitor	What, demes þou till oure dukes that doole schulde be	
	dight?	
Judas	Nay sir, so saide I noght.	184a
	If I be callid to counsaille þat cause schall be knawen	185
	Emang þat comely companye, to clerke and to knyght.	
Janitor	Byde me here bewchere or more blore be blowen,	
	And I schall buske to þe benke wher baneres are bright	
	And saie vnto oure souereynes, or seede more be sawen,	
	Þat swilke a seege as þiselff sewes to þer sight.	190
	My lorde nowe of witte þat is well,	
	I come for a cas to be kydde.	
Pilatus	We, speke on and spare not þi spell.	
Cayphas	Ȝa, and if vs mystir te mell,	
	Sen ȝe bere of bewté þe bell,	195
	Blythely schall we bowe as ȝe bidde.	f.127ˣ

	Sir, withoute þis abatyng þer houes as I hope	
Janitor	A hyne helte-full of ire, for hasty he is.	
Pilatus	What comes he fore?	
Janitor	I kenne hym noght, but he is cladde	
	in a cope,	
	He cares with a kene face vncomely to kys.	200
Pilatus	Go gete hym þat his greffe we grathely may grope,	
	So no oppen langage be goyng amys.	
Janitor	Comes on bylyue to my lorde and if þe liste to lepe,	
	But vttir so thy langage that þou lette noght þare blys.	
Judas	That lorde, sirs, myght susteyne ȝoure seele	205
	Þat floure is of fortune and fame.	
Pilatus	Welcome, thy wordis are but wele.	
Cayphas	Say, harste þou knave, can þou not knele?	
Pilatus	Loo, here may men faute in you fele,	
	Late be sir youre scornyng, for schame.	210

	Bot bewshere, be noȝt abayst to byde at þe bar.	
Judas	Before you sirs to be brought abowte haue I bene,	
	And allway for youre worschippe.	
Anna	Say, wotte þou any were?	
Judas	Of werke sir þat hath wretthid ȝou I wotte what I meene,	

183. drawen] *TS; MS* drawe
184a. *Extra-metrical; see Note*
191–2. *Ruled off from 190 and misassigned Judas; misassignment deleted*
194. te] *This ed; TS* to (*conj*)
197. withoute þis] *K* withouten
198. *Erroneously ruled off from 197 (main scribe)*
   hyne] *Conj TS (glossary); MS* hyve
211. bar] *TS; MS* bay

f.128

But I wolde make a marchaundyse youre myscheffe to marre.

Pilatus   And may þou soo?

Judas   Els madde I such maistries to mene. 216

Anna   Þan kennes þou of som comberaunce oure charge for to
                                                    chere?

For cosyne, þou art cruell.

Judas   My cause sir is kene.

For if ȝe will bargayne or by,
      Jesus þis tyme will I selle ȝou.   220

I Doctor   My blissing sone haue þou forthy –
      Loo, here is a sporte for to spye.

Judas   And hym dar I hete ȝou in hye,
      If ȝe will be toward I telle ȝou.

Pilatus   What hytist þou?

Judas   Judas Scariott.

Pilatus   Þou art a juste man   225
      Þat will Jesus be justified by oure jugement.
      But howe-gates bought schall he be? Bidde furthe thy
                                                    bargayne.

Judas   But for a litill betyng to bere fro þis bente.

Pilatus   Now what schall we pay?

Judas   Sir, thirti pens and plete, no more þan.

Pilatus   Say, ar ȝe plesid of this price he preces to present?   230

II Doctor Ellis contrarie we oure consciens, consayue sen we can f.128ᵛ
      Þat Judas knawes hym culpabill.

Pilatus   I call ȝou consent.

      But Judas, a knott for to knytt,
            Wilte þou to þis comenaunt accorde?

Judas   Ȝa, at a worde.

Pilatus   Welcome is it.   235

II Miles   Take þerof, a traytour tyte.

I Miles   Now, leue ser, late no man wete
      How þis losell laykis with his lord.

Pilatus   Why, dwellis he with þat dochard whos dedis hase us drouyd?

I Miles   Þat hase he done ser and dose, no dowte is þis day.   240

Pilatus   Than wolde we knawe why þis knave þus cursidly contryued.

II Miles   Enquere hym, sen ȝe can best kenne if he contrarie.

Pilatus   Say man, to selle þi maistir what mysse hath he moved?

Judas   For of als mekill mony he made me delay,
      Of ȝou as I resayue schall but right be reproued.   245

216. mene] *TS; MS* meve
226. justified] *An otiose b follows*
227. *Erroneously ruled off from 226 (main scribe)*
232. hym] *TS; MS* hm
236. þerof] *This ed; TS* þee of *(conj)*
242. contrarie] *TS conj* contraye, *He* gaynsaye

Anna	I rede noght þat ȝe reken vs oure rewle so to ray,
	For þat þe false fende schall þe fang.
I Miles	When he schall wante of a wraste.
I Doctor	To whome wirke we wittandly wrang.
II Doctor	Tille hym bot ȝe hastely hang.
III Doctor	Ȝoure langage ȝe lay oute to lang.
	But Judas, we trewly þe trast,

f.129

250

For truly þou moste lerne vs that losell to lache,
    Or of lande thurgh a lirte that lurdayne may lepe.

Judas	I schall ȝou teche a token hym tyte for to take
	Wher he is thryngand in þe thrang, withouten any threpe.
I Miles	We knawe hym noght.
Judas	Take kepe þan þat caytiffe to catche
	The whilke þat I kisse.
II Miles	Þat comes wele þe, curious, I cleepe!

255

But ȝitt to warne vs wisely allwayes muste ȝe wacche.
Whan þou schall wende forthwith we schall walke a wilde
                                    hepe,

	And therfore besye loke now þou be.
Judas	Ȝis, ȝis, a space schall I spie vs
	Als sone as þe sonne is sette, as ȝe see.
I Miles	Go forthe, for a traytoure ar ȝe.
II Miles	Ȝa, and a wikkid man.
I Doctor	Why, what is he?
II Doctor	A losell ser, but lewté shuld lye vs.

261

265

He is trappid full of trayne, þe truthe for to trist,
    I holde it but folye his faythe for to trowe.

Pilatus	Abide in my blyssing and late youre breste,
	For it is beste for oure bote in bayle for to bowe.
	And Judas, for oure prophite we praye þe be prest.
Judas	Ȝitt hadde I noght a peny to purvey for my prowe.
Pilatus	Þou schalte haue delyueraunce belyue at þi list,
	So þat þou schall haue liking oure lordschipp to loue.
	And therfore Judas mende þou thy mone
	And take þer þi siluere all same.
Judas	Ȝa, nowe is my grete greffe ouere-gone.
I Miles	Be lyght þan.
Judas	Ȝis, latte me allone,
	For tytte schall þat taynte be tone
	And þerto jocounde and joly I am.

f.129ᵛ

270

275

280

247. false] *Ho¹; MS, TS* fales
    fende] *TS; MS* frende
250. hastely hang] *TS; MS* hastely hym hang
252–4. *Original assignment to Pilatus deleted by a later hand; see the Note*
268. faythe] *Suppl TS*
269. late] *Ha* late be
275. *Lineation TS; two lines in MS*
280. Caret hic *in a first later hand to right;* Janitor & Judas *to right of this in hand of J.
    Clerke*

Pilatus	Judas, to holde þi behest be hende for oure happe,
	And of vs helpe and vpholde we hete þe to haue.
Judas	I schall bekenne ʒou his corse in care for to clappe.
Anna	And more comforte in þis case we coveyte not to craue.
I Miles	Fro we may reche þat rekeles his ribbis schall we rappe, 285
	And make þat roy or we rest for rennyng to raffe. f.130
Pilatus	Nay sirs, all if ʒe scourge hym ʒe schende noʒt his schappe,
	For if þe sotte be sakles vs sittis hym to saue.
	Wherfore when ʒe go schall to gete hym
	Vnto his body brew ʒe no bale. 290
II Miles	Our liste is fro leping to lette hym,
	But in youre sight sownde schall ve sette hym.
Pilatus	Do flitte nowe forthe till ʒe fette hym
	With solace all same to youre sale.

XXVII The Bakers

The Last Supper

Jesus	Pees be both be day and nyght	f.131ᵛ
	Vntill þis house and till all þat is here.	
	Here will I holde as I haue hight	
	The feeste of Paas with frendis in feere.	
Marcelus	Maistir, we haue arayed full right	5
	Seruise þat semes for youre sopere.	
	Oure lambe is roste and redy dight,	
	As Moyses lawe will lely lere.	
Jhesus	That is, ilke man þat has	
	Pepill in his awne posté	10
	Shall roste a lambe at Paas,	
	To hym and his meyné.	

284.   Caret hic *to right in a later hand*
292.   ve] *This ed; TS* we *(conj)*
294+   Finis *added by J. Clerke. Bottom half of f.130 blank; ff.130ᵛ 131 blank*

   1.   Jesus] *Suppl TS. Originally unassigned; J. Clerke has inserted* Deus *above the first line. At top right corner of leaf in a later hand* caret hic principio

Andreas	Maistir, þe custome wele we knawe
	That with oure elthers euer has bene,
	How ilke man with his meyné awe
	To roste a lambe and ete it clene.
Jesus	I thanke ȝou sothtly of youre sawe,
	For ȝe saye as youreselffe has sene.
	Thcrfore array ȝou all on rawe,
	Myselfe schall parte itt ȝou betwene.
	Wherfore I will þat ȝe
	Ette þerof cucre-ilkone,
	The remelaunt parted schall be
	To þe poure þat purueyse none.

15

20

Of Moyses lawes here make I an ende   25
    In som party, but noght in all.
My comaundement schall othirwise be kende
    With þam þat men schall craftely call.
But þe lambe of Pase þat here is spende,   f.132
    Whilke Jewes vses grete and small,   30
Euere forward nowe I itt deffende
    Fro Cristis folke what so befall.
        In þat stede schall he sette
            A newe lawe vs bytwene,
        But who þerof schall ette   35
            Behoues to be wasshed clene.

For þat new lawe whoso schall lere,
 •In harte þam bus be clene and chaste.
Marcelle myn awne discipill dere,
    Do vs haue watir here in hast.   40

Marcellus	Maistir, it is all redy here,
	And here a towell clene to taste.
Jesus	Commes forthe with me all in feere,
	My wordis schall noght be wroght in waste.
	Settis youre feete fourth, late see,
	They schall be wasshen sone.
Petrus	A, lorde, with þi leue, of þee
	Þat dede schall noȝt be done.

45

I schall neuere make my membres mete,
    Of my souerayne seruice to see.   50

Jesus	Petir, bott if þou latte me wasshe þi feete
	Þou getis no parte in blisse with me.
Petrus	A, mercy lorde and maistir swete,
	Owte of þat blisse þat I noght be —
	Wasshe on my lorde to all be wete,
	Both hede and hande, beseke I þe.

55

28+ *Catchword* But þe lambe of pase
29. *Quire R begins*
        Pase] *This ed;* TS Pasc

Jesus	Petir, þou wotiste noȝt ȝitt
	What þis werke will bemene.
	Hereaftir schall þou witte,
	And so schall ȝe all bedene.

f.132ᵛ
60

Tunc lauat manus.

Ȝoure lorde and maistir ȝe me call,
  And so I am, all welthe to welde.
Here haue I knelid vnto ȝou all,
  To wasshe youre feete as ȝe haue feled.
Ensaumple of me take ȝe schall   65
  Euer for to ȝeme in ȝouþe and elde,
To be buxsome in boure and hall,
  Ilkone for to bede othir belde.
    For all-if ȝe be trewe
      And lele of loue ilkone,   70
    Ȝe schall fynde othir ay newe
      To greue whan I am gone.

Jacobus	Now sen oure maistir sais he schall
	Wende and will not telle vs whedir,
	Whilke of vs schall be princepall?
Jesus	Late loke now whils we dwell togedir.
	I wotte youre will both grete and small,

75

I wotte youre will both grete and small,
  And youre high hartis I here þam hedir;
To whilke of ȝou such fare schulde fall
  Þat myght ȝe carpe when ȝe come thedir,   80
    Where it so schulde be tyde
      Of such materes to melle.
    But first behoues ȝou bide
      Fayndyngis full ferse and felle.

Here schall I sette ȝou for to see   85
  Þis ȝonge childe for insaumpills seere,
Both meke and mylde of harte is he,
  And fro all malice, mery of chere;
So meke and mylde but if ȝe be
    [· · ·   · · ·
  · · ·   · · ·
    · · ·   · · ·
      · · ·   · · ·
        · · ·   · · ·
          · · ·   · · ·
            · · ·   · · ·]

[A leaf is missing from the MS at this point. The play is likely to have
gone on to deal with the episode of the bread and the wine, the

60+   *SD added to right by J. Clerke*
61.   Deus *written to right by J. Clerke*

institution of the Eucharist, perhaps implying reference to the doctrinally sensitive issue of Transubstantiation. The leaf could for this reason have been deliberately removed during the religious controversies of the sixteenth century. Assuming that the metrical scheme remained the same, it is probable that 53 lines have been lost: seven to complete the fragmentary stanza beginning at line 85, ten preceding the fragmentary stanza ending at line 91, and three complete stanzas. The text resumes at the point where Jesus has said 'One of you shall betray me'. Lines 90–1 are the words spoken by Jesus to Judas in John xiii. 27, just after he has indicated the betrayer by giving him the sop.]

[. . .   . . .
     . . .   . . .
  . . .   . . .
     . . .   . . .
     . . .   . . .
        . . .   . . .
  . . .   . . .
     . . .   . . .
        . . .   . . .
     . . .   . . .]

[*Jesus*]	*Quod facis fac cicius:*	f.133
	Þat þou schall do, do sone.	91

Thomas	Allas, so wilsom wightis as we	
	Was neuere in worlde walkand in wede,	
	Oure maistir sais his awne meyné	
	Has betrayed hym to synfull seede.	95
Jacobus	A, Jhon, sen þou sittist nexte his kne,	
	We pray þe spire hym for oure spede.	
Johannes	*Domine, quis est qui tradit te?*	
	Lord, who schall do þat doulfull dede?	
	Allas, oure playe is paste,	100
	Þis false forward is feste.	
	I may no lenger laste,	
	For bale myn herte may breste.	

Judas	Now is tyme to me to gang,	
	For here begynnes noye all of newe.	105
	My fellaws momellis þame emang	
	Þat I schulde alle þis bargayne brewe –	
	And certis þai schall noȝt wene it wrang.	
	To þe prince of prestis I schall pursue,	
	And þei schall lere hym othir ought long	110
	That all his sawes sore schall hym rewe.	
	I wotte whedir he remoues	
	With his meyné ilkone,	

96. *Jacobus*] *TS; MS Jacobus Maior*
       Jhon] *K; MS, TS* I hope
100. is] *TS; MS* is is

I schall telle to þe Jewes
And tyte he schalle be tane.   115

Jesus   I warne ȝou nowe my frendis free,
Sese to ther sawes þat I schall say:
The fende is wrothe with ȝou and me
And will ȝou marre if þat he may.
But Petir, I haue prayed for þe,   120
So þat þou schall noȝt drede his dray;   f.133ᵛ
And comforte þou þis meyné
And wisse hem whan I am gone away.

Petrus   A, lorde, where wilte þou lende?
I schall lende in þat steede,   125
And with þe schall I wende
Euermore in lyffe and dede.

Andreas   No wordely drede schall me withdrawe
That I schall with þe leue and dye.
Thomas   Certis, so schall we all on rawe,   130
Ellis mekill woo were we worthy.
Jesus   Petir, I saie to þe þis sawe
Þat þou schalte fynde no fantasie:
Þis ilke nyght or þe cokkys crowe
Shall þou thre tymes my name denye,   135
And saye þou knewe me neuere
Nor no meyné of myne.

Petrus   Allas lorde, me were lever
Be putte to endles pyne.

Jesus   As I yow saie so schall it bee,   140
Ye nedis non othir recours to craue.
All þat in worlde is wretyn of me
Shall be fulfilled, for knyght or knave.
I am þe herde, þe schepe are ȝe,
And whane þe herde schall harmes haue   145
The flokke schall be full fayne to flee,
And socoure seke þameselffe to saue.
Ȝe schall whan I am slayne
In grete myslykyng lende,   f.134
But whanne I ryse agayne   150
Þan schall youre myrthe be mende.

Ȝe haue bene bowne my bale to bete,
Therfore youre belde ay schall I be.
And for ȝe did in drye and wete
My comaundementis in ilke contré,   155

124.   wilte þou] *K* þou wilte
148.   slayne] *He; MS, TS* allone
151.   mende] *TS; MS* mened

The kyngdome of heuen I you behete
Euen as my fadir has highte itt me.
With gostely mete þere schall ʒe mete
And on twelffe seeges sitte schall ʒe,
For ʒe trewlye toke ʒeme   160
In worlde with me to dwell,
There shall ʒe sitte to deme
Xij kyndis of Israell.

But firste ʒe schall be wille of wone,
And mo wathes þen ʒe of wene   165
Fro tyme schall come þat I be tone,
Þan schall ʒe turne away with tene.
And loke þat ʒe haue swerdis ilkone,
And whoso haues non ʒou bytwene
Shall selle his cote and bye hym one,   170
Þus bidde I þat ʒe do bedene.
Satcheles I will ʒe haue,
And stones to stynte all striffe,
Youreselffe for to saue
In lenghyng of youre liff.   175

Andreas   Maistir, we haue here swerdis twoo
Vs with to saue on sidis seere.
Jesus   Itt is inowe, ʒe nedis no moo,
For fro all wathis I schall ʒou were.   f.134ᵛ
Butt ryse now vppe, for we will goo,   180
By þis owre enemyes ordand are;
My fadir saide it schall be soo,
His bidding will I noʒt forbere.
Loke ʒe lere forthe þis lawe
Als ʒe haue herde of me,   185
Alle þat wele will itt knawe
Ay blessid schall þei bee.

158. ʒe] *K; MS, TS* we
162. to deme] *Ha; MS* by dene, *TS* be-deme
173. stones] *TS; MS* stones *or* stoues, *K* swordes
176. we] *TS; MS* ʒe
177. Vs] *TS; MS* Vis
187. Hic caret *to left in a first later hand;* novo loquela *added subsequently by J. Clerke*
187+ *Bottom half of f.134ᵛ blank; ff.135, 135ᵛ blank*

The Agony in the Garden and the Betrayal

Jesus	Beholde, my discipulis þat deyne is and dere,	f.136
	My flesshe dyderis and daris for doute of my dede.	
	Myne enemyes will newly be neghand full nere	
	With all þe myght if þei may to marre my manhede.	
	But sen ȝe are forwakid and wanderede in were,	5
	Loke ȝe sette ȝou doune rathely and reste ȝoue, I reede.	
	Beis noȝt heuy in ȝoure hertis, but holde yow even here	
	And bidis me a stounde stille in þis same steede.	
	Beeis witty and wyse in youre wandyng	
	So þat ȝe be wakand alway,	10
	And lokis nowe prestely ȝe pray	
	To my fadir, þat ȝe falle in no fandyng.	
Petrus	Ȝis lorde, at thy bidding full baynly schall we abide,	
	For þou arte boote of oure bale and bidis for þe best.	
Johannes	Lorde, all oure helpe and oure hele, that is noght to hyde,	15
	In þe – oure faythe and oure foode – all hollye is feste.	
Jacobus	Qwat way is he willid in þis worlde wyde,	
	Whedir is he walked, estewarde or weste?	
Petrus	Ȝaa sirs, I schall saye ȝou, sittis vs doune on euery ilka side,	
	And late vs nowe rathely here take oure reste;	f.136ᵛ
	My lymmys are heuy as any leede.	21
Johannes	And I muste slepe, doune muste I lye.	
Jacobus	In faithe felawes, right so fare I,	
	I may no lenger holde vppe my hede.	
Petrus	Oure liffe of his lyolty his liffe schall he lose,	25
	Vnkyndely be crucified and naylyd to a tree.	
Jesus	Baynly of my blissing youre eghen ȝe vnclose,	
	So þat ȝe falle in no fandyng for noght þat may be,	
	But prayes fast.	
Johannes	Lorde, som prayer þou kende vs,	30
	That somwhat myght mirthe vs or mende vs.	

    1. *Jesus*] *Suppl TS*
      De nouo facto *added to right by a later hand*
  27. of] *K* in
  30. kende] *He; MS, TS* kenne. *? also read* prayer I wolde þou

Jacobus	Fro all fandyng vnfaythfull þou fende vs
	Here in þis worlde of liffe whille we laste.

Jesus I schall kenne ȝou and comforte ȝou and kepe ȝou from
care.
ȝe schall be broughte, wete ȝe wele, fro bale vnto blisse.35
Petrus ȝaa, but lorde, and youre willis were witte wolde we more,
Of this prayer so precious late vs noȝt mys
We beseke þe.
Johannes For my felows and me all in feere,
Some prayer þat is precious to lere. 40
Jacobus Vnto thy fadir þat moste is of poure
Som solace of socoure to sende þe.

[A leaf is wanting in the MS at this point, conjugate with the one lost between lines 89 and 90 of the preceding play. It probably carried some 40 lines, but the precise subject matter is open to question. Lines 30ff. depart from the usual narrative of the Agony in the Garden by introducing the disciples' request that Jesus teach them a prayer, and this he presumably goes on to do in the lost passage. The playwright may have had in mind the incident related in Luke xi. 2–4, where the disciples make just such a request and Jesus responds by teaching them the Lord's Prayer. In lines 43ff. Jesus is once more alone, praying to the Father.]

[Jesus] Þe nowys þat me neghed hase it nedis not to neuen, f.137
For all wate ȝe full wele what wayes I haue wente.
Instore me and strenghe with a stille steuen, 45
I pray þe interly þou take entent
Þou menske my manhed with mode.
My flessh is full dredand for drede,
For my jorneys of my manhed
I swete now both watir and bloode. 50

Þes Jewes hase mente in þer mynde full of malice
And pretende me to take withouten any trespasse.
But fadir, as þou wate wele, I mente neuere amys,
In worde nor in werk I neuer worthy was.
Als þou arte bote of all bale and belder of blisse 55
And all helpe and hele in thy hande hase,
Þou mensk thy manhede, þou mendar of mysse,
And if it possible be this payne myght I ouerpasse.
And fadir, if þou se it may noght,
Be it worthely wrought 60

38. *He would assign to Johannes*
49. my'] *K* þe
54. worthy] *He* unworthy
57. thy] *K* my
60. *He would omit*

Euen at thyne awne will,
Euermore both myldely and still,
With worschippe allway be it wroght.

Vnto my discipillis will I go agayne,
Kyndely to comforte þam þat kacchid are in care.   65
What, are ȝe fallen on slepe now euerilkone
And þe passioun of me in mynde hase no more?   f.137ᵛ
What, wille ȝe leue me þus lightly and latte me allone
In sorowe and in sighyng þat sattillis full sore?
To whome may I meue me and make nowe my mone?   70
I wolde þat ȝe wakened, and your will wore.
Do Petir sitte vppe nowe, late se,
Þou arte strongly stedde in þis stoure.
Might þou noght þe space of an owre
Haue wakid nowe mildely with me?   75

Petrus   Ȝis lorde, with youre leue nowe will we lere
Full warely to were ȝou fro alle wandynge.
Jesus   Beeis wakand and prayes faste all in fere
To my fadir, þat ȝe falle in no fanding,
For þe euelle spirit is neghand full nere   80
That will ȝou tarie at þis tyme with his tentyng.
And I will wende þer I was withouten any were,
But bidis me here baynly in my blissing.
Agayne to þe mounte I will gang
Ȝitt eftesones where I was ere,   85
But loke þat ȝe cacche ȝow no care,
For lely I schall noȝt dwelle lange.

Þou fadir þat all formed hase with fode for to fill,
I fele by my ferdnes my flessh wolde full fayne
Be torned fro this turnement and takyn þe vntill,   90
For mased is manhed in mode and in mayne.
But if þou se sothly þat þi sone sill
Withouten surffette of synne þus sakles be slayne,
Be it worthly wroght even at thyne awne will,
For fadir, att þi bidding am I buxum and bayne.   95
Now wightely agayne will I wende   f.138
Vnto my discipilis so dere.
What, slepe ȝe so faste all in fere?
I am ferde ȝe mon faile of youre frende.

But ȝitt will I leue ȝou and late you allone   100
And eftesones þere I was agayne will I wende.

80. þe] *Suppl Ho¹*
spirit] *Ho¹; MS, TS* spiritis
91. is manhed] *K* is my manhed
95+ *Catchword* Now wightly agayne
96. *Quire S begins*

Vnto my fadir of myght now make I my mone,
  As þou arte saluer of all sore som socoure me sende.
Þe passioun they purpose to putte me vppon,
  My flesshe is full ferde and fayne wolde defende. 105
At þi wille be itt wrought worþely in wone;
  Haue mynde of my manhed my mode for to mende,
    Some comforte me kythe in þis case.
And fadir, I schall dede taste, I will it noȝt deffende –
  Ȝitt yf thy willis be, spare me a space. 110

[And seis . . .   . . . yght
  With rappes full rudely . . .   . . . the rode rente]

Angelus   Vnto þe maker vnmade þat moste is of myght
  Be louyng ay-lastand in light þat is lente.
Thy fadir þat in heuen is moste he vppon highte, 115
  Thy sorowes for to sobir to þe he hase me sente.
For dedis þat man done has thy dede schall be dight,
  And þou with turmentis be tulyd – but take nowe entente,
    Thy bale schall be for þe beste,
      Thurgh þat mannys mys schall be mende. f.138ᵛ
      Þan schall þou withouten any ende 121
    Rengne in thy rialté full of reste.

Jesus   Now if my flessh ferde be, fadir I am fayne
  Þat myne angwisshe and my noyes are nere at an ende.
Vnto my discipilis go will I agayne, 125
  Kyndely to comforte þam þat mased is in þer mynde.
Do slepe ȝe nowe sauely, and I schall ȝou sayne.
  Wakyns vppe wightely and late vs hens wende,
For als tyte mon I be taken with tresoune and with trayne;
  My flesshe is full ferde and fayne wolde deffende. 130
    Full derfely my dede schall be dight,
      And als sone as I am tane
      Þan schall ȝe forsake me ilkone,
    And saic neuere ȝe sawe me with sight.

Petrus   Nay sothely, I schall neuere my souereyne forsake, 135
  If I schulde for þe dede darfely here dye.
Johannes   Nay, such mobardis schall neuere man vs make,
  Erste schulde we dye all at onys.
Jacobus   Nowe in faith felows, so shulde I.
Jesus   Ȝa, but when tyme is betydde þanne men schalle me take,
  For all ȝoure hartely hetyng ȝe schall hyde ȝou in hy.f.139
Lyke schepe þat were scharid away schall ȝe schake, 141
  Þer schall none of ȝou be balde to byde me þan by.

104. Þe] *K* Of þe
111–2. *Erased, but partially recoverable under u-v light*
113. *Angelus*] and archangels *added by the 'Cutler-Nandicke' hand*
115. he] *Hoᶦ* hegh

Petrus	Nay sothely, whils I may vayle þe
	I schall were þe and wake þe,
	And if all othir forsake þe 145
	I schall neuere fayntely defayle þe.
Jesus	A, Petir, of swilke bostyng I rede þou late bee,
	For all thy kene carpyng full kenely I knawe.
	For ferde of myne enmyse þou schalte sone denye me
	Thries ȝitt full thraly or the cokkes crowe; 150
	For ferde of my fomen full fayne be for to flee,
	And for grete doute of þi dede þe to withdrawe.
Anna	Sir Cayphas, of youre counsaille do sone late vs now see,
	For lely it langes vs to luke vnto oure lawe.
	And therfore sir prestely I pray ȝou, 155
	Sen þat we are of counsaille ilkone,
	That Jesus þat traytoure wer tane;
	Do sone late se sir I pray ȝou.
Cayphas	In certayne sir, and sone schall I saye ȝou, f.139ᵛ
	I wolde wene by my witte þis werke wolde be wele. 160
	Late vs justely vs june tille Judas þe gente,
	For he kennes his dygnites full duly ilke a dele,
	ȝa, and beste wote I warande what wayes þat he is wente.
Anna	Now þis was wisely saide, als euer haue I seele;
	And sir, to youre saiyng I saddely will assente, 165
	Therfore take vs of oure knyghtis that is stedfast as stele
	And late Judas go lede þam belyffe wher that he last lente.
Cayphas	Full wele sir.
	Nowe Judas dere neghbour, drawe nere vs.
	Lo Judas, þus in mynd haue we ment: 170
	To take Jesus is oure entent,
	For þou muste lede vs and lere vs.
Judas	Sirs, I schall wisse you þe way euen at youre awne will—
	But loke þat ȝe haue many myghty men 174
	That is both strang and sterand, and stedde hym f.140
	stone stille.
Anna	ȝis Judas, but be what knowlache shall we þat corse kenne?

---

143. *Lineation TS. 143 written between 139 and 140 in the MS; between 142 and 144* ȝis
sothly quod Petir *(see the Note)*
þe] *TS; MS* þe I
148. For] *TS; MS* Fo
154. lawe] *TS; MS* lawys
158. se] *Interlined*
166–72. *Lineation TS; MS reverses the speeches of Anna and Cayphas*
168. *Taken as part of 169 in TS; separate line in MS*
173–81. *Lineation partially after TS. MS places 179–80 to away before 173–5 (ruling off
both sets of lines and assigning them 'Judas'). I schrew you all* þenne *(180) follows*
Why nay Judas *in MS (i.e., 181, assigned to Cayphas)*

Judas   Sirs, a tokenyng in þis tyme I schall telle ȝou vntill,
       But lokis by youre lewty no liffe ȝe hym lenne:
       Qwhat man som I kys þat corse schall ye kyll,
       And also beis ware þat he wil not away — I schrew you all
                                            þenne.

Cayphas   Why nay Judas,   181
       We purpose þe page schall not passe.
       Sir knyghtis in hy.

I Miles   Lorde, we are here.

Cayphas   Calles fourth youre felaws in feere
       And gose justely with gentill Judas.   185

I Miles   Come felaws, by youre faith, come forthe all faste
       And carpis with sir Cayphas, he comaundis me to call.

II Miles   I schrewe hym all his liffe þat loues to be last.

III Miles   Go we hens þan in hy and haste vs to þe halle.

IV Miles   Lorde, of youre will worthely wolde I witte what was't?   190

Cayphas   To take Jesus þat sawntrelle all same, þat ȝe schall.

I Miles   Lorde, to þat purpose I wolde þat we paste.

Anna   Ȝa, but loke þat ȝe be armed wele all,   f.140ᵛ
       The moste gentill of þe Jury schalle gyde ȝou.

Cayphas   Ȝa, and euery ilke a knyght in degré   195
       Both armed and harneysed ȝe be,
       To belde ȝou, and baynely go byde ȝou.

Anna   Ȝa, and þerfore sir Cayphas ȝe hye ȝou,
       Youre wirschippe ȝe wynne in þis cas.
       As ȝe are a lorde most lofsom of lyre   200
       Vndir sir Pilate þat lyfis in þis empire,
       Ȝone segger þat callis hymselffe a sire
       With tresoure and tene sall we taste hym.
       Of ȝone losell his bale schall he brewe,
       Do trottes on for þat traytoure apas   205
         In haste.

Cayphas   Nowe sirs, sen ȝe say my poure is most beste
       And hase all þis werke þus to wirke at my will,
       Now certayne I thinke not to rest,
       But solempnely youre will to fulfille   210
         Riȝt sone.

       Full tyte þe traytoure schall be tane —
       Sirs, knyghtis, ȝe hye ȝou ilkone,

---

183. *Character-designations TS; MS assigns first half to I Miles, second half to II Miles*
197. byde] *TS; MS* by
199. *Hic caret to right in a later hand*
204–6. *Ruled off from 203 by red line (main scribe), but not assigned*
204. he] *Suppl TS*
206. *Written to right of 204–5 in MS; TS treats as part of 210*
211. *Written to right of 209 in MS; TS treats as part of 209*

For in certayne þe losell schall be slane.
Sir Anna, I praye ȝou haue done.   215

Anna   Full redy tyte I schall be boune
                Þis journay for to go till.
              Als ȝe are a lorde of grete renoune
                ȝe spare hym not to spill,
                  Þe devill hym spede.   220
                    Go we with oure knyghtis in fere,
                    Lo, þay are arrayed and armed clere.
                    Sir knyghtis, loke ȝe be of full gud chere,
                Where ȝe hym see on hym take hede.

I Judeus   Goode tente to hym lorde schall we take,   f.141
                He schall banne þe tyme þat he was borne.   226
              All his kynne schall come to late,
                He schall noght skape withouten scorne
                  Fro vs in fere.
II Judeus   We schall hym seke both even and morne,   230
                Erly and late with full gode chere
                  Is oure entente.

III Judeus Stye nor strete we schall spare none,
                Felde nor towne, þus haue we mente
                  And boune in corde.   235

Cayphas   Malcus!
Malcus   A, ay, and I schulde be rewarde,
              And right als wele worthy were,
              Loo, for I bere light for my lorde.
Cayphas   A, sir, of youre speche lette, and late vs spede
              A space and of oure speche spare.   240
              And Judas, go fande þou before
              And wisely þou wisse þam þe way,
              For sothely sone schall we saye
              To make hym to marre vs no more.

Jesus   Now will þis oure be neghand full nere   245
                That schall certefie all þe soth þat I haue saide.
Cayphas   Go, fecche forth þe freyke for his forfette.
Judas   All hayll maistir, in faith, and felawes all in fere,
                With grete gracious gretyng on grounde be ȝe graied.
              I wolde aske you a kysse maistir, and youre willes were, 250
                For all my loue and my likyng is holy vppon ȝou layde.

214. slane] a *altered from* o *by a later hand*
227. to late] ? *read* to lack
230. We schall hym] *K* Hym for to
236. *Cayphas*] *Suppl this ed*
247. *Cayphas*] *Suppl this ed; see the Note*
249. ȝe] *Ho'; MS, TS* he

Jesus	Full hartely Judas, haue it even here,
	For with þis kissing is mans sone betrayed.
I Miles	Whe, stande traytoure, I telle þe for tane. f.141ᵛ
Cayphas	Whe, do knyghtis, go falle on before. 255
II Miles	3is maistir, moue þou no more,
	But lightly late vs allone.
III Miles	Allas, we are loste for leme of þis light.
Jesus	Saye 3e here, whome seke 3e? Do saye me, late see.
I Judeus	One Jesu of Nazareth I hope þat he hight. 260
Jesus	Beholdis all hedirward, loo here, I am hee.
I Miles	Stande dastarde, so darfely thy dede schall be dight,
	I will no more be abasshed for blenke of thy blee.
I Judeus	We, oute, I ame mased almost in mayne and in myght.
II Judeus	And I am ferde be my feyth and fayne wolde I flee, 265
	For such a si3t haue I not sene.
III Judeus	Þis leme it lemed so light,
	I saugh neuer such a si3t,
	Me meruayles what it may mene.
Jesus	Doo, whame seke 3e all same 3itt I saye? 270
I Judeus	One Jesus of Nazareth, hym wolde we neghe nowe.
Jesus	And I am he sothly.
Malcus	And þat schall I asaie,
	For þou schalte dye, dastard, sen þat it is þowe. f.142
Petrus	And I schall fande be my feythe þe for to flaye,
	Here with a lusshe, lordayne, I schalle þe allowe. 275
Malcus	We! Oute! All my deueres are done.
Petrus	Nay
	Traytoure, but trewly I schall trappe þe I trowe.
Jesus	Pees, Petir, I bidde þe,
	Melle þe nor move þe no more.
	For witte þou wele, and my willis were, 280
	I myght haue poure grete plenté
	Of aungellis full many to mustir my myght.
	Forthy putte vppe þi swerde full goodely agayne,
	For he þat takis vengeaunce all rewlid schall be right
	With purgens and vengeaunce þat voydes in vayne. 285
	Þou man þat is þus derede and doulfully dyght,
	Come hedir to me sauely and I schalle þe sayne.
	In þe name of my fadir þat in heuene is most vpon hight,
	Of thy hurtis be þou hole in hyde and in hane,
	Thurgh vertewe þi vaynes be at vayle. 290
Malcus	What, ille hayle, I hope þat I be hole –
	Nowe I schrewe hym þis tyme þat gyvis tale
	To touche þe for þi trauayle.

272b. *Malcus] Suppl K; MS, TS, assign whole line to Jesus*
276. *Lineation as conj TS; Nay begins 277 in MS*
278. *Jesus] Suppl by a later hand (? J. Clerke)*
285. purgens] *Ha* violence

I Judeus	Do felaws, be youre faithe, late vs fange on in fere, f.142ᵛ
	For I haue on þis hyne [. . . . . .] 295
II Miles	And I haue a loke on hym nowe – howe felawes, drawe nere.
III Miles	ʒis, by þe bonys þat þis bare, þis bourde schall he banne.
Jesus	Euen like a theffe heneusly hurle ʒe me here;
	I taught you in youre tempill, why toke ʒe me noʒt
	þanne?
	Now haues merkenes on molde all his power. 300
I Judeus	Do, do, laye youre handes belyue on þis lourdayne.
III Judeus	We, haue holde þis hauk in þi hende.
Malcus	Whe, ʒis felawes, be my faith he is fast.
IV Judeus	Vnto sir Cayphas I wolde þat he past.
	Farewele, for, iwisse, we will wende. 305

XXIX The Bowers and Fletchers

Christ before Annas and Caiaphas

Cayphas	Pees bewshers, I bid no jangelyng ʒe make, f.144
	And sese sone of youre sawes and se what I saye,
	And trewe tente vnto me þis tyme þat ʒe take,
	For I am a lorde lerned lelly in youre lay.
	By connyng of clergy and casting of witte 5
	Full wisely my wordis I welde at my will,
	So semely in seete me semys for to sitte
	And þe lawe for to lerne you and lede it by skill,
	Right sone.
	What wyte so will oght with me 10
	Full frendly in feyth am I foune;

295. *Latter half of line missing*
300. merkenes] *Ho'; MS, TS* mekenes
302. hende] *He; MS, TS* handis
304. past] *TS; MS* passen
305. iwisse] *K; MS, TS* I wisse
  wende] *He; MS, TS* wenden
305+ *Rest of f.142ᵛ blank; ff.143, 143ᵛ blank*

  1. *Cayphas] Suppl by J. Clerke*
  9. *To right of 7 in MS; added to 10 in TS*

Come of, do tyte late me see
  Howe graciously I shall graunte hym his bone.

Ther is nowder lorde ne lady lerned in þe lawe,
  Ne bisshoppe ne prelate þat preued is for pris,   15
Nor clerke in þe courte þat connyng will knawe,
  With wisdam may were hym in worlde is so wise.

I haue þe renke and þe rewle of all þe ryall,
  To rewle it by right als reasoune it is.
All domesmen on dese awe for to dowte me   20
  That hase thaym in bandome in bale or in blis;
    Wherfore takes tente to my tales, and lowtis vnto me.

And therfore sir knyghtis –
Tunc dicunt Lorde.
I charge you chalange youre rightis,
To wayte both be day and by nyghtis   25
  Of þe bringyng of a boy into bayle.

I Miles	Yis lorde, we schall wayte if any wonderes walke,
	And freyne howe youre folkis fare þat are furth ronne.
II Miles	We schall be bayne at youre bidding and it not to-balk
	Yf þei presente you þat boy in a bande boune. 30
Anna	Why syr, and is þer a boy þat will noght lowte to youre
	bidding?
Cayphas	Ya sir, and of þe coriousenesse of þat karle þer is carping,

	But I haue sente for þat segge halfe for hethyng.	
Anna	What wondirfull werkis workis þat wighte?	f.144ᵛ
Cayphas	Seke men and sori he sendis siker helyng –	35
	And to lame men – and blynde he sendis þer sight.	

Of croked crepillis þat we knawe
  Itt is to here grete wondering,
How þat he helis þame all on rawe,
  And all thurgh his false happenyng.   40

I am sorie of a sight
  Þat egges me to ire,
Oure lawe he brekis with all his myght,
  Þat is moste his desire.

---

18. ryall] *TS conj* ryalté
22–6. *For conjectures see Ha, He, Ho¹*
23+ *SD added to right by J. Clerke*
29. to-balk] *This ed; TS* to balk
35–6. *For conjectures see K, Ho³, Ho⁴*

	Oure Sabott day he will not safe	45
	But is aboute to bringe it downe,	
	And therfore sorowe muste hym haue	
	May he be kacched in felde or towne,	
	For his false stevyn,	
	He defamys fowly þe Godhed	50
	And callis hymselffe God sone of hevene.	

Anna   I haue goode knowlache of þat knafe:
          Marie me menys his modir highte,
          And Joseph his fadir as God me safe
          Was kidde and knowen wele for a wrighte.   55

          But o thyng me mervayles mckill ouere all,
          Of diuerse dedis þat he has done –
Cayphas With wicche-crafte he fares withall
          Sir, þat schall ʒe se full sone.

          Oure knyghtis þai are furth wente   60
          To take hym with a traye,
          By þis I holde hym shente,
          He can not wende away.

Anna   Wolde ʒe, sir, take youre reste –
          This day is comen on hande –   65
          And with wyne slake youre thirste?
          Þan durste I wele warande   f.145

          ʒe schulde haue tithandis sone
          Of þe knyghtis þat are gone,
          And howe þat þei haue done   70
          To take hym by a trayne.

          And putte all þought away
          And late youre materes reste.
Cayphas I will do as ʒe saie,
          Do gette vs wyne of þe best.   75

I Miles My lorde, here is wyne þat will make you to wynke,
          Itt is licoure full delicious my lorde, and you like.
          Wherfore I rede drely a draughte þat ʒe drynke,
          For in þis contré, þat we knawe, iwisse ther is none slyke,
                Wherfore we counsaile you this cuppe sauerly for to
                                                                kisse.

Cayphas Do on dayntely and dresse me on dees   81
          And hendely hille on me happing,

75–6.   Hic caret *in a first later hand to right of* 76, *deleted.* Hic *to left of* 76, *and* Hic For
be we ones well wett / The better we will reste *to right of* 75–6, *in Clerke's hand*
80.   *Lineation this ed; two lines in MS, TS*

And warne all wightis to be in pees
For I am late layde vnto napping.

Anna   My lorde, with youre leue, and it like you, I passe.   85
Cayphas Adiew be unte, as þe manere is.

Mulier   Sir knyghtys, do kepe þis boy in bande,
For I will go witte what it may mene,
Why þat yone wighte was hym folowand
Erly and late, morne and ene.   90

He will come nere, he will not lette,
He is a spie, I warand, full bolde.
III Miles It semes by his sembland he had leuere be sette   f.145ᵛ
By þe feruent fire to fleme hym fro colde.

Mulier   Ya, but and ȝe wiste as wele as I   95
What wonders þat þis wight has wrought,
And thurgh his maistir sorssery,
Full derfely schulde his deth be bought.

IV Miles Dame, we haue hym nowe at will
Þat we haue longe tyme soughte,   100
Yf othir go by vs still
Þerfore we haue no thought.

Mulier   Itt were grete skorne þat he schulde skape
Withoute he hadde resoune and skill,
He lokis lurkand like an nape,   105
I hope I schall haste me hym tille.

Thou caytiffe, what meves þe stande
So stabill and stille in þi thoght?
Þou hast wroght mekill wronge in londe
And wondirfull werkis haste þou wroght.   110

A lorell, a leder of lawe,
To sette hym and suye has þou soght.
Stande furth and threste in yone thrawe,
Thy maistry þou bryng vnto noght.

Wayte nowe, he lokis like a brokke   115
Were he in a bande for to bayte,

85–6. *Lineation this ed; four lines in MS, TS*
87. *Mulier] This ed; MS, TS I Mulier; see the Note*
87ff. *Stanzas no longer indicated from this point to end of play in TS. For discussion, see He, p. 23, whose proposed arrangement is in part followed here*
88. *mene] He preue (reading eue in 90)*
90. *ene] Conj TS; MS eue or ene*
97. *And] K All*

   Or ellis like an nowele in a stok
    Full preualy his pray for to wayte.

Petrus Woman, thy wordis and thy wýnde þou not waste,
    Of his company never are I was kende.   120
   Þou haste þe mismarkid, trewly be traste,
    Wherfore of þi misse þou þe amende.

Mulier Þan gaynesaies þou here þe sawes þat þou saide,
    How he schulde clayme to be callid God sonne,
   And with þe werkis þat he wrought whils he walked f.146
    Baynly at oure bydding alway to be bonne.   126

Petrus I will consente to youre sawes, what schulde I saye more?
    For women are crabbed – þat comes þem of kynde.
   But I saye as I firste saide, I sawe hym neuere are, 129
    But as a frende of youre felawschippe shall ye me aye
                   fynde.

Malchus Herke, knyghtis þat are knawen in this contré as we kenne,
    Howe yone boy with his boste has brewed mekill bale.
   He has forsaken his maistir before ȝone womenne,
    But I schall preue to ȝou pertly and telle you my tale.

   I was presente with pepull whenne prese was full prest 135
    To mete with his maistir with mayne and with myght,
   And hurled hym hardely and hastely hym arreste,
    And in bandis full bittirly bande hym sore all þat nyght.

   And of tokenyng of trouth schall I telle yowe
    Howe yone boy with a brande brayede me full nere – 140
   Do move of thez materes emelle yowe –
    For swiftely he swapped of my nere.

   His maistir with his myght helyd me all hole,
    That by no syne I cowthe see no man cowþe it witten, f.146ᵛ
   And þan badde hym bere pees in euery-ilke bale, 145
    For he þat strikis with a swerd with a swerde schall be
                 smitten.

   Late se whedir grauntest þou gilte:
    Do speke oon and spare not to telle vs

124+ *Catchword* And þe werkis þat he wroght
125. *Quire T begins*
   walked] *He;* MS, TS walketh in þis flodde
128. þat] *TS;* MS þat þat, þat² *deleted*
130. youre] *He;* MS, TS oure
144. witten] *He* witte (*reading* smitte *in 146*)
145. þan] *TS;* MS þon
146. smitten] *Ha;* MS, TS streken, *He* smitte
147. grauntest þou] *K* þou grauntest þi

Or full faste I schall fonde þe flitte,
The soth but þou saie here emelle vs.   150

Come of, do tyte late me see nowe,
In sauyng of thyselffe fro schame
[. . .   . . .]
3a, and also for beryng of blame.

Petrus   I was neuere with hym in werke þat he wroght,
          In worde nor in werke, in will nor in dede.   155
          I knawe no corse þat 3e haue hidir brought,
          In no courte of this kith, yf I schulde right rede.

Malchus   Here sirs howe he sais, and has forsaken
          His maistir to þis woman here twyes,
          And newly oure lawe has he taken—   160
          Thus hath he denyed hym thryes.

Jesus   Petir, Petir, þus saide I are
          When þou saide þou wolde abide with me
          In wele and woo, in sorowe and care,
          Whillis I schulde thries forsaken be.   165

Petrus   Alas þe while þat I come here,
          That euere I denyed my lorde in quarte,
          The loke of his faire face so clere
          With full sadde sorrowe sheris my harte.

III Miles Sir knyghtis, take kepe of þis karll and be konnand   170
           Because of sir Cayphas, we knowe wele his þoght.
           He will rewarde vs full wele, þat dare I wele warand,
           Whan he wete of oure werkis how wele we haue wroght.
IV Miles   Sir, þis is Cayphas halle here at hande,
           Go we boldly with þis boy þat we haue here broght.   175
III Miles Nay sirs, vs muste stalke to þat stede and full still stande,f.147
           For itt is nowe of þe nyght, yf þei nappe oght.
               Say, who is here?
I Miles   Say who is here?
III Miles   I, a frende,
           Well knawyn in þis contré for a knyght.
II Miles   Gose furthe, on youre wayes may yee wende,   180
           For we haue herbered enowe for tonyght.

152+   *Line missing; no gap in MS*
153.   Caret hic *to right in a later hand*
163.   þou . . . þou] *This ed;* TS you . . . you
176.   III Miles] *Suppl* K
       still stande] stast, *deleted, between*
177.   nowe] *K* none
178.   I Miles] *Suppl this ed (gap for omitted character-designation between first and second
       instances of* Say who is here *in MS)*
178c. III Miles] *This ed;* 178c-179 *assigned to* I Miles *in MS, TS; see the Note*

I Miles	Gose abakke bewscheres, ȝe bothe are to blame
	To bourde whenne oure busshopp is boune to his bedde.
IV Miles	Why sir, it were worthy to welcome vs home, 184
	We haue gone for þis warlowe and we haue wele spedde.
II Miles	Why, who is þat?
III Miles	The Jewes kyng, Jesus by name.
I Miles	A, yee be welcome, þat dare I wele wedde,
	My lorde has sente for to seke hym.
IV Miles	Loo, se here þe same.
II Miles	Abidde as I bidde and be noght adreed. 189
	My lorde, my lorde, my lorde, here is layke and ȝou list.
Cayphas	Pees, loselles. Leste ȝe be nyse?
I Miles	My lorde, it is wele and ye wiste.
Cayphas	What, nemen vs no more, for it is twyes.
	Þou takist non hede to þe haste that we haue here on honde,
	Go frayne howe oure folke faris that are furth ronne. 195
II Miles	My lorde, youre knyghtis has kared as ye þame commaunde
	And thei haue fallen full faire.
Cayphas	Why, and is þe foole fonne?
I Miles	Ya lorde, þei haue brought a boy in a bande boune. f.147ᵛ
Cayphas	Where nowe sir Anna, þat is one and able to be nere?
Anna	My lorde, with youre leue me behoues to be here. 200
Cayphas	A, sir, come nere and sitte we bothe in fere.
Anna	Do sir bidde þam bring in þat boy þat is bune.
Cayphas	Pese now sir Anna, be stille and late hym stande,
	And late vs grope yf þis gome be grathly begune.
Anna	Sir, þis game is begune of þe best, 205
	Nowe hadde he no force for to flee þame.
Cayphas	Nowe in faithe I am fayne he is fast,
	Do lede in þat ladde, late me se þan.
II Miles	Lo sir, we haue saide to oure souereyne,
	Gose nowe and suye to hymselfe for þe same thyng. 210
III Miles	Mi lorde, to youre bidding we haue ben buxom and bayne,
	Lo, here is þe belschere broght þat ye bad bring.
IV Miles	My lorde, fandis now to fere hym.
Cayphas	Nowe I am fayne,
	And felawes, faire mott ye fall for youre fynding.
Anna	Sir, and ye trowe þei be trewe withowten any trayne, 215
	Bidde þayme telle you þe tyme of þe takyng.

198. *I Miles*] *Suppl He*

199. *Cayphas*] *Altered from main scribe's I Miles by a later hand (not Clerke's)*
     sir] *TS; MS* s + *two minims* + r

200–7. *Assignments to Anna and Cayphas reversed in original rubrics; all corrected by same*
     later hand as at 199

203. stande] *Ha* reste

210. Gose] *Also written immediately beneath in red (main scribe)*

211. ben] *Suppl He*

213. I] *Superimposed on another letter*

213–4. *Lineation TS;* And felawes *at end of 213 in MS*

Cayphas	Say felawes, howe wente ye so nemely by nyȝt?
III Miles	My lorde, was þere no man to marre vs ne mende vs.
IV Miles	My lorde, we had lanternes and light f.148
	And some of his company kende vs. 220

Anna	But saie, howe did he, Judas?
III Miles	A, sir, full wisely and wele,
	He markid vs his maistir emang all his men
	And kyssid hym full kyndely his comforte to kele,
	By cause of a countenaunce þat karll for to kenne.
Cayphas	And þus did he his deuere?
IV Miles	Ya lorde, euere-ilke a dele, 225
	He taughte vs to take hym the tyme aftir tenne.
Anna	Nowe be my feith a saynte frende myght he þer fele.
III Miles	Sire, ye myght so haue saide hadde ye hym sene þenne.
IV Miles	He sette vs to þe same þat he solde vs
	And feyned to be his frende as a faytour, 230
	This was þe tokenyng before þat he tolde vs.
Cayphas	Nowe trewly, þis was a trante of a traytour.

Anna	Ȝa, be he traytour or trewe geue we neuer tale,
	But takes tente at þis tyme and here what he telles.
Cayphas	Now sees þat oure howsolde be holden here hole, 235
	So þat none carpe in case but þat in court dwellis.
III Miles	A, lorde, þis brethell hath brewed moche bale.
Cayphas	Therfore schall we spede vs to spere of his spellis.
	Sir Anna, takis hede nowe and here hym.
Anna	Say ladde, liste þe noght lowte to a lorde? 240
IV Miles	No sir, with youre leue we schall lere hym. f.148ᵛ

Cayphas	Nay sir, noght so, no haste,
	Itt is no burde to bete bestis þat are bune.
	And therfore with fayrenes firste we vill hym fraste
	And sithen forþer hym furth as we haue fune. 245
	And telle vs som tales truly to traste.
Anna	Sir, we myght als wele talke tille a tome tonne.
	I warande hym witteles, or ellis he is wrang wrayste,
	Or ellis he waitis to wirke als he was are wonne.
III Miles	His wonne was to wirke mekill woo 250
	And make many maystries emelle vs.
Kayphas	And some schall he graunte or he goo,
	Or muste yowe tente hym and telle vs.
IV Miles	Mi lorde, to witte þe wonderes þat he has wroght,
	For to telle you the tente it wolde oure tonges tere. 255

226. take hym] he, *deleted, between*
227. fele] *He; MS, TS* fynde
228. hym] *This ed; TS* hymn
237. hath]*This ed; TS* has
241. *IV Miles] Suppl TS*
242. *Cayphas] Altered from main scribe's IV Miles by a later hand (? J. Clerke)*
255. tere] *K; MS, TS* stere

Kayphas	Sen þe boy for his boste is into bale broght	
	We will witte or he wende how his werkis were.	
III Miles	Oure Sabott day we saye saves he right noght,	
	That he shulde halowe and holde full dingne and full dere.	
IV Miles	No sir, in þe same feste als we the sotte soughte	260
	He salued þame of sikenesse on many sidis seere.	
Cayphas	What þan, makes he þame grathely to gange?	f.149
III Miles	ȝa lorde, even forthe in euery-ilke a toune	
	He þame lechis to liffe aftir lange.	
Cayphas	A, this makes he by the myghtis of Mahounde.	265

IV Miles	Sir, oure stiffe tempill þat made is of stone,	
	That passes any paleys of price for to preyse,	
	And it were dounc to þe erth and to þe gronde gone	
	This rebalde he rowses hym it rathely to rayse.	
III Miles	ȝa lorde, and othir wonderis he workis grete wone,	270
	And with his lowde lesyngis he losis oure layes.	
Cayphas	Go lowse hym, and levis þan and late me allone,	
	For myselfe schall serche hym and here what he saies.	
Anna	Herke, Jesus of Jewes, we will haue joie	
	To spille all thy sporte for thy spellis.	275

Cayphas	Do meve, felawe, of thy frendis þat fedde þe beforne,	
	And sithen, felowe, of thi fare forþer will I freyne;	
	Do neven vs lightly. His langage is lorne!	
III Miles	My lorde, with youre leve, hym likis for to layne,	
	But and he schulde scape skatheles it wer a full skorne,	280
	For he has mustered emonge vs full mekil of his mayne.	
IV Miles	Malkus youre man, lord, þat had his ere schorne,	
	This harlotte full hastely helid it agayne.	
Cayphas	What, and liste hym be nyse for þe nonys,	
	And heres howe we haste to rehete hym.	285
Anna	Nowe by Beliall bloode and his bonys,	
	I holde it beste to go bete hym.	

Cayphas	Nay sir, none haste, we schall haue game or we goo.	f.149ᵛ
	Boy, be not agaste if we seme gaye.	
	I coniure þe kyndely and comaunde þe also,	290
	By grete God þat is liffand and laste schall ay,	
	Yf þou be Criste, Goddis sonne, telle till vs two.	
Jesus	Sir, þou says it þiselffe, and sothly I saye	
	Þat I schall go to my fadir þat I come froo	
	And dwelle with hym wynly in welthe allway.	295

261. þame] K men
many sidis] TS; MS many sere sidis
262. Cayphas] Suppl by J. Clerke
272. Cayphas] Altered from main scribe's IV Miles by Clerke
274–5. Hic caret to right in a later hand
274. we] Suppl this ed

Cayphas	Why, fie on þe faitoure vntrewe,
	Thy fadir haste þou fowly defamed.
	Now nedis vs no notes of newe,
	Hymselfe with his sawes has he schamed.
Anna	Nowe nedis nowdir wittenesse ne counsaille to call, 300
	But take his sawes as he saieth in þe same stede.
	He sclaunderes þe Godhed and greues vs all,
	Wherfore he is wele worthy to be dede –
	And therfore sir, saies hym þe sothe.
Cayphas	Sertis so I schall.
	Heres þou not, harlott? Ille happe on thy hede! 305
	Aunswere here grathely to grete and to small
	And reche vs oute rathely som resoune, I rede.
Jesus	My reasouns are not to reherse,
	Nor they þat myght helpe me are noȝt here nowe.
Anna	Say ladde, liste þe make verse? 310
	Do telle on belyffe, late vs here nowe.
Jesus	Sir, if I saie þe sothe þou schall not assente,
	But hyndir, or haste me to hynge.
	I prechid wher pepull was moste in present,
	And no poynte in priuité to olde ne ȝonge. 315
	And also in youre tempill I tolde myne entente;
	Ye myght haue tane me þat tyme for my tellyng
	Wele bettir þan bringe me with brondis vnbrente,
	And þus to noye me be nyght, and also for nothyng.
Cayphas	For nothyng, losell? Þou lies! f.150
	Thy wordis and werkis will haue a wrekyng. 321
Jesus	Sire, sen þou with wrong so me wreyes,
	Go spere thame þat herde of my spekyng.
Cayphas	A, þis traitoure has tened me with tales þat he has tolde,
	Ȝitt hadde I neuere such hething of a harlott as hee. 325
I Miles	What, fye on the, beggar, who made þe so bolde
	To bourde with oure busshoppe? Thy bane schalle I bee.
Jesus	Sir, if my wordis be wrange or werse þan þou wolde,
	A wronge wittenesse I wotte nowe ar ȝe;
	And if my sawes be soth þei mon be sore solde, 330
	Wherfore þou bourdes to brode for to bete me.
II Miles	My lorde, will ȝe here? For Mahounde,
	No more now for to neven þat it nedis.
Cayphas	Gose dresse you and dyng ȝe hym doune,
	And deffe vs no more with his dedis. 335

308–11. *Lineation TS; MS reverses order of speeches of Jesus and Anna. To right of 307 in hand of J. Clerke* Sir my reason is not to rehers – Jesus
313. to] *Suppl TS*
318. vnbrente] *Ho¹, K on* bente
325. hething of] *K; MS, TS* hething as of
336. estate] *He; MS, TS* estatis

Anna	Nay sir, þan blemysshe yee prelatis estate,
	ȝe awe to deme no man to dede for to dynge.
Cayphas	Why sir? So were bettir þan be in debate,
	Ye see þe boy will noȝt bowe for oure bidding.
Anna	Nowe sir, ye muste presente þis boy vnto sir Pilate 340
	For he is domysman nere and nexte to þe king,
	And late hym here all þe hole, how ye hym hate,
	And whedir he will helpe hym or haste hym to hyng
I Miles	My lorde, late men lede hym by nyght,
	So schall ye beste skape oute o skornyng. 345
II Miles	My lorde, it is nowe in þe nyght,
	I rede ȝe abide tille þe mornyng.
Cayphas	Bewschere, þou sais þe beste and so schall it be– f.150ᵛ
	But lerne yone boy bettir to bende and bowe.
I Miles	We schall lerne yone ladde, be my lewté, 350
	For to loute vnto ilke lorde like vnto yowe.
Cayphas	ȝa, and felawes, wayte þat he be ay wakand.
II Miles	ȝis lorde, þat warant will wee,
	Itt were a full nedles note to bidde vs nappe nowe.
III Miles	Sertis, will ye sitte and sone schall ye see
	Howe we schall play popse for þe pages prowe. 355
IV Miles	Late see, who stertis for a stole?
	For I haue here a hatir to hyde hym.
I Miles	Lo, here is one full fitte for a foole,
	Go gete it and sette þe beside hym.
II Miles	Nay, I schall sette it myselffe and frusshe hym also. 360
	Lo here a shrowde for a shrewe, and of shene shappe.
III Miles	Playes faire in feere, and þer is one and þer is–ij;
	I schall fande to feste it with a faire flappe–
	And ther is–iij; and there is–iiij.
	Say nowe with an nevill happe, 365
	Who negheth þe nowe? Not o worde, no!
IV Miles	Dose noddill on hym with neffes that he noght nappe.
I Miles	Nay, nowe to nappe is no nede,
	Wassaille! Wassaylle! I warande hym wakande.
II Miles	ȝa, and bot he bettir bourdis can byde 370
	Such buffettis schall he be takande.

344. by nyght] *K* by lyght *or* anon ryght
352. *Lineation He; two lines in MS, TS*
     he] *He* ye
355. popse] *This ed; TS* papse
359. *Ruled off in red from 358 (main scribe), but not assigned*
362–63. *Lineation as conj TS; MS* Playes faire . . . feste it / With a . . . is–ij
364. iiij] *He* four therto, *Hoʹ* four lo
365. *Ruled off from 364, assignment to III Miles repeated*
368. nede] *Hoʹ* tide
370. byde] *K* bede

III Miles	Prophete, Y saie, to be oute of debate,
	Quis te percussit, man? Rede, giffe þou may. f.151
IV Miles	Those wordes are in waste, what wenes þou he wate?
	It semys by his wirkyng his wittes were awaye. 375
I Miles	Now late hym stande as he stode in a foles state,
	For he likis noȝt þis layke my liffe dare I laye.
II Miles	Sirs, vs muste presente þis page to ser Pilate,
	But go we firste to oure souerayne and see what he saie.
III Miles	My lorde, we haue bourded with þis boy 380
	And holden hym full hote emelle vs.
Cayphas	Thanne herde ye some japes of joye?
IV Miles	The devell haue þe worde, lorde, he wolde telle vs.
Anna	Sir, bidde belyue þei goo and bynde hym agayne,
	So þat he skape noght, for þat were a skorne. 385
Cayphas	Do telle to sir Pilate oure pleyntes all pleyne,
	And saie þis ladde with his lesyngis has oure lawes lorne.
	And saie þis same day muste he be slayne
	Because of Sabott day þat schal be tomorne,
	And saie þat we come oureselffe for certayne, 390
	And for to fortheren þis fare, fare yee beforne.
I Miles	Mi lorde, with youre leve, vs muste wende,
	Oure message to make as we maye.
Cayphas	Sir, youre faire felawschippe we betake to þe fende,
	Goose onne nowe, and daunce forth in þe deuyll way.

372.   Y saie] *Ho¹; MS, TS* ysaie

373.   *Quis te] K; MS* In iuste, *TS* Iniuste
      þou] *This ed; TS* you

379.   saie] *He; MS, TS* saies

394.   *Cayphas] Substituted by J. Clerke for main scribe's Anna, which is deleted; TS retains
      Anna*

395.   *Ruled off from 394 and assigned to Cayphas (main scribe); so TS*

395+   Finis *added by Clerke; ff.151ᵛ, 152 blank*

Christ before Pilate 1: The Dream of Pilate's Wife

Pilatus	Yhe cursed creatures þat cruelly are cryand,	f.152ᵛ

Pilatus Yhe cursed creatures þat cruelly are cryand, f.152ᵛ
  Restreyne you for stryuyng for strengh of my strakis;
Youre pleyntes in my presence vse plately applyand,
  Or ellis þis brande in youre braynes sone brestis and brekis.
  Þis brande in his bones brekis, 5
    What brawle þat with brawlyng me brewis,
  That wrecche may not wrye fro my wrekis,
  Nor his sleyghtis noʒt slely hym slakis;
    Latte þat traytour noʒt triste in my trewys.

For sir Sesar was my sier and I sothely his sonne, 10
  That exelent emperoure exaltid in hight
Whylk all þis wilde worlde with wytes had wone,
  And my modir hight Pila þat proude was o plight;
  O Pila þat prowde, Atus hir fadir he hight.
    This 'Pila' was hadde into 'Atus'— 15
  Nowe renkis, rede yhe it right?
  For þus schortely I haue schewid you in sight
    Howe I am prowdely preued 'Pilatus'.

Loo, Pilate I am, proued a prince of grete pride.
  I was putte into Pounce þe pepill to presse, 20
And sithen Sesar hymselffe with exynatores be his side
  Remytte me to þer remys þe renkes to redresse.
  And yitte am Y graunted on grounde as I gesse
    To justifie and juge all þe Jewes.
  A, luffe, here lady? No lesse? 25

---

1. Pilatus] *Centred, in same inking and script as dialogue*
4. sone] *Conj TS; MS* schalle
7. wrekis] *TS; MS* werkis
9. trewys] s *added by a later hand*
12. wilde] *K* wide
13. plight] *Hoᶦ; MS, TS* pight
14. prowde, Atus] *K; MS, TS* prowde and Atus
21. exynatores] *Hoᶦ* þe synatores
22. þer] *This ed; MS, TS* þe
23–4. *Lineation TS; reversed in MS*
25. here] *Hoᶦ* dere

> Lo sirs, my worthely wiffe, þat sche is,
> So semely, loo, certayne scho schewys.

Vxor Was nevir juge in þis Jurie of so jocounde generacion,
    Nor of so joifull genologie to gentrys enioyned
As yhe, my duke doughty, demar of dampnacion   f.153
    To princes and prelatis þat youre preceptis perloyned.   31
    Who þat youre preceptis pertely perloyned,
      With drede into dede schall ye dryffe hym;
    By my trouthe, he vntrewly is troned
    Þat agaynste youre behestis hase honed;   35
      All to ragges schall ye rente hym and ryue hym.

    I am dame precious Percula, of prynces þe prise,
      Wiffe to ser Pilate here, prince withouten pere.
    All welle of all womanhede I am, wittie and wise,
      Consayue nowe my countenaunce so comly and clere.   40
    The coloure of my corse is full clere
      And in richesse of robis I am rayed,
    Ther is no lorde in þis londe as I lere,
    In faith, þat hath a frendlyar feere
      Than yhe my lorde, myselffe þof I saye itt.   45

Pilatus Nowe saye itt may ye saffely, for I will certefie þe same.
Vxor   Gracious lorde, gramercye, youre gode worde is gayne.
Pilatus Yhitt for to comforte my corse me muste kisse you madame.
Vxor   To fulfille youre forward my fayre lorde I am fayne.
Pilatus Howe, howe, felawys! Nowe in faith I am fayne   50
    Of theis lippis so loffely are lappid
    In bedde is full buxhome and bayne.
Domina Yha sir, it nedith not to layne,
    All ladise we coveyte þan bothe to be kyssid and clappid.

Bedellus My liberall lorde, o leder of lawis,   55
    O schynyng schawe þat all schames escheues,
I beseke you my souerayne, assente to my sawes,   f.153ᵛ
    As ye are gentill juger and justice of Jewes.

26. Lo sirs] *Lineation TS; written to right of 24–5 in MS*
28. Vxor] *MS (twice), TS Vxor Pilati*
30. Vxor Pilaty *added again (main scribe)*
32. preceptis] *This ed; TS* perceptis
34. troned] *This ed; MS, TS* stonyed
45. Than . . . lorde] *Lineation TS; written to right of 43 in MS*
    þof] *This ed; TS* yof
46. itt may] *Conj TS; MS* itt save may
49. lorde I] *Conj TS; MS* lorde in faith I
52. is full] *Ho¹ scho is. Punctuation of 50–2 uncertain*

Domina	Do herke howe þou, javell, jangill of Jewes.
	Why, go bette horosonne boy, when I bidde þe. 60
Bedellus	Madame, I do but þat diewe is.
Domina	But yf þou reste of thy resoune þou rewis,
	For all is acursed, carle – hase in, kydde þe!

Pilatus	Do mende you madame, and youre mode be amendand,
	For me semys it wer sittand to se what he sais. 65
Domina	Mi lorde, he tolde nevir tale þat to me was tendand,
	But with wrynkis and with wiles to wend me my weys.
Bedellus	Gwisse, of youre wayes to be wendand itt langis to oure
	lawes.
Domina	Loo lorde, þis ladde with his lawes!
	Howe, thynke ye it prophitis wele his prechyng to prayse?
Pilatus	Yha luffe, he knawis all oure custome, 71
	I knawe wele . . .

Bedellus	My seniour, will ye see nowe þe sonne in youre sight,
	For his stately strengh he stemmys in his stremys?
	Behalde ovir youre hede how he heldis fro hight 75
	And glydis to þe grounde with his glitterand glemys.
	To þe grounde he gois with his bemys
	And þe nyght is neghand anone.
	Yhe may deme aftir no dremys,
	But late my lady here with all hir light lemys 80
	Wightely go wende till hir wone; f.154

	For ye muste sitte sir þis same nyght, of lyfe and of lyme.
	Itt is noȝt leeffull for my lady by the lawe of this lande
	In dome for to dwelle fro þe day waxe ought dymme, 84
	For scho may stakir in þe strete but scho stalworthely
	stande.
	[. . . . . .]
	Late hir take hir leve whill þat light is.
Pilatus	Nowe wiffe, þan ye blythely be buskand.
Domina	I am here sir, hendely at hande.
Pilatus	Loo, þis renke has vs redde als right is.

59. javell, jangill] *Ha* javell and jangill
62–3. *Lineation TS; three lines in MS, dividing after* resoune *and* acursed
63. acursed] *TS; MS* a cursed. *Ho' would read* For als a cursed carle hastou kydde þe
68. lawes] *TS conj* layes. *For conjectural reconstructions of 68–72 see* He, Ho'
71–2. *So in MS; TS divides after* knawis
75–6. *Lineation TS; three lines in MS;* how he . . . þe grounde / Behalde . . . hede / with . . . glemys
75. heldis] *This ed; TS* holdis
79. deme] *This ed; TS* dome
80+ *Catchword* Wightely go wende
81. *Quire V begins*
85+ *Line missing; no gap in MS*
89. þis renke] *This ed; TS* þis is renke

| Domina | Youre comaundement to kepe to kare forþe Y caste me. | 90 |

Domina   Youre comaundement to kepe to kare forþe Y caste me.   90
          My lorde, with youre leue, no lenger Y lette yowe.
Pilatus   Itt were a repreue to my persone þat preuely ȝe paste me,
          Or ye wente fro this wones or with wynne ȝe had wette
                                                              yowe.
          Ye schall wende forthe with wynne whenne þat ȝe haue
                                                        wette yowe.
              Gete drinke! What dose þou? Haue done!   95
          Come semely, beside me, and sette yowe.
          Loke, nowe it is even here þat I are behete you,
              Ya, saie it nowe sadly and sone.

Domina   Itt wolde glad me my lorde if ȝe gudly begynne.   99
Pilatus   Nowe I assente to youre counsaille so comely and clere.
          Nowe drynke madame – to deth all þis dynne.
Domina   Iff it like yowe, myne awne lorde, I am not to lere –
          This lare I am not to lere.
Pilatus   Yitt efte to youre damysell madame.   f.154ᵛ
Domina   In thy hande, holde nowe and haue here.   105
Ancilla   Gramarcy, my lady so dere.
Pilatus   Nowe fares-wele, and walke on youre way.

          [. . .   . . .
              . . .   . . .]
Domina   Now farewele þe frendlyest, youre fomen to fende.
Pilatus   Nowe farewele þe fayrest figure þat euere did fode fede,
          And farewele ye damysell, indede.   110
Ancilla   My lorde, I comande me to youre ryalté.
Pilatus   Fayre lady, here is schall you lede.
          Sir, go with þis worthy in wede,
              And what scho biddis you doo loke þat buxsome you be.

Filius   I am prowde and preste to passe on apasse,   115
          To go with þis gracious hir gudly to gyde.

---

90.   forþe] *TS; MS* for þe
92.   a repreue] *K; MS, TS* appreue
97.   Loke, nowe] *TS; MS* Loke what dose þou haue done nowe
97–8. *Lineation TS;* þat I . . . and sone *one line in MS*
100.   clere] *TS; MS* clene
101.   drynke madame] *TS* drynke [ȝe] madame
104.   Yitt] *K* Yiff it. *For conjectural reconstructions of 103–7, see He, K*
107+   *First two lines of stanza missing; no gap in MS*
108.   þe] *This ed; TS* ye
109.   þe] *This ed; TS* ye
110.   *Ruled off from 109, but not assigned (main scribe)*
112.   here is] *This ed; MS, TS* he þis
113.   wede] *K; MS, TS* dede
115.   Filius] *TS; MS Secundus Filius, and so in all instances to 180; thereafter Primus Filius (see the Note)*

Pilatus   Take tente to my tale þou turne on no trayse,
  Come tyte and telle me yf any tythyngis betyde.
Filius   Yf any tythyngis my lady betyde,
  I schall full sone sir witte you to say. 120
 This semely schall I schewe by hir side
 Belyffe sir, no lenger we byde.
Pilatus   Nowe fares-wele, and walkes on youre way.

 Nowe wente is my wiffe, yf it wer not hir will, 124
  And scho rakis tille hir reste as of nothyng scho rought.
 Tyme is, I telle þe, þou tente me vntill;
  And buske þe belyue, belamy, to bedde þat Y wer broght
 [. . .   . . .]
  And loke I be rychely arrayed.
Bedellus   Als youre seruaunte I haue sadly it sought, f.155
 And þis nyght, sir, newe schall ye noght, 130
  I dare laye, fro ye luffely be layde.

Pilatus   I comaunde þe to come nere, for I will kare to my couche.
 Haue in thy handes hendely and heue me fro hyne,
 But loke þat þou tene me not with þi tastyng, but tendirly
        me touche.
Bedellus   A, sir, yhe whe wele.
Pilatus   Yha, I haue wette me with wyne. 135
 [. . .   . . .]
  Yhit helde doune and lappe me even here,
 For I will slelye slepe vnto synne.
 Loke þat no man nor no myron of myne
  With no noyse be neghand me nere.

Bedellus   Sir, what warlowe yow wakens with wordis full wilde, 140
 Þat boy for his brawlyng were bettir be vnborne.
Pilatus   Yha, who chatteres, hym chastise, be he churle or childe,
 For and he skape skatheles itt were to vs a grete skorne –
 Yf skatheles he skape it wer a skorne.
 What rebalde þat redely will rore, 145
 I schall mete with þat myron tomorne
 And for his ledir lewdenes hym lerne to be lorne.
Bedellus   Whe! So sir, slepe ye, and saies no more.

Domina   Nowe are we at home. Do helpe yf ye may,
 For I will make me redye and rayke to my reste. 150

127+ *Line missing; no gap in MS*
128+ *At the bottom left-hand corner of the leaf* plato (? *for* pilato, *or* prelato) *in an early
  hand (? s. xv)*
135. *Bedellus* A . . . wele] *Added later by the main scribe in the left margin*
  me with] *This ed;* TS *with* me
135+ *Line missing; no gap in MS*
136. here] *Suppl* TS

Ancilla	Yhe are werie madame, for-wente of youre way,
	Do boune you to bedde, for þat holde I beste.
Filius	Here is a bedde arayed of þe beste. f.155ᵛ
Domina	Do happe me, and faste hense ye hye.
Ancilla	Madame, anone all dewly is dressid. 155
Filius	With no stalkyng nor no striffe be ye stressed.
Domina	Nowe be yhe in pese, both youre carpyng and crye.

Diabolus	Owte! Owte! Harrowe! 157a
	Into bale am I brought, this bargayne may I banne,
	But yf Y wirke some wile in wo mon I wonne.
	This gentilman, Jesu, of cursednesse he can, 160
	Be any syngne þat I see þis same is Goddis sonne.
	And he be slone oure solace will sese,
	He will saue man saule fro oure sonde
	And refe vs þe remys þat are rounde.
	I will on stiffely in þis stounde 165
	Vnto ser Pilate wiffe pertely and putte me in prese.

	O woman, be wise and ware, and wonne in þi witte
	Ther schall a gentilman, Jesu, vnjustely be juged
	Byfore thy husband in haste, and with harlottis be hytte.
	And þat doughty today to deth þus be dyghted, 170
	Sir Pilate, for his prechyng, and þou,
	With nede schalle ye namely be noyed.
	Youre striffe and youre strenghe schal be stroyed,
	Youre richesse schal be refte you þat is rude,
	With vengeaunce, and þat dare I auowe. 175

Domina	A, I am drecchid with a dreme full dredfully to dowte.
	Say childe, rise vppe radly and reste for no roo,
	Thow muste launce to my lorde and lowly hym lowte,
	Comaunde me to his reuerence, as right will Y doo.
Filius	O, what, schall I trauayle þus tymely þis tyde? 180
	Madame, for the drecchyng of heuen,
	Slyke note is newsome to neuen
	And it neghes vnto mydnyght full even f 156
Domina	Go bette boy, I bidde no lenger þou byde,

	And saie to my souereyne þis same is soth þat I send hym:
	All naked þis nyght as I napped 186
	With tene and with trayne was I trapped,

157a. *Lineation this ed; written as one line with first half-line of 158 in MS, TS*
168. Jesu . . . juged] *Ho'* vnjustely be juged, Jesus
170. to . . . dyghted] *Ho'* be dyght to deth þus
171. *He* For his prechyng, sir Pilate and þou
173. striffe] tr *doubtful*
187. trayne] *Ha* traye

          With a sweuene þat swiftely me swapped
              Of one Jesu, þe juste man þe Jewes will vndoo.   189

          She prayes tente to þat trewe man, with tyne be noȝt trapped,
            But als a domesman dewly to be dressand,
              And lelye delyuere þat lede.

Filius   Madame, I am dressid to þat dede —
              But firste will I nappe in þis nede,
          For he hase mystir of a morne-slepe þat mydnyght is   195
                              myssand.

Anna   Sir Cayphas, ye kenne wele this caytiffe we haue cached
            That ofte-tymes in oure tempill hase teched vntrewly.
        Oure meyné with myght at mydnyght hym mached
            And hase drevyn hym till his demyng for his dedis
                              vndewly;
              Wherfore I counsaile þat kyndely we care   200
                Vnto ser Pilate oure prince, and pray hym
                That he for oure right will arraye hym —
                This faitour — for his falsed to flay hym;
            For fro we saie hym þe soth he schall sitte hym full sore.

Cayphas   Sir Anna, þis sporte haue ye spedely aspied,   205
            As I am pontificall prince of all prestis.
        We will prese to ser Pilate, and presente hym with pride
            With þis harlott þat has hewed oure hartis fro oure brestis
              Thurgh talkyng of tales vntrewe.   f.156$^\text{v}$
          And þerfor ser knyghtis —

Milites   Lorde.   210
Cayphas   Sir knyghtis þat are curtayse and kynde,
              We charge you þat chorle be wele chyned.
              Do buske you and grathely hym bynde
              And rugge hym in ropes his rase till he rewe.

I Miles   Sir, youre sawes schall be serued schortely and sone.   215
            Yha, do felawe, be thy feith; late vs feste þis faitour full
                              fast.

II Miles   I am douty to þis dede, delyuer, haue done;
            Latte vs pulle on with pride till his poure be paste.
I Miles   Do haue faste and halde at his handes.
II Miles   For this same is he þat lightly avaunted,   220
            And God sone he grathely hym graunted.

200.   care] *TS; MS* carie
204.   he] *K; MS, TS* I
210.   *Milites] This ed; TS* I Miles. *Lineation this ed (the line is extrametrical);* And . . .
        knyghtis *one line in MS,* Lorde *a second; so in TS*
220.   lightly] *Ho¹* highly

I Miles	He bese hurled for þe highnes he haunted –
	Loo, he stonyes for vs, he stares where he standis.
II Miles	Nowe is the brothell boune for all þe boste þat he blawe,
	And þe laste day he lete no lordynges myȝt lawe hyme. 225
Anna	Ya, he wende þis worlde had bene haly his awne.
	Als ye are dowtiest today tille his demyng ye drawe hym,
	And þan schall we kenne how þat he canne excuse hym.
I Miles	Here, ye gomes, gose a-rome, giffe vs gate,
	We muste steppe to yone sterne of astate. 230
II Miles	We muste yappely wende in at þis yate,
	For he þat comes to courte, to curtesye muste vse hym.

f.157

I Miles	Do rappe on the renkis þat we may rayse with oure rolyng.
	Come forthe sir coward, why cowre ye behynde?
Bedellus	O, what javellis are ye þat jappis with gollyng? 235
I Miles	A, goode sir, be noȝt wroth, for wordis are as þe wynde.
Bedellus	I saye, gedlynges, gose bakke with youre gawdes.
II Miles	Be sufferand I beseke you,
	And more of þis matere yhe meke yowe.
Bedellus	Why, vnconand knaves, an I cleke yowe, 240
	I schall felle yowe, be my faith, for all youre false
	frawdes.

Pilatus	Say childe, ill cheffe you! What churlles are so claterand?
Bedellus	My lorde, vnconand knaves þei crye and þei call.
Pilatus	Gose baldely beliffe and þos brethellis be batterand, 244
	And putte þam in prisoune vppon peyne þat may fall.
	Yha, spedely spir þam yf any sporte can þei spell –
	Yha, and loke what lordingis þei be.
Bedellus	My lorde þat is luffull in lee,
	I am boxsom and blithe to your blee. 249
Pilatus	And if they talke any tythyngis come tyte and me tell.

Bedellus	Can ye talke any tythandis, by youre faith, my felawes?
I Miles	Yha sir, sir Cayphas and Anna ar come both togedir

---

224. *II Miles] Suppl by a later hand*
       blawe] *He; MS, TS* blowne
225. lawe] *TS; MS* lawne
226. awne] *He* awe
227. dowtiest today] þis day, *deleted, between*
233. *I Miles] In what may be another hand, over erasure of original character-designation; and so at 236*
244. batterand] *Ha; MS, TS* battand
248–9. *Lineation TS; one line in MS*
249. your] *TS; MS* yor + r *suprascript*
251. *As conj TS; MS* My felawes by youre faith can ye talke any tythandis
252. sir²] *This ed; om TS*

To sir Pilate o Pounce and prince of oure lawes;
And þei haue laughte a lorell þat is lawles and liddir. f.157

Bedelus   My lorde, my lorde!

Pilatus   Howe?   255

Bedellus   My lorde, vnlappe yow belyve where ye lye.
Sir Cayphas to youre courte is caried,
And sir Anna, but a traytour hem taried.
Many wight of þat warlowe has waried,
They haue brought hym in a bande his balis to bye. 260

Pilatus   But are thes sawes certayne in soth þat þou saies?

Bedellus   Yha lorde, þe states yondir standis, for striffe are they
stond.

Pilatus   Now þan am I light as a roo, and ethe for to rayse.
Go bidde þam come in both, and the boye þey haue boune.

Bedellus   Siris, my lorde geues leue inne for to come.   265

Cayphas   Hayle prince þat is pereles in price,
Ye are leder of lawes in þis lande,
Youre helpe is full hendely at hande.

Anna   Hayle, stronge in youre state for to stande,   269
Alle þis dome muste be dressed at youre dulye deuyse.

Pilatus   Who is there, my prelates?   f.158

Cayphas   Yha lorde.

Pilatus   Nowe be ȝe welcome
iwisse.

Cayphas   Gramercy my souerayne. But we beseke you all same
Bycause of wakand you vnwarly be noght wroth with þis,
For we haue brought here a lorell – he lokis like a lambe.

Pilatus   Come byn, you bothe, and to þe benke brayde yowe.

Cayphas   Nay gud sir, laugher is leffull for vs.   276

Pilatus   A, sir Cayphas, be curtayse yhe bus.

Anna   Nay goode lorde, it may not be þus.

Pilatus   Sais no more, but come sitte you beside me in sorowe
as I saide youe.

Filius   Hayle, þe semelieste seeg vndir sonne sought,   280
Hayle, þe derrest duke and doughtiest in dede.

Pilatus   Now bene-veneuew beuscher, what boodworde haste þou
brought?

---

253.   lawes] *He; MS, TS* lawe
255.   *Lineation TS (the line is extra-metrical); two lines in MS*
262.   stond] *K; MS, TS* stonden
264.   boune] *K* bond
265.   leue] *An otiose i follows. Lineation this ed (the line is extra-metrical); two lines in MS, TS*
271.   there] *TS; MS* the *+ four minims +* e

Filius	Hase any langour my lady newe laught in þis leede?
	Sir, þat comely comaundes hir youe too,
	And sais, al nakid þis nyght as sche napped 285
	With tene and with traye was sche trapped,
	With a sweuene þat swiftely hir swapped
	Of one Jesu, þe juste man þe Jewes will vndo.

	She beseches you as hir souerayne þat symple to saue,
	Deme hym noght to deth for drede of vengeaunce. 290
Pilatus	What, I hope þis be he þat hyder harlid ʒe haue.
Cayphas	Ya sir, þe same and þe selffe – but þis is but a f.158ᵛ
	skaunce,
	He with wicchecrafte þis wile has he wrought.
	Some feende of his sand has he sente
	And warned youre wiffe or he wente. 295
Pilatus	Yowe! Þat schalke shuld not shamely be shente,
	Þis is sikir in certayne, and soth schulde be sought.

Anna	Yha, thurgh his fantome and falshed and fendes-craft
	He has wroght many wondir where he walked full wyde,
	Wherfore, my lorde, it wer leeffull his liffe were hym rafte.
Pilatus	Be ye neuere so bryme ye boþe bus abide 301
	But if þe traytoure be taught for vntrewþe,
	And þerfore sermones you no more.
	I will sekirly sende hymselffe fore,
	And se what he sais to þe sore. 305
	Bedell, go brynge hyme, for of þat renke haue I rewþe.

Bedellus	This forward to fulfille am I fayne moued in myn herte.
	Say, Jesu, þe juges and þe Jewes hase me enioyned
	To bringe þe before þam even bounden as þou arte.
	Yone lordyngis to lose þe full longe haue þei heyned, 310
	But firste schall I wirschippe þe with witte and with will.
	This reuerence I do þe forthy, f.159
	For wytes þat wer wiser þan I,
	They worshipped þe full holy on hy
	And with solempnité sange Osanna till. 315

I Miles	My lorde þat is leder of lawes in þis lande,
	All bedilis to your biding schulde be boxsome and bayne,
	And ʒitt þis boy here before yowe full boldely was bowand
	To worschippe þis warlowe – methynke we wirke all in
	vayne.

283. leede] *Altered to* hede *by a later hand; TS* hede
293. *He would om* He
296. *Pilatus] Suppl Ha*
297. soth] *TS; MS* soh
302. vntrewþe] *Ho'; MS, TS* vntrewe
307. moued . . . herte] *TS; MS* in myn herte moued
310. heyned] *Probably an error for* hoyned *(MED)*
315. Osanna till] *He* Osanna þe till

II Miles	Yha, and in youre presence he prayed hym of pees,
	In knelyng on knes to þis knave $\qquad$ 321
	He besoughte hym his seruaunte to saue.
Caiphas	Loo lord, such arrore amange þem þei haue
	It is grete sorowe to see, no seeg may it sese.

It is no menske to youre manhed þat mekill is of myght   325
To forbere such forfettis þat falsely are feyned,
Such spites in especiall wolde be eschewed in your sight.

Pilatus	Sirs, moves you noȝt in þis matere but bese myldely demeaned,
	For yone curtasie I kenne had som cause.
Anna	In youre sight sir þe soth schall I saye, $\qquad$ 330
	As ye are prince take hede I you praye,
	Such a lourdayne vnlele, dare I laye,
	Many lordis of oure landis might lede fro oure lawes.

Pilatus	Saye losell, who gaue þe leve so for to lowte to yone ladde
	And solace hym in my sight so semely þat I saw? $\quad$ f.159ᵛ
Bedellus	A, gracious lorde, greue you noght for gude case I hadde.
	Yhe comaunded me to care, als ye kenne wele and knawe,
	To Jerusalem on a journay, with seele;
	And þan þis semely on an asse was sette
	And many men myldely hym mette, $\qquad$ 340
	Als a God in þat grounde þai hym grette,
	Wele semand hym in waye with worschippe lele.

'Osanna' þei sange, 'þe sone of Dauid',
Riche men with þare robes þei ranne to his fete,
And poure folke fecched floures of þe frith $\qquad$ 345
And made myrthe and melody þis man for to mete.

Pilatus	Nowe gode sir, be þi feith, what is 'Osanna' to saie?
Bedellus	Sir, constrew it we may be langage of þis lande as I leue,
	It is als moche to me for to meue –
	Youre prelatis in þis place can it preue – $\qquad$ 350
	Als, 'oure sauiour and souerayne þou saue vs we praye'.

Pilatus	Loo senioures, how semes yow? Þe soþe I you saide.
Cayphas	Yha lorde, þis ladde is full liddir, be þis light.
	Yf his sawes wer serchid and sadly assaied,
	Saue youre reuerence, his resoune þei rekenne noȝt with right.
	This caytiffe þus cursedly can construe vs. $\qquad$ 356

330. *Character-designation in a different ink, perhaps in a different hand; and so at 336, 352*
337. kenne] *Ho¹; MS, TS* kende
349. meue] u *altered to* v
351. sauiour] a *superimposed on another letter*

Bedellus	Sirs, trulye þe trouþe I haue tolde	
	Of þis wighte ȝe haue wrapped in wolde.	
Anna	I saie, harlott, thy tonge schulde þou holde,	f.160
	And noght agaynste þi maistirs to meve þus.	360

Pilatus	Do sese of youre seggyng, and I schall examyne full sore.	
Anna	Sir, demes hym to deth or dose hym away.	
Pilatus	Sir, haue ye saide?	
Anna	Yha lorde.	
Pilatus	Nowe go sette you with	
	sorowe and care,	
	For I will lose no lede þat is lele to oure lay.	
	But steppe furth and stonde vppe on hight	365
	And buske to my bidding, þou boy,	
	And for þe nones þat þou neven vs a noy.	
Bedellus	I am here at youre hande to halow a hoy,	
	Do move of youre maistir for I shall melle it with myȝt.	

Pilatus	Cry 'Oyas'.	
Bedellus	Oyas.	
Pilatus	Yit efte, be þi feithe.	
Bedellus	Oyas! [*Alowde.*	370

Pilatus	Yit lowdar, that ilke lede may lithe –	
	Crye pece in this prese, vppon payne þervppon,	
	Bidde them swage of þer sweying bothe swiftely and swithe	
	And stynte of þer stryuyng and stande still as a stone.	
	Calle Jesu þe gentill of Jacob, þe Jewe.	375
	Come preste and appere,	
	To þe barre drawe þe nere,	
	To þi jugement here,	
	To be demed for his dedis vndewe.	

I Miles	Whe, harke how þis harlott he heldis oute of harre,	f.160ᵛ
	This lotterelle liste noght my lorde to lowte.	381
II Miles	Say beggar, why brawlest þou? Go boune þe to þe barre.	
I Miles	Steppe on thy standyng so sterne and so stoute.	
II Miles	Steppe on thy standyng so still.	
I Miles	Sir cowarde, to courte muste yhe care –	385
II Miles	A lessoune to lerne of oure lare.	
I Miles	Flitte fourthe, foule myght þou fare.	
II Miles	Say warlowe, þou wantist of þi will.	

---

364. lay] *Ho¹; MS, TS* law
370. *Lineation this ed (the line is extra-metrical); four lines in MS, one line in TS (with first half-line of 371). Alowde conj as SD by TS*
371. *The second half-line (after* lowdar) *ruled off from the first; hic caret to right in a later hand*
  Yit] *This ed; MS, TS* Pilatus yit
  lithe] *Ho⁶; MS, TS* light
386. lare] *TS; MS* lawe

Filius	O Jesu vngentill, þi joie is in japes,	
	Þou can not be curtayse, þou caytiffe I calle þe,	390
	No ruthe were it to rug þe and ryue þe in ropes.	
	Why falles þou noȝt flatte here, foule falle þe,	
	For ferde of my fadir so free?	
	Þou wotte noght his wisdome iwys,	
	All thyne helpe in his hande þat it is,	395
	Howe sone he myght saue þe fro þis.	
	Obeye hym, brothell, I bidde þe.	

Pilatus	Now Jesu, þou art welcome ewys, as I wene,	
	Be noȝt abasshed but boldely boune to þe barre;	
	What seyniour will sewe for þe sore I haue sene.	400
	To wirke on þis warlowe, his witte is in warre.	
	Come preste, of a payne, and appere,	
	And sir prelatis, youre pontes bes prevyng.	
	What cause can ye caste of accusyng?	
	Þis mater ye marke to be meving,	405
	And hendly in haste late vs here.	

Cayphas	Sir Pilate o Pounce and prince of grete price,	
	We triste ye will trowe oure tales þei be trewe,	f.161
	To deth for to deme hym with dewly device.	
	For cursidnesse yone knave hase in case, if ye knew,	410
	In harte wolde ye hate hym in hye.	
	For if it wer so	
	We mente not to misdo;	
	Triste, ser, schall ye þerto,	
	We hadde not hym taken to þe.	415

Pilatus	Sir, youre tales wolde I trowe but þei touche none entente.	
	What cause can ye fynde nowe þis freke for to felle?	
Anna	Oure Sabbotte he saues not, but sadly assente	
	To wirke full vnwisely, þis wote I riȝt wele,	
	[. . . . . .]	
	He werkis whane he will, wele I wote,	420
	And þerfore in herte we hym hate.	
	Itt sittis you to strenghe youre estate	
	Yone losell to louse for his lay.	

Pilatus	Ilke a lede for to louse for his lay is not lele.	
	Youre lawes is leffull, but to youre lawis longis it	425

389. *Filius] This ed; MS, TS Junior Filius*
401. warre] *TS; MS* waste
404. accusyng] *TS; MS* accusy *+ three minims +* g
412–5. *Lineation TS; two lines in MS*
412. wer] *K* ner
415. to þe] *Ho¹* þe nye
419+ *Line missing; no gap in MS*

Þis faitoure to feese wele with flappes full fele,
   And woo may ye wirke hym be lawe, for he wranges it.
     Therfore takes vnto you full tyte,
       And like as youre lawes will you lede
       Ye deme hym to deth for his dede.   430

Cayphas   Nay, nay sir, þat dome muste vs drede,
      [. . .   . . .]

It longes noȝt till vs no lede for to lose.
Pilatus   What wolde ye I did þanne? Þe deuyll motte you drawe!
Full fewe are his frendis but fele are his fooes.
     His liff for to lose þare longes no lawe,   435
       Nor no cause can I kyndely contryue
       Þat why he schulde lose þus his liffe.
Anna   A, gude sir, it raykes full ryffe   f.161ᵛ
       In steedis wher he has stirrid mekill striffe
       Of ledis þat is lele to youre liffe.   440

Cayphas Sir, halte men and hurte he helid in haste,
     The deffe and þe dome he delyuered fro doole
By wicchecrafte, I warande – his wittis schall waste –
     For þe farles þat he farith with loo how þei folowe yone
                                          fole,
       Oure folke so þus he frayes in fere.   445
Anna   The dede he rayses anone –
       Þis Lazare þat lowe lay allone
       He graunte hym his gates for to gone,
     And pertely þus proued he his poure.

Pilatus Now goode siris, I saie, what wolde yhe seme?   450
Caiphas   Sir, to dede for to do hym or dose hym adawe.
Pilatus Yha, for he dose wele his deth for to deme?
     Go layke you sir, lightly; wher lerned ye such lawe?
       This touches no tresoune I telle you.
       Yhe prelatis þat proued are for price,   455
       Yhe schulde be boþe witty and wise
       And legge oure lawe wher it lyse,
     Oure materes ye meve þus emel you.

Anna   Misplese noȝt youre persone, yhe prince withouten pere,
     It touches to tresoune þis tale I schall tell: 460

428. takes] *Ho¹* takes hym
431+ *Line missing; no gap in MS*
437. Þat why] *He* Why þat
446. dede] *He; MS, TS* dethe
450. seme] *Suppl He*
451. do . . . dose] *Ho¹* deme . . . do
454. no] *K* to
457. oure] *Ho¹* youre
458. Oure] *Ho¹* Youre

Yone briboure, full baynly he bed to forbere
The tribute to þe emperoure, þus wolde he compell
Oure pepill þus his poyntis to applye.

Cayphas   The pepull he saies he schall saue,
And Criste garres he calle hym, yone knave,   465
And sais he will þe highe kyngdome haue –   f.162
Loke whethir he deserue to dye.

Pilatus   To dye he deserues yf he do þus indede,
But Y will se myselffe what he sais.
Speke Jesu, and spende nowe þi space for to spede.   470
Þez lordyngis þei legge þe þou liste noȝt leve on oure lays,
They accuse þe cruelly and kene;
And þerfore as a chiftene Y charge þe,
Iff þou be Criste þat þou telle me,
And God sone þou grughe not to graunte þe,   475
For þis is þe matere þat Y mene.

Jesus   Þou saiste so þiselue. I am sothly þe same
Here wonnyng in worlde to wirke al þi will.
My fadir is faithfull to felle all þi fame;
Withouten trespas or tene am I taken þe till.   480
Pilatus   Loo busshoppis, why blame ye þis boye?
Me semys þat it is soth þat he saies.
Ye meve all þe malice ye may
With youre wrenchis and wiles to wrythe hym away,
Vnjustely to juge hym fro joie.   485

Cayphas   Nought so sir, his seggyng is full sothly soth,
It bryngis oure bernes in bale for to bynde.
Anna   Sir, douteles we deme als dewe of þe deth
Þis foole þat ye fauour – grete fautes can we fynde
This daye for to deme hym to dye.   490
Pilatus   Saie losell, þou lies be þis light!
Naie, þou rebalde, þou rekens vnright.
Cayphas   Avise you sir, with mayne and with myght,
And wreke not youre wrethe nowe forthy.

Pilatus   Me likes noȝt his langage so largely for to lythe.   495
Caiphas   A, mercy lorde, mekely, no malice we mente.   f.162ᵛ

465+   *Catchword* And sais he will
466.   *Quire X begins*
471.   lays] *He; MS, TS* lawes
475.   þe] *This ed; TS* ye
482.   saies] *He* dose saie
486/8. *For conjectures to restore rhyme, see He, Ho¹*
488.   of] *TS; MS* als
489.   Þis] *K* In þis *(with different punctuation)*
492.   Naie] *K; MS, TS* Saie
495.   his] *TS* [t]his
       lythe] *He; MS, TS* lye

Pilatus	Noo done is it douteles, balde be and blithe,
	Talke on þat traytoure and telle youre entente.
	Yone segge is sotell ye saie;
	Gud sirs, wer lerned he such lare? 500
Cayphas	In faith, we can not fynde whare.
Pilatus	Yhis, his fadir with some farlis gan fare
	And has lered þis ladde of his laie.

Anna	Nay, nay sir, we wiste þat he was but a write,
	No sotelté he schewed þat any segge saw. 505
Pilatus	Thanne mene yhe of malice to marre hym of myght,
	Of cursidnesse convik no cause can yhe knawe.
	Me meruellis ye malyngne o mys.
Cayphas	Sir, fro Galely hidir and hoo
	The gretteste agayne hym ganne goo, 510
	Yone warlowe to waken of woo,
	And of þis werke beres witnesse ywis.

Pilatus	Why, and hase he gone in Galely, yone gedlyng ongayne?
Anna	Yha lorde, þer was he borne, yone brethelle, and bredde.
Pilatus	Nowe withouten fagyng, my frendis, in faith I am fayne, 515
	For now schall oure striffe full sternely be stede.
	Sir Herowde is kyng þer ye kenne,
	His poure is preued full preste
	To ridde hym or reue hym of rest.
	And þerfore, to go with yone gest 520
	Yhe marke vs oute of þe manliest men.

Cayphas	Als witte and wisdome youre will schal be wroght,
	Here is kempis full kene to þe kyng for to care.
Pilatus	Nowe seniours, I saie yow sen soth schall be soght, f.163
	But if he schortely be sente it may sitte vs full sore. 525
	And þerfore sir knyghtis –
Milites	Lorde.
Pilatus	Sir knyghtis þat are cruell and kene,
	That warlowe ye warrok and wraste,
	And loke þat he brymly be braste
	[. . . . . .]
	Do take on þat traytoure you betwene. 530

---

497. be and] *This ed; MS, TS* and be
500. wer] *This ed; TS* wher
503. laie] *TS; MS* lare
504. we . . . write] *TS; MS* was but a write þat we wiste
509. and] *Ha* on
514. and bredde] *Added to right by J. Clerke; main scribe* and borne
524. Pilatus] *This ed; TS* Anna (conj)
526. *Milites] Suppl this ed. Lineation this ed (the line is extra-metrical); one line in MS,*
Lorde *separated from* knyghtis *by a red flourish. TS places between* 529 *and* 530,
omitting lorde *and adding* [in haste]
529+ *Line missing; no gap in MS*

Tille Herowde in haste with þat harlott ye hye,
　　Comaunde me full mekely vnto his moste myght.
Saie þe dome of þis boy, to deme hym to dye,
　　Is done vpponne hym dewly, to dresse or to dight
　　Or liffe for to leue at his liste.   535
　　　　Say ought I may do hym indede,
　　　　His awne am I worthely in wede.
I Miles　　　My lorde, we schall springe on a-spede.
　　Come þens! To me þis traitoure full tryste.

Pilatus　Bewe sirs, I bidde you ye be not to bolde,   540
　　But takes tente for oure tribute full trulye to trete.
II Miles　Mi lorde, we schall hye þis beheste for to halde
　　And wirke it full wisely in wille and in witte.
Pilatus　　So sirs me semys itt is sittand.
I Miles　　　Mahounde, sirs, he menske you with myght –   545
II Miles　　　And saue you sir, semely in sight.
Pilatus　　　Now in þe wilde vengeaunce ye walke with þat wight,
　　And fresshely ye founde to be flittand.

XXXI The Litsters

Christ before Herod

Rex　　Pes, ye brothellis and browlys in þis broydenesse inbrased,   f.164
　　And freykis þat are frendely your freykenesse to frayne,
Youre tounges fro tretyng of triffillis be trased,
　　Or þis brande þat is bright schall breste in youre brayne.
　　Plextis for no plasis but platte you to þis playne,   5
　　　　And drawe to no drofyng but dresse you to drede,
　　　　With dasshis.

533–4.　*Lineation (with emendation) TS; two lines in MS, dividing (and reading)* . . . *dye is done / Done vpponne* . . .
533.　deme] e *altered from* o
539.　þens] *Ho'* hens
　　to me] *TS conj* dome, *K, Ho³ with*
　　tryste] *Ho'*; *MS, TS* tyte
548+　finis *added by J. Clerke; f.163ᵛ blank*
　1.　Rex] *Suppl TS*

Traueylis noȝt as traytours þat tristis in trayne,
  Or by þe bloode þat Mahounde bledde with þis blad
                                  schal ye blede.
Þus schall I brittyn all youre bones on brede,   10
  Ȝae, and lusshe all youre lymmys with lasschis.

Dragons þat are dredfull schall derke in þer dennes
  In wrathe when we writhe, or in wrathenesse ar wapped.
Agaynste jeauntis ongentill haue we joined with ingendis, 14
  And swannys þat are swymmyng to oure swetnes schall
                                be suapped,
  And joged doune þer jolynes oure gentries engenderand.
  Whoso repreue oure estate we schall choppe þam in
                                  cheynes,
  All renkkis þat are renand to vs schall be reuerande.

Therfore I bidde you sese or any bale be,
  Þat no brothell be so bolde boste for to blowes.   20
And ȝe þat luffis youre liffis, listen to me
  As a lorde þat is lerned to lede you be lawes.
And ye þat are of my men and of my menȝe,
  Sen we are comen fro oure kyth as ȝe wele knawes,
And semlys all here same in þis cyté,   25
  It sittis vs in sadnesse to sette all oure sawes.

I Dux   My lorde, we schall take kepe to youre call
         And stirre to no stede but ȝe steuen vs,
      No greuaunce to grete ne to small.
Rex   Ya, but loke þat no fawtes befall.   30
II Dux   Lely my lord so we shall,
      Ye nede not no more for to nevyn vs.

                                       f.164ᵛ
I Dux   Mounseniour, demene you to menske in mynde what I mene
    And boune to youre bedward, for so holde I best,
For all þe comons of þis courte bene avoyde clene,   35
  And ilke a renke, as resounc as, are gone to þer reste –
  Wherfore I counsaile, my lorde, ȝe comaunde you a
                               drynke.
Rex   Nowe certis, I assente as þou sais.
      Se ych a qwy is wente on his ways
      Lightly withouten any delayes.   40

---

11. *Lineation this ed;* Ȝae *at end of 10 in MS, TS*
12. dennes] *He; MS, TS* denne
14–5. *Lineation TS; reversed in MS*
20. blowes] *He* blawe *(and corresponding rhymes at 22, 24, 26)*
24. knawes] *TS; MS* knawe
29. No] *K* Nor do
33. to] *Ha; MS, TS* in
34. bedward] *This ed; MS, TS* bodword
36. as²] *This ed; TS* is *(conj)*

>   Giffe vs wyne wynly and late vs go wynke,
>   And se þat no durdan be done.

       Tunc bibit Rex

I Dux	My lorde, vnlase you to lye,
	Here schall none come for to crye.
Rex	Nowe spedely loke þat þou spie 45
	Þat no noyse be neghand þis none.

I Dux   My lorde, youre bedde is new made, you nedis noȝt for to
                                                    bide it.

Rex   Ya, but as þou luffes me hartely, laye me doune softely,
     For þou wotte full wele þat I am full tendirly hydid.

I Dux   Howe lye ȝe my goode lorde?

Rex   Right wele, be þis light,   50
        All hole at my desire.
        Wherfore I praye ser Satan oure sire,
        And Lucifer moste luffely of lyre,
        He sauffe you all sirs, and giffe you goode nyght.

I Miles	Sir knyght, ye wote we ar warned to wende 55
	To witte of þis warlowe what is þe kyngis will.
II Miles	Sir, here is Herowde all even here at oure hende,
	And all oure entente tyte schall we tell hym vntill.
I Miles	Who is here? f.165
I Dux	Who is there?
I Miles	Sir, we are knyghtis kende
	Is comen to youre counsaill þis carle for to kill. 60
I Dux	Sirs, but youre message may myrthis amende,
	Stalkis furthe be yone stretis or stande stone still.
II Miles	Yis certis ser, of myrthis we mene,
	The kyng schall haue matteres to melle hym.
	We brynge here a boy vs betwene, 65
	Wherfore to haue worschippe we wene.
I Dux	Wele sirs, so þat it turne to no tene,
	Tentis hym and we schall go telle hym.

        My lorde, yondir is a boy boune þat brought is in blame,
        Haste you in hye, þei houe at youre ȝate.   70

Rex   What, and schall I rise nowe, in þe deuyllis name,
        To stighill amang straungeres in stales of astate?

42+ *SD added to right of 42 by J. Clerke*
47–50. *Lineation this ed; eight lines in MS, TS*
57. here²] *K* nere
66. to] *Suppl Ho¹*
69. *Previous character-designation repeated*
70. ȝate] *He; MS, TS* ȝates

	But haue here my hande, halde nowe,	
	And se þat my sloppe be wele sittande.	
I Dux	My lorde, with a goode will Y wolde youe,	75
	No wrange will I witte at my wittande.	

	But my lorde, we can tell ȝou of vncouthe tythande.	
Rex	Ȝa, but loke ye telle vs no tales but trewe.	
II Dux	My lorde, þei bryng you yondir a boy boune in a bande	
	Þat bodus outhir bourdyng or bales to brewe.	80
Rex	Þanne gete we some harrowe full hastely at hande.	
I Dux	My lorde, þer is some note þat is nedfull to neven you of	
	new.	
Rex	Why, hoppis þou þei haste hym to hyng?	f.165ᵛ
II Dux	We wotte noght þer will nor þer wenyng,	
	But boodword full blithely þei bryng.	85
Rex	Nowe do þan and late vs se of þere sayng.	
II Dux	Lo sirs, ye schall carpe with þe kyng,	
	And telles to hym manly youre menyng.	

I Miles	Lorde, welthis and worschippis be with you alway.	
Rex	What wolde you?	
II Miles	A worde, lorde, and youre willes were.	90
Rex	Well, saye on þan.	
I Miles	My lorde, we fare foolys to flay	
	Þat to you wolde forfette.	
Rex	We, faire falle you þerfore.	
I Miles	My lorde, fro ȝe here what we saie	
	Itt will heffe vppe youre hertis.	
Rex	Ȝa, but saie what heynde haue ȝe þore?	
II Miles	A presente fro Pilate, lorde, þe prince of oure lay.	95
Rex	Pese in my presence, and nemys hym no more.	
I Miles	My lorde, he woll worschippe you faine.	
Rex	I consayue ȝe are ful foes of hym.	
II Miles	My lorde, he wolde menske you with mayne,	
	And therfore he sendis you þis swayne.	100
Rex	Gose tyte with þat gedlyng agayne,	
	And saie hym a borowed bene sette I noght be hym.	

I Dux	A, my lorde, with youre leve, þei haue faren ferre,	f.166
	And for to fraiste of youre fare was no folye.	
II Dux	My lorde, and þis gedlyng go þus it will greue werre,	105
	For he gares growe on þis grounde grete velanye.	
Rex	Why, menys þou þat þat myghtyng schulde my myghtes	
	marre?	
I Dux	Nay lorde, but he makis on þis molde mekill maystrie.	

77. tythande] *He; MS, TS* tythandes
90. you] *This ed; TS* þou
92. Þat] *TS; MS* Yt
94. heynde] y *over two minims*

Rex	Go ynne, and late vs see of þe sawes ere,	109
	And but yf þei be to oure bordyng, þai both schalle abye.	
II Miles	My lorde, we were worthy to blame	
	To brynge you any message of mysse.	
Rex	Why þan, can ye nemyn vs his name?	
I Miles	Sir, Criste haue we called hym at hame.	
Rex	O, þis is þe ilke selue and þe same—	115
	Nowe sirs, ye be welcome ywisse.	

	And in faith I am fayne he is fonne,	
	His farles to frayne and to fele;	
	Nowe þes games was grathely begonne.	
II Miles	Lorde, lely þat likis vs wele.	120

Rex	Ya, but dar ӡe hete hartely þat harlott is he?	
I Miles	My lorde, takis hede and in haste ye schall here howe.	
Rex	Ya, but what menys þat þis message was made vnto me?	
II Miles	My lorde, for it touches to tresoune I trowe.	
I Miles	My lorde, he is culpabill kende in oure contré	125
	Of many perillus poyntis, as Pilate preues nowe.	
II Miles	My lorde, when Pilate herde he had gone thurgh	f.166ᵛ
	Galylé	
	He lerned vs þat þat lordschippe longed to ӡou,	
	And or he wiste what youre willis were,	
	No ferther wolde he speke for to spille hym.	130
Rex	Þanne knawes he þat oure myghtis are þe more?	
I Miles	Ӡa, certis sir, so saie we þore.	
Rex	Nowe sertis, and oure frenschippe þerfore	
	We graunte hym, and no greuaunce we will hym.	

	And sirs, ye are welcome ywisse as ye wele awe,	135
	And for to wende at youre wille Y you warande,	
	For I haue coueite kyndely þat comely to knawe,	
	For men carpis þat þe carle schulde be konnand.	
II Miles	My lorde, wolde he saie you soth of his sawe,	
	Ӡe saugh neuir slik selcouth, be see nor be sande.	140
Rex	Nowe gois abakke both and late þe boy blowe,	
	For I hope we gete some harre hastely at hande.	
I Miles	Jerusalem and þe Jewes may haue joie	
	And hele in ther herte for to here hym.	
Rex	Saie, beene-venew in bone fay,	145
	Ne plesew & a parle remoy?	
II Miles	Nay my lorde, he can of no bourdyng, þis boy.	
Rex	No sir? With þi leue we schall lere hym.	

109. ere] *Ho'* nerre
111. were] *Suppl TS*
132. *Ho' would read* sawe *for* saie, *or* saide he *for* saie we
139. he] *K* we

I Filius	Mi lorde, se ther knyghtis þat knawe and are kene,
	How þai come to youre courte withoutyn any call. 150
Rex	ȝa sone, and musteris grete maistries, what may þis bymene?
I Dux	My lorde, for youre myghtis are more þan þei all f.167
	They seke you as souerayne, and sertis þat is sene.
Rex	Nowe certis, sen ȝe saie so, assaie hym I schall,
	For I am fayner of þat freyke þen othir fiftene, 155
	ȝae, and hym þat firste fande, faire myght hym fall.
I Miles	Lorde, lely we lereth you no legh,
	Þis liffe þat he ledis will lose hym.
Rex	Wele sirs, drawes you adrygh,
	And bewscheris, bryngis ȝe hym nygh, 160
	For yif all þat his sleghtis be slye
	ȝitte or he passe we schalle appose hym.
	O, my harte hoppis for joie
	To se nowe þis prophette appere.
	Wc schall haue goode game with þis boy— 165
	Takis hede, for in haste ȝe schall here.
	I leve we schall laugh and haue likyng
	To sc nowe þis lidderon her he leggis oure lawis.
II Dux	Harke cosyne, þou comys to karpe with a kyng,
	Take tente and be conande, and carpe as þou knowis. 170
I Dux	Ya, and loke þat þou be not a sotte of thy saying,
	But sadly and sone þou sette all þi sawes.
Rex	Hym semys full boudisch, þat boy þat þei bryng.
II Dux	Mi lorde, and of his bordyng grete bostyng men blawes.
Rex	Whi, þerfore haue I soughte hym to see. 175
	Loke, bewsheris, ye be to oure bodis boune.
I Dux	Knele doune here to þe kyng on thy knee.
II Dux	Naye, nedelyngis yt will not be.
Rex	Loo sirs, he mekis hym no more vnto me f.167ᵛ
	Þanne it were to a man of þer awne toune. 180
I Dux	Whe! Go, lawmere, and lerne þe to lowte
	Or þai more blame þe to-bring.
Rex	Nay, dredeles withouten any doute
	He knawes noȝt þe course of a kyng.
	And her beeis in oure bale, bourde or we blynne— 185
	Saie firste at þe begynnyng withall, where was þou borne?

---

149. knawe and are] *K* kant are and

152+ *Pen trials by the 'Cutler-Nandicke' hand in the right margin on f.167 (gild name and character-designations)*

152. þei] *This ed; MS* ye + i *suprascript, TS* ye, *Ho'* þere

168. nowe] ? *read* howe
her he] *Ho'* ther he, *K* her þat

174. II Dux] *This ed; om TS*

180. þer] *He* his

Do felawe, for thy faith, latte vs falle ynne.
Firste of þi ferleis, who fedde þe beforne?
What, deynes þou not? Lo sirs, he deffis vs with dynne.
Say, whare ledde ȝe þis lidrone? His langage is lorne.   190

I Miles   My lorde, his mervaylis to more and to myne
Or musteres emange vs both mydday and morne.

II Miles   Mi lorde, it were to fele
Of wonderes, he workith þam so wightely.

I Miles   Whe man, momelyng may nothyng avayle,   195
Go to þe kyng and tell hyme fro toppe vnto tayle.

Rex   Do bringe vs þat boy vnto bale,
For lely we leffe hym noȝt lightly.

I Dux   This mop mennes þat he may marke men to þer mede;
He makes many maistries and mervaylcs emange.   200

II Dux   V ml. folke faire gon he feede
With fyve looffis and two fisshis to fange.

Rex   Howe fele folke sais þou he fedde?

II Dux   V ml. lorde, þat come to his call.

Rex   ȝa boye? Howe mekill brede he þem bedde?   205

I Dux   But v looffis dare I wele wedde.   f.168

Rex   Nowe be þe bloode þat Mahounde bledde,
What, þis was a wondir at all.

II Dux   Nowe lorde, ij fisshis blissid he efte
And gaffe þame, and þer none was forgetyn.   210

I Dux   ȝa lorde, and xij lepfull þer lefte
Of releue whan all men had eten.

Rex   Of such anodir mangery no man mene may.

II Dux   Mi lorde, but his maistries þat musteris his myght.

Rex   But saie sirs, ar þer sawis soth þat þei saie?   215

II Miles   ȝa lorde, and more selcouth were schewed to oure sight.
One Lazar, a ladde þat in oure lande lay,
Lay loken vndir layre fro lymme and fro light,
And his sistir come rakand in rewfull arraye.
And lorde, for þer raryng he raysed hym full right,   220
And fro his grath garte hym gang
Euere forthe, withouten any evill.

189.   deffis] *Ho¹;* MS, TS dethis
190.   Say, whare] *He;* MS, TS Say deynis þou not whare
192.   Or musteres] *He* Er mustered, *K* He musteres
196.   tell hyme] *Interlined by J. Clerke*
199.   This] *TS;* MS Thus
       mennes] n¹ *altered to* y *by a later hand*
201.   *II Dux] Added by a later hand (? Clerke's)*
202.   two] *In a later hand (? Clerke's) over erasure*
214.   þat] *TS;* MS þat þat
215.   *Rex] Added to right in what may be another early hand; original character-designation, I Dux, deleted*
218.   light] *Altered from* lithe *by a later hand*
221.   grath] *He* grave

Rex	We, such lesyngis lastis to lange.
I Miles	Why lorde, wene ȝe þat wordis be wronge?
	Þis same ladde leuys vs emange. 225
Rex	Why, there hope Y be dedis of þe deuyll.

Why schulde ȝe haste hym to hyng
That sought not newly youre newys?

II Miles	My lorde, for he callis hym a kyng
	And claymes to be a kyng of Jewis. 230

Rex	But saie, is he kyng in his kyth wher he come froo?
I Miles	Nay lorde, but he callis hym a kyng his caris to kele.
Rex	Thanne is it litill wondir yf þat he be woo, f.168ᵛ

For to be weried with wrang sen he wirkis wele;
But he schalle sitte be myselfe sen ȝe saie soo. 235
Comes nerre, kyng, into courte. Saie, can ȝe not knele?
We schalle haue gaudis full goode and games or we goo.
Howe likis þa, wele lorde? Saie. What, deuyll, neuere a
dele?

I faute in my reuerant in otill moy,
I am of fauour, loo, fairer be ferre. 240
Kyte oute yugilment. Vta! Oy! Oy!
Be any witte þat Y watte it will waxe werre.

Seruicia primet,
Such losellis and lurdaynes as þou, loo,
Respicias timet. 245
What þe deuyll and his dame schall Y now doo?

Do carpe on, carle, for Y can þe cure.
Say, may þou not here me? Oy man, arte þou woode?
Nowe telle me faithfully before howe þou fore.
Forthe, frende. Be my faith, þou arte a fonde foode. 250

I Dux	My lorde, it astonys hym, youre steuen is so store
	Hym had leuere haue stande stone still þer he stode.
Rex	And whedir þe boy be abasshid of Herrowde byg blure
	That were a bourde of þe beste, be Mahoundes bloode.
II Dux	My lorde, Y trowe youre fauchone hym flaies 255
	And lettis hym.
Rex	Nowe lely I leue þe,

And therfore schall Y waffe it away
And softely with a septoure assaie.

---

224. þat] *K* þes
225. leuys] *This ed; TS* lenys *(MS* u *or* n*)*
243–6. *Lineation this ed; two lines in MS, TS*
243. *Hoᵗ Sevitia perimet; (MS* pᵗmet*)*
245. timet] *Hoᵗ* temet
255. hym flaies] *Hoᵗ* does hym flaie
256–60. *Lineation TS; in MS,* And lettis hym *written as part of 255, the rest three lines dividing after* away *and* assaie

Nowe sir, be perte Y þe pray,
   For none of my gromys schall greue þe.   260

Si loqueris tibi laus,
   Pariter quoque prospera dantur;
Si loqueris tibi fraus,
   Fell fex et bella parantur.
   Mi menne, ʒe go menske hym with mayne,   265
     And loke yhow þat it wolde seme.

I Dux   Dewcus fayff ser and sofferayne.
II Dux   Sir vdins amangidre demayne.
Rex   Go aunswer thaym grathely agayne.
     What, deuyll, whedir dote we or dreme?   270

I Miles   Naye we gete noʒt o worde, dare Y wele wedde,   f.169
     For he is wraiste of his witte or will of his wone.
Rex   ʒe saie he lakkid youre lawis as ʒe þat ladde ledde?
II Miles   ʒa lorde, and made many gaudis as we haue gone.
Rex   Nowe sen he comes as a knave and as a knave cledde,   275
     Wherto calle ye hym a kyng?
I Dux   Nay lorde, he is none,
   But an harlotte is hee.
Rex   What, deuyll, Y ame harde stedde,
   A man myght as wele stere a stokke as a stone.
I Filius   My lorde, þis faitour so fouly is affrayde,
     He loked neuere of lorde so langly allone.   280
Rex   No sone, þe rebalde seis vs so richely arayed
     He wenys we be aungelis euere-ilkone.
II Dux   My lorde, Y holde hym agaste of youre gaye gere.
Rex   Grete lordis augh to be gay.
     Here schall no man do to þe dere,   285
     And therfore yit nemyne in my nere –
     For by the grete god, and þou garre me swere
     Þou had neuere dole or this day.

   Do carpe on tyte, karle, of thy kynne.
I Dux   Nay, nedelyngis he neuyns you with none.   290
Rex   Þat schalle he bye or he blynne –
II Dux   A, leves lorde.
Rex   Lattis me allone.

I Dux   Nowe goode lorde, and ye may, meue you no more,
     Itt is not faire to feght with a fonned foode,

---

260. gromys] r *suprascript*
261–4. *Lineation this ed; two lines in MS, TS*
266. yhow] *Ho'* how
267–8. Dewcus *and* Sir vdins *taken as parts of character-designations in TS*
267. fayff] *He* sayff
270. dreme] *He;* MS, TS dremys
276–7. *Lineation TS; three lines in MS, dividing after* kyng *and* hee
278. as²] *He* or

	But gose to youre counsaille and comforte you þere.	295
Rex	Thou sais soth. We schall see yf so will be goode,	f.169ᵛ
	For certis oure sorowes are sadde.	
II Filius	What a deuyll ayles hym?	
	Mi lorde, I can garre you be gladde,	
	For in tyme oure maistir is madde.	300
	He lurkis, loo, and lokis like a ladde,	
	He is wode lorde, or ellis his witte faylis hym.	

III Filius   Mi lorde, ȝe haue mefte you as mekill as ȝe may,

    For yhe myght menske hym no more were he Mahounde;

And sen it semys to be soo, latte vs nowe assaie.   305

Rex   Loke, bewscheris, ȝe be to oure bodis boune.

I Dux   Mi lorde, howe schulde he dowte vs? He dredis not youre

                                   dray.

Rex   Nowe do fourthe, þe deuyll myght hym droune!

And sen he freyms falsed and makis foule fraye,

  Raris on hym rudely, and loke ȝe not roune.   310

I Filius   Mi lorde, I schall enforce myselffe sen ȝe saie soo.

    Felawe, be noȝt afferde nor feyne not þerfore,

But telle vs nowe some truffillis betwene vs twoo,

  And none of oure men schall medill þam more.

      And þerfore by resoune array þe,   315

        Do telle vs some poynte for thy prowe.

      Heris þou not what Y saie þe?

      Þou mummeland myghtyng, I may þe

        Helpe, and turne þe fro tene as Y trowe.

II Filius   Loke vppe ladde, lightly, and loute to my lorde here,   320

    For fro bale vnto blisse he may nowe þe borowe.

Carpe on, knave, kantely, and caste þe to corde here,

  And saie me nowe somwhat, þou sauterell, with sorowe.

      Why standis þou as stille as a stone here?

        Spare not, but speke in þis place here   325

      Þou gedlyng, it may gayne þe some grace here.

III Filius   My lorde, þis faitour is so ferde in youre face   f.170

                                   here

None aunswere in þis nede he nevyns you with none

                                   here.

303. mcftc] *This ed; TS* meste

307. dray] *He; MS, TS* drays

308. Nota *to left in a later hand*

    droune] *This ed; MS* drawe, *TS* drawe [sonne], *He* drawe downe

309. freyms] *This ed; MS, TS* freyins

    fraye] *He; MS, TS* frayes

310. Hic *to right in a later hand*

    roune] *This ed; TS* ronne

319. Nota *to left in a later hand,* hic *to right in a later hand*

322. kantely] *This ed; TS* cautely

326+ *Catchword* Mi lorde þis faitour

327. *Quire Y begins*

    III Filius] *This ed (at foot of f.169ᵛ); om TS*

Do bewsher, for Beliall bloode and his bonys,
  Say somwhat – or it will waxe werre.   330
I Filius   Nay, we gete nouȝt one worde in þis wonys.
II Filius   Do crie we all on hym at onys.
Al chylder Oȝes! Oȝes! Oȝes!
Rex   O, ȝe make a foule noyse for þe nonys.
III Filius Nedlyng my lorde, it is neuere þe nerre.

I Filius   Mi lorde, all youre mutyng amendis not a myte,   335
  To medill with a madman is meruaille to me.
  Comaunde youre knyghtis to clothe hym in white
    And late hym carre as he come to youre contré.
Rex   Lo sirs, we lede you no lenger a lite,
  Mi sone has saide sadly how þat it schuld be –   340
  But such a poynte for a page is to parfite.
I Dux   Mi lorde, fooles þat are fonde þei falle such a fee.
Rex   What, in a white garmente to goo,
      Þus gayly girde in a gowne?
II Dux   Nay lorde, but as a foole forcid hym froo.   345
Rex   How saie ȝe sirs, schulde it be soo?
Al chylder Ȝa lord.
Rex   We, þan is þer no more,
    But boldely bidde þam be boune.

  Sir knyghtis, we caste to garre you be gladde,
    Oure counsaile has warned vs wisely and wele.   350
  White clothis we saie fallis for a fonned ladde,
    And all his foly in faith fully we feele.

I Dux   We will with a goode will for his wedis wende,
    For we wotte wele anowe what wedis he schall were.
II Dux   Loo, here is an haterell here at youre hende   f.170ᵛ
    Alle faciound þerfore foolis to feere.   356

I Miles   Loo here a joppon of joie,
    All such schulde be gode for a boy.
I Dux   He schalle be rayed like a roye,
    And schall be fonne in his folie.   360

329. *Ruled off from 328 and previous character-designation repeated.* Nota *to right in a later hand,* Pylatus *to left in a later hand*
  bewsher] *K; MS, TS* bewsheris
333. *Al chylder*] *Suppl this ed*
  Lineation this ed; Oȝes . . . Oȝes *to right of 332 in MS, TS*
334. Nota *to right in a later hand*
336. me] *TS; MS* mene
347–8. *Lineation TS (see next note)*
347. *Al chylder*] *In same script and inking as dialogue in MS; as character-designation in TS. This and* ȝa lorde *to right of 346 in MS*
  We . . . more *(TS* moo, *conj) one line with 348 in MS*
355. hende] *He; MS, TS* hente

II Dux	We, thanke þam, euyll motte þou the.
I Miles	Nay, we gete noȝt a worde wele Y warand.
II Miles	Man, mustir some meruaile to me.
I Dux	What, wene ȝe he be wiser þan we?

Leffe we and late þe kyng see 365
  Howe it is forcyd and farand.

Mi lorde, loke yf ȝe be paied,
  For we haue getyn hym his gere.

Rex Why, and is þis rebalde arayed?
  Mi blissing, bewscheris, ȝe bere. 370

Gose, garre crye in my courte and grathely garre write
  All þe dedis þat we haue done in þis same degré.
And who fyndis hym greued late hym telle tyte,
  And yf we fynde no defaute hym fallis to go free.

I Dux Oȝes! Yſ any wight with þis wriche any werse wate 375
  Werkis beris wittenesse who so wirkis wrang,
Buske boldely to þe barre his balis to abate,
  For my lorde, be my lewté, will not be deland lang.
My lorde, here apperes nonc to appeyre his estate.

Rex Wele þanne, fallis hym goo free. 380
  Sir knyghtis, þanne grathis you goodly to gange,
And repaire with youre present and saie to Pilate
  We graunte hym oure frenschippe all fully to fang.

I Miles My lorde, with youre leue þis way schall we lere, f.171
  Vs likis no lenger here to abide. 385

II Miles Mi lorde, and he worþe ought in were,
  We come agayne with goode chere.

Rex Nay bewscheris, ȝe fynde vs not here,
  Oure leue will we take at þis tyde

And rathely araye vs to reste, 390
  For such notis has noyed vs or nowe.

I Dux Ȝa, certis lorde, so holde Y beste,
  For þis gedlyng vngoodly has greued you.

II Dux Loke ȝe bere worde as ye wotte,
  Howe wele we haue quitte vs þis while. 395

I Miles We, wise men will deme it we dote
  But if we make ende of oure note.

373. *Lineation TS;* late ... tyte *at beginning of 374 in MS*
375. *Post* Rex *added to right of character-designation, ? by J. Clerke*
  Oȝes] *This ed; TS* O yes
  wriche] *K* wreche
376. *K* Of his werkis beris witenesse, what so he wirkis wrang
378. lang] *Suppl He*
380. *? Extra-metrical; He would suppl* us emang
382. *Ruled off from 381, erased character-designation to right (main scribe)*
385. here to abide] *TS; MS* to abide here
390. rathely] *TS; MS* ȝathely

Rex	Wendis fourth, þe deuyll in þi throte,
	We fynde no defaute hym to file.

Wherfore schulde we flaye hym or fleme hym   400
    We fynde noȝt in rollis of recorde;
And sen þat he is dome, for to deme hym,
    Ware þis a goode lawe for a lorde?

Nay losellis, vnlely ȝe lerned all to late,   404
    Go lere þus lordingis of youre londe such lessons to lere.
Repaire with youre present and saie to Pilate
    We graunte hym oure poure all playne to appere,
And also oure greuaunce forgeue we algate
    And we graunte hym oure grace with a goode chere.
As touchyng þis brothell þat brawlis or debate,   410
    Bidde hym wirke as he will, and wirke noght in were.
    Go telle hym þis message fro me,
        And lede fourth þat mytyng, euyll motte he the.

I Miles	Mi lorde, with youre leue, late hym be,	
	For all to longe ledde hym haue we.	415
II Miles	What, ȝe sirs, my lorde, will ȝe see?	

Rex	What, felawes? Take ȝe no tente what I telle you	f.171ᵛ
	And bid you? Þat yoman ye ȝeme.	
II Miles	Mi lorde, we schall wage hym an ill way.	
Rex	Nay bewscheris, be not so bryme.	420
	Fare softely, for so will it seme.	
I Miles	Nowe sen we schall do as ye deme,	
	Adewe sir.	
Rex	Daunce on, in þe deuyll way.	

399. file] *Ho'; MS, TS* slee
418. ȝeme] *He* ȝeme amelle you
423+   *Rest of f.171ᵛ blank; f.172 blank*

XXXII The Cooks and Waterleaders

The Remorse of Judas

Pilatus	Pees, bewscheres, I bidde you, þat beldis here aboute me, f.172ᵛ

Pees, bewscheres, I bidde you, þat beldis here aboute me,   f.172ᵛ
   And loke þat ȝe stirre with no striffe but stande stone still,
Or by þe lorde þat me liffe lente I schall garre you lowte me,
   And all schall byde in my bale þat wirkis noȝt my will.
      Ye rebaldis þat regnys in þis rowte,   5
      Ȝe stynte of youre steuenyng so stowte,
      Or with þis brande þat dere is to doute
        All to dede I schall dryue you þis day.

For sir Pilate of Pounce as prince am Y preued,
   As renke moste royall in richeste array,   10
Þer is no berne in þis burgh has me aboute heuyd,
   But he sekis me for souereyne, in certayne Y saie,
     To knawe.
      Therfore take hede to youre lordis estate,
      Þat none jangill nor jolle at my ȝate,   15
      Nor no man to grath hym no gate
     Tille I haue seggid and saide all my sawe.

For I ame þe luffeliest lappid and laide,
   With feetour full faire in my face,
My forhed both brente is and brade   20
   And myne eyne þei glittir like þe gleme in þe glasse.

And þe hore þat hillis my heed
   Is even like to þe golde wyre,
My chekis are bothe ruddy and reede
   And my coloure as cristall is cleere.   25

Ther is no prince preuyd vndir palle
   But I ame moste myghty of all to behold,
Nor no kyng but he schall come to my call,
   Nor grome þat dare greue me for golde.

Sir Kayphas, thurgh counsaill þi clergy is kid,   30
   For thy counsaille is knowyn for connand and clere;

---

  1. me] *Deleted in MS; retained by TS*
  3. lowte me] *TS; MS* lorde me, me *deleted*
13. *Lineation this ed; to right of* 10 *in MS, TS*
27. *Lineation this ed; to* behold *written to right of* 25 *by J. Clerke in MS; not incorporated in text by TS*

And sir Anna, þyn aunswer aught not to be hidde,
For þou is one and is abill and aught to be nere
In parlament playne.
And I am prince pereles youre poyntis to enquere: 35
How saie ȝe Jues of Jesus, þat swayne?
Haue done sirs, sais on youre sawis,
What tytill nowe haue ȝe vntill hym   f.173
And lely ȝe loke vppon youre lawes?
Saye, why sente ȝe so sone for to spille hym?   40

Anna   Sir, þat is prince and lorde of oure laye,
That traitour vntrewe þat ye of telle vs,
Nowe certayne and sone þe soth schall I saie
It is Jesus þat japer þat Judas ganne selle vs.
He marres oure men in all þat he may,   45
His merueylis full mekill is mustered emelle vs,
That faitoure so false.
He dois many derffe dedis on oure Sabotte day,
Þat vnconnand conjeon he castis hym to quelle vs,
Fro man onto man he will compelle vs   50
And vndo you and ourselffe als.
Youreselffe he will fordo
And he halde furth þis space,
And all þis Jurie to
Yf þat ye graunte hym grace.   55

Pilatus   Sir Anna, þis aunswere allow I no thyng,
I halde it but hatereden, þis artikill hale;
And therfore ser busshoppe, at my biddyng,
Do telle me nowe trewly þe texte of þis tale.
Do termyne it trewly and tyte   60
And lely ȝe lede it by þe lawe;
Felonye or falsed euyn here I defie it —
Saie me sadly þe soth, for loue or for awe.

Kayphas   Sir Pilate, þe talis þe traitoure has tolde,
It heuys vs in harte full haly to here þam.   65
Þe warlowe with his wilis he wenys þam to wolde,
Þe ladde with his lesyngis full lightly gan lere þam.
Full tyte will he take þam vntill hym
And he þus forth go with his gaudis,
Or speche ouersprede — ȝa, bettir is to spille hym,   70
The faitoure is so felle with his false fraudis.

Pilatus   Youre aunsweres is hedouse and hatefull to here.   f.173ᵛ
Hadde I not herde hym and myselfe had hym sene

38.   vntill] *He; MS, TS* vnto
46.   His] *TS; MS* This
47.   *Lineation as in MS; TS places between 49 and 50 (conj)*
52–5.   *Lineation TS; two lines in MS*
73.   not] *He; MS, TS* nowe

Yitt ȝe myght haue made me to trowe you intere;
But faute in hym I fynde none, but conande and clene. 75
For conande and clene can I clere hym,
No faute can I fynde to reffuse hym,
I hope yitt in haste ȝe schall here hym
Whanne he comys to racleyme – þan may ȝe cuse hym.

I Miles Lorde, fele of his ferles in faith haue we fonne, 80
Yone harlotte heuys oure hartis full of hate ire.
He sais hymselffe þat he is Goddis sone
And schall sitte on þe right hande beside his awne sire.
II Miles Þer talis is full trewe þat we telle.
On þe raynebowe þe rebalde it redis, 85
He sais he schall haue vs to heuene or to hell
To deme vs aday aftir oure dedis.

Pilatus To deme vs, in þe deuyll name? Say whedir? Saie whedir,
to þe deuyll?
What, dastardis, wene ye be wiser þan we?
I Miles Mi lorde, with youre leue, we neuen it for non ill, 90
He has mustered his mervayles to mo þan to me.
Mi soueraync lorde, yone sauterell he sais
He schall caste doune oure tempill, noȝt for to layne,
And dresse it vppe dewly within thre daies
Als wele as it was, full goodely agayne. 95

Anna Ȝa sir, and on oure awne Sabott day
Þanne werkis he werkis full wele.
Pilatus We, fye on hym, faitour, for ay,
For þei are darke dedis of þe deuyll.
Kayphas Sir, a noysomemare note newly is noysed 100
Þat greuis me more þan any kynne thyng,
He claymes hym clerly till a kyngdome of Jewes f.174
And callis hymselffe oure comelicst kyng.

Pilatus Kyng, in þc dcuillis name? We, fye on hym, dastard.
What, wenys þat woode warlowe ouere-wyn vs þus wightly?
A begger of Bedlem, borne as a bastard? 106
Nowe by Lucifer, lach I þat ladde I leue hym not lightly.
Anna Sir, þe harlotte is at Heroudes hall euyn her at your
hande.
Pilatus I sente to hym þat warlowe, þe deuyll myght hym wery.

76. clere] *He; MS, TS* clepe
89. wene ye] *K* wenes he
90. neuen it] *TS; MS* neuenist
97. wele] *Ha* yll
100. *He would read* Newly is noysed noysomare newes
105. wightly] *He; MS, TS* lightly
107. lach] *Ha; MS, TS* lath
109. hym¹] *Suppl K*

Kaiphas	It langis to youre lordschippe be lawe of þis land	110
	As souerayne youreselffe to sitte of enquery.	

Anna	Sir, þe traitoure has tolde vs mo trufullis truly	
	Wolde tene you full tyte and we you þam tolde.	
Pilatus	Nowe be Beliall bonis þat boy schall abie	
	And bring on his bak a burdeyne of golde.	115
I Filius	Mi lorde þat is ledar of lawis of þis lande,	
	3e sente hym youreselfe to Herowde þe kyng	
	And sais, 'Ðe dome of þat doge lies holy in your hande,	
	To deme hym or lose hym at youre likyng'.	

And þus 3e comaunded youre knyghtis for to saie;   120
For sir Heroude will serche hym full sore,
So þat he wende with no wilis away –
And þerfore, my goode lorde, moue you no more.

Kaiphas	Nowe certis þis was wele saide.	
	But sir, wille 3e sese nowe and we schall se syne?	125
Pilatus	Sir Kayphas and Anna, right so nowe I thynke.	
	Sittis, in Mahoundis blissing, and aske vs þe wyne –	
	3e knyghtis of my courte, comaundis vs to drynke.	

Judas	Allas for woo þat I was wrought	
	Or euere I come be kynde or kynne,	130
	I banne þe bonys þat me furth brought,	f.174ᵛ
	Woo worthe þe wombe þat I bredde ynne.	
	So may I bidde,	
	For I so falsely did to hym	
	Ðat vnto me grete kyndnesse kidde.	135

Ðe purse with his spens aboute I bare,
Ðer was none trowed so wele as I.
Of me he triste, no man mare,
And I betrayed hym traytourly
With a false trayne.   140
Sakles I solde his blessid body
Vnto Jues for to be slayne.

To slaa my souereyne assente I
And tolde þem þe tyme of his takyng,

110.   land] *Added by J. Clerke*
118.   sais] *Ho'* said
123.   *Lineation TS; between 120 and 121 in MS*
124–5.   *Lineation as in MS; TS treats as one line. 124 perhaps extra-metrical*
128.   *Additions to right, (ii) and (iii) possibly by J. Clerke, made at different times: (i)* Hic caret; *(ii)* loquela de primo filio; *(iii)* et aliis
134.   hym] *Ho' would suppl* ginne *or* winne
134–5.   *Lineation TS; one line in MS*
141–2.   *Lineation TS; one line in MS*
144.   takyng] *Ho'* taying

Shamously myselfe þus schente I   145
So sone for to sente to his slayng.
    Nowe wiste I howe he myght passe þat payne;
    To loke þat howe beste bote myght be
Vnto þe Jues I will agayne
    To saue hym – he myght passe free,   150
        Þis ware my will.
    Lorde, welthe and worschippe mot with yow be.
Pilatus   What tythandis, Judas, tellis þou vs till?

Judas   My tydyngis are tenefull, I telle ʒou
                Sir Pilate, þerfore I you praye,   155
            My maistir þat I gune selle ʒou,
                Gode lorde, late hym wende on his way.
Kaiphas   Nay, nedelyngis Judas, þat we denye.
                What mynde or mater has moued þe þus?
Judas   Sir, I haue synned full greuously,   160
                Betraied þat rightwisse bloode, Jesus
                And maistir myne.
Kayphas   Bewscher, what is þat till vs?
                Þe perill and þe plight is thyne.

            Thyne is þe wronge, þou wroughte it.   165
                Þou hight vs full trulye to take hym,
            And oures is þe bargayne, we boughte it –
                Loo, we are alle sente for to slee hym.
Judas   Allas, þat may me rewe full ill   f.175
                Giffe ʒe assente hym for to slaa.   170
Pilatus   Why, what wolde þou þat we did þertill?
Judas   I praie you goode lorde, late hym gaa,
                And here is of me youre paymente playne.
Kayphas   Naie, we will noght so,
                We bought hym for he schulde be slayne.   175

            To slee hym þiselffe þou assentit,
                Þis wate þou wondirly wele.
            What right is nowe to repente it?
                Þou schapist þiselffe vnseele.
Anna   Do waie Judas, þou dose for noght,   180
                Thy wordis I warne þe are in waste.

148. loke þat howe beste] *TS* loke howe beste þat *(conj)*
        bote myght be] *TS; MS* myght be bote
150. hym – he] *Ho¹* hym þat he
153–4. Hic caret loquela magna et diversa *to left in a later hand*
167. it] *TS; MS* hym
169. Judas] *Added by a later hand*
173. playne] *TS; MS* hale. *Ho¹, K would restore metre by reading* And here is playne / (Of
        me) youre payment. *Kayphas* Naie . . . so
176. assentit] *This ed; MS, TS* assente it
178. it] *Suppl TS*

Thyselffe to selle hym whanne þou vs sought,
Þou was agaynste hym þanne þe moste
Of vs ilkan.

Kayphas   We schall be venged on hym in haste,   185
Whedir þat euere he wille or none.

Pilatus   Þer wordis þat þou nenys noght nedis it,
Þou onhanged harlott, harke what I saie;
Spare of thy spekyng, noght spedis it,
Or walke oute at þe dore in þe deuill way.   190

Judas   Why will ye þanne noȝt latte hym passe
And haue of me agayne youre paie?

Pilatus   I telle þe traytoure, I wille it noght.

Judas   Allas, þanne am I lorne
Boþe bone and bloode.   195
Allas þe while so may I saie,
That euere I sente to spille his bloode.

To saue his bloode sirs, I saie youe,
And takes you þare youre payment hole.
Spare for to spille hym I praye youe,   f.175ᵛ
Ellis brewe ȝe me full mekill bale.   201

Pilatus   Nay, heriste þou Judas, þou schall agayne,
We will it nouȝt. What deuyll art þou?
When þou vs sought þou was full fayne
Of þis money. What aylis þe nowe   205
For to repente?

Judas   Agayne sirs here I giffe it you,
And saue hym þat he be noȝt schent.

Pilatus   To schende hym thyselfe has þe schamed,
Þou may lathe with þi liffe þat þou ledis,   210
Fondely as a false foole þiselffe has famed,
Therfore þe deuyll þe droune for thy darfe dedis.

Judas   I knawe my trespasse and my gilte,
It is so grete it garres me grise;
Me is full woo he schulde be spilte,   215
Might I hym saue of any wise
Wele were me þan.
Saue hym sirs – to youre seruise
I will me bynde to be your man.

Youre bondeman, lorde, to be   220
Nowe euere will I bynde me.

191. passe] *He* go
193. wille it noght] *He* wille noght so
194. lorne] *TS would suppl* this day, *K for* ay
194–5. *Lineation TS; one line in MS*
197. spille his bloode] *Ho*ᵗ felle *(or* file) þis foode

	Sir Pilate, ye may trowe me,	
	Full faithfull schall ʒe fynde me.	
Pilatus	Fynde þe faithfull? A, foule mot þe falle	
	Or þou come in oure companye,	225
	For by Mahoundes bloode þou wolde selle vs all.	
	Thi seruice will we noght, forthy	
	Þou art vnknowen.	
	Fals tiraunte, for þi traitoury	
	Þou art worþi to be hanged and drawen.	230

	Hanged and drawen schulde þou be, knave,	
	And þou had right, by all goode reasoune.	
	Thi maistirs bloode þou biddist vs saue	
	And þou was firste þat did hym treasoune.	
Judas	I cry ʒou mercy lorde, on me rewe,	235
	Þis werryd wight þat wronge has wrought.	f.176
	Haue mercy on my maistir trewe	
	Þat I haue in youre bandome brought	
	[. . . . . .]	
Pilatus	Goo jape þe Judas, and neuen it noght,	
	Nor move vs of þis matere more.	240

Anna	No more of þis matere þou move þe,	
	Þou momeland mytyng emell,	
	Oure poynte expresse her reproues þe	
	Of felonye falsely and felle.	
Kaiphas	He grucchis noʒt to graunte his gilte,	245
	Why schonnys þou noʒt to shewe þi schame?	
	We bought hym for he schulde be spilte,	
	All same we were consente to þe same	
	And þiselffe als.	
	Þou feyned noʒt for to defame,	250
	Þou saide he was a traytoure fals.	

Pilatus	ʒaa, and for a false faitoure	
	Thyselffe full fully gon file hym—	
	O þat was a trante of a traytour,	
	So sone þou schulde goo to begile hym.	255
I Miles	What, wolde þou þat we lete hym ga,	
	Yone weried wight þat wrought such wronge?	
	We will noght lose oure bargayne swaa,	
	So lightely for to late hym gang.	
	And reson why?	260

227. forthy] *TS; MS* for it
230. worþi] *TS; MS* woþi
231. knave] *TS; MS* knowen
238. Caret hic *to right in a later hand, deleted*
238+ *Line missing; TS suppl* I cry ʒou sore
253. fully] *Ho'* foully
file] *Ho'; MS, TS* selle
260. *To right of 257 by main scribe; repeated to right of 259 by J. Clerke, there deleted*

Latte we þat lotterell liffe ought long
It will be fonde, in faith, foly.

II Miles   Yone folte, for no fooles schall he fynde vs.
We wotte all full wele howe it was
His maistir whanne he gune bringe vs,   265
He praied yow my goode lord late hym not passe.
Pilatus   Nay, sertis, he schalle noȝt passe free
Þat we for oure mony has paied.
Judas   Take it agayne þat ȝe toke me   f.176ᵛ
And saue hym fro þat bittir braide,   270
Þan were I fayne.
Anna   Itt serues of noght þat þou has saide,
And therfore takis it tyte agayne.

Pilatus   Tyte agayne, traytoure, þou take it,
We wille it noght welde within oure wolde.   275
Ȝitt schalte þou noȝt, sawterell, þus sune forsake it,
For I schall sers hym myselffe sen þou has hym solde.
Kaiphas   Forsake it in faith, þat he ne schall,
For we will halde hym þat we haue.
The payment chenys þe withall,   280
The thar no nodir comenaunte craue
[. . .   . . .]
Judas   Sen ȝe assente hym for to slaa,
Vengeaunce I crie on you ilkone.

Ilkane I crie, þe deuill fordo youe,
And þat myghte I both here and see.   285
Herde heuenyng here I wnto youe,
For sorowe onsought ye on me se.

Kaiphas   Whe, fye on the, traytoure attaynte, at þis tyde,
Of treasoune þou tyxste hym þat triste þe for trewe.
Do buske þe henne, brothell, no lenger þou abide,   290
For if þou do, all þi respouns sare schall þe rewe.
Say, wote þou noght who is I?
Nowe be my nociens, myght I negh nere þe,
In certayne, ladde, yitt schulde I lere þe
To lordis to speke curtaisely.   295

Pilatus   Go thy gatis, geddlyng, and greue vs no more.
Leffe of þi talke, þe deuill mot þe hange.

263.   fooles] *K; MS, TS* foole
265.   bringe] *He* binde, *Ho'* minde
276.   þus] *He; MS, TS* þu
281+   *Line missing, no gap in MS; TS suppl* Nor mercy none
282.   *He would read* Sen for to sla hym assente ȝe haue
286.   here] *K* hete

Judas	Þat att ȝe toke me, take it you þere,	
	Ther with youre maistrie make yowe emange	
	And clayme it you clene,	300
	Me lathes with my liff, so liffe I to lang,	f.177
	My traitourfull torne he turment my tene.	

Sen for my treasoune haue I tane vnto me,
  Me thare aske no mercy, for none mon Y gete.
Therfore in haste myselffe schall fordo me,   305
  Allas þe harde while þat euere ete I meete.
    Thus schall I marke my mytyng meede
    And wirke me wreke with harte and will,
  To spille myselffe nowe wille I spede,
  For sadly haue I seruyd þertill.   310
      So walaway
  Þat euere I was in witte or wille
  Þat tristy trewe for to betraye.

Allas, who may I meue to,
  Shall I me take non othir reede?   315
Miselffe in haste I schall fordoo
  And take me nowe vnto my dede.

Kaiphas	Haue done nowe sir Pilate, late se what ȝe saie	
	As touchyng þis money þat we here haue,	
	Þat Judas in a wreth has wauyd away	320
	And keste vs crabbidly, þat cursed knave.	
	Howe saie ȝe þerby?	
Anna	Sir, sen he it slang we schall it saue.	
Kayphas	Tite truste it tille oure tresorie.	

Pilatus	Nay sir, noght soo.	
Kaiphas	Why sir, how þan?	325
Pilatus	Sir, it schall nouȝt combre vs nor come in oure corbonan.	
Kayphas	No, tille oure tresory certayne farther schall it nought.	
Pilatus	And se youreselffe soth certayne and skill	
	It is price of þe bloode þat we with it boght,	
	Therfore some othir poynte I purpose it till,	330
	And þus I deuyse:	
	A spotte of erthe for to by wayte nowe I will,	f.177ᵛ
	To berie in pilgrimes þat by þe wey dies.	

Pilgrimes and palmeres to putte þere –
  Sir Kaiphas and Anna, assente ȝe þerto? –
                                        335

298. take] t *and* k *superimposed on other letters*
302. he turment my] *He* me turmentis with
303. Sen for] *Ho'* For sen
314. meue] *or* mene
325+ *Perhaps a line missing between 325 and 326*
326. *Lineation He; two lines in MS, TS*
328. *Pilatus*] *Suppl this ed; suppl at 332 in TS, at 330 by He*
    skill] *TS; MS* skall

	And oþere false felons þat we forfare.	
Anna	As ʒe deme lorde, so wille we doo.	
Armiger	Hayle sir Pilate perles, and prince of þis empire,	
	Haile þe gaiest on grounde in golde þer ʒe glide,	
	Haile þe louffeliest lorde of lyme and of lyre,	340
	And all þe soferans semely þat sittith þe beside.	

Pilatus	What wolde þou?	
Armiger	A worde lorde, and wende.	
Pilatus	Nowe þou arte welcome iwisse.	

	But delyuere þe lightly withouten any lette,	
	We haue no tome all day to tente onto þe.	345
Armiger	A place here-beside lorde wolde I wedde-sette.	
Pilatus	What title has þou þerto? Is it þyne awne free?	
Armiger	Lorde, fre be my fredome me fallis it,	
	Þis tale is full trewe þat I telle ʒou,	
	And Caluary-locus men callis it.	350
	I wolle it wedde-sette, but not for to selle ʒou.	

Pilatus	What wolde þou borowe, bewshire? Belyve late me se.	
Armiger	If it ware youre lekyng, my lorde, for to lene it,	
	xxx^{ti} pens I wolde ʒe lente onto me.	
Kayphas	Yis bewshire, þat schall þou haue.	355
Pilatus	Shewe vs thi dedis and haue here þi mony.	f.178
Armiger	Haue her gode lord, but loke ʒe þame saue.	

Pilatus	Ʒis certis, we schall saue þame full soundely,	
	And ellis do we noght dewly oure deuere.	
	Faste, freke, for thy faith, on thy fote fonde þe,	360
	For fro þis place, bewschere, I soile þe foreuere.	
Armiger	Now sorowe on such socoure as I haue soght,	
	For all my tresoure thurgh tresoune I tyne.	

	I tyne it vntrewly by tresoune,	
	Þerfore nowe my way will I wende,	365
	For ʒe do me no right nor no resoune	
	I betake you all to þe fende.	
Pilatus	Nowe certis we are serued att all,	
	Þis place is purchesed full propirly.	
	The Felde of Bloode loke ʒe it call,	370
	I you comaunde ilkone forthy.	

Kaiphas	Sir, as ʒe comaunde vs call it schall we soo.	
	But my lorde, with youre leue, we may lende her no lengar,	

339. Hic caret *added to left by a later hand*
355+ *Catchword* Shew vs thy dedis
356. *Quire 3 begins*
361. Hic caret *to right in a first later hand;* loquela *added later beneath by J. Clerke*

But faste late vs founde to fang on oure foo,
3one gedlyng ongodly has brewed vs grete angir. 375

Anna   Do way sir busshoppe, and be not abaste,
For loste is all oure lekyng, lepe he so light.

Kaiphas   Nay sir, he schall not trusse so tite, and þat be 3e traste,
For it wynnes vs no worschippe þe werkis of yone wight,
But grete angir. 380
Forthy late vs dresse vs his deth for to dite,
And late we þis lotterell leue her no lengar.

f.178ᵛ

Pilatus   Sir Kayphas, thurgh counsaile comaunde we our knyghtis
To wacche on yone warlowe what way þat he wendis.
Do dresse 3ou nowe dewly, to yone doderon 3ou dightis 385
And lette no3t to laite hym in lande where he lendis,
Nor leuys hym no3t lightly.

II Miles   In faith we schall fette hym full farre fro his frendis.
Pilatus   Nowe walkis on in þe wanyand and wende youre way
wightely.

XXXIII The Tilemakers

Christ before Pilate 2: The Judgement

Pilatus   Lordyngis þat are lymett to þe lare of my liaunce,   f.180
3e schappely schalkes and schene for to schawe,
I charge 3ou as 3our chiftan þat 3e chatt for no chaunce,
But loke to youre lord here and lere at my lawe –
As a duke I may dampne 3ou and drawe. 5
Many bernys bolde are aboute me,
And what knyght or knave I may knawe
Þat list no3t as a lord for to lowte me,
I sall lere hym

389+ Finis *added by Clerke. Bottom half of f.178ᵛ blank; ff.179, 179ᵛ blank*
  1. *Pilatus*] *Same script and inking as dialogue, centred*

In the deueles name, þat dastard, to dowte me— 10
3a, who werkis any werkes withoute me,
   I sall charge hym in chynes to chere hym.

Tharfore 3e lusty ledes within þis lenght lapped,
  Do stynte of 3oure stalkyng and of stoutnes be stalland.
What traytoure his tong with tales has trapped, 15
  That fende for his flateryng full foull sall be falland.
  What broll ouere-brathely is bralland
    Or vnsoftely will sege in þer sales,
Þat caysteffe þus carpand and calland
    As a boy sall be broght vnto bales. 20
      Þerfore
    Talkes not nor trete not of tales,
    For þat gome þat gyrnes or gales,
      I myself sall hym hurte full sore.

Anna   3e sall sytt hym full sore, what sege will assay 3ou; 25
    If he like not youre lordshippe, þat ladde, sall 3e lere hym
As a pereles prince full prestly to pay 3ou,
  Or as a derworth duke with dyntes sall 3e dere hym.
Cayphas 3aa, in faythe 3e haue force for to fere hym,
    Thurgh youre manhede and myght bes he marred. 30
No chyualrus chiftan may chere hym
    Fro that churll with charge 3e haue charred
    [. . .   . . .]
    In pynyng payne bees he parred.
Anna   3aa, and with schath of skelpys yll scarred
    Fro tyme þat youre tene he haue tasted. 35

Pilatus Now certes, as me semes, whoso sadly has soght 3ou, f.180ᵛ
    3oure praysyng is prophetable 3e prelates of pees.
Gramercy 3oure goode worde, and vngayne sall it no3t you
  That 3e will say the sothe and for no sege cese.
Cayphas Elles were it pité we appered in þis prees— 40
  But consayue how 3oure knyghtes ere command.
Anna   3a my lord, þat leve 3e no lese,
    I can telle you 3ou tydes sum tythand
      Ful sadde.
Pilatus Se, they bring 3oone brolle in a bande. 45
  We sall here nowe hastely at hand
    What vnhappe before Herowde he had.

---

15. traytoure] *He; MS, TS* traytoures
24. hym] *TS; MS* hyn
32+ *Line missing, no gap in MS; TS suppl* And chasted
33. *Ruled off, and previous character-designation repeated (main scribe)*
35. tasted] d *added later*
36. *Pilatus*] *This ed; om TS*
42. my] *TS; MS* my my
43. tythand] *He; MS, TS* tythandis

I Miles	Hayll louelyest lorde þat euere lawe led ʒitt,
	Hayll semelyest vndre sylke on euere ilka syde,
	Hayll stateliest on stede in strenghe þat is sted ʒitt, 50
	Hayll liberall, hayll lusty to lordes allied.
Pilatus	Welcome, what tydandis þis tyde?
	Late no langgage lightly nowe lette ʒou.
II Miles	Sir Herowde ser, it is noght to hyde,
	As his gud frende grathely he grete yowe 55
	Foreuere.
	In what manere þat euere he mete ʒou,
	By hymselfe full sone wille he sette ʒou
	And sais þat ʒe sall not disseuer.

Pilatus	I thanke hym full thraly; and ser, I saie hym þe same — 60
	But what meruelous materes dyd þis myron þer mell?
I Miles	For all þe lordis langage his lipps, ser, wer lame;
	For any spirringes in þat space no speche walde he spell,
	Bot domme as a dore gon he dwell.
	Þus no faute in hym gon he fynde, 65
	For his dedis to deme hym to qwell,
	Nor in bandis hym brathely to bynde;
	And þus
	He sente hym to youreself, and assynde f.181
	Þat we, youre knyghtis, suld be clenly enclyned 70
	And tyte with hym to you to trus.

Pilatus	Syrs, herkens, here ʒe not what we haue oppon hand?
	Loo howe þere knyghtes carpe þat to þe kyng cared.
	Syr Herowde, þai say, no faute in me fand,
	He fest me to his frenschippe, so frendly he fared. 75
	Moreover sirs, he spake — and noght spared —
	Full gentilly to Jesu, þis Jewe,
	And sithen to ther knyghtis declared
	How fawtes in hym fande he but fewe
	To dye. 80
	He taste hym, I telle ʒou for trewe,
	For to dere hym he demed vndewe,
	And sirs, ye sothly saie I.

Caiphas	Sir Pilate oure prince, we prelatis nowe pray ʒou
	Sen Herowde fraysted no ferþer þis faitour to flaye, 85
	Resayue in ʒour sall þer sawes þat I saie ʒou,
	Late bryng hym to barre and at his berde sall we baye.
Anna	ʒa, for and he wende þus by wiles away
	I wate wele he wirke will vs wondre.

49.   vndre sylke on] *Ha; MS, TS* vndre on, *Ho'* vndre sonne
83.   ye] *This ed; TS* þe, *Ho'* þis
      sothly] *He* sothe, *K* same
85.   flaye] *This ed; TS* slaye (*MS long s- or f-*)

   Oure menȝé he marres þat he may,   90
    With his seggynges he settes þam in sondre,
     With synne;
    With his blure he bredis mekill blondre.
    Whills ȝe haue hym nowe haldes hym vndir –
    We sall wery hym away yf he wynne.   95

Cayphas Sir, no tyme is to tarie þis traytour to taste.
    Agayne ser Cesar hymselfe he segges, and saies
   All þe wightis in this world wirkis in waste
   Þat takis hym any tribute – þus his teaching outrayes.
    Ȝitt forther he feynes slik affraies,   100
    And sais þat hymself is God son.
    And ser, oure lawe leggis and layes
     In what faytour falsed is fon
      Suld be slayne.
Pilatus   For no schame hym to shende will we shon. 105
Anna   Sir, witnesse of þis wanes may be wonne, f.181ᵛ
    Þat will telle þis withowten any trayne.

Cayphas I can reken a rable of renkes full right,
    Of perte men in prese fro this place ar I pas,
   Þat will witnesse, I warande, þe wordis of þis wight, 110
   How wikkidly wrought þat þis wrecche has:
   Simon, Ȝarus and Judas,
    Datan and Gamaliell,
   Neptalim, Leui and Lucas,
    And Amys þis maters can mell   115
     Togithere.
    Þer tales for trewe can they telle
    Of this faytour þat false is and felle,
     And in legyng of lawes ful lithre.

Pilatus Ȝa, tussch for youre tales, þai touche not entente. 120
    Þer witnesse I warande þat to witnesse ȝe wage,
   Some hatred in ther hartis agaynes hym haue hent
    And purpose be this processe to putt doun þis page.
Caiphas Sir, in faith vs fallith not to fage,
    Þai are trist men and true þat we telle ȝou. 125
Pilatus Youre swering, seris, swiftely ȝe swage,
    And no more in this maters ye mell ȝou
     I charge.
Anna   Sir, dispise not þis speche þat we spell you.
Pilatus If ȝe feyne slike frawdis I sall felle ȝou, 130
    For me likis noght youre langage so large.

---

 106. *To right of character-designation (foot of f.181), ? Memorandum, or perhaps merely a*
    pen-trial, by a later hand
 108. *Cayphas] Suppl by J. Clerke*
 112-5. *Lineation TS; two lines in MS*
 117. they] *K* we

Caiphas   Oure langage is to large, but ȝoure lordshipp releue vs.
        Ȝitt we both beseke you late brynge hym to barre;
        What poyntes þat we putte forth latt your presence
                                appreue vs—
        Ȝe sall here how þis harlott heldes out of herre.   135
Pilatus   Ȝa, butt be wise, witty, and warre.
Anna   Ȝis sir, drede ȝou noȝt for nothyng we doute hym.
Pilatus   Fecche hym, he is noght right ferre—
        Do bedell, buske þe abowte hym.
Preco   I am fayne   140
        My lorde for to lede hym or lowte hym.   f.182
        Vncleth hym, clappe hym and clowte hym
        If ȝe bid me I am buxhome and bayne.

        Knyghtis, ȝe er commaundid with þis caityf to care,
        And bryng hym to barre, and so my lord badd.   145
I Miles   Is þis thy messege?
Preco   Ȝa sir.
I Miles   Þan moue þe no mare,
        For we ar light for to leppe and lede forthe þis ladd.
II Miles   Do steppe furth; in striffe ert þou stadde,
        I vphalde full euyll has þe happed.
I Miles   O man, thy mynde is full madde,   150
        In oure clukis to be clowted and clapped
          And closed.
II Miles   Þou bes lassched, lusschyd and lapped.
I Miles   Ȝa, rowted, russhed and rapped,
        Þus thy name with noye sall be noysed.   155

II Miles   Loo this sege her, my souerayne, þat ȝe for sente.
Pilatus   Wele, stirre noȝt fro þat stede, but stande stille þare.
        Bot he schappe som shrewdnesse with shame bese he shente,
        And I will frayst in faith to frayne of his fare.
Caiphas   We! Outte! Stande may I noȝt, so I stare.   160
Anna   Ȝa, harrowe of this traytour with tene.
Pilatus   Say renkes, what rewth gars you rare?
        Er ye woode or wittles I wene?
         What eyles ȝou?
Caiphas   Out, slike a sight suld be sene.   165
Anna   Ȝa, allas, conquered ar we clene.
Pilatus   We, ere ȝe fonde, or youre force fayles ȝou?

138. *Pilatus] Suppl Ho¹*
141. *Previous character-designation repeated (main scribe)*
146. *Preco, I Miles²] Suppl TS*
147. *þis] This ed; MS þs, TS þe*
155. *name] He; MS, TS named*
159. *his] He; MS, TS hir*
163. *Er ye] Ho¹ Ye er*

Caiphas	A, ser, saugh ȝe noȝt þis sight, how þat þer schaftes schuke,
	And thez baneres to this brothell þai bowde all on brede?
Anna	Ȝa, ther cursed knyghtes by crafte lete them croke f.182ᵛ
	To worshippe þis warlowe vnworthy in wede. 171
Pilatus	Was it dewly done þus indede?
Caiphas	Ȝa, ȝa sir, oureselfe we it sawe.
Pilatus	We, spitte on them, ill mott þai spede –
	Say dastardes, þe deuyll mote ȝou drawe, 175
	How dar ȝe
	Þer baners on brede þat her blawe
	Lat lowte to þis lurdan so lawe?
	O faytouris, with falshed how fare ȝe?

III Miles	We beseke you and tho senioures beside ȝou sir sitte, 180
	With none of oure gouernaunce to be greuous and gryll,
	For it lay not in oure lott þer launces to lett,
	And þis werke þat we haue wrought it was not oure will.
Pilatus	Þou lise – harstow lurdan? – full ille.
	Wele þou watte if þou witnes it walde. 185
IV Miles	Sir, oure strengh myght noȝt stabill þam stille,
	They hilded for ought we couthe halde,
	Oure vnwittyng.
V Miles	For all oure fors in faith did þai folde
	As þis warlowe worschippe þai wolde – 190
	And vs semid, forsoth, it vnsittyng.

Caiphas	A, vnfrendly faytours, full fals is youre fable,
	Þis segge with his suttelté to his seett haþ you sesid.
VI Miles	Ȝe may say what you semes ser, bot þer standerdes to stabill
	What freyke hym enforces full foull sall he be fesid. 195
Anna	Be þe deuyllis nese, ȝe ar doggydly diseasid –
	A, henne-harte, ill happe mot ȝou hente.
Pilatus	For a whapp so he whyned and whesid,
	And ȝitt no lasshe to þe lurdan was lente.
	Foul fall ȝou. 200
III Miles	Sir, iwisse no wiles we haue wente.
Pilatus	Shamefully ȝou satt to be shente,
	Here combred caystiffes I call ȝou.

IV Miles	Sen ȝou lykis not, my lord, oure langage to leve, f.183
	Latte bryng the biggest men þat abides in þis land 205
	Propirly in youre presence þer pousté to preve;
	Beholde þat they helde nott fro þei haue þaim in hand.
Pilatus	Now ȝe er ferdest þat euere I fand,
	Fy on youre faynte hertis in feere.

175. dastardes] *He; MS, TS* dastard
198. he] *K* ye
202. *Pilatus] This ed; om TS*
204. *Character-designation given twice (main scribe)*

Stir þe, no langer þou stande   210
Þou bedell, þis bodworde þou bere
   Thurgh þis towne,
Þe wyghtest men vnto were
And þe strangest þer standerdis to stere,
   Hider blithely bid þam be bowne.   215

Preco   My souerayne, full sone sall be serued youre sawe,
   I sall bryng to þer baneres right bigg men and strange.
A company of keuellis in this contré I knawe
   That grete ere and grill, to þe gomes will I gange.
Say, ye ledis botht lusty and lange,   220
   Ʒe most passe to ser Pilate apace.

I Miles   If we wirke not his wille it wer wrang,
   We ar redy to renne on a race
      And rayke.

Preco   Then tarie not, but tryne on a trace   225
And folow me fast to his face.

II Miles   Do lede vs, vs lykes wele þis lake.

Preco   Lorde, here are þe biggest bernes þat bildis in þis burgh,
   Most stately and strange if with strenght þai be streyned.
Leve me ser, I lie not, to loke þis lande thurgh,   230
   Þai er myghtiest men with manhode demened.

Pilatus   Wate þou wele, or ellis has þou wenyd?

Preco   Sir, I wate wele withoute wordis moo.

Caiphas   In thy tale be not taynted nor tenyd.   f.183ᵛ

Preco   We, nay ser, why shuld I be soo?   235

Pilatus   Wele þan,
   We sall frayst or they founde vs fer fro
To what game þai begynne for to go.
   Sir Cayphas, declare þam Ʒe can.

Caiphas   Ʒe lusty ledis, nowe lith to my lare,   240
   Schappe Ʒou to þer schaftis þat so schenely her schyne.
If Ʒon baners bowe þe brede of an hare
   Platly Ʒe be putte to perpetuell pyne.

I Miles   I sall holde þis as even as a lyne.

Anna   Whoso schakis with schames he shendes.   245

II Miles   I, certayne I saie as for myne,
   Whan it sattles or sadly discendis
      Whare I stande –
When it wryngis or wronge it wendis,
   Outher bristis, barkis, or bendes –   250
   Hardly lat hakke of myn hande.

219. þe] *Ho¹* þer
242. Ʒon] *This ed; TS* Ʒou
     baners] *Craigie (in Furnivall Miscellany, p. 57); MS, TS* barnes
     of] *TS; MS* of of
250. barkis] *He* brekis

Pilatus	Sirs, waites to þer wightis þat no wiles be wrought,
	Þai are burely and brode, þare bost haue þai blowen.
Anna	To neven of þat nowe ser it nedis right noght,
	For who curstely hym quytes he sone sall be knawen. 255
Cayphas	3a, þat dastard to dede sall be drawen,
	Whoso fautis he fouly sall falle.
Pilatus	Nowe knyghtis, sen þe cokkis has crowen,
	Haue hym hense with hast fra this halle
	His wayes. 260
	Do stiffely steppe on þis stalle,
	Make a crye, and cantely þou call
	Euene like as ser Annay þe sais.

Anna	Oyes. Jesu, þou Jewe of gentill Jacob kynne,
	Þou nerthrist of Nazareth, now neuend is þi name. 265
	Alle creatures þe accuses. We commaunde þe comme in f.184
	And aunswer to þin enemys; deffende now thy fame.

Et Preco, semper post Annam, recitabit judicatur Jesus.

Cayphas	We! Out! We are shente alle for shame,
	Þis is wrasted all wrange as I wene.
Anna	For all þer boste 3one boyes are to blame. 270
Pilatus	Slike a sight was neuere 3it sene.
	Come sytt,
	My comforth was caught fro me clene –
	I vpstritt, I me myght no3t abstene
	To wirschip hym in wark and in witte. 275

Cayphas	Þerof meruayled we mekill what moued 3ou in mynde
	In reuerence of þis ribald so rudely to ryse.
Pilatus	I was past all my powre þogh I payned me and pynd,
	I wrought not as I wolde in no maner of wise.
	Bot syrs, my spech wele aspise: 280
	Wightly his wayes late hym wende,
	Þus my dome will dewly deuyse,
	For I am ferde hym in faith to offende
	In sightes.
Anna	Þan oure lawe were laght till an ende 285
	To his tales if 3e treuly attende –
	He enchaunted and charmed oure knyghtis.

Cayphas	Be his sorcery, ser – youreselffe þe soth sawe –
	He charmed oure chyualers and with myscheffe
	enchaunted.

262.   cantely] *This ed; TS* cautely
264.   Oyes] *Added to left by J. Clerke*
      iewe] *This ed; TS* rewe
265.   nerthrist] *He* netherist
267+   SD *(main scribe) in red, to right of 266–7*
274.   me] *TS; MS* my
289.   charmed] *K; MS, TS* charmes

	To reuerence hym ryally we rase all on rowe;	290
	Doutles we endure not of þis dastard be daunted.	
Pilatus	Why, what harmes has þis hatell here haunted?	
	I kenne to convyk hym no cause.	
Anna	To all gomes he God son hym graunted	
	And liste not to leve on oure lawes.	295
Pilatus	Say man,	
	Consayues þou noȝt what comberous clause	f.184ᵛ
	Þat þis clargye accusyng þe knawse?	
	Speke, and excuse þe if þou can.	

Jesus	Euery man has a mouthe þat made is on molde	300
	In wele and in woo to welde at his will,	
	If he gouerne it gudly like as God wolde	
	For his spirituale speche hym thar not to spill.	
	And what gome so gouerne it ill,	
	Full vnhendly and ill sall he happe;	305
	Of ilk tale þou talkis vs vntill	
	Þou accounte sall, þou can not escappe.	
Pilatus	Sirs myne,	
	Ȝe fonne in faithe, all þe frappe,	
	For in þis lede no lese can I lappe	310
	Nor no poynte to putt hym to pyne.	

Caiphas	Withoute cause ser we come not þis carle to accuse hym,	
	And þat will we ȝe witt as wele is worthy.	
Pilatus	Now I recorde wele þe right ȝe will no raþere refuse hym	
	To he be dreuen to his dede and demed to dye;	315
	But takes hym vnto you forthé,	
	And like as youre lawe will you lere,	
	Deme ȝe his body to abye.	
Anna	O, sir Pilate withouten any pere,	
	Do way,	320
	Ȝe wate wele withouten any were	
	Vs falles not, nor oure felowes in feere,	
	To slo no man – youreself þe soth say.	

Pilatus	Why suld I deme to dede þan withoute deseruyng in dede?	
	But I haue herde al haly why in hertes ȝe hym hate.	325
	He is fautles, in faith, and so God mote me spede	
	I graunte hym my gud will to gang on his gate.	
Caiphas	Nought so ser, for wele ȝe it wate,	
	To be kyng he claymeth, with croune,	f.185

---

293. convyk] *TS;* MS covyk
299. excuse] *Ho¹* expurge
303. thar] *Suppl TS*
309. fonne] *This ed;* TS foune
      þe] *This ed;* TS ȝe
323. man] *TS;* MS nan

	And whoso stoutely will steppe to þat state	330
	ȝe suld deme ser, to be dong doune	
	And dede.	
Pilatus	Sir, trulye þat touched to treasoune,	
	And or I remewe he rewe sall þat reasoune,	
	And or I stalke or stirre fro þis stede.	335

Sir knyghtis þat ar comly, take þis caystiff in keping,
Skelpe hym with scourges and with skathes hym scorne.
Wrayste and wrynge hym to, for wo to he be wepyng,
And þan bryng hym before vs as he was beforne.

I Miles	He may banne þe tyme he was borne,	340
	Sone sall he be serued as ȝe saide vs.	
Anna	Do wappe of his wedis þat are worne.	
II Miles	All redy ser, we haue arayde vs.	
	Haue done,	
	To þis broll late vs buske vs and brayde vs	345
	As ser Pilate has propirly prayde vs.	
III Miles	We sall sette to hym sadly sone.	

IV Miles	Late vs gete of his gere, God giffe hym ille grace.	
I Miles	Þai ere tytt of tite lo, take þer his trasshes.	
III Miles	Nowe knytte hym in þis corde.	
II Miles	I am cant in þis case.	350
IV Miles	He is bun faste – nowe bete on with bittir brasshis.	
I Miles	Go on, lepis, harȝé lordingis, with lasshes,	
	And enforce we, þis faitour, to flay hym.	
II Miles	Late vs driffe to hym derfly with dasshes,	
	Alle rede with oure rowtes we aray hym	355
	And rente hym.	
III Miles	For my parte I am prest for to pay hym.	
IV Miles	Ȝa, sende hym sorow, assaye hym.	
I Miles	Take hym þat I haue tome for to tente hym.	

II Miles	Swyng to this swyre to swiftely he swete.	f.185ᵛ
III Miles	Swete may þis swayne for sweght of our swappes.	361
IV Miles	Russhe on this rebald and hym rathely rehete.	
I Miles	Rehete hym I rede you with rowtes and rappes.	
II Miles	For all oure noy þis nygard he nappes.	
III Miles	We sall wakken hym with wynde of oure whippes.	365
IV Miles	Nowe flynge to þis flaterer with flappes.	
I Miles	I sall hertely hitte on his hippes	
	And haunch.	
II Miles	Fra oure skelpes not scatheles he skyppes.	
III Miles	Ȝitt hym list not lyft vp his lippis	370
	And pray vs to haue pety on his paunch.	

350. cant] *This ed; TS* caut
352. harȝé] *This ed; TS* har ȝe
360. this] t *added later*
361. Swete] eʳ *interlined*

IV Miles	To haue petie of his paunche he propheres no prayere.
I Miles	Lorde, how likes you þis lake and þis lare þat we lere ȝou?
II Miles	Lo, I pull at his pilche, I am prowd payere. 374
III Miles	Thus youre cloke sall we cloute to clence you and clere ȝou.
IV Miles	I am straunge in striffe for to stere ȝou.
I Miles	Þus with choppes þis churll sall we chastye.
II Miles	I trowe with þis trace we sall tere you.
III Miles	All þin vntrew techyngis þus taste I,
	Þou tarand. 380
IV Miles	I hope I be hardy and hasty.
I Miles	I wate wele my wepon not wast I.
II Miles	He swounes or sweltes I swarand. f.186

III Miles	Late vs louse hym lightyly, do lay on your handes.
IV Miles	Ȝa, for and he dye for this dede vndone ere we all. 385
I Miles	Nowe vnboune is þis broll and vnbraced his bandes.
II Miles	O fule, how faris þou now? Foull mott þe fall!
III Miles	Nowe because he oure kyng gon hym call
	We will kyndely hym croune with a brere.
IV Miles	Ȝa, but first þis purpure and palle 390
	And þis worthy wede sall he were,
	For scorne.
I Miles	I am prowd at þis poynte to apper.
II Miles	Latte vs clethe hym in þer clothes full clere,
	As a lorde þat his lordshippe has lorne. 395

III Miles	Lange or þou mete slike a menȝé as þou mett with þis morne.
IV Miles	Do sette hym in þis sete as a semely in sales.
I Miles	Now thryng to hym thrally with þis þikk þorne.
II Miles	Lo, it heldes to his hede þat þe harnes out hales.
III Miles	Thus we teche hym to tempre his tales — 400
	His brayne begynnes for to blede.
IV Miles	Ȝa, his blondre has hym broght to þer bales.
	Now reche hym and raught hym in a rede
	So rounde,
	For his septure it serues indede. 405
I Miles	Ȝa, ıt ıs gode inowe in þis nede,
	Late vs gudly hym grete on þis grounde.

    Aue, riall roy and *rex judeorum*,
        Hayle, comely kyng þat no kyngdom has kende.   f.186ᵛ
    Hayll vndughty duke, þi dedis ere dom,   410
        Hayll, man vnmyghty þi menȝé to mende.

---

373. you] *This ed; TS* thou

374. payere] *Ho'* playere

382+ *Line 383 first written here then deleted in red. Catchword* He swounes or sweltis

383. *Quire & (i.e., Tironian nota) begins. First line on leaf is a repetition of 382, deleted in red*

403. a] *Interlined by a later hand*

III Miles	Hayll, lord without lande for to lende,	
	Hayll kyng, hayll knave vnconand.	
IV Miles	Hayll, freyke without forse þe to fende,	
	Hayll strang, þat may not wele stand	415
	To stryve.	
I Miles	We, harlott, heve vp thy hande,	
	And vs all þat þe wirschip are wirkand	
	Thanke vs, þer ill mot þou þryve.	

II Miles	So late lede hym belyve and lenge her no lenger,	420
	To ser Pilate oure prince oure pride will we prayse.	
III Miles	ʒa, he may synge or he slepe of sorowe and angir,	
	For many derfe dedes he has done in his dayes.	
IV Miles	Now wightly late wende on oure wayes,	
	Late vs trusse vs, no tyme is to tarie.	425
I Miles	My lorde, will ʒe listen oure layes?	
	Here þis boy is ʒe bade vs go bary	
	With battis.	
II Miles	We ar combered his *corpus* for to cary,	
	Many wightis on hym wondres and wary –	430
	Lo, his flessh al beflapped þat fat is.	

Pilatus	Wele, bringe hym before vs as he blisshes all bloo;	
	I suppose of his seggyng he will cese euermore.	
	Sirs, beholde vpon hight and *ecce homoo*	
	Þus bounden and bette and broght you before.	435
	Me semes þat it sewes hym full sore,	
	For his gilte on this grounde is he greuyd;	
	If ʒou like for to listen my lore	
	[. . . . . .]	
	In race	
	[.	
	. . . . . .	
	. . . . . .]	

[A leaf is missing from the MS here. It probably contained some 54 lines: four complete stanzas, the four lines needed to complete the fragment ending with line 439, and the two lines required before 440. The incidents covered no doubt included the call by the Jews to crucify Jesus, Pilate's offer that Jesus be the prisoner customarily released at the Passover, and the decision to release Barabbas instead. In lines 44off. the dramatist is following St Matthew's account: And Pilate seeing that he nothing preuailed, but rather tumult was toward, taking water he washed his hands before the people . . . (Matt. xxvii. 24).]

> [. . .   . . .
> . . .   . . .]

419. þer] *He* or
431. al beflapped] *Ho¹; MS, TS* al be beflapped
432. as] *This ed;* s *added by a later hand in MS; TS* A!

[*Pilatus*]	For propirly by þis processe will I preve f.187
	I had no force fro þis felawshippe þis freke for to fende.
Preco	Here is all, ser, þat ȝe for sende. 442
	Wille ȝe wasshe whill he þe watir is hote?

      Tunc lavat manus suas.

Pilatus	Nowe this Barabas bandes ȝe vnbende,
	With grace late hym gange on his gate 445
	Where ȝe will.
Barabas	Ȝe worthy men þat I here wate,
	God encrece all youre comely estate
	For þe grace ȝe haue graunt me vntill.

Pilatus	Here þe jugement of Jesu, all Jewes in þis stede: 450
	Crucifie hym on a crosse and on Caluerye hym kill.
	I dampne hym today to dy þis same dede,
	Þerfore hyngis hym on hight vppon þat high hill.
	And on aythir side hym I will
	Þat a harlott ȝe hyng in þis hast – 455
	Methynkith it both reasoune and skill
	Emyddis, sen his malice is mast,
	Ȝe hyng hym;
	Þen hym turmente, som tene for to tast.
	Mo wordis I will not nowe wast, 460
	But blynne not to dede to ȝe bryng hym.

Caiphas	Sir, vs semys in oure sight þat ȝe sadly has saide.
	Now knyghtis þat are conant with þis catyf ȝe care,
	The liffe of þis losell in youre list is it laide.
I Miles	Late vs one my lorde, and lere vs na lare. 465
	Siris, sette to hym sadly and sare,
	All in cordis his coorse vmbycast.
II Miles	Late vs bynde hym in bandis all bare.
III Miles	Here is one, full lange will it laste.
IV Miles	Lay on hande here. 470
V Miles	I powll to my poure is past.
	Nowe feste is he felawes, ful fast; f.187ᵛ
	Late vs stere vs, we may not long stand here.

Anna	Drawe hym faste hense, delyuere ȝou, haue done.
	Go, do se hym to dede withoute lenger delay, 475
	For dede bus hym be nedlyng be none.
	All myrthe bus vs move tomorne þat we may,

---

441. fende] *Ha; MS, TS* lende
443+ *Line 444 written out first as if part of Preco's speech, deleted in red. SD added to right by J. Clerke*
445. gate] *TS; MS* gatis
446. ȝe] *He* he
465. one] *So main scribe; deleted and* alone *interlined by a later hand; TS* alone

Itt is sothly oure grette Sabott day —
No dede bodis vnberid sall be.

VI Miles   We see wele þe soth ȝe vs say.   480
We sall traylle hym tyte to his tree,
Þus talkand.

IV Miles   Farewele, now wightely wende we.
Pilatus   Nowe certis ȝe are a manly menȝe,
Furth in þe wylde wanyand be walkand.   485

XXXIV The Shearmen

The Road to Calvary

Primus miles incipit: f.189

Pees, barnes and bachillers þat beldis here aboute,
Stirre noȝt ones in þis stede but stonde stone stille,
Or be þe lorde þat I leue on I schall gar you lowte.
But ȝe spare when I speke youre speche schall I spille
Smertely and sone,   5
For I am sente fro sir Pilate with pride
To lede þis ladde oure lawes to abide,
He getis no bettir bone.

Therfore I comaunde you on euere ilke a side,
Vppon payne of enprisonment þat no man appere   10
To suppowle þis traytoure, be tyme ne be tyde,
[. . .   . . .]
Nought one of þis prees,
Nor noght ones so hardy for to enquere,
But helpe me holly alle þat are here
Þis kaitiffe care to encrees.   15

Therfore make rome and rewle you nowe right,
That we may with þis weried wight
Wightely wende on oure waye.

485+   Finis *added by J. Clerke. Bottom half of f.187ᵛ blank, ff.188, 188ᵛ blank*

11+   *Line missing, no gap in MS*
13.   ones so] *Ho¹* ones be so
18.   waye] *TS; MS* wayes

He napped noght of all þis nyght,
And þis daye schall his deth be dight –   20
   Latte see who dare saie naye?
    Because tomorne is prouyde
For oure dere Sabbott day,
   We wille no mysse be moued,
But mirthe in all þat euere men may.   25

We haue bene besie all þis morne
To clothe hym and to croune with thorne,
   As falles for a fole kyng,
And nowe methynkith oure felawes skorne,
They highte to haue ben here þis morne   30
   Þis faitour forthe to bring.
    To nappe nowe is noȝt goode –
   We, howe! High myght he hyng!

II Miles   Pees man, for Mahoundes bloode,
   Why make ȝe such crying?   35

I Miles Why, wotte þou noght als wele as I,
Þis carle burde vnto Caluery
   And þere on crosse be done?
II Miles Sen dome is geuen þat he schall dy   f.189ᵛ
Late calle to vs more companye,   40
   And ellis we erre oure-fone.
I Miles   Oure gere behoues to be grayde
And felawes sammed sone,
   For sir Pilate has saide
Hym bus be dede be none.   45

Wher is sir Wymond, wotte þou oght?
II Miles He wente to garre a crosse be wroght
   To bere þis cursed knave.
I Miles That wolde I sone wer hyder broght,
For sithen schall othir gere be soght   50
   That vs behoues to haffe.
II Miles   Vs bus haue sties and ropes
To rugge hym tille he raue,
   And nayles and othir japes
If we oureselue wille saue.   55

I Miles To tarie longe vs were full lathe,
But Wymond come it is in wathe
   But we be blamed all three.
We, howe, sir Wymond wayteskathe.

---

37. burde] *He* bud
56. lathe] a *altered from* o
58. But] *He* And, *K* Þat
59. wayteskathe] *This ed; TS* wayt e[s] skathe

II Miles	We, howe, sir Wymond, howe.
III Miles	I am here – what saie ʒe bathe? 60
	Why crye ʒe so on me?
	I haue bene garre make
	Þis crosse, as yhe may see,
	Of þat laye ouere þe lake –
	Men called it þe kyngis tree. 65
I Miles	Nowe sekirly I þought þe same,
	For þat balke will no man vs blame
	To cutte it for þe kyng.
II Miles	This karle has called hym kyng at hame, f.190
	And sen þis tre has such a name 70
	It is accordyng thyng
	Þat his rigge on it may reste,
	For skorne and for hethyng.
III Miles	Methoughte it semyd beste
	Tille þis bargayne to bryng. 75
I Miles	It is wele warred, so motte I spede,
	And it be lele in lenghe and brede
	Þan is þis space wele spende.
III Miles	To loke þeraftir it is no nede,
	I toke þe mesure or I yode, 80
	Bothe for þe fette and hende.
II Miles	Beholde howe it is boorede
	Full euen at ilke an ende.
	This werke will wele accorde,
	It may not be amende. 85
III Miles	Nay, I haue ordande mekill more,
	ʒaa, thes theues are sente before
	Þat beside hym schall hyng.
	And sties also are ordande þore
	With stalworthe steeles as mystir wore, 90
	Bothe some schorte and some lang.
I Miles	For hameres and nayles
	Latte see sone who schall gang.
II Miles	Here are bragges þat will noght faile,
	Of irnne and stele full strange. 95
III Miles	Þanne is it as it aweth to bee –
	But whiche of yowe schall beere þis tree,
	Sen I haue broughte it hedir?

60. *Lineation this ed; two lines in MS, TS. Alternatively, 6oa may be extra-metrical*
81. hende] *He;* MS, TS hande
92. and nayles] *This ed;* TS and [for] nayles
94. will noght faile] *He* þat noght fayles
97. beere] *This ed;* TS bere *(conj)*

I Miles	Be my feithe, bere it schall hee
	Þat þeron hanged sone schall bee, 100
	And we schall teeche hym whedir.
II Miles	Vppon his bakke it schalle be laide, f.190ᵛ
	For sone we schall come thedir.
III Miles	Loke þat oure gere be grayede
	And go we all togedir. 105

Johannes   Allas for my maistir þat moste is of myght,
That ʒister-even late, with lanternes light,
    Before þe busshoppe was brought.
Bothe Petir and I we saugh þat sight
And sithen we wente oure wayes full wight, 110
    When þe Jewes wondirly wrought.
      At morne þei toke to rede
    And soteltes vpsoght,
      And demed hym to be dede
    Þat to þam trespassed noght. 115

Allas for syte what schall I saie?
My worldly welthe is wente for ay,
    In woo euere may I wende.
My maistir þat neuere lakke in lay
Is demed to be dede þis day, 120
    Ewen in hys elmys hende.
      Allas for my maistir mylde
    That all mennys mysse may mende,
      Shulde so falsely be filed
    And no frendis hym to fende. 125

Allas for his modir and oþir moo,
Mi modir and hir sisteres alsoo,
    Sittes samen with sighyngis sore.
Þai wate nothyng of all þis woo,
Forthy to warne þam will I goo 130
    Sen I may mende no more.
      Sen he schall dye as tyte
    And þei vnwarned wore,
      I ware worthy to wite—
    I will go faste therfore. 135

But in myn herte grete drede haue I
Þat his modir for dole schall dye,
    When she see ones þat sight.
But certis I schal not wande forthy
To warne þat carefull company 140

112–5. *Lineation TS; two lines in MS*
119. lakke] *This ed; TS* lakke[d]

Or he to dede be dight.

[. . .   . . .
. . .   . . .
. . .   . . .
. . .   . . .]

[A leaf conjugate with the one missing between lines 439 and 440 of the preceding play is wanting here. If the metre remained the same, it probably contained five complete stanzas, four lines required to complete the fragmentary stanza beginning at line 136, and other lines belonging with the irregular fragment beginning at line 142. In the Towneley version (which continues in the same metre as York), John goes and greets the three Marys with the news of the impending execution of Jesus, and conducts them to where he is.]

	Sen he fro vs will twynne	f.191
	I schall þe neuere forsake.	
	Allas þe tyme and tyde,	
	I watte wele þe day is come	145
	Þat are was specified	
	Of prophete Symeoun in prophicie:	
	The swerde of sorowe schulde renne	
	Thurghoute þe herte, sotelly.	
II Maria	Allas þis is a sithfull sight,	150
	He þat was euere luffely and light	
	And lorde of high and lawe,	
	Oo, doulfully nowe is he dight.	
	In worlde is none so wofull a wighte	
	Ne so carefull to knawe.	155
	Þei that he mended moste	
	In dede and als in sawe,	
	Now haue they full grete haste	
	To dede hym for to drawe.	
Jesus	Doughteres of Jerusalem cytté,	160
	Sees, and mournes no more for me,	
	But thynkes vppon this thyng:	
	For youreselfe mourne schall ʒee,	
	And for þe sonnes þat borne schal be	
	Of yowe, bothe olde and yonge.	165
	For such fare schall befalle,	
	That ʒe schall giffe blissyng	
	To barayne bodies all,	
	That no barnes forthe may brynge.	
	For certis ʒe schall see suche a day,	170
	That with sore sighyng schall ʒe saye	
	Vnto þe hillis on highte,	

149. sotelly] *He* sotelly

'Falle on vs mountaynes, and ȝe may,
And couere vs fro þat felle affraye
  That on vs sone schall light'.   175
    Turnes home þe toune vntill,   f.191ᵛ
  Sen ȝe haue seen þis sight.
    It is my fadirs will,
  Alle þat is done and dighte.

III Maria   Allas, þis is a cursed cas.   180
He þat alle hele in his hande has
  Shall here be sakles slayne.
A, lorde, beleue lete clense thy face –
Behalde howe he hath schewed his grace,
  Howe he is moste of mayne!   185
    This signe schalle bere witnesse
  Vnto all pepull playne,
    Howe Goddes sone here gilteles
  Is putte to pereles payne.

I Miles   Saie, wherto bide ȝe here aboute?   190
Thare quenys with þer skymeryng and þer schoute
  Wille noght þer stevenis steere.
II Miles   Go home casbalde, with þi clowte,
Or be þat lorde we loue and loute,
  Þou schall abye full dere.   195
III Maria   This signe schall vengeaunce calle
  On yowe holly in feere.
III Miles   Go, hye þe hense withalle,
  Or ille hayle come þou here.

Johannes   Lady, youre gretyng greues me sore.   200
Maria Sancta John, helpe me nowe and eueremore,
  That I myght come hym tille.
Johannes   My lady, wende we forthe before,
To Caluery when ȝe come thore
  Þan schall ȝe saie what ȝe will.   205
I Miles   What a deuyll is þis to sayc,   f 192
  How longe schall we stande stille?
    Go, hye you hens awaye,
  In þe deuylis name, doune þe hill.

177. seen] *Suppl Ho¹*
198. withalle] *TS; MS* with ille
201. euere-] *He; MS, TS* neuere
204. thore] *Conj TS; MS* thedir
205. Þan] *TS; MS* Þ + n *or* u *suprascript*
     saie] *He* see
205+ *Catchword* What deuyl is þis
206. *Quire* con *begins (the signature is an elaborated form of the Latin abbreviation for the syllable 'con'; ex inf. Peter Meredith)*
     I Miles] Suppl by different later hands, one of them (in red) that of J. Clerke
208. Go] *TS; MS* To

II Miles	Ther quenes vs comeres with þer clakke.	210
	He schall be serued for þer sake,	
	With sorowe and with sore.	
III Miles	And þei come more such noyse to make,	
	We schall garre lygge þame in þe lake	
	Yf þei were halfe a skore.	215
I Miles	Latis nowe such bourdyng be.	
	Sen oure tooles are before,	
	Þis traitoure and þis tree	
	Wolde I full fayne were þore.	

II Miles	We schall no more so stille be stedde,	220
	For nowe þer quenes are fro vs fledde	
	Þat falsely wolde vs feere.	
III Miles	Methynkith þis boy is so forbledde	
	With þis ladde may he noght be ledde;	
	He swounes, þat dare I swere.	225
I Miles	It nedis noȝt harde to harle	
	Sen it dose hym slike dere.	
II Miles	I se here comes a karle	
	Shall helpe hym for to bere.	

III Miles	Þat schall ȝe see sone one assaye.	230
	Goode man, whedir is þou away?	
	Þou walkis as þou were wrothe.	
Symon	Sir, I haue a grete journay	
	Þat bus be done þis same day,	f.192ᵛ
	Or ellis it may do skathe.	235
I Miles	Þou may with litill payne	
	Eease thyselffe and vs bathe.	
Symon	Goode sirs, þat wolde I fayne,	
	But to dwelle were me lathe.	

II Miles	Nay beuscher, þou schall sone be spedde,	240
	Loo here a ladde þat muste be ledde	
	For his ille dedis to dye.	
III Miles	And he is brosid and all forbledde,	
	That makis vs here þus stille be stedde.	
	We pray þe sir, forthy,	245
	That þou wilte take þis tree	
	And bere it to Caluerye.	
Symon	Goode sirs, þat may nouȝt be,	
	For full grete haste haue I.	

	My wayes are lang and wyde,	250
	And I may noght abide	
	For drede I come to late,	
	For sureté haue I hight	

243.   *III Miles] Suppl by a later hand*

Muste be fulfillid þis nyght,
  Or it will paire my state. 255
    Therfore sirs, by youre leue,
  Methynkith I dwelle full lang.
    Me were loth you for to greue—
  Goode sirs, ȝe late me gang,

  No lenger here now may I wone. 260

I Miles Nay, certis, þou schalte noȝt go so sone
  For ought þat þou can saye.
  Þis dede is moste haste to be done,
  For þis boy muste be dede by none
    And nowe is nere myddaye. 265
    Go helpe hym in þis nede
  And make no more delaye.

Symon   I praye yowe dose youre dede f.193
  And latis me wende my waye,

  And sirs, I schall come sone agayne 270
  To helpe þis man with all my mayne,
    And even at youre awne will.

II Miles What, wolde þou trusse with such a trayne?
  Nay faitour, þou schalte be fayne
    Þis forwarde to fullfille, 275
    Or be myghty Mahounde
  Þou schalte rewe it full ille.

III Miles   Late dyng þis dastarde doune
  But he goo tyte þertill.

Symon Sertis sir, þat wer nought wisely wrought 280
  To bete me but I trespassid ought,
    Outhir in worde or dede.

I Miles Vppon his bakke it schall be brought
  To bere it, whedir he wille or noght—
    What, deuyll, whome schulde we drede? 285
    Go, take it vppe belyve
  And bere it forthe goode spede.

Symon   It helpis noȝt here to striue,
  Bere it behoues me nede,

  And þerfore sirs, as ȝe haue saide, 290
  To bere þis crosse I holde me paied
    Right as ȝe wolde it wore.

II Miles Ȝaa, nowe are we right arraied.
  Loke þat oure gere be redy grayed
    To wirke whanne we come þore. 295

III Miles   I warand all redy,

296—9. *Lineation TS: two lines in MS*

          Oure tooles bothe lesse and more.
             Late hym goo hardely
          Forthe with þe crosse before.

I Miles   Sen he has his lade nowe late hym gang,   300
          For with þis warlowe wirke we wrang   f.193ᵛ
             And we þus with hym yode.
II Miles   And nowe is noght goode to tarie lang,
          What schulde we done more vs emang?
             Say sone, so motte þou spede.   305
III Miles   Neuen vs no nodir noote
          Tille we haue done þis dede.
I Miles   Weme, methynke we doote,
          He muste be naked, nede.

          All yf he called hymselffe a kyng   310
          In his clothis he schall noʒt hyng,
             But naked as a stone be stedde.
II Miles   That calle I accordand thyng —
          But tille his sidis I trowe þei clyng
             For bloode þat he has bledde.   315
III Miles   Wheder þei clynge or cleue
          Naked he schalle be ledde,
           And for þe more myscheue
          Buffettis hym schall be bedde.

I Miles   Take of his clothis beliffe, latte see —   320
          A ha, þis garment will falle wele for mee
             And so I hope it schall.
II Miles   Nay sir, so may it noght be,
          Þame muste be parte amonge vs thre,
             Take euen as will fall.   325
III Miles   ʒaa, and sir Pilate melle hym
          Youre parte woll be but small.
I Miles   Sir, and ʒe liste go telle hym,
          ʒitt schall he noght haue all,

          Butte even his awne parte and no more.   f.194
II Miles   ʒaa, late þame ligge stille here in stoore   331
             Vntill þis dede be done.
III Miles   Latte bynde hym as he was before
          And harle on harde þat he wer þore,
             And hanged or it be none.
                        335
I Miles   He schall be feste as fee,
          And þat right sore and sone.

304. done] *He* do; *or alternatively, with Ho'*, be *for* we
308. Weme] *This ed; MS, TS* We me
326. melle] *He; MS, TS* medill
336. as] *He; MS, TS* of

II Miles	So fallis hym for to be,
	He gettis no bettir bone.

III Miles	Þis werke is wele nowe I warand,	340
	For he is boune as beeste in bande	
	That is demed for to dye.	
I Miles	Þanne rede I þat we no lenger stande,	
	But ilke man feste on hym a hande	
	And harle hym hense in hye.	345
II Miles	Ʒaa, nowe is tyme to trusse	
	To alle oure companye.	
III Miles	If anye aske aftir vs,	
	Kenne þame to Caluarie.	

XXXV The Pinners

The Crucifixion

	Crucifixio Christi	f.195
I Miles	Sir knyghtis, take heede hydir in hye,	
	This dede on dergh we may noght drawe.	
	Ʒee wootte youreselffe als wele as I	
	Howe lordis and leders of owre lawe	
	Has geven dome þat þis doote schall dye.	5
II Miles	Sir, alle þare counsaile wele we knawe.	
	Sen we are comen to Caluarie	
	Latte ilke man helpe nowe as hym awe.	
III Miles	We are alle redy, loo,	
	Þat forward to fullfille.	10
IV Miles	Late here howe we schall doo,	
	And go we tyte þertille.	
I Miles	It may noʒt helpe her for to hone	
	If we schall any worshippe wynne.	
II Miles	He muste be dede nedelyngis by none.	15

349+ finis *added by J. Clerke; f.194ᵛ blank*

1— *Title by main scribe*
9—12. *Lineation TS; two lines in MS*

III Miles	Þanne is goode tyme þat we begynne.
IV Miles	Late dynge hym doune, þan is he done –
	He schall nought dere vs with his dynne.
I Miles	He schall be sette and lerned sone,
	With care to hym and all his kynne.
II Miles	Þe foulest dede of all
	Shalle he dye for his dedis.
III Miles	That menes crosse hym we schall.
IV Miles	Behalde, so right he redis.

I Miles	Thanne to þis werke vs muste take heede,
	So þat oure wirkyng be noght wronge.
II Miles	None othir noote to neven is nede,
	But latte vs haste hym for to hange.
III Miles	And I haue gone for gere goode speede,
	Bothe hammeres and nayles large and lange.
IV Miles	Þanne may we boldely do þis dede.
	Commes on, late kille þis traitoure strange.
I Miles	Faire myght ȝe falle in feere
	Þat has wrought on þis wise.
II Miles	Vs nedis nought for to lere
	Suche faitoures to chastise.

III Miles	Sen ilke a thyng es right arrayed,
	The wiselier nowe wirke may we.
IV Miles	Þe crosse on grounde is goodely graied
	And boorede even as it awith to be.
I Miles	Lokis þat þe ladde on lenghe be layde
	And made me þane vnto þis tree.
II Miles	For alle his fare he schalle be flaied,
	That one assaie sone schalle ye see.
III Miles	Come forthe þou cursed knave,
	Thy comforte sone schall kele.
IV Miles	Thyne hyre here schall þou haue.
I Miles	Walkes oon – now wirke we wele.

Jesus	Almyghty God, my fadir free,
	Late þis materes be made in mynde:
	Þou badde þat I schulde buxsome be
	For Adam plyght for to be pyned.
	Here to dede I obblisshe me
	Fro þat synne for to saue mankynde,
	And soueraynely beseke I þe
	That þai for me may fauoure fynde.
	And fro þe fende þame fende,
	So þat þer saules be saffe

Line numbers in right margin: 20, 25, f.195ᵛ, 31, 35, 40, 45, 50, 55

19. lerned] *K* serued
42. me þane] *Ho'*, *Ca* be tane
50. made] *K, Ca* marked

In welthe withouten ende— f.196
I kepe nought ellis to craue. 60

I Miles We, herke sir knyghtis, for Mahoundis bloode,
Of Adam-kynde is all his þoght.
II Miles Þe warlowe waxis werre þan woode,
Þis doulfull dede ne dredith he noght.
III Miles Þou schulde haue mynde, with mayne and moode, 65
Of wikkid werkis þat þou haste wrought.
IV Miles I hope þat he hadde bene as goode
Haue sesed of sawes þat he vppe-sought.
I Miles Thoo sawes schall rewe hym sore
For all his saunteryng sone. 70
II Miles Ille spede þame þat hym spare
Tille he to dede be done.

III Miles Haue done belyue boy, and make þe boune,
And bende þi bakke vnto þis tree.
IV Miles Byhalde, hymselffe has laide hym doune 75
In lenghe and breede as he schulde bee.
I Miles This traitoure here teynted of treasoune,
Gose faste and fetter hym þan ʒe thre;
And sen he claymeth kyngdome with croune,
Even as a kyng here hange schall hee. 80
II Miles Nowe, certis, I schall noʒt fyne
Or his right hande be feste.
III Miles Þe lefte hande þanne is myne—
Late see who beres hym beste.

IV Miles Hys lymmys on lenghe þan schalle I lede, 85
And even vnto þe bore þame bringe.
I Miles Vnto his heede I schall take hede, f.196ᵛ
And with myne hande helpe hym to hyng.
II Miles Nowe sen we foure schall do þis dede 4 wounds
And medill with þis vnthrifty thyng, 90
Late no man spare for speciall speede
Tille that we haue made endyng.
III Miles Þis forward may not faile;
Nowe are we right arraiede.
IV Miles This boy here in oure baile 95
Shall bide full bittir brayde.

I Miles Sir knyghtis, saie, howe wirke we nowe?
II Miles ʒis, certis, I hope I holde þis hande,

78. fetter] *K, Ca; MS, TS, Be* fette
80. hange] *K, Ca; MS, TS, Be* haue
81. fyne] *He, Ca; MS, TS, Be* feyne
97. howe] *Ca* nowe
nowe] *He, Ca* oght
98. *II Miles*] *Wallis (see the Note); MS, TS* + *III Miles*

	And to þe boore I haue it brought	
	Full boxumly withouten bande.	100
I Miles	Strike on þan harde, for hym þe boght.	
II Miles	ȝis, here is a stubbe will stiffely stande,	
	Thurgh bones and senous it schall be soght —	
	This werke is wele, I will warande.	
I Miles	Saie sir, howe do we þore?	105
	Þis bargayne may not blynne.	
III Miles	It failis a foote and more,	
	Þe senous are so gone ynne.	

IV Miles	I hope þat marke amisse be bored.	
II Miles	Þan muste he bide in bittir bale.	110
III Miles	In faith, it was ouere-skantely scored,	
	Þat makis it fouly for to faile.	
I Miles	Why carpe ȝe so? Faste on a corde	
	And tugge hym to, by toppe and taile.	
III Miles	ȝa, þou comaundis lightly as a lorde;	115
	Come helpe to haale, with ille haile.	
I Miles	Nowe certis þat schall I doo —	f.197
	Full snelly as a snayle	
III Miles	And I schall tacche hym too,	
	Full nemely with a nayle.	120

	Þis werke will holde, þat dar I heete,	
	For nowe are feste faste both his hende.	
IV Miles	Go we all foure þanne to his feete,	
	So schall oure space be spedely spende.	
II Miles	Latte see what bourde his bale myght beete,	125
	Tharto my bakke nowe wolde I bende.	
IV Miles	Owe, þis werke is all vnmeete —	
	This boring muste all be amende.	
I Miles	A, pees man, for Mahounde,	
	Latte no man wotte þat wondir,	130
	A roope schall rugge hym doune	
	Yf all his synnous go asoundre.	

II Miles	Þat corde full kyndely can I knytte,	
	Þe comforte of þis karle to kele.	
I Miles	Feste on þanne faste þat all be fytte,	135
	It is no force howe felle he feele.	
II Miles	Lugge on ȝe both a litill ȝitt.	
III Miles	I schalle nought sese, as I haue seele.	

101.	*I Miles*] *Wallis, Ca, Be; MS II Miles, TS ?IV Miles*
102.	*II Miles*] *TS ?I Miles*
105.	*I Miles*] *TS II Miles, Be III Miles (conj)*
107.	*III Miles*] *Be I Miles (conj)*
116.	haale, with] *Ho¹, Ca* haale him, with
118.	snelly] *Ca; MS, TS, Be* suerly, *Ha* snelle
122.	hende] *He, Ca; MS, TS, Be* handis

IV Miles	And I schall fonde hym for to hitte.
II Miles	Owe, haylle!
IV Miles	Hoo nowe, I halde it wele.
I Miles	Haue done, dryue in þat nayle,
	So þat no faute be foune.
IV Miles	Þis wirkyng wolde noȝt faile
	Yf foure bullis here were boune.

140

I Miles	Ther cordis haue evill encressed his paynes,
	Or he wer tille þe booryngis brought.
II Miles	Ȝaa, assoundir are bothe synnous and veynis
	On ilke a side, so haue we soughte.
III Miles	Nowe all his gaudis nothyng hym gaynes,
	His sauntering schall with bale be bought.
IV Miles	I wille goo saie to oure soueraynes
	Of all þis werkis howe we haue wrought.
I Miles	Nay sirs, anothir thyng
	Fallis firste to youe and me,
	Þei badde we schulde hym hyng
	On heghte þat men myght see.

f.197ᵛ
146

150

155

II Miles	We woote wele so ther wordes wore,
	But sir, þat dede will do vs dere.
I Miles	It may not mende for to moote more,
	Þis harlotte muste be hanged here.
II Miles	The mortaise is made fitte þerfore.
III Miles	Feste on youre fyngeres þan, in feere.
IV Miles	I wene it wolle neuere come þore —
	We foure rayse it noȝt right to-yere.
I Miles	Say man, whi carpis þou soo?
	Thy liftyng was but light.
II Miles	He menes þer muste be moo
	To heve hym vppe on hight.

160

165

III Miles	Now certis, I hope it schall noght nede
	To calle to vs more companye.
	Methynke we foure schulde do þis dede
	And bere hym to ȝone hille on high.
I Miles	It muste be done, withouten drede.
	No more, but loke ȝe be redy,
	And þis parte schalle I lifte and leede;
	On lenghe he schalle no lenger lie.
	Therfore nowe makis you boune,
	Late bere hym to ȝone hill.
IV Miles	Thanne will I bere here doune,
	And tente his tase vntill.

170

f.198
176

180

154. and] *Suppl Ho¹, Ca, Be*
155. Þei] *Ho¹, Ca, Be; MS, TS* I

II Miles	We twoo schall see tille aythir side,
	For ellis þis werke wille wrie all wrang.
III Miles	We are redy.
IV Miles	Gode sirs, abide,
	And late me first his fete vp fang.
II Miles	Why tente ȝe so to tales þis tyde? 185
I Miles	Lifte vppe!
IV Miles	Latte see!
II Miles	Owe, lifte alang.
III Miles	<u>Fro all þis harme he schulde hym hyde</u>
	And he war God.
IV Miles	Þe deuill hym hang!
I Miles	For-grete harme haue I hente,
	My schuldir is in soundre. 190
II Miles	And sertis I am nere schente,
	So lange haue I borne vndir.
III Miles	This crosse and I in twoo muste twynne,
	Ellis brekis my bakke in sondre sone.
IV Miles	Laye downe agayne and leue youre dynne, 195
	Þis dede for vs will neuere be done.
I Miles	Assaie sirs, latte se yf any gynne
	May helpe hym vppe withouten hone,
	For here schulde wight men worschippe wynne,
	And noght with gaudis al day to gone. 200
II Miles	More wighter men þan we
	Full fewe I hope ȝe fynde.
III Miles	Þis bargayne will noght bee, f.198ᵛ
	For certis me wantis wynde.
IV Miles	So wille of werke neuere we wore — 205
	I hope þis carle some cautellis caste.
II Miles	My bourdeyne satte me wondir soore,
	Vnto þe hill I myght noght laste.
I Miles	Lifte vppe, and sone he schall be þore,
	Therfore feste on youre fyngeres faste. 210
III Miles	Owe, lifte!
I Miles	We, loo!
IV Miles	A litill more.
II Miles	Holde þanne!
I Miles	Howe nowe?
II Miles	Þe werste is paste.
III Miles	<u>He weyes a wikkid weght.</u>
II Miles	So may we all foure saie,
	Or he was heued on heght 215
	And raysed in þis array.
IV Miles	He made vs stande as any stones,
	So boustous was he for to bere.

183–4. *Added later to right by main scribe*
183. *IV Miles] Wallis; MS III, TS, Be* in, *om Ca*
215. *Ruled off from 214, but not assigned (main scribe)*

I Miles	Nowe raise hym nemely for þe nonys	
	And sette hym be þis mortas heere,	220
	And latte hym falle in alle at ones,	
	For certis þat payne schall haue no pere.	
III Miles	Heue vppe!	
IV Miles	Latte doune, so all his bones	
	Are asoundre nowe on sides seere.	
I Miles	Þis fallyng was more felle	225
	Þan all the harmes he hadde.	
	Nowe may a man wele telle	f.199
	Þe leste lith of þis ladde.	

III Miles	Methynkith þis crosse will noght abide	
	Ne stande stille in þis morteyse ȝitt.	230
IV Miles	Att þe firste tyme was it made ouere-wyde;	
	Þat makis it wave, þou may wele witte.	
I Miles	Itt schall be sette on ilke a side	
	So þat it schall no forther flitte.	
	Goode wegges schall we take þis tyde	235
	And feste þe foote, þanne is all fitte.	
II Miles	Here are wegges arraied	
	For þat, both grete and smale.	
III Miles	Where are oure hameres laide	
	Þat we schulde wirke withall?	240

IV Miles	We haue þem here euen atte oure hande.	
II Miles	Gyffe me þis wegge, I schall it in dryue.	
IV Miles	Here is anodir ȝitt ordande.	
III Miles	Do take it me hidir belyue.	
I Miles	Laye on þanne faste.	
III Miles	Ȝis, I warrande.	245
	I thryng þame same, so motte I thryve.	
	Nowe will þis crosse full stabely stande,	
	All-yf he raue þei will noght ryve.	
I Miles	Say sir, howe likis you nowe,	
	Þis werke þat we haue wrought?	250
IV Miles	We praye youe sais vs howe	
	Ȝe fele, or faynte ȝe ought.	

Jesus	Al men þat walkis by waye or strete,	
	Takes tente ȝe schalle no trauayle tyne.	f.199ᵛ
	Byholdes myn heede, myn handis, and my feete,	255
	And fully feele nowe, or ȝe fyne,	
	Yf any mournyng may be meete,	
	Or myscheue mesured vnto myne.	
	My fadir, þat alle bales may bete,	
	Forgiffis þes men þat dois me pyne.	260

230. morteyse] *TS+; MS* moteyse
248. you] *This ed (also conj Ho', Ca); TS, Be* þou

    What þei wirke wotte þai noght;
    Therfore, my fadir, I craue,
    Latte neuere þer synnys be sought,
    But see þer saules to saue.

I Miles   We, harke, he jangelis like a jay.   265
II Miles   Methynke he patris like a py.
III Miles   He has ben doand all þis day,
    And made grete meuyng of mercy.
IV Miles   Es þis þe same þat gune vs say
    That he was Goddis sone almyghty?   270
I Miles   Therfore he felis full felle affraye,
    And demyd þis day for to dye.
II Miles   Vath, *qui destruis templum!*
III Miles   His sawes wer so, certayne.
IV Miles   And sirs, he saide to some   275
    He myght rayse it agayne.

I Miles   To mustir þat he hadde no myght,
    For all the kautelles þat he couthe kaste.
    All-yf he wer in worde so wight,
    For all his force nowe he is feste.   280
    Als Pilate demed is done and dight,
    Therfore I rede þat we go reste.
II Miles   Þis race mon be rehersed right,
    Thurgh þe worlde both este and weste.
III Miles   Ʒaa, late hym hynge here stille   f.200
    And make mowes on þe mone.   286
IV Miles   Þanne may we wende at wille.
I Miles   Nay goode sirs, noght so sone,

    For certis vs nedis anodir note:
    Þis kirtill wolde I of you craue.   290
II Miles   Nay, nay sir, we will loke be lotte
    Whilke of vs foure fallis it to haue.
III Miles   I rede we drawe cutte for þis coote –
    Loo, se howe sone – alle sidis to saue.
IV Miles   The schorte cutte schall wynne, þat wele ʒe woote,   295
    Whedir itt falle to knyght or knave.
I Miles   Felowes, ʒe thar noght flyte,
    For þis mantell is myne.

264.   In welth without end / I kepe noght elles to crave *added to right by J. Clerke*
266.   patris] *Be* pratis
268.   meuyng] *or* menyng
272.   And demyd] *He* And is demyd
273.   Vath] *This ed; TS* + Vah
     destruis] *TS* +; *MS* destruit
284.   both] *Ca, Be; TS* þoth
284+ *Catchword* Ʒaa late hym hyng
285.   *Quire xxvj^u begins*
292.   it] *Ca, Be; TS* to

II Miles Goo we þanne hense tyte,
Þis <u>trauayle</u> here we tyne &c.   300

XXXVI The Butchers
The Death of Christ

Mortificacio Christi   f.201

Pilatus Sees, seniours, and see what I saie,
Takis tente to my talkyng enteere.
Devoyde all þis dynne here þis day,
And fallis to my frenschippe in feere.
Sir Pilate, a prince withowten pere,   5
My name is full neuenly to neuen,
And domisman full derworth in dere
Of gentillest Jewry full euen
Am I.
Who makis oppressioun   10
Or dose transgressioun,
Be my discressioun
Shall be demed dewly to dy.

To dye schall I deme þame, to dede,
Þo rebelles þat rewles þame vnright.   15
Who þat to ȝone hill wille take heede
May se þer þe soth in his sight,
Howe doulfull to dede þei are dight
That liste noȝt owre lawes for to lere.
Lo, þus be my mayne and my myght   20
Tho churles schalle I chasteise and cheere,
Be lawe.

300. &c] *This ed; om TS+*
300+ *Bottom half of f.200 blank; f.200ᵛ blank*
   1- *Title in red (main scribe)*
   6. neuenly] *Ho'* nemely, *Be* evenly
   7. in] *He* and
           dere] *TS; MS, Be* dede
  14. to dede] *He* indede
  20. myght] *Altered from* myne *by a later hand*

Ilke feloune false
Shall hynge be þe halse.
Transgressours als   25
On the crosse schalle be knytte for to knawe.

To knawe schall I knytte þame on crosse,
To schende þame with schame schall I shappe.
Ther liffis for to leese is no losse,
Suche tirrauntis with teene for to trappe.   30
Þus leelly þe lawe I vnlappe
And punyssh þame pitously.
Of Jesu I holde it vnhappe
Þat he on yone hill hyng so hye
For gilte.   35
His bloode to spille
Toke ye you tille,
Þus was youre wille
Full spitously to spede he were spilte.

Caiphas   To spille hym we spake in a speede,   f.201ᵛ
For falsed he folowde in faie.   41
With fraudes oure folke gan he feede
And laboured to lere þame his laye.
Anna   Sir Pilate, of pees we youe praye—
Oure lawe was full lyke to be lorne.   45
He saued noȝt oure dere Sabott daye,
And þat—for to scape it—were a scorne,
By lawe.
Pilatus   Sirs, before youre sight,
With all my myght   50
I examynde hym right,
And cause non in hym cowthe I knawe.

Caiphas   Ȝe knawe wele þe cause sir, in cace;
It touched treasoune vntrewe.
Þe tribute to take or to trace   55
Forbadde he, oure bale for to brewe.
Anna   Of japes ȝitt jangelid yone Jewe,
And cursedly he called hym a kyng.
To deme hym to dede it is diewe,
For treasoune it touches, þat thyng,   60
Indede.
Caiphas   Ȝitt principall,
And worste of all,
He garte hym call
Goddes sonne—þat foulle motte hyme speede. 65

Pilatus   He spedis for to spille in space,
So wondirly wrought is youre will.
His bloode schall youre bodis enbrace,
For þat haue ȝe taken you till.

Anna	Þat forwarde ful fayne to fulfille	70
	Indede schall we dresse vs bedene.	
	Ʒone losell hym likis full ille,	
	For turned is his trantis all to teene,	
	I trowe.	
Cayphas	He called hym kyng,	f.202
	Ille joie hym wring.	76
	Ʒa, late hym hyng	
	Full madly on þe mone for to mowe.	

Anna	To mowe on þe moone has he mente.	
	We, fye on þe, faitour, in faye!	80
	Who, trowes þou, to þi tales toke tente?	
	Þou saggard, þiselffe gan þou saie,	
	Þe tempill distroie þe todaye,	
	Be þe thirde day ware done ilka dele	
	To rayse it þou schulde þe arraye.	85
	Loo, howe was þi falsed to feele,	
	Foule falle þe.	
	For thy presumpcyoune	
	Þou haste thy warisoune.	
	Do faste come doune,	90
	And a comely kyng schalle I calle þee.	

Cayphas	I calle þe a coward to kenne,	
	Þat meruaylles and mirakills made.	
	Þou mustered emange many menne;	
	But, brothell, þou bourded to brade.	95
	Þou saued þame fro sorowes, þai saide—	
	To saue nowe þiselffc late vs see.	
	God sonne if þou grathely be grayde,	
	Delyuere þe doune of þat tree	
	Anone.	100
	If þou be funne	
	To be Goddis sonne,	
	We schalle be bonne	
	To trowe on þe trewlye ilkone.	

Anna	Sir Pilate, youre pleasaunce we praye,	105
	Takis tente to oure talkyng þis tide,	
	And wipe ʒe yone writyng away,	
	It is not beste it abide.	
	It sittis youe to sette it aside	f.202ᵛ
	And sette þat he saide in his sawe,	110

75. *Cayphas*] *Suppl by J. Clerke*
82-4. *For conjectures see Ho¹, K, Ho²*
95. brade] a *altered from* o; *TS* + brede
102. To] *Ho¹; MS, TS* + Þou
105. pleasuance] *TS* +; *MS* pleasaune

As he þat was prente full of pride:
'Jewes kyng am I', comely to knawe,
Full playne.

Pilatus   *Quod scripci, scripci.*
Ʒone same wrotte I;   115
I bide þerby,
What gedlyng will grucche thereagayne.

Jesus Þou man þat of mys here has mente,
To me tente enteerly þou take.
On roode am I ragged and rente,   120
Þou synfull sawle, for thy sake;
For thy misse amendis wille I make.
My bakke for to bende here I bide,
Þis teene for thi trespase I take.
Who couthe þe more kyndynes haue kydde   125
Than I?
Þus for thy goode
I schedde my bloode.
Manne, mende thy moode,
For full bittir þi blisse mon I by.   130

Maria Allas for my swete sonne I saie,
Þat doulfully to dede þus is diʒt.
Allas, for full louely he laye
In my wombe, þis worthely wight.
Allas þat I schulde see þis sight   135
Of my sone so semely to see.
Allas, þat þis blossome so bright
Vntrewly is tugged to þis tree.
Allas,
My lorde, my leyffe,   140
With full grete greffe
Hyngis as a theffe.
Allas, he did neuer trespasse.

Jesus Þou woman, do way of thy wepyng,
For me may þou nothyng amende.   145
My fadirs wille to be wirkyng,
For mankynde my body I bende.

Maria Allas, þat þou likes noght to lende,   f.203
Howe schulde I but wepe for thy woo?
To care nowe my comforte is kende.   150
Allas, why schulde we twynne þus in twoo
Foreuere?

Jesus   Womanne, instede of me,

---

114. *scripci, scripci]* Be *scripsi, scripsi*
126. *Added to right of 125 by J. Clerke*
133. *he]* Ho'; *MS, TS* + þou

Loo, John þi sone schall bee.
John, see to þi modir free,   155
For my sake do þou þi deuere.

Maria   Allas sone, sorowe and siȝte,
               Þat me were closed in clay.
             A swerde of sorowe me smyte,
               To dede I were done þis day.   160
Johannes   A, modir, so schall ȝe noght saie.
                 I praye youe be pees in þis presse,
               For with all þe myght þat I maye
                 Youre comforte I caste to encresse,
                 Indede.   165
                     Youre sone am I,
                     Loo, here redy;
                     And nowe forthy
                 I praye yowe hense for to speede.

Maria   My steuen for to stede or to steere,   170
                 Howe schulde I, such sorowe to see,
               My sone þat is dereworthy and dere
                 Thus doulfull a dede for to dye?
Johannes   A, dere modir, blynne of þis blee,
                 Youre mournyng it may not amende.   175
Maria Cleophe A, Marie, take triste vnto þe,
                 For socoure to þe will he sende
                     Þis tyde.
Johannes   Fayre modir, faste
                     Hense latte vs caste.   180
Maria   To he be paste
                 Wille I buske here baynly to bide.

Jesus   With bittirfull bale haue I bought,
                 Þus, man, all þi misse for te mende.   f.203ᵛ
               On me for to looke lette þou noȝt,   185
                 Howe baynly my body I bende.
               No wiȝhte in þis worlde wolde haue wende
                 What sorowe I suffre for thy sake.
               Manne, kaste þe thy kyndynesse be kende,
                 Trewe tente vnto me þat þou take,   190
                 And treste.
                     For foxis þer dennys haue þei,
                     Birdis hase ther nestis to paye,
                     But þe sone of man this daye
                 Hase noȝt on his heed for to reste.   195

155. to] *Interlined*
157. sone, sorowe] *He* sone, for sorowe
158. *For conjectures see He, K, Ho²*
189. thy] *He* my
195. on his heed] *K* his heed on

Latro a Sinistris	If þou be Goddis sone so free,
	Why hyng þou þus on þis hille?
	To saffe nowe thyselffe late vs see,
	And vs now, þat spedis for to spille.
Latro a Dextris	Manne, stynte of thy steuen and be stille, 200
	For douteles thy God dredis þou noȝt.
	Full wele are we worthy thertill,
	Vnwisely wrange haue we wrought,
	Iwisse.
	Noon ille did hee 205
	Þus for to dye.
	Lord, haue mynde of me
	Whan þou art come to þi blisse.

Jesus	Forsothe sonne, to þe schall I saie,
	Sen þou fro thy foly will falle, 210
	With me schall dwelle nowe þis daye,
	In paradise place principall.
	Heloy, heloy!
	My God, my God full free,
	Lama zabatanye, 215
	Wharto forsoke þou me
	In care?
	And I did neuere ille
	Þis dede for to go tille,
	But be it at þi wille. 220
	A, me thristis sare.

Garcio	A drinke schalle I dresse þe, indede,
	A draughte þat is full dayntely dight.
	Full faste schall I springe for to spede,
	I hope I schall holde þat I haue hight. 225
Caiphas	Sir Pilate þat moste is of myght, f.204
	Harke, 'Heely' now harde I hym crye.
	He wenys þat þat worthely wight
	In haste for to helpe hym in hye
	In his nede. 230
Pilatus	If he do soo
	He schall haue woo.
Anna	He wer oure foo
	If he dresse hym to do vs þat dede.

Garcio	Þat dede for to dresse yf he doo, 235
	In sertis he schall rewe it full sore.

197.   hyng] *Ho'* hynges
199.   now] *Ho'* two
208.   Whan] *Ha; MS, TS* + What
211.   schall dwelle] *Ho'* schall þou dwelle
213–6.   *Lineation TS; two lines in MS*
235.   *Garcio] Against 239 in Be (conj)*

Neuereþelees, if he like it noght, loo,
 Full sone may he couere þat care.
Now swete sir, youre wille yf it ware,
 A draughte here of drinke haue I dreste,   240
To spede for no spence þat 3e spare,
 But baldely ye bib it for þe beste.
  For-why
   Aysell and galle
   Is menged withalle;   245
   Drynke it 3e schalle—
  Youre lippis I halde þame full drye.

Jesus   Þi drinke it schalle do me no deere,
 Wete þou wele, þerof will I none.
Nowe fadir, þat formed alle in fere,   250
 To thy moste myght make I my mone:
Þi wille haue I wrought in þis wone,
 Þus ragged and rente on þis roode,
Þus doulffully to dede haue þei done.
 Forgiffe þame be grace þat is goode,   255
  Þai ne wote no3t what it was.
  My fadir, here my bone,
  For nowe all thyng is done.
  My spirite to þee right sone
  Comende I, *in manus tuas*.   260

Maria   Now dere sone, Jesus so jente,
 Sen my harte is heuy as leede,
O worde wolde I witte or þou wente.
 Allas, nowe my dere sone is dede,   f.204ᵛ
 Full rewfully refte is my rede.   265
  Allas for my darlyng so dere.
Johannes   A, modir, 3e halde vppe youre heede,
 And sigh no3t with sorowes so seere
  I praye.
Marie Cleophe   It dose hir pyne   270
   To see hym tyne.
   Lede we her heyne,
  Þis mornyng helpe hir ne maye.

Caiphas   Sir Pilate, parceyue I you praye,
 Oure costemes to kepe wele 3e canne.   275
Tomorne is oure dere Sabott daye,
 Of mirthe muste vs meve ilke a man.

---

241. spare] *TS+; MS* aware
254. for why *added to right by J. Clerke*
256. *Ho¹ would substitute* Þeir trespas
259. þee] *Altered from* me
272. Hic caret *to right in a later hand*

    Ʒone warlous nowe waxis full wan
      And nedis muste þei beried be.
    Delyuer þer dede sir, and þane   280
      Shall we sewe to oure saide solempnité
      Indede.

Pilatus   It schalle be done
          In wordis fone.
          Sir knyghtis, go sone,   285
    To Ʒone harlottis you hendely take heede.

    Þo caytiffis þou kille with þi knyffe–
    Delyuere, haue done þei were dede.

Miles   Mi lorde, I schall lenghe so þer liffe
    Þat þo brothelles schall neuere bite brede.   290

Pilatus   Ser Longeus, steppe forthe in þis steede;
      Þis spere, loo, haue halde in thy hande.
    To Jesus þou rake fourthe I rede,
      And sted nouƷt, but stiffely þou stande
      A stounde.   295
        In Jesu side
        Schoffe it þis tyde.
        No lenger bide,
      But grathely þou go to þe grounde.

Longeus latus   O maker vnmade, full of myght,   300
    O Jesu so jentill and jente   f.205
    Þat sodenly has sente me my sight,
      Lorde, louyng to þe be it lente.
      On rode arte þou ragged and rente,
        Mankynde for to mende of his mys.   305
      Full spitously spilte is and spente
        Thi bloode, lorde, to bringe vs to blis
        Full free.
          A, mercy my socoure,
          Mercy, my treasoure,   310
          Mercy, my sauioure,
        Þi mercy be markid in me.

Centurio   O wondirfull werkar iwis,
      Þis weedir is waxen full wan.
    Trewe token I trowe þat it is   315
      Þat mercy is mente vnto man.
    Full clerly consayue þus I can
      No cause in þis corse couthe þei knowe,
    Ʒitt doulfull þei demyd hym þan

---

288. done þei] *K* done, þat þei
294. sted] *K* ster
302. sente] *Ho¹; MS, TS +* lente
313. *Centurio] Be; MS, TS Centerio*

To lose þus his liffe be þer lawe, 320
 No riȝte.
  Trewly I saie,
  Goddis sone verraye
  Was he þis daye,
  Þat doulfully to dede þus is diȝt. 325

Joseph Þat lorde lele ay-lastyng in lande,
 Sir Pilate, full preste in þis presse,
 He saue þe be see and be sande,
 And all þat is derworth on deesse.

Pilatus Joseph, þis is lely, no lesse, 330
 To me arte þou welcome iwisse.
 Do saie me þe soth or þou sesse,
 Thy worthyly wille what it is
  Anone.

Joseph   To þe I praye, 335
  Giffe me in hye
  Jesu bodye,
  In gree it for to graue al alone.

Pilatus Joseph sir, I graunte þe þat geste,
 I grucche noȝt to grath hym in grave. 340
 Delyuer, haue done he were dreste, f.205ᵛ
 And sewe, sir, oure Sabott to saffe.

Joseph With handis and harte þat I haue
 I thanke þe in faith for my frende.
 God kepe þe þi comforte to craue, 345
 For wightely my way will I wende
  In hye.
   To do þat dede
   He be my speede
   Þat armys gun sprede, 350
   Mannekynde be his bloode for to bye.

Nichodemus Weill mette, ser. In mynde gune I meffe
 For Jesu þat juged was vnjente.
 Ye laboured for license and leve
 To berye his body on bente? 355

Joseph Full myldely þat matere I mente,
 And þat for to do will I dresse.

Nichodemus Both same I wolde þat we wente
 And lette not for more ne for lesse,
  For-why 360
  Oure frende was he,
  Faithfull and free.

---

335. praye] *He* crie
352. Nichodemus] *TS+ (and so in subsequent instances); MS Nichomedis (and so in
 subsequent instances)*
 I] *Suppl TS+*
358. we] *Suppl He, Be*

Joseph　　　　　　　　Þerfore go we
　　　　　　　　　　To berie þat body in hye.

　　　　　　　All mankynde may marke in his mynde　　365
　　　　　　　　To see here þis sorowfull sight.
　　　　　　　No falsnesse in hym couthe þei fynde
　　　　　　　　Þat doulfully to dede þus is dight.
Nichodemus　He was a full worthy wight,
　　　　　　　　Nowe blemysght and bolned with bloode.　370
Joseph　　　3a, for þat he mustered his myght,
　　　　　　　　Full falsely þei fellid þat foode
　　　　　　　　I wyne.
　　　　　　　　　Bothe bakke and side　　　　f.206
　　　　　　　　　Has woundes wide,　　　　　375
　　　　　　　　　Forþi þis tyde
　　　　　　　　Take we hym doune vs betwene.

Nichodemus　Betwene vs take we hym doune
　　　　　　　　And laie hym on lenthe on þis lande.
Joseph　　　Þis reuerent and riche of rennoune,　　380
　　　　　　　　Late vs halde hym and halse hym with hande.
　　　　　　　A graue haue I garte here be ordande
　　　　　　　　Þat neuer was in noote, it is newe.
Nichodemus　To þis corse it is comely accordande,
　　　　　　　　To dresse hym with dedis full dewe　　385
　　　　　　　　Þis stounde.
Joseph　　　　　A sudarye,
　　　　　　　　　Loo here, haue I.
　　　　　　　　　Wynde hym forthy,
　　　　　　　　And sone schalle we graue hym in grounde.　390

Nichodemus　In grounde late vs graue hym and goo;
　　　　　　　　Do liffely latte vs laie hym allone.
　　　　　　　Nowe sauiour of me and of moo,
　　　　　　　　Þou kepe vs in clennesse ilkone.
Joseph　　　To thy mercy nowe make I my moone:　　395
　　　　　　　　As sauiour be see and be sande,
　　　　　　　Þou gyde me þat my griffe be al gone,
　　　　　　　　With lele liffe to lenge in þis lande,
　　　　　　　　And esse.
Nichodemus　　　Seere oynementis here haue I　　400
　　　　　　　　Brought for þis faire body.
　　　　　　　　I anoynte þe forthy
　　　　　　　With myrre and aloes.

---

365. *Ruled off from 364 but not assigned (main scribe)*
371. mustered] *Be; TS* maistered
375. Has] *He; MS, TS +* His
395. To] *TS +; MS* Do

Joseph	Þis dede it is done ilke a dele,	
	And wroughte is þis werke wele iwis.	405
	To þe, kyng, on knes here I knele,	f.206ᵛ
	Þat baynly þou belde me in blisse.	
Nichodemus	He highte me full hendely to be his	
	A nyght whan I neghed hym full nere.	
	Haue mynde lorde, and mende me of mys,	410
	For done is oure dedis full dere	
	Þis tyde.	
Joseph	Þis lorde so goode	
	Þat schedde his bloode,	
	He mende youre moode,	415
	And buske on þis blis for to bide.	

XXXVII The Saddlers

The Harrowing of Hell

Jesus	Manne on molde, be meke to me,	f.207ᵛ
	And haue thy maker in þi mynde,	
	And thynke howe I haue tholid for þe	
	With pereles paynes for to be pyned.	
	The forward of my fadir free	5
	Haue I fulfillid, as folke may fynde,	
	Þerfore aboute nowe woll I bee	
	Þat I haue bought for to vnbynde.	
	Þe feende þame wanne with trayne	
	Thurgh frewte of erthely foode;	10
	I haue þame getyn agayne	
	Thurgh bying with my bloode.	

404.   *Joseph*] *Be; MS Joshep*
410.   mende] *TS+; MS wende*
416.   þis] *Hoᵗ his*
416+   finis *added by J. Clerke. Rest of f.206ᵛ blank except for faint scribbles in brown crayon;*
           f.207 blank

  1.   *Jesus*] *Suppl by a later hand*
 10.   frewte] *T fraude*

And so I schall þat steede restore
  For whilke þe feende fell for synne,
Þare schalle mankynde wonne euermore   15
  In blisse þat schall neuere blynne.
All þat in werke my werkemen were,
  Owte of thare woo I wol þame wynne,
And some signe schall I sende before
  Of grace, to garre þer gamys begynne.   20
    A light I woll þei haue
      To schewe þame I schall come sone.
    My bodie bidis in graue
      Tille alle thes dedis be done.

My fadir ordand on þis wise   25
  Aftir his will þat I schulde wende,
For to fulfille þe prophicyes,
  And als I spake my solace to spende.
My frendis þat in me faith affies,
  Nowe fro ther fois I schall þame fende,   30
And on the thirde day ryght vprise,
  And so tille heuen I schall assende.
    Sithen schall I come agayne
      To deme bothe goode and ill   f.208
    Tille endles joie or peyne;   35
      Þus is my fadris will.

    Tunc cantent.

Adame   Mi bretheren, harkens to me here,
  Swilke hope of heele neuere are we hadde;
Foure thowsande and sex hundereth ȝere
  Haue we bene heere in þis stedde.   40
Nowe see I signe of solace seere,
  A glorious gleme to make vs gladde,
Wherfore I hope oure helpe is nere
  And sone schall sesse oure sorowes sadde.
Eua   Adame, my husband hende,   45
    Þis menys solas certayne.
    Such light gune on vs lende
      In paradise full playne.

Isaiah   Adame, we schall wele vndirstande –
  I, Ysaias, as God me kende,   50

14. For¹] *TS conj, Si* Fro
17. werke] *K* worlde
27. prophicyes] *He, Si; MS, TS* prophicye
33+ *Catchword* To deme both goode
34. *Quire xxvijᵗⁱ begins; f.208 is a singleton pasted to the stub of a cancel*
36+ *SD added (to right of 35–6) by a later hand*
40. in þis stedde] *T* in darknes stad
49. *Isaiah*] *TS+; MS* Isaac
    we] *Si conj* ȝe; *T* thou

I prechid in Neptalym, þat lande,
  And Zabulon, even vntill ende.
I spake of folke in mirke walkand
  And saide a light schulde on þame lende.
This lered I whils I was leuand,   55
  Nowe se I God þis same hath sende.
    Þis light comes all of Criste,
      Þat seede to saue vs nowe.
    Þus is my poynte puplisshid –
      But Symeon, what sais þou?   60

Symeon   Þhis, my tale of farleis feele,
  For in þe temple his frendis me fande.
I hadde delite with hym to dele
  And halsed homely with my hande.
I saide, 'Lorde, late thy seruaunt lele   65
  Passe nowe in pesse to liffe lastand,
For nowe myselfe has sene thy hele   f.208ᵛ
  Me liste no lengar to liffe in lande'.
    Þis light þou hast purueyed
      To folkes þat liffis in leede,   70
    Þe same þat I þame saide
      I see fulfillid in dede.

Johannes Baptista   Als voyce criand to folke I kende
  Þe weyes of Criste als I wele kanne.
I baptiste hym with bothe my hende   75
  Euen in þe floode of flume Jordanne.
Þe holy goste fro heuene discende
  Als a white dowue doune on hym þanne;
The fadir voice, my mirthe to mende,
  Was made to me euen als manne: 80
    'This is my sone', he saide,
      'In whome me paies full wele'.
    His light is on vs laide,
      He comes oure cares to kele.

Moyses   Of þat same light lernyng haue I: 85
  To me, Moyses, he mustered his myght,
And also vnto anodir, Hely,
  Wher we were on an hille on hight.
Whyte as snowe was his body,
  And his face like to þe sonne to sight;   90

---

58. seede] *Tolkien (in Si, glossary) conj* deede
59. puplisshid *Si conj* puplist
61. Þhis] *Si; TS* Yhis
62. þe] *Ho�, after T* the; *MS, TS* þis, *Si conj* his
64. halsed homely] *K* halsed hym homely, *so T*
75. hende] *Hoᵗ, conj Si, so T; MS, TS* hande
83. laide] a *altered from* e

No man on molde was so myghty
Grathely to loke agaynste þat light.
Þat same light se I nowe
Shynyng on vs sarteyne,
Wherfore trewly I trowe   95
We schalle sone passe fro payne.

I Diabolus   Helpe, Belsabub, to bynde þer boyes—
                  Such harrowe was neuer are herde in helle.
II Diabolus   Why rooris þou soo, Rebalde? Þou royis—   f.209
                  What is betidde, canne þou ought telle?   100
I Diabolus   What, heris þou noȝt þis vggely noyse?
                  Þes lurdans þat in Lymbo dwelle,
                  Þei make menyng of many joies
                  And musteres grete mirthe þame emell.
II Diabolus   Mirthe? Nay, nay, þat poynte is paste,   105
                  More hele schall þei neuer haue.
I Diabolus   Þei crie on Criste full faste
                  And sais he schal þame saue.

Belsabub   Ȝa, if he saue þame noght, we schall,
                  For they are sperde in speciall space.   110
                  Whils I am prince and principall
                  Schall þei neuer passe oute of þis place.
                  Calle vppe Astrotte and Anaball
                  To giffe þer counsaille in þis case,
                  Bele-Berit and Belial,   115
                  To marre þame þat swilke maistries mase.
                  Say to Satan oure sire,
                  And bidde þame bringe also
                  Lucifer, louely of lyre.
I Diabolus   Al redy, lorde, I goo.   120

Jesus   *Attollite portas, principes,*
                  Oppen vppe, ȝe princes ol paynes sere,
                  Et eleuamini eternales,
                  Youre yendles ȝatis þat ȝe haue here.
Sattan   What page is þere þat makes prees   125
                  And callis hym kyng of vs in fere?
Dauid   I lered leuand, withouten lees,
                  He is a kyng of vertues clere,
                  A lorde mekill of myght
                  And stronge in ilke a stoure,   130
                  In batailes ferse to fight   f.209ᵛ
                  And worthy to wynne honnoure.

97.   *I Diabolus*] T Rybald
99.   *II Diabolus*] *Suppl by another hand; T Belzabub*
105. poynte] *Si; TS* þoynte
113. Anaball] *Si; TS* A

Sattan	Honnoure? In þe deuel way! For what dede?
	All erthely men to me are thrall.
	Þe lady þat calles hym lorde in leede 135
	Hadde neuer ʒitt herberowe, house, ne halle.
I Diabolus	Harke Belsabub, I haue grete drede,
	For hydously I herde hym calle.
Belliall	We, spere oure ʒates, all ill mot þou spede,
	And sette furthe watches on þe wall – 140
	And if he calle or crie
	To make vs more debate,
	Lay on hym þan hardely
	And garre hym gange his gate.
Sattan	Telle me what boyes dare be so bolde 145
	For drede to make so mekill draye.
I Diabolus	Itt is þe Jewe þat Judas solde
	For to be dede þis othir daye.
Sattan	Owe, þis tale in tyme is tolde,
	Þis traytoure traueses vs alway. 150
	He schall be here full harde in holde,
	Loke þat he passe noght, I þe praye.
II Diabolus	Nay, nay, he will noʒt wende
	Away or I be ware,
	He shappis hym for to schende 155
	Alle helle or he go ferre.
Sattan	Nay faitour, þerof schall he faile,
	For alle his fare I hym deffie.
	I knowe his trantis fro toppe to taile,
	He leuys with gaudis and with gilery. 160
	Þerby he brought oute of oure bale
	Nowe late Lazar of Betannye; f.210
	Þerfore I gaffe to þe Jewes counsaille
	Þat þei schulde alway garre hym dye.
	I entered in Judas 165
	Þat forwarde to fulfille,
	Þerfore his hire he has
	Allway to wonne here stille.
Belsabub	Sir Sattanne, sen we here þe saie
	Þat þou and þe Jewes wer same assente, 170
	And wotte he wanne Lazar awaye
	Þat tille vs was tane for to tente,
	Trowe þou þat þou marre hym maye,
	To mustir mightis what he has mente?

135.   lady þat calles hym] *T* lad that thou callys
150.   traueses] *Si, cf T* trauesses; *MS, TS* traues
154.   I] *T* it
170.   þe] *Si, cf T* the; *MS, TS* ʒe

<table>
<tr><td></td><td>If he nowe depriue vs of oure praye,</td><td>175</td></tr>
<tr><td></td><td>We will ȝe witte whanne þei are wente.</td><td></td></tr>
<tr><td>*Sattan*</td><td>I bidde ȝou be noȝt abasshed,</td><td></td></tr>
<tr><td></td><td>But boldely make youe boune</td><td></td></tr>
<tr><td></td><td>With toles þat ȝe on traste,</td><td></td></tr>
<tr><td></td><td>And dynge þat dastard doune.</td><td>180</td></tr>
</table>

<table>
<tr><td>*Jesus*</td><td>*Principes, portas tollite,*</td><td></td></tr>
<tr><td></td><td>Vndo youre ȝatis, ȝe princis of pryde,</td><td></td></tr>
<tr><td></td><td>*Et introibit rex glorie,*</td><td></td></tr>
<tr><td></td><td>Þe kyng of blisse comes in þis tyde.</td><td></td></tr>
<tr><td>*Sattan*</td><td>Owte, harrowe! What harlot is hee</td><td>185</td></tr>
<tr><td></td><td>Þat sais his kyngdome schall be cryed?</td><td></td></tr>
<tr><td>*Dauid*</td><td>Þat may þou in my Sawter see,</td><td></td></tr>
<tr><td></td><td>For þat poynte I prophicied.</td><td></td></tr>
<tr><td></td><td>I saide þat he schuld breke</td><td></td></tr>
<tr><td></td><td>Youre barres and bandis by name,</td><td>190</td></tr>
<tr><td></td><td>And on youre werkis take wreke –</td><td></td></tr>
<tr><td></td><td>Nowe schalle ȝe see þe same.</td><td></td></tr>
</table>

<table>
<tr><td>*Jesus*</td><td>Þis steede schall stonde no lenger stoken:</td><td>f.210ᵛ</td></tr>
<tr><td></td><td>Opynne vppe, and latte my pepul passe.</td><td></td></tr>
<tr><td>*I Diabolus*</td><td>Owte! Beholdes, oure baill is brokynne,</td><td>195</td></tr>
<tr><td></td><td>And brosten are alle oure bandis of bras –</td><td></td></tr>
<tr><td></td><td>Telle Lucifer alle is vnlokynne.</td><td></td></tr>
<tr><td>*Belsabub*</td><td>What þanne, is Lymbus lorne? Allas,</td><td></td></tr>
<tr><td></td><td>Garre Satan helpe þat we wer wroken;</td><td></td></tr>
<tr><td></td><td>Þis werke is werse þanne euere it was.</td><td>200</td></tr>
<tr><td>*Sattan*</td><td>I badde ȝe schulde be boune</td><td></td></tr>
<tr><td></td><td>If he made maistries more.</td><td></td></tr>
<tr><td></td><td>Do dynge þat dastard doune</td><td></td></tr>
<tr><td></td><td>And sette hym sadde and sore.</td><td></td></tr>
</table>

<table>
<tr><td>*Belsabub*</td><td>Ȝa, sette hym sore – þat is sone saide,</td><td>205</td></tr>
<tr><td></td><td>But come þiselffe and serue hym soo.</td><td></td></tr>
<tr><td></td><td>We may not bide his bittir braide,</td><td></td></tr>
<tr><td></td><td>He wille vs marre and we wer moo.</td><td></td></tr>
<tr><td>*Sattan*</td><td>What, faitours, wherfore are ȝe flayd?</td><td></td></tr>
<tr><td></td><td>Haue ȝe no force to flitte hym froo?</td><td>210</td></tr>
<tr><td></td><td>Belyue loke þat my gere be grathed,</td><td></td></tr>
<tr><td></td><td>Miselffe schall to þat gedlyng goo.</td><td></td></tr>
</table>

177. abasshed] *Si conj* abaste
185. What harlot] *Suppl TS+, from T*
188. I prophicied] *Si; MS, TS* of prophicie
195. *I Diabolus*] *I suppl this ed*
     baill] *Interlined by a later hand*
196. of] *Interlined by a later hand*
209. flayd] *Hoʼ, after T* flayd; *MS, TS+* ferde
211. *To the left in J. Clerke's hand, deleted,* nota caret nova loquela

Howe, belamy, abide,
With al thy booste and bere,
And telle to me þis tyde   215
What maistries makes þou here?

Jesus   I make no maistries but for myne,
Þame wolle I saue I telle þe nowe.
Þou hadde no poure þame to pyne,
But as my prisounes for þer prowe   220
Here haue þei soiorned, noght as thyne,
But in thy warde – þou wote wele howe.

Sattan   And what deuel haste þou done ay syne   f.211
Þat neuer wolde negh þame nere or nowe?

Jesus   Nowe is þe tyme certayne   225
Mi fadir ordand before,
Þat they schulde passe fro payne
And wonne in mirthe euer more.

Sattan   Thy fadir knewe I wele be sight,
He was a write his mette to wynne,   230
And Marie me menys þi modir hight –
Þe vttiremeste ende of all þi kynne.
Who made þe be so mekill of myght?

Jesus   Þou wikid feende, latte be thy dynne.
Mi fadir wonnys in heuen on hight,   235
With blisse þat schall neuere blynne.
I am his awne sone,
His forward to fulfille,
And same ay schall we wonne
And sundir whan we wolle.   240

Sattan   God sonne? Þanne schulde þou be ful gladde,
Aftir no catel neyd thowe crave!
But þou has leued ay like a ladde,
And in sorowe as a symple knave.

Jesus   Þat was for hartely loue I hadde   245
Vnto mannis soule, it for to saue;
And for to make þe mased and madde,
And by þat resoune þus dewly to haue
Mi Godhede here, I hidde
In Marie modir myne,   250
For it schulde noȝt be kidde
To þe nor to none of thyne.

---

220. as] *T* in
   prisounes] *Ho', conj Si; TS* prisonne, *Si* prisoure, *T* pryson
237–8. *Lineation TS; one line in MS*
242. neyd thowe crave] *Added to right by J. Clerke; main scribe* þus þe I telle
244. as] *Interlined by a later hand (? Clerke's, and so next)*
   knave] *Interlined by a later hand over main scribe's* braide

Sattan.

A, þis wolde I were tolde in ilke a toune.　　　　f.211ᵛ
　　So, sen þou sais God is thy sire,
I schall þe proue be right resoune　　　　　　　　255
　　Þou motes his men into þe myre.
To breke his bidding were þei boune,
　　And, for they did at my desire,
Fro paradise he putte þame doune
　　In helle here to haue þer hyre.　　　　　　　260
　　　　And thyselfe, day and nyght,
　　　　　　Has taught al men emang
　　　　To do resoune and right,
　　　　　　And here werkis þou all wrang.

Jesus

I wirk noght wrang, þat schal þow witte,　　　　265
　　If I my men fro woo will wynne.
Mi prophetis playnly prechid it,
　　All þis note þat nowe begynne.
Þai saide þat I schulde be obitte,
　　To helle þat I schulde entre in,　　　　　　270
And saue my seruauntis fro þat pitte
　　Wher dampned saulis schall sitte for synne.
　　　　And ilke trewe prophettis tale
　　　　　　Muste be fulfillid in mee;
　　　　I haue þame boughte with bale,　　　　275
　　　　　　And in blisse schal þei be.

Sattan

Nowe sen þe liste allegge þe lawes,
　　Þou schalte be atteynted or we twynne,
For þo þat þou to wittenesse drawes
　　Full even agaynste þe will begynne.　　　　280
Salamon saide in his sawes
　　Þat whoso enteres helle withynne
Shall neuer come oute, þus clerkis knawes—
　　And þerfore felowe, leue þi dynne.
　　　　Job, þi seruaunte, also　　　　　　285
　　　　　　Þus in his tyme gune telle
　　　　Þat nowthir frende nor foo　　　　f.212
　　　　　　Shulde fynde reles in helle.

Jesus

He saide full soth, þat schall þou see,
　　Þat in helle may be no reles,　　　　　　290
But of þat place þan preched he
　　Where synffull care schall euere encrees.

253.　*Appears as last line on f.211 and first line on f.211ᵛ; first instance deleted in red (main scribe)*

254.　So] *TS+; MS* Fo

268.　þat nowe] *Ho'* þat I nowe, *after T*

274.　in] *Interlined*

275.　boughte] *Si; TS* broughte

And in þat bale ay schall þou be
  Whare sorowes sere schall neuer sesse,
And for my folke þerfro wer free,   295
  Nowe schall þei passe to þe place of pees.
    Þai were here with my wille,
      And so schall þei fourthe wende,
    And þiselue schall fulfille
      Þer wooe withouten ende.   300

Sattan   Owe, þanne se I howe þou menys emang
  Some mesure with malice to melle,
Sen þou sais all schall noȝt gang,
  But some schalle alway with vs dwelle.

Jesus   Ȝaa, witte þou wele, ellis were it wrang,   305
  Als cursed Cayme þat slewe Abell,
And all þat hastis hemselue to hange,
  Als Judas and Archedefell,
    Datan and Abiron,
      And alle of þare assente,   310
    Als tyrantis euerilkone
      Þat me and myne turmente.

And all þat liste noght to lere my lawe
  Þat I haue lefte in lande nowe newe—
Þat is my comyng for to knawe,   315
  And to my sacramente pursewe,
Mi dede, my rysing, rede be rawe—
  Who will noght trowe, þei are noght trewe. f.212ᵛ
Vnto my dome I schall þame drawe,
  And juge þame worse þanne any Jewe.   320
    And all þat likis to leere
      My lawe and leue þerbye,
    Shall neuere haue harmes heere,
      But welthe, as is worthy.

Sattan   Nowe here my hande, I halde me paied,   325
  Þis poynte is playnly for oure prowe.
If þis be soth þat þou hast saide
  We schall haue moo þanne we haue nowe.
Þis lawe þat þou nowe late has laide
  I schall lere men noȝt to allowe;   330
Iff þei it take þei be betraied,
  For I schall turne þame tyte, I trowe.
    I schall walke este and weste,
      And garre þame werke wele werre.

Jesus   Naye, feende, þou schall be feste,   335
    Þat þou schalte flitte not ferre.

301. menys] *K, Si, after T* menys; *MS, TS* mouys
308. Archedefell] *T* Architophelle

Sattan	Feste? Þat were a foule reasoune –
	Nay bellamy, þou bus be smytte.
Jesus	Mighill myne aungell, make þe boune
	And feste yone fende þat he noght flitte. 340
	And, Deuyll, I comaunde þe go doune
	Into thy selle where þou schalte sitte.
Sattan	Owt! Ay herrowe! Helpe, Mahounde!
	Nowe wex I woode oute of my witte.
Belsabub	Sattan, þis saide we are, 345
	Nowe schall þou fele þi fitte.
Sattan	Allas for dole and care,
	I synke into helle pitte.
Adame	A, Jesu, lorde, mekill is þi myght,
	That mekis þiselffe in þis manere, f.213
	Vs for to helpe as þou has hight, 351
	Whanne both forfette, I and my feere.
	Here haue we leuyd withouten light
	Four thousand and vi c ȝere;
	Now se I be þis solempne sight 355
	Howe thy mercy hath made vs clere.
Eue	A, lorde, we were worthy
	Mo turmentis for to taste,
	But mende vs with mercye
	Als þou of myght is moste. 360
Baptista	A, lorde, I loue þe inwardly,
	That me wolde make þi messengere
	Thy comyng in erth for to crye,
	And teche þi faith to folke in feere;
	And sithen before þe for to dye 365
	And bringe boodworde to þame here,
	How þai schulde haue thyne helpe in hye.
	Nowe se I all þi poyntis appere
	Als Dauid, prophete trewe,
	Ofte tymes tolde vntill vs; 370
	Of þis comyng he knewe,
	And saide it schulde be þus.
Dauid	Als I haue saide, ȝitt saie I soo,
	Ne derelinquas, domine,
	Animam meam in inferno, 375
	Leffe noght my saule, lorde, aftir þe
	In depe helle where dampned schall goo;
	Ne suffre neuere saules fro þe be,

347.   dole] *TS +; MS* dolee
354.   vi c] *Si* six hundred
356.   clere] *TS +; MS* clene
375.   in] *Suppl TS, after T*
378.   saules fro þe be] *T* thi sayntes to se

The sorowe of þame þat wonnes in woo
Ay full of filthe, þat may repleye. 380

Adame We thanke his grete goodnesse
He fette vs fro þis place.
Makes joie nowe, more and lesse. f.213ᵛ

Omnis We laude God of his grace.

Tunc cantent.

Jesus Adame, and my frendis in feere, 385
Fro all youre fooes come fourth with me.
ʒe schalle be sette in solas seere
Wher ʒe schall neuere of sorowes see.
And Mighill, myn aungell clere,
Ressayue þes saules all vnto þe 390
And lede þame als I schall þe lere,
To paradise with playe and plenté.
Mi graue I woll go till,
Redy to rise vpperight,
And so I schall fulfille 395
That I before haue highte.

Michill Lorde, wende we schall aftir þi sawe,
To solace sere þai schall be sende.
But þat þer deuelis no draught vs drawe
Lorde, blisse vs with þi holy hende. 400

Jesus Mi blissing haue ʒe all on rawe,
I schall be with youe wher ʒe wende,
And all þat lelly luffes my lawe,
Þai schall be blissid withowten ende.

Adame To þe, lorde, be louyng, 405
Þat vs has wonne fro waa.
For solas will we syng
Laus tibi cum gloria etc.

---

380. þat may repleye] *T and may not fle*
384. Omnis] *Si; MS, TS place in dialogue*
384+ *SD added (to right of 384) by a later hand, ? J. Clerke*
400. hende] eʳ *altered to* o *by a later hand*
408+ finis *added by Clerke; ff.214, 214ᵛ blank*

XXXVIII The Carpenters

The Resurrection

Pilatus	Lordingis, listenys nowe vnto me:	f.215
	I comaunde ʒou in ilke degré	
	Als domesman chiffe in þis contré,	
	For counsaill kende,	
	Atte my bidding ʒou awe to be	5
	And baynly bende.	
	And sir Cayphas, chiffe of clergye,	
	Of youre counsaill late here in hye.	
	By youre assente sen we dyd dye	
	Jhesus þis day,	10
	Þat ʒe mayntayne, and stande þerby	
	Þat werke allway.	
Cayphas	Ʒis sir, þat dede schall we mayntayne,	
	By lawe it was done all bedene,	
	Ʒe wotte youreselue withouten wene	15
	Als wele as we.	
	His sawes are nowe vppon hym sene	
	And ay schall be.	
Anna	Þe pepull, sir, in þis same steede,	
	Before ʒou saide with a hole-hede	20
	Þat he was worthy to be dede,	
	And þerto sware.	
	Sen all was rewlid by rightis rede	
	Nevyn it no more.	
Pilatus	To neuyn methinketh it nedfull thyng.	25
	Sen he was hadde to beriyng	
	Herde we nowthir of olde ne ʒing	
	Thithynges betwene.	
Cayphas	Centurio, sir, will bringe thiding	
	Of all bedene.	30

---

1. *Pilatus*] *Suppl by a later hand*
9. youre] *He, K, Ca; MS, TS, Ma* oure
11. ʒe] *K, Ca; MS, TS, Ma* we
19. sir] *Ma, Ca; MS, TS,* sirs
23. rightis] *Ha, Ma* rightwis
29. bringe thiding] *Ho', Ca; MS, TS* bringe thidings, *Ma* tidingis bringe

344

We lefte hym þere for man moste wise,
If any rebelles wolde ought rise
Oure rightwise dome for to dispise
  Or it offende,
To sese þame till þe nexte assise   35
  And þan make ende.

Centurio   A, blissid lorde Adonay,
What may þes meruayles signifie
Þat her was schewed so oppinly
  Vnto oure sight,   40
Þis day whanne þat þe man gune dye
  Þat Jesus highte?

Itt is a misty thyng to mene,   f.215ᵛ
So selcouth a sight was neuere sene,
Þat oure princes and prestis bedene   45
  Of þis affray
I woll go weten withouten wene,
  What þei can saye.

God saue ȝou sirs on ilke a side,
Worschippe and welthe in worldis wide;   50
With mekill mirthe myght ȝe abide
  Both day and nyght.
Pilatus   Centurio, welcome þis tide,
  Oure comely knyght.

ȝe haue bene miste vs here among.   55
Centurio   God giffe you grace grathely to gang.
Pilatus   Centurio, oure frende full lang,
  What is your will?
Centurio   I drede me þat ȝe hauc done wrang
  And wondir ill.   60

Cayphas   Wondir ill? I pray þe, why?
Declare it to þis company.
Centurio   So schall I sirs telle ȝou trewly
  Withowten trayne:
Þe rightwise mane þannc mene I by   65
  Þat ȝe haue slayne.

Pilatus   Centurio, sesse of such sawe,
Þou arte a lered man in þe lawe,
And if we schulde any witnes drawe
  Vs to excuse,   70
To mayntayne vs euermore þe awe,
  And noȝt reffuse.

52. Both] *K, Ma, Ca; MS, TS* Boght. *The whole line added to the right by a later hand*
68. Hic deficit *added to left by a later hand*

Centurio	To mayntayne trouthe is wele worþi.
	I saide ȝou whanne I sawe hym dy
	Þat he was Goddis sone almyghty 75
	Þat hangeth þore;
	Ȝitt saie I soo, and stande þerby
	For euermore.

Cayphas	Ȝa sir, such reasouns may ȝe rewe.
	Ȝe schulde noght neueyn such note enewe f.216
	But ȝe couthe any tokenyngis trewe 81
	Vnto vs tell.
Centurio	Such woundirfull cas neuere ȝitt ȝe knewe
	As now befell.

Anna	We praye þe telle vs of what thyng. 85
Centurio	All elementis, both olde and ȝing,
	In ther maneres þai made mornyng
	In ilke a stede,
	And knewe be countenaunce þat þer kyng
	Was done to dede. 90

Þe sonne for woo he waxed all wanne,
Þe mone and sterres of schynyng blanne,
Þe erthe tremeled and also manne
   Began to speke;
Þe stones þat neuer was stered or þanne 95
   Gune asondir breke,

	And dede men rose, both grete and small.
Pilatus	Centurio, beware withall,
	Ȝe wote oure clerkis þe clipsis þei call
	Such sodayne sight. 100
	Both sonne and mone þat sesoune schall
	Lak of þer light.

Cayphas	Ȝa, and if dede men rose bodily
	Þat myght be done thurgh socery,
	Þerfore we sette nothyng þerby 105
	To be abaiste.
Centurio	All þat I tell for trewthe schall I
	Euermore traste.

In þis ilke werke þat ȝe did wirke
Nought allone þe sonne was mirke, 110

76. hangeth] *K, Ma* hanged
79+ *Catchword* Ȝe schulde not nevyn
80. *Quire xxviij* begins
   note enewe] *T* notes newe
93. *T* And erthe it tremlyd as a man
109. In] *Ma* For, *T* Not for

	But howe youre vaile raffe in youre kirke,	
	That witte I wolde.	
Pilatus	Swilke tales full sone will make vs irke	
	And þei be talde.	

Anna	Centurio, such speche withdrawe,	115
	Of all þes wordes we haue none awe.	
Centurio	Nowe sen ȝe sette noght be my sawe	
	Sirs, haue gode day.	
	God graunte you grace þat ȝe may knawe	
	Þe soth alway.	120

Anna	Withdrawe þe faste sen þou þe dredis,	
	For we schall wele mayntayne oure dedis.	
Pilatus	Such wondir reasouns as he redis	
	Was neuere beforne.	
Caiphas	To neven þis noote no more vs nedis,	f.216ᵛ
	Nowþere even ne morne.	126

Þerfore loke no manne make ille chere,
All þis doyng may do no dere.
But to beware ȝitt of more were
   Þat folke may fele, 130
We praye you sirs, of þes sawes sere
   Avise ȝou wele.

And to þis tale takes hede in hye,
For Jesu saide even opynly
A thyng þat greues all þis Jury, 135
   And riȝte so may:
Þat he schulde rise vppe bodily
   Within þe thirde day.

And be it so, als motte I spede,
His lattar deede is more to drede 140
Þan is the firste if we take hede
   Or tente þerto.
To neuyn þis noote methynke moste nede
   And beste to do.

| *Anna* | Ȝa sir, if all þat he saide soo, | 145 |

He has no myght to rise and goo
But if his menne stele hym vs froo
   And bere away.
Þat were tille us and oþer moo
   A foule fraye, 150

---

119. God] *Om TS (misprint); suppl as emendation by later edd.*
127. ille] *Proposed as emendation by Ho¹, Ma, Ca; TS* ilke
145. if all] *Ma* all if

For þanne wolde þei saie euere-ilkone
Þat he roose by hymselffe allone.
Therfore latte hym be kepte anone
   With knyghtes hende,
Vnto thre daies be comen and gone   155
   And broght till ende.

Pilatus   In certayne sirs right wele ʒe saie,
For þis ilke poynte nowe to purvaye
I schall ordayne if I may.
   He schall not ryse,   160
Nor none schalle wynne hym þens away
   On nokyns wise.

Sir knyghtis, þat are in dedis dowty,
Chosen for chiffe of cheualrye,
As we ay in youre force affie   165
   Boþe day and nyght,
Wendis and kepis Jesu body
   With all youre myghte.

And for thyng þat euere be maye
Kepis hym wele to þe thirde day,   170
And latis no man take hym away
   Oute of þat stede —
For and þei do, suthly I saie
   ʒe schall be dede.

I Miles   Lordingis, we saie ʒou for certayne,   f.217
We schall kepe hym with myghtis and mayne.   176
Þer schall no traitoures with no trayne
   Stele hym vs froo.
Sir knyghtis, takis gere þat moste may gayne
   And lates vs goo.   180

II Miles   ʒis, certis, we are all redy bowne,
We schall hym kepe till oure rennowne,
On ilke a side latte vs sitte doune
   Nowe all in fere,
And sone we schall crake his croune   185
   Whoso comes here.

---

158. to] *Suppl TS+, after T* to
159. if I] *K, Ma* if that I
163. Lorde *interlined by a later hand between* knyghtis *and* þat
171. take] *Ho', Ma, Ca; MS, TS* takis
175. I Miles] *Suppl by a later hand; so assigned in T*
176. myghtis] *K, Ma, Ca* myght
185. sone we schall crake] *K, Ma* fownde we schall to crake, *after T* shalle fownde to
     crake

Tunc 'Jesus resurgente'.

I Maria	Allas, to dede I wolde be dight,
	So woo in werke was neuere wight,
	Mi sorowe is all for þat sight
	Þat I gune see, 190
	Howe Criste my maistir moste of myght
	Is dede fro me.

Allas þat I schulde se his pyne
Or yit þat I his liffe schulde tyne,
Of ilke a myscheue he was medicyne   195
   And bote of all,
Helpe and halde to ilke a hyne
   Þat on hym wolde call.

II Maria   Allas, who schall my balis bete
Whanne I thynke on his woundes wete.   200
Jesu, þat was of loue so swete
   And neuere did ill,
Es dede and grauen vnder þe grete,
   Withouten skill.

III Maria   Withowten skill þe Jewes ilkone   205
Þat louely lorde has newly slayne,
And trespasse did he neuere none
   In nokyn steede.
To whome nowe schall I make my mone
   Sen he is dede?   210

I Maria   Sen he is dede my sisteres dere,
Wende we will on mylde manere
With oure anoynementis faire and clere
   Þat we haue broght,
To noynte his wondis on sides sere   215
   Þat Jewes hym wroght.

II Maria   Goo we same my sisteres free,   f.217ᵛ
Full faire vs longis his corse to see.
But I wotte noght howe beste may be,
   Helpe haue we none.   220
And who schall nowe here of vs thre
   Remove þe stone?

187– *SD by main scribe, in red. To right in hand of J. Clerke* Tunc Angelus cantat
     'Resurgens'
188. werke] *T* warlde, *Ma* worlde
189. Memorandum *added to right by a later hand*
195. was] *Hoˡ after T* was; *MS, TS+* is
198. on hym wolde] *Conj TS; Ma, Ca. MS* hym on wolde
217. II] *TS+; MS* Prima. *T assigns to Maria Jacobi (= II Maria in Y)*
218. faire] *T* sore, *Ma* sare

III Maria	Þat do we noght but we wer moo,	
	For it is huge and heuy also.	
I Maria	Sisteris, a ȝonge childe, as we goo	225
	Makand mornyng,	
	I see it sitte wher we wende to,	
	In white clothyng.	

II Maria	Sistirs, sertis it is noght to hide,	
	Þe heuy stone is putte beside.	230
III Maria	Sertis, for thyng þat may betyde	
	Nere will we wende,	
	To layte þat luffely and with hym bide	
	Þat was oure frende.	

Angelus	Ȝe mournand women in youre þought,	235
	Here in þis place whome haue ȝe sought?	
I Maria	Jesu, þat to dede is brought,	
	Oure lorde so free.	
Angelus	Women, certayne here is he noght,	
	Come nere and see.	240

	He is noght here þe soth to saie,	
	Þe place is voide þat he in laye,	
	Þe sudary here se ȝe may	
	Was on hym laide.	
	He is resen and wente his way,	245
	As he ȝou saide.	

	Euen as he saide so done has hee,	
	He is resen thurgh grete poostee,	
	He schall be foune in Galilé	
	In flesshe and fell.	250
	To his discipilis nowe wende ȝe	
	And þus þame tell.	

I Maria	Mi sisteres dere, sen it is soo	
	Þat he is resen dede þus froo,	
	As þe aungell tolde me and yow too—	255
	Oure lorde so fre—	
	Hens will I neuer goo	
	Or I hym see.	

II Maria	Marie, vs thare no lenger lende,	
	To Galilé nowe late vs wende.	f.218

237. to] *K, Ma* unto, *after T* vnto
 is] *Ma* was, *after T* was
245. his] *TS+; MS* his his
254. Et hic deficit *to left in a later hand, deleted*
259. lende] *Conj TS; Ma, Ca. MS* layne

I Maria	Nought tille I see þat faithfull frende	261
	Mi lorde and leche,	
	Þerfore all þis my sisteres hende,	
	Þat ȝe forth preche.	

III Maria	As we haue herde so schall we saie.	265
	Marie oure sistir, haue goode daye.	
I Maria	Nowe verray God as he wele maye—	
	Man most of myght—	267a
	He wisse you, sisteres, wele in youre waye	
	And rewle ȝou right.	

Allas, what schall nowe worþe on me.   270
Mi kaytiffe herte will breke in three
Whenne I thynke on þat body free,
   How it was spilte.
Both feete and handes nayled tille a tre,
   Withouten gilte.   275

Withouten gilte þe trewe was tane,
For trespas did he neuere none,
Þe woundes he suffered many one
   Was for my misse.
It was my dede he was for slayne   280
   And nothyng his.

How might I, but I loued þat swete,
Þat for my loue tholed woundes wete
And sithen be grauen vndir þe grete,
   Such kyndnes kithe?   285
Þer is nothing to þat we mete
   May make me blithe.

I Miles	What, oute allas, what schall I saie?	
	Where is þe corse þat herein laye?	
II Miles	What ayles þe man? Is he awaye	290
	Þat we schulde tent?	
I Miles	Rise vppe and see.	
II Miles	Harrowe, for ay	
	I telle vs schente.	

III Miles	What deuill is þis, what aylis ȝou twoo,	
	Such noyse and crye þus for to make too?	295
I Miles	Why is he gone?	

---

264. *T* Loke that ye preche
267a. *Suppl TS+, from T. MS has* A weryed wight *added by J. Clerke to right of 270*
280. dede] *T* gylt
294–8. *For conjectural reconstructions see Ho', Ma*

III Miles	Allas, whare is he þat here laye?
IV Miles	Whe, harrowe! Deuill, whare is he away?

III Miles   What, is he þus-gatis fro vs wente,   f.218ᵛ
            Þat fals traitour þat here was lente,   300
            And we trewly here for to tente
                Had vndirtane?
            Sekirlie, I telle vs schente
                Holy ilkane.

I Miles   Allas, what schall we do þis day,   305
            Þat þus þis warlowe is wente his waye?
            And sauely sirs I dare wele saie
                He rose allone.
II Miles   Witte sir Pilate of þis affraye
                We mon be slone.   310

III Miles	Why, canne none of vs no bettir rede?
IV Miles	Þer is not ellis but we be dede.
II Miles	Whanne þat he stered oute of þis steede

                None couthe it kenne.
I Miles   Allas, harde happe was on my hede   315
                Amonge all menne.

            Fro sir Pilate witte of þis dede,
            Þat we were slepande whanne he ȝede,
            He will forfette withouten drede
                All þat we haue.   320
II Miles   Vs muste make lies, for þat is nede,
                Oureselue to saue.

III Miles	Ȝa, that rede I wele, also motte I goo.
IV Miles	And I assente þerto alsoo.
II Miles	An hundereth schall I saie, and moo,

                Armed ilkone,   325
            Come and toke his corse vs froo
                And vs nere slayne.

I Miles   Nay; certis I halde þere none so goode
                As saie þe soth even as it stoode,   330
            Howe þat he rose with mayne and mode
                And wente his way.
            To sir Pilate if he be wode
                Þis dar I saie.

---

299.   *III Miles*] Ma; *TS, Ca* II Miles
305.   *I Miles*] M, *after* T; MS, TS, Ca III Miles
319.   He will] *T* We mon
323.   that rede] *This ed; TS* that I rede
        also] *T* so, *Ho'* als
325.   hundereth] *T* thousand
326.   Armed] *T, K* Welle armed

II Miles	Why, dare þou to sir Pilate goo	335
	With thes tydingis and saie hym soo?	
I Miles	So rede I; if he vs sloo	
	We dye but onys.	
III Miles	Nowe he þat wrought vs all þis woo	
	Woo worthe his bonys.	340

IV Miles	Go we þanne, sir knyghtis hende,	f.219
	Sen þat we schall to sir Pilate wende.	
	I trowe þat we schall parte no frende	
	Or þat we passe.	
I Miles	And I schall hym saie ilke worde tille ende,	345
	Even as it was.	

Sir Pilate, prince withouten pere,
Sir Cayphas and Anna in fere,
And all ȝe lordyngis þat are here
   To neven by name,   350
God saue ȝou all on sidis sere
   Fro synne and schame.

Pilatus	Ȝe are welcome, oure knyghtis kene,	
	Of mekill mirthe nowe may ȝe mene,	
	Therfore some tales telle vs betwene	355
	Howe ȝe haue wroght.	
I Miles	Oure wakyng, lorde, withouten wene,	
	Is worthed to noȝt.	

Cayphas	To noght? Allas, sesse of such sawe.	
II Miles	Þe prophete Jesu þat ȝe wele knawe	360
	Is resen and gone for all oure awe,	
	With mayne and myght.	
Pilatus	Þerfore þe deuill hymselffe þe drawe,	
	Fals recrayed knyght.	

	Combered cowardis I you call,	365
	Haue ȝe latten hym goo fro you all?	
III Miles	Sir, þer was none þat did but small	
	When þat he ȝede.	
IV Miles	We wer so ferde downe ganne we falle	
	And dared for drede.	370

Anna	Hadde ȝe no strenghe hym to gaynestande?
	Traitoures, ȝe myght haue boune in bande

---

337. I; if] *K, Ma* I, for, if
339. *T assigns to III Miles et Omnes*
343. frende] *K, Ma, Ca, after T* freynde; *MS, TS* frendes
345. I Miles] *Suppl by a later hand; so assigned in T*
351. God] *T* Mahowne

Bothe hym and þame þat ȝe þer fande,
And sessid þame sone.

I Miles Þat dede all erthely men leuand   375
Myght noȝt haue done.

II Miles We wer so radde euerilkone
Whanne þat he putte beside þe stone,
We wer so stonyed we durste stirre none,
And so abasshed.   380

Pilatus What, rose he by hymselfe allone?
I Miles Ȝa sir, þat be ȝe traste.

IV Miles We herde never sen we were borne,
Nor all oure faderes vs beforne,   f.219ᵛ
Suche melodie mydday ne morne   385
As was made þere.

Cayphas Allas, þanne is oure lawes lorne
For eueremare.

II Miles What tyme he rose goode tente I toke,
Þe erthe þat tyme tremylled and quoke,   390
All kyndely force þan me forsoke
Tille he was gone.

III Miles I was aferde, I durste not loke
Ne myght had none,

I myght not stande, so was I starke.   395
Pilatus Sir Cayphas, ȝe are a connyng clerke:
If we amysse haue tane oure merke,
I trowe same faile—
Þerfore what schalle worþe nowe of þis werke?
Sais your counsaille.   400

Cayphas To saie þe beste forsothe I schall
That schall be prophete to vs all.
Ȝone knyghtis behoues þere wordis agayne-call,
Howe he is miste.
We nolde for thyng þat myght befall   405
Þat no man wiste.

Anna Now sir Pilate, sen þat it is soo
Þat he is resynne dede us froo,
Comaundis youre knyghtis to saie wher þei goo
Þat he was tane   410
With xxᵗⁱ ml. men and mo,
And þame nere slayne,

382. *I Miles*] *Suppl by a later hand*
395. Stet *added by a later hand to right*
408. dede] *Ma* [in-]dede

	And therto of our tresorie	
	Giffe to þame a rewarde forthy.	
Pilatus	Nowe of þis purpose wele plesed am I,	415
	And forther þus:	
	Sir knyghtis þat are in dedis dowty,	
	Takes tente to vs,	

And herkenes what þat ȝe schall saie
To ilke a man both nyȝt and daye,   420
That ten ml. men in goode araye
   Come ȝou vntill,
With forse of armys bare hym awaye
   Agaynst your will.

Thus schall ȝe saie in ilke a lande,   425
And þerto on þat same comenaunde
A thousande pounde haue in youre hande
   To your rewarde –
And frenschippe sirs, ȝe vndirstande,
   Schall not be spared.   430

Caiphas	Ilkone youre state we schall amende,	
	And loke ȝe saie as we ȝou kende.	f.220
I Miles	In what contré so ȝe vs sende	
	Be nyght or daye,	
	Wherso we come wherso we wende	435
	So schall we saie.	

Pilatus	Ȝa, and whereso ȝe tarie in ilke contré,	
	Of oure doyng in no degré	
	Dois þat no manne þe wiser be	
	Ne freyne beforne,	
	Ne of þe sight þat ȝe gonne see	440
	Nevynnes it nowþere even ne morne.	

For we schall mayntayne ȝou alwaye,
And to þe pepull schall we saie
It is gretely agaynste oure lay   445
   To trowe such thing.
So schall þei deme both nyght and day
   All is lesyng.

Thus schall þe sothe be bought and solde
And treasoune schall for trewthe be tolde,   450
Þerfore ay in youre hartis ȝe holde
   Þis counsaile clene.
And fares nowe wele both yonge and olde,
   Haly bedene.

431. *Caiphas] Supp by J. Clerke*
454+ *Finis added by J. Clerke. Bottom half of f.220 blank, ff.220ᵛ, 221 blank*

Christ's Appearance to Mary Magdalene

Maria	Allas, in þis worlde was neuere no wight	f.221ᵛ
	Walkand with so mekill woo.	
	Thou dredfull dede, drawe hythir and dight	
	And marre me as þou haste done moo.	
	In lame is it loken, all my light,	5
	Forthy on grounde onglad I goo;	
	Jesus of Nazareth he hight,	
	The false Jewes slewe hym me froo.	

Mi witte is waste nowe in wede,
  I walowe, I walke, nowe woo is me,   10
For laide nowe is þat lufsome in lede,
  The Jewes hym nayled vntill a tree.
My doulfull herte is euere in drede,
  To grounde nowe gone is all my glee.
I sporne þer I was wonte to spede,   15
  Nowe helpe me God in persones three.

Thou lufsome lede in ilke a lande,
  As þou schope both day and nyght,
Sonne and mone both bright schynand,
  Þou graunte me grace to haue a sight   20
Of my lorde, or ellis his sande.

Jesus Thou wilfull woman in þis waye,
  Why wepis þou soo als þou wolde wede,
Als þou on felde wolde falle doune faie?
  Do way, and do no more þat dede.   25
Whome sekist þou þis longe daye?
  Say me þe sothe, als Criste þe rede.
Maria Mi lorde Jesu and God verray,
  Þat suffered for synnes his sides bleede.

Jesus I schall þe saie, will þou me here,   30
  Þe soth of hym þat þou hast sought:
Withowten drede, þou faithfull fere,
  He is full nere þat mankynde bought.   f.222
Maria Sir, I wolde loke both ferre and nere
  To fynde my lorde — I se hym noght.   35

3. drawe] *He; MS, TS* drawen

Jesus   Womane, wepe noght, but mende thy chere,
       I wotte wele whedir þat he was brought.
Maria   Swete sir, yf þou hym bare awaye,
         Saie me þe sothe and thedir me leede
       Where þou hym didde, withouten delay   40
         I schall hym seke agayne goode speede.

       Therfore, goode gardener, saie þou me,
         I praye þe for the prophetis sake,
       Of thez tythyngis þat I aske þe.
       For it wolde do my sorowe to slake   45
       When Goddis body founden myght be,
         Þat Joseph of þe crosse gonne take.
       Might I hym fange vnto my fee,
         Of all my woo he wolde me wrake.

Jesus   What wolde þou doo with þat body bare   50
         Þat beried was with balefull chere?
       Þou may noght salue hym of his sare,
         His peynes were so sadde and seere.
       But he schall cover mankynde of care,
         Þat clowded was he schall make clere,   55
       And þe folke wele for to fare
         Þat fyled were all in feere.
Maria   A, myght I euere with þat man mete,
         Þe whiche þat is so mekill of myght,
       Drye schulde I wype þat nowe is wete;   60
         I am but sorowe of worldly sight.

Jesus   Marie, of mournyng amende thy moode,
         And beholde my woundes wyde.   f.222ᵛ
       Þus for mannys synnes I schedde my bloode
         And all þis bittir bale gonne bide.   65
       Þus was I rased on þe roode
         With spere and nayles that were vnride.
       Trowe it wele, it turnes to goode
         Whanne men in erthe þer flcssh schall hyde.

Maria A, Rabony, I haue þe sought,   70
         Mi maistir dere, full faste þis day.
Jesus   Goo awaye Marie, and touche me noȝt,
         But take goode kepe what I schall saie:
       I ame hee þat all thyng wroght,
         Þat þou callis þi lorde and God verraye.   75
       With bittir dede I mankynde boght,
         And I am resen as þou se may.

46. When] *He; MS, TS* Wher
67. vnride] *K; MS, TS* vnrude

And therfore, Marie, speke nowe with me,
 And latte þou nowe be thy grctte.

Maria Mi lorde Jesu, I knowe nowe þe,   80
 Þi woundes þai are nowe wette.

Jesus Negh me noght, my loue, latte be
 Marie my doughtir swete.
To my fadir in Trinité
 Forþe I stigh noȝt yette.   85

Maria A, mercy, comely conquerour,
 Thurgh þi myght þou haste ouercome dede.
Mercy, Jesu, man and saueour,
 Thi loue is swetter þanne þe mede.
Mercy, myghty confortour,   90
 For are I was full wille of rede.
Welcome lorde, all myn honnoure,
 Mi joie, my luffe, in ilke a stede.

Jesus Marie, in thyne harte þou write   f.223
 Myne armoure riche and goode: 95
Myne actone couered all with white
 Als cors of man behewede,
With stuffe goode and parfite
 Of maydenes flessh and bloode;
Whan thei ganne thirle and smyte   100
 Mi heede for hawberke stoode.

Mi plates wer spredde all on brede,
 Þat was my body vppon a tree;
Myne helme couered all with manhede,
 Þe strengh þerof may no man see;   105
Þe croune of thorne þat garte me blede,
 Itt bemenes my dignité.
Mi diademe sais, withouten drede,
 Þat dede schall I neuere be.

Maria A, blessid body þat bale wolde beete, 110
 Dere haste þou bought mankynne.
Thy woundes hath made þi body wete
 With bloode þat was þe withinne.
Nayled þou was thurgh hande and feete,
 And all was for oure synne.   115
Full grissely muste we caitiffis grete –
 Of bale howe schulde I blynne?

To se þis ferly foode
 Þus ruffully dight,

85. Hic deficit *to left in a later hand*

Rugged and rente on a roode,   120
    Þis is a rewfull sight;
And all is for oure goode,
    And nothyng for his plight.
Spilte þus is his bloode,
    For ilke a synfull wight.   125

Jesus To my God and my fadir dere,   f.223ᵛ
    To hym als-swithe I schall assende,
For I schall nowe noȝt longe dwelle here,
    I haue done als my fadir me kende;
And therfore loke þat ilke man lere   130
    Howe þat in erthe þer liffe may mende.
All þat me loues I schall drawe nere
    Mi fadirs blisse þat neuere schall ende.

Maria Alle for joie me likes to synge,
    Myne herte is gladder þanne þe glee,   135
And all for joie of thy risyng
    That suffered dede vpponne a tree.
Of luffe nowe is þou crouned kyng,
    Is none so trewe levand more free.
Thy loue passis all erthely thyng,   140
    Lorde, blissed motte þou euere bee.

Jesus To Galilé schall þou wende
    Marie, my doghtir dere,
Vnto my brethir hende,
    Þer þei are all in fere.   145
Telle þame ilke worde to ende
    Þat þou spake with me here.
Mi blissing on þe lende,
    And all þat we leffe here.

131. þat] *Ho¹* þai
149+ *Catchword* Þat lorde þat me lente

The Supper at Emmaus

I Perigrinus	That lorde þat me lente þis liffe for to lede,	f.224
	In my wayes þou me wisse þus will of wone.	
	Qwen othir men halfe moste mirthe to þer mede,	
	Þanne als a mornand manne make I my mone.	
	For douteles nowe may we drede vs–	5
	Allas, þei haue refte vs oure rede,	
	With doole haue þei dight hym to dede,	
	Þat lorde þat was leeffe for to lede vs.	
II Perigrinus	He ledde vs full lelly þat lorde, nowe allas,	
	Mi lorde for his lewté his liffe has he lorne.	10
I Perigrinus	Saye, who comes þere claterand?	
II Perigrinus	Sir, I, Cleophas;	
	Abide, my leffe broþere, to bale am I borne.	
	But telle me whedir þou bounes?	
I Perigrinus	To Emax, þis castell beside vs.	
	Ther may we bothe herber and hyde vs,	15
	Þerfore late vs tarie at no townes.	
II Perigrinus	Atte townes for to tarie take we no tent,	
	But take vs tome at þis tyme to talke of sume tales,	
	And jangle of þe Jewes and of Jesu so gente,	
	Howe þei bette þat body was bote of all bales.	20
	With buffettis þei bete hym full barely,	
	In sir Cayphas hall garte þei hym call;	
	And hym before sir Pilate in his hall	
	On þe morne þan aftir, full arely.	
I Perigrinus	Full arely þe juggemen demed hym to dye;	25
	Both prestis and prelatis to Pilate made preysing,	

1. *Quire xxix^li begins*
   Perigrinus] So in MS, passim; TS Peregrinus, passim
   þat] This ed; om TS
5. *Ruled off from 4 by a later hand (? J. Clerke, and so at 6, 10, 11), hic de nouo facto added to right*
6. Hic caret *to right in a later hand, deleted*
10. Hic de nouo facto *to right in a later hand*
11. De novo facto *to right in a later hand*
11–12. *Lineation TS, Sir. . .broþere one line in MS*
18. tales] s *added by another hand*
20. bales] s *added by another hand*
23. hym] Ho³ *would om*

And alls cursid caytiffis and kene on Criste gan þei crie,
And on þat lele lorde made many a lesyng.
Þei spitte in his face to dispise hym,   29
  To spoile hym nothyng þei spared hym,   f.224ᵛ
  But natheles baynly þei bared hym,
  With scourges smertly goyng þei smote hym.

II Perigrinus Þei smotte hym full smertely þat þe bloode oute braste,
Þat all his hyde in hurth was hastely hidde.   34
A croune of thorne on his heede full thraly þei thraste,
Itt is grete dole for to deme þe dedis þei hym dide.
  With byndyng vnbaynly and betyng,
  Þane on his bakke bare he þame by
  A crosse vnto Caluery;
  Þat swettyng was swemyed for swetyng.   40

I Perigrinus For all þe swette þat he swete with swyngis þei hym swang,
And raffe hym full rewfully with rapes on a rode.
Þan heuyd þei hym highly on hight for to hang,
  Withouten misse of þis man, þus mensked þai his mode
  Þat euere has bene trewest in trastyng.   45
  Methynkith myn herte is boune for to breke,
  Of his pitefull paynes when we here speke,
  So frendfull we fonde hym in fraistyng.

II Perigrinus In frasting we fonde hym full faithfull and free,
In his mynde mente he neuere mysse to no man.   50
Itt was a sorowe, forsoth, in sight for to see
Whanne þat a spetyffull spere vnto his harte ranne.
  In baill þus his body was beltid,
  Into his harte thraly þei thraste;
  Whan his piteffull paynes were paste,   55
  Þat swet thyng full swiftely he sweltid.

I Perigrinus He sweltid full swithe in swonyng, þat swette.
Allas for þat luffely þat laide is so lowe,
With granyng full grissely on grounde may we   f.225
                                                    grette,
  For so comely a corse canne I none knowe.   60
  With dole vnto dede þei did hym
  For his wise werkis þat he wroght þame,
  Þes false folke, whan þei beþoughte þame,
  Þat grette vnkyndynesse þei kidde hym.

II Perigrinus Vnkyndynesse þei kidde hym, þo caitiffis so kene,   65
And als vnwitty wightis wrought þei hym wrake.

29, 32. *For conjectures (to restore rhyme) see He, Ho'*
50. In] *Ho'; MS, TS* And
56. swet thyng] *This ed; MS, TS* swetthyng
66. wrake] *He; MS, TS* wreke

Jesus	What are þes meruailes þat ȝe of mene
	And þus mckill mournyng in mynde þat ȝe make,
	Walkyng þus wille by þes wayes?
II Perigrinus	Why, arte þou a pilgryme and haste bene　　　70
	At Jerusalem, and haste þou noght sene
	What dole has ben done in þes daies?

Jesus	In ther daies, dere sir, what dole was þer done?
	Of þat werke wolde I witte, and youre will were,
	And therfore I pray you telle me now sone,　　75
	Was þer any hurlyng in hande? Nowe late me here.
I Perigrinus	Why, herde þou no carpyng nor crying
	Att Jerusalem þer þou haste bene,
	Whenne Jesu þe Nazarene
	Was doulfully dight to þe dying?　　　　　　80

II Perigrinus	To þe dying þei dight hym þat defte was and dere,
	Thurgh prokering of princes þat were þer in prees.
	Forthy as wightis þat are will þus walke we in were,
	For-pechyng als pilgrymes þat putte are to pees.
	For mornyng of oure maistir þus morne wee,　　85
	As wightis þat are wilsome þus walke we,
	Of Jesus in telling þus talke we,　　　　f.225ᵛ
	Fro townes for takyng þus turne we.

I Perigrinus	Þus turne we fro townes, but take we entent
	How þei mourthered þat man þat we of mene.　　90
	Full rewfully with ropis on rode þei hym rente
	And takkid hym þertill full tyte in a tene.
	Vpperightis full rudely þei raised hym,
	Þanne myghtely to noye hym withall,
	In a mortaise faste lete hym fall –　　　　95
	To pynne hym þei putte hym and peysed hym.

II Perigrinus	Thei peysed hym to pynne hym, þat pereles of pese;
	Þus on þat wight þat was wise wroȝt þei grete wondir,
	Ȝitt with þat sorowe wolde þei noȝt sesse –　　99
	They schogged hym and schotte hym his lymes all in
	sondir,
	His braynes þus brake þei and braste hym.
	A blynde knyght, such was his happe,
	Inne with a spere-poynte atte þe pappe
	To þe harte full thraly he thraste hym.

79.　þe] *This ed; MS, TS* of; *K* Crist þe, *Ho²* þe gente
83.　Forthy] *TS; MS* For they
85.　mornyng] *Ho¹* monyng
　　　of] *TS; MS* of of
87-8.　*MS assigns to I Perigrinus; reassigned to II P. by TS*
92.　takkid] *TS; MS* talkid
96.　and peysed hym] *TS; MS places before* þei

I Perigrinus	Thei thraste hym full thraly, þan was þer no threpyng,
	Þus with dole was þat dere vnto dede dight.　106
	His bak and his body was bolned for betyng—
	Itt was, I saie þe forsoth, a sorowfull sight.
	But ofte-sithes haue we herde saie,
	And we trowe as we herde telle,　110
	That he was to rawsoune Israell;
	But nowe is þis þe thirde daye.

II Perigrinus	Þes dayes newe owre wittis are waxen in were,
	For some of oure women for certayne þei saide
	That þai sawe in þer sightis solas full seere,　f.226
	Howe all was lemand light wher he was laide.　116
	Þei called vs, euer myght þei thriffe,
	For certayne þei saugh it in sight,
	A visioune of aungellis bright,
	And tolde þame þer lorde was alyue.　120

I Perigrinus	On lyue tolde þei þat lorde leued hir in lande;
	Þez women come lightly to warne, I wene.
	Some of oure folke hyed forthe, and faste þei it fande
	Þat all was soth þat þei saide þat sight had þei sene.
	For lely þei loked þer he laye　125
	Þei wende þer þat foode to haue fonne;
	Þanne was his toumbe tome as a tonne—
	Þanne wiste þei þat wight was away.

II Perigrinus	Awaye is þat wight þat wonte was vs for to wisse.
Jesus	A, fooles þat are fauty and failes of youre feithe,　130
	Þis bale bud hym bide and belde þame in blisse—
	But ȝe be lele of youre laye youre liffe holde I laith.
	To prophetis he proued it and preched,
	And also to Moyses gan he saie
	Þat he muste nedis die on a day,　135
	And Moyses forth talde it and teched,

	And talde it and teched it many tymes þan.
I Perigrinus	A, more of þis talking we pray you to telle vs.
II Perigrinus	Ȝa sir, be youre carping full kyndely we kenne
	Ȝe meene of oure maistir of whome þat we melle vs. 140
I Perigrinus	Ȝa, goode sir, see what I saie ȝou,

105.	thraste] *This ed; TS* thaste
111.	Israell] *TS; MS* Iraell
120.	And] *K* Þat
122.	lightly] *Ho¹* wightly
131.	and] *He* to
132+	*134 first written in error, deleted*
135-6.	*Lineation TS: reversed in MS*

Se ȝe þis castell beside her?
All nyght we thynke for to bide here;   f.226ᵛ
Bide with vs sir pilgrime, we praye ȝou.

We praye ȝou, sir pilgrime, ȝe presse noȝt to passe.   145
Jesus   Ȝis sir, me bus nede.
I Perigrinus   Naye sir, þe nyght is ovir-nere.
Jesus   And I haue ferre for to founde.
II Perigrinus   I hope wele þou has.
I Perigrinus We praye þe sir, hartely, all nyght holde þe here.
Jesus   I thanke youe of þis kyndinesse ȝe kydde me.
I Perigrinus   Go in sir, sadly and sone.   150
II Perigrinus   Sir, daunger dowte noȝt, haue done.
Jesus   Sir, I muste nedis do as ȝe bid me.

Ȝe bidde me so baynly I bide for þe beste.
I Perigrinus   Lo, her is a sege goode sir, I saie ȝou.
II Perigrinus With such goode as we haue glad we oure geste.   155
I Perigrinus   Sir, of þis poure pitaunce take parte now we pray yow.

[. . .   . . .
    . . .   . . .]
Jesus   Nowe blisse I þis brede þat brought is on þe borde.
              Fraste þeron faithfully, my frendis, you to feede.

I Perigrinus [. . .   . . .] vnterly haue we tane entent—
              Ow, I trowe some torfoyr is betidde vs!   160
              Saie, wher is þis man?
II Perigrinus   Away is he wente—
              Right now satte he beside vs.

I Perigrinus Beside vs we both sawe hym sitte,
              And by no poynte couthe I parceyue hym passe.   f.227
II Perigrinus Nay, be þe werkis þat he wrought full wele myght we witte
              Itt was Jesus hymselffe—I wiste who it was.   166

I Perigrinus Itt was Jesus þus wisely þat wrought,
              Þat raised was and rewfully rente on þe rode.
              Of bale and of bittirnesse has he vs boght,
              Boune was and betyn þat all braste on bloode.   170

II Perigrinus All braste on bloode, so sore was he bette,
              With þer wickid Jewes þat wrethfull was euere;

---

151. dowte] *Ho¹; MS, TS* dowe
156+ *Two lines missing; cf. He, Ho¹*
159-60. *Lineation TS; reversed in MS*
159. *First words missing; TS conj* To feed þeron
          vnterly] *K* enterly *or* vtterly
161-2. *Lineation TS;* Away. . .vs *one line in MS*

With scourges and scharpe thornes on his heede sette,
 Suche torfoyr and torment of telle herde I neuere.

I Perigrinus Of telle herde I neuere of so pitefull peyne   175
 As suffered oure souerayne hyngand on highte;
Nowe is he resen with myght and with mayne,
 I telle for sikir, we saugh hym in sight.

II Perigrinus We saugh hym in sight, nowe take we entent
 Be þe brede þat he brake vs so baynly betwene,   180
Such wondirfull wais as we haue wente
 Of Jesus þe gente was neuere none seene.

I Perigrinus Sene was þer neuere so wondirfull werkes,
 Be see ne be sande, in þis worlde so wide.
Menskfully in mynde þes materes now merkis,   185
 And preche we it prestly on euery ilke side.

II Perigrinus On euery ilke side prestely prechis we –
 Go we to Jerusaleme þes tydingis to telle.
Oure felawes fro fandyng nowe fraste we,
 More of þis mater her may we not melle.   190

I Perigrinus Here may we notte melle more at þis tyde,   f.227ᵛ
 For prossesse of plaies þat precis in plight.
He bringe to his blisse on euery ilke side,
 Þat sofferayne lorde þat moste is of myght.

---

175. peyne] *He; MS, TS* peynes
181. wais] i *interlined*
186. preche] *Altered from* prechid
it] *Interlined*
187. prechis] *This ed;* s *superimposed on another letter; TS* prech it
191. melle more] *TS* melle [of] more
193. bringe] ? *read* bringe us *or* you
194+ Finis *added by J. Clerke. Rest of f.227ᵛ and ff.228–231ᵛ, originally blank, now occupied by play XVII (q v.) in Clerke's hand. On f.231ᵛ (end of quire xxixᵈ), the original catchword erased (cf. XVII 432+, textual note). For ff.232 and 233, see textual notes at XVII 433, 460+, and XLI 1–*

The Incredulity of Thomas

Petrus	Allas, to woo þat we wer wrought,	f.233
	Hadde never no men so mekill þought,	
	Sen that oure lorde to dede was brought	
	With Jewes fell;	
	Oute of þis steede ne durste we noght,	5
	But here ay dwelle.	
Johannes	Here haue we dwelte with peynes strang;	
	Of oure liffe vs lothis, we leve to lange,	
	For sen the Jewes wrought vs þat wrong	
	Oure lorde to sloo,	10
	Durste we neuere come þame emang,	
	Ne hense to goo.	
Jacobus	Þe wikkid Jewes hatis vs full ille,	
	And bittir paynes wolde putte vs till.	
	Therfore I rede þat we dwelle stille	15
	Here þer we lende,	
	Vnto þat Criste oure lorde vs wille	
	Some socoure sende.	
Deus	Pees and reste be with yowe.	
Petrus	A, brethir dere, what may we trowe?	20

1– *Fol. 233 is a loose singleton bearing a catchword at the foot of the verso (see 84, textual note). It was originally inserted by the main scribe to replace a cancel, the first leaf of quire* xxx^{ti}, *and was pasted on to the stub. Subsequently, John Clerke detached f.233 and pasted a second singleton (f.232) in its place, in order to complete his interpolation of play XVII; see the textual notes to lines 433 and 460+ thereof*

1. to] *Sy* the
   wer] *Sy* are
5. ne] *Sy* sens
8. *Sy* And wyth owr lyvys owr lath we lyff so long
9. For sen the] *Sy* Sens þat thes
   vs þat] *Sy* this
11. Durste] *Sy* Sens drust
12. to] *Om Sy*
13. Þe] *Sy* Þes
14. wolde] *Sy* thay
15. þat] *Om Sy*
16. þer] *Sy* þat
17–18. *Sy* Tyll þat Cryst vs some socor send
19. Deus] *Sy* Iesus (*and so throughout, respectively*)
   with] *Sy* vnto

What was this sight þat we saughe nowe
　　Shynand so bright,
And vanysshed þus and we ne wote how,
　　Oute of oure sight?

Johannes	Oute of oure sight nowe is it soghte,	25

Itt makith vs madde, þe light it broght,
What may it be?

Jacobus 　　　　　　　　Sertis, I wotte noght,
　　But sekirly
Itt was vanyté in oure þought,
　　Nought ellis trowe I it be. 　　　　　　30

Deus 　Pees vnto yowe euermore myght be,
Drede you noȝt, for I am hee.
Petrus 　On Goddis name, *benedicite!*
　　What may þis mene?
Jacobus 　Itt is a sperite forsothe, thynketh me, 　　35
　　Þat dose vs tene.

Johannes 　A sperite it is, þat trowe I right,
All þus appered here to oure sight. 　　　f.233ᵛ
Itt makis vs madde of mayne and myght,
　　So is vs flaied; 　　　　　　　　40
Ȝone is þe same þat broughte þe light
　　Þat vs affraied.

Deus 　What thynke ȝe, madmen, in youre thought?
What mournyng in youre hertis is brought?
I ame Criste, ne drede ȝou noght; 　　　　45
　　Her may ȝe se
Þe same body þat has you bought
　　Vppon a tre.

21. this] *Sy* þe
23. vanysshed þus and] *Sy* thus ys wanysshyd
　　　we ne wote] *Sy* we wayt not
25. oure] *Ho¹, after Sy* owr; *MS, TS* youre
27–8. *Lineation and assignments this ed;* What...be *placed between 28 and 29 and assigned to Jacobus in TS; Sy* it may.
　　　Sertis...sekirly *one line in MS: om Sy*
29. was vanyté] *Sy* ys some vanytes
30. it be] *Om Sy*
35. *Sy* A sprett for soth so thynke me
38. All] *Sy* Þat
40. So is vs] *This ed; MS* Sois *or* Dois vs, *TS* Dois vs; *Sy* So yt vs
41. Ȝone] *Sy* Yt
44. brought] *Sy* wroght
45. I] *Sy* For I
46. may] *TS, after Sy* may; *MS* nay
48. *An otiose* v *to the left*

Þat I am comen ȝou here to mete,
Behalde and se myn handis and feete,   50
And grathely gropes my woundes wete
     Al þat here is.
Þus was I dight youre balis to beete,
     And bring to blis.

For yowe þer gatis þanne haue I gone.   55
Felys me grathely euerilkone,
And se þat I haue flessh and bone.
     Gropes me nowe,
For so ne has sperite none,
     Þat schall ȝe trowe.   60

To garre ȝou kenne and knowe me clere
I schall you schewe ensaumpillis sere.
Bringe nowe forthe vnto me here
     Some of youre mette,
If ȝe amange you all in fere   65
     Haue ought to ete.

Jacobus Þou luffand lorde þat laste schall ay,
Loo, here is mette þat þou ete may,
A hony kombe þe soth to saye,
     Roste fecche þertill.   70
To ete þerof here we þe praie
     With full goode will.

Deus Nowe sen ȝe haue broughte me þis mete,
To make youre trouthe stedfast and grete,
And for ȝe schall wanhope forgete   75
     And trowe in me,
With youe þan here wol I ete,
     Þat ȝe schalle see.

Nowe haue I done, ȝe haue sene howe,
Boldely etyng here with youe.   80
Stedfastly loke þat ȝe trowe
     Yitt in me efte,

50. and²] *Sy* my
55. þer gatis] *Cawley, LSE, vii–viii, (1952), p. 59; TS* þusgatis
          þanne] *Sy* þus
56. Felys] *This ed, after Sy* Felys; *MS, TS* Folous
59. sperite] *Sy* sprettis
68. þat] *Sy* yf
70. Roste fecche] *Sy* Rochfych
71. here we þe] *Sy* we wold ye
77. þan here] *Sy* now here þen
80. Boldely etyng here] *Sy* Bodely here etyn
81. Stedfastly] *Sy* Now stedfastly

And takis þe remenaunte sone to you
  Þat her is lefte.

For ʒoue þus was I reuyn and rayst,   f.234
Þerfore some of my peyne ʒe taste;   86
And spekis now nowhare my worde waste,
  Þat schall ʒe lere,
And vnto ʒou þe holy goste
  Resave yow here.   90

Beis now trewe, and trowes in me,
And here I graunte youe in youre posté:
Whome þat ʒe bynde, bounden schall be
  Right at youre steuene,
And whome þat ʒe lowys, losed schal be   95
  Euermore in heuene.

Thomas   Allas for sight and sorowes sadde,
Mornyng makis me mased and madde;
On grounde nowe may I gang vngladde
  Boþe even and morne.   100
Þat hende þat I my helpe of hadde
  His liffe has lorne.

Lorne I haue þat louely light,
Þat was my maistir moste of myght.
So doulfully as he was dight   105
  Was neuere no man;
Such woo was wrought of þat worthy wighte
  With wondis wan.

Wan was his wondis and wonderus wette,
With skelpis sore was he swongen, þat swette,   110

83. remenaunte sone to] *Sy* remland vnto
84. *Fol. 233ᵛ (cf. textual note at 1-) carries a catchword* For ʒou þus was I
85. reuyn] *Sy* rent
 rayst] *He, after Sy* rayst; *MS, TS* dreste
86. peyne] *Sy* panys
87. now no-] *Sy* nore
 my worde] *Sy* your wordis i
88. Þat schall ʒe] *K* Þat ʒe schall; *Sy* Here that ye
90. Resave] *He, after Sy* Resave; *MS, TS* Releffe
92. youe] *Om Sy*
93. bynde] *Sy* bound
95. lowys] *This ed, after Sy* lowys; *MS, TS* lesid
97. sorowes] *Sy* sorow
99. gang] *Sy* goo
101. hende] *Sy* hynd
109. Wan was his] *This ed, after Sy* Wan was his; *MS, TS* Whan lo as
 wonderus] *This ed, after Sy* wonderus; *MS, TS* wondis
110. skelpis] *Sy* swapis

All naked nailed thurgh hande and feete.
  Allas, for pyne,
Þat bliste, þat beste my bale myght bete,
  His liffe schulde tyne.

Allas, for sorowe myselffe I schende   115
When I thynke hartely on þat hende,
I fande hym ay a faithfull frende,
  Trulie to telle.
To my brethir nowe wille I wende
  Wherso þei dwell.   120

So wofull wyghtis was neuere none,
Oure joie and comforte is all gone.
Of mournyng may we make oure mone
  In ilka lande.
God blisse you brether, bloode and bone,   125
  Same þer 3e stande.

Petrus   Welcome Thomas, where has þou bene?
Wete þou wele withouten wene
Jesu oure lorde þan haue we sene
  On grounde her gang.   130
Thomas   What saie 3e men? Allas, for tene,
  I trowe 3e mang.

Johannes Thomas, trewly it is noght to layne,   f.234ᵛ
Jesu oure lorde is resen agayne.
Thomas   Do waie, thes tales is but a trayne   135
  Of fooles vnwise.
He þat was so fully slayne,
  Howe schulde he rise?

Jacobus   Thomas, trewly he is on lyue
Þat tholede þe Jewes his flessh to riffe,   140
He lete vs fele his woundes fyue,
  Oure lorde verray.

111. hande] *Sy* handis
113. bale] *Sy* ballis
116. on] *Sy* of
119. To] *Sy* Vnto
120. Wherso] *Sy* Whersome
121. So wofull wyghtis] *This ed, after Sy* So wofull wyghtis; *MS, TS* A blistfull sight
122. and] *Sy* owr
128. Wete] *Sy* For wete
131. men] *Sy* man
133. *Johannes*] *Suppl from Sy by TS*
134. resen] *Sy* resyng
135. a trayne] *Ha, after Sy* a trayne; *MS, TS* attrayne
137. He] *Sy* For he, *so TS*
139. trewly] *Sy* lely
142. Oure] *Sy* Þat

Thomas	That trowe I nought, so motte I thryue,	
	Whatso ȝe saie.	
Petrus	Thomas, we saugh his woundes wette,	145
	Howe he was nayled thurgh hande and feete;	
	Hony and fisshe with vs he eette,	
	Þat body free.	
Thomas	I laye my liff it was some sperit	
	Ȝe wende wer hee.	150
Johannes	Nay Thomas, þou haste misgone,	
	Forwhy he bad vs euerilkon	
	To grope hym grathely, bloode and bone	
	And flesh to feele.	
	Such thyngis, Thomas, hase sperite none,	155
	Þat wote thou wele.	
Thomas	What, leue felawes, late be youre fare.	
	Tille þat I see his body bare	
	And sithen my fyngir putte in thare	
	Within his hyde,	160
	And fele the wounde þe spere did schere	
	Riȝt in his syde,	
	Are schalle I trowe no tales betwene.	
Jacobus	Thomas, þat wounde haue we seene.	
Thomas	Ȝa, ȝe wotte neuere what ȝe mene,	165
	Youre witte it wantis.	
	Ye muste thynke no syne me þus to tene	
	And tule with trantis.	
Deus	Pees, brethir, be vnto you;	
	And Thomas, tente to me takis þou,	170

144. Whatso ȝe say] *Sy* Why sa ye say
146. hande] *Sy* handis
150. wer] *Sy* was
155. sperite] *Sy* spretis
156. thou] *This ed, after Sy* thou; *MS, TS* ȝe
157. What, leue] *Sy* Now
158. his] *Sy* þat
159. fyngir] *Sy* fyngers
161. þe] *Sy* this
163. tales betwene] *Sy* talis vs betwene
164. wounde haue] *Sy* wond þen haue
166. witte it] *Sy* wyttis
167. Ye muste] *Om Sy*
     no syne] *This ed, after Sy* no syne; *MS, TS* sen ȝe
     me þus] *Sy* thus me
     to] *Suppl from Sy, this ed*
168. tule] *Sy* tyll
169. brethir] *Sy* and rest

Putte forthe thy fyngir to me nowe.
　Myn handis þou see,
Howe I was nayled for mannys prowe
　Vppon a tree.

Beholde my woundis are bledand;　　　　　　　175
Here in my side putte in þi hande,　　　　　　f.235
And fele my woundis and vndirstande
　Þat þis is I,
And be no more mistrowand,
　But trowe trewly.　　　　　　　　　　　　180

Thomas　　Mi lorde, my God, full wele is me.
A, blode of price, blessid mote þou be;
Mankynd in erth, behold and see
　Þis blessid blode.
Mercy nowe lorde ax I the,　　　　　　　　185
　With mayne and mode.

Deus　　Thomas, for þou haste sene þis sight,
Þat I am resen as I the hight,
Þerfore þou trowes it – but ilka wight,
　Blissed be they euere　　　　　　　　　190
Þat trowis haly in my rising right,
　And saw it neuere.

My brethir, fonde nowe forthe in fere,
Ouereall in ilke a contré clere.
My rising both ferre and nere　　　　　　　195
　Preche it schall ȝe;
And my blissyng I giffe ȝou here,
　And my menȝe.

171.　fyngir] *Sy* fyngers
175.　are bledand] *Sy* ar all bledhand
177.　my woundis] *Sy* this wond
178.　þis] *Sy* yt
179.　more mistrowand] *Sy* morre so mystrowand, *so TS*
183.　*Suppl from Sy by TS*
185.　nowe lorde] *Sy* lord now
188.　resen] *Sy* resyng
　　　the] *This ed, after Sy* the; *MS* you *or* þou, *TS* you
189.　þou] *Om Sy*
　　　but ilka] *Sy* euerylk
190.　they] *This ed, after Sy* they; *MS, TS* þou
194.　clere] *Sy* sere
196.　Preche it] *Ho'; MS, TS* and preche it, *Sy* Preched
　　　ȝe] *Sy* be
198.　my] *Sy* this
198+　*Bottom half of f.235 blank; ff.235ᵛ, 236 blank*

XLII The Tailors

The Ascension

Petrus	O mightfull God, how standis it nowe,	f.236^v

Petrus   O mightfull God, how standis it nowe,   f.236ᵛ
　　　　In worlde þus will was I neuere are;
　　Butte he apperes, bot I ne wote howe –
　　　　He fro vs twynnes whanne he will fare.
　　And ȝitt may falle þat for oure prowe,   5
　　　　And alle his wirkyng lesse and mare.
　　A, kyng of comforte, gudde arte þou
　　　　And lele, and likand is thy lare.

Johannes   The missing of my maistir trewe
　　　　That lenghis not with vs lastandly,   10
　　Makis me to morne ilke a day newe
　　　　For tharnyng of his company.
　　His peere of gudnes neuere I knewe,
　　　　Of myght ne wisdome ȝit any.
Petrus   That we hym tharne sore may vs rewe,   15
　　　　For he luffed vs full faithfully.

　　Bot ȝitt in all my mysselykyng
　　　　A worde þat Criste saide comfortis me:
　　Oure heuynes and oure mournyng,
　　　　He saide, to joie turned schuld be.   20
　　Þat joie, he saide in his hetyng,
　　　　To reue vs none schulde haue no posté,
　　Wherefore abouen all othir thyng
　　　　That joie me longis to knowe and see.

Maria   Þou Petir, whanne my sone was slayne   25
　　　　And laide in graue, ȝe wer in were
　　Whedir he schulde rise, almoste ilkane;
　　　　But nowe ȝe wotte thurgh knowyng clere.
　　Some þat he saide schulde come is gane,
　　　　And some to come; but ilkane sere,   f.237
　　Whedir it be to come or none,   31
　　　　Vs awe to knowe it all in fere.

3.   Butte] *K* Ofte
6.   And] *K* As
8.   *Lineation TS;* and lele *at end of 7 in MS (where it is deleted).* And leill *to left of 8 in a later hand* (? *J. Clerke*)
14. ȝit any] *Ho³; MS, TS* it anly
29. Some] *Ha; MS, TS* Come
     come] *Suppl He*

373

Jesus   Almyghty God, my fadir free,
     In erthe þi bidding haue I done
And clarified þe name of þe;   35
     To thyselffe clarifie þe sone.
Als þou haste geuen me pleyne posté
     Of ilke a flesh, graunte me my bone,
Þat þou me gaffe myght lyffand be
     In endles liffe and with þe wonne.   40

Þat liffe is þis þat hath none ende,
     To knawe þe, fadir, moste of myght;
And me thy sone, whame þou gon sende
     To dye for man withouten plight.
Mankynde was thyne, whome þou bekende   45
     And toke me to my ȝemyng right.
I died for man, mannes misse to mende,
     And vnto spitous dede was dight.

Thy wille vnto þem taughte haue I,
     Þat wolde vnto my lare enclyne.   50
Mi lare haue they tane buxsomly,
     Schall none of them þer trauaile tyne.
Þou gaffe þem me but noght forthy,
     Ȝitt are they thyne als wele as myne;
Fleme þem not fro oure companye,   55
     Sen thyne are myne and myne er thyne.

Sen they are oures, if þame nede ought
     Þou helpe þem, if it be thy will;
And als þou wate þat I þame boght,
     For faute of helpe latte þem not spill.   60
Fro þe worlde to take þem pray I noght,   f.237ᵛ
     But þat þou kepe þame ay fro ill,
All þois also þat settis þare þoght
     In erthe my techyng to fulfill.

Mi tythandis tane has my menȝe   65
     To teche þe pepull wher they fare,
In erthe schall þei leue aftir me
     And suffir sorowes sadde and sare.
Dispised and hatted schall þei be,
     Als I haue bene, with lesse and mare,   70
And suffer dede in sere degré,
     For sothfastnesse schall none þem spare.

Þou halowe þame fadir, forthy,
     In sothfastnes so þat þei may

43. whame] *This ed; TS* whanne
46. my] *He; MS, TS* þi
71. suffer] *TS; MS* suffered

Be ane as we ar, þowe and I,   75
    In will and werke, both nyght and day,
And knawe þat I ame verilye
    Both sothfastnes and liffe alway,
Be the whilke ilke man þat is willy
    May wynne þe liffe þat laste schall ay.   80

Bot ȝe, my postelis all bedene
    Þat lange has wente abowte with me,
In grete wanne-trowyng haue ȝe bene,
    And wondir harde of hartis ar ȝe.
Worthy to be reproued, I wene,   85
    Ar ȝe forsothe, and ȝe will see
In als mekill als ȝe haue sene
    My wirkyng proued and my posté.

Whan I was dede and laide in graue
    Of myne vpryse ȝe were in doute,   90
And some for myne vprysing straue
    When I was laide als vndir clowte
So depe in erthe. But sithen I haue
    Ben walkand fourty daies aboute,   f.238
Eten with ȝou, youre trouthe to saue,   95
    Comand emange ȝou inne and oute.

And þerfore beis no more in were
    Of myne vpperysing, day nor nyght.
Youre misbelcue leues ilkone seere,
    For witte ȝe wele, als man of myght   100
Over whome no dede may haue poure,
    I schall be endles liffeand right.
Bot for to schewe you figure clere,
    Schewe I me þusgatis to youre sight

Howe man by cours of kynde schall ryse,   105
    Allþogh he be roten ontill noȝt.
Oute of his graue in þis same wise
    At þe daye of dome schall he be broght
Wher I schall sitte as trewe justise,
    And deme man aftir he has wroght,   110
Þe wikkid to wende with þer enmyse,
    Þe gode to blisse þei schall be broght.

Anodir skill forsoth is þis:
    In a tre man was traied thurgh trayne;

75.   þowe] *This ed; TS* yowe
92.   clowte] *Ho¹; MS, TS* lowte
102. liffeand] *He; MS, TS* liffe and
105. Howe] *K* Nowe (*with* sight. *in 104*)
107. same] *TS; MS* sane

Ane man, forthy, to mende þat misse   115
   On a tree boght mankynde agayne,
In confusioune of hym and his
   Þat falsely to forge þat frawde was fayne,
Mankynde to bringe agayne to blisse,
   His foo, þe fende, till endles peyne.   120

Þe thirde skille is, trewly to tell,
   Right als I wende als wele will seme,
So schall I come in flessh and fell
   Atte þe day of dome, whan I schall deme
Þe goode in endles blisse to dwell,   125
   Mi fomen fro me for to fleme
Withouten ende in woo to well,
   Ilke leuand man here to take yeme.   f.238ᵛ

But intill all þe worlde wendand,
   Þe gospell trewly preche schall ȝe   130
Tille ilke a creatoure liffand.
   Who trowes, if that he baptised be
He schall, als yhe schall vndirstande,
   Be saued, and of all thraldome free.
Who trowis it not, as mistrowand   135
   For faute of trouthe dampned is he.

But all ther tokenyngis bedene
   Schall folowe þam þat trowis it right,
In my name deuellis crewell and kene
   Schall þei oute-caste of ilka wight,   140
With newe tongis speke, serpentis vnclene
   Fordo; and if þei day or nyght
Drinke venym wik, withouten wene,
   To noye þame schall it haue no myght.

On seke folke schall þei handes lay   145
   And wele schall þei haue sone at welde,
Þis poure schall þei haue alway,
   My menȝhe, bothe in towne and felde;
And witte ȝe wele, so schall þei
   Þat wirkis my wille in youthe or elde —   150
A place for þame I schall purveye
   In blisse with me ay in to belde.

Nowe is my jornay brought till ende,
   Mi tyme þat me so lang was lente.

---

115. Ane] *This ed (cf. K); MS, TS* I *(numeral)*
129. wendand] *Ho¹; MS, TS* weldand
133. He schall] *Deleted by a later hand but subsequently re-inked.* I am *to left in a later hand
(? J. Clerke), deleted*
154. so] *He* to
lente] *TS; MS* lende

To my fadir nowe vppe I wende,   155
  And youre fadir þat me doune sente—
Mi God, youre God, and ilk mannes frende
  That till his techyng will consente,
Till synneres þat no synne þame schende,
  Þat mys amendis and will repente.   160

But for I speke þes wordis nowe
  To you, youre hartis hase heuynes.   f.239
Fullfillid all be it for youre prowe
  Þat I hense wende, als nedfull is.
And butte I wende comes noght to yowe   165
  Þe comforteoure of comforteles,
And if I wende ȝe schall fynde howe
  I schall hym sende, of my goodnesse.

Mi fadirs will fullfillid haue I,
  Therfore fareswele ilkone seere;   170
I goo make youe a stede redye
  Endles to wonne with me in feere.
Sende doune a clowde, fadir, forthy
  I come to þe my fadir deere.
Þe fadir blissing moste myghty   175
  Giffe I you all þat leffe here.

Tunc cantat angelus 'Ascendo ad patrem meum'.

Maria   A, myghtfull God, ay moste of myght,
  A selcouth sight is þis to see,
Mi sone þus to be ravisshed right
  In a clowde wendande vppe fro me.   180
Bothe is my herte heuy and light,
  Heuy for swilke twynnyng schulde be,
And light for he haldis þat he hight
  And þus vppe wendis in grette posté.

His hetyngis haldis he all bedene,   185
  Þat comfortis me in all my care.
But vnto whome schall I me mene?
  Þus will in worlde was I neuere are,
To dwelle amonge þes Jewes kene—
  Me to dispise will þei not spare.   190
Johannes All be he noght in presens seene,
  ȝitt is he salue of ilka sare.

---

166. comforteoure] *TS; MS* comforte oure
176+ *SD. A first later hand wrote (to right of 176)* Tunc cantat angelus *(TS* cantant angeli) gloria in excelsys deo. *Subsequently, J. Clerke deleted the last four words and substituted* Ascendo ad patrem meum
188. are] *Suppl He*

But lady, sen þat he betoke
  Me for to serue you as youre sonne,
зou nedis nothyng, lady, but loke   195
  What thyng in erthe зe will haue done.   f.239ᵛ
I ware to blame if I forsoke
  To wirke youre wille, midday or none,
Or any tyme зitt of þe woke.
Maria   I thanke þe John, with wordis fune: 200

Mi modirhed, John, schall þou haue,
  And for my sone I wolle þe take.
Johannes Þat grace, dere lady, wolde I craue.
Maria   Mi sone sawes will I neuere forsake,
Itt were not semand þat we straue   205
  Ne contraried noзt þat he spake;
But John, tille I be broght in graue,
  Schall þou never see my sorowe slake.

Jacobus   Owre worthy lorde, sen he is wente
  For vs, lady, als is his will,   210
We thanke hym þat vs þe hath lente
  With vs on lyue to lenge her stille.
I saie for me with full concente,
  Þi likyng all will I fulfille.
Andreas   So wille we all with grete talent,   215
  Forthy lady, giffe þe noght ill.

I Angelus зe men of þe lande of Galilé,
  What wondir зe to heuene lokand?
Þis Jesus whome зe fro youe see
  Vppe-tane, зe schall wele vndirstande,   220
Right so agayne come doune schall he.
  When he so comes with woundes bledand,
Who wele has wrought full gladde may be,
  Who ill has leved full sore dredand.

II Angelus зe þat has bene his seruauntis trewe   225
  And with hym lengand nyght and day,   f.240
Slike wirkyng als зe with hym knew
  Loke þat зe preche it fourthe alway.
Youre mede in heuene beis ilke day newe,
  And all þat seruis hym wele to paye.   230
Who trowes you noght it schall þame rewe,
  Þei mon haue peyne encresand ay.

Jacobus   Loued be þou lorde ay moste of myght,
  Þat þus, in all oure grete disease,

206. noзt] *Ho'* oзt
212. on] *TS; MS* no

    Vs comfortist with thyne aungellis bright.   235
     Nowe aught þer Jewes þare malise meese,
    Þat sawe þameselue þis wondir sight
     Þus nere þame wroght vndir þer nese—
    And we haue mater day and nyght
     Oure God more for to preyse and plese.   240

Andreas   Nowe may þer Jewes be all confused
     If þai on-thinke þame inwardly,
    Howe falsely þci haue hym accused
     And sakles schente thurgh þer envy.
    Þer falsed, þat þei longe haue vsed,   245
     Nowe is it proued here opynly;
    And they were of þis mater mused
     Itt schulde þame stirre to aske mercy.

Petrus   Þat wille þei noʒt Andrewe, late be,
     For þei are full of pompe and pride.   250
    Itt may noʒt availe to þe ne me
     Ne none of vs with þame to chide.
    Prophite to dwelle can I none see,
     Forthy late us no lenger bide,
    But wende we vnto seere contré   255
     To preche thurgh all þis worlde so wide.

Johannes   Þat is oure charge, for þat is beste,
     Þat we lenge nowe no lenger here,
    For here gete we no place of reste
     To lenge so nere þe Jewes poure.   260
    Vs to fordo þei will þame caste,   f.240ᵛ
     Forthy come forthe my lady dere
    And wende vs hense; I am full preste
     With you to wende with full goode chere.

    Mi triste is nowe euer ilk a dele   265
     In yowe, to wirke aftir youre counsaill.
Jacobus   Mi lady dere, þat schall ʒe fele
     In oght þat euere vs may availe.
    Oure comforte, youre care to kele,
     Whill we may leue we schall not faile.   270
Maria   Mi brethir dere, I traste itt wele,
     Mi sone schall quyte ʒou youre trauaile.

Petrus   To Jerusalem go we agayne
     And loke what fayre so aftir fall,
    Oure lorde and maistir moste of mayne   275
     He wisse youe, and be with youe all.

236. aught] *This ed; TS* might
238. nese] *TS; MS* nose
261. to fordo] *K; MS, TS* for to do
263–4. *Lineation TS; three lines in MS:* And . . . hense / I . . . wende / with . . . chere
269. comforte, youre] *Ho¹* comforte is youre
276+ *Bottom half of f.240ᵛ blank except for catchword* Brethir takis tente

XLIII The Potters

Pentecost

Petrus	Brethir, takes tente vnto my steuen,	f.241
	Þanne schall ʒe stabily vndirstande	
	Oure maistir hende is hente to heuyn,	
	To reste þere on his fadirs right hande.	
	And we are leued alyue elleuyn,	5
	To lere his lawes lely in lande;	
	Or we begynne vs muste be even	
	Ellis are owre werkis noght to warande.	
	For parfite noumbre it is none	
	Off elleuen for to lere,	10
	Twelue may be asoundir tone	
	And sett in parties seere.	

Nobis precepit dominus predicare populo, et testificare
quia prope est iudex viuorum et mortuorum.

Oure lord comaunded vs more and lesse
   To rewle vs right aftir his rede,
He badde vs preche and bere wittenesse   15
   That he schulde deme bothe quike and dede.
To hym all prophettis preuys expresse
   All þo þat trowis in his Godhede,
Off synnes þei schall haue forgiffenesse,
   So schall we say . . . mekill rede.   20
      And senne we on þis wise
         Schall his counsaile discrie,
      Itt nedis we vs avise
      Þat we saye noʒt serely.

Johannes   Serely he saide þat we schulde wende   25
   In all þis worlde his will to wirke,
And be his counsaile to be kende
   He saide he schulde sette haly kirke.

1. *Quire xxxj^{li} begins*
   Petrus] No character-designation by main scribe. Deus suppl by a first later hand; this
   deleted and Petrus substituted by J. Clerke; TS Peter
3. hente] *This ed;* TS hence
12. sett] *He; MS,* TS settis
12+ *Lines in Latin throughout play in red; here and at 192+ they are extra-metrical*
   iudex] *Interlined by a later hand*
13–14. *To right in hand of J. Clerke* Nota a newe clause mayd for the eleccion *(TS*
   eleuen) of an apostle to make the number of xij
20. *Word or words missing between* say *and* mekill *(K)*

But firste he saide he schulde doune sende
  His sande, þat we schuld noȝt be irke,   30
His haly gaste on vs to lende
  And make vs to melle of materes mirke.   f.241ᵛ
    Vs menis he saide vs þus
      Whan þat he fared vs froo:
      'Cum venerit paraclitus   35
      Docebit vos omnia'.

Jacobus   Ȝa, certaynely he saide vs soo,
  And mekill more þanne we of mene:
'Nisi ego abiero',
  Þus tolde he ofte-tymes vs betwene.   40
He saide, forsoth, 'But if I goo
  Þe holy goste schall not be sene,
Et cum assumptus fuero
  Þanne schall I sende ȝou comforte clene'.
    Þus tolde he holy howe   45
      Þat oure dedis schulde be dight,
    So schall we trewly trowe
      He will holde þat he vs highte.

IV Apostolus   He highte vs fro harme for to hyde
  And holde in hele both hede and hende,   50
Whanne we take þat he talde þat tyde,
  Fro all oure foois it schall vs sende.
But þus in bayle behoues vs bide
  To tyme þat sande till vs be sende;
Þe Jewis besettis vs in ilke a side   55
  Þat we may nowdir walke nor wende.

V Apostolus   We dare noȝt walke for drede
      Or comforte come vs till,
    Itt is moste for oure spede
      Here to be stokyn still.   60

Maria   Brethir, what mene ȝe ȝou emelle,
  To make mournyng at ilk a mele?
My sone þat of all welthe is well,
  He will ȝou wisse to wirke full wele,   f.242
For þe tente day is þis to telle   65
  Sen he saide we schull fauoure fele.
Leuys wele þat lange schall it not dwell,
  And therfore drede you neuere a dele,
    But prayes with harte and hende
      Þat we his helpe may haue,   70
    Þanne schall it sone be sende,
      Þe sande þat schall vs saue.

35–6. *Lineation TS; one line in MS. To right, III Apostolus joined by red line to omnia
(main scribe) as if character-designation; taken as such by TS (refers to Jacobus, 37)*
43. *cum] He; MS, TS dum*

I Doctor	Harke maistir, for Mahoundes peyne,
	Howe þat þes mobbardis maddis nowe.
	Þer maistir þat oure men haue slayne
	Hase garte þame on his trifullis trowe. 75
II Doctor	Þe lurdayne sais he leffis agayne;
	Þat mater may þei neuere avowe,
	For as þei herde his prechyng pleyne
	He was away, þai wiste noȝt howe. 80
I Doctor	They wiste noȝt whenne he wente,
	Þerfore fully þei faile,
	And sais þam schall be sente
	Grete helpe thurgh his counsaille.

II Doctor	He myghte nowdir sende clothe nor clowte, 85
	He was neuere but a wrecche alway –
	But samme oure men and make a schowte,
	So schall we beste yone foolis flaye.
I Doctor	Nay, nay, þan will þei dye for doute.
	I rede we make noȝt mekill dray, 90
	But warly wayte when þai come oute
	And marre þame þanne, if þat we may.
II Doctor	Now certis, I assente þertille, f.242ᵛ
	Yitt wolde I noght þei wiste,
	Ȝone carles þan schall we kill 95
	But þei liffe als vs liste.

Angelus tunc cantare 'Veni creator spiritus'.

Maria	Honnoure and blisse be euer newe,
	With worschippe in þis worlde alwaye,
	To my souerayne sone Jesu,
	Oure lorde allone þat laste schall ay. 100
	Nowe may we triste his talis ar trewe,
	Be dedis þat here is done þis day;
	Als lange as ȝe his pase pursue
	Þe fende he fendis yow for to flay.
	For his high hali gaste 105
	He lattis here on ȝou lende,
	Mirthis and trewthe to taste
	And all misse to amende.

Petrus	All mys to mende nowe haue we myght,
	Þis is þe mirthe oure maistir of mente. 110
	I myght noȝt loke, so was it light –
	A, loued be þat lorde þat itt vs lente.

96+   *SD. Angelus . . . cantare by main scribe, in red; 'Veni . . . spiritus' added by a later hand*
   (? J. Clerke)
97.   *Maria] Suppl by a later hand*
   newe] Co; MS, TS nowe
104.   *he] Conj TS (glossary), He; MS, TS (text) ne*

Now hase he holden þat he vs highte, *seized*
  His holy goste here haue we hente;
Like to þe sonne itt semed in sight,   115
  And sodenly þanne was itt sente.

II Apostolus   Hitt was sente for oure sele, *health*
      Hitt giffis vs happe and hele,
    Methynke slike forse I fele
      I myght felle folke full feele.   120

III Apostolus We haue force for to fighte in felde
  And fauour of all folke in feere,   f.243
With wisdome in þis worlde to welde
  Be knowing of all clergye clere.

IV Apostolus We haue bewteis to be oure belde *support*   125
  And langage nedis vs none to lere,
Þat lorde vs awe ȝappely to ȝelde *promptly*
  Þat vs has ȝemed vnto þis ȝere. *cared (for)*

V Apostolus   This is þe ȝere of grace
      Þat musteris vs emang,   130
    As aungellis in þis place
      Þat sais þus in þer sange.

I Apostolus In þare sigging saide þei þus,
  And tolde þer talis betwene þem two:
  '*Veni creator spiritus,*   135
    Mentes tuorum visita'.
Þei praied þe spirite come till vs
  And mende oure myndis with mirthis ma, *prophecy*
Þat lered þei of oure lorde Jesus, *fulfilled*
  For he saide þat itt schulde be swa.   140

II Apostolus   He saide he schulde vs sende
      His holy goste fro heuyn,
    Oure myndis with mirthe to mende –
      Nowe is all ordand euyn.

III Apostolus Euen als he saide schulde to vs come   145
  So has bene schewid vnto oure sight:
  '*Tristicia impleuit cor vestrum*' –
    Firste sorowe in herte he vs hight;
  '*Sed conuertetur in gaudium*'.
    Sen saide he þat we schulde be light.   150
Nowe þat he saide vs, all and summe,
  Is mefid emange vs thurgh his myght.

IV Apostolus   His myght with mayne and mode
      May comforte all mankynde.   f.243ᵛ

131. As] *K* Twa *(punctuating as* grace; / emang / place, *in 129–31)*
133. *Petrus added after I Apostolus by a later hand*
    sigging] *Ho'* singing
135–6. *Lineation TS; one line in MS*
150. we] *Ho'*; MS, TS he

I Doctor	Harke man, for Mahoundes bloode,	155
	Þer men maddis oute of mynde.	

Þei make carpyng of ilke contré,
  And leris langage of ilk a lande.

II Doctor   They speke oure speche als wele as we,
  And in ilke a steede it vndirstande.   160

I Doctor   And alle are noȝt of Galilee
  Þat takis þis hardinesse on hande?
  Butt þei are drounken, all þes menȝe,
  Of muste or wyne, I wolle warande.

II Doctor   Nowe certis þis was wele saide,   165
  Þat makis þer mynde to marre;
  Ȝone faitours schall be flaied
  Or þat þei flitte aught ferre.

IV Apostolus   Harke brethir, waites wele aboute,
  For in oure fayre we fynde no frende.   170
  Þe Jewes with strengh are sterne and stoute
  And scharpely schapes þem vs to schende.

I Apostolus   Oure maistir has putte all perellis oute
  And fellid þe falsed of þe fende.
  Vndo youre dores and haues no doute,   175
  For to ȝone warlowes will we wende.

II Apostolus   To wende haue we no drede,
  Noght for to do oure dette
  For to neuyn þat is nede
  Shall none on lyve vs lette.   180

Petrus   Ȝe Jewez þat in Jerusalem dwelle,
  Youre tales are false, þat schall ȝe fynde.
  Þat we are dronken we here you telle
  Because ȝe hope we haue bene pynnyd.
  A prophette preued, his name is Johell,   185
  A gentill Jewe of youre awne kynde,   f.244
  He spekis þus in his speciall spell
  And of þis matere makis he mynde.
  Be poyntis of prophicie
  He tolde full ferre before,   190
  Þis may ȝe noȝt denye,
  For þus his wordis wore:
  'Et erit in nouissimis diebus, dicit dominus,
  effundam de spiritu meo super omnem carnem'.

173.   De novo facto *to left in hand of J. Clerke, deleted*
177.   Hic de nouo facto *to left in hand of J. Clerke, deleted*
178.   Noght] *K* Nor
192+   *See textual note to 12+*
       nouissimis] *He; MS, TS* nouissimus

III Apostolus	Loo, losellis, loo, þus may ye lere
	Howe youre elders wrotte alway.
	Þe holy goste haue we tane here
	As youre awne prophettis prechid ay.
IV Apostolus	Hitt is þe myght of oure maistir dere,
	All dedis þat here are done þis daye;
	He giffis vs myght and playne power
	To conclude all þat ȝe can saie.
I Doctor	There men hase mekill myght
	Thurgh happe þei here haue tone.
II Doctor	Wende we oute of þer sight
	And latte þem even allone.
I Apostolus	Nowe, brethir myne, sen we all meffe
	To teche þe feithe to foo and frende,
	Oure tarying may turne vs to mischeffe,
	Wherfore I counsaille þat we wende
	Vntille oure lady and take oure leue.
II Apostolus	Sertis, so woll we with wordis hende.
	Mi lady, takis it noght to greue,
	I may no lenger with you lende.
	[. . . . . .
	. . . . . .
	. . . . . .
	. . . . . .]
Maria	Nowe Petir, sen itt schall be soo
	Þat ȝe haue diuerse gatis to gang,
	Ther schall none dere you for to doo
	Whils my sone musteris you emang.
	Butt John and Jamys, my cosyns twoo,
	Loke þat ȝe lenge not fro me lange.
Johannes	Lady, youre wille in wele and woo,
	Itt schall be wroght, ellis wirke we wrang.
Jacobus	Lady, we bothe are boune
	Atte youre biddyng to be.
Maria	The blissing of my sone
	Be boith with you and me.

195

200

205

210

215

f.244ᵛ

220

193. Nota *to left in a later hand*
212+ *Four lines missing, no gap in MS*
223. Hic caret *to left in a later hand*
224. Loquela de novo facta *to left in hand of J. Clerke*
224⫟ *Beneath last line in Clerke's hand:* That with his grace ye may endewe / And bryng yowe to his companye. *Bottom half of f.244ᵛ blank; f.245 blank*

XLIV The Drapers
The Death of the Virgin

Gabriel	Hayle, myghfull Marie, Godis modir so mylde,	f.245ᵛ

<table>
<tr><td>Gabriel</td><td>Hayle, myghfull Marie, Godis modir so mylde,</td><td>f.245ᵛ</td></tr>
</table>

Gabriel   Hayle, myghfull Marie, Godis modir so mylde,   f.245ᵛ
    Hayle be þou, roote of all reste, hayle be þou, ryall.
Hayle floure and frewte noȝt fadid nor filyd,
    Haile, salue to all synnefull. Nowe saie þe I schall
        Thy sone to þiselue me has sente,   5
        His sande, and sothly he saies
        No lenger þan þer thre dayes
    Here lefte þe þis liffe þat is lente.

And þerfore he biddis þe loke þat þou blithe be,
    For to þat bigly blisse þat berde will þe bring,   10
There to sitte with hymselue, all solas to see,
    And to be crowned for his quene and he hymselue kyng
        In mirthe þat euere schall be newe.
        He sendis to þe worþely iwis
        Þis palme oute of paradise,   15
    In tokenyng þat it schall be trewe.

Maria   I thanke my sone semely of all his sandis sere;
    Vnto hym lastandly be ay louyng
Þat me þus worþely wolde menske on þis manere,
    And to his bigly blisse my bones for to bringe.   20
        But gode ser, neuenes me þi name.
Gabriell   Gabriell, þat baynly ganne bringe
        Þe boodworde of his bering –
    Forsothe lady, I ame þe same.

Maria   Nowe Gabriell þat sothly is fro my sone sent,   25
    I thanke þe þer tythyngis þou tellis me vntill,
And loued be þat lorde of the lane þat has me lente
    [. . .   . . .]
        And dere sone, I beseke þe
        Grete God, þou graunte me þi grace,
        Thyne appostelis to haue in þis place,   30
    Þat þei at my bering may be.

---

8. lente] *TS; MS* lentthe *(? lente the)*
12. kyng] *TS; MS* leyng
12–15. *Lineation TS; three lines in MS:* And . . . quene / And . . . newe / He . . .
    paradise
27+ *Line missing, no gap in MS*
28–31. *Lineation TS; two lines in MS*

Gabriell	Nowe foode faireste of face, most faithfull and fre,
	Þyne askyng þi sone has graunte of his grace,
	And saies all same in sight ʒe schall see
	All his appostelis appere in þis place, f.246
	To wirke all þi will at þi wending. 36
	And sone schall þi peynes be paste,
	And þou to be in liffe þat schall laste
	Euermore withouten any ending.

Johannes	Marie my modir, þat mylde is and meke 40
	And cheffe chosen for chaste, nowe telle me, what chere?
Maria	John, sone, I saie þe forsothe I am seke.
	Mi swete sone sonde I hente, right nowe it was here,
	And douteles he saies I schall dye.
	Within thre daies iwis, 45
	I schall be beldid in blisse
	And come to his awne company.

Johannes	A, with þi leue lady, þou neuene it me noght,
	Ne telle me no tydingis to twynne vs in two,
	For be þou, blissid birde, vnto bere broght 50
	Euermore whils I wonne in þis worlde will me be full woo,
	Therfore lete it stynte and be still.
Maria	Nay John, sone, myselue nowe I see
	Atte Goddis will moste it nedis be,
	Þerfore be it wroght at his will. 55

Johannes	A, worthy, when þou art wente will me be full woo—
	But God giffe þe appostelis wiste of þi wending.
Maria	ʒis John, sone, for certayne schall it be so,
	All schall þei hardely be here at myne ending.
	The sonde of my sone saide me þis, 60
	Þat sone schall my penaunce be paste
	And I to be in liffe þat euere schall laste,
	Than baynly to belde in þat blisse.

Petrus	O God omnipotent, þe giffer of all grace,
	Benedicite dominus, a clowde now full clere 65
	Vmbelappid me in Judé prechand as I was,
	And I haue mekill meruayle how þat I come here.

Jacobus	A, sesse, of þis assemelyng can I noʒt saie
	Howe and in what wise þat we are here mette, f.246ᵛ
	Owthir myrþe or of mornyng mene wele it maye, 70
	For sodenly in sight here sone was I sette.

43. hente] *Ha; MS, TS* hete
44-7. *Lineation TS; two lines in MS*
60. þis] *This ed; MS, TS* þus
66. Vmbelappid] *TS; MS* Vnbelappid
70-1. *Lineation this ed, as MS; TS reverses (see the Note)*

Andreas	A, bredir, be my wetand and iwisse so wer we,
	In diuerse landes lely I wotte we were lente,
	And how we are semelid þus can I noȝt see,
	But as God of his sande has vs same sente. 75
Johannes	A, felawes, late be youre fare,
	For as God will it moste nedis be,
	Þat pereles is of posté,
	His myȝt is to do mekill mare.

For Marie þat worthy schall wende nowe I wene,   80
   Vnto þat bigly blisse þat high barne baynly vs boght;
Þat we in hir sight all same myght be sene
   Or sche disseuer vs froo, hir sone sche besoght.
      And þus has he wroght atte hir will,
         Whanne sche schal be broght on a bere,   85
         That we may be neghand hir nere
      This tyme for to tente hir vntill.

Maria	Jesu my darlyng þat ding is and dere,

I thanke þe my dere sone of þi grete grace
Þat I all þis faire felawschip atte hande nowe has here,   90
   Þat þei me some comforte may kythe in þis case.
      Þis sikenes it sittis me full sare;
         My maidens, take kepe nowe on me
         And caste some watir vppon me –
      I faynte, so febill I fare.   95

I Ancilla	Allas for my lady þat lemed so light,
	That euere I leued in þis lede þus longe for to lende,
	That I on þis semely schulde se such a sight.
II Ancilla	Allas, helpe, sche dyes in oure hende.

   A, Marie, of me haue þou mynde   100
   [. . .   . . .]
   Some comforte vs two for to kythe,
   Þou knowes we are comen of þi kynde.

Maria	What ayles yow women for wo þus wynly to wepe?

Yhe do me dere with youre dynne, for me muste   f.247
                                     nedis dye
Yhe schulde, whenne ȝe saw me so slippe on slepe,   105
   Haue lefte all youre late and lette me lye.
      John, cosẏne, garre þame stynte and be still.

76-9. *Lineation TS; two lines in MS*
81. high] *Ho'* hir
82. hir] *TS; MS* high
90. felawschip] *TS; MS* felawschp
100+ *Line missing, no gap in MS*
103. wynly] *TS conj (glossary)* wanly
104. for] *TS; MS* fo
105. on] *This ed; MS, TS* and

Johannes   A, Marie þat mylde is of mode,
When þi sone was raised on a rode
To tente þe he toke me þe till,   110

And þerfore at þi bidding full bayne will I be.
Iff þer be oght, modir, þat I amende may,
I pray þe, myldest of mode, meue þe to me,
And I schall, dereworþi dame, do it ilke a daye.

Maria   A, John, sone, þat þis peyne were ouere-paste!   115
With goode harte ȝe alle þat are here
Praies for me faithfully in feere,
For I mon wende fro you as faste.

I Judeus   A, foode fairest of face, moste faithfull to fynde,
Þou mayden and modir þat mylde is and meke,   120
As þou arte curtaise and comen of oure kynde
All our synnes for to sesse þi sone þou beseke,
With mercy to mende vs of mys.

II Judeus   Sen þou, lady, come of oure kynne,
Þou helpe vs nowe þou veray virginne,   125
Þat we may be broght vnto blisse.

Maria   Jesu my sone, for my sake beseke I þe þis,
As þou arte gracious and grete God þou graunte me þy
                                         grace.
Þei þat is comen of my kynde and amende will þere mys,
Nowe specially þou þame spede and spare þame a spacc,
And be þer belde, if þi willis be.   131
And dere sone, whane I schall dye,
I pray þe þan for þi mercy
Þe fende þou latte me noȝt see.

And also my blissid barne, if þi will be,   f.247ᵛ
I sadly beseke þe my sone, for my sake,   136
Men þat are stedde stiffely in stormes or in see
And are in will wittirly my worschippe to awake,
And þanne nevenes my name in þat nede,
Þou late þame not perissh nor spille.   140
Of þis bone my sone, at þi will,
Þou graunte me specially to spede.

Also my bliste barne þou graunte me my bone,
All þat are in newe or in nede and nevenes me be name,
I praie þe sone for my sake þou socoure þame sone,   145
In alle þer schoures þat are scharpe þou shelde þame
                                         fro schame.

114. daye] a *altered from* e *and another letter*
122. beseke] *TS; MS* besoke
128. þy] *He; MS, TS* my

And women also in þare childing,
Nowe speciall þou þame spede,
And if so be þei die in þat drede
To þi blisse þane baynly þou þame bringe.   150

Jesus   Marie my modir, thurgh þe myght nowe of me
For to make þe in mynde with mirthe to be mending,
Þyne asking all haly here heete I nowe þe.
But modir, þe fende muste be nedis at þyne endyng
In figoure full foule for to fere þe.   155
Myne aungelis schall þan be aboute þe,
And þerfore dere dame þou thar noȝt doute þe,
For douteles þi dede schall noȝt dere þe.

And þerfore my modir come myldely to me,
For aftir þe sonne my sande will I sende,   160
And to sitte with myselfe all solas to se
In ay-lastand liffe in likyng to lende.
In þis blisse schall be þi bilding,
Of mirth schall þou neuere haue missing
But euermore abide in my blissing,   165
All þis schall þou haue at þi welding.

Maria   I thanke þe my swete sone, for certis I am seke,   f.248
I may noȝt now meve me for mercie almoste
To þe, sone myne þat made me, þi maiden so meke;
Here thurgh þi grace, god sone, I giffe þe my goste.   170
Mi sely saule I þe sende
To heuene þat is highest on heghte,
To þe, sone myne þat moste is of myght,
Ressayue it here into þyne hende.

Jesus   Myne aungellis louely of late, lighter þan þe levene,   175
Into þe erþe wightly I will þat ȝe wende
And bringe me my modir to þe highest of heuene,
With mirthe and with melody hir mode for to mende,
For here schall hir blisse neuer be blynnande.
Mi modir schall myldely be me   180
Sitte nexte þe high trinité,
And neuere in two to be twynnand.

I Angelus   Lorde, atte þi bidding full bayne will I be,
Þat floure þat neuere was fadid full fayne will we fette.
II Angelus And atte þi will, gode lorde, wirke will we   185
With solace on ilke side þat semely vmsitte.

164-6. *Lineation TS; 166 before 164 in MS*
169.   þe] *TS; MS* þie *(apparently)*
174.   hende] *He; MS, TS* hande
186.   on] *This ed; TS* in

III *Angelus* Latte vs fonde to hir faste hir fors to deffende,
Þat birde for to bringe vnto þis blis bright.
Body and sawle we schall hir assende
To regne in þis regally be regentté full right.   190
IV *Angelus*   To blisse þat birde for to bringe
Nowe Gabriell late vs wightly be wendand.
This maiden mirthe to be mendand
A semely song latte vs sing.

Cum vno diabolo.

Et cantant antiphona, scilicet 'Aue regina celorum'.

XLIVA

The Funeral of the Virgin ('Fergus')

No trace of the play on the subject of the Funeral of the Virgin is to be found either here (its appropriate place in the sequence) or elsewhere in the Register. Mention of its existence occurs in documents between 1415 and 1432, and 1476 and 1518; see the Note

187. hir fors] *This ed; TS* fors hir; *K* hir for
191. *Lineation TS; after 186 in MS*
194. sing] *TS; MS* see
194+ *Cum . . . diabolo*] *In red (main scribe) to right of 194. SD (main scribe) in red. Fol. 248ᵛ blank except for catchword* In waylyng and weping

The Assumption of the Virgin

Thomas	In waylyng and weping, in woo am I wapped,	f.249
	In site and in sorowe, in sighing full sadde.	

Mi lorde and my luffe, loo, full lowe is he lapped,
Þat makes me to mourne nowe full mate and full madde.
What harling and what hurlyng þat hedesman he hadde,   5
    What breking of braunches ware brosten aboute hym,
What bolnyng with betyng of brothellis full badde;
    Itt leres me full lely to loue hym and lowte hym,
        That comely to kenne.
            Goddis sone Jesus   10
            He died for vs,
            Þat makes me þus
        To mourne amange many men.

Emange men may I mourne for þe malice þei mente
    To Jesus þe gentillest of Jewes generacioun.   15
Of wisdome and witte were þe waies þat he wente
    Þat drewe all þo domesmen derffe indignacioun,
For douteles full dere was his diewe dominacioun.
    Vnkyndely þei kidde þem þer kyng for to kenne
With carefull comforth and colde recreacioun,   20
    For he mustered his miracles amonge many men
    And to þe pepull he preched.
        But þe Pharases fers
        All his resouns revers,
        And to þer hedesmen rehers   25
    Þat vntrewe were þe tales þat he teched.

He teched full trewe, but þe tirauntes were tened.
    For he reproued þer pride þai purposed þame preste
To mischeue hym, with malis in þere mynde haue þei menyd,
    And to accuse hym of cursednesse þe caistiffis has caste.   30
Ther rancoure was raised, no renke might it reste,
    Þai toke hym with treasoune, þat turtill of treuthe,
Þei fedde hym with flappes, with fersnesse hym feste,
    To rugge hym, to riffe hym; þer reyned no rewthe.
        Vndewly þei demed hym: f.249ᵛ
        Þei dusshed hym, þei dasshed hym,   36

---

  1. *Quire xxxijᵗⁱ begins*
      Thomas] *MS, TS Thomas Apostolus; see the Note*
  17. domesmen derffe] *K* domesmen to derffe

Þei lusshed hym, þei lasshed hym,
Þei pusshed hym, þei passhed hym,
All sorowe þei saide þat it semed hym.

Itt semed hym all sorowe, þei saide in þer seggyng.   40
Þei skippid and scourged hym – he skapid not – with
                                                  scornes;
Þat he was leder and lorde in þere lawe lay no leggyng,
  But thrange on and thristed a croune of thik thornes.
  Ilk tag of þat turtill so tatterid and torne es
    That þat blissid body blo is and bolned for betyng,   45
  Ʒitt þe hedesmen to hynge hym with huge hydous hornes
    As brothellis or bribours were belyng and bletyng:
      'Crucifie hym' þei cried.
        Sone Pilate in parlement
        Of Jesus gaffe jugement,   50
        To hynge hym þe harlottis hym hente;
      Þer was no deide of þat domesman denyed.

Denyed not þat domesman to deme hym to dede,
  Þat frendly faire foode þat neuere offended.
Þei hied þame in haste þan to hynge vppe þere heede,   55
  What woo þat þei wroghte hym no wiʒt wolde haue
                                                  wende it.
  His true titill þei toke þame no tome for to attende it,
    But as a traitour attcynted þei toled hym and tuggid hym,
  Þei schonte for no schoutis his schappe for to schende it,
    Þei rasid hym on rode als full rasely þei rugged hym. 60
      Þei persed hym with a spere,
        Þat þe blode riall
        To þe erþe gun fall,
        In redempcion of all
      Þat his lele lawes likis to lere.   65

To lere he þat likis of his lawe þat is lele
  Mai fynde in oure frende here full faithfull feste,
Þat wolde hynge þus on hight to enhaunce vs in hele
  And by vs fro bondage by his bloode þat is beste.
  Þan þe comforte of oure companye in kares were keste, 70
    But þat lorde so allone wolde not leffe vs full longe.
  On þe thirde day he rose riʒt with his renkis to reste,

40. þei . . . þer] *He; MS, TS* þe . . . þe
41. skippid] *Ha* strippid, *Ho¹* skelpid
   with] *He* without
43. But thrange] *Ho¹* But þei thrange
47. were] *TS; MS* we
62-3. *Originally om, but added later by main scribe to left*

Both flessh and fell fersly þat figour gon fange
And to my brethir gonne appere. f.250
Þai tolde me of þis 75
Bot I leued amys,
To rise flesshly iwis
Methought þat it paste mans poure.

But þe poure of þat prince was presiously previd
Whan þat souerayne schewed hymselffe to my siȝt. 80
To mene of his manhode my mynde was all meued,
But þat reuerent redused me be resoune and be riȝt.
Þe woundes full wide of þat worthy wight
He frayned me to fele þame my faith for to feste,
And so I did douteless, and doune I me diȝt – 85
I bende my bak for to bowe and obeyed hym for beste.
So sone he assendid
Mi felaus in feere
Ware sondered sere,
If þai were here 90
Mi myrthe were mekill amendid

Amendid were my mirthe with þat meyné to mete.
Mi felaus in fere for to fynde woll I fonde,
I schall nott stedde in no stede but in stall and in strete
Grath me be gydis to gette þame on grounde. 95
O souerayne, how sone am I sette here so sounde!
Þis is þe Vale of Josophat in Jury so gente.
I will steme of my steuene and sted here a stounde,
For I am wery for walkyng þe waies þat I wente
Full wilsome and wide. 100
Þerfore I kaste
Here for to reste,
I halde it beste
To buske on þis banke for to bide.

| Song 1: | *Surge proxima mea* (first version; see Appendix 1) | f.250ᵛ |

I Angelus	Rise Marie, þou maiden and modir so milde.	f.251
II Angelus	Rise, lilly full lusty, þi luffe is full likand.	106
III Angelus	Rise, chefteyne of chastité in chering þi childe.	
IV Angelus	Rise, rose ripe redolent, in reste to be reynand.	
V Angelus	Rise, douffe of þat domesman all dedis is demand.	
VI Angelus	Rise turtour, tabernacle, and tempull full trewe.	110
VII Angelus	Rise, semely in sight, of þi sone to be semande.	
VIII Angelus	Rise, grathed full goodely in grace for to grewe.	
IX Angelus	Rise vppe þis stounde.	
X Angelus	Come chosen childe.	
XI Angelus	Come Marie milde.	115

78. poure] TS pou[e]re
104+ *Fol. 250ᵛ, music (eight staves)*

XII Angelus	Come floure vnfiled.	
VIII Angelus	Come vppe to þe kyng to be crouned.	

Song 2:   *Veni de Libano* (first version; see Appendix 1)

Thomas	O glorious God what glemes are glydand,	f.251ᵛ
	I meve in my mynde what may þis bemene?	
	I see a berde borne in blisse to be bidand	120
	With aungelus companye, comely and clene.	
	Many selcouth sitis in sertis haue I sene,	
	But þis mirthe and þis melody mengis my mode.	
Maria	Thomas, do way all þi doutes bedene,	
	For I ame foundynge fourthe to my faire fode	125
	I telle þe þis tyde.	
Thomas	Who, my souerayne lady?	
Maria	ȝa, sertis I saie þe.	
Thomas	Whedir wendes þou I praye þe?	
Maria	To blisse with my barne for to bide.	130

Thomas	To bide with thy barne in blisse to be beldand?
	Hayle jentilest of Jesse in Jewes generacioun,
	Haile welthe of þis worlde all welthis is weldand,
	Haile hendest, enhaunsed to high habitacioun,
	Haile, derworth and dere is þi diewe dominacioun, 135
	Haile floure fressh florisshed, þi frewte is full felesome,
	Haile sete of oure saveour and sege of saluacioun,
	Haile happy to helde to, þi helpe is full helesome.
	Haile pereles in plesaunce,
	Haile precious and pure, 140
	Haile salue þat is sure,
	Haile lettir of langure,
	Haile bote of oure bale in obeyesaunce.

Maria	Go to þi brethir in bale are abiding,	
	And of what wise to welthe I ame wendande	f.252
	Withoute tarying þou telle þame þis tithynge,	146
	Þer mirthe so besse mekill amendande.	
	For Thomas, to me were þei tendande	
	Whanne I drewe to þe dede, all but þou.	
Thomas	Bot I lady? Whillis in lande I ame lendande	150
	Obeye þe full baynly my bones will I bowe.	
	Bot I, allas!	
	Whare was I þanne	
	When þat barette beganne?	
	An vnhappy manne	155
	Both nowe and euere I was.	

117+   *Bottom half of f.251, music (four staves)*
120.   berde] *Conj TS; MS* babbe
131.   beldand] *K; MS, TS* bidand
151.   Obeye] *He* To obeye

Vnhappy, vnhende am I holden at home;
What drerye destonye me drewe fro þat dede?

Maria   Thomas, sesse of thy sorowe for I am sothly þe same.   159
Thomas   Þat wote I wele, þe worthiest þat wrapped is in wede.
Maria   Þanne spare nott a space nowe my speche for to spede,
Go saie þem sothely þou sawe me assendinge.
Thomas   Now douteles, derworthy, I dare not for drede,
For to my tales þat I telle þei are not attendinge,
For no spelle þat is spoken.   165
Maria   I schall þe schewe
A token trewe
Full fresshe of hewe,
My girdill, loo, take þame þis tokyn.

Thomas   I thanke þe as reuerent rote of oure reste,   170
I thanke þe as stedfast stokke for to stande,
I thanke þe as tristy tre for to treste,
I thanke þe as buxsom bough to þe bande,
I thanke þe as leefe þe lustiest in lande,   f.252ᵛ
I thanke þe as bewteuous braunche for to bere,   175
I thanke þe as floure þat neuere is fadande,
I thanke þe as frewte þat has fedde vs in fere,
I thanke þe for euere.
If thay repreue me
Now schall þei leue me.   180
Þi blissinge giffe me
And douteles I schall do my deuere.

Maria   Thomas, to do þanne thy deuere be dressand,
He bid þe his blissinge þat beldis aboven.
And in siȝtte of my sone þer is sittand   185
Shall I knele to þat comely with croune,
Þat who in dispaire be dale or be doune
With pitevous playnte in perellis will pray me,
If he swynke or swete in swelte or in swoune,
I schall sewe to my souerayne sone for to say me   190
He schall graunte þame þer grace.
Be it manne in his mournyng
Or womanne in childinge,
All þes to be helpinge
Þat prince schall I praye in þat place.   195

Thomas   Gramercy þe goodliest grounded in grace,
Gramercy þe lufliest lady of lire,
Gramercy þe fairest in figure and face,
Gramercy þe derrest to do oure desire.

187. who in] *This ed; MS, TS* what
189. swynke] *He; MS, TS* synke

Maria	Farewele, nowe I passe to þe pereles empire.	200
	Farewele Thomas, I tarie no tyde here.	
Thomas	Farewele þou schynyng schappe þat schyniste so schire,	
	Farewele þe belle of all bewtes to bide here,	
	Farewele þou faire foode.	
	Farewele þe keye of counsaile,	f.253
	Farewele all þis worldes wele,	206
	Farewele our hope and oure hele,	
	Farewele nowe, both gracious and goode.	

Song 3:   *Veni electa* (first version; see Appendix 1)

Thomas	That I mette with þis may here my mirthe is amend.	
	I will hy me in haste and holde þat I haue hight,	210
	To bere my brethir þis boodeword my bak schall I bende	
	And saie þame in certayne þe soth of þis sight.	
	Be dale and be doune schall I dresse me to diȝt	
	To I fynde of þis felawschippe faithfull in fere,	
	I schall renne and reste not to ransake full right.	215
	Lo, þe menȝe I mente of I mete þame even here	f.253ᵛ
	At hande.	
	God saffe ȝou in feere,	
	Say brethir, what chere?	
Petrus	What dois þou here?	220
	Þou may nowe of þi gatis be gangand.	

Thomas	Why dere brethir, what bale is begune?	
Petrus	Thomas, I telle þe þat tene is betidde vs.	
Thomas	Me forthinkith for my frendis þat faithfull are foune.	
Jacobus	ȝa, but in care litill kyndnes þou kid vs.	225
Andreas	His bragge and his boste is he besie to bid vs,	
	But and þer come any cares he kepis not to kenne.	
	We may renne till we raue or any ruth rid vs	
	For þe frenschippe he fecched vs, be frith or be fenne.	
Thomas	Sirs, me meruailes, I saie yowe,	230
	What mevis in youre mynde.	
Johannes	We can wele fynde	
	Þou art vnkynde.	
Thomas	Nowe pees þanne, and preue it I praye yowe.	234

Petrus	Þat þou come not to courte here vnkyndynes þou kid vs,	
	Oure treuth has of-turned vs to tene and to traye.	
	Þis yere haste þou rakid, þi reuth wolde not ridde vs,	
	For witte þou wele þat worthy is wente on hir waye.	
	In a depe denne dede is scho doluen þis daye,	
	Marie þat maiden and modir so milde.	240
Thomas	I wate wele iwis.	f.254
Jacobus	Thomas, do way.	

217. *Lineation this ed; continuous with 216 in MS, TS*
236. has of-] *Ho'; MS, TS* of has

Andreas	Itt forse noȝt to frayne hym, he will not be filde.
Thomas	Sirs, with hir haue I spoken
	Lattar þanne yee.
Johannes	Þat may not bee.
Thomas	Yis, knelyng on kne.
Petrus	Þanne tite can þou telle vs some token?

245

Thomas	Lo þis token full tristy scho toke me to take youe.
Jacobus	A, Thomas, whare gate þou þat girdill so gode?
Thomas	Sirs, my message is meuand some mirthe for to make youe,
	For founding flesshly I fande hir till hir faire foode,
	And when I mette with þat maiden it mendid my mode.
	Hir sande has scho sente youe, so semely to see.
Andreas	Ya, Thomas, vnstedfaste full staring þou stode—
	Þat makis þi mynde nowe full madde for to be.
	But herken and here nowe;
	Late vs loke where we laid hir,
	If any folke haue affraied hir.
Johannes	Go we groppe wher we graued hir,
	If we fynde ouȝte þat faire one, in fere nowe.

249

255

260

Petrus	Behalde nowe hidir youre hedis in haste,
	Þis glorious and goodely is gone fro þis graue.
Thomas	Loo, to my talking ye toke youe no tente for to traste.
Jacobus	A, Thomas, vntrewly nowe trespassed we haue.
	Mercy full kyndely we crie and we craue.
Andreas	Mercye, for foule haue we fautid in faye.
Johannes	Mercye we praye þe, we will not depraue.
Petrus	Mercye for dedis we did þe þis daye.
Thomas	Oure saueour so swete
	Forgiffe you all,
	And so I schall.
	Þis tokyn tall
	Haue I brought yowe youre bales to beete.

265

f.254ᵛ

270

Petrus	Itt is welcome iwis fro þat worthy wight,
	For it was wonte for to wappe þat worthy virgine.
Jacobus	Itt is welcome iwis fro þat lady so light,
	For hir wombe scho wrappe with it and were it with wynne.
Andreas	Itt is welcome iwis fro þat saluer of synne,
	For scho bende it aboute hir with blossome so bright.
Johannes	Itt is welcome iwis fro þe keye of oure kynne,
	For aboute þat reuerent it rechid full right.

275

280

---

250. message] *Ho¹; MS, TS* messages
  meuand] *or* menand
252. mendid] *This ed; TS* mengid
256. *Lineation TS; after 258 in MS*
262. goodely] *This ed; TS* goddely
280. keye] *This ed; TS* kepe

Petrus	Nowe knele we ilkone
	Vpponne oure kne.
Jacobus	To þat lady free.
Andreas	Blissid motte sche be, 285
	3a, for scho is lady lufsome allone.

Thomas	Nowe brethir, bese besie and buske to be bownand.
	To Ynde will I torne me and trauell to teche.
Petrus	And to Romans so royall þo renkis to be rownand
	Will I passe fro þis place my pepull to preche. 290
Jacobus	And I schall Samaritanus so sadly enserche,
	To were þam be wisdome þei wirke not in waste.
Andreas	And I to Achaia full lely þat lede for to leche f.255
	Will hy me to helpe þame and hele þame in haste.
Johannes	Þis comenaunt accordis; 295
	Sirs, sen 3e will soo
	Me muste nedis parte youe froo,
	To Assia will I goo.
	He lede 3ou, þat lorde of all lordis.

Thomas	The lorde of all lordis in lande schall he lede youe 300
	Whillis 3e trauell in trouble þe trewthe for to teche.
	With frewte of oure feithe in firthe schall we fede youe
	For þat laboure is lufsome ilke lede for to leche.
	Nowe I passe fro youre presence þe pepull to preche,
	To lede þame and lere þame þe lawe of oure lorde.
	As I saide, vs muste asoundre and sadly enserche 306
	Ilke contré to kepe clene and knytte in o corde
	Off oure faithe.
	Þat frelye foode
	Þat died on rode 310
	With mayne and moode
	He grath yowe be gydis full grath.

Song 4:   *Surge propera mea* (second version; see Appendix 1)   f.256

Song 5:   *Veni de Libano*   ⎫
Song 6:   *Veni electa*   ⎭ (second versions; see Appendix 1)   f.256ᵛ

293. I] *Suppl this ed*
306. enserche] *He* beseche
312+ *Rest of f.255 blank; f.255ᵛ blank except for running-title and* Surge *faintly in a later hand. Fol. 256ʳ⁻ᵛ, music (eighteen staves); at foot of f.256ᵛcatchword* Myne aungellis þat are

The Coronation of the Virgin

Jesus	Myne aungellis þat are bright and schene,	f.257
	On my message take ye þe waye	
	Vnto Marie, my modir clene,	
	Þat berde is brighter þan þe daye.	
	Grete hir wele haly bedene,	5
	An to þat semely schall ʒe saye	
	Off heuene I haue hir chosen quene,	
	In joie and blisse þat laste schall aye.	

I wille ʒou saie what I haue þoughte
    And why þat ʒe schall tille hir wende,   10
I will hir body to me be brought
    To beilde in blisse withouten ende.

Mi flesshe of hir in erþe was tone;
    Vnkindely thing it were iwis,
Þat scho schulde bide be hire allone   15
    And I beilde here so high in blis.

Forthy tille hir þan schall ʒe fare
    Full frendlye for to fecche hir hedir,
Þere is no thyng þat I loue more,
    In blisse þanne schall we belde togedir.   20

I Angelus	O blisfull lorde nowe moste of myght,	
	We are redye with all oure myght	
	Thy bidding to fulfille,	
	To þi modir þat maiden free,	
	Chosen cheffe of chastité,	25
	As it is thy wille.	

II Angelus	Off þis message we are full fayne,	
	We are redy with myght and mayne,	
	Bothe be day and be nyght.	
	Heuene and erthe nowe gladde may be,	30
	Þat frely foode nowe for to see	
	In whome þat þou did light.	f.257ᵛ

---

1. *Quire xxxiijᵗⁱ begins. Above and to right of first line, in later hands,* caret *and* memorandum
5. haly] *K* halyly

III Angelus	Lorde Jesu Criste, oure gouernoure,
	We are all boune atte þi bidding,
	With joie and blisse and grete honnoure, 35
	We schall þi modir to þe bringe.

IV Angelus Hayle, þe doughtir of blissid Anne,
Þe whiche consayued thurgh þe holy goste,
And þou brought forthe both God and manne,
The whiche felled doune þe fendis boste. 40

V Angelus Haile, roote of risse, þat fourthe brought
Þat blissid floure oure saueoure,
The whiche þat made mankynde of noght
And brought hym vppe into his toure.

VI Angelus Of þe allone he wolde be borne 45
Into þis worlde of wrecchidnesse,
To saue mankynde þat was forlorne
And bringe þame oute of grete distresse.

I Angelus Þou may be gladde bothe day and nyght
To se thy sone oure saucoure, 50
He will þe croune nowe, lady bright,
Þou blissid modir and faire floure.

II Angelus Marie, modir and mayden clene,
Chosen cheffe vnto þi childe,
Of heuene and erþe þou arte quene; 55
Come vppe nowe lady, meke and mylde.

III Angelus Þi sone has sente vs aftir þe
To bringe þe nowe vnto his blisse,
Þer schall þou belde and blithe be, f.258
Of joie and mirthe schall þou noȝt misse. 60

IV Angelus For in his blisse withouten ende,
Þere schall þou alkynnc solas see,
Þi liffe in likyng for to lende
With þi dere sone in trinité.

Maria A, blissid be God, fadir all-weldand, 65
Hymselffe wottith best what is to doo.
I thanke hym with harte and hande,
Þat þus his blisse wolde take me too,

And ȝou also his aungellis bright
Þat fro my sone to me is sente, 70

---

44. hym] *Ho'* þam

I am redy with all my myght
For to fulfille his comaundement.

V Angelus Go we nowe þou worþi wight
Vnto þi sone þat is so gente,
We schall þe bringe into his sight   75
To croune þe quene, þus hase he mente.

VI Angelus Alle heuene and erþe schall worschippe þe
And baynnely be at þi biddinge,
Thy joie schall euere incressid be,
Of solas sere þan schall þou synge.   80

Cantando.

I Angelus Jesu, lorde and heueneis kyng,
Here is þi modir þou aftir sente,
We haue her brought at þi biddynge,
Take hir to þe as þou haste mente.

Maria Jesu my sone, loved motte þou be,   85
I thanke þe hartely in my þought   f.258ᵛ
Þat þis wise ordand is for me,
And to þis blisse þou haste me broght.

Jesus Haile be þou Marie, maiden bright,
Þou arte my modir and I thy sone,   90
With grace and goodnesse arte þou dight,
With me in blisse ay schall þou wonne.

Nowe schall þou haue þat I þe hight,
Thy tyme is paste of all þi care,
Wirschippe schall þe aungellis bright,   95
Of newe schall þou witte neuere more.

Maria Jesu my sone, loued motte þou be,
I thanke þe hartely in my þoȝt,
Þat on þis wise ordand is for me,
And to this blisse þou has me broght.   100

Jesus Come forth with me my modir bright,
Into my blisse we schall assende
To wonne in welthe, þou worþi wight,
That neuere more schall it haue ende.

80+ SD *(main scribe) to left in red*
87. ordand is] *He; MS, TS* ordandis
94. Thy] *K* The
99. ordand is] *He; MS, TS* ordandis

Thi newis, modir, to neuen þame nowe,   105
    Are turned to joie, and soth it is
All aungellis bright þei schall þe bowe
    And worschippe þe worþely iwis.
For mekill joie, modir, had þou
    Whan Gabriell grette þe wele be þis,   110
And tolde þe tristely for to trowe
    Þou schulde consayue þe kyng of blisse.

Nowe maiden meke and modir myne,
    Itt was full mekill myrþc to þe
Þat I schuld ligge in wombe of þine   f.259
    Thurgh gretyng of an aungell free.   116
The secounde joie, modir, was syne
    Withouten payne whan þou bare me;
The thirde aftir my bittir peyne
    Fro dede on lyve þou sawe me be.   120

The fourthe was when I stied vppe right
    To heuene vnto my fadir dere –
My modir, when þou saugh þat sight,
    To þe it was a solas seere.
Þis is þe fifte þou worthy wight,   125
    Of þe jois þis has no pere,
Nowe schall þou belde in blisse so bright
    For euer and ay, I highte þe here,

For þou arte cheffe of chastité,
    Off all women þou beris þe floure;   130
Nowe schalle þou, lady, belde with me
    In blisse þat schall euere indowre
Full high on highte in magesté,
    With all worshippe and all honnoure,
Wher we schall euere samen be   135
    Beldand in oure bigly boure.

Alle-kynnys swetnesse is þerin
    Þat manne vppon may thynke, or wiffe,
With joie and blisse þat neuere schall blynne
    Þer schall þou, lady, lede thy liffe.   140

Þou schalte be worshippid with honnoures
    In heuene blisse þat is so bright,

113–60. *Ruled off in red every fourth line; to 144, assigned I–VI, I–III Angelus seriatim,
      and so in TS. Assignment of whole speech to Jesus, this ed*
120. lyve þou] *Ho¹* lyve whan þou
126. þe] *Ho¹* þi
134. honnoure] *This ed; MS, TS* honnoures
136. boure] *This ed; MS, TS* boures

With martiris and with confessouris,   f.259ᵛ
   With all virginis, þou worthy wight.
Before all oþere creatours   145
   I schall þe giffe both grace and might,
In heuene and erþe to sende socoures
   To all þat seruis þe day and nyght.

I graunte þame grace with all my myght
   Thurgh askyng of þi praier,   150
Þat to þe call be day or nyght
   In what disease so þat þei are.

Þou arte my liffe and my lekyng,
   Mi modir and my mayden schene;
Ressayue þis croune my dere darlyng,   155
   Þer I am kyng þou schalte be quene.

Myne aungellis bright, a songe ȝe singe
   In þe honnoure of my modir dere,
And here I giffe ȝou my blissing
   Haly nowe, all in fere.   160

XLVIA

The Coronation of the Virgin

(later fragment)

Hayle, fulgent Phebus and fader eternall,   f.267
Parfite plasmator and God omnipotent,
Be whos will and power perpetuall
All thinges hath influence and beyng verament.
To the I giffe louyng and laude right excellent,   5

144.   þou] *K; MS, TS* þat
147.   socoures] *He; MS, TS* socoure
160+   *Rest of f.259ᵛ blank; ff.260, 260ᵛ blank*

And to the sperite also, graunter of all grace,
Whilke by thi woorde and thi warke omnipotent
I am thi sonne and equale in that case.
O *sapor suauitatis*, o succour and solace,
O life eternall and luffer of chastité,   10
Whome aungels abowne and þe erthe in his grete space
And all thinges create loues in magesté.
Remembre, fader meke, in thi solempnyté
The woundes of thi sonne, whilke by thy providence
Þou made discende frome thyne equalité   15
Into the wombe of Marye, be meke obedience.
Of a virgin inviolate for mans iniquyté,
Whilke for his synne stoode mekill fro þi grace,
Be hoole assente of thi solempnité
Þou made me incarnate, and trulie man I was.   20
Wherefore too spede me here in this space,
Þou here me fader, hertely I the praye,
As for my moder truely in this case
Þou here þi sonne, and herk what I shall saye.
Me semes mysilfe it is right grete offence   25
My moder wombe in erthe sulde putrifye,
Sen hir flessh and myne were bothe oone in escence,
I had none othir bot of hir truely.
She is my moder to whome *legem adimpleui*
Whilke þou has ordinate as by thi prouidence.   30
Graunte me thi grace, I the beseke hertely,
As for the tyme of hir meke innocence,   f.267ᵛ
In woorde ne dede thoght the neuer to offende,
Sho myght be assumpt, I pray thyne excellence,
Vnto thi troone, and so to be commende,   35
In bodye and saule euer withoutyn ende
With the to reyne in thyne eternyté,
Fro sorrowe and sadnesse synners to offende.
O flagraunt fader, graunte yt myght so be.

Responcio Patris ad Filium:
O lampe of light, o *lumen* eternall,   40
O coequale sonne, o verrey sapience,
O mediator ande meen and lyfe perpetuall,
In whome of derk clowedes may haue none accidence –
Thoue knawes right wele by thy providence
I haue commyt my powere generall,   45
Tibi data potestas, ande plenall influence.
Thou ert my sonne. . .

27. oone] *Added to right, with caret mark*
47+ *Bottom half of f.267ᵛ blank except for* Tibi data potestas *in a later hand (? the 'Cutler-Nandicke' hand). Fol. 268 originally blank; at head of page,* Corpus Christi playe *in a later hand, and beneath this (in imitation)* Corpus Cristi playe Thomas Cutler Richarde Nandicke. *Fol. 268ᵛ blank*

XLVII The Mercers

The Last Judgement

Deus incipit:

Firste when I þis worlde hadde wroght—
   Woode and wynde and wateris wan,
And all-kynne thyng þat nowe is oght—
   Fulle wele meþoght þat I did þanne.
Whenne þei were made, goode me þame þoght;   5
   Sethen to my liknes made I man
And man to greue me gaffe he noght,
   Þerfore me rewis þat I þe worlde began.

Whanne I had made man at my will,
   I gaffe hym wittis hymselue to wisse,   10
And paradise I putte hym till
   And bad hym halde it all as his.
But of þe tree of goode and ill
   I saide, 'What tyme þou etis of þis,
Manne, þou spedes þiselue to spill—   15
   Þou arte broght oute of all blisse'.

Belyue brak manne my bidding.
   He wende haue bene a god þerby;
He wende haue wittyne of all-kynne thyng,
   In worlde to haue bene als wise as I.   20
He ete þe appill I badde schulde hyng,
   Þus was he begilid thurgh glotony;
Sithen both hym and his ospring
   To pyne I putte þame all forthy.

To lange and late meþoghte it goode   25
   To catche þois caitiffis oute of care.
I sente my sone with full blithe moode
   Till erþe, to salue þame of þare sare.
For rewþe of þame he reste on roode
   And boughte þame with his body bare;   30
For þame he shedde his harte-bloode—
   What kyndinesse myght I do þame mare?

4. I] *Interlined*
8. þe worlde] *K, Ma om*
16. all blisse] *K, Ca* all thi blisse
31. harte-bloode] *Ho¹, Ma; MS, TS, Ca* harte and bloode

Sethen aftirwarde he heryed hell
   And toke oute þois wrecchis þat ware þareinne;
Þer faughte þat free with feendis feele   35
   For þame þat ware sounkyn for synne.   f.261ᵛ
Sethen in erthe þan gonne he dwelle,
   Ensaumpill he gaue þame heuene to wynne,
In tempill hymselffe to teche and tell,
   To by þame blisse þat neuere may blynne.   40

Sethen haue þei founde me full of mercye,
   Full of grace and forgiffenesse,
And þei als wrecchis, wittirly,
   Has ledde þer liffe in lithirnesse.
Ofte haue þei greued me greuously,   45
   Þus haue þei quitte me my kyndinesse;
Þerfore no lenger, sekirlye,
   Thole will I þare wikkidnesse.

Men seis þe worlde but vanité,
   Ʒitt will no manne beware þerby;   50
Ilke a day þer mirroure may þei se,
   Ʒitt thynke þei noʒt þat þei schall dye.
All þat euere I saide schulde be
   Is nowe fulfillid thurgh prophicie,
Therfore nowe is it tyme to me   55
   To make endyng of mannes folie.

I haue tholed mankynde many a ʒere
   In luste and likyng for to lende,
And vnethis fynde I ferre or nere
   A man þat will his misse amende.   60
In erthe I see butte synnes seere,
   Therfore myne aungellis will I sende
To blawe þer bemys, þat all may here
   The tyme is comen I will make ende.

Aungellis, blawes youre bemys belyue,   65
   Ilke a creatoure for to call,
Leerid and lewde, both man and wiffe,
   Ressayue þer dome þis day þei schall,
Ilke a leede þat euere hadde liffe —
   Bese none forgetyn, grete ne small.   70
Ther schall þei see þe woundes fyve   f.262
   Þat my sone suffered for þem all.

And sounderes þame before my sight,
   All same in blisse schall þei not be.
Mi blissid childre, as I haue hight,   75
   On my right hande I schall þame see;

37. erthe] *Interlined by a later hand*
49. worlde but] *Ca* worlde is but

Sethen schall ilke a weried wight
  On my lifte side for ferdnesse flee.
Þis day þer domys þus haue I dight
  To ilke a man as he hath serued me.   80

I Angelus   Loued be þou, lorde of myghtis moste,
  Þat aungell made to messengere.
Thy will schall be fulfillid in haste,
  Þat heuene and erthe and helle schalle here.
Goode and ill, euery-ilke a gaste,   85
  Rise and fecche youre flessh þat was youre feere,
For all þis worlde is broght to waste.
  Drawes to youre dome, it neghes nere.

II Angelus   Ilke a creature, bothe olde and yhing,
  Belyue I bidde ȝou þat ȝe ryse;   90
Body and sawle with ȝou ȝe bring,
  And comes before þe high justise.
For I am sente fro heuene kyng
  To calle ȝou to þis grette assise,
Þerfore rise vppe and geue rekenyng   95
  How ȝe hym serued vppon sere wise.

I Anima Bona   Loued be þou lorde, þat is so schene,
  Þat on þis manere made vs to rise,
Body and sawle togedir, clene,
  To come before þe high justise.   100
Of oure ill dedis, lorde, þou not mene,
  That we haue wroght vppon sere wise,
But graunte vs for thy grace bedene
  Þat we may wonne in paradise.

II Anima Bona   A, loued be þou, lorde of all,   f.262ᵛ
  Þat heuene and erthe and all has wroght,   106
Þat with þyne aungellis wolde vs call
  Oute of oure graues hidir to be broght.
Ofte haue we greued þe, grette and small,
  Þeraftir lorde þou deme vs noght,   110
Ne suffir vs neuere to fendis to be thrall,
  Þat ofte in erþe with synne vs soght.

I Anima Mala   Allas, allas, þat we were borne,
  So may we synfull kaytiffis say;
I here wele be þis hydous horne   115
  Itt drawes full nere to domesday.
Allas, we wrecchis þat are forlorne,
  Þat never ȝitt serued God to paye,

85. euery] *Ma* euer
    a gaste] *He, Ma, Ca; MS, TS* agaste
98. vs] *TS+; MS* vis

But ofte we haue his flessh forsworne —
    Allas, allas, and welaway.   120

What schall we wrecchis do for drede,
    Or whedir for ferdnes may we flee,
When we may bringe forthe no goode dede
    Before hym þat oure juge schall be?
To aske mercy vs is no nede,   125
    For wele I wotte dampned be we,
Allas, þat we swilke liffe schulde lede
    Þat dighte vs has þis destonye.

Oure wikkid werkis þei will vs wreye,
    Þat we wende nevcr schuld haue bene weten,   130
Þat we did ofte full pryuely,
    Appertly may we se þem wreten.
Allas, wrecchis, dere mon we by —
    Full smerte with helle fyre be we smetyn.
Nowe mon neuere saule ne body dye,   135
    But with wikkid peynes euermore be betyne.

Allas, for drede sore may we quake,
    Oure dedis beis oure dampnacioune.   f.263
For oure mys menyng mon we make,
    Helpe may none excusacioune.   140
We mon be sette for oure synnes sake
    Foreuere fro oure saluacioune,
In helle to dwelle with feendes blake,
    Wher neuer schall be redempcioune.

II Anima Mala   Als carefull caitiffis may we ryse,   145
    Sore may we wringe oure handis and wepe;
For cursidnesse and for covetise
    Dampned be we to helle full depe.
Rought we neuere of Goddis seruise,
    His comaundementis wolde we noȝt kepe,   150
But ofte þan made wc sacrafise
    To Satanas when othir slepe.

Allas, now wakens all oure were,
    Oure wikkid werkis may we not hide,
But on oure bakkis vs muste þem bere —   155
    Thei wille vs wreye on ilke a side.
I see foule feendis þat wille vs feere,
    And all for pompe of wikkid pride.
Wepe we may with many a teere,
    Allas, þat we þis day schulde bide.   160

129. Nota *to left in a later hand*
139. mys menyng] *Ma, Ca; TS* mys-meuyng
156. vs] *Interlined*

Before vs playnly bese fourth brought   f.266ᵛ
Þe dedis þat vs schall dame bedene;
Þat eres has herde, or harte has þoght,
Sen any tyme þat we may mene,
Þat fote has gone or hande has wroght,   165
That mouthe hath spoken or ey has sene –
Þis day full dere þanne bese it boght;
Allas, vnborne and we hadde bene.

III Angelus   Standis noght togedir, parte you in two!   f.263
All sam schall ȝe noght be in blisse;   170
Oure fadir of heuene woll it be soo,
For many of yowe has wroght amys.
Þe goode on his right hande ȝe goe,
Þe way till heuene he will you wisse;
ȝe weryed wightis, ȝe flee hym froo   175
On his lefte hande as none of his.

Deus   Þis woffull worlde is brought till ende,
Mi fadir of heuene he woll it be;
Þerfore till erþe nowe will I wende   f.263ᵛ
Miselue to sitte in magesté.   180
To deme my domes I woll descende;
Þis body will I bere with me –
Howe it was dight, mannes mys to mende,
All mankynde þere schall it see.

Mi postelis and my darlyngis dere,   185
Þe dredfull dome þis day is dight.
Both heuen and erthe and hell schall here
Howe I schall holde þat I haue hight:
That ȝe schall sitte on seetis sere
Beside myselffe to se þat sight,   190
And for to deme folke ferre and nere
Aftir þer werkyng, wronge or right.

I saide also whan I you sente
To suffre sorowe for my sake,
All þo þat wolde þame right repente   195
Shulde with you wende and wynly wake;

161–8.   *Reference mark (large black cross) and* nota *in a later hand to right of 160. The stanza constituted by 161-8 originally om, but later added by main scribe after the closing SD on f. 266ᵛ (380+), where there is a similar reference mark*
169.   *III Angelus] T I Angelus cum gladio*
170.   sam] *Originally* samen, *last two letters deleted*
171.   Oure] *He, Ma, Ca, after T* Oure; *MS, TS* Mi
fadir] *TS, Ca; He, Ma* lord *after T* lord
173.   Þe] *TS, Ca; MS* Þe *or* Ye, *Ma* Ye
177.   Deus] *Ca* Jesus, *as in T*
185.   *Previous character-designation repeated*

And to youre tales who toke no tente
  Shulde fare to fyre with fendis blake.
Of mercy nowe may noȝt be mente,
  Butt, aftir wirkyng, welth or wrake.   200

My hetyng haly schall I fullfille,
  Therfore comes furth and sittis me by
To here þe dome of goode and ill.

I Apostolus   I loue þe, lord God allmyghty;
Late and herely, lowde and still,   205
  To do thy bidding bayne am I.
I obblissh me to do þi will
  With all my myght, als is worthy.

II Apostolus   A, myghtfull God, here is it sene
  Þou will fulfille þi forward right,   210
And all þi sawes þou will maynteyne.
  I loue þe, lorde, with all my myght,   f.264
Þat for vs þat has erthely bene
  Swilke dingnitees has dressed and dight.

Deus   Comes fourthe, I schall sitte ȝou betwene,   215
  And all fullfille þat I haue hight.

Hic ad sedem iudicij cum cantu angelorum.

I Diabolus   Felas, arraye vs for to fight,
  And go we faste oure fee to fange.
Þe dredefull dome þis day is dight –
  I drede me þat we dwelle full longe.   220

II Diabolus   We schall be sene euere in þer sight
  And warly waite, ellis wirke we wrange,
For if þe domisman do vs right,
  Full grete partie with vs schall gang.

III Diabolus   He schall do right to foo and frende,   225
  For nowe schall all þe soth be sought.
All weried wightis with vs schall wende,
  To payne endles þei schall be broght.
[. . .   . . .
  . . .   . . .
. . .   . . .
  . . .   . . .]

203. *To left in a later hand* What thay shall haue for þer folly, *with reference marks either side of 204*
205-7. *Bracketed to left; to right in hand of J. Clerke* hic caret o soverand savyour de novo facto
209. *To right in Clerke's hand* de novo facto
213. Þat for] *Ho¹, K, Ma, Ca; MS, TS* Þer fore
216+ *SD (main scribe) in same script and inking as dialogue*
228+ *Four lines missing. To right of 228* hic caret *and* de novo facto *added by a later hand or hands*

Deus
　　　　　Ilke a creature, takes entent
　　　　　　　What bodworde I to you bringe:　　　　　230
　　　　　Þis wofull worlde away is wente,
　　　　　　　And I am come as crouned kynge.
　　　　　Mi fadir of heuene, he has me sente
　　　　　　　To deme youre dedis and make ending.
　　　　　Comen is þe day of jugement;　　　　　235
　　　　　　　Of sorowe may ilke a synfull synge.

　　　　　The day is comen of kaydyfnes,
　　　　　　　All þam to care þat are vnclene,
　　　　　Þe day of bale and bittirnes –
　　　　　　　Full longe abedyn has it bene;　　　　　240
　　　　　Þe day of drede to more and lesse,
　　　　　　　Of ire, of trymbelyng, and of tene,
　　　　　Þat ilke a wight þat weried is
　　　　　　　May say, 'Allas, þis daye is sene'.　　　f.264ᵛ

　　　　　Here may ȝe see my woundes wide,　　　　245
　　　　　　　Þe whilke I tholed for youre mysdede.
　　　　　Thurgh harte and heed, foote, hande and hide,
　　　　　　　Nought for my gilte, butt for youre nede.
　　　　　Beholdis both body, bak and side,
　　　　　　　How dere I bought youre brotherhede.　　250
　　　　　Þes bittir peynes I wolde abide –
　　　　　　　To bye you blisse þus wolde I bleede.

　　　　　Mi body was scourged withouten skill,
　　　　　　　As theffe full thraly was I thrette;
　　　　　On crosse þei hanged me, on a hill,　　　255
　　　　　　　Blody and bloo, as I was bette,
　　　　　With croune of thorne throsten full ill.
　　　　　　　Þis spere vnto my side was sette –
　　　　　Myne harte-bloode spared noght þei for to spill;
　　　　　　　Manne, for thy loue wolde I not lette.　　260

　　　　　Þe Jewes spitte on me spitously,
　　　　　　　Þei spared me no more þan a theffe.
　　　　　Whan þei me strake I stode full stilly,
　　　　　　　Agaynste þam did I nothyng greue.
　　　　　Behalde, mankynde, þis ilke is I,　　　265

229–31. *Additions to right by J. Clerke, apparently made at different times:* (i) Alas that I
　　　　was borne dixit prima anima mala et ijᵃ anima mala; (ii) *de nouo facta*
230. you bringe] *K* you shall bringe, *cf T* I shalle you bryng
242. ire] *This ed;* care *interlined, so TS +*
254. I] *Suppl TS +, after T* I
259. noght þei] *Ho',* Ma þei noght, *after T* thai not
263. full] *TS +* would om; *not in T*
264. greue] u *altered to* v *by another hand*

Þus was I dight for thy folye —
Man, loke, thy liffe was to me full leffe.

Þus was I dight þi sorowe to slake;
Manne, þus behoued þe to borowed be.   270
In all my woo toke I no wrake,
Mi will itt was for þe loue of þe.
Man, sore aught þe for to quake,
Þis dredfull day þis sight to see.
All þis I suffered for þi sake —   275
Say, man, what suffered þou for me?

My blissid childre on my right hande,   f.265
Youre dome þis day ȝe thar not dredc,
For all youre comforte is command,
Youre liffe in likyng schall ȝe lede.   280
Commes to þe kyngdome ay-lastand
Þat ȝou is dight for youre goode dede,
Full blithe may ȝe be where ȝe stande,
For mekill in heuene schall be youre mede.

Whenne I was hungery ȝe me fedde,   285
To slake my thirste youre harte was free;
Whanne I was clothles ȝe me cledde,
Ȝe wolde no sorowe vppon me see.
In harde presse whan I was stedde,
Of my payns ȝe hadde pitee;   290
Full seke whan I was brought in bedde,
Kyndely ȝe come to coumforte me.

Whanne I was wille and werieste
Ȝe herbered me full hartefully;
Full gladde þanne were ȝe of youre geste,   295
And pleyned my pouerté piteuously.
Bclyue ȝe brought me of þe beste
And made my bedde full esyly,
Þerfore in heuene schall be youre rcste,
In joie and blisse to be me by.   300

I Anima Bona Whanne hadde we, lorde þat all has wroght,
Meete and drinke þe with to feede,
Sen wc in erþe hadde neuere noght
But thurgh þe grace of thy Godhede?

---

268. to] *Interlined. TS, Ma would om; not in* T
273. sore aught þe for] *Ca om* for; T *for sorow aght the*
276+   *Catchword* Mi blissid childre
277. *Quire* xxxiiijᵗⁱ *begins (four leaves only)*
289. presse] T *prison, so* He, Ma, Ca
290. payns] *Interlined by a later hand over main scribe's* penaunce; T *penance*
293. wille] *This ed;* TS+ wikke; T *wille*

II Anima Bona   Whanne waste þat we þe clothes brought,   305
    Or visite þe in any nede,
Or in þi sikenes we þe sought?   f.265ᵛ
    Lorde, when did we þe þis dede?

Deus   Mi blissid childir, I schall ʒou saye
    What tyme þis dede was to me done: 310
When any þat nede hadde, nyght or day,
    Askid ʒou helpe and hadde it sone.
Youre fre hartis saide þem neuere nay,
    Erely ne late, mydday ne none,
But als ofte-sithis as þei wolde praye,   315
    Þame thurte but bide and haue þer bone.

ʒe cursid caytiffis of Kaymes kynne,
    Þat neuere me comforte in my care,
I and ʒe foreuer will twynne,
    In dole to dwelle for euermare.   320
Youre bittir bales schall neuere blynne
    Þat ʒe schall haue whan ʒe come þare;
Þus haue ʒe serued for youre synne,
    For derffe dedis ʒe haue done are.

Whanne I had mistir of mete and drynke,   325
    Caytiffis, ʒe cacched me fro youre ʒate.
Whanne ʒe wer sette as sirs on benke,
    I stode þeroute, werie and wette;
Was none of yowe wolde on me thynke,
    Pyté to haue of my poure state,   330
Þerfore till hell I schall you synke—
    Weele are ʒe worthy to go þat gate.

Whanne I was seke and soriest
    ʒe visitte me noght, for I was poure;
In prisoune faste whan I was feste   335
    Was none of you loked howe I fore.   f.266
Whenne I wiste neuere where for to reste,
    With dyntes ʒe draffe me fro your dore,
Butte euer to pride þanne were ʒe preste,
    Mi flessh, my bloode, ofte ʒe forswore.   340

Clothles whanne I was ofte, and colde,
    At nede of you, ʒede I full naked;
House ne herborow, helpe ne holde
    Hadde I none of you, þof I quaked.

317. *Deus added as character-designation (in black) by another hand here and at 325, 333*
    and 341. This hand supplies all further character-designations in the play
327. benke] *T* bynke, *so Ca*
337. for] *Om Ma; not in T*

Mi mischeffe sawe ye manyfolde,   345
 Was none of you my sorowe slaked,
Butt euere forsoke me, yonge and alde,
 Þerfore schall ȝe nowe be forsaked.

I Anima Mala Whan had þou, lorde þat all thing has,
 Hungir or thirste, sen þou God is?   350
Whan was þat þou in prisoune was?
 Whan was þou naked or herberles?
II Anima Mala Whan was it we sawe þe seke, allas?
 Whan kid we þe þis vnkyndinesse?
Werie or wette to late þe passe,   355
 When did we þe þis wikkidnesse?

      Caȝt oȝȝ
Deus   Caistiffis, als ofte als it betidde
 Þat nedfull aught askid in my name,
ȝe herde þem noght, youre eris ȝe hidde,
 Youre helpe to þame was noȝt at hame.   360
To me was þat vnkyndines kyd,
 Þerefore ye bere þis bittir blame;
To leste or moste whan ȝe it did,   f.266ᵛ
 To me ȝe did þe selue and þe same.

Mi chosen childir, comes vnto me,   365
 With me to wonne nowe schall ȝe wende
Þere joie and blisse schall euer be,
 ȝoure liffe in lyking schall ȝe lende.
ȝe cursed kaitiffis, fro me ȝe flee,
 In helle to dwelle withouten ende,   370
Þer ȝe schall neuere butt sorowe see
 And sitte be Satanas þe fende.

Nowe is fulfillid all my forþoght,
 For endid is all erthely thyng.
All worldly wightis þat I haue wroght,   375
 Aftir þer werkis haue nowe wonnyng.
Thei þat wolde synne and sessid noght,
 Of sorowes sere now schall þei syng,
And þei þat mendid þame whils þei moght
 Shall belde and bide in my blissing.   380

Et sic facit finem, cum melodia angelorum transiens a loco ad locum.

351. þat] *Suppl Ho¹, Ma after T* that; *Ca* it
362. ye] *Suppl Ho¹, Ma, Ca after T* ye
363. or moste . . . it] *T of* myne . . . oght, *so He, Ma*
364. þe²] *Om Ma; not in T*
372. *To left in a later hand (?J. Clerke) nota miscremini etc*
380+ *SD (main scribe) in red; below, the stanza om after 160 (see 161–8, textual note). For ff.267–268ᵛ, see play XLVIA and its textual note at 47+*

Notes

I The Fall of the Angels

Text
Together with plays II and IIIA, play I is the work of Scribe A, whose hand appears in the first quire, and nowhere else in the manuscript. There is evidence to suggest that this quire (which is unsigned) was prepared in the first place by the main scribe of the manuscript. It was pricked according to his practice, but Scribe A pricked the sheets again to provide a larger frame within which to write. The running-title (see below) was also inserted by the main scribe. It appears likely that the quire as a whole was prepared by the main scribe, but then (apart from the running-titles to no. I) either left blank or handed over to Scribe A. Offsets on f.4 from f.3^v indicate that the quire was already in the form of a booklet when Scribe A came to write.

Play I has unusually long character-designations, some of which embody a kind of stage-direction. For this reason the text is printed in a format which differs slightly from that used for the rest of the cycle, each character-designation occupying a line to itself at the head of the speech. In the manuscript, the stage-directions are in red and the beginnings of some of the stanzas are marked with red paraphs to the left. The scribe himself made minor corrections in lines 39 and 42, but he omitted a character-designation at 129, which was supplied by a later hand.

Versification
The eight-line alliterative stanza, abab$_4$cddc$_3$, is also found in play XLIV and in the first part play of XL.

Running-title
'The Barker(e)s' was written at the head of each leaf by the main scribe of the manuscript (see above). The Barkers, also known as Tanners, were engaged in the conversion of hides into leather, by 'tanning' them with oak-bark in water.

II The Creation

Text
This, the second play in the first quire of the manuscript, was copied by Scribe A (see the preceding Note). Two lines were written as one throughout, and the division between them was often indicated by a *punctus elevatus*. The stanzas were haphazardly marked in several ways: by paraph signs to the left of the first line, by a horizontal red line

between stanzas, or by slightly enlarged initial letters. Though Miss Toulmin Smith printed the text in stanzas, she numbered the lines according to the double lineation of the manuscript. Each line has been given its own number in this edition.

The scribe made minor corrections to his own work in several places (see lines 1, 69, 77 and 171), but he omitted the only character-designation necessary, at the beginning. It was later supplied by John Clerke, who also made an interlineation in line 150.

Versification
The twelve-line stanza, $abababab_4cbcb_3$, appears nowhere else in the cycle.

Title
'Playsterers' was written at the head of the first page only (f.4ᵛ) in a large ornamental script, by Scribe A.

III The Creation of Adam and Eve

Text
Two copies of the text were registered, one presumably by mistake. The first copy, on folios 6ᵛ–8, occupies the latter part of the first (unsigned) quire, and is the work of Scribe A. The second, on folios 9–10, is the first play copied by Scribe B, the main scribe of the Register, and it stands at the beginning of quire A. How this duplication arose can only be guessed at, but it seems that the unsigned quire, though prepared by the main scribe (see the Note on play I), was at some time separated from the rest of the manuscript whilst Scribe A worked on it: this scribe would scarcely have made his copy of III if Scribe B's copy was before him. The unsigned quire, it should be noted, carries no catchword.

The two copies may be conveniently referred to here and in the Textual Notes as *A* and *B*. It is beyond doubt that both were made from the same 'original'. Miss Toulmin Smith rightly judged *B* to be slightly superior textually, and printed it alone in the *editio princeps*. *A* was subsequently printed by P. E. Dustoor, *Allahabad University Studies*, xiii (1937), pp. 25–8, who pointed out that the *A* scribe preserves the northern complexion of the language to a much greater extent than that of *B*. The text printed in this edition is *A*, corrected in several places from *B*. *B* is also collated in the textual notes for substantive but not for orthographical and dialectal variants; D^3 signifies readings and emendations proposed by Dustoor, *loc. cit.*

The *A* copy of III is more elaborately decorated than the two preceding texts by the same hand, rubrication being used primarily as a metrical indication: stanzas are ruled off in red, rhyme brackets added to the right and paraph marks to the left. *B*, exceptionally in the main scribe's work, has each speech beginning with a red *littera notabilior*.

At line 44 in both *A* and *B* there are additions by John Clerke. Though the wording differs, the burden of both passages is the same, emphasizing the subjection of Eve to Adam. Beneath the last lines of both copies there are also added inscriptions which prove to be similar to one another. The addition at the end of *A* is faint, having been largely erased; it was probably in Clerke's hand. The one at the end of *B* is undoubtedly in Clerke's hand, and reads 'The Fullers pagyant / Adam and Eve this is the place – Deus.' It refers forward to the next play, giving the first line and the identity of the first speaker. These additions, which are best interpreted as a kind of cue or *aide-mémoire* to the user of the Register, are elucidated by an episode in the later history of the play. In 1529 it was ordained that plays III and IV were to be amalgamated: 'Item the said presens haith ordred that the Walkers [i.e. Fullers] & Cardemakers of this City fromehensfurth shall ioyne bothe thayre paiauntes in oone & ichone of the saides Craftes to be like charged in euery behalff with the paiaunt Torches & play' (*REED: York*, pp. 249–50. For further discussion of Clerke's annotations in no. III see P. Meredith, *LSE*, NS, xii (1981) pp. 255–7).

It is not possible to enter here into the details of how this amalgamation might have been effected, but Clerke's additions suggest that in his day the first line of IV followed immediately upon the last line of III. (A comparable arrangement may once have prevailed in the case of plays XIV and XV, and erased 'cue' being still partially visible in the manuscript after the last line of XIV; see the Note on no. XIV, below.)

Versification
Cross-rhyming four-stress quatrains are used throughout. No. III is the only play written throughout in this metre, which occurs sporadically elsewhere in the cycle.

Title, running-title
A has a large heading in ornamental script, 'Cardmakers', followed by 'this is entryd afterwardes' in the hand of John Clerke; there are no running-titles. *B* has 'The Cardemakers' as running-title throughout, in the main scribe's usual manner. The Cardemakers were manufacturers of combs, known as cards, used for straightening the fibres of wool prior to spinning.

IV Adam and Eve in Eden

Text
The main scribe was not supplied with copy for this play, but he knew of its existence and made provision for it by leaving a series of blank leaves (ff.11–13) with suitable headings (see below). These leaves remained blank until 1557–9. In 1557 it was ordered that 'suche pageantz as be not registered in the Cite booke shall be called in to be registred by discrecion of my lord mayor', and in 1559 the Chamberlains' accounts record as follows: 'Item payd to Iohn Clerke for entryng in the Regyster the Regynall of the pagyant pertenyng to Craft of Fullars whiche was never before Regestred xijd.' (*REED: York*, pp. 324, 330). When he came to write, Clerke began work on f.10ʳ, supplying his own heading (see below). His reason for ignoring the main scribe's heading on f.11 and beginning the play on the preceding blank page was no doubt to bring no. IV into close proximity with no. III, which ended on f.10. As has

been explained in the preceding Note, plays III and IV had been amalgamated in 1529, and Clerke later added the first line of IV beneath the last line of III as a further indication of how the performance should run.

Versification
The play is in a ten-line stanza, $aa_4b_3cc_4bdbdb_3$, found nowhere else in the cycle. Play XXXIV uses a similarly shaped stanza, but the rhymes differ.

Title, running-title
On f.11 the main scribe wrote 'The regynall pertynyng to the Crafte of Fullers', and on ff.11ᵛ and 12 he wrote 'The Fullers', leaving those leaves otherwise blank. Later, for reasons mentioned above, Clerke supplied his own title when he began the play on f.10ᵛ: 'The regynall of the Fullers pagyant'. The Fullers, who were also known as Walkers, were engaged in the trade of fulling cloth, that is, beating it to clean and thicken it.

V The Fall of Man

Text
At this point in his work the main scribe had not yet settled upon the layout for the plays which he used more or less consistently for the bulk of the manuscript. He was at first somewhat confused by the elaborate stanza in which the play is written, and both the lineation and the character-designations are erratic near the beginning. Miss Toulmin Smith observed that 'many of the lines in the first five stanzas are written very confusedly in the MS; they are corrected here without indicating each one' (*York Plays*, p. 22, n.1). With one exception (lines 6–7) her lineation is followed here. As to the character-designations, some were written at the same time as the dialogue, but not always in the correct place. Others were added later in red, in an ornamental script, some of them duplicates of those already there. After line 137, all are in red. Against lines 1 and 25 John Clerke later added further otiose character-designations. The stage-directions were all written at the same time as the dialogue. The main scribe omitted several lines: 159 he himself later added in red, in an ornamental script. Line 16 was added by a later hand in a gap left by the main scribe, and line 170 similarly inserted by John Clerke.

Versification
The eleven-line stanza, $abab_4c_2bc_4 dcdc_3$, also appears in lines 79–166 of play XIII.

Running-title
'The Cowpers (Coupers)': The Coopers were concerned with the manufacture and repair of such items as barrels, tubs and buckets.

VI The Expulsion

Text
After some metrical confusion on the first page (f.16ᵛ) the rest of this play is copied in the format which the main scribe attempted to use consistently throughout the bulk of the manuscript. Exceptional in VI are the red capitulum marks preceding new speeches on ff.17–18, and an unfilled space for a *littera notabilior* at the beginning of line 77. John Clerke later attempted to elucidate a line (69), and he was possibly responsible for the character-designation at 161.

Versification
The six-line 'Burns' stanza, $aaa_4b_2a_4b_2$, also appears in plays XXII, XXXVIII and XLI. Several instances of five-line stanzas (the sense being unaffected) should be noted: lines 13–17, 36–40, 41–5, 58–62, 141–4; see A. C. Cawley, *LSE*, vii–viii (1952), pp. 60–1.

Title, running-title
The scribe headed the first page 'The Origenall Perteynyng to þe Crafte of Armourrers' and subsequent pages 'The Armourrers'. The Armourrers, who were also sometimes known as Furbers, manufactured and maintained armour and weaponry.

VII Cain and Abel

Text
This play is seriously defective owing to the loss from the manuscript of two leaves. See the discussion in the text, between lines 70 and 71. The text was prepared with some care by the main scribe, who noted and corrected errors at the rubrication stage (see lines 7 and 34–7). John Clerke was active in rectifying the major loss, but any insertion of new leaves he may have made has also disappeared.

Versification
The eleven-line stanza, $ababbc_4 dbcc_4d_{2/3}$, is found nowhere else in the cycle. The fragmentary stanza formed by lines 100–6 and the last stanza (129–39) agree in showing a slight variation on the usual rhyme scheme.

Title, running-title
At the head of the first page is 'The Originall perteynyng to the Craft of Gloueres' and beneath this 'Sacrificium Cayme et Abell', one of the rare titles in the manuscript. Subsequent pages are headed 'The Gloueres'. As well as manufacturing leather gloves, the Glovers made other small leather goods such as bags, purses and key bands.

VIII The Building of the Ark

Text
Play VIII is distinguished from all the others in the cycle in that the text has been carefully examined, and altered in many small particulars, by a

later hand. The handwriting suggests that John Clerke was responsible for many or all of the changes. Details of all the alterations, which include erasures, erasures with substitutions and interlineations, are set out in the Textual Notes and there designated as 'by later hand'. In a number of cases they are clearly identifiable as Clerke's work, but in others (including of course the simple erasures) there is insufficient evidence to provide identification. Apart from the interlineations 'yit' (line 122) and 'at' (126), which are evidently aimed at improving the metre, the alterations are generally in the direction of modernizing the dialect and the orthography of the main scribe's work. For instance, in line 29 'not' is suggested for 'noght', in 59 'swnkyn' is altered to 'sownkyn', and in 99 'must' is suggested for 'bud'–an alteration evidently made in full in 122, 124 and 127. In 81 and 83 the main scribe's 'lang' and 'strang' are altered to 'long' and 'strong', violating other rhymes, but in 119 'bowde' is altered to 'bollde' to restore a rhyme. Alterations at lines 102–3 and 131 show that the main scribe made some attempt to correct his own work whilst rubricating the manuscript, but a line is missing after 104, and 110 can scarcely be correct as it stands in the manuscript.

Versification
The eight-line alternately rhyming stanza, with four stresses to the line, also appears in the Annunciation episode of no. XII, throughout no. XLVII and also in Nos. XX, XXXIX, XLIII and XLVI.

Running-title
'The Shipwrites'.

IX The Flood

Text
The text was copied with close attention to the layout of the large stanzas, and there are only minor mislineations in lines 263–4 and 303–4. The main scribe corrected his own work whilst rubricating at line 80, and later hands made additions or corrections at 106, 134, 221, 294 and 266+ (a stage-direction added). None of these appear to be the work of John Clerke.

Versification
The fourteen-line stanza, $ababababab_4cdcccd_3$, exhibits a moderate amount of ornamental alliteration. It is found in a fully alliterative form in plays XXVI and XXXI.

Running-title
'The Fysshers (Fisshers) and Marynars (Marinars)'. The Mariners, who were also known as Shipmen, were principally a distributive trade, handling especially the river traffic between York and Hull.

X Abraham and Isaac

Text

Play X is in a fairly good state of preservation, though there are several places where the metre is uncertain, and some of them attracted the attention of annotators and correctors. The main scribe corrected his own work whilst rubricating (lines 108 and 327), and there are later marginalia and alterations at lines 15, 90, 108, 164–5 (itself an error), 235–8, 282–4, 297–30. Many of these are probably the work of John Clerke, whose hand certainly appears at 145 and 266–8; see further P. Meredith, *LSE*, NS, xii (1981), p. 269, n.28.

Versification

The bulk of the play is in the twelve-line stanza, $ababab_1cdcd_3$, which appears in eleven other plays in the cycle. It was also the metre used throughout the *Middle English Metrical Paraphrase of the Old Testament*, on which parts of play X were based (see R. Beadle, *Yearbook of English Studies*, xi (1981), pp. 178–87). Passages in other metres are as follows: first, lines 25–8, 235–8 and 297–300 are three-stress cross-rhyming quatrains. The second instance has been bracketed off by a later annotator, and 'hic' written in the margin; 'hic' is also added against the third. The passages seem unexceptionable from the point of view of the sense. Second, lines 221–8 and 301–8 are four-stress octaves with alternate rhymes, and, like the stanzas in the first group, they could be regarded as components of the basic twelve-line stanzas of the piece. Third, lines 229–34 are a tail-rhyme stanza $aa_3b_1cc_3b_1$. Finally, lines 263–72 constitute an imperfect passage involving both cross-rhyme quatrain and tail-rhyme, impossible to categorize. The arrangement adopted in the text at that point is *ad hoc,* and there can be no doubt that material has been lost. This fact did not escape John Clerke, who made repeated attempts to rectify the omission, but his suggestions cannot be incorporated in any obvious way. Apart from the last case, it is not easy to say whether the departures from the basic metrical scheme are due to revision or to deterioration of the text in the process of transmission. It may be noted that in two instances, 229–34 and 297–300, the changes of metre coincide with moments of particular emotional and dramatic tension, namely the final embrace of Abraham and Isaac, and the instant when the sword descends.

Running-title

'The Parchemyners (-ars) and Bokebynders (-ars)' .The Parchment-makers manufactured the fine membranes for the writing of documents and the making up of books, and the Bookbinders (known after the rise of printing as Stationers) later sold books, as well as binding them.

XI Moses and Pharaoh

Text

Another copy of this play is to be found in the Towneley manuscript, and its readings (denoted by *T* in the Textual Notes) sometimes throw light on difficulties in the York text. Pollard, *The Towneley Plays*, pp. xv–xvii, discusses the main differences between the two.

On ff.38–40 of the Register the presentation of the text is unusual in that two lines are often written as one, separated by a red virgule. This edition follows Miss Toulmin Smith's in restoring the stanzaic pattern. Rhyme-bracketing appears sporadically on ff.38–40, largely disappears on ff.40^v–42, but is fully supplied on f.42^v. The main scribe's handwriting is markedly smaller here than elsewhere in the manuscript, and is characterized by a 'splayed' effect and by attention to calligraphic detail. These features are also found on ff.180–87^v, which contain play XXXIII, and the two texts doubtless belonged to the same stint of copying.

The scribe had particular trouble with the character-designations, and there were still several to correct when the manuscript left his hands. Corrections by John Clerke appear at lines 159, 183, 284 and 289, and it is possible that he was also responsible for some of the other alterations attributed in the Textual Notes to 'later hands' (lines 32, 41, 42, 197, 342, 345, 351). At line 21 the first of a number of characters designated 'Cons.' in plays XI, XVI and XIX appears. Miss Toulmin Smith and later editors believed the correct expansion of the abbreviation to be 'Consoles' or 'Consules', 'king's officers'. However, at line 219 of XI the scribe misassigned a speech and, exceptionally, wrote out the character-designation in full: 'Consolator'. Arthur Brown argued that the intended sense of the word was 'flatterer' (*Early English and Norse Studies presented to A. H. Smith*, pp. 2–3), but perhaps more likely is an out-of-the-way spelling of 'consulator', meaning 'counsellor'. (See Latham, *Revised Medieval Latin Word-List*, s.v. consul/-ator. The *Ordo Paginarum* of 1415 refers to the characters thus designated in play XVI as 'consiliarij'; *REED: York*, p. 19).

Versification
The twelve-line stanza, ababab$_4$cdcd$_3$, is found in eleven other plays in the cycle.

Running-title
'The Hosers (Hoseers, Hoosers)'.

XII The Annunciation and the Visitation

Text
This play falls into three distinct episodes: the speech of the Doctor, the Annunciation, and the Visitation. All three are distinguished from one another by their metres (see below) and the Visitation (lines 193–240) is copied on a single extra leaf added at the end of quire E. The handwriting and layout of the Visitation do not however differ from what goes before, and the play seems all to have been copied at one time.

The first word of every new speech and of each Latin quotation in the play was intended to receive a *littera notabilior*, and a few have been roughly supplied by a later hand or hands. John Clerke supplied the character-designation for the speaker of the first 144 lines of the play (misinterpreted by Miss Toulmin Smith – see *York Plays*, p. 93, n.1, and pp. xv–xvi). He also added two stage-directions and made other alterations. These facts indicate that he was familiar with the registered version of the play, but at some time, presumably later, he also wrote 'this matter is / newly made wherof / we have no coppy' at the top of the first page. This would seem to indicate that the play, or perhaps the first part of it, was substantially revised whilst the manuscript was accessible to Clerke. Another later hand had already inserted a missing line (168).

Versification

The first episode, the prologue of the Doctor (lines 1–144) consists of twelve twelve-line stanzas of the type found in eleven other plays in the cycle, $ababab_4cdcd_3$. It is perhaps worth noting that the play attributed to the Spicers was originally described in the *Ordo Paginarum* of 1415 as follows: 'Spicers: Mary, the Angel greeting her, Mary greeting Elizabeth', but a different or later hand has added before the first 'Mary', 'A learned man declaring the sayings of the prophets concerning the future birth of Christ' (see *REED: York*, p. 18; transl. quoted from p. 704). This addition may well refer to the passage in the twelve-line stanza, which could either have been accidentally omitted by the compiler of the *Ordo Paginarum*, or have been composed and added to a still extant 'Annunciation and Visitation' play between 1415 and the time it was registered (1463–77). The episode of the Annunciation and the first stanza of the Visitation (lines 145–99) consist of seven four-stress alternately rhyming octaves, with ornamental alliteration, of the type also found throughout plays VII and XLVII, and also in plays XX, XXXIX, XLIII and XLVI. The rest of the Visitation (lines 200–40) is in three-stress alternately rhyming octaves, a stanza found elsewhere briefly in no. XXXIX.

Running-title

The running-titles were the object of a curious error on the scribe's part. Examination under ultra-violet light shows that 'The Spicers and Foundours' was originally written at the top of each page. The latter two words were later erased, but only after the manuscript had been rubricated. The scribe seems simply to have confused the ownership of this play with that of the next in the cycle. The Spicers dealt in the various substances used extensively in the preservation and enrichment of food and wine during the medieval period.

XIII Joseph's Trouble about Mary

Text

A. Hohlfeld, *Anglia*, xi (1889), pp. 254–5, pointed out that reminiscences of a number of scattered lines in this play also appear in a corresponding episode of play X in the Towneley manuscript: certainly Y30/T250, Y103/T195, Y106/T206, Y158/T186, Y196/T169 and Y291/T181; possibly Y68/T324, Y92/T180, Y159/T187 and Y188/T204 (cf. England and Pollard, *The Towneley Plays*, pp. 88–97).

More than one later user of the Register has scrutinized the text of no. XIII. John Clerke certainly supplied line 116, and his may be the hand responsible for some of the more minor alterations, such as the altering of earlier and dialectal *a* to *o* in the rhymes in a number of places; see also in lines 11, 31, 91 and 224. Line 235 was supplied by another later hand, but a further line missing after 221 went undetected. The line-numbering in this edition differs from that in Miss Toulmin Smith's, as she gave the two halves of line 178 consecutive numbers.

Versification
Lines 1–70, 167–75 and 187–304 are in a ten-line stanza, abab$_4$ccbccb$_3$, not found elsewhere in the cycle. Lines 79–166 are in the eleven-line stanza, abab$_4$c$_2$bc$_4$dcdc$_3$, used throughout play V. Lines 71–8 are two cross-rhyming quatrains and lines 176–86 are in no particular stanzaic form, consisting of four pairs of couplets and two rhyming tags. The passage may be corrupt.

Running-title
'The Pewtere(r)s and Foundours'. The Founders manufactured and repaired commonplace metal objects such as candlesticks, pans and kettles. Pewter was the usual material for items of everyday household use, such as plates and mugs, amongst the better off.

XIV The Nativity

Text
Apart from a faint and insignificant addition by another hand against line 4, this play is entirely devoid of the kinds of marginalia and alterations to the text which accompany most other plays in the manuscript. Its position with regard to the following play also calls for comment, as it appears that nine blank leaves were originally left between the end of no. XIV (f.56) and the beginning of no. XV (f.59). Two leaves, originally the inner bifolium of quire G, have since been lost, and only five blank pages are now to be seen. The leaving of nine blank pages between XIV and XV contrasts with the scribe's practice elsewhere, which was usually to leave two or three blank pages between plays. In other places where nine blanks are left it is clear that provision was being made for plays not to hand at the time of copying, as the scribe inserted the name of the gild from whom a text was expected (see the Notes on nos. IV, XXIIA and XXIIIA). The large gap between XIV and XV, together with another which originally occurred between nos. XL and XLI are enigmatic, as there is no evidence that anything is missing from the cycle in either of these places. It has been suggested that these gaps were left by the scribe with the vague idea that the *Purification* and the *Funeral of the Virgin* belonged in the respective vicinities – both were apparently 'laid apart' from the rest of the cycle when the Register was compiled (see the Notes on nos. XVII and XLIVA, and R. Beadle and P. Meredith, *LSE*, NS, xi (1980), pp. 52–3 for further discussion). In the event, John Clerke later inserted the *Purification* in the space between nos. XL and XLI, ignoring the potentially better position between XIV

and XV, though it is possible that the inner bifolium of quire G had gone by his time, leaving inadequate space.

An alternative possibility is that the gap between nos. XIV and XV has some bearing on the relationship between those two plays, there being both bibliographical and documentary evidence to suggest that it was at one time very close. The indications are that XIV and XV may, at some time after the Register had been compiled, have been performed 'in tandem', much in the way that the Masons and Goldsmiths can be shown to have performed no. XVI in the period when they were both associated with it (see the Note on no. XVI). Only very generalized statements can be made about this development, owing to the scanty and difficult nature of the evidence. The earliest descriptions of the two plays in the *Ordo Paginarum* of 1415 have been lost, and the entries have been rewritten by a later hand over erasure. (*Ex inf.* Mr Peter Meredith; cp. *REED: York,* p. 18. This fact calls for revision of my recent statement that the registered copy of no. XIV dates from between 1415 and 1463–77; see *Philological Essays . . . presented to A. McIntosh,* p. 234, n.11, where I follow J. W. Robinson, *JEGP,* lxx (1971), p. 241, n.2.) In the briefer list of the plays which accompanies the document dated 1415, the relevant entries give no reason to suppose that the two plays were performed in any way other than normal, that is, as separate units: 'Tilers: Bethlehem with the new-born boy'; 'Chandlers: The offering of the shepherds' (*REED: York,* translation on p. 710; cf. p. 25). It is to be suspected that the lost entries of 1415 reflected the same circumstances, which still seem to have been in force when the two plays were registered as discrete units between 1463 and 1477 – though with the anomalous gap between them discussed above. However, annotations by later hands near the last line of no. XIV in the Register, taken together with the rewriting of the *Ordo* entry and other documentary evidence, suggest (i) that no. XIV was wholly or partially revised at some time after 1477, and (ii) that in performance it became closely connected with no. XV. The two developments perhaps occurred simultaneously, but this need not necessarily have been the case. The re-written entries for nos. XIV and XV in the *Ordo Paginarum* are:

Tilers: Mary   Joseph, the midwife, the new-born boy lying in a manger between the cow and the ass, the angel speaking to the shepherds and the players in the following pageant.

Chandlers: Shepherds speaking to one another, the star in the East, the angel announcing the joy over the new-born boy to the shepherds.

(After the translation in *REED: York,* p. 704; cf. p. 18.) It is clear that the entry for no. XIV does not describe the play that is in the Register, which has no midwife and no angel, and, as it stands, no relationship with the following play. It is therefore possible that the *Nativity* was wholly or partially revised after 1477 to include a part for an angel whose words were audible to the actors in the *Shepherds* on the next pageant-wagon, the angel of the latter being, presumably, one and the same character, in spite of intervening dialogue exclusive to the shepherds. That the end of XIV (whatever form the play had assumed) and the beginning of XV were at some late date brought into close proximity is further betrayed by the annotations of three later hands by the last line of the *Nativity:* 'Br.th.r with haste' (erased, but legible under ultra-violet light; the beginning of XV 1); 'hic caret pastoribus'; 'sequitur postea'. (The situation in the Register after the amalgamation of plays III and IV in 1529 should be compared, both copies of III carrying the first line of IV at the end, as a kind of cue; see the Note on III.) Finally, it is relevant to note an instruction issued to John Clerke by the civic authorities in 1567, to the effect that he should enter into the Register all those plays which had never before been registered, including 'of the Tylars the lattr part of their pageant' (*REED: York,* p. 351). This is unlikely to refer to the version of the Tilethatchers' play in the Register, which is clearly a self-contained piece, and it appears that Clerke was being instructed to enter the 'ending' of a new version of the *Nativity* which post-dated it. (It is also possible that the instruction of 1567 may have some bearing on the observation 'Here wantes the conclusyon of this matter', written by John Clerke beneath the last line of no. XV; see the next Note.) The absence of marginalia and annotations by later hands bearing on the extant text of XIV is also significant. Elsewhere in the manuscript the same feature emerges in connection with plays which were re-written, or were removed from the cycle: see the Notes on nos. XIX, XLIV, XLV and XLVI.

Versification
The seven-line stanza, abab$_4$c$_2$b$_4$c$_2$, is also found in play XV, lines 37–85, and throughout plays XXI and XXV.

Running-title
'The Tille thek(k)ers'. As well as laying tiles the Tilethatchers also engaged in other branches of the building-trade such as plastering and bricklaying, eventually joining themselves into a composite gild with the Plasterers and Bricklayers.

XV The Shepherds

Text
The main scribe left the character-designations in an unsatisfactory state, and later hands (including John Clerke's) supplied and corrected in various places. There are corrections in the dialogue at lines 20 (main scribe) and 78 (later hand), and at line 85 the main scribe noted an omitted word in the margin whilst rubricating; it was later inserted in the text by John Clerke.

The main problem in the text is the lacuna between lines 55 and 56, occasioned by the loss or removal of a single leaf which had been interpolated between the sixth and seventh leaves of quire G. The lacuna remained undetected by Miss Toulmin Smith and later editors of the play, and I have recently discussed the bibliographical evidence elsewhere (see *Philological Essays. . .presented to A. McIntosh,* pp. 229–35). Briefly, a stub which must have keyed the missing singleton between the sixth and seventh leaves of quire G is to be seen amongst the blank leaves occurring between the end of no. XIV and the beginning of no. XV (between ff.57^v and 58, the second and third leaves of quire G). The 'stanza' constructed by Miss Toulmin Smith and her successors from the last five lines on f.59^v (lines 51–5) and the first two on f.60 (lines 56–7) conceals a loss of some 60 lines. The reason for the interpolation remains open to conjecture, though the belated recognition of a defective exemplar or an accidental omission on the copyist's part are the kinds of cause which suggest themselves from a bibliographical point of view. The subsequent disappearance of the leaf is equally puzzling. If it had taken place by Clerke's time he made no allusion to it, though he did draw attention to other shortcomings in the text.

A particular point of interest is that the first of the 'Shrewsbury Fragments', consisting of the part of III Pastor from a vernacular Shepherds' play containing liturgical chants from the *Officium Pastorum*, runs parallel to the York text from around line 42 to the end (see N. Davis, *Non-Cycle Plays and Fragments*, pp. 1–2; F. H. Miller, *MLN*, xxxiii (1918) p. 92). The first few lines of the fragment give some idea of what must be missing from between lines 55 and 56 of the York play, but the arrangement of the lines and the versification (see below) are different. The nature of the relationship between the York and Shrewsbury texts is unknown, though it may be noted that the Shrewsbury manuscript is considerably the earlier, being dated by Professor Davis in the early fifteenth century.

As has been explained in the Note on the preceding play, the original description of no. XV in the *Ordo Paginarum* of 1415 was rewritten, probably after 1477, owing to a revision of this part of the cycle. This may have involved the staging of XIV and XV 'in tandem'. Play XIV was certainly revised or rewritten, perhaps as part of the new staging arrangements, but it is not possible to say whether the same is true of XV, there being no significant discrepancy between the rewritten *Ordo Paginarum* description of the episode and the extant text – given that the material missing between lines 55 and 56 did include the angel: 'Chandlers: Shepherds speaking to one another, the star in the East, the angel announcing the joy over the new-born boy to the shepherds' (*REED: York*, translation on p. 704; cf. p. 18). On the other hand, there are a significant number of later marginal annotations by John Clerke and others suggesting that the registered copy was unsatisfactory by the sixteenth century (see at lines 64, 99, 108, 120). Particularly arresting in this respect is the partially erased inscription by John Clerke beneath the last line: 'Here wantes the conclusyon of this matter'.

Versification
The first three and the last three stanzas (lines 1–36, 96–131) have the twelve-line form abababab$_4$cdcd$_3$ found in eleven other plays in the cycle. Lines 86–95 rhyme ababab$_4$cdcd$_3$, and are possibly a fragment. The intervening passage (lines 37–85) and probably also the missing material are or were in the seven-line stanza, abab$_4$c$_2$b$_4$c$_{2-1}$, which also appears in plays XIV, XXI and XXV.

Running-title
'The Chaundelers'. Chandlers made not only a wide variety of candles for ecclesiastical use and for lighting amongst the better off, but also wax images for religious purposes.

XVI Herod / The Magi

The editorial problems posed by this play are of singular complexity, and it is impossible, in approaching them, not to enter into the histories of the gilds which at different times had responsibility for different parts of the performance. It is also necessary to consider the manner in which the play may have been staged before sense can be made of the scribe's presentation of the text in the manuscript. Before 1432–3 the Goldsmiths by themselves presented a play which may well have consisted of all the extant text as printed above, except the first Herod 'scene'. It is also possible that the production involved the use of two pageant-wagons at one station, 'Jerusalem' and 'Bethlehem' respectively. In 1432–3 responsibility for the performance was divided between the Goldsmiths and the Masons, the Masons taking over Herod's 'Jerusalem', and the Goldsmiths retaining 'Bethlehem' and the Three Kings. At or soon after this time an additional Herod 'scene' was composed for the Masons and placed at the beginning of the play. From 1432–3 to 1477 it appears that the play was performed by the two gilds in association with one another. In 1477 the Masons were reassigned to no. XVII (see the following Note), and the Register was apparently obsolete, as far as the assignment of the Herod episodes of no. XVI were concerned, shortly after it was completed. The play nevertheless continued to be performed, as later annotations in the manuscript show. No evidence, however, survives to indicate which gild or gilds, if any, took over the material attributed in the Register to the Masons. This is the case until 1561, when it is recorded that the gild of Minstrels assumed responsibility for what was previously performed by the Masons. For the period between 1477 and 1561 an obvious possibility is that the Goldsmiths once more brought forth the entire episode, as had been the case prior to 1432–3: a Goldsmiths' order of 1561, that 'neither the Corones nor gownes [? costumes of the Three Kings] be lent to any vnder viij d a pece' suggests as much (*REED: York*, p. 334).

The presentation of the text in the Register reflects the situation between 1432–3 and 1477, when the play was divided between the Masons and the Goldsmiths. It is convenient, though anachronistic, to refer to the variously apportioned sections of the piece as 'scenes'. The main scribe, it appears, was faced with two 'originals', one giving two scenes where the Masons were involved, and the other three scenes in which the Goldsmiths were concerned. These two groups he entered in the Register as if they were separate plays, heading them 'Masons' and 'Goldsmiths' respectively. However, the second scene attributed to the Goldsmiths proves to be practically identical with the second scene already registered in the name of the Masons. The duplicated scene consists of 143 lines, and dramatizes the visit of the Three Kings to Herod's court at Jerusalem. It is difficult to conceive circumstances in which it would be necessary or desirable for the Goldsmiths to follow the Masons in performance, giving a play which is in large part identical to its predecessor in the cycle, though this is what the manuscript appears to imply in its presentation of the text. Miss Toulmin Smith, noting the duplication, speculated that the Masons' and the Goldsmiths' plays were perhaps alternatives, and she printed the Goldsmiths' text (her no. XVII) in its entirety, giving the first scene only of the Masons' (her no.

XVI; see *York Plays,* p. 125, n.1). The repetition of identical scenes in what the manuscript presents as successive plays, is, however, only apparent. As will be suggested in more detail below, the duplication of the part where Herod comes face to face with the Three Kings was necessary because both the Masons and the Goldsmiths were involved in putting it on, and both gilds would therefore have held originals containing the same scene.

The present edition, assembled partly with the help of evidence not accessible to Miss Toulmin Smith, seeks to reconstitute what was in effect a single play. Accordingly, the plays numbered XVI and XVII in Miss Toulmin Smith's edition have here become one play, XVI. The reconstruction rests to some extent on the assumption that the staging of the episode was not orthodox. Both textual and bibliographical evidence appear to call for an interpretation which indicates that two pageant-wagons were used at one station – the Masons' Herod at 'Jerusalem' and the Goldsmiths' Holy Family at 'Bethlehem', as suggested above – with the Three Kings moving between the two *loci,* perhaps on horseback. The use of two pageant-wagons at one station may not have been unique. It appears that plays III and IV were somehow combined after 1529, and quite possibly plays XIV and XV at some time after 1477 (see the Notes above).

The four 'scenes' of play XVI are: (i) lines 1–56, Herod boasting and being flattered by his courtiers and son (Masons only, ff.62ᵛ–63ᵛ line 2). (ii) lines 57–128, the Three Kings meeting and resolving to seek Herod's permission to look for the new-born Saviour (Goldsmiths only, ff.68–9 line 11). (iii) lines 129–272, duplicated, the coming of a messenger to Herod's court telling him of the Three Kings; the interview between Herod and the Three Kings, and his attempt to trick them; the departure of both parties (Masons' copy, f.63ᵛ line 4–f.66; Goldsmiths' copy f.69 line 12–f.71ᵛ line 20). (iv) lines 273–392, the Three Kings making their offerings to the Holy Family at Bethlehem; the warning of the Three Kings by the Angel not to return to Herod (Goldsmiths only, f.71ᵛ line 21–f.73ᵛ). The bibliographical evidence which suggests that this was the manner in which the play was performed is as follows.

The material copied by the scribe under the heading 'Masons' consists of scene (i) and the first copy of scene (iii), lines 1–56 and 129–272. Between 56 and 129, and given a line to themselves, are the words 'his wille', which Miss Toulmin Smith subjoined to the stanza ending with line 56, though they are clearly out of place there as regards both sense and metre. Holthausen (*Archiv,* lxxxv (1890), p. 414) pointed out that 'his wille' are the last words of the last line of what is here printed as scene (ii), lines 57–128, 'Wende we and witte his wille'. This scene is the first part of the text entered by the scribe under the heading 'Goldsmiths'.

At this point it is necessary to mention the annotations by a later hand or hands, as much light is thrown on how what appears in the Register was read and understood, and on how the play was staged. All the marginal annotations appear at points of transition between the scenes as described above: between scene (i) and the Masons' copy of scene (iii); at the beginning of scene (ii), of the Goldsmiths; and at the end of both the Masons' and the Goldsmiths' copies of scene (iii). Several of the annotations have been erased, but most of the writing is legible under ultra-violet light. It may well be that all are the work of John Clerke (so Peter Meredith, *LSE*, NS, xii (1981), pp. 262–4), though owing to the erasures it is not possible to be absolutely certain.

The first additions appear in the vicinity of the ending of the Masons' scene (i). To the right of line 56 and of 'his wille' just beneath is a largely irrecoverable erased inscription, including the word 'caret' and a reference mark in the form of Maltese cross. (The offset from the cross is clearly visible between the first two words of the text on the opposite page). Beneath and to the left of 'his wille', against the first line of the Masons' copy of scene (iii) (129), were the words 'sequitur postea', now erased, but recoverable. From these additions it is clear that a hiatus was recognized in the text attributed to the Masons, probably by John Clerke, though at what date and under what circumstances he made the discovery is more difficult to say. The reason for the erasure of the additions is also obscure. It is however possible to suggest why they were originally inserted. The erased Maltese cross after line 56 is answered by an identical symbol added by a later hand immediately to the left of line 57, the first line attributed to the Goldsmiths and the opening line of what has here been termed scene (ii). The lost inscription, including 'caret', probably explained in more detail what was 'wanting' here, namely the first part of the Goldsmiths' text. As has been noted above, scene (ii) ends with the line 'wende we and witte his wille' (128), and the 'his wille' standing before the first line of the copy of scene (iii) attributed to the Masons may therefore be explained as a cue. The reason for 'sequitur postea' to the left of this first line was perhaps to signal that the third scene 'followed after' what did not appear in the Masons' text between lines 56 and 129.

If the interpretation of the bibliographical evidence to this point is sound, then it may be possible to visualize the first three scenes being played as follows. Scene (i), lines 1 to 56, presented from 1432–3 to 1477 by the Masons, and consisting of Herod boasting and being flattered by his son and courtiers: this was probably presented on a pageant-wagon, representing Jerusalem. Scene (ii), lines 57 to 128, the Goldsmiths playing the Three Kings meeting and resolving to seek Herod's permission to look for the new-born Saviour: the Kings speak of themselves as travelling, and it is possible that the scene was played in the street. They could have been on foot, but artistic and dramatic traditions suggest that they are more likely to have been on horseback. In the third scene, lines 129 to 272, the Three Kings of the Goldsmiths go to the Herod's court presented by the Masons, and the reason for the duplication of this part of the text in the manuscript becomes apparent: because both the Masons and the Goldsmiths were involved in the production of the third scene, the same dialogue would be found in the originals surrendered by the two gilds to the main scribe for registration.

The end of the third scene also calls for comment, as both the Masons' and the Goldsmiths' copies have significant later annotations at this point. The scene is brought to an end by the departure of the Three

Kings, who promise to return and tell Herod if they find the child. Herod congratulates himself on the subtlety of his deceit (lines 261 ff.), and amongst his closing remarks makes the following proposal:

> Go we nowe till þei come agayne
> To playe vs in som othir place (267–8)

This signals the end of what was originally the Masons' part in the play, and shortly after the same point in the Goldsmiths' copy of scene (iii) John Clerke observed in the margin: 'Nota: the Harrode passeth and the iij Kynges commyth agayn to make there offerynges' (272+). Taken together with the preceding dialogue, there is perhaps sufficient evidence here to suggest that Herod and his court on the 'Jerusalem' pageant-wagon did literally depart at this moment, presumably making their way to the next station to begin the performance again. As has been explained above, the text attributed to the Masons breaks off at this point, but John Clerke added beneath the last line the opening words of the fourth scene, where the Goldsmiths play the oblation: 'Hic caret / I Rex / Alake forsoth what shall I say / we lake þat syne þat we haue soght / sequitur postea' (erased, but legible under ultra-violet light). Lines 273–4, as originally registered, run

I Rex   A, sirs, for sight what shall I say?
             Whare is oure syne? I se it noth.

The final scene, performed by the Goldsmiths alone, calls for no comment here beyond the fact that the Nativity scene at Bethlehem is likely to have been mounted on the gild's own pageant-wagon, and it is to this that the Three Kings go when they 'commyth agayn' after line 272.

   This, in outline, is the justification for the manner in which play XVI has been printed in this edition. The situation before 1432 seems to have been that the Goldsmiths by themselves produced a play in most essentials the same as the one which now appears in the Register, except for scene (i) and a speech adapted slightly for Herod's son in what was later the Masons' part of scene (iii). In the *Ordo Paginarum* of 1415, the play then attributed to the Goldsmiths is described thus: 'Orfevers, Goldbeaters, Moneymakers: The three Kings coming from the East, Herod asking them about the boy Jesus, and two councillors and a messenger, Mary with the boy and the star above and the three Kings offering gifts'. It was no doubt as a result of the dividing up of the play in 1432–3 that 'Masons' was added to the list of gilds by a later hand. The interlineation of 'and the son of Herod' for insertion between 'Jesus' and 'and the two councillors' may indicate that scene (i) was composed at or soon after this time (see *REED: York*, p. 19 and p. 704 for the translation quoted). Herod's son appears in the first scene, which is in a different metre from the rest of the play (see below), and in lines 181–4 of the Masons' copy of scene (iii), which are quite clearly an adaptation of the corresponding lines in the Goldsmiths' copy. This was probably the pre-1432 text, and there the lines are attributed to Herod himself. The adaptation was made simply by changing the character-designation and the pronouns.

The reasons for the dividing of the play between the two gilds are set out in a document preserved in the city's A/Y Memorandum Book (*REED: York*, pp. 47–8, but note the corrected dating in *LSE*, NS, xi (1980), p. 56, n.4). The Goldsmiths claimed they had fallen on hard times, and were unable to sustain what were described as 'two pageants' (and, later in the document, 'both their pageants'), though both the *Ordo* of 1415 and the briefer accompanying list of the plays agree with one another in attributing one play only to them. They petitioned for relief. The Masons meanwhile were dissatisfied with having to produce a play on the subject of the Funeral of the Virgin (see below, no. XLIVA), and were happy to take over 'one of their pageants, i.e. that of Herod'. In York at this date the word 'pageant' could refer either to a play or to the vehicle on which a play was performed. It is certainly possible that before 1432 the Goldsmiths were already using two pageant-wagons in their production, and this obviously has some bearing on the foregoing analysis of how the text was later presented in the Register. (See also A. F. Johnston, *Speculum*, l (1975), p. 68, n.2, for earlier remarks on the possibility that the Goldsmiths originally employed two pageant-wagons.)

It is not possible to say how no. XVI was performed between 1477, when the Masons took over the *Purification* (no. XVII) and 1561, when their Herod 'pageant' is found to be the new responsibility of the Minstrels. In that year the Herod pageant is described as being 'somtyme brought forth by the late Masons of the. . .Citie' (*REED: York*, p. 334). It appears highly unlikely that the Masons continued to be involved with play XVI after 1477. They had always been an eccentrically constituted body, and they began to decline rapidly in the later years of the fifteenth century, probably dying out in the mid-sixteenth. (See Palliser, *Tudor York*, pp. 171–2, who discusses the reasons for their decline, and *VCH: City of York*, p. 115, for evidence of their increasingly rare appearances on the Freeman's Roll in this period.)

Text
The text has been printed in the order of performance suggested above:
(i) *olim* Masons, later Minstrels, lines 1–56;
(ii) Goldsmiths, lines 57–128;
(iii) both copies, in parallel; *olim* Masons, later Minstrels, on the left hand page, Goldsmiths on the right, lines 129–272;
(iv) Goldsmiths, lines 272–392.
The main scribe did little to correct his work, and left the character-designations in a particularly poor state in places (see at lines 1, 42, G135, MG187, MG209, MG213, MG225, MG233, G261). John Clerke's hand appears with corrections in both copies of lines 129–272 (G176, G213, M219), and the interlineation in line 19 is probably attributable to him.

The stanza formed by lines 369–80 also appears in the Towneley *Magi* play (see England and Pollard, *The Towneley Plays*, p. 159, lines 595–606; cf. Hall, *EStn*, ix (1886), p. 448, and Herttrich, *Studien zu den York Plays*, p. 4).

For the characters designated 'Consolator', see the Note above on play XI.

Versification

Lines 57 to 392, scenes (ii) to (iv), and probably the play belonging to the Goldsmiths alone before 1432–3, is in the twelve-line stanza also found in eleven other plays in the cycle: $ababab_4cdcd_3$. Scene (i), lines 1–56, which may have been composed in or soon after 1432–3 to provide additional material for the Masons, consist of five stanzas in the long alliterative line: lines 1–22, two eleven-line stanzas, $ababbcbc_1d_2cd_1$; lines 23–30, an alternately rhyming octave; lines 31–56, two thirteen-line stanzas, $ababab_4c_2ddd_3c_{3/4}$. None of these stanza forms appears elsewhere in the cycle.

Running-titles

On ff 62^v–66, 'The Masonns'. To the right of the first instance John Clerke wrote 'Mynstrells'. The last running-title in the Masons' section (f.66) is odd: after 'The Masonns' the scribe has added a character consisting of a vertical stroke with a hook to the left at the top and a horizontal bar through the shaft. A Tironian nota was possibly intended. The red frame added to emphasize and decorate the running-title has here been partially erased. On ff.68–73^v the running-title is 'The Gold(e) Smythis' or 'The Goldsmythis'.

XVII The Purification

Text

Users of Miss Toulmin Smith's edition will be familiar with the fact that this play was inserted in the Register, by a later hand, between the plays now numbered XL and XLI. As she was unaware of this before the first half of her text had gone to press, she was unable to include the play where it properly belongs in the sequence, and accordingly printed it as no. XLI, with the comment 'The play should, rightly, have been numbered XVIII and have been placed between the Adoration and the Flight into Egypt' (p. 433, n.1; see also p. xxi, n.4). In the present edition, the *Purification* has been set in this position and numbered XVII, since the plays previously numbered XVI and XVII now appear as one, XVI. As is explained below, Miss Toulmin Smith's nos. XLII to XLVIII have now been re-numbered XLI to XLVII.

Play XVII was entered in the Register in or soon after 1567, the year in which the governing body of the city ordered that such plays as were not already in the book should be copied therein by John Clerke, and amongst those listed was 'the Labrors the Purificacion of our lady' *REED: York,* p. 351). The play accordingly appears in Clerke's hand on a series of blank leaves left by the main scribe between plays XL and XLI, to which Clerke added a singleton (f.232) in order to give himself space to complete the work. To explain why the play appeared in the Register when and where it did, it is necessary to look into its history and to consider certain bibliographical evidence. Not all the problems which are revealed prove to be soluble.

A play on the subject of the *Purification* is first heard of in a largely unaltered entry in the *Ordo Paginarum* of 1415. It was not at that time played by a gild, but by a religious house: '(formerly) the House of St Leonard (now Masons): Mary with the boy, Joseph, Anna, the midwife with the young doves, Simeon receiving the child into his arms, and the two sons of Simeon' (*REED: York*, p. 19, quoted in translation from p. 705; the words in brackets were added by a later hand). The body originally responsible for the play was the hospital of St Leonard, in its time a large and important institution, but decaying in the fifteenth century (*VCH: Yorkshire*, iii, pp. 336–45). The change of ownership implied in the addition by the later hand is known to have taken place in 1477, record of it surviving in both the A/Y Memorandum Book and a Chamberlains' Book of the period: 'That the pagiant of the purificacion of our lady from nowe furth shalbe plaed yerely in the fest of corpus christi as other pageantes and vppon that it was agreid that the Masons of this Cite for tyme beyng bere the charge and expensez of the pageant aforsaid. . .' (*REED: York*, p. 115; cf. pp. 112–13). Why and precisely when St Leonards had relinquished control of its play does not appear, but the implication of what is said in 1477 may well be that the *Purification* was not at that time being played annually as part of the cycle.

The Register itself undoubtedly throws some light on the situation. It was evidently not part of the main scribe's plan to include the *Purification* in the volume at all, and the best way of explaining this is to repeat in part what has been said above, in the Note on play XIV, regarding the scribe's procedure when he was not supplied with copy for a given play. His usual practice was to leave a series of blank pages, the first few of which he headed with the name of the gild which had failed to produce the expected play. No such provision was made between nos. XVI and XVIII, where there is only a single leaf (f.74), originally blank. From this it has been inferred that not only was the Register compiled before the Masons changed their affiliation from *Herod* (see no. XVI) to the *Purification* in 1477, but also, as has been hinted above, that the *Purification* was not felt to be a regular component of the cycle when the Register was being compiled. It has however been suggested that the unexplained sequence of blank leaves between plays XIV and XV (see the Note on XIV) may have been vaguely intended by the scribe to receive a play which was perhaps defunct whilst he was at work, but possibly liable to revival at an undeterminable date in the future. It might indeed have been expected that Clerke would have inserted the play in that position when he came to copy it a century later. However, the loss of two blank leaves between the present ff.58 and 59 could have occurred by his time, reducing the available space and causing him to look elsewhere in the manuscript. For further discussion of these points see R. Beadle and P. Meredith, *LSE*, NS, xi (1980), pp. 52–3.

Though Clerke may have been unable or was for some reason unwilling to enter the *Purification* in the blank space between plays XIV and XV (the end of whatever the Tilers were playing as no. XIV was being called for registration in 1567; see the Note thereon), he indicated where the play was to be found, as follows. On f.74, the blank between plays XVI and XVIII, in the position where No XVII would rightly have come, he wrote:

> Hatmakers Maysons and Laborers / purificacio Marie | the Laborers is assigned to bryng furth this pagyant | It is entryd in the Latter end of this booke / next after the Sledmen or | palmers / and it begynnyth (by the preest) All myghty god in heven | so hye /

Though this cross-reference (the first word of which was written at a different time from the rest) indicates where play XVII belongs, and where it is to be found, the matter unfortunately does not rest there. Folio 74 is a palimpsest, and the visible inscription by Clerke is in part over the erasure of an earlier inscription, also attributed to Clerke by Peter Meredith (*LSE*, NS, xii (1981) p.257). It is partially recoverable under ultra-violet light, and reads:

> Maria et Joseph offerentes. . . . . .templo. . . | . . .templo. . . . . .Symeon. . . . . .in | vlnas suas Anna prophetissa et angelus /| The Maysons and Laborers bryngyth | furth this matter. It is nowe broght | forth by the Comon Chambre of York | This matter lakkys & it begynnyth almyghty god in heven | so hee / by the preest

It is not yet clear what construction is to be placed on the vernacular part of this inscription, and as it is an issue which bears more on the histories of the bodies concerned than on the text, no further discussion is offered here. It is however clear that the erased description of the play here relates to the text actually registered by Clerke, and contrasts with the description of the episode in the *Ordo Paginarum* of 1415. In 1415 the cast included a midwife and the two sons of Simeon, characters who do not appear in the registered version of 1567, which in its turn has a priest and an angel not mentioned in 1415. The play was either substantially revised or completely replaced at some time in the intervening period.

Turning to the text itself, the number of very obvious corrections necessary where the rhymes betray scribal errors indicates that the *Purification* has reached us in a state of what appears to be considerable corruption. It is possible that the dialect or the orthography of the exemplar were, by Clerke's day, old-fashioned or difficult, but, as hinted in the remarks below concerning the versification, much of what is to be found wanting may go back to the actual composition of the piece. Even where corruption is not indicated by loss of rhyme, the apparently defective sense or rhythm of a great many lines invites improvement, an invitation not resisted by Herttrich, Holthausen and Kölbing in the articles referred to in the Textual Notes. The silence of the Textual Notes on this play does not imply that the editor believes all the manuscript readings to be readily defensible.

Versification
A medley of stanza-forms to be found, including passages in quatrains and octaves, together with a variety of variable stanzas of a somewhat *ad*

hoc character. A nine-line stanza, $abab_4c_2ddd_3c_2$, and a tail-rhyme stanza, aaabcccb, appear frequently. The play may have been patched together from different sources, but it is to be feared that mere ineptitude is the likelier explanation.

Heading
There are no running-titles, but Clerke has given as the heading in a large ornamental script 'hatmakers Masons & laborers'. The presence of the Hatmakers in this heading remains to be explained. The same word was not written at the same time as the rest of the inscription in Clerke's cross-reference on f.74 (see above).

XVIII The Flight into Egypt

Text
Some 24 lines scattered between lines 37 and 229 of the play have parallels in play XV of the Towneley cycle. Herttrich, *Studien zu den York Plays,* p. 6, prints the corresponding passages; cf. England and Pollard, *The Towneley Plays,* pp. 160–5.

Near the beginning John Clerke wrote 'This matter is mayd of newe after anoþer form', but it was later deleted. The marginal observation by a later hand near line 33, 'Maria ad huc' is obscure; Mary's speech, which begins on the recto of f.75 appears to continue uninterruptedly on the verso of the leaf.

Between plays XVIII and XIX the main scribe left a blank leaf, the recto of which Clerke later headed 'Mylners'. This has been deleted. As far as is known, the Millers never had any connection with either of these plays.

Versification
The twelve-line stanza $ababcc_4dde_2fef_3$ is not found anywhere else in the cycle. The stanza formed by lines 37–50 has two extra 'ab' lines, and 231 is an extra line in the final stanza.

Running-title
'The Marchallis,-es'. The Marshals were farriers, dealing with all aspects of the management of horses.

XIX The Slaughter of the Innocents

Text
It appears from John Clerke's note at the head of the blank page preceding the one on which the play begins (f.79'), that the registered version of the *Slaughter of the Innocents* was by his day obsolete, or at least became so whilst the manuscript was in his hands: 'This matter of the gyrdlers agreyth not with the Coucher in no poynt, it begynnyth, Lysten lordes vnto my lawe'. As a coucher was invariably a large volume it would appear that he was referring to the Register itself. He may well have perceived that the Girdlers had a new play whilst 'keeping the Register'

at the first station during a performance, and noted the *incipit*. It is
worth remarking that the extant text, apart from the insertion of the
first speaker's name, shows no evidence of correction or annotation by
any later hand, in spite of some glaring deficiencies in the text. There is
a line missing after 193, and character-designations are wanting at lines
90, 91, 223, 274 and 276. The speeches beginning at lines 167 and 176
have been assigned respectively to I and II Consolator, but Herod's
remarks from 163 onwards are clearly addressed to the Milites, and the
designations are therefore corrected here. (For the term 'Consolator' see
the Note on play XI, above.) Lines 63–9 are obscure, and probably
corrupt. They are printed as they stand in the manuscript, apart from a
rhyme emendation.

Versification
The eight-line stanza, ababcaac, with three stresses to the line, is not
found anywhere else in the cycle.

Running-title
'The Girdillers (Gyrdillers) and Naylers (Nayllers)'. Both gilds special-
ized in the manufacture of a variety of small metal objects. As well as the
studded belts from which they took their name, the Girdlers also made
such miscellaneous things as dog-collars, book-clasps and decorative
bullions.

XX Christ and the Doctors

Text
The plays on this subject from the Coventry and Chester cycles and in
the Towneley manuscript all show in varying degrees the influence of a
Christ and the Doctors play which probably originated in York. The
relationships have been examined by Greg in *Bibliographical and Textual
Problems*, chapter III, and *Studies in the Chester Cycle*, pp. 101–20. Greg
believed that the extant York play preserves the piece in its most original
form and that the Towneley version, which for the most part runs
parallel to York from line 73 onwards, was 'copied from a close relative
of Y, possibly the very "original" in the hands of the Sporiers and
Lorimers of York from which Y also derived, more probably from a
defective copy of the same' (*Bibliographical and Textual Problems*, pp. 87,
93–4, 100). The Chester and Coventry versions differ substantially, but
contain lines and phrases from the York ancestor. Towneley (*T* in the
Textual Notes) throws light on difficulties in the extant York text and
may preserve early features not recorded in the registered copy, e.g.
stage-directions at lines 48+ and 192+ (Y 72+, 204+) and an
extra-metrical line in Latin at 86+ (Y 114+); see England and Pollard,
The Towneley Plays, no. XIV. A substantial contrast between York and
Towneley resides in the treatment of the Decalogue (Y 145–92, T 117–
76), where Towneley has a different version of the last eight command-
ments, derived from *Speculum Christiani:* see A. C. Cawley, *LSE*, NS, viii
(1975), pp. 137–40, showing that the exemplar from which Towneley
was derived was not necessarily, as Greg believed, defective.

An odd feature of the York text concerns the character-designations. At line 129 the characters previously designated 'Magister' all become 'Doctor', though they are undoubtedly the same persons. Towneley has 'Magister' throughout. At the end of the York play the scribe, exceptionally, copied a list of the *dramatis personae* mentioning three doctors. At line 65 II Magister points out that he and his fellows are 'doctours' as well as masters.

No. XX attracted relatively little attention from later annotators: there is a marginal note at line 20, and a minor correction at 253–4.

Versification
The twelve-line stanza, abababab$_4$ cdcd$_3$, is found in eleven other plays in the cycle. Lines 217–40 consist of three four-stress alternately rhyming octaves, which Greg (*op.cit.* p. 87, n.2) believed to be fragments of the main stanza of the piece, the three-stress sections having dropped out after 224, 232 and 240. The sense, however, seems satisfactory, and the shorter stanzas are not ill-suited to the dramatic temperature of the episode.

Running-title
"The Sporiers and lorimers(-ymers): Both trades supplied metal objects connected with horses and riding, such as spurs, bits, bridles, harness and so forth.

XXI The Baptism

Text
The lacunae indicated by the metrical defects at lines 71ff. and 84ff., together with the main scribe's elaborate correction of his own work at the rubrication stage (lines 141–4), suggest that the copy for this play was difficult or defective. The main scribe also corrected himself in lines 52 and 131.

John Clerke's comment beneath the last line shows that the registered version of the *Baptism* was superseded in his time: 'This matter is newly mayd and devysed, wherof we haue no coppy regystred'. Earlier, he had corrected the surviving text, shown by: 'Her wantes a pece newely mayd for saynt John Baptiste' (near line 49), and his substitution of a word in line 101. 'Hic caret' at 71 and 'De nouo facto' at 84 are probably also his work, and may relate to the metrically unsound passages in these places. At line 59 it was apparently he who inserted an erroneous character-designation, later correcting himself.

Versification
The seven-line stanza, abab$_4$c$_2$b$_4$c$_2$ was also employed throughout plays XIV and XXV, and in the central section of play XV.

Running-title
'The Barbours'.

XXII The Temptation

Text
Apart from the 'stage-direction' added by John Clerke near line 91, play XXII has survived very much as it left the main scribe's pen. The scribe corrected his own work in lines 154 and 192.

Versification
The six-line stanza, $aaa_4b_2a_4b_2$ also appears in plays VI, XXXVIII and XLI.

Running-title
Originally 'The Smythis' throughout. A later hand has inserted 'Lokk' above the first instance, on f.95. A document of 1530 records an agreement of the (Black) smiths and Locksmiths to take joint responsibility for 'their pageants of Corpus Christi'. The plays referred to are no. XVIII and the present one, the Smiths having already officially combined with the Marshals to produce the Slaughter of the Innocents in 1480 (*REED: York,* pp. 123–4, 252).

XXIIA The Marriage at Cana

This play was never registered, though the main scribe knew of its existence and made provision for it by leaving a series of blank leaves (ff.97ᵛ–101ʳ) between nos. XXII and XXIII, two of which he headed 'The Vinters' (ff.98ᵛ and 99). In 1567 the civic authorities ordered that 'the Pageantes of Corpus christi suche as be not allready Registred shalbe with all convenyent spede be fayre wrytten by Iohn Clerke in the old Registre yerof viz. of Vyntenors the Archetricline . . .' (*REED: York,* p. 351). At some time Clerke was able to record what are probably the opening line-and-a-half of the play, perhaps because he heard them whilst 'keeping the Register' at the first station during a performance.

   In the *Ordo Paginarum* of 1415 a play attributed to the Vintners was described as follows: 'Jesus, Mary, the bridegroom with the bride, the steward with his servant with six jars of water when the water was turned into wine'. Both the *Ordo* and the second list of plays which accompanies it in the A/Y Memorandum Book agree in listing the *Marriage* between the *Baptism* (no. XXI) and the *Temptation* (no.XXII), whereas the Register has the events in their scriptural order. A series of guide-letters to the left of the descriptions of the three plays in the *Ordo* corrects the running-order (*REED: York,* pp. 19, 25; translation quoted from p. 705).

XXIII The Transfiguration

Text
The text of no. XXIII calls for little comment. The main scribe had some difficulty with the lineation and omitted a character-designation at line 145, which was supplied by a later hand. There are other minor additions by later hands at lines 13, 169 and 180.

Versification
The twelve-line stanza, ababab$_4$cdcd$_3$, is to be found in eleven other plays in the cycle.

Running-title
'The Curiours'. The Curriers were a secondary branch of the leather trade, engaged in the dressing and colouring of hides and skins.

XXIIIA Jesus in the House of Simon the Leper

This play was never registered, though the main scribe knew of it and left a series of blank leaves (ff.106^v–10^v) where it should appear. On f.107 he wrote 'The Ironmongers' at the top, and a later hand subsequently added the same words at the head of the preceding page, in an ornamental script. In 1567 the civic authorities announced that John Clerke should make copies of all the plays still missing from the Register, and included in the list was 'thyron mongars Marie Magdalene wasshyng the Lordes feete &c.' (*REED: York*, p. 351). At some time Clerke inserted beneath the main scribe's heading on f.107 a description of the missing episode. It has since been erased, but is legible with the assistance of ultra-violet light:

> This matter lakkes, videlicet:
> Jesus, et Symon leprosus rogans eum vt
> manducaret cum eo, duo discipuli, Maria
> Magdalena lauans pedes Jesu lacrimis et capillis
> suis tergens.

This description is derived almost verbatim from the one in the *Ordo Paginarum* of 1415: see *REED: York*, p. 20.

XXIV The Women Taken in Adultery / The Raising of Lazarus

Text
As is explained at the relevant points in the text, this play has considerable defects owing to the removal or loss of two leaves, the conjugate pair constituting the third and the sixth leaves of quire O. There is no indication in the manuscript of when this loss might have taken place, though it was evidently after the time when John Clerke had access to it (see below).

The *Ordo Paginarum* of 1415 and the second list of plays which accompanies it in the A/Y Memorandum Book show the *Woman Taken in Adultery* and the *Raising of Lazarus* as separate plays staged by different gilds, the first by the Plumbers and Pattenmakers (Plumbers only in the second list), the second by the Pouchmakers, Bottlemakers and Capmakers (Hartshorners only in the second list) (*REED: York*, pp. 20, 25). By the time the Register was compiled in the third quarter of the fifteenth century the two episodes are found as one play in the ownership of the 'Capmakers &c.', as the Register has it, but there are no documents known which show how or when this development took place. A vestige of the earlier circumstances appears at the head of f.112^v, where the scribe has inserted the title 'Lazare mortus' in red (after line 80), though the Lazarus episode does not begin until line 98. The metre of the piece is the same throughout (see below).

Marginalia at lines 50 ('Hic deficit') and 186 ('Nota quia non concordat' and 'novo addicio facto') are probably the work of John Clerke. The episode may well have been revised or rewritten by his time, a civic order of 1567 calling for the Cappers' 'original' to be 'examined with the Register & reformed', but the wording of the document is obscure (*REED: York*, p. 351).

Versification
The twelve-line stanza, abababab$_4$ cdcd$_3$, is used in eleven other plays in the cycle.

Running-title
The first two running-titles are 'The Cap(p)makers &c' (ff.111, 111^v) to the first of which Clerke has added 'and Hatmakers'. Subsequently, the main scribe wrote variously 'The Capperes' and 'The Cappemakers'. A document of 1569 records that the Hatmakers were from then on to be 'Likewyse contributories with the Cappers towardes bryngyngfurth of there pagyant of the play callyd Corpuscristy' (*REED: York*, p. 356).

XXV The Entry into Jerusalem

Text
There are various alterations, corrections and additions by later users of the manuscript. John Clerke added a character-designation at line 85, altered a word at 248 and altered the position of a line at 382. Stage-directions, or observations which read like stage-directions, were added by later hands at 287+ and 540+, and 'hic caret' inserted against 359.

Versification
The seven-line stanza abab$_4$c$_2$b$_4$c$_2$, is also found throughout plays XIV and XXI and in the central section of play XV.

Running-title
'The Skynners'. The Skinners dealt in and prepared the pelts, skins and furs of a large variety of animals, prior to dressing and manufacture into garments and objects.

XXVI The Conspiracy

Text
This is the first of a number of plays in the long alliterative line, and the manner in which the texts are presented changes in various ways at this point in the manuscript. The usual format of the single column of verse

is retained, but the long lines are in general divided between the second and third stressed words, the second half-line being copied beneath the first, with an initial capital letter. This division into half-lines has been ignored in the present edition, in order that the stanzas may be set out in the way in which they were conceived. The first 48 lines of no. XXVI occupy the last leaf of quire P, and the scribe attempted to rubricate what he had written according to the pattern used in the first half of the manuscript. Rhyme-brackets are employed, but owing to the new layout of the verse, they bear no relation to the real rhymes. With the beginning of quire Q (line 49, f.124) rhyme-bracketing is abandoned, and the red lines separating the speeches are drawn differently. This change of format holds for the rest of the manuscript, with exception of ff.180–7ᵛ (play XXXIII), where both the handwriting and the rubrication are in the manner of the early part of the volume.

Compared with some of the plays in the long alliterative line which follow, the text of no. XXVI is relatively well-preserved. Lines 247 to 254, however, appear unsatisfactory as to both sense and metre. The passage is here reproduced as it stands in the manuscript, a variety of conjectural reconstructions being possible. The intended assignment of speeches in this passage is not clear. A new speech appears to begin with line 252 and the main scribe indeed assigned it to 'Pilatus', but the name has been deleted by a later hand. The 'III Doctor' of line 251 appears nowhere else in the play. It is possible that Cayphas was originally intended, as he has not spoken since Pilate's rebuke at 209–10, and no further dialogue is assigned to him in the play as it stands.

The text attracted the attention of John Clerke and other later users of the manuscript. Character-designations have been added or altered at lines 1, 191 and 252, and a designation added by Clerke at 117 has been corrected, it appears, by another late hand. At lines 280 and 284 'Caret hic' has been written in the margin, and near the first instance Clerke has added 'Janitor & Judas', perhaps indicating a missing exchange between those two characters, though the text as it stands looks intact.

Versification
A fourteen-line stanza is used: abababab₄cdcccd₃. The same rhyme-scheme appears in play IX, where the line is scanned syllabically, and again in the alliterative form in play XXXI. Line 184a is best regarded as extra-metrical. It may be compared with lines 58 and 104, which have been overloaded by the introduction of colloquial interjections.

Running-title
'The Cutteleres'.

XXVII The Last Supper

Text
As is explained in the text, this play is defective owing to the removal or loss of a leaf from the manuscript, and some 53 lines are missing between lines 89 and 90. It is not possible to say precisely when the leaf disappeared, but it was probably after the time when the manuscript was

in John Clerke's hands, as he has noted defects elsewhere in the piece. Marginal notes near lines 1 and 187 suggest that revisions had taken place by the mid-sixteenth century. Clerke also added what appears to be an erroneous 'stage-direction', or observation about what was taking place in performance, at line 60+.

Versification
The twelve-line stanza, $ababab ab_4 cdcd_3$, is found in eleven other plays in the cycle.

Running-title
'The Baxter(e)s'.

XXVIII The Agony in the Garden and the Betrayal

Text
This play must have reached the main scribe in state of considerable confusion, and the lineation is often doubtful. Where Miss Toulmin Smith found 301 lines, the present edition has 306, but such is the confusion in the manuscript that alternatives are open to an editor in a number of places.

The deficiencies of the text as set down by the main scribe have since been augmented by the loss of a leaf, carrying away some 40 lines, between lines 42 and 43; see the note at that point. This leaf was conjugate with the one lost in the preceding play, as explained in the Note above and at XXVII 89. If the loss occurred whilst John Clerke or any other sixteenth-century annotator had the opportunity to note it, they did not do so.

The play was probably in one metre throughout when originally composed, and must have been made up of some 25 to 30 twelve-line stanzas in the long alliterative line, $ababab ab_4 cddc_3$. Only nine of those extant conform to this scheme, though several others may be restored with only minor adjustments to the manuscript lineation. The scribe or a predecessor made a revealing error between lines 142 and 144 (see 143, Textual Note) in copying an actor's cue into the verse. It is possible that the scribe himself was faced with the task of recompiling from loose papers containing actors' parts, or that he was copying from an exemplar where this process had been imperfectly carried out. (On the presence of a cue in another play, see the Note on no. XVI.) Several lines or groups of lines are displaced, misassigned or written confusedly in the manuscript, e.g. 168–72, 179–80, 206, 211, 236 and 247. The stanzaic pattern breaks down altogether between lines 198 and 244, and the sense is suspect at several places in this vicinity. Particularly problematic is line 247, which is not part of the stanza where it occurs, and nor is it attributable to Jesus, who is speaking. In this edition it is taken as a prose interruption by Cayphas, who is sending Judas from his own group to Jesus's. Later, line 304 suggests that the two groups have been standing at some distance from one another.

Given the palpable and extensive shortcomings of the text of no. XXVIII, it is surprising that later hands do not appear more often than they do with marginal comments and corrections. Possibly 'De nouo facto' against line 1 was sufficient. 'Hic caret' appears near line 199, at the beginning of the long metrically defective passage mentioned above. The hand which added a character-designation at 278 was probably John Clerke's.

Versification
See above. The predominant stanza is a twelve-line form abab-abab$_4$cddc$_3$, using the long alliterative line, but there are a number of corrupt or variant stanzas together with a long passage where no regular metre is discernible. The twelve-line stanza occurs nowhere else in the cycle.

Running-title
'The Cordewaneres'. Cordwainers were makers of leather shoes.

XXIX Christ before Annas and Caiaphas

Text
The text of play XXIX is scarcely better preserved than its immediate predecessor in the cycle. Once again the scribe's copy must have been poor or confusing, but here later users of the manuscript have taken steps to correct and supplement what was originally written. The metre is also in a poor state of preservation, and Miss Toulmin Smith abandoned the attempt to distinguish stanzas after line 87 of her edition. The sudden and apparently arbitrary variations in line-length in the early part of the play were particularly confusing to the scribe. The present edition disagrees with Miss Toulmin Smith's as to the lineation in several places, yielding 395 lines as against her 398.

Numerous additions and alterations show that the text was examined quite closely by John Clerke and probably by others in the sixteenth century. For instance, character-designations have been supplied or improved at lines 1, 199, 200–7, 242, 262, 272 and 394. 'Hic caret' appears in several places (75–6, 153, 274–5) and in one of these instances and once elsewhere Clerke has supplied what he considered were missing parts of the text (75 6, 307). An observation couched like a stage-direction appears in Clerke's hand near line 23. The play has been the object of much textual criticism. Passages where the sense or the metre, or both, are particularly difficult will be found at lines 18–26, 35–6, 125 and 266–75, along with references to more or less drastic proposals for improvement.

Two points call for more detailed comment. At line 87 the scribe's character-designation refers to the woman who taunts Peter as 'I Mulier', though subsequent speeches are merely designated 'Mulier'. Though Matt. xxvi 69–71 refers to two women, and line 133 of the play implies the presence of more than one woman, there appears to have been only one speaking part. An addition to the description of the play in the *Ordo Paginarum* of 1415 has the expression 'mulier accusans Petrum' (see below). At lines 178–9 a different problem arises. Once the character-designations have been correctly established it is clear that a speciality of staging is involved. III and IV Miles are 'without' and I and II Miles 'within'. The passage may be compared with another arising at XXXI 59, where a similar situation occurs, and the scribe has succeeded in representing the author's intentions correctly.

Versification
Lines 1–169 are mostly cross-rhyming quatrains with either three or four stressed and alliterating syllables to the line, but there are several places where corruption is evident, or the intended metre is difficult to discern (e.g. 18–22, 31–2, 45–51). At line 170 the metre changes to a long-lined alliterative version of the twelve-line stanza used commonly elsewhere in the cycle, ababababₐcdcdₐ. This continues to the end of the play, but again with patches of irregularity or corruption. It will be noticed that the change of metre coincides with a turn in the action. Lines 1–169 deal with the High Priests' grievances against Jesus and Peter's denial. With line 170 the soldiers take Jesus to Cayphas's 'hall' and the trial scene begins. The description of a play attributed to the Bowers and Fletchers in the *Ordo Paginarum* of 1415 originally read 'Bowers and Fletchers: Jesus, Annas, Caiaphas, and four Jews striking and buffeting', to which has been added by a different or later hand 'Jesus, Peter, the woman accusing Peter, and Malchus' (After *REED: York*, p. 706 (translation); cf. p. 21). It is possible that some connection exists between the addition to the *Ordo* and the passage preceding the change of metre in the play.

Running-title
'The Bowers and Fleccher(e)s'. These two crafts were connected in the manufacture of bows and arrows, the name 'Fletchers' referring in particular to the feathered flights of arrows.

XXX Christ before Pilate 1: The Dream of Pilate's Wife

Text
In common with several other plays in this part of the manuscript, no. XXX probably owes its poor state of preservation to the scribe's struggles with difficult or confusing copy. The lineation, in particular, was the cause of many problems, and although Miss Toulmin Smith made most of the necessary corrections, further suggestions are embodied in the present edition, giving a total of 548 lines as against her 546. A number of lines are best regarded as extra-metrical (see below). Lines appear to be missing after 85, 107, 127, 135, 419, 431 and 529, and lines 185–95 are probably the relics of two stanzas. The main scribe added line 135 later, but otherwise seems to have done little to correct his work. Character-designations were supplied by later hands at 224, 233, 236, 330, 336 and 352, but they remained the object of confusion at 28, 30 and 110. Alterations or additions to the dialogue occur in lines 9, 283 and 514, and 'hic caret' was written near line 371. Many of the later insertions are probably to be attributed to John Clerke. Amongst the places where the sense remains unclear are lines 50–3, 68–72, 486 and 539.

Two other points call for comment. The character introduced at line 115 is at first designated 'Secundus Filius' and after line 180 as 'Primus Filius'; at 389 he is 'Junior Filius'. One and the same individual is undoubtedly concerned throughout, and he is simply designated 'Filius' in this edition. The second point concerns the stage-direction at line 370, the only original one in English in the cycle. The main scribe probably mistook it for part of the dialogue.

Versification
Two varieties of stanza are found in the play. The first part, to line 157, is in a nine-line stanza employing the long alliterative line, abab₁bcbbc₃. It is found nowhere else in the cycle. From line 158, where the Devil enters, there is a second nine-line stanza, abab₁cdddc₃, also in the long alliterative line, and also not to be found elsewhere in the cycle. Lines 185–95 do not conform to this pattern, and may be fragments of the complete stanza. A number of lines cannot be accommodated within the regular metrical scheme, and have been regarded as extra-metrical: 157a, 210, 255, 265, 370, 526.

The change of metre at line 158 may have some bearing on the fact that the play attributed to the Tapiters and Couchers in the *Ordo Paginarum* of 1415 was described in somewhat laconic terms: 'Jesus, Pilate, Annas, Caiaphas, two councillors, and four Jews accusing Jesus' (after *REED: York*, p. 707 (translation); cf. p. 21). As Miss Toulmin Smith remarked (pp. xxiv–xxv, n.1) 'It is curious that no mention is made . . . of dame Percula, Pilate's wife, nor any of the other personages in the first scenes, which must have been prominent and popular'. The silence of the *Ordo* on this point, and the discrepancy between its description and the extant text as regards the 'four Jews', are facts sufficient to suggest that the play in the Register is the result of a substantial revision or a complete rewriting of the episode after 1415 and before 1463–77.

Running-title
'The Tapite(e)res and Coucher(e)s (Cowchers)'. The Tapiters worked figured cloths, especially counterpanes and wall-hangings, and the Couchers made bedding and the ornamental hangings which surrounded beds.

XXXI Christ before Herod

Text
The text of play XXXI is in a poor state of preservation, and its metrical irregularity poses special problems for the editor. The commonest stanza is one of fourteen lines, though quatrains also appear frequently. There are on the other hand numerous irregular or variant stanza-forms, most only occurring once and many of them perhaps relics of an original fourteener. How this state of affairs came about it is not possible to say, but a combination of revision and careless transmission may well have contributed to the confusion. The lineation is very doubtful in several places, and there are alternative ways of constituting a number of the stanzas. Consequently, the present edition offers a play running to

423 lines, whilst Miss Toulmin Smith's gives 406, our main disagree-
ments being over lines 47–50, 243–6 and 261–4. There is no evidence
that the main scribe went back and attempted to improve upon what he
had written, but there are a few alterations and additions by later hands.
John Clerke added an observation expressed like a stage-direction after
line 42, and his hand also appears elsewhere (196, 201, 202). Other
alterations occur at lines 215 and 218, and a series of marginal
annotations (mostly 'Nota' and 'Hic') is found between lines 308 and 334.

Two points call for further comment. At line 347, where Herod's sons
speak in unison, the words 'Al chylder' are written as if they are part of
the dialogue. Miss Toulmin Smith rightly decided that they were
(though, exceptionally, in English) a character-designation. The same
words are supplied with the same function at line 333 in this edition, an
unassigned speech where the boys also speak in unison. The second
point arises at lines 375–6, where the Duke formally calls upon persons
with a grievance against Jesus to appear. The text at this point is corrupt,
and to the right John Clerke has written 'Post Rex'. It is not clear what
this signifies, but the situation might be compared with that in play
XXXIII, at line 269, where the Beadle is called upon in a stage-direction
to recite an announcement phrase by phrase after Annas, 'post Annam'.

Versification
About half the play is in a fourteen-line stanza, usually abab-
abab$_4$cdcccd$_3$, in the long alliterative line, and this may have been the
original metre of the piece as a whole. The same stanza is also found in
no. XXVI and (in a non-alliterative form) in no. IX. Interspersed
amongst the fourteen-line stanzas are fourteen cross-rhyming quatrains,
some with three and some with four stresses to the line. The remainder
of the play can be resolved into a variety of stanza-forms, only one of
which occurs more than once, abab$_1$cdcccd$_3$ (four instances). These and
other irregular stanzas have the appearance of being fragments of the
predominant fourteener.

Running-title
'The Littisteres (Lysteres, Lyttisters).' The Litsters were dyers of cloth.

XXXII The Remorse of Judas

Text
Like several of the immediately preceding plays in the cycle, no. XXXII
is preserved in a somewhat confused and corrupt condition. Once again
the main scribe must have been faced with difficult and unsatisfactory
copy, and a modern editor can expect only limited success in reproduc-
ing the text in print. Although the present edition arrives at the same
total number of lines as Miss Toulmin Smith's, the lineation differs from
hers in a number of places (see at 13, 27, 47, 124–5 and 326). Elsewhere,
lines have been lost (see at 238+, 281+ and 325+), but there are on the
other hand some which cannot be fitted into any metrical scheme (124,
325–6, 342–3). Though two main stanza-forms may be distinguished,
interspersed amongst them are passages in a variety of metres.

There are a number of corrections and marginal observations by later hands. John Clerke supplied parts of the text at lines 28 and 110, and attempted to alter the layout at line 260. Near line 128 he made a series of marginal observations suggesting that material known to him was missing at this point. A note of similar intent but by another later hand appears against lines 153–4 ('Hic caret loquela magna et diversa'), and at 361, where a later hand first wrote 'Hic caret', Clerke added 'loquela'. These inscriptions indicate either that the shortcomings of the text as originally registered were noted at an early period, or that the play had by the time of the annotators been revised to some extent. A deleted 'Caret hic' also appears against line 238 (the next line is missing) and 'Hic caret' at 339 (note the apparently extra-metrical lines just below, 342–3).

Versification
Lines 55–128 and 334 to 371 (excepting 352–63) are mostly in an eight-line stanza, $abab_4cdcd_3$, using the long alliterative line. Lines 143–324 (excepting 284–302) and 372–82 are in an eleven-line stanza, $abab_4cdcdede_3$, likewise in the long alliterative line. Neither of the two main stanzas of the play are found elsewhere in the cycle. The remainder of the play consists of a variety of stanzaic forms. There are a number of quatrains, two instances of an eight-line stanza $abab_4cccd_3$, four instances of a seven-line stanza $ababcbc_3$ and several other forms which occur only once. As Miss Toulmin Smith remarked, given the degree of corruption in the text and the variousness of the metres, no. XXXII 'must have undergone some vicissitudes'.

Running-title
'The Co(o)kis and Watirleder(e)s, (-ars)'. The Waterleaders were responsible for the drawing and distribution of fresh water around the city before piped water became available.

XXXIII Christ before Pilate 2: The Judgement

Text
Play XXXIII exhibits markedly less textual and metrical corruption than its immediate predecessors in the cycle. The appearance of the main scribe's handwriting and the pattern of rubrication (including the use of rhyme-brackets) share the characteristics of an earlier part of the manuscript, particularly play XI and its immediate vicinity (see the Note on XI for details). It is clear that no. XXXIII was copied at a different time from the other plays in the Passion section. Its main defect is the lacuna, occasioned by the loss of a leaf, between lines 438–9 and 440, and the missing material has been discussed at that point in the text. It is not possible to say for sure when the loss took place, but it is likely to have been after the time when the manuscript was in the hands of John Clerke, who worked over the text and noted some less major defects. The main scribe made some attempt to check his work at the rubrication stage, correcting an error concerning lines 382 and 383, and the repetition of line 444. He missed the loss of a line after 32 and left errors and omissions in the character-designations (33, 108, supplied by

Clerke, 138, 146, 204). John Clerke later found a word to add in the text at line 264 and also added an observation expressed as a stage-direction at 443+.

Versification
A twelve-line stanza, using the long alliterative line, appears throughout: abab$_4$bcbc$_3$dccd$_3$. It is not found elsewhere in the cycle.

Running-title
'The Tillemakers, (Tyllemakers)'. In five places this original running-title has been deleted and 'Mylners' substituted by John Clerke. The history of this entire episode of the Passion, and of its affiliations with various gilds, is uncommonly complicated. The documentary evidence has recently been discussed in an illuminating article by Peter Meredith: see *LSE*, NS, xi (1980), pp. 59–73. In the first surviving documentary references (1417–22), the events of the extant play, together with other incidents which have not survived, are found as separate plays, each owned by a different gild. Between this time and the period when the Register was compiled (1463–77) a single play came into being, though exact details of its scope, and the date at which it took its present form are not clear. The initial act of amalgamation may however be dated to 1422–3. The new play appears to have developed through more than one phase, and as it did so it came increasingly under the control of the Tilemakers, to whom the other gilds originally concerned were or became contributory. The situation reflected in the Register, with the Tilemakers having exclusive responsibility for the actual production of the play, prevailed until 1515, when they were described as 'ruynous and dekayed'. In that year the Millers took the play over, a change later indicated again in Clerke's alterations to the running-titles.

XXXIV The Road to Calvary

Text
Herttrich, *Studien zu den York Plays,* pp. 4–5, pointed out that the following lines of York XXXIV also appear in play XXII in the Towneley collection, and prints the relevant passages in parallel: 106–15, 126–35, 190–9, 216–9, 226–49; cf. England and Pollard, *The Towneley Plays,* pp. 252–7.

As is explained in a note at the relevant point in the text, a leaf has been lost or removed from the manuscript between lines 141 and 142. It was conjugate with the one missing in play XXXIII (see the preceding Note). Though John Clerke and perhaps other early users of the manuscript made minor corrections to the text, no indication of a missing leaf was given, if the loss had occurred by the mid-sixteenth century. The passage which follows the lacuna is unsatisfactory as to both sense and metre, and lines 142–9 have been printed as they stand in the manuscript. The surviving part of the text is much better preserved than is the case with most other plays in the manuscript dealing with the Passion. A line has dropped out after line 11, and the character-designations were later corrected at lines 206 and 243, probably by John Clerke.

Versification
Apart from the first two stanzas and lines 142–9 (see above), the play is in a ten-line stanza, aa₁b₃aa₁bcbcb₃. It occurs nowhere else in the cycle, though the stanza of no. IV is similarly shaped, but with different rhymes. Lines 1 to 16 are two eight-line stanzas, abab₁c₂dd₁c₃, in the long alliterative line, also not to be found elsewhere in the cycle.

Running-title
'The Shearmen'. The Shearmen were a branch of the cloth trade, engaged in 'shearing' the nap from woollen cloths.

XXXV The Crucifixion

Text
No. XXXV is in a comparatively good state of preservation as far as the dialogue is concerned, but the relationship between the actions which it implies and the character-designations had deteriorated by the main scribe's time, and remains doubtful in places. At lines 183–4 the main scribe corrected his own work, adding material earlier missed out in the right-hand margin. John Clerke also gave attention to the text and made a curious addition at line 264, the end of Jesus's second long speech in the play, quoting the last two lines of the *first* long speech by the same character (lines 59–60). It is possible that the similarity of lines 58 and 264 caused him to confuse the two speeches.

In the stanza composed of lines 97–108 it is particularly difficult to establish the relationship between the actions and the characters who perform them, the character-designations in the manuscript being confused. The present edition follows the arrangement suggested by J. P. R. Wallis, *MLR*, xii (1917), pp. 494–5, who glosses as follows:

> I Miles is clearly in charge of the party: he orders the other three to bring the cross (78) and then stations himself at the head, whence he directs the work. II Miles takes the right hand (81–2), III Miles the left (83) and IV Miles the legs (85) . . . the action runs thus: the knight in charge calls the party to the work in hand (97). II Miles takes the right hand and brings it to the bore (98–100). The leader bids him fix it (101) which is done (102–4). The first knight turns to him who has charge of the left arm (III Miles) and asks him how matters stand with him (105–6), who answers that the left hand is 'a foote and more' short of the 'bore' (107–8).

A minor feature of the text which remains to be explained is the 'etcetera' found at the end of the last line of the play.

Versification
The twelve-line stanza, ababababab₄cdcd₃, is found in eleven other plays in the cycle.

Title, running-title
No. XXXV is one of the few plays in the manuscript to bear a title; it was probably carried over from the exemplar. The running-title is 'The Pynneres (-ares)', but in the first instance on f.195 the words 'and paynters' have been added by John Clerke. A document of 1422 records

that a play of 'The Stretching Out and Nailing of Christ', performed by the Painters and Stainers, was being amalgamated with 'The Raising of Christ on the Mountain', for which the Pinners and Latteners were responsible. The latter two gilds were to have principal charge of the new play, with the former pair as financial contributors. (For the document proposing the amalgamation, with details of why it should take place, see *REED: York*, pp. 37–8 and 722–4.) The Pinners made small metal objects, mostly with sharp points, such as pins, fishhooks and buckles.

XXXVI The Death of Christ

Text
A. Hohlfeld, *Anglia*, xi (1889), pp. 254–5, pointed out that lines 114–5 and 117 of play XXXVI are paralleled in the Towneley play on the same subject. See England and Pollard, *The Towneley Plays*, p. 275, lines 555–7. The text of the play as a whole is fairly well preserved, though some passages remain which resist acceptable emendation: see lines 82–4 and 158. An oddity which has been corrected throughout from line 352 is the main scribe's character-designation 'Nichomedis' for the usual 'Nichodemus'. 'Hic caret' was written by a later hand against line 272, but nothing discernible in the manuscript appears to be wrong in the vicinity. John Clerke supplied a character-designation at line 75 and a missing line (126). His 'for why' against line 254 is possibly an attempt to substitute for line 256, which is metrically irregular, but the sense is not improved; cf. line 243.

Versification
The thirteen-line stanza, ababbcbc₄deee₂d₃, employing the long alliterative line, is very similar but not identical to the stanza of no. XLV.

Title and running-title
The play has a title, an uncommon feature in the manuscript, probably carried over from the exemplar. The running-title is 'The Bocheres (Boocheres)'.

XXXVII The Harrowing of Hell

Text
Another copy of this play exists in the Towneley manuscript, and its readings (*T* in the Textual Notes) occasionally assist with difficulties in the York text. The two copies are substantially the same. There is a detailed comparison in W. R. Cozart's unpublished dissertation *The Northern Middle English Harrowing of Hell Plays of the York and Towneley Cycles*, pp. 144–53.

The leaf containing lines 34 to 66 (f.208) is a singleton substituted for a cancel, but the text appears to be unaffected and the substitution was probably the result of mismanagement on the scribe's part. The scribe checked his work whilst filling in the rubrication, and finding line 253 inadvertently repeated, deleted it.

John Clerke probably added many of the later marginalia and corrections appearing in the manuscript: see at lines 1, 36+, 195–6. His hand certainly appears in lines 242 and 244 with corrections to the text, and near 384 he added an observation expressed as a stage-direction. Against line 211 he made a marginal comment to the effect that a new speech was wanting at that point, but it has been deleted. Inconsistent character-designations amongst the devils, however, were not cleared up. The York dialogue and the Towneley readings indicate that I Diabolus is called 'Ribald' and II Diabolus 'Belsabub', the latter name also appearing as an alternative designation at line 109 and thereafter.

Versification
The twelve-line stanza, abababab$_4$cdcd$_3$, is found in eleven other plays in the cycle.

Running-title
'The Sadiller(e)s'.

XXXVIII The Resurrection

Text
A variant copy of this play appears in the Towneley manuscript, and in the passages where it runs parallel to York, T may be used to throw light on the York text. For the Towneley text see England and Pollard, *The Towneley Plays*, pp. 306–25, with comparative remarks on York and Towneley on pp. xviii–xx. Broadly speaking, T runs parallel to Y from just before the entry of the Centurion (Y31) to the end, at which point T has an additional 76 lines dealing with the appearance of Jesus to Mary Magdalene in the garden. This is the subject of the following play in the York cycle, and there are no parallels. The main differences in detail between Y and T are: after Y42, T has 25 lines not in Y, an extension of the soliloquy by the Centurion; after Y186, T has 122 lines not in Y, consisting first of a few more lines of conversation amongst the soldiers, but mostly of an address to mankind by the risen Jesus; from Y187, where Y merely distinguishes the three Marys numerically, the rubrics in T distinguish them as Mary Magdalene, Mary the mother of James and Mary Salome; and at Y225, where a single 'childe' appears at the sepulchre, T mentions 'two . . . /In whyte clothyng'. It is interesting to note that Y and T have a corrupt passage in common: Y294–8 must be the relic of a stanza (here printed as it appears in the manuscript) and T is likewise defective at the corresponding point.

John Clerke and perhaps others have paid close attention to the text of no. XXXIX. Clerke was certainly responsible for the character-designation supplied at line 431, for elucidating the main scribe's stage-direction at 186+ and for attempting to provide for the line missing after 267 (the T reading proves more satisfactory). He may also have been involved in other alterations and additions: the supply of character-designations left wanting by the main scribe at lines 1, 175 and 345; dialogue at 52 and 163; 'hic deficit' near 68 and 254 (deleted), though nothing appears to be wrong in the immediate vicinities, and T preserves similar readings.

At line 189 'Memorandum' was inserted later, but again the purpose is obscure, though it may be significant that T has between Y186 and 187 the long passage spoken by the risen Jesus, of which Y has no trace. The fact that this passage in T continues uninterruptedly in the same metre as used in Y has led to the suggestion that Jesus's speech was once part of the York Play (see England and Pollard, *The Towneley Plays,* p. xix). Near line 395 is what appears to be an early instance of the term 'stet', but what it refers to is not clear.

Versification
The six-line stanza, $aaa_4b_2a_4b_2$ is also found in plays VI, XXII and XLI.

Running-title
'The Carpenteres'.

XXXIX Christ's Appearance to Mary Magdalene

Text
The text calls for little comment. A later hand wrote 'hic deficit' near line 85, but it is not clear what this refers to. A scrawled inscription by a later hand beneath the last line of the play cannot now be read.

Versification
The bulk of the play is in octaves with alternate rhymes, some stanzas with three and some with four accents to the line. Exceptions are: lines 17–21, perhaps a fragment of an octave; lines 30–41 and 50–61, which are in a twelve-line stanza $abababab cdcd_1$; see the discussion by Miller, *MLN,* xxxv (1920), pp. 379–80. For comparable metres elsewhere in the cycle see plays VIII, XLII, XLVII and the latter part of XII.

Running-title
Play XXXIX ends well down f.223^v, which is the last page of quire xxviij^{ti}, and play XL begins on f.224, the first page of quire xxix^{ti}. The scribe here departs from his usual habit of leaving up to three blank leaves between plays, and this fact is probably at the bottom of the series of apparent errors which plagues the running-titles, and therefore to some extent our knowledge of the ownership of plays XXXIX and XL. The running-title 'The Wynedraweres' was originally inserted by the main scribe not only at the head of each page of no. XXXIX, but also throughout no. XL, *The Supper at Emmaus.* The impression given by the Register may be interpreted in two ways. Taking into account the anomalous disposition of the two plays in relation to one another, without the usual gap between, there is the suggestion that XXXIX and XL are all one play in the ownership of the Winedrawers. On the other hand, it may be that the absence of the usual gap was not a problem to the main scribe and later users of the manuscript, in which case it appears that two plays were attributed to the Winedrawers at the time the Register was compiled. There is no documentary evidence from the period of registration either to confirm or to dispel either of these

impressions, and information about the later history of both episodes is extremely scanty. The *Ordo Paginarum* of 1415, and the second list of plays which accompanies it, are however clear in distinguishing two plays, as follows: *Ordo:* 'Winedrawers: Jesus, Mary Magdalene with spices'; 'Brokers, Woolpackers, (Wadmen) (*added later*): Jesus, Luke and Cleophas dressed as pilgrims'. Second list: 'Winedrawers: The appearance of Christ to Mary Magdalene'; 'Woolpackers: The appearance of Christ to the pilgrims' (After *REED: York* pp. 708, 711 (translations); cf. pp. 22–3, 26. Both entries in the *Ordo* have alterations by later hands). Apart from what is found in the Register, there appears to be no other information concerning the Winedrawers and their play of Jesus and Mary Magdalene. As regards the Woolbrokers' play of Christ and the pilgrims, the Register has in no. XL a play on the subject, but no mention of any of the gilds connected with it in the *Ordo*. For the period between the *Ordo* and the compilation of the Register there is a single documentary reference from 1428, mentioning the pageant-money of the 'Broggos lanarum' (*REED: York,* p. 46), but nothing is said of what play, if any, the Woolbrokers were at that time performing.

It is possible that the main scribe was correct in inserting 'Wine-drawers' as running-title to play XXXIX and to play XL, and that that gild was indeed performing both plays, or conceivably an amalgamation of the two, at the time when the Register was compiled. This seems, however, a remote possibility. The ground taken here, and it is admittedly hypothetical, is that the Winedrawers were responsible for no. XXXIX only, and that no. XL was in fact still the responsibility of the Woolpackers and the Woolbrokers, as it had been in 1415, and probably in 1428. The main scribe was therefore mistaken in using 'Winedrawers' as running-title in no. XL, perhaps having been misled by its apparent contiguity to no. XXXIX. His mistake proved to be a source of confusion to later users of the manuscript, principally John Clerke, who noted changes in the ownership of no. XL as if they had happened to no. XXXIX.

The head of the first page of no. XXXIX (f.221ʳ) is a palimpsest reflecting changes in the ownership of play XL. At an unknown date prior, probably, to 1535 the Sledmen took over responsibility for no. XL, presumably from the Woolpackers, Woolbrokers and Woadmen. The words 'The Sledmen' and 'Sledmens' (now erased, but visible under ultra-violet light) and 'Sledmen' (now deleted) all appear around the heading of the first page of no. XXXIX, which originally read 'The Wynedraweres.' The position of this heading is now occupied by the following inscription in John Clerke's hand, since erased, but still legible: 'Wevers assygnyd in / Aᵒdni Mˡ Dˡⁱⁱʲᵗⁱ William / Cowplande then maior'. The change in ownership of no. XL, evidently from the Sledmen to the Weavers, was only temporary, and by 1554 the Weavers were once again bringing forth their usual play, no. XLV. To the right of Clerke's inscription is the word 'palmers' in another later hand. This appears to refer to the subject matter of no. XL, traditionally known as the 'peregrini' or pilgrims to Emmaus.

For further discussion and documentation of the ownership of play XL, see the next Note. For a different explanation of the annotations at the beginning of no. XXXIX see P. Meredith, *LSE*, NS, xii (1981), pp. 260–1.

XL The Supper at Emmaus

Text
The text is in general fairly well preserved. Some material has been lost, and the lines extant are written confusedly in the vicinity of 156–9, shortly after the change of metre at 153 (see below). The main scribe corrected himself at 132+, but failed to note the transposition of lines 135 and 136. Against lines 5, 6, 10 and 11 there is a series of marginal annotations, probably by John Clerke, which implies that the opening of the play, at least, had been revised or replaced.

Versification
Lines 1–152 are in a heavily alliterative eight-line stanza, abab₁cddc₃. The last line of each stanza is partially reiterated in the first line of the one following. The same stanza also appears in plays I and XLIV, but without the reiteration. From line 153 to the end of the play cross-rhyming quatrains in the long alliterative line are found, and the linking of stanzas continues. The change of metre occurs where the characters enter the 'castell' (line 14), where Jesus is shortly to vanish, and sit down.

Running-title
For reasons set out in the Note on the preceding play, it may be suggested that the main scribe by mistake wrote 'The Wynedraweres' at the head of each page in this piece, as well as in no. XXXIX. The *Ordo Paginarum* of 1415 assigns a play on the subject of the travellers to Emmaus to the Woolbrokers and Woolpackers, to whom the Woadmen have been added by a later hand. The more succinct list of the gilds and plays which accompanies the *Ordo* assigns it to the Woolpackers, and there is a reference to the Woolbrokers' financial arrangements for a play in 1428 (*REED: York*, pp. 23, 26, 46). None of these gilds is mentioned in the Register, either with regard to no. XL, or elsewhere. The main scribe's 'Winedrawers' running-titles were treated as follows, the alterations being in the hand of John Clerke: all but the last were deleted, and the first five have 'Sledmen' substituted. The Sledmen, operators of horsedrawn sleds used for moving goods around the city, are first heard of as having responsibility for a play in 1535 – though as this pre-dates Clerke's association with the Register, there can be no absolute certainty that the play they were then associated with was no. XL (*REED: York*, pp. 258, 261, 679). As has also been explained in the Note on the preceding play, 'Sledmen(s)' and 'The Sledmen' were later written at the head of the first page of no. XXXIX, possibly in the belief that the *Supper at Emmaus* began at that point. In the same place there is also an inscription by John Clerke recording the fact that the Weavers supplanted the Sledmen in the ownership of their play in 1553, whilst no. XLV was temporarily suspended. The Weavers returned to performing no. XLV in 1554, but nothing more is heard as to whether

no. XL continued to be performed, or who had responsibility for it. (See the Note on no. XLV for further discussion and documentation.)

The main scribe originally left a series of eight blank pages between plays XL and XLI (ff.228–31ᵛ). In or soon after 1567 John Clerke made use of this space (adding a leaf, f.232) to insert a copy of the *Purification* play, no. XVII in this edition. See the Note on no. XVII.

XLI The Incredulity of Thomas

Text
A second manuscript of this play exists. York, Yorkshire Museum, Sykes MS, consists of four vellum leaves of the second quarter of the sixteenth century, containing a copy of the Scriveners' play only. It is believed to be a late copy of the gild's own 'original' of their play. For an exhaustive discussion and critical edition, including extensive comparison with the copy in the Register, see A. C. Cawley, *LSE*, vii–viii (1952), pp. 45–80. In the present edition, the Sykes MS as printed by Cawley has been collated for substantive variants (*Sy* in the Textual Notes), and is occasionally used to correct the registered copy. According to Cawley (p. 47) Sy is not likely to have been copied from the Register, though two of the corrections in it by a later hand may derive from the earlier manuscript.

It appears that the main scribe of the Register was guilty of some sort of mismanagement near the beginning of the play. The original first leaf of quire xxxⁱⁱ was cancelled and a singleton (f.233) carrying the first 84 lines of the play substituted. It carries a catchword at the foot of the verso, and was later detached from its stub by John Clerke when he inserted the preceding leaf to complete the copying of no. XVII. As a result, it is not properly bound into the manuscript, and is rather loose to the touch.

Apart from the additions in the vicinity of the first running-title (see below) there are no marginalia or alterations by later hands – an unusual feature.

Versification
The six-line stanza, $aaa_4b_2a_4b_2$, is also found in plays VI, XXII and XXXVIII.

Running-title
'The Escreueneres'. On the first page, f.233, the original running-title was deleted, but has been re-inked. To the right is 'Escreveners' in a later hand, probably John Clerke's, and to the right of this and slightly higher another added word, now erased and irrecoverable. To the left of the running-title are first the letters 'Skr. . .' and then another word, now erased and also irrecoverable. The Scriveners and allied trades copied and decorated books and documents.

XLII The Ascension

Text
A. Hohlfeld, *Anglia*, xi (1899), p. 255, observes that lines 137–46 of this play are echoed in a play on the same subject in the Towneley manuscript; see England and Pollard, *The Towneley Plays*, p. 357, lines 130–9. The text is in a relatively good state of preservation. The scribe was uncertain of the lineation in 263–4, and it may be suspected that a character-designation, 'Maria', has dropped out between 'hence' and 'I' in 263. A marginal comment expressed like a stage-direction was added by a later hand near line 176. Peter Meredith has recently suggested that this may be the hand of Miles Newton, Common Clerk of York from 1519 to 1550 (*LSE,* NS, xii (1981) pp. 258–9). The addition was subsequently amended by John Clerke to specify a different piece of music sung by the angel. Clerke also corrected the main scribe's lineation at line 8, and it was also probably he who attempted some sort of amendment at 133, but it has been deleted.

Versification
Alternately rhyming four-stress octaves are used, similar to those found in play VIII, the Annunciation episode of play XII, and in plays XXXIX and XLVII.

Running-title
'The Tailoures'. Beside the first running-title on f.236ᵛ a later hand wrote 'Potters' (now deleted). The Potters were responsible for the next play in the cycle, XLIII, and are not known to have had any connection with no. XLII. It is possible that the later annotator was confused by the fact that the main scribe omitted his usual blank leaves between XLII and XLIII. No. XLII ends about half-way down f.240ᵛ (the last page of quire xxxᵗⁱ), whilst XLIII begins immediately afterwards on f.241 (the first page of quire xxxjᵗⁱ). The scribe usually left up to three blank pages between plays, and his departure from the norm may have given the impression that XLII and XLIII were one continuous piece. (Compare the situation with regard to nos. XXXIX and XL, as discussed in the Notes above.)

XLIII Pentecost

Text
A special feature of this play is the series of passages in Latin, for which the main scribe made provision, leaving gaps at the first stage of copying and filling in the Latin in red later on. The character-designations are inconsistent, the manuscript sometimes giving the apostles their names, and sometimes referring to them numerically. 'I Apostolus' is Peter, 'II Apostolus' is John, 'III Apostolus' is James; IV and V Apostoli are not identified.

  Later users of the manuscript found much to amend, supply and comment upon. Character-designations were supplied or elucidated at lines 1 (probably by John Clerke), 97 and 133, and a missing word was supplied in a Latin passage at 12+. At 96+ a later hand inserted an observation expressed like a stage-direction to which John Clerke made an addition. Other later annotations were 'Nota' near line 193 and 'Hic caret' near 233. The latter is elucidated by one of the marginalia certainly attributable to John Clerke. His note against lines 13–14 indicates that the opening of the play, concerning the election of a twelfth apostle, had been revised by his time. Near the end, where 'Hic caret' had already been written, he added 'Loquela de novo facta', and, presumably later, gave two verses he considered were wanting at the end of the play (224, 224+). On the other hand, other marginal observations suggesting revision, near lines 173 and 177, have been deleted.

Versification
The twelve-line stanza, $abababab_4cdcd_3$, is also found in eleven other plays in the cycle.

Running-title
'The Potteres'.

XLIV The Death of the Virgin

Text
Apart from the loss of two lines (after 27 and 100 respectively), the text of this play is fairly well preserved, though the lineation gave the scribe considerable trouble: see at 12, 28, 44, 76, 164, 191. Miss Toulmin Smith was able to resolve the difficulties in these places, but at 70–1 she reversed the manuscript lineation, joining 68–71 on to 64–7 to manufacture a stanza similar but not identical to the rest. In this edition the manuscript lineation is preserved and the two groups of lines regarded as independent quatrains. (Note another quatrain made up of lines 183–6.) Apart from the feature discussed below in connection with the running-title, there are no additions or alterations by later hands. This is unusual, and may be connected with the later history of the play, and of the other two Marian plays.

Versification
Apart from three cross-rhyming quatrains in the alliterative long line, an eight-line alliterative stanza, $abab_4cddc_3$, is employed. It also appears in plays I and XL.

Running-title
'The Draperes'. The first running-title (f.245ᵛ) is preceded by a cross like a plus sign inserted by a later hand, a feature also shared by the two other Marian plays in the manuscript, nos. XLV and XLVI. Its probable explanation lies in the histories of these three plays in the mid-sixteenth century. In 1548 it was decided that plays XLIV, XLV and XLVI should not be performed, and though no reason was given in the minute recording the decision, it is to be suspected that their subject matter was no longer acceptable in the changed religious climate of the day. In 1551 it was recorded that the Drapers were discharged of the financial responsibility for their play, but later references in the documents

appear to imply that XLIV, XLV and XLVI were restored to the cycle temporarily from 1554. In 1561 another minute is found, recording their renewed suspension in terms similar to those used in 1548 (*REED: York*, pp. 291–2, 293, 297, 331–2).

XLIVA The Funeral of the Virgin ('Fergus')

This play was never registered, and in compiling the manuscript the main scribe made no provision for it in the way he did elsewhere when the copy he was expecting failed to appear. In such cases he left a longer series of blank pages than usual between plays, and headed several of them with the name of the gild whose play was expected for registration (see the Notes on plays IV, XXIIA and XXIIIA). Where the *Funeral of the Virgin* might have been expected to appear, between the present nos. XLIV and XLV, the main scribe proceeded as follows. He finished copying no. XLIV on the penultimate page of quire xxxj^{ii} (f.248) and inserted a catchword at the foot of the last page (f.248^v) referring forward to the beginning of play XLV on the first page of quire xxxij^{ii} (f.249). He therefore effectively precluded the insertion of further material between nos. XLIV and XLV, and this further confirms that his plan for the Register did not include any provision for the *Funeral*, at least in its proper place in the running-order.

There are, furthermore, no allusions by later annotators to the absence of this episode from the Register, a fact no doubt connected with the chequered history of the play. Before 1432 the *Funeral*, or 'Fergus' as it was popularly known, was the responsibility of the Masons, but in that year they gave it up in favour of the Herod episodes of play XVI (see the Note on XVI, above, and *REED: York*, pp. 47–8). No more is heard of the play until 1476, when it was taken over by the Linenweavers, an abortive association lasting until 1485, though a document of 1517–8, referring to the play and the gild in terms suggesting that a performance might still be contemplated, should not be overlooked (*REED: York*, pp. 110, 123, 136, 143, 216).

It has been argued that the main scribe was vaguely aware of the existence of the *Funeral*, but at the time he compiled the Register the play was in some sense in abeyance or defunct. This may conceivably account for an inaccurately placed series of four originally blank leaves (ff.228–31^v) between plays XL and XLI, without anticipatory running-titles, now occupied by John Clerke's copy of no. XVII. For further discussion see Beadle and Meredith, *LSE*, NS, xi (1980), pp. 51–3.

XLV The Assumption of the Virgin

Text

Play XLV is distinguished by the presence in the manuscript of musical settings of the songs performed at three points in the action. A discussion, with transcriptions of the pieces, will be found in Appendix 1, by Professor John Stevens. If the copying of the settings was not the work of the main scribe, then it is clear that he must have collaborated closely with the copyist of the music, judging by the way in which accurate provision was made for the staves in the dialogue on ff.250ᵛ, 251 and 253. Alternative settings of the three songs were placed on ff.256–256ᵛ, separated from the end of the play by a blank page. Apart from the feature mentioned below in connection with the running-title, play XLV is also distinguished from most of the others by the absence of marginalia or alterations to the text by later hands – a fact probably connected with the later history of the play (see below). The main scribe corrected his own work, inserting lines 62–3 later, but left the lineation confused at 217 and 256. A character-designation, possibly 'Johannes', may be wanting at line 286.

Versification
The thirteen-line stanza, ababbcbc₄deee₂d₃, in the long alliterative line, is found nowhere else in the cycle, though the metre of no. XXXVI is very similar. In many cases, the last line of the stanza is partially reiterated in the first line of the stanza which follows.

Heading, running-title
The first character-designation, 'Thomas Apostolus', is written at the head of the first page in a larger ornamental script than usual, rather in the manner of a title. The regular running-title is 'The Wefferes'. On its first appearance (f.249) the running-title is preceded by a cross like a plus sign in a later hand. Identical crosses precede the first running-titles of nos. XLIV and XLVI, and the feature is probably connected with the suspension of the Marian plays in 1548 or 1561; see the Note on no. XLIV, above. At the time when the main scribe was at work, the running-title he inserted is likely to have embraced both Woollen-weavers and Linenweavers, but the relationship between the two groups of craftsmen was troubled and complicated. A formal severance took place in 1517–8, the Linenweavers already having made a move in that direction with their temporary espousal of the *Funeral of the Virgin* play between 1476 and 1485 (see the preceding Note). The two groups were reunited in 1549. In 1553, play XLV having been suspended from the cycle five years previously, the Weavers temporarily took control of play XL from the Sledmen. In 1554 it appears that they reverted to no. XLV, which remained part of the cycle in performance until 1561, when the earlier ban on the Marian plays was reimposed. (See the Notes to nos. XXXIX and XL above; *REED: York*, pp. 293, 307, 310, 331–2; Raine, *York Civic Records*, v, p. 9.)

XLVI and XLVIA The Coronation of the Virgin (and later fragment)

Texts
In addition to the text registered under the heading 'Hostlers' (otherwise 'Innholders'), the Register contains further material attributed to the same body, added later on an originally blank leaf (f.267) after play XLVII. It is in a sixteenth-century hand found nowhere else in the manuscript. The passage consists of a dialogue between God the Father and God the Son, apparently the opening of a play, with the Son asking the Father whether the Virgin might not be 'assumpt'. It is

numbered XLVIA in this edition, and printed immediately after no.
XLVI.

As to the text of play XLVI itself, its most curious feature is
undoubtedly the assignment of lines 113 to 160 to a series of angels. The
content of the passage, however, suggests that it is a continuation of the
speech begun by Jesus at line 101, and it is here assigned to him. Apart
from the points to be dealt with in connection with the running-title,
below, there are no marginal additions or alterations to the text by later
hands.

Versification

In no. XLVI, lines 1–8, 105–36 and 141–8 are four-stress octaves, with
alternate rhymes. Lines 9–20, 33–104, 137–140 and 149–160 are
four-stress quatrains with alternate rhymes. Lines 21 to 32 are in
tail-rhyme $aa_4b_3cc_4b_3$. No. XLVIA does not seem to have been framed
with any particular metrical principles in mind. The numbers of syllables
and stresses in the line vary, and though a continuous rhyme-scheme is
evident, there is no stanzaic pattern.

Running-title

The main scribe's running-title in no. XLVI is 'The Osteleres'. Against
the first instance there is a cross in the form of a plus sign added by a
later hand. Similar crosses appear against the first running-titles in nos.
XLIV and XLV, and the feature is probably linked with the suspension
of the Marian plays from the cycle in 1548 or 1561 (see the Note on no.
XLIV, above). To the right of the first running-title are the words 'Alias
Inholders' in the hand of John Clerke. Nearby are the words 'Caret'
(probably Clerke) and, apparently, 'Memorandum' (not Clerke). On
f.267 no. XLVIA has the heading 'The Inholders' in a hand different
from that of the text beneath, and also not that of John Clerke.

The history of no. XLVI is unusual, and, in its later period, possibly
throws light on the reasons for the presence of no. XLVIA in the
Register. Dr Dorrell has shown that a play on the subject of the
coronation of the Virgin was the responsibility of the mayor and his
brethren, the governing body of the city, in the period prior to 1463. At
an unknown date between 1463 and 1468 responsibility was handed
over to the Hostelers, who enjoyed a subsidy from civic funds towards
the bringing forth of the play (see *LSE*, NS, v (1971), pp. 35–45). In
1548, no. XLVI was suspended from the cycle along with the other
Marian plays still being performed at that time. Further confirmation of
the suspension was made in 1551, but later references suggest that
XLIV, XLV and XLVI were restored to the cycle between 1554 and
1561 (see the Note on no. XLIV, above, and references there). In 1557 it
was ordered that 'suche pageantz as be not registred in the Cite booke
shall be called in to be registred by discrecion of my lord mayor' (*REED:
York*, p. 324). It is difficult to see how this need have affected the
Innholders if their version of the *Coronation* in the Register was still
current. However, the following record appears soon afterwards, in an
entry in the Chamberlains' Book for May 1559: 'Mr Thomas Glason
promysed before my Lord Maiour to bryng in the Regynall of the

Inholdrs pagyant that it may be Regestred before mydsomer next'; a later marginal note adds 'he apperyd the xx of Iuly (?*read* Iune) and haith ferther day geve to the xxvij of Iune' (*REED, York*, pp. 330–1; Glason was doubtless the innholder of that name admitted to the freedom of the city in 1543–4, see Dorrell, *op. cit*, p. 44, n.31). It is possible that Glason eventually complied, and, given that the Innholders' 'original' was a *Coronation* play, the whole episode may account for the presence of no. XLVIA in the Register – though it should be added that the handwriting of the piece is more characteristic of the earlier half of the sixteenth century than of the period of Glason's activities. The marginal annotations by later hands at the very beginning of XLVI may be relevant here: John Clerke's 'Caret' and what appears to be 'Memorandum' inserted by somebody else. It has been suggested that no. XLVIA was a later composition rectifying the omission of material at the beginning of no. XLVI (See A. J. Mill, *PMLA*, lxv (1950), p. 873, n.29), but in the absence of fuller evidence there can be no certainty about this.

XLVII The Last Judgement

Text
Lines 145–84 and 229–372 of this play also appear in the Last Judgement play in the Towncley manuscript, which otherwise differs considerably from the York version. The first group of York lines is found scattered in Towneley, but the second group runs consecutively. The parallel Towneley passages were printed at the foot of the page in Miss Toulmin Smith's edition, and were later discussed by England and Pollard, *The Towneley Plays*, pp. xx–xxi. Towneley readings (*T* in the Textual Notes) occasionally help with difficulties in the York text.

The first part of XLVII occupies the latter half of quire xxxiij[ii], as usual an eight, and the copying was completed on a quire of four leaves only, xxxiiij[ii]. To the signature on the second leaf of this short quire (f.266) was added a +, drawing attention to the anomaly and signalling the end of the manuscript.

The play differs in layout from most of its predecessors in the cycle, and is in places confused. Red capitulum marks appear from time to time in the left-hand margin, denoting the beginnings of stanzas (ff.261, 261[v], 262, 263[v], 264[v], 265). In several places the stanzas are ruled off from one another as if they were separate speeches, the following groups of lines being divided up in this way: 113–44, 145–60, 185–200, 309–48, 357–80. The main scribe for some reason abandoned the insertion of character-designations towards the end of the play, and from line 317 onwards they are all supplied by another hand, in black. He also originally omitted lines 161–8, adding them later at the end of the play and inserting a reference mark in their intended position. Four lines are also wanting after line 228, an omission which attracted the attention of later annotators, though there is no gap in the manuscript. John Clerke apparently attempted to supply some of the missing material, but also wrote 'de nouo facta' nearby at another time (see at 228+, 229–31). The provision of new material in the vicinity of lines

203–7 was also noted by Clerke and (it appears) another annotator, and Clerke's addition near 372 may have arisen for a similar reason. It is evident that the play had been to some extent revised by the mid-sixteenth century. Nevertheless, there are later alterations to the registered text in lines 37, 242 and 290.

Versification
The four-stress, eight-line stanza with alternate rhymes also appears in plays VIII, XXXIX, XLII and in part of play XII.

Running-title
'The Merceres'.

Appendix 1

The music of play XLV: The Assumption of the Virgin
edited by
John Stevens
Fellow of Magdalene College, Cambridge

Introduction

Play XLV of the York cycle is unique in the surviving medieval English drama: it contains polyphonic music fully written out with Latin words set to it. There are directions for music scattered throughout the plays of the four main mystery cycles; two English songs survive in T. Sharp's early nineteenth-century transcript of the 'true-Coventry' plays;[1] and a short fragment of measured music for one voice in the Chester cycle.[2] These songs are in a later style; the York music is our only written record of fifteenth-century musical presentation of the plays.[3]

The manuscript contains six pieces (not five as has sometimes been stated): *Surge proxima mea* (two settings), *Veni de Libano sponsa* (two settings), and *Veni electa mea* (two settings). The first setting of each piece is given in the course of the text of the play; the other settings follow at the end (ff.256–256ᵛ) in a group. The identification of the sixth piece rests on two words only: *Veni* (Voice I, bars 1–5) and *tuam* (Voice II, bars 26–7); there are no further words to the song, but these are conclusive. It looks as if a hurried scribe entered the first and last words specifically for the purpose of ready identification.

1 T. Sharp, *A Dissertation on the Pageants or Dramatic Mysteries Anciently Performed at Coventry* (Coventry, 1825; repr. Wakefield, 1973), pp. 115–18. The music is not included in Hardin Craig's standard edition, *Two Coventry Corpus Christi Plays*, EETS, ES LXXXVII (2nd edn, 1957).
2 That is 'pricksong', not plainsong, as erroneously described on p. 81 of the first paper cited in n. 3 below.
3 The subject of 'Music in Medieval Drama' is discussed in the author's paper, read to the Royal Musical Association in May 1958, and published in the *Proceedings*, 84th session (1957–8), pp. 81–95. The York music is described on pp. 93–4. I thank the Council of the Association for permission to quote from it here.

Since this Appendix was first drafted, for another purpose, Carolyn Wall has published 'York Pageant XLVI and its Music', *Speculum*, xlvi (1971), pp. 689–712; pp. 698–712 consist of a 'Note on the Transcriptions' and transcriptions of all the music by Ruth Steiner. Dr Steiner's work is, as one would expect, extremely well considered; it is only a pity that she has allowed Dr Wall to perpetrate one serious error which affects the dating of the music. It is not true that 'the presence of red notes suggests strongly that all six pieces were composed before the middle of the fifteenth century, when the change from black to white notation took place'. The two manuscripts which I cite in my third paragraph (not to mention the *O Quam Suavis* choirbook, *c.* 1500, and other early Tudor manuscripts) totally invalidate her argument proposing 1430–40 as the most likely date for the Register of the plays (p. 694, n.28). On notational grounds there is no reason why a date in the second half of the century should not be correct.

The music of the songs is well-written in a professional hand accustomed to writing music. The scribe, perhaps one of the cantors of the cathedral, fully understood the notation he was using, with its complicated system of ligatures and coloured notes. The general style of the York notation is similar to that found in the first part of the Ritson MS (London, British Library, Additional MS 5665), a late fifteenth-century collection of polyphonic carols and processional music from the neighbourhood of Exeter. The use of black and red notation, which was gradually being replaced by void notation both in England and on the Continent, continued in use here until the early years of the sixteenth century (see, for example, London, British Library, Additional MS 5465).

These Latin songs have several points in common with the later English medieval carol: the use of score for presentation, their 'gymel' style, their predominantly rhythmical relationship between words and music, and, indeed, their general musical idiom. The use of score (as distinct from partbook or other method of presentation) is an old-fashioned feature. We find it in nos. 1–3. Nos. 4–6 are written in a variety of 'choirbook' notation, each part being written out separately at length and not aligned with its fellow. Score notation was associated particularly with church-music of the *conductus* type, predominantly chordal music for use in processions, moving note-against-note with a freely composed melody in the tenor (the underneath) part. Of this music the carol and these dramatic songs are a late survival. The provision of words to the lower voice only is another characteristic which they share with the earlier *conducti*.

'Gymel' is a name given to a particular kind of 'duet' – or 'twin'-song (*cantus gemellus*) – such as often occurs in the English music of this period. In 'gymel' the two voices wind in and out and interweave their melodies. This is the style of many carol-verses, written for two soloists (e.g. *Ave Maria*).[4] But there is this difference: the carols never seem to employ *two* voices of alto (or counter-tenor) range together. The usual combination is of tenor and alto or of two tenors.

The relationship between words and music, it should be noted, is not an expressive one. In singing or hearing these Latin songs we are not conscious of any quality in the music appropriate either to the spiritual 'appearance' of Our Lady or to the fervent words which recall the *Song of Songs*. Nor is any particular word in the text 'pointed' by the music as a post-Reformation composer might have pointed it (*Surge*, for instance). The words, in effect, do not provide matter for delicate commentary, but supply a purely physical 'roughage' which enables the singers to give additional pulse to the words.

It is perhaps misleading to suggest simply that these dramatic songs share a general musical idiom with the later polyphonic carols. The truth is that both are written in a characteristic fifteenth-century style with long melodies, a strong metrical pulse and marked cross-rhythms. The carols have rather more balance of phrase, reflecting the metrical balance of their texts.

An interesting but puzzling question arises about the relationship

4 Musica Britannica, iv (2nd edn, 1958), no. 36.

between the different settings of each text. The relationship is not close, but it may be observed that one of the later settings (later in the manuscript and probably later in composition) is not only more ornate but is, basically, an ornamented version of the other setting. The opening phrase of Song 4 freely expands that of Song 1 (to the word *Surge*). The process continues throughout the piece: *vasculum vitae* is imitated almost note for note, but the composer's usual method is to start each phrase by recalling the opening notes from the earlier piece, to diverge freely, and finally to come to a cadence on the same note (the cadence Song 1 bar 8 and Song 4 bar 14 is an exception to this). Songs 2 and 5, 3 and 6 are only very loosely related.

The relationship between the two groups of settings has not only a musical but a dramatic aspect. Were they alternatives for performance, according to the skill of the available singers? Do the more ornate settings represent the taste of a slightly later generation and were they therefore to supersede the old? Or were *both* sets sung in the same production? These questions are impossible to answer; but a 'yes' to the third seems unlikely.

An easier but more important question brings this Introduction to a close. What dramatic purpose did these relatively 'churchy' pieces serve in the play? Music is used here, as so often in the medieval drama, *to symbolize heaven:*

> When God appears on a 'scaffold' between two angels or more playing musical instruments, we know that God is in his heaven. All may not be right with the world, but at least heaven is depicted as a place of order and of harmony. . . . the sense of a divine order, a cosmic symphony, was tangibly conveyed to the ears. . . . Singing angels represent a higher harmony, a more complete order than we can know on earth. Music is a mirror or *speculum* (to use their favourite image) of the God-created Universe. . . .

> The gracious intervention of the Virgin Mary in the affairs of Thomas is symbolized by music, as it should be. God's intervention and man's response are the *raison d'être* of music in the plays.[5]

The music of the angels is not introduced for dramatic 'atmosphere'; it is a representation of the great truth which inspired the religious cycles – 'God with us'.

Editorial Note

The songs have been edited in accordance with the general principles employed in *Medieval Carols*, Musica Britannica, vol. iv (1952; revised edn, 1958), with the aim of producing a musical text which will serve both scholarly and practical purposes. The prefatory stave gives the first sounding note and the original time- and 'key'-signatures. All the material in square brackets is editorial. The *signum congruentiae* (:S:) of the manuscript has been replaced in the transcription by the pause sign (⌒) when it clearly has that meaning. All such changes and all other editorial

5 'Music in Medieval Drama', *Proceedings of the Royal Musical Association*, lxxxiv (1957–8), pp. 94–5.

alterations are recorded in the footnotes. These refer first to the bar, then to the voice-part, then to the note in question. Thus, '9 I 2C' refers to the second C of the voice occupying the highest stave in bar 9. The information which follows the colon in manuscript values, e.g. 'MS semibreve' means that instead of the note given in the transcription (say, a quaver) the MS has a semibreve (which would be a crotchet if left uncorrected).

The songs are well-written on five-line staves, of which the lines and clef-signs are generally in red. This has no musical significance. The colours of the red and black notes, on the other hand, are functional. Red notes (coloration) are indicated by ⌐ ⌐. Ligatures are marked ⌐ ⌐. 'Directs', or note-guides, have been omitted. There are no regular bar-lines in the manuscript. Double-bar lines in the transcription represent the single lines in the manuscript marking off the sections. 'Longs' at the ends of phrases are conventionalized.

All words in italics are editorial. The underlay has been conservatively rearranged. The singer should not be put off by the repetition of a note without change of syllable (e.g. Song 1, bars 5–6, Voice I); this is a common feature of pre-Reformation vocal writing, as is also breaking into a word or syllable with a musical rest. It cannot be assumed that the almost entire absence of words under the notes of Song 6 means that the music was performed instrumentally. The text was available from Song 3; it was the singer's business to know how to fit it to the music.

Song 1

1 Prefatory stave II: clef written twice, once correctly as shown, once on the bottom line / **2** I flat: MS places at beginning of stave which contains measures 1–8 / **4** text *proxima*: Version II corrects to read *propera* / **7** II second note F: void note; all other semi-minims are red (except Song 5, 17 II G) / **9** I A: MS sharp before this note refers to the B which follows / **24**: these longs are ornamented in the MS.

Song 2

Ve — — ni — de Li - ba - no spon — sa,

Ve — — ni — de Li - ba - no spon — sa,

ve — — — — ni, co — — — ro —

ve — — — ni, co — — — ro —

na — — — — be — — — ris.

na — — — — be — — — ris.

2 No notes

Song 3

3 4 I and II: MS longs / 26 I and II: MS longs with *signa congruentiae* instead of the usual pauses / 26 underlay: *-am*, the syllable is presumably to be repeated.

Song 4

Sur — — — — — — — — ge,

Sur — — — — — — — — ge,

pro-pe-ra me — — — — — — a,

pro-pe-ra me — — — — — — a,

co-lum-ba me — — — — — a, ta-ber-

co-lum-ba me — — — — — a, ta-ber-na

na — cu-lum glo — ri —

— cu-lum glo — ri —

— e, vas-cu-lum vi — te, tem-plum

— e vas-cu-lum vi — te tem-plum

ce — — les — — te

ce — — les — — te

Song 5

4 This piece is not in score: Voice II begins stave 6 of f.256 / 19 II *tabernaculum*: the MS words break off after the third syllable, as shown, for no apparent reason / 25 II coloured notes: *minor color* / 27 I pause: MS *signum congruentiae* / 37 I 2G: MS long with pause / 37 II 2G: MS long without pause.

5 This piece is not in score: Voice II begins near the end of the second stave of f.251 and takes over its clef from Voice I / 5 I pause: MS *signum* / 6: MS gives o [¾] time-signature in both voices / 11 II pause: MS *signum* / 13–13 II F pause: MS *signum* / 12–13 I GC, II CG: the form 𝄢 may be the unfamiliar and obsolescent breve-long ligature, or it may be a sign for *divisi*. I have transcribed it as a ligature, because the coloration suggests a rhythmic group, but suggest tying over the notes to avoid the discordant bare fourth on the third chord. / 15 II E: written as minim in MS and corrected to be first note of a two-semibreve ligature / 22 II pause: MS omits.

Song 6

6 This piece is not in score and is unclearly set out. Voice I begins in the middle of stave 4, taking over the clef from Voice II of the preceding song; it has the single word, *veni*. Voice II begins early in stave 7, immediately following on the end of Voice I; there is no text underlaid except for the last word, *tuam* (in red). / 4 I 2C: MS semibreve / 6 II C: MS dots this note (? *punctum divisionis*) / 17 II E: MS minim / 19 I pause: MS ? *signum* / 20 double-bar: indicated in MS by bar-line in II only / 24 II rests: MS 3 semibreve rests.

474

Appendix 2

Summary of versification

As part of the Introduction to her edition Miss Toulmin Smith gave a 'Sketch Analysis of the Metres' of the plays (pp. li–lii). This Appendix follows the arrangement of her analysis, but gives a somewhat more detailed breakdown when more than one stanza-form appears in a play. Further comments will be found under the heading 'Versification' in the Notes on the plays. There are no entries for no. XVII (see the Note), and passages where the stanza-form has been lost, or where minor irregularities appear, have been ignored.

Four-line stanzas:
Syllabic
abab$_3$ see XXIX 1–169.
abab$_4$ III throughout; II 1–4, XIII 71–8; see also XXIX 1 169, XXXI, XLVI.
Alliterative
abab$_4$ XL 153–94, XLIV 64–71, 183–6; see also XXIX 1–169, XXXI.

Six-line stanza:
Syllabic
aaa$_4$b$_2$a$_4$b$_2$ VI, XXII, XXXVIII and XLI throughout.

Seven-line stanza:
Syllabic
abab$_4$c$_2$b$_4$c$_2$ XIV, XXI and XXV throughout; XV 37–85.

Eight-line stanzas:
Syllabic
ababcaac$_3$ XIX throughout.
ababab$_3$ XII 200–40; see XXXIX.
abababab$_4$ VIII, XLVII throughout; XII 145–99, XX 217–40; see XXXIX, XLIII and XLVI.
Alliterative
abababab$_4$ XVI 23–30.
abab$_4$cddc$_3$ I throughout; XL 1–152, XLIV 1–63, 72–182, 187–94.
abab$_4$cdcd$_3$ see XXXII.
abab$_4$c$_2$dd$_4$c$_3$ XXXIV 1–15.

Nine-line stanzas:
Alliterative
abab$_4$bcbbc$_3$ XXX 1–157.
abab$_4$cdddc$_3$ XXX 158–548.

Ten-line stanzas:
Syllabic
$aa_4b_3cc_4bdbdb_3$ IV throughout.
$aa_4b_3aa_4bcbcb_3$ XXXIV 16–349.
$abab_4ccbccb_3$ XIII 1–70, 167–75, 187–304.

Eleven-line stanzas:
Syllabic
$abab_4c_2bc_4dcdc_3$ V throughout; XIII 79–166.
$ababbc_4dbcc_4d_{2/3}$ VII throughout except for interpolations.
Alliterative
$ababbcbc_4d_2cd_4$ XVI 1–22
$abab_4cdcdede_3$ see XXXII

Twelve-line stanzas:
Syllabic
$abababab_4cbcb_3$ II throughout.
$abababab_4cdcd_3$ X, XI, XX (except 217–40), XXIII, XXIV, XXVII,
XXXV, XXXVII, XLIII throughout; XII 1–144, XV
1–36, 96–131, XVI 57–392.
$ababababcdcd_4$ XXXIX 30–41, 50–61.
$ababcc_4dde_2fef_3$ XVIII throughout.
Alliterative
$abababab_4cddc_3$ see XXVIII.
$abababab_4cdcd_3$ XXIX 170–395.
$abab_4bcbc_3dccd_3$ XXXIII throughout.

Thirteen-line stanzas:
Alliterative
$abababab_4c_2ddd_3c_{3/4}$ XVI 31–56.
$ababbcbc_4deee_2d_3$ XXXVI throughout.
$ababbcbc_4deee_2d_3$ XLV throughout.

Fourteen-line stanzas:
Syllabic
$abababab_4cdcccd_3$ IX throughout.
Alliterative
$abababab_4cdcccd_3$ XXVI throughout; see XXXI.

Glossary

The Glossary is intended principally to elucidate words whose meaning or appearance may be unfamiliar to the modern reader. Obvious northern dialectal spellings of familiar words have not in general been glossed, e.g. *ga* 'go', *nane* 'none', *fute* 'foot', *halde* 'hold', as their meanings are almost invariably clear from the context.

In the ordering, *ȝ* follows *g* and *þ* is placed with *th*. Vocalic *y* is treated like *i*, but initial *y* with consonantal value is in the usual place after *w*.

A number of very commonly occurring words are glossed without line-references. Like much verse of the period, the plays contain numerous phatic expressions and rhyming-tags, e.g. *down and dale, firth and fell, more and myne*. Such phrases are not always easy to gloss, nor is it necessary to gloss them once the reader is aware of their metrical or non-expressive function. Consequently, they are illustrated by line-reference only (after the signification of any unfamiliar component word has been given) and signalled by *in phatic phr.*

a *prep.* (out) of 10.115

abaiste, abayst, abass(h)ed, -id, abast(e) *v. p.p., adj.* frightened, afraid 5.80, 11.135, 26.211, 30.399; upset, perturbed 7.59, 16.237

abaites *see* **abate**

abakke *adv.* away 29.182; back, aside 31.141

abass(h)ed, -id, abast(e) *see* **abaiste**

abate, abatte *v. tr.* diminish, reduce 3.27; put an end to 31.377; *intr.* diminish; **abaites** *3sg. pr.* 17.144

abatyng *vbl. n.* hesitation 26.197

abedyn *see* **abide**

aby(e), abie *v.* pay (the penalty) for 13.111, 31.110, 32.114; **dere abye** pay for dearly 6.54, 19.135, 24.17

abide, abidde *v.* wait, await, remain; endure (the severity of) 34.7; remain firm 35.229; **abydande** *pres. p.* 1.7; **abedyn** *p.p.* 47.240

aboute, abowte *prep.* (*with* **is, be**) busy, engaged 26.212, 29.46, 37.7

abowne *adv.* above 46A.11, higher 1.87

abstene *v.* restrain 33.274

accept *v. p.p.* accepted, received 17.289

accidence *n.* temporary effect 46A.43

accordand(e), accordyng *ppl. adj.* fitting, suitable 34.71, 313, 36.384

accorde *v.* agree 16.127, 209, 26.234;

acordys, accordis *3sg. pr.* is suitable (for a purpose) 3.15, 45.295

accounte *n.* financial reckoning; **till accounte** in financial terms 9.132

accounte *v.* explain, justify 33.309

achesoune *n.* reason 15.80

acordys *see* **accorde**

actone *n.* padded jerkin worn under mail or armour 39.96

aday *n.* (on) a certain day 32.87

adawe *adv.* to death; **dose hym adawe** put him to death 30.451

ado *n.* dealings, intercourse 13.169

adred, adreed *ppl. adj.* frightened 22.189, 29.189

adrygh *adv.* aside; **drawes you adrygh** stand aside 31.159

aferde, afferde *ppl. adj.* frightened 9.306, 11.367, 23.207

affecte *v.* aspire (to an opinion) 26.18

affie *v.* place faith (in), trust 38.165; **affies** *3sg. pr.* 37.29

affray(e), affraie *n.* assault, attack 34.174; outrage 7.117; trouble, difficulty 5.152, 11.324; **affraies, afrayse** *pl.* 11.38, 33.100

affraied *v. pa.t.* terrified 41.42; *p.p.* disturbed 45.258

after, -yr, -ir, efter, -yr, -ir *adv.* according to 1.125, 11.10, 24.52; behind 37.376; for 37.242

477

after-warkes *n. pl.* later works, subsequent creations 1.152

agayn(e)(s) *prep.* against 6.12, 11.222, 25.480; before, in front of 25.15; towards, to meet 25.251, 30.510; in readiness for 21.33

agayne-call *v.* take back, revoke 38.403

agayneward *adv.* back 20.39

agaynste *prep.* towards, at

agaste *ppl. adj.* afraid 9.91, 29.289, 31.283

ay, I *interj.* yea, yes 5.71, 9.185, 28.237, 33.246

ay(e) *adv.* ever, all the time, always 3.67, 10.350, 14.86; **for anes and ay** once and for all 10.250; **ay newe** continually 27.71

ay(e)-lastand(e), ay-lastyng *adj.* everlasting, eternal 1.24, 9.1, 18.63, 36.326

ay-lastandly *adv.* eternally 2.4

ayles, -is, -eth, eyles *v.* 3sg., pl. pr. trouble(s) vex(es) 20.18, 32.205, 33.164; **what ayles . . . at?** what [does he, do they] have against . . . ? 18.67, 135

ayre *adv. see* **are** *adv.*

aysell *n.* vinegar 36.244

ay-where, -whare *adv.* everywhere 3.66, 23.211

ay(e)-whils *adv.* as long as 1.40, 19.201

alang *adv.* lengthwise 35.186

al-beledande *adj.* all-protecting 1.21

alde *see* **elde**

algate *adv.* in every respect 31.408

alkyn(ne), all(e)-kyn(nys) *adj.* of every kind, all kinds of 2.110, 5.70, 6.9, 46.62, 137

all *n. see* **hall**

all *adv. (as conj.)* for all that, even though 42.191

allegge *v.* expound, set forth, cite 20.56, 37.277; **alleggis** *3sg. pr.* 20.193

alle redy *adj. phr.* (I am) willing, ready 5.168

all-yf, -if *conj.* even though, notwithstanding 2.8, 8.47, 27.69, 35.248

all(e)-kyn(nys) *see* **alkyn(ne)**

all-myghtfull *adj.* almighty 21.106

allone *adj.* only, exclusively 1.57

allowe *v.* approve, act in conformity with 37.330; repay 28.275

all-weldand *adj.* all-wielding, almighty 14.1, 16.69, 46.65

als *adv.* also, as well; *conj.* as, just as

also, alswa *adv.* also; as, like 24.19, 38.93

als-swithe *adv.* as soon as possible 39.127

alther, -ir *adv.* of all; **alther best, mast** the very best, most of all 13.252, 269

alway, allway *adv.* always; continually; perpetually; regardless 37.164

amange *see* **emang(e)(s)** *prep.*

amende *v.* improve; change (usually for the better) 5.81, 31.61; cure, heal 11.256; **amendis** *3pl. pr.* repents of 42.160; **amendand(e)** *pres.p.* 30.64, 45.147; **amend(e)** *p.p.* 34.85, 35.128, 45.209; atoned for 2.17; improved the lot of 9.22; **þou þe amende** be disabused 29.122

amys(se), amisse, omys *adv.* wrong, wrongly 1.139, 25.179, 38.397, 45.76; out of place 35.109; malevolently 26.92

an, and *conj.* if

and *adv.* then 7.19, 8.6

ane *pron.* one, me 1.103

ane *adj.* one 42.115

anes, ones, onys *adv.* once 9.301, 10.250, 13.125, 38.338

angrys, -is *n.pl.* tribulations, afflictions 8.147, 13.274

anlepy *adj.* solitary 13.40

anodyr, -ir *adj.* another

anoynementis *n.pl.* unguents 38.213

anoynte *v. pa.t.* anointed 26.133

anone *adv.* soon, forthwith 7.72, 30.78, 155

anowe *see* **inowe** *adv.*

apayd *ppl.adj.* contented, satisfied; **hold you apayd** be contented 4.81

apas, apasse *adv.* apace, quickly 28.205, 30.115

aperte *adv.* plainly, openly 21.26

appeyre *v.* harm, impugn 31.379

appert(e)ly *adv.* openly, publicly 21.133, 47.132

applye *v.* put into action 30.463; **applyand** *pres. p.* setting forth (grievances) 30.3

appose *v.* question, interrogate 16.143, 31.162

appostita *n.* apostate 26.76

araye *v. see* **array(e)** *v.*

are, arr, ayre *adv.* before, beforehand 9.259, 10.340, 17.297, 18.42

arly, arely *adv.* early 22.124, 25.416, 40.24; *in phatic phr.* **arly and late**

a-rome *adv.* to a distance; **gose a-rome** stand aside 30.229

arow *adj.* afraid 21.142

arr *adv. see* **are** *adv.*

array(e) *n.* fashion, manner 31.219, 35.216; clothes, robes 16.147

array(e), araye *v.* prepare, provide for 27.19, 30.202, 31.390; **ar(r)ayed, arraiede** *p.p.* 27.5, 35.37, 94; **array þe** apply yourself, co-operate 31.315

arreste *v. pa.t.* arrested, captured 29.137

arrore *n.* error, false belief 30.324

artikill *n.* matter, business 32.57

as *v. see* **asse** *v.*; **asaie** *n. and v. see* **assaie, assaye** *n. and v.*

asarme(s) *interj.* to arms 19.207, 276

asent *n. and v. see* **assent(e)** *n. and v.*

asith *n.* reparation 25.453
aske, askis *see* **asse** *v.*
asoundre *v.* part company 45.306
a-spede *adv.* speedily 30.538
aspise *v.* consider 33.280; **aspied** *p.p.* detected 30.205
assaie, asaie *n.* trial, test; **on(e) as(s)aie** by trial 15.61; put to the test 35.44
assaye, as(s)aie, assesaye *v.* test, put to the test 10.67, 31.154; make attempt, try 22.40, 31.258; venture upon, undertake, begin 2.53, 5.22, 8.96; **assaied** *p.p.* 30.354; **assaye þe see** take a sounding 9.195
asse, ax, axke *v.* ask 3.68, 22.158, 41.185; deserve, demand 11.7; **as, aske, askis** *3sg. pr.* 15.118, 25.77, 31.36
assemelyng *vbl.n.* coming together 44.68
assende *v.* (*tr.*) take up, waft away 44.189
assent(e), asent *n.* will 2.90; **at asent** ? at the appointed time or place 13.27; **of þare assente** of like mind 37.310
assente *v.* *3sg.pr.* is willing 30.418; **asent, assent(e) assentit** *pa.t.* 2.9, 18, 32.143, 176; **assent(e)** *p.p.* agreed 10.235, 37.170
assewe *v.* follow 25.401
assynde *v. pa.t.* ordained, appointed 33.69
assise *n.* sitting (of law court) 38.35, 47.94
assumpt *v. p.p.* assumed (into heaven) 46A.34
astate *see* **estate**
astonys *v. 3sg. pr.* stupefies 31.251
at(t) *rel. pron.* that, which 1.73, 97, 32.298; *conj.* that 17.288; *prep.* of, from 21.121
at *adv.* (*with inf.*) to 1.12, 20, 22, 11.282, 13.140; *see the verbs*
at(t) all *adv.phr.* in every respect 31.208, 32.368
ather *see* **owther**
attaynte, atteynted *v. p.p., adj.* convicted, proven 32.288, 37.278, 45.58
avayle *v.* help, benefit, be the better 22.144, 31.195; **avaylls** *3sg.pr.* 17.400
avaunted *v. pa.t.* boasted 30.220
augh *see* **awe** *v.*; **aughen** *see* **awne** *n.*, *adv. see* **ought(e)** *n.*, *adv.*
aught *v.* ought; (*quasi-impers.*) **þe aught** it behoves you, you ought 21.62, 22.165
avise *v.* (*usu. refl.*) consider; **avise you** (*sg.*) **3ou** (*pl.*) 25.202, 30.493; **þe avise** 10.76, 11.235; **me avise** 22.128 bethink yourself, -selves, myself
aungelus *n. gen.pl.* angels' 45.121
avoyde *v. p.p.* gone away 31.35
avowe *n.* oath, promise 19.180
avowe *v.* confirm, prove 43.78
avowt(e)ry *n.* adultery 24.15, 35
auter *n.* altar 10.159
awdir *see* **owther**

awe *n.* fear 11.73, 23.90, 32.63
awe, augh, aghe *v.* ought 10.53, 11.12, 16.367, 31.284; **aweth, -ith** *3sg.pr.* 35.40, 34.96; (*quasi-impers.*) **me . . . awe** 20.128, 21.74; **awe vs** 23.49, **vs awe** 25.261; **þe aghe, awe** 25.332, 38.71 it behoves me, us, you; I, we you ought; **awe** *3sg.pr.* owes (in obedience) 16.10; **oght** *p.p.* (is) owed; requires, needs 2.158
awne, aughen nawe *adj.* own 10.240, 12.202, 25.226, 27.10
ax, axke *see* **asse** *v.*

bachillers *n.pl.* retainers 34.1
bad(d)(e) *see* **byd(d)(e)** *v.*, **bide** *v.*
bay *v.'* submit, be obedient 3.79
baye *v.²* bark, shout coarsely 33.87
bayle, -ile, -yll, bale *n.'* captivity, custody 11.247, 17.377, 32.4, 35.95, 37.161
baill *n.²* prison wall 37.195
bayle, baill *n.* misery, evil etc. *see* **bale**
bayne *adj.* obedient, complaisant, willing 6.94, 8.136, 10.194, 21.63
baynly, bayn(n)ely *adv.* willingly, readily 1.20, 160, 40.31; obediently 1.35, 20.284, 47.78
bait *v.'* undo, release 17.377
bayte *v.²* bait (an animal) 29.117
bak *n.* clothing 18.165
balde *adj. see* **bold(e); baldely** *adv. see* **boldly**
bale, bayle, -ill *n.* evil deeds 26.26; pain, misery, misfortune, evil 1.102, 6.39, 37.275, 293
balé *n.* belly, womb 2.152
balefull *adj.* sad 39.51
balke *n.* piece of timber 34.67
balme *n.* ointment 25.520
ban *see* **bane** *n.'*
bande *n.* bond, that which binds; piece of string 15.112; rope 16.192, 29.30; **bandis** *pl.* 10.214; metal bands 37.190, 196
bande *v. see* **binde**
bandome *n* power of control 29.21, 32.238
bane, ban *n.'* bone 3.35, 9.95
bane *n.²* destroyer, killer 29.327
banne *v.* curse 5.127, 11.257, 13.21
baptyme *n.* baptism 21.95; **baptyme-watir** holy water 21.102
baptiste *v. p.p.* baptised 21.97
bar, barre *n.* rail in front of judge's seat 26.211, 30.377, 31.377; **barres** *pl.* bars, defences 37.190
baran, barayne, barrane *adj.* barren, infertile 10.31, 12.184, 34.168
bare *v. pa.t. see* **bere** *v.*
bared *v. pa.t.* stripped naked 40.31
barely *adv.* utterly, to the utmost 26.37, 40.21

baren-broche *n.* child's brooch, trinket 15.103

barenhede *n.* childhood 10.5

barett(e) *n.* strife, trouble 22.27 45.154

bargayne, bargan(n)(e) *n.* transaction, deal 13.23, 35, 26.140; undertaking, state of affairs, business 5.119, 9.130, 19.279; behaviour, goings-on 9.126, 13.111

bary *v.* beat 33.427

barkis *v. 3sg.pr.* splinters 33.250

barme *n.* bosom 11.153

barne, berne *n.* child 10.34, 13.73, 96; man, person 32.10; **barnes, bernes** *pl.* 6.71, 30.487; boys, servants 10.374

barres *see* **bar**

bathe, boith *adj., conj.* both

batterand *v. pres.p.* beating 30.244

battis *n.pl.* blows 33.428

bawdery *n.* sexual misdemeanour 24.17

be *prep.* by; for 22.126; concerning, about 14.105

be *v.* be, *occas. written* **by** 3.52, 11.72, 275, 15.12; **es, his, bees** *3sg.pr.* 2.49, 123, 3.47, 12.84; **er(r)(e)** *pl.pr.*; **beese, beis, -ith, bes(s)e** *ipv.* 9.103, 203, 11.97, 45.147, 287; **at be here, at here be** to be here 1.20, 22

beat *v. see* **bete** *v.*²

bed *v. pa.t. see* **byd(d)(e)** *v.*

bede, bid, byde *v.* give, offer 9.170, 11.74, 29.370, 45.184; **bedde** *pa.t.* 31.205; *p.p.* 34.319

bedell *n.* beadle 30.306; **bedilis** *pl.* 30.317

bedene *see* **bydene**

bedward *adv.* towards bed 31.34

beede *n.* prayer 24.141

beelde *n. and v. see* **belde** *n. and v.*

beeldyng, bilding *vbl.n.* dwelling place 1.38, 44.163

beene-venew *see* **bene-veneuew**

beere *v. see* **bere** *v.*; **bees(e)** *see* **be** *v.*

beflapped *ppl.adj.* flogged, bruised 33.431

before, beforn(e) *adv. (time)* beforehand, in advance 1.142, 37.19; *(place)* in the presence of; **me beforne, hym before, vs beforn** in my, his, our presence 1.106, 23.14, 25.301; *prep. (place)* above 3.56, 82

begynne *v.* begin, act, come about; **begonne, bygonne, -une** *p.p.* 2.105, 14.62, 16.81

behest(e) *n.* promise 26.281; command 30.542

beheste *v. pa.t.* promised 25.201; **beheest** *p.p.* 25.233

behete *v.* assure 10.273, 15.57; promise 27.156; **behete** *pa.t.* 30.97

behewede *ppl.adj.* coloured, of the colour 39.97

beholden *v.* adhere to, abide by 11.77

behoues, bus(e), bud *v. 3sg.pr. (impers.)* must, ought, should; it is needful that . . . ; **me bus, bus me; yow bus, behoues þe, 3ou; vs bus** I, you, we needs must 8.148, 9.64, 10.128, 151, 231, 27.83; **bud** *pa.t. as pr.* 8.99, 26.3; **bud** *pa.t.* it was needful to, had to 40.131

beilde, beylde *n. and v. see* **belde** *n. and v.*

beyldly *adj.* sheltering, protecting 17.336

beis, -ith *see* **be** *v.*

bekenne *v.* deliver 26.283; **bekende** *pa.t.* entrusted 42.45

bel(l)amy *n.* good friend 30.127, 37.213, 338

belde, beelde, beylde, bilde *n.* support, help 17.364, 27.68, 43.125; one who aids or supports 8.119, 14.76, 24.166; happiness, comfort 16.13, 17.304, 318

belde, beelde, beylde, -ilde, bylde *v. intr.* dwell, remain, be 9.244, 13.8, 18.61, 46.12; *refl.* **belde vs** shelter 14.14; *at* **beelde vs** to flourish 1.47; *tr.* support 10.34; protect, defend 8.89, 17.313, 28.197; place, establish, create 1.35, 36.407; save, redeem 16.289; **bildis** *3pl.pr.* 33.228; **beldand, beeldand(e)** *pres.p.* 1.61, 87, 45.131; **beldid, beelded** *p.p.* 1.107, 44.46

belder *n.* defender, protector 28.55

beleves *v. ipv.pl.* remain, rest 20.269

belyng *v. pres.p.* bellowing 45.47

belyue, -ffe, -ve, bylyue *adv.* quickly, forthwith 19.150, 20.67, 26.203, 28.167

bell(e) *n.* bell; paragon 45.203; **bere . . . þe bell** excel, claim the prize 26.195

belschere *see* **bews(c)her(e)**

beltid *v. p.p.* encompassed, embraced 40.53

bemene *v.* signify 27.58, 45.119; **bemenes** *3sg.pr.* 39.107

bemes *n.*¹ *pl.* beams, rays 1.50, 16.13

bemys *n.*² *pl.* trumpets 47.63

bende *v.*¹ extend, stretch out 36.123, 147; obey 38.6; **bende** *pa.t.* bent, bowed 45.86; **bente** *p.p.* ? inclined towards 12.46

bende *v.*² *pa.t.* wrapped 45.279; *p.p.* tied up, bound 16.312

bene *n.* bean 31.102

bene-veneuew, beene-venew *interj.* greetings 30.282, 31.145

benke *n.* bench, elevated seat 26.188, 30.275, 47.327

bente *n.* place 26.228; *in phatic phr.* **on bente** 36.355

bente *v. p.p. see* **bende** *v.*¹; **berande** *see* **bere** *v.*

berde *n.* beard 26.167, 33.87

berde *n.* lady, lord *see* **birde**

bere *n.*¹ commotion, clamour 37.214
bere *n.*² bier 44.50
bere, beere *v.* bear, carry 11.75, 18.162, 34.97; take to 5.81; *refl.* **beres hym** acquits himself 35.84; **berande** *pres.p.* behaving 1.40; **bare** *pa.t.* 40.38; **borne** *p.p.* carried away, plunged into 40.12
beryng, -ing *vbl.n.* birth 17.458, 44.23; funeral 44.31
berk *v.* shout offensively 26.167
berne *see* **barne**; **bese** *see* **be** *v.*
beseke *v.* beseech, pray 10.233, 18.30, 30.57; **besoght** *pa.t.* 44.83
besettis *v.* *3pl.pr.* assail, harrass 43.55
beside *adv.* aside 38.378
besye, -ie *adj.* busy, active, solicitous 26.261, 45.226
besoght *see* **beseke**; **besse** *see* **be** *v.*
best(e) *n.* animal, creature 3.14, 25.38
beswyked *v.* *p.p.* deceived, betrayed 6.69
betake *v.* entrust 29.394; commit 32.367; **betoke** *pa.t.* 42.193
betande *see* **bete** *v.*²
betaught *v.* *p.p.* entrusted 26.5
bete *v.*¹ beat, scourge, flog; **bettis** *3sg.pr.* beats down (like rain) 11.316; **betis** *ipv.pl.* 16.133; **bete, bette** *pa.t.* 40.20, 21; **betyn(e), bette** *p.p.* 16.192, 33.435, 40.170, 47.136
bete, beat, beete *v.*² remedy, relieve, assuage 16.333, 17.88, 35.125; **betande** *pres.p.* kindling 1.102
beþoughte *v.* *pa.t.*, *refl.* contrived, plotted 40.63
betyde *v.* happen, befall; (of time) come 18.151; **betyde** *pa.t.* 26.80; **betydde, -idde** *p.p.* 5.132, 28.139, 40.160
betyme *adv.* promptly 16.370
betyne *see* **bete** *v.*¹
betyng *vbl.n.*¹ whipping 45.45
betyng *vbl.n.*² reward 26.228
betoke *see* **betake**; **bett(e)** *v.* *p.p. see* **bete** *v.*¹
bette *n.* that which makes amends, comforter 19.211
bette *adv.* quickly; **go bette** begone, make haste 30.60, 184
bettir *v.* enhance 26.12
bettis *v. see* **bete** *v.*¹
betwene *adv.* in the meantime 38.28, 355, 40.180
bews(c)her(e), bewcher(e), belschere, beuscher *n.* good sir, (my) good man 26.187, 29.212, 348, 30.282, 31.329; **bewe sirs** *pl.* 30.540
bewté *n.* beauty 26.195; **bewteis, bewtes** *pl.* moral virtues 43.125, 45.203
by *adv.* nearby, at hand 5.35
by *v.* 'to be' *see* **be** *v.*

by(e) *v.* buy 26.219, 27.170; redeem, ransom 15.19; pay (the penalty) for 1.119, 6.67, 30.260; **bought(e)** *pa.t.* 9.272; suffered for 19.228; *p.p.* 22.22
bib *v.* drink 36.242
byd(d)(e), bid(d)(e) *v.* pray, ask for, request, tell, command; beg for mercy 5.126; **bad(d)e, bed** *pa.t.* 6.8, 7.17, 30.461; **bidde furthe** make known 26.227
bid, byde give *see* **bede** *v.*
bide, bidde *v.* stay, remain, abide 14.36, 20.287, 25.431; suffer, undergo, endure 10.188, 13.53; **biddis** *ipv.pl.* 23.41; **bidand** *pres.p.* 12.4, 45.120; **bade, bode** *pa.t.* 23.192; lived long enough 14.90
bidde *v. see* **byd(d)(e)** *or* **bide**
bidding, biding *vbl.n.* instruction(s), command(s) 29.31, 30.317, 37.257; request 20.284; commandment 20.145
bydene, bydeyne, bedene *adv.* forthwith, immediately 1.14, 7.8; altogether, all told, indeed 2.52, 6.132; *often phatic* 10.292, 17.202
biding *vbl.n. see* **bidding**
bygged *v.* *p.p.* formed, made; **bygged with þe beste** one of the most beautiful 1.68
bigly, bygg(e)ly *adj.* perfect, commodious 6.42, 125, 44.10, 20
bygly *adv.* firmly, securely 1.70
bygonne, -gune *see* **begynne**
bying *vbl.n.* redemption 37.12
bilde *n. and v. see* **belde** *n. and v.*; **bilding** *see* **beeldyng**; **bylyue** *see* **belyue**
byn *adv.* in 30.275
binde *v.* bind, tie, incarcerate; *refl.* oblige 32.221; **bande, boune** *pa.t.* 29.138; obliged 45.173; **bonne, boone, bounden, boune, bowne, bun(e)** *p.p.* (*also adj.*) 7.114, 16.334, 20.17, 23.130, 29.202; frostbound 2.107; obliged (in duty, gratitude) 10.10, 23.44
birde, byrde, berde *n.* maiden, lady 10.372, 13.78, 17.209, 44.50; lord 44.10
byrnande, byrne *see* **brenne**
birrall *n.* beryl 25.504
birthe *n.* child 12.179
bittilbrowed *adj.* beetle-browed 26.169
bittir *adj.* cruel, severe, grievous; *adv.* cruelly 36.130
bittirful *adj.* grievous 36.183
bittirly(e) *adv.* wickedly 5.116; severely 11.274
blad *n.* blade 31.9
blayne *n.* boil, pustule 11.316
blake *adj.* black 47.143; **blakkeste** *spv.* 1.101
blame *n.* fault 25.83; censure 26.19
blanne *see* **blynne**
blastis *n.pl.* blasts (of wind) 16.4

blawe *see* **blowe**

ble, blee *n.* colour, appearance (of face), countenance 1.5, 26.20, 28.263, 30.249; condition, attitude 36.174

bledand *v. pres.p.* bleeding, wet with blood 41.175, 42.222

blemysshe *v.* dishonour, tarnish (a reputation) 29.336; **blemysght** *ppl.adj.* fatally wounded 36.370

blende *v.¹ p.p.* mingled, mixed 2.153, 11.258

blendyng *v.¹² pres.p.* ? dazzling *or* suffusing (*as v.¹*) 1.5

blenke *n.* radiance 28.263

bletyng *v. pres.p.* crying out 45.47

blynne *v. intr.* end, cease, leave off 19.158, 24.12, 37.16; *tr.* put an end to 9.165, 18.107; **blynnande** *pres.p.* 44.179; **blanne** *pa.t.* 38.92; **blyne** *p.p.* 11.197

blisshes *v. 3sg.pr.* blushes 33.432

blisse *v.* bless 25.13, 37.400; **blyst** *pa.t.* 12.111; **bliste, blyste, blissid** *p.p., adj.* 9.257, 12.36, 37.404

blyssyng, blissing *vbl.n.* blessing 37.401; invocation 1.20, 147; **my blyssyng o ble** the blessing of my countenance 1.5

blyste, bliste *ppl.adj. as n.* blessed one 12.84, 41.113; *see* **blisse**

blistfull *adj.* holy, sacred 8.89

blithe *adj.* glad, ready, willing 11.395, 19.42, 30.497; *adv.* readily, willingly 7.50

blythely *adv.* gladly, readily 26.196

blithes *v. 3sg.pr.* gladdens 16.13

blo(o) *adj.* dark, discoloured, livid 33.432, 45.45; **blakkeste and blo** utterly discoloured 1.101

blonderande *v. pres.p.* churning about 16.4

blondre *n.* confusion 33.93; stirring up of trouble 33.402

bloode, blode, blude *n.* blood 11.264, 41.182; person 32.161

blore, blure *n.* wailing, lamentation 11.294; bluster, boasting 26.187, 33.93; loud voice 31.253

blowe, blawe *v.* blow 47.63; breathe 31.141; wave 33.177; **blowes** *(? as inf.)* give vent to 31.20; **blowes** *2sg.pr.* 26.169; **blawe** *pa.t.* 30.224; **blowen** *p.p.* 26.187

blude *see* **bloode; blure** *see* **blore**

bodis *n.¹ pl.* commands 31.176

bodis *n.² pl.* bodies; **youre bodis** you 36.68

bodus *v. 3sg.pr.* forebodes 31.80

bod(e)word(e), boodword(e) *n.* tidings, message 11.132, 12.159, 17.166; command 10.66

boy *n.* knave, rascal, fellow 19.89, 29.26, 289; **boyes** *pl.* 11.247, 37.97, 145

boyste *n.* box 26.131

boith *see* **bathe**

bokes *n.pl.* books, authorities 20.151

bold(e), balde, bowde *adj.* sure (of something), confident 8.119, 17.218, 344, 30.497

boldly, baldely, bowdly *adv.* boldly 5.80, 8.63, 30.244, 36.242

bolned *v. p.p., adj.* swollen 36.370, 40.107, 45.45

bolnyng *vbl.n.* swelling 45.7

bondeman *n.* servant 32.220

bone, boone *n.* petition, request, desire 10.252, 11.350, 16.354, 25.340; command 23.163; reward 26.12

bone *adj. see* **boune** *ppl.adj.*; **bonne** *v. p.p. see* **binde; boodword(e)** *see* **bod(e)word(e); boone** *n. see* **bone** *n.*; **boone** *v. p.p. see* **binde; boore** *see* **bore**

boorede *ppl.adj.* with holes bored in 35.40

booryngis *see* **boring; booste** *see* **boste** *n.*; **boote** *see* **bo(o)te; bordand** *see* **bourde** *v.*; **borde** *n.* jest *see* **burde** *n.¹*; **borde** *n.* table *see* **burde** *n.²*; **bordyng** *see* **bourdyng**

bore, boore *n.* hole 35.86, 99

boring *vbl.n.* hole 35.128; **booryngis** *pl.* 35.146

borne *see* **bere** *v.*

borowe *v.* obtain upon a pledge 32.352; redeem, save 6.40, 31.321; **borowed** *p.p.* 47.270

boste, booste *n.* boasting, proud or arrogant words 26.169, 29.132, 37.214

bot *see* **but**

bo(o)t(e), bute *n.* help, one who helps, benefit 9.170, 16.334, 24.166; remedy, cure 20.206, 32.148, 38.196; fortune 11.96

botment *n.* remedy 19.90

boudisch *adj.* peevish, sullen 31.173

bough, bugh, bowe *n.* bough, branch 4.73, 25.388, 45.173; **bowis** *pl.* 2.70

bought(e) *see* **by(e)** *v.*; **bounden** *see* **binde**

boune, bone, bowne *ppl. adj. (see* **binde)** ready, prepared 9.68, 10.283, 16.386; willing 7.49, 11.397. 19.14; ready to go 10.113; en route 25.309

boune *v. (often refl.)* go, betake (oneself) 30.152, 31.34; **bounes** *2sg.pr.* 40.13; **bownand** *pres.p.* 45.287

boune *v. pa.t., p.p. see* **binde**

bountith *n.* ? a good deed 15.118

bourde *n. see* **burde** *n.¹*

bourde, bowrde *v.* play, jest, speak lightly, play the fool 9.66, 29.183, 327, 31.185; **bordand** *pres.p.* 20.80; **bourded** *p.p.* 29.380; **burdis (bourdes) to brode** speak out of turn 19.89; act hastily 29.331; **bourded to brade** spoke thoughtlessly 36.95

bourdeyne *n.* burden 35.207

bourdyng, bordyng *vbl.n.* sport, pleasure 31.80, 110, 147; idle talk 31.174, 34.216

boure *n.* small room; house, dwelling 17.336, 27.67; **boures** *pl.* 46.136; **Jesse boure** house (i.e. lineage) of Jesse 12.76; *in phatic phr.* **boure and hall** 27.67

boustous *adj.* awkward, heavy 35.218

bowde *n. see* **bold(e); bowde** *v. pa.t. see* **bowe** *v.*; **bowdly** *see* **boldly**

bowe *n.¹* rainbow 9.284

bowe *? n.²* bow (of a vessel) 8.110

bowe *n.* bough *see* **bough**

bowe *v.* submit, comply 10.68, 26.196, 29.339; **bowes** *3sg.pr.* 25.493; **bowand** *pres.p.* bowing 30.318; **bowde** *pa.t.* bowed 33.169

bowis *n. pl. see* **bough; bownand** *see* **boune** *v.*; **bowne** *v. p.p., adj. see* **binde** *v. or* **boune** *ppl. adj.*; **bowrde** *see* **bourde** *v.*

bowrdyng *vbl.n.* jesting, facetious talk 20.89

bowsom, boxsom(e) *see* **buxom; box(s)omly, -sumly** *see* **bux(s)umly**

brace *v.* radiate 16.13

brade *adj., adv. see* **brode** *adj., adv.*

bragges *n. pl.* large nails, spikes 34.94

brayede *v. pa.t.* chopped 29.140

brayde, braide *n.* rash act 5.127; blow, onslaught, assault 23.192, 37.207; affliction, torment 10.188, 32.270, 35.96

brayde *v.* hasten 30.275, 33.345

braythe *see* **brathe; brake** *v. pa.t. see* **breke; bralland** *see* **brawlest**

brande *n.* sword 29.140, 30.4, 31.4; **brondis** *pl. ?* torches 29.318

bras *n.* brass 37.196

brasshis *n. pl.* blows 33.351

braste *see* **brest(e)** *v.*

brathe, braythe *adj.* angry 26.37; eager 26.132

brathely *adv.* severely 33.67

braunche *n.* descendant 45.175; **braunches** *pl.* sticks 45.6

brawle *see* **broll(e)**

brawlest *v. 2sg.pr.* disobey 30.382; **brawlis** *3sg.pr.* wrangles 31.410; **brawlyng, bralland** *pres.p.* squabbling 16.38; causing a commotion 33.17

brawlyng *vbl.n.* noisy behaviour 30.141

brede *n.¹* bread 22.57, 31.205, 36.290

brede, breede *n.²* breadth 33.242, 34.77, 35.76; **on brede** spread out 2.70, 20.142; in every place 31.10; on every side 33.169

brede *v.* breed 2.152; grow, come forth 12.76; **bredde** *pa.t.* grew, was nurtured 32.132; **bredde** *p.p.* brought about, caused 12.31

breder, -ir *see* **brodyr**

bredde *v. pa.t., p.p. see* **brede** *v.*; **breede** *n. see* **brede** *n.²*

breke *v.* violate, disobey 37.257; **brak(e)** *pa.t.* 47.17; crushed 40.101; broke 40.180

brenne, byrne, bryne *v.* burn 10.110, 179, 292; **byrnande, brynande** *pres.p.* 1.102; shining 1.50; **brent(e)** *p.p.* 1.107, 123, 10.195

brente *adj.* steep, high 32.20

brere *n.* wild rose 26.20; garland of thorns 33.389

brest(e) *v. intr.* burst 26.4, 27.103; **bristis** *3sg.pr.* shivers, shatters 33.250; **braste** *pa.t.* 40.33; *tr.* smash into, burst 31.4; crush, shatter 16.38; **brestis** *3sg.pr.* 30.4; **braste** *pa.t.* 40.101; **braste, brosten** *p.p.* 37.196, 45.6; constrained 30.529; **all braste on bloode** (he) was drenched in blood 40.170, 171

breste *n.¹* complaining, clamour 26.269

brestis *n.² pl.* breasts (as seat of emotion) 30.208; breastplates 26.4

brethell *n.* wretch 26.179, 29.237

brether, -ir, breþere *see* **brodyr**

breue *adj.* brief, short 25.62

brew(e) *v.* brew (trouble), bring about 8.20, 26.131, 290; **brewis** *3sg.pr.* 30.6; **brewed** *p.p.* 29.132

bribour(e) *n.* villain, scoundrel 26.169, 30.461

bryg(e) *n.* dispute 16.238G *(M version* **brigge)**; predicament, plight 5.143

brighthede, -hode *n.* brilliance, splendour 1.50, 68

bryme *adj.* fierce, impatient 24.53, 30.301, 31.420

brymly *adv.* fiercely 30.529

brynande, bryne *see* **brenne; bristis** *v. 3sg.pr. see* **brest(e)** *v.*

brittyn *v.* hack to pieces 31.10; **brittynd** *p.p.* 10.195

bro *n.* unpleasant business *(lit.* stew) 19.135

brode, brade *adj.* broad, big 32.20, 33.253; wide, expansive 3.58

brode, brade *adv.* unrestrainedly, improperly 19.89, 29.331, 36.95

brodyr, -ir *n.* brother 23.112, 25.50; **breder, -ir, brether, -ir, breþere** *pl.* 15.86, 23.105, 25.274, 39.144, 41.125

broydenesse *n.* spacious area 31.1

brokke *n.* badger 29.115

broll(e), brawle, browle *n.* wretch, miserable creature 16.38, 30.6, 33.17, 45; **browl(y)s** *pl.* 31.1; children, brats 19.196

brondis *see* **brande**

brosid *ppl.adj.* bruised 34.243

brosten *see* **brest(e)** *v.*

brothell *n.* wretch 19.265, 30.224

brotherhede *n.* group, fellowship; **youre brotherhede** all believers 47.250

browle, browl(y)s *see* **broll(e); bud** *v. see* **behoues**

buffettis *n.pl.* blows 29.371, 34.319

bugh *see* **bough; bun(e)** *see* **binde**

burde, borde, bourde *n.¹* sport, amusement 29.243; prank, frivolous trick 26.117, 28.297; **burdis, bordis, bourdis** *pl.* 19.246, 29.370; marvels 23.86

burde, borde *n.²* board, plank 8.97; table 40.157; **burdes** *pl.* 8.75

burde *v. pa.t. as pr.* is obliged (to go), must (go) 34.37

burden *n.* birth 16.165M

burdis *v. 2sg.pr. see* **bourde** *v.*

burely *adj.* burly, hefty 33.253

burgeis *n.pl.* burgesses, prominent citizens 25.484

burgh *n.* town 15.13, 87, 32.11

burgvns *n.pl.* blossoms 2.80

bus(e) *see* **behoues**

busk *n.* bush 11.101

busk(e) *v.* prepare 36.416; undertake, endeavour 36.182, 45.104; move quickly, hasten 13.8, 26.188; *ipv.* 30.127, 33.139; **buskand** *pres.p.* going on your way 30.87

busshopp(e) *n.* high priest 29.183, 327, 32.58

but, bot *conj.* but; **but if** unless 11.312, 18.102

bute *see* **bo(o)t(e)**

buxom, bowsom, boxsom(e), buxhome, buxsome, buxsum *adj.* obedient 6.73, 27.67, 28.95, 30.249; humble 24.141; willing, eager 30.52

bux(s)umly, box(s)omly, -umly *adv.* obediently 1.40, 2.66, 4.52, 35.100, 42.51

cace *see* **cas(s)(e); cacche, cac(c)hed** *see* **catche**

caytiff(e), caityf, caystiffe, -effe *n.* wretch, scoundrel 26.74, 115, 33.19, 144; **caytiffe, kaitiffe** *gen.sg.* 26.60, 34.15

cald *n.* the cold, frost 2.107

calde *adj. see* **colde**

calland *v. pres.p.* shouting 33.19

can *v. see* **con**

cankerd *ppl.adj.* rotten, worthless 7.98

cant *adj.* bold, keen 33.350; cruel 22.183

cantely, kantely *adv.* boldly 31.322, 33.262

care, carre, kare *v.¹* go, proceed 30.90, 200, 31.338; **caris** *2sg.pr.* 26.171, **cares** *3sg.pr.* 26.200 come(s); **kared** *p.p.* 29.196

care, kare *v.²* *intr.* care; fear 17.259; *tr.* cause suffering to 47.238

carefull *adj.* grievous 13.145, 45.20; griev-

ing 34.140; burdened with sorrow, sorrowful 34.155, 47.145

caried *v. p.p.* **is caried** has proceeded 30.257

carl(e), karle, karll *n.* man, fellow, person 29.32, 170, 30.63, 31.60; **carls** *pl.* slaves 11.192

carpe, karpe *v.* speak, tell 11.201, 16.45, 31.169; **carpand** *pres.p.* 16.138, 22.184; **at carpe** to tell 13.140

carping, -yng *vbl.n.* words, talk 19.5, 69, 22.85, 29.32; **make carpyng** speak the language 43.157

carre *v. see* **care** *v.¹*

cas(s)(e) *n.* circumstance, matter, business; predicament 11.196, 13.145; cause, reason 30.336; **in cace** in this case 36.53; **hase in case** is devising 30.410

casbalde *n. term of abuse;* ? baldhead 34.193

cast(e), kast(e) *v.* throw, hurl, put from *(often fig.);* cast a spell 35.278; prepare, endeavour 30.90, 31.322, *(refl.)* 36.189; put forward (a case) 30.404; hasten, go 36.180; calculate, compute 24.123; **casten, kest(e)** *p.p.* 6.147, 26.116, 45.70; formed 2.79

casting *vbl.n.* application, use 29.5

catche, cac(c)he *v.* catch; snatch, remove 47.26; *(refl.)* fall into 28.86; drive 16.201; **cac(c)hed, kacched, -id** *pa.t., p.p.* 29.48, 30.196, 47.326; pursued 13.254; cast into 28.65

catel *n.* goods, property 37.242; **catelles** *pl.* animals 9.172

catteraks *n.pl.* the floodgates of heaven 9.190

cause *n.* way; **by cause of** by way of 29.224

cautellis, kautellis *n.pl.* magical tricks, spells 35.206, 278

cele *see* **sele**

certayne, -eyne, sartayne, -eyne *etc. adv.* assuredly, certainly

certes, -is, sertis *adv.* certainly, surely, indeed 1.81, 6.127, 9.233; **in sertis** for sure 45.122

certifie *v.* tell, declare 26.29; vouch for 30.46, 28.246

ceté *see* **cité; chaas** *see* **chase**

chalange *v.* be aware of, be alive to 29.24

chance, chaunce *n.* circumstance 17.361; **for no chaunce** under no circumstances 33.3

charge *n.* concern 26.217; punishment 33.32

charge *v.* instruct 25.18; command 30.473; bind, fetter 33.12; *(ipv.)* load 11.393; **no3t to charge** not to be taken into account, irrelevant 20.120

charmed *v. pa.t.* practised magic upon 33.287

charred *see* **chere** *v.*²

chase, chaas *v. pa.t.* chose 18.29, 23.29

chastye *v.* punish 33.377

chaunce *see* **chance; cheere** *n. see* **che(e)re** *n.*; **cheere** *v. see* **chere** *v.*²

cheff, chiffe *adj.* highest ranking, chief 25.94, 111, 38.3

cheffe *n.* paragon 46.25; **chiffe of clergie** high priest 38.7

cheffe *adv.* especially 46.54

cheffe *v.* befall; **ill cheffe you** a curse on you 30.242

chefteyne, chiftan, chiftene *n.* paragon 30.493, 33.3, 45.107

cheynes, chynes *n.pl.* chains 31.17, 33.12

chenys *v. 3sg.pr.* binds 32.280; **chined** *p.p.* chained, shackled 30.212

che(e)re *n.* frame of mind, mood, disposition 3.27, 9.103, 20.21; mien 25.349; **make ille chere** be downcast 38.127; **what cheere** what is the matter 9.99; **what chere (with þe)** how are you 13.92, 14.85

chere *v.*¹ comfort, console 33.31; **chering** *pres.p.* nursing 45.107

chere, cheere *v.*² arouse 26.217; thwart, punish 33.12, 36.21; **charred** *p.p.* 33.32

chesoune *n.* reason; **by chesoune** for a good reason 25.77

cheualrye *n.* chivalry, knighthood 38.164

cheueleres, chyualers *n.pl.* knights 16.51, 33.289

chide, -yde *v.* wrangle, dispute 26.180, 42.252

chiffe *adj. and n. see* **cheff** *adj.*, **cheffe** *n.*; **chiftan, -ene** *see* **chefteyne**

childe *n.* man 30.242, 38.225; knight 30.142

childe *v.* shield; **God childe** God forbid 13.69

childing(e) *vbl.n.* childbirth 44.147, 45.193

childir *n.pl.* children 10.109, 131, 20.114; descendants 11.118; **childre** *gen.* 20.120

chined *see* **chenys** *v. 3sg.pr.*; **chynes** *n.pl. see* **cheynes** *n.pl.*; **chyualers** *see* **cheueleres**

choppe *v.* clap (in chains), imprison 31.17

choppes *n.pl.* blows 33.377

churle, chorle *n.* knave, low-born person 26.180, 30.142, 212

cité, citee, ceté *n.* city 20.4, 25.283, 544

cytte *see* **syte**

clay *n.* earth 17.134, 36.158; *in phatic phr.* **in clay** 17.305

clakke *n.* clamour 34.210

clappe *v.* beat 33.142; enfold, embroil 26.283; **clapped** *pa.t.* wrapped 16.1; **clapped, -id** *p.p.* 33.151; embraced 30.54

clargy(e) *see* **clergy(e)**

clarifie *v.* make known 23.67; transfigure 42.36; **clarified** *p.p.* glorified 42.35

clatterand *v. pres.p.* making a noise, chattering 30.242, 42.11

clause *n.* allegation 33.297

cledde *v. pa.t.* clad, clothed 47.287; *p.p.* 12.29, 31.275

cleepe *v.* say 26.258

cleyne *see* **clene** *adj., adv.*

cleyngked *v. p.p.* clenched, made fast; *(shipbuilding)* clinkered 8.106

cleke *v.* seize, catch 30.240

clematis *n.pl.* regions of the earth 16.1

clence *v.* clean 33.375

clene, cleyne *adj.* perfect, sinless, good 2.48, 7.5, 13.59; *as n.* sinless one 16.315

clene, cleyne *adv.* cleanly (according to religious precept) 27.16; neatly 8.73; completely, utterly 11.45, 23.201, 31.35

clenly *adv.* in a seemly manner 33.70

clennesse *n.* purity, sinlessness 36.394

cle(e)re *adj.* radiant, glorious, beautiful 1.23, 7.5, 37.128; free, unobstructed 2.115

cle(e)re *adv.* clearly, for sure 5.3, 41.61; openly, manifestly 12.63

clerenes *n.* splendour 16.1

clergy(e), clargy(e) *n.* knowledge, learning, understanding 20.70, 24.26, 29.5; learned men 16.316; prelates 33.298, 38.7; learned disputation 20.54

clerkis *n.pl.* learned men 11.64

clerly *adj.* clear (of sin), pure 15.9

cleuc *v.* stick 34.316

clipsis *n.pl.* eclipses 38.99

cloghe *n.* valley 15.52

cloke *n.* cloak 33.375

closed *v. p.p.* enveloped, enclosed 12.29; buried 36.158

cloth *n.* bedclothes 14.24

clothles *adj.* naked 47.287, 341

cloumsed *v. pa.t.* stunned 23.201

cloute *v. see* **clowte** *v.*

clowded *ppl.adj.* obscure 39.55

clowte *n.*¹ (piece of) cloth 34.193; rag 43.85; swaddling clothes 19.152; shroud 42.92

clowte *n.*² blow, box on the ear 9.120

clowte, cloute *v.* hit 33.142, 375; **clowted** *p.p.* 33.151

clukis *n.pl.* clutches 33.151

cobill-notis *n.pl.* hazelnuts 15.112

cobittis *see* **cubyttis**

coequal *adj.* equal (in rank) 46A.41

colde, calde *adj.* distressing, dire 6.46, 9.10

com(m)an(n)d(e) *v. pres.p. see* **come**

comaunde *v.* command; commend 30.111, 179; **comaundes** *3sg.pr.* 30.284; **co-**

m(m)aunde *pa.t.* 25.268, 29.196; **comaundis vs to drinke** send for drinks for us 32.128

comberous *adj.* serious 33.297

comberaunce *n.* trouble 26.217

combered *ppl. adj.* miserable, fainthearted 33.203, 38.365; *see next*

combre *v.* burden 32.326; **comeres** *3pl.pr.* annoy, inconvenience 34.210; **combered** *p.p.* 26.171

come *v.* come; **comys** *ipv.pl.* 3.94; **comes** *3sg.pr.* becomes, is appropriate to 26.258; **com(m)an(n)d(e)** *pres.p.* 9.8, 22.209, 42.96; **come** *pa.t.* 23.211; is descended 25.239; **comen** *p.p.* 18.53, 19.48, 41.49; **come of** *expr. of encouragement,* come along 29.12; **comen on hande** almost over 29.65

comely *adj.* worthy, gracious 26.186; **comeliest** *spv.* 32.103; *as n.* gracious person 25.261, 30.284

comely, comly *adv.* properly 16.45, 17.397, 36.384

comen *adj. see* **comon** *adj.*; **comen** *v.p.p. see* **come**

comenaunt(e), comenaunde *n.* agreement 26.234, 32.281, 38.426, 45.295

comeres *see* **combre**

comforte, comforth *v. pa.t.* comforted 17.445, 47.318

comforteles *adj. as n.* those in despair 42.166

comly *adv. see* **comely** *adv.*; **comman(n)d(e)** *see* **come**; **commaunde** *v.pa.t. see* **comaunde** *v.*

commyt *v. p.p.* entrusted 46A.45

commende *v. p.p.* worshipped 46A.35

commodrys *n.pl.* gossips, close friends 9.143

comon, comen *adj.* common, for the use of the community 25.57, 193

comons *n.pl.* common people 26.116, 31.35

compellis *v. 3pl.pr.* enjoin, require 26.87

complete *v. p.p.* completed 3.3

con, can, -(n)(e), kon, kan, -(n)(e) *v. (as auxil. + inf.)* can, know how to; *(as intensive)* can justifiably, do indeed 25.216; understand, know, be able (to) 8.47, 11.26, 12.68, 25.219; know in theory 3.75; **couthe, -þe, kouthe, cowde** *pa.t.* 6.88, 9.35, 25.148, 304

conande, conant *see* **connyng** *adj.*

conclude *v.* refute 43.200

confessouris *n.pl.* confessors, holy persons 46.143

confounde *v.* destroy 11.45

coniure *v.* request, enjoin 29.290

conjeon *n.* blockhead 32.49

connandly *adv.* wisely 20.132

connyng *vbl.n.* competence, expertise 29.5

connyng, · conande, conant, konnand *ppl.adj.* wise, skilled, clever 15.117, 16.31, 29.170, 33.463

consayte *n.* intent 25.246

consayue *v.* understand, perceive, see 25.126, 26.231, 30.40; conceive (a child) 46.112; **consayued** *pa.t.* 46.38

consent(e) *v. p.p., adj.* agreed, consented, agreeable 26.232, 32.248

consume *v.* destroy 26.56

construe, constrew *v.* translate 30.348; expound 30.356

contek *n.* strife, combat 19.235

contene *v.* remain so, continue 1.15

contynewe *v.* continue; remain (in good health) 25.362

contynuaunce *n.* period of time 26.102

contrarie *v.* conflict with 26.231; offend 26.242; **contraried** *pa.t.* went against 42.206

contré, cuntré *n.* country, place

contryue *v.* fabricate 30.436; **contryued** *p.p.* plotted 26.241

conversacion *n.* way of life 17.65

convik, -yk *v.* (to) find guilty 30.507, 33.293

coote *n.* garment 35.293

cope *n.* cloak 26.199

corbonan *n.* treasury 32.326

corde *n.¹* agreement; **bounde in corde** agreed, decided 28.235; **in o corde** state of unity 45.307

corde *n.²* rope 35.113, 133

corde *v.* come to an agreement 31.322; **cordis** *3sg.pr.* agrees 25.226

corse, coorse *n.* body, person 17.397, 26.283, 33.467; **my corse** myself 30.48

cosyne *n.* cousin 26.218, 31.169; **cosyn(e)s** *pl.* relatives 9.143, 43.217

coste *n.* place 26.171

costemes *n.pl.* customs 36.275

coveyte *v.* long for 25.256, 26.284, 30.54; covet 20.190; **covaites** *2sg.pr.* wish 24.122; **coveytande** *pres.p.* 16.60 **coveyte, -ite** *pa.t.* 12.198; *p.p.* 23.13, 31.137

cover, couere *v.* deliver (from) 39.54; be relieved of 36.238; **coueres** *3sg.pr.* 26.101; **couered** *p.p.* 24.199

couetise, covetise *n.* covetousness 22.131, 47.147

counsail(l)(e) *n.* counsel, advice 6.153, 10.208, 37.114; wisdom 24.26, 45.205; court, assembly 31.60; conference 26.185; advisers 31.295; **of counsaille** in agreement 28.156

countenaunce *n.* appearance 38.89; **by cause of a countenaunce** by way of a sign 29.224

cours(e), courese *n.* course, orbit (of heavenly body) 1.155, 24.123; custom, legal procedure 24.50, 31.184; **curs(s)is, -es** *pl.* 2.115, 3.6; ebb and flow 2.34; stages (in a procedure) 3.3; **cours of kynde** natural process 42.105

courte *n.* place of meeting 45.235

couthe, -þe, cowde *see* **con**

cowre *v.* cower, cringe 30.234

crabbed *ppl.adj.* perverse, ill-tempered 9.213, 29.128

crafte *n.* skill; (? *also* vessel) 8.150

craftely *adj.* wise 27.28

crake *v.*[1] crack, break 38.185

crakid *v.*[2] *p.p.* trilled 15.67

craue, crave *v.* ask, demand, seek, make enquiry 12.47, 16.182, 37.242

creat *v. pa.t.* created 17.6

creaturis, creatours *n.pl.* creations 2.48, 111; beings 46.145

crepillis *n.pl.* cripples 29.37

crie, crye *v.* cry, proclaim, shout; beg 45.265; **criand, cryand** *pres.p.* 30.1, 37.73; **crie on** call upon, for 34.61, 37.107

croke *v.* bow 20.240, 33.170

croked *ppl.adj.* (*see prec.*) crooked, bowed by infirmity 29.37

crosse *v.* crucify 35.23

crouchis *see* **crucchys**

croune, crowne *n.* crown; head 7.88, 16.43, 38.185

crucchys, crouchis *n.pl.* crutches 25.376, 380

cruelly *adv.* fiercely 30.1

cubyttis, -ittis, cobittis *n.pl.* cubits (units of length, about 18 inches) 8.81, 83, 9.201

culpabill *adj.* blameworthy 31.125

cure *v.* take care of 31.247

cuntré *see* **contré**

curious *adj. as n.* singular person, odd fellow 26.258

coriousenesse *n.* cleverness 29.32

cursednesse, -idnesse, curstnesse *n.* wickedness, malice 26.171, 30.160, 410

cursidly, curstely *adv.* wickedly, maliciously 26.73, 241, 33.255

curs(s)is, -es *see* **cours(e)**

curstnesse *see* **cursednesse**

curtayse *adj.* worthy, noble 19.163, 30.211; genteel, respectable 15.101

cuse *v.* accuse 32.79

cutte *n.* straw 35.295; **drawe cutte** draw lots 35.293

daylls *see* **dale** *n.*[1]

dayne *n.* insult 26.66

daynetethly *adv.* bountifully 1.78

dayntely *adv.* in a seemly manner, adroitly 29.81, 36.223

dayntys *n.pl.* wonderful things 4.97

day warke, daies dede *n.* day's work 1.158, 8.51

dale *n.*[1] valley 2.59, 104; **daylls** *pl.* 17.401; *in phatic phr.* **dale or . . . doune** 45.187

dale *n.*[2] gift (of grace) 1.78

dame *n.* wife 31.246; lady 44.157

dame, dampne *v.* damn, condemn 33.5, 47.162; **dampned** *p.p., adj.* 24.65, 37.272; *as n.* the damned 37.377

damysell *n.* maiden 10.365; lady-in-waiting 30.104

dampne, dampned *see* **dame** *v.*

dare *v.* fear, be afraid 18.105, 19.6; **daris** *3sg.pr.* shrinks with fear 28.2; **dared for drede** cowered with fright 38.370

darfe *see* **derf(f)e; darfely** *see* **derf(e)ly**

darlyng *n.* beloved 10.311; **darlynges** *pl.* the beloved of God 23.79

dase *n.pl.* days; **alde dase** old age 13.11

dasshis, -es *n.pl.* blows 31.7, 33.354

dasshed *v. pa.t.* rained blows upon 45.36

dastard(e) *n.* wretch, worthless person 16.130, 19.275, 28.262

daunce *n.* business, affair 11.225, 19.96

daunce *v.* go, proceed; **daunce (forth, on) in the deuel way** *see* **deuel(l)**

daunger *n.* power 11.212; subjection, bondage 11.186; peril 40.151

daunted *v. p.p.* intimidated 33.291

deare *adj. see* **dere** *adj.*[1]

debate *v. 3sg.pr.* disputes 31.410

declare *v.* instruct 33.239

ded *v. pa.t. see* **do(o)**

dede, ded *n.*[1] death 10.83, 24.20, 35.21

dede, deyd, deide *n.*[2] deed, action, feat, event 4.72, 10.266, 45.52; **dede** *pl.* doings, activities 11.66, 76; **dedis** documents (in a property transaction) 32.356

dede *adj.* dead 3.32, 6.160, 18.60, 37.148 (*as p.p. of 'slay'*)

ded(e)yned *v. pa.t.* expressed indignation 5.6; (*impers.*) **dedyned me** I was offended 5.11

deere *n. see* **dere** *n.*; **dees(se)** *see* **dese**

defayle *v.* desert 28.146

def(f)ame *n.* predicament 16.193; disgrace 24.43

defame *v.* denounce, traduce 13.52; **defamys** *3sg.pr.* 29.50; **defamed** *p.p.* 29.297

defaute *n.* error, failing 20.58, 71; offence 31.374; **defautys** *pl.* misfortunes 11.374

def(f)ende *v.* forbid 25.384, 27.31; resist 28.105, 109; **defende** *pa.t.* 5.45; **defende . . . of** protect from 11.198

deffe *n.* deaf people 25.132, 30.442

deffe *v.* deafen, stupify 29.335; **defes** *3sg.pr.* overcomes, overwhelms 5.129; **deffis** deafens 31.189

defte *n.* ? noble, exalted 1.92; gentle 40.81

degree, degré *n.* rightful place, due order 2.114, 10.356, 20.65; manner, way 9.275, 314, 10.164; stage (in a series of events) 3.92; order of beings 5.5; privilege 23.219; **in no degré** not at all 10.125, 38.438; **in all degré** in every respect 22.82

deyd, deide *see* **dede** *n.²*; **deyne** *adj. see* **ding** *adj.*

deynes *v. 2sg.pr.* deign, condescend 31.189

delay *n.* the action of witholding (money); **made me delay** witheld from me 26.244

deland *vbl.n.* dealing, changing money 26.89

deland(e) *pres.p. see* **dele** *v.*

dele *n.* bit, piece, portion; **(euer) ilk(e) (a) dele** every bit, entirely, completely 1.158, 6.114, 8.106, 9.200; **sum dele** somewhat, a little (more) 10.82; **no dele, neuere a dele** not at all 16.353, 20.234, 43.68

dele *v.* associate, have to do with 12.234, 37.63; **deland(e)** *pres.p.* bestowing 1.78; sitting in judgement 31.378

delfe *v.* dig, labour 11.75; **doluen** *p.p., adj.* buried 24.89, 45.239

delyueraunce *n.* payment 26.273

delyuere *v.* release, free 30.192, *(refl.)* 36.99; **delyuer(e)** *ipv.* hasten, make haste 30.217, *(refl.)* 33.474; **delyuere þe** express yourself, speak 32.344

demar *n.* judge 30.30; **demers** *pl.* 23.142

deme *v.* judge 12.68, 47.181; consider, think about 40.36; form opinions 10.126; **demes** *ipv.pl.* 24.51; **demys** *3sg.pr.* tells 20.113; **demand** *pres.p.* 45.109; **demed** *pa.t.* instructed 19.250; was judged 35.272

demene *v.* condescend *(refl.)* 31.33; **demeaned, demened** *p.p.* ? endowed 33.231; disposed 30.328

demers *see* **demar**

demyng *vbl.n.* power of judgement 20.66; trial (in court) 30.199, 227

denay *v.* disbelieve 17.15; **denyed** *pa.t.* failed 45.53; **denyed** *p.p.* not carried out 45.52

denn(e) *n.* den 26.90; grave 45.239

departid *v. p.p.* distributed 26.143

depraue *v.* cavil, disparage 45.266

deraye, dray(e) *n.* confusion, disorder 9.78; outcry, clamour 37.146, 43.90; violent threat, assault 27.121, 31.307

dere, deere *n.* harm, injury, distress 1.64, 26.183, 36.248

dere, deare *adj.¹* worthy, excellent, noble; pleasurable, pleasing 4.97; **derrest** *spv.*

30.281, 45.199; *as n.* good person 18.121; beloved one 40.106

dere *adj.²* dangerous, dire 32.7, 45.18

dere *adv.* dearly, at great cost 6.54, 67, 19.228

dere *v.* harm, injure 22.35, 33.28; frighten 10.280; annoy 13.304; **derand** *pres.p.* 1.37; **derede** *p.p.* 27.286

dereworthy, -þi *adj.* fine, excellent 36.172, 44.114; *as n.* **derworthy** worthy one 45.163

derf(f)e, darfe *adj.* wicked, sinful, cruel 32.48, 212, 33.423, 45.17

derfenes *n.* irreverence, sacrilege 26.90

derf(e)ly, darfely *adv.* cruelly 28.131, 262, 33.354; miserably, wretchedly 5.165, 13.148

dergh *n.* length (of time); **on dergh ... drawe** put off, delay 35.2

derke, durk *v.* shrink back, hide 18.105; lurk 31.12

derrest *see* **dere** *adj.¹*

derworth *adj.* worthy, estimable 1.92, 33.28, 36.329; **derworth in dere** capable in difficult circumstances 36.7

derworthy *see* **dereworthy**

dese, dees(se) *n.* dais 29.20, 81, 36.329

destanye, -onye *n.* destiny, fate 11.68, 45.158, 47.128

dette *n.* debt, obligation, duty 16.340, 43.178

dcuel(l), -yl(l) *n.* devil; **what (a) deuel** what the devil 11.47, 31.298; **þe deuyll motte you drawe** the devil take you 30.433; **in the deuel way** in the devil's name 16.177, 37.133, *intensified as* **daunce (on, forth) in the deuel way** hence, away ... 7.52, 29.395, 31.423

deuer(e), deyuer *n.* duty, appointed task 1.156, 24.157, 36.156; **deueres** *pl.* deeds 28.276

device, deuyse *n.* judgement (in law) 30.270, 409

deuyse *v.* prescribe, give instruction 7.79, 33.282

devoyde *v.* put aside, cease 36.3

dewe *n.* duty 17.272

dewe, diewe *adj.* due, appropriate, rightful 17.280, 30.61, 45.18; **dewe of** deserving 30.488

dewell *v.* dwell, live 2.128, 3.64; **dewlland** *pres.p.* 2.140

dewes *n. (interj.)* God 1.92

dewly *adj. see* **dulye**

dewly, diewly *adv.* duly, accordingly

didde *see* **do(o)**

dyderis *v. 3sg.pr.* trembles 28.2

dye *v.* put to death 38.9

diewe *see* **dewe** *adj.*; **diewly** *see* **dewly** *adj.*

dight(e), dyght(e), dite *v. (many transf. and fig. senses)* determine, direct, ordain 10.38, 13.202, 14.49, 32.381; condemn 30.534; strike 39.3; *refl.* **ʒou dightis** go, betake yourselves 32.385; **dight(e), dyght(e), diʒt, dyghted** *p.p.* 1.98, 109, 30.170, 47.267; prepared 17.232, 21.32; dressed, adorned 25.115, 517; put (to death) 10.83, 16.55, 36.132; made, done 1.11, 2.88, 17.46, 26.184; dealt with 37.262; treated 47.183

dygnyté, dyngnité *n.* rank, estate, exalted place 1.11, 3.55; **dygnites, dingnitees** *pl.* 47.214; rights, authority (to do something) 28.162

dying *vbl.n.* death 40.80, 81

dyke *v.* dig 11.75

dill *adj.* foolish 5.149

dym(m)e *adj.* obscure 25.152; dark 30.84

dyn(n)(e) *n.* noise, clamour 35.18; **leue, lat be thy dyn** be quiet 8.80, 9.271, 18.148

ding, deyne, dingne *adj.* worthy 28.1, 29.259, 44.8

dyng(e) *v.* smite, strike 11.399, 16.39, 29.334; **dyngis** *ipv.pl.* 16.133; **dong** *p.p.* 33.331

dyngnité *see* **dygnyté**

dyns *v. 3sg.pr.* resounds with noise 6.114

dynte *n.* blow 7.128

discouer *v.* reveal (a plot), divulge 26.135

discrie *v.* proclaim, reveal 43.22

disease, -easse, -esse *n.* afflicition 42.234, 46.152; injury 25.70, 16.42

disease, dyseas *v.* displease 15.127; disturb 17.150; **diseasid** *p.p.* afflicted 33.196

dispite, dispitte *n.* malice 16.130, 19.133, 25.465

disputuously *adv.* cruelly 19.230

dyssende *v. pa.t.* descended 25.8

disseuer *v.* part company 33.59, 44.83

dite *see* **dight(e)**

dyuers(e) *adj.* diverse, various 1.14, 8.124, 127

do(o) *v.* do; **doand** *pres.p.* doing so 35.267; **didde, ded** *pa.t.* 19.259; put 39.40; **do(o), does, -is** *ipv.* do, perform 1.156, 29.367; cause, provide, ensure 27.40, 38.439; **do way** cease, enough of this 5.60, 6.144, 13.101; **do f(o)urth** begin, perform, get on 8.80, 25.98; **do(o) to dede, dose ... adawe** put to death 18.55, 104, 30.451; **to done** necessary 25.92; **done downe** thwarted 26.7

dochard *n.* fool 26.239

doderon *n.* wretch, miserable creature 32.385

doggydly *adv.* accursedly 33.196

doyf *see* **douf(f)e; dois** *see* **do(o)**

dole, dode, doulle, dule *n.* grief, misery, evil 1.98, 6.25, 11.289, 19.121

doluen *see* **delfe**

dom(m)(e) *adj.* dumb 31.402, 33.64; idle, useless 33.410; *as n.* dumb people 25.132, 30.442

dome *n.* judgement 20.60, 30.533; court 30.84

domysman, -isman *n.* judge 25.538, 29.341; **domesmen** *pl.* 29.20

don(e) *see* **do(o); dong** *see* **dyng(e)** *v.*

dongon *n.* dungeon 1.98; **þat dongeoun hell** 23.128

doole *see* **dole; dose** *see* **do(o)**

do(o)te *n.* fool 26.65, 35.5

do(o)te *v.* speak or behave foolishly 31.270, 34.308; **dotist** *2sg.pr.* 13.179

douf(f)e, doyf, dowue *n.* dove 9.237, 17.248, 37.78 45.109

do(u)ghtir *n.* daughter *as term of affection,* dear wife 14.20, 85, 18.84

doughty, douty *adj.* bold, resolute 25.503, 30.30, 217; **doughtiest, dowtiest** *spv.* 30.227, 281; *as n.* worthy person 30.170

doulfull *adj.* terrible 27.99; grieving 39.13; *as adv.* cruelly 36.18, 319

doulf(f)ully *adv.* grievously 34.153, 36.254

doulle *see* **dole; doune** *n. see* **downe** *n.*

doune-commyng *vbl.n.* descent 12.88

doute *n.* fear 28.2

douty *see* **doughty**

downe, doune *n.* hill; *in phatic phr.* **down(es) and dale(s), dale or ... doune** 2.59, 17.401, 45.187

dowte *v.* fear, worry, 1.64 *(refl.),* 25.541, 30.176

dowtiest *see* **doughty; dowue** *see* **douf(f)e; draffe** *v. pa.t. see* **dryue**

dragons *n. gen.sg.* devil's 21.157

dray(e) *see* **deraye**

draught *n.* trick; **no draught vs drawe** play no trick on us 37.399

drawe *v.* fetch, bring; draw *(sc.* sometimes as a form of punishment) 11.75, 23.128, 33.5, 37.317; cite 38.69; **drawes** *2sg.pr.* 37.279; *3sg.pr.* falls into 16.50; **drawe** *ipv.* incline 31.6; **drewe** *pa.t* caused, incited to 45.17; **drawen** *p.p.* 26.183

drecchid *v. p.p.* frightened 30.176

drecchyng *vbl.n.* (act of) troubling, disturbing; **for the drecchyng of heuen** for heaven's sake 30.181

dredand(e) *ppl.adj.* afraid 10.210, 28.48, 42.224

drede *n.* fear, doubt 7.129, 11.326; *in phatic phr.* **withouten drede** 9.104, 11.400

drede *v.* fear 11.68; *(refl.)* **þou þe dredis** you are afraid 38.121

dredles *adv.* doubtless 13.90

drely *adv.* earnestly 29.78

drerye *adj.* sad, lamentable 45.158; wicked 5.128

dresse *v. (many transf. and fig. senses)* direct, ordain, constitute 2.62, 13.202, 22.201; prepare, endeavour, undertake 29.334 (*refl.*), 31.6, 36.235; place, lay 29.81; correct 20.59, 30.534; **dresand** *pres.p.* 30.191; **dreste** *p.p.* 26.8, 36.240; **I am dressid** I am on my way (to do) 30.193; **dresse vs . . . oure way** let us go 17.228, 271; **dresse þe downe** get out of the way 7.52; **dresse the furth** go forth 17.341; **dresse . . . vppe** build 32.94

dreuen, drevyn *see* **dryue**

drewry *n.* treasure, ornamentation 25.517

dry(e) *adj.* shrivelled, bloodless 11.295; (of sticks) dead 13.28

drynes *n.* dry area 2.61; **in drynesch** as dry land 2.60

dryue, dryff(e) *v. tr.* drive, thrust forth, impel 13.19, 19.16, 30.33; **dryues** *3sg.pr.* tramples down 16.339; **draffe** *pa.t.* 47.338; **dreuen, drevyn** *p.p.* 17.426, 30.199, 33.315; *intr.* **dryffe** *3sg.pr.* drives (as mist, rain etc.) 11.315; **till hethyng . . . dryff** hold up to scorn 13.151

drofyng *vbl.n.* commotion 31.6

drouyd *v. p.p.* vexed 26.239

droune *v.* drown 19.269, 31.308, 32.212

dubbyng *vbl.n.* investment with a title; **dubbyng of my dingnité** rights by virtue of my title 26.7

dugeperes *n.pl.* famous knights (in general) 26.8; leaders 26.183

dule *see* **dole**

dulye, dewly *adj.* lawful 30.270, 409

durdan *n.* uproar, commotion 31.42

dure *v.* last, endure 12.66; **durand** *pres.p.* 11.343

durk *see* **derke**

durst(e) *v. pa.t.* dared 24.14, 41.11; *used in pr. sense* dare 24.153, 41.5; *1sg.pr. subj.* should I dare 29.67

dusshed *v. pa.t.* struck (him) down 45.36

ease, eease *v.* oblige, satisfy 22.111, 34.237

eette *see* **ete**

efte *adv.* likewise, also 30.104, 31.209; again, a second time 30.370; subsequently 41.82

efter, -yr, -ir *see* **after**

eftesones *adv.* another time, again 28.85, 101

eyles *see* **ayles**

egges *v. 3sg.pr.* incites, moves 29.42

eyne, eghen, eghne *n.pl.* eyes 10.288, 18.20,

28.27, 32.21; **hye** *sg.* **giffis gode hye** take heed 25.329

eyre *n.* air 23.172

eke *conj.* also 5.82

eke *v.* increase 2.35; aggravate 26.36

elde, eelde, alde, olde *n.* age 8.91, 10.55, 17.385; old age 12.182; seniority 16.307; coming of age 11.7

elementis *n.pl.* elements, substances of which universe is composed 6.118, 38.86

elleuyn, -en *adj.* eleven 43.5, 10

ellis *adj.* else; **somwhat ellis** something else 9.84, 15.36; **not ellis** no alternative 38.312

ellis *conj.* provided that; **and ellis if** so long as 26.36

elmys *n. gen.pl.* enemies' 34.121

elthers *n.pl.* forefathers 27.14

emang(e) *adv.* continually, thus, 6.158, 37.262, 301

emang(e)(s), amange, in-mange, omange *prep.* among 2.33, 4.45, 12.236, 41.65; in amongst 13.31

eme *see* **yeme**

emel(l)(e) *prep.* between 19.21; amongst 11.30, 29.381; in the midst of 1.146

emell *adv.* thus, in this way 22.9

emyde, emyddis *adv.* in the midst 16.2; in the middle 33.457

enbrace, inbrace *v.* embrace 17.388; pertain to, be upon 36.68; **enbraste** *p.p.* entangled in 13.275; **inbrased** *p.p. (quasi-adj.)* surrounded, on all sides 31.1

encheson *n.* reason 23.208

enclyne *v.* submit 10.245, 42.50; **enclyned** *p.p.* (of manner) disposed 33.70

encresand *ppl.adj.* growing 42.232

encrese *n.* family, pedigree 26.60

endles *adv.* eternally 42.172

endower *v.* endeavour 4.26

endowre *n.* livelihood, way of life 4.30

endurand *ppl.adj.* continuing, endless 6.25

ene *n.* ? e'en, i.e. evening; *cf.* **even** *n.* 29.90

enewe *adv.* again 38.80

enforce *v., refl.* attempt, endeavour 31.311, 33.353; **enforces** *3sg.pr.* 33.195

engenderand *v. pres.p.* giving rise to, causing 31.16

enhance, enhaunce *v.* comfort 17.362; improve, increase 45.68; **enhaunsed** *p.p.* exalted 45.134

enioyned *v. p.p.* united 30.29

enmyse *n.pl.* enemies 42.111

enquere *v.* ask 34.13; **enquered** *pa.t.* asked of 23.34

enquery *n.* investigation; **sitte of enquery** preside over investigations 32.111

ensampelys, ensaumpillis, insaumpillis

n.pl. tokens, prophecies 25.170; signs 41.62; models, patterns 27.86

enserche *v.* seek out 45.291

enspyre *v.* fill, imbue 1.18

enteere, intere *adv.* entirely, wholeheartedly 32.74, 36.2

entent(e) *n.* intention, purpose 10.54, 13.72, 29.316; point (of an argument) 30.416, 33.122; frame of mind, disposition 4.50; attention, heed 7.9, 20.49; **give, take entent** pay attention 2.100, 25.282

entere, entier *adj.* sincere, passionate 7.102; **with herte entere** devoutly 10.309, 14.152

enterly, enteerly, interly *adv.* carefully 7.9; wholly, fully 10.232, 25.151, 28.46; wholeheartedly 36.119

entreand *v. pres.p.* entering, penetrating 12.214

equalité *n.* equality; **thyne equalité** the state of being equal to you 46A.15

equité *n.* state of righteousness 25.393

er, ere, erre *see* **be** *v.*

erbes, -is, -ys *n.pl.* plants, vegetation 2.67, 105, 4.4

erste *adv.* first 28.198

erth(e)ly *adj.* on earth, of this world 4.62, 12.168, 47.213

es *see* **be** *v.*

escheues *v. 3sg.pr.* shuns 30.56; **eschewed** *p.p.* 30.327

esse *n.* ease, convenience 25.40, 36.399

estate, astate *n.* position 30.422, 31.17; standing 31.379; dignity 29.336; high rank 30.230; **stales of astate** court 31.72

ete, eette *v. pa.t.* ate 32.306, 41.147; **eten** *p.p.* 42.95

ethe *adj.* well disposed 30.263

even *n.* evening 25.512, 38.126

euen, even *adj.* equal (in status) 12.19; of an even number 43.7

euen, even, ewen, -yn *adv.* indeed, truly 34.121, 37.76; accordingly, properly 2.29, 43.144; **full euen** almost 30.183; accurately 34.83; equally 37.280

euere *adv.* all the time, continually 6.158

euerelastande *adj.* everlasting 16.57

ever-ylk, euerilka, euere-ilke euery-ilke (a) *etc., adj.* each and every 8.106, 17.60, 19.276, 20.60

euerilkone, -ane *pron.* each and every one, all 6.118, 37.311

evill *adv.* cruelly 35.145

ewen *see* **euen** *adv.*; **ewys(se)** *see* **iwys**

excluded *v. p.p.* nullified, suppressed 15.32

excusacioune *n.* attempt at explanation 47.140

excuse *v.* defend, justify 13.162

exynatores *n.pl.* senators 30.21

expres(se) *adv.* deliberately 22.203; openly, explicitly 23.222, 32.243, 43.17

faciound *v. p.p.* made 31.356

fade *v., tr.* waste, dim the light of 1.60; corrupt, weaken 1.132; *intr.* **faded** *pa.t.* became dim 1.148; **fadande** *pres.p.* withering 45.176

fadir *n.* forefather 12.163; **fader, -yr** *gen.sg.* father's 11.40, 37.79

fage *v.* lie, deceive 33.124

fagyng *vbl.n.* deception; **withouten fagyng** truly 30.515

fay(e), faie *n.* faith; *in phatic phr.* **in fay(e), faie** 17.94, 444, 36.41

fayd *adj.* troublesome, untrustworthy 9.257

faie *n.* dead 39.24

faile *v.* fall short 35.112; fall into disarray 43.82; **failis** *3sg.pr.* 35.107; **fayles** *3pl.pr.* (of faculties) fail, cease functioning 24.154

fayland *ppl.adj.* fickle, weak 9.228, 23.210

faynde *see* **fonde** *v.*; **fayndyngis** *see* **fandyng**

fayne, faughe *adj.* glad, joyful, happy 6.95, 11.360, 16.109; pleasing, enjoyable 4.34; eager of, desirous 30.49; **fayner** *cpv.* 31.155

fayne *adv.* gladly, eagerly 5.135, 10.185, 25.220

faynte *adj.* untrustworthy 29.227

faire, fayre *n. see* **fare** *n.*

faire, fare *adv.* politely 25.191; properly, in an orderly fashion 8.131

fayrear *adj.* splendid, handsome 1.53

fayrhede *n.* physical beauty 1.66, 129

fays *see* **foo**

faythely *adv.* indeed, truly 1.19

faitour(e), faytor, faytour(e) *n.* liar, deceiver, cheat 11.213, 16.27, 26.47, 37.157

fall(e) *v.* happen, come about 11.374, 15.107, 16.208; desist, repent 36.210; *impers.* **falles, -is** is appropriate, befits 19.12, 24.47, 31.351; **me falles** I deserve 15.45; **falle** *3pl.pr.* are allotted 31.342; **falland(e)** *pres.p.* falling 1.94; subsiding 9.243; **falle** *pr. subj.* should belong, pertain 26.55; **fallis** *ipv.pl.* incline 36.4; **foule falle þe, fowll myght thowe fall** a curse on you 7.97, 30.392; **faire falle þe, faire mott ye fall** a blessing on you 16.49, 29.214; **fallen full faire** prospered 29.197; **fallen fra** turned away from 6.18; **falle ynne** begin 31.187; **falle on hande** be put aside 16.194

false *n.* treachery 26.170

falsed *n.* falsehood, wickedness 16.387, 30.203, 31.309

falsely *adj.* wicked, sinful 32.244

famed *v. p.p.* proclaimed 32.211

fande *v.* attempt *see* **fonde** *v.*; **fande** *v.* go *see* **founde**; **fande** *v. p.p. see* **finde**

fandelyng *n.* brat 19.157; **fondelyngis** *pl.* 19.193

fandyng *n.* temptation 28.12, 32; trouble 40.189; **fandyngis, fayndyngis** trials, tribulations 6.47, 27.84

fang(e) *v.* take, catch, have 11.355, 19.128, 39.48; partake of (food) 5.79, 9.227, 31.202; gain 26.47; **fanges** *ipv.pl.* assume responsibility for 9.174; **fanged** *pa.t.* acquired, won 26.17; **fang(e) on** go, proceed 28.294; resume dealings with 32.374

fantasie, -ye, -sy *n.* untruth, lie 13.142, 27.133; apparition 23.99; **in fantasyes fell** became deluded 1.129

fantyse *n.* treachery, deceit 11.82

fantome *n.* guile 30.298

farand *see* **fare** *v.*

fare, faire, -yre *n.* business, matter 9.90, 11.374, 42.274; behaviour, practices 13.100, 29.277, 37.158

fare *adv. see* **faire** *adv.*

fare *v.* go, depart 5.173, 11.183, 16.101; fare, continue, live 11.292; **fares** *3sg.pr.* is concerned 29.58; **faren** *3pl.pr.* 11.303; **farand** *pres.p.* 31.366; **fared, fore, fure** *pa.t.* 11.292, 31.249, 43.34, 47.336; **faren** *p.p.* 23.232, 31.103; **we fare** we make it our business 31.91; **gan fare** was involved 30.502; **how fare 3e** what are you doing 24.28

farly, farle(i)s, farlis *n. see* **ferly** *n.*; **farly** *adj. see* **ferly** *adj.*

farrar *adv.* further 11.62, 80

fast *adj.* (held) firm 28.303

fast(e) *adv.* tightly, firmly 8.108, 9.24, 10.214; vigourously, earnestly 11.118, 24.129, 25.319; **as faste** very soon 44.118

faste *v.* fasten *see* **fest(e)** *v.*

fastande *v. pres.p.* fasting, suffering deprivation 1.80

fauchone *n.* large sword 31.255

faughe *adj. see* **fayne** *adj.*; **faute** *n. see* **fawte**

faute *v.* lack, want of 31.239; **fautis** *3sg.pr.* offends 33.257

fauty, fawté *adj.* misguided, mistaken 26.83, 40.130

fawlde *see* **folde** *v.*

fawte, faute *n.* fault, failing, sin 10.219, 246, 26.209; want, lack 42.60, 135

fawté *see* **fauty**; **feare** *n. see* **fere** *n.²*

febyll, -ill *n.* infirmity, weakness 17.94, 18.18

febyll, -ill *adj.* immoral, evil 13.100; insignificant, base 3.31; weak through sickness 44.95; of weak faith 17.42, **febill of faithe** 23.169

febilly *adv.* aimlessly 24.160

fecche *n.* fish 41.70

fecched *v. pa.t.* brought 45.229

fe(e)de *v.* feed 47.302; nourish, bring up 13.185; eat 30.109; **fedde** *pa.t.* 29.276, 31.188; **fedd, fede** *p.p.* spiritually nourished 1.76; **fedd/Be tyne** deceived 12.25

fedrys *n.pl.* feathers 2.141

fee *n.¹* beasts, livestock 4.13, 11.58; sheep 15.35; property 47.218; **feste as fee** trussed up like an animal 34.336; **fange vnto my fee** have in my keeping 39.48

fee *n.²* reward 31.342

feele *adj. see* **fele** *adj.*

feele, feill, fel(l)(e) *v.¹* perceive, know, see 8.138, 10.78, 19.157, 25.150; discover 9.127; enquire into, examine 31.118; think 26.18; **felys** *ipv.pl.* touch 41.56; **felande** *pres.p.* tasting 1.79; **felde, feled** *p.p.* 10.225, 27.64

feele, feylle *v.²* cover, conceal 8.108, 9.202

feende *see* **fende** *n.*

feere *n.* fear 10.42

feere *n.* companion *see* **fere** *n.¹*; **feere** *n.* company *see* **fere** *n.²*

feere *v.* suit, befit 31.356

feere *v.* frighten *see* **fere** *v.¹*

feese *v.* prosecute 16.40; punish 30.426; **fesid** *p.p.* upset, discomfited 33.195

feeste *n. see* **feste** *n.*

feetour *n.pl.* features 32.19

feill *v.* perceive *see* **feele** *v.¹*; **feylle** *v.* cover *see* **feele** *v.²*

feyndes *n.pl. see* **fende** *n.*

feyne *v.* invent, fabricate 5.24; hesitate, hold back 25.249, 31.312; **feynes** *3sg.pr.* 33.100; *2pl.pr.* 13.142; **feyned** *pa.t.* pretended 29.230; refrained 32.250; **feyned** *p.p.* 30.326

feyned *ppl.adj.* treacherous 16.387 *(see prec.)*

fekyll *adj.* fickle, untrustworthy 7.63

felawe, felowe *n.* fellow *(often contemptuous)* 24.3, 37.284; **felas, felaus** *pl.* 45.88, 47.217

felaws(c)hippe *n.* company, group 29.130, 33.441, 45.214

felde *n.* field 22.146; *in phatic phr.* **in þe felde, on felde** 25.377, 39.24

felde *v. p.p. see* **feele** *v.¹*

fele, feele, felle *adj.* many, numerous 19.256, 26.111, 31.203, 43.120

fele *adv.* in large numbers, frequently 20.183

fele *adj.* fierce *see* **fell(e)** *adj.*; **fele, feled, felys** *v. see* **feele** *v.¹*

felesome *adj.* pleasant (to the taste) 45.136

felyng *vbl.n.* ? perception *or* defilement 1.60

fell *n.¹* skin; **flessh(e) and fell** bodily form 38.250, 40.123, 45.73

fell *n.²* hill, upland; *in phatic phr.* **firth and fell** 2.126

fell(e), fele *adj.* cruel, grievous 6.47, 34.174, 41.4; fierce, horrible 2.134, 22.173; malicious 32.71, 244; **fellest** *spv.* (of frost) keenest 14.72

fell(e) *v.* overthrow 11.28, 12.116, 15.31; knock down 30.241; kill 16.53, 30.417; put an end to 16.193; **fellid** *pa.t.* 36.372; *p.p.* 43.174; **fell/Tille offerand** make sacrifice of 10.205

fell(e) *v.* perceive *see* **feele** *v.¹*; **felle** *adj.* many *see* **fele** *adj.*

felle *adv.* sharply, grievously 35.136

felly *adv.* burdened with sin 6.64

felonye, felouné *n.* treachery 16.34, 32.62, 244

felons *n.pl.* criminals 32.336

felons, felowns *adj.* deceitful, wicked 11.39, 363

felouné *see* **felonye; felowe** *see* **felawe**

fende, feende *n.* fiend, devil, Satan 12.24, 25, 44.154

fende *v.* defend 10.62, 11.368; prevent 2.19; assail 30.108

fendes-craft *n.* diabolical contriving 30.298

fenne *n.* marshland; *in phatic phr.* **fenne or frith, frith or . . . fenne** 7.127, 45.229

ferde *n.* fear 10.270, 30.393

ferde *ppl.adj.* afraid 10.211, 28.99, 31.327; **ferdest** *spv.* 33.208

ferdnes(se) *n.* fear, terror 28.89, 47.78

fere, feer(e) *n.¹* companion, spouse 3.37, 17.187; equal, peer 26.18

fere, feare, feer(e) *n.²* company; **in fere** *etc.* together, all together, as a group 2.58, 9.144, 12.206 *(often phatic);* **all fe(e)re** 16.142

fere, feere *v.* frighten, intimidate 11.134, 29.213, 44.155; distract 34.222

ferly, farly *n.* wonder, marvel 8.40; **ferlis, -eis, farles, -is, -eis** *pl.* 25.128, 30.443, 502, 31.188, 37.61, **had farly** were amazed, marvelled 21.22

ferly, farly *adj.* wondrous, extraordinary 10.78, 13.253, 25.394

ferre *adv.* far, a long way, away 9.58, 31.103, 37.156; **ferre** *cpv.* further 11.333; **ferre before** long ago 43.190

fers(e) *adj.* ferocious 2.134; violent, dangerous 37.131; cruel 45.23

fersly *adv.* boldly 17.121

fersly *adv.* freshly *see* **fresshely**

fersnesse *n.* cruel force 45.33

feruent *adj.* warm 29.94

fesid *see* **feesc**

fest *ppl.adj.* firm, sure 13.247 *(see next)*

fest(e), faste *v.* secure, make fast, place 8.108, 29.363, 45.84; tie 35.113; fetter,

imprison 11.308; **fest** *pa.t.* united 33.75; **fest(e)** *p.p.* 1.66, 35.122, 37.335

feste, feest *n.* feast day, holy day 25.20, 29.260; feast, revelry 15.44; spiritual nourishment 45.67

festynde *v. p.p.* combined, united 2.58

fetys, fettis *adj.* handsome, well-formed 1.55, 65, 16.49

fett(e) *v.* fetch 16.336, 25.63, 44.184; **fette** *pa.t.* brought out, rescued 37.382

fette *n.pl. see* **fote; fettis** *see* **fetys**

fewell *n.* fuel 14.44

fewle, fewll *see* **fowle** *n.;* **fewne** *see* **fone** *n.* (*as adj.*)

fy(e), fie *interj., expr. of disapproval, indignation etc.* 11.67, 217, 19.115, 29.296

fye *v.* denounce, execrate 24.38

figure, fygure, figour(e) *n.* aspect, expression (of the face) 26.161, 45.198; appearance, likeness 1.140, 44.155; being, human being 30.109, 45.73; sign, prefiguration 42.103; **figuris** *pl.* heavenly bodies 2.101

fygured *v. p.p.* fashioned, shaped 1.65

filde *ppl.adj.⁽¹⁾* polite, courteous of speech 45.242

file *v.* blame, find guilty, traduce 31.399, 32.253; **filed, -id, -yd, fyled** *etc.,* **fylde** *p.p., adj.⁽²⁾ (see prec.)* 34.124; violated, corrupted, defiled 12.173, 13.106, 44.3; sinful 39.57; polluted 17.39, 48

filth, fylth(e) *n.* impurity, corruption, sin 1.60, 132; rubbish, ordure 1.106

find(e), fynd(e) *v.* discover, find; support, nourish spiritually 16.309; **fand(e), fonde** *pa.t.* 11.50, 20.134, 40.48, 45.351; **fon(n)(e), founden, fun(n)(e), fundyn** *p.p.* 2.101, 126, 7.100, 10.12, 306, 11.39, 20.183, 23.100, 31.117, 33.103, 36.101

fynde *ppl.adj.* ripe 2.81

fyne *n.* fin 2.129

fyne *adv.* fittingly 26.142

fyne *v. intr.* stop, pause 9.51, 35.81; pass by, go away 35.256; *tr.* put an end to 17.460; **fynyd** *p.p.* 9.287

fyrd *v. p.p.* rejected, put aside 17.248

fyrste *n.* first; **in þe fyrste** in the beginning 1.19; **at firste** for the first time 9.127

firth, fyrth(e) *see* **frith**

fitte *n.* harrowing experience; **fele þi fitte** undergo your appointed punishment 37.346

fitte, fytt *adj.* ready, suitable 35.161; handsome, becoming 1.65

flagraunt *adj.* ? radiant, glorious 46A.39

flay(e) *v.* frighten, intimidate 31.91, 43.88; punish 30.203, 31.400; put to flight 28.274; **flaies** *3sg.pr.* 31.255; **flaied, flayed** *p.p.* 24.4, 41.40

flappe *n.* blow 29.363
flaterer *n.* liar, deceiver 33.366
fleme *v.* escape 29.94 *(refl.)*; condemn 31.400; banish 42.55 *(ipv.)*, 126; **flemyd** *p.p.* 18.98
flenge *see* **flynge**
flesh *n.* human being 42.38
flesshly *adv.* in bodily form 45.77, 251
flet *v.* swim 2.129
flighte *v. see* **flyte**
flynge, flenge *v.* fly 25.381; **flynge to** flail at 33.366
flyte, flighte *v.* argue, wrangle 16.132, 35.297
flitte *v. intr.* go, depart, escape 11.307, 15.34, 16.389; move, remove 9.58, 11.271; *tr.* expel 37.210; **flittand** *pres.p.* 30.548
floode, flode, flowyd *n.* flood 8.27; river 21.53; waters 37.76
florisshand *ppl.adj.* blooming 25.496
florisshed *ppl.adj.* blooming 45.136
floscampy *n.* flower of the field 17.366
floure *n.* flower 25.496, 26.206
flowyd *see* **floode**
flume *n.* river 37.76
fode *see* **foode** *n.*[1], *n.*[2]
folde *n.* earth; *in phatic phr.* **on folde** 16.17
folde, fawlde *v.* bend over 33.189; fail, grow weak 8.113
fole, fule *n.* fool 30.444, 33.387, 34.28
folye *n.* folly, wickedness 25.69; **with folye** committing sin 24.3
folowand *v. pres.p.* to come, to be 20.264
folte *n.* idiot, blockhead 32.263
fomen *n.pl.* enemies 28.151, 42.126
fon(e) *v. p.p. see* **find(e)**
fonde, fonned *adj., ppl.adj.* foolish, deranged 31.250, 294, 33.167
fonde, faynde, fande, founde *v.* try, attempt, endeavour 5.18, 24, 10.205, 9.80 *(absol.)*; seek 16.156, 28.241; find out 20.264; **fandis** *ipv.pl.* 20.152
fonde *v.* go *see* **founde**
fondely *adv.* stupidly 32.211
fondelyngis *see* **fandelyng**
fone *n.* few 19.256, 26.11; *as adj.* **fewne, fone, fune** 21.72, 36.284, 42.200
fonn(e) *v. p.p. see* **find(e)**
fonne *v.* act madly, behave foolishly 33.309; **fonnes** *2sg.pr.* 9.89
fonned *see* **fonde** *adj.*
foo *n.* foe 26.91, 36.233; **fays** *pl.* 11.198
foode, fode, fudde *n.*[1] food, nourishment 1.106, 11.262, 37.10; spiritual sustenance 1.76, 22.77
foode, fode *n.*[2] baby, child 14.91, 15.78, 18.201; person 16.40, 31.250, 45.54
foole *n.* foal 25.22

for *prep.* because 5.36, 23.14; because of 1.129, 23.170; in spite of 2.19, 38.361; in order that 23.78; as if for 33.198; in respect of 42.91; by 29.332
for *prep.* from *see* **fro**
for *adv.* forth 19.100; beforehand 13.286
forbede *v.* forbid 21.109; **forbed** *pa.t.* 6.33; **forbyd** *p.p.* 4.79
forbere *v.* withold 30.461; tolerate 30.326; neglect, fail to perform 27.183
forbledde *ppl.adj.* weakened by loss of blood 34.223, 243
force, forse *n.* strength, power 2.19, 8.113, 11.28; constraint 10.225; **no force** irrelevant 35.136; **make no force** consider insignificant 11.211
fordede *n.* favour 21.107
fordele *n.* advantage 15.107
fordo *v.* destroy, kill, ruin 11.66, 18.121, 32.52; **fordone** *p.p.* 8.22
fore *v. pa.t. see* **fare** *v.*
fore-reyner *n.* precursor 21.16
foreswore *v. pa.t.* denied 47.340; **forsworne** *p.p.* abjured 47.119
forfare *v.* wreak vengeance 18.140; put to death 32.336
forfette *n.* punishment 28.247; **forfettis** *pl.* offences 30.26
forfette *v.* transgress, offend 31.92; confiscate, deprive of 38.319; **forfette** *pa.t.* 21.119, 37.352
forgange *v.* relinquish 18.101
forge *v.* plot, contrive 42.118; **forges** *3sg.pr.* 16.34
forgetyn *v. p.p.* overlooked 31.210
for-grete *adj.* excessive 35.189
forlorne *ppl.adj.* damned 47.117
for-marryde *ppl.adj.* utterly destroyed 1.139
forme *n.* outward appearance 1.66
forme-faders, -yrs, -res *n.pl.* forefathers 9.14, 12.110, 15.5, 23.181
former *n.* maker 17.454
forne *prep.* on behalf of 22.15
fornicacioun *n.* fornication (as distinct from adultery) 24.34
for-pechyng *v. pres.p.* panting excessively, breathing hard 40.84
forsake *v.* turn from 42.204; **forsoke** *pa.t.* omitted, failed 42.197; left 38.391; **forsaked** *p.p.* abandoned to destruction 47.348
forse *n. see* **force**
forse *v. 3sg.pr.* signifies, helps 45.242
forsoke *see* **forsake**
forsoth(e) *adv.* truly, indeed 15.92, 25.11 *(often phatic)*
forsworne *v. p.p. see* **foreswore**
forth(e), furth(e), fourth(e) *adv.* forth, away, out; **do furthe** begin 8.80

forthe *v. ipv.* obey, proceed 31.250
fortheraunce *n.* support, favour 36.47
forþer, fortheren *v.* expedite 29.391; proceed with 29.245; **fortheres** *3sg.pr.* profits, is as well 18.168
forthi, forthy, forþi *conj.* therefore, for that reason
forthinkith *v. 3sg.pr., impers.* **me forthinkith** I am sorry 45.224
forthinking *ppl.adj.* repentant 9.279
forþoght *n.* plan 2.150, 47.373
forty *adj.* fortieth 17.38
forwakid *ppl.adj.* tired with watching 28.5
forwandered *ppl.adj.* exhausted with wandering 13.250
forward(e) *n.* promise, agreement, covenant 10.212, 16.249, 37.166
forward *adv.* hereafter 20.14; **euere forward** henceforth forever 27.31
for-wente *ppl.adj.* tired; **for-wente of youre way** tired out by your journey 30.151
for-why *adv.* since, because 4.86, 36.360; wherefore 26.119, 36.243
fostyr *v.* nourish 2.65
fote *n.* foot; **fette** *pl.* 25.483, 34.81
fouchesaffe, fouchest saffe *see* **vowchesaffe**
foul(l)e, fowll *adv.* unfortunately, unluckily 36.65; **foule/fowll myght thowe fare/fall, foule falle** þe a curse on you 7.97, 30.387, 392
foulis, -ys *see* **fowle**
founde, fande, fonde *v.* go, go along with, proceed, leave 6.96, 30.548, 32.374, 40.147; **fonde/fande** þe hasten, betake yourself 18.149, 32.360; **foundynge** *pres.p.* 45.125
founde *v.* attempt *see* **fonde** *v.*; **founden, foune** *see* **find(e)**
founding *vbl.n.* walking, going 45.251
foure *adv.* four times 11.308
fourme *v.* create 1.142
fourth(e) *see* **forth(e)**
fowle, fewle, fewll *n.* bird 4.13, 20, 9.205, 17.236; **foulis, -ys** *pl.* 2.139, 3.10
fowly, fully *adv.* wickedly, treacherously 29.50, 297, 32.253
fowll *adv. see* **foul(l)e**
fray(e) *n.* breach of the peace 38.150; offence 31.309; trouble, difficulty 17.267, 347
frayes *v. 3sg.pr.* dismays 30.445
frayne, freyne *v.* ask, enquire (about, into) 9.90, 10.185, 16.107; ? learn 31.2; **frayned** *pa.t.* 45.84; **frayne/At** ask of 10.353; **freyne beforne** enquire into it 38.440
fraiste, -yste, frast(e) *v.* try, attempt, endeavour 2.141, 15.35, 40.158; en-

deavour to help 40.189; discover, find out 7.63, 16.239, 31.104; question, examine 29.244; **fraysted** *pa.t.* sought 33.85
fraistyng, frasting *vbl.n.* trial, being put to the test 40.48, 49
frappe *n.* crowd; **all** þe **frappe** all of you 33.309
frast(e) *see* **fraiste; frasting** *see* **fraistyng**
frawde *n.* deceit, piece of trickery 42.118; **frawdis** *pl.* falsehoods 33.130
fre(e) *adj.* willing 2.116, 47.286; (of land tenure) freehold 32.347, 348; gracious, worthy 16.231, 18.35; *as n.* worthy person 25.105, 47.35
freele *adj.* frail 21.84
freese *n.* frost 14.72
freyke *see* **freke**
freykenesse *n.* ? courage, boldness 31.2
freyms *v. 3sg.pr.* devises, concocts 31.309
freyne *see* **frayne**
freke, freyke *n.* man, person 28.247, 30.417
frekly *adv.* speedily 11.394
frely(e) *adj.* noble, worthy 15.78, 19.110, 45.309
frendis *n.pl.* relatives, kinsmen 20.270, 37.62
frendfull *adj.* loving 40.48
frendlye *adv.* lovingly 46.18
fressh *adv.* brightly 45.136
fresshe *adj.* bright 45.168
fresshely, fersly *adv.* briskly 30.548; afresh, anew 45.73
frewte *see* **fruyt(e)**
frith, firth, fyrth(e) *n.* wood; field 30.345; *in phatic phr.* **frith or fenne, felde; firth and fell** 2.126, 13.9, 17.93, 45.229
fro *prep.* from, *sometimes written* **for**, 2.142, 9.267; from the time that, when 11.364, 26.285, 30.84
froo *adv.* away 37.210
frosshis *n.pl.* frogs 11.271
fruyt(e), frewte, frute, fruth *n.* fruit 2.72, 4.4, 74, 5.28, 45.136; reward 37.10; offspring 25.164
frusshe *v.* hit 29.360
frute, fruth *see* **fruyt(e); fudde** *see* **foode** *n.¹*
fule *n. see* **fole**
ful(l)fill(e), fulfyll *v.* carry out, comply with (a request, command, promise) 3.80, 4.71, 10.119, 16.249, 30.307; replenish, fill 1.140, 8.12; satisfy 16.88; **fulfillid** *p.p.* ended, completed 2.123
fulgent *adj.* radiant 46A.1
full *adv.* very
full *v.* befoul, corrupt 1.60
fully *adv.* together 25.104
fully *adv.* foully *see* **fowly**

fuls *v. 3sg.pr.* tramples down, oppresses 11.118

fun(n)(e) *see* find(e); **fune** *adj. see* **fone** *n. (as adj.)*; **fundyn** *see* find(e); **fure** *v. pa.t. see* **fare** *v.*; **furth(e)** *see* forth(e) *adv.*

gab(be) *v.* lie, prevaricate 13.48, 141
gabbyngis *vbl.n.* idle talk 20.26
gadir, gedir *v.* gather, collect up 10.376, 13.300, 19.149
gadlyng, gedlyng *n.* scoundrel, knave 19.63, 68, 26.157
gaffe *see* **giue**
gay(e) *adj.* richly attired 20.232, 31.284; sumptuous 31.283; merry 29.289
gayly *adv.* (of attire) richly 25.115, 31.344
gayne *adj.* pleasing, agreeable 30.47; **gaynest, ganeste** *spv.* (of routes, ways) most direct, quickest 10.90, 373
gayne *v.* be useful, profit 8.140, 11.248, 38.179; *impers.* **ʒow, hym gaynes** it profits you, him 26.106, 35.149
gaynesaye, -saie *v.* oppose 10.198, 25.29; contradict 24.32; **gaynesaies** *3sg.pr.* 29.123
gaynest, ganeste *see* **gayne** *adj.*
gaynestande *v.* withstand, oppose 38.371; **gaynestandyng** *pres.p.* 10.55
gales *v. 3sg.pr.* complains 33.23
game, gamme, gome *n.* joy, pleasure, sport 6.7, 17.103; happening, matter 23.104, 29.204; **gamys** *pl.* rejoicings 37.20; **grettest of game** the noblest, most accomplished 26.10
gan(e), gon(e), gun(e) *v. pa.t.* did
ganeste *see* **gayne** *adj.*
gang(e) *v.* go, depart, move 2.114, 6.161, 22.1; fare, prosper 38.56; **gangand** *pres.p.* 45.221; travelling 23.16
gar(r)(e) *v.* cause, make; **gar(e)s** *3sg.pr.* 1.103, 18.55; **garte** *pa.t.* 5.142, 8.52, 25.137
gast(e) *n.* spirit 3.41, 12.239, 21.14
gate, gatte *n.* way, thoroughfare 9.98, 11.228, 25.402; **gates, -is** *pl.* 1.155, 10.373; things, matters 12.48; **gatis most nedis be gone** painful deed must be done 10.197; **gatis . . . haue I gone** sufferings I have endured 41.55
gate *v. pa.t.* begat, conceived upon 13.73
gawde *n.* deceitful trick 13.137; **gaudes, -is, gawdes** *pl.* 11.37, 22.122, 37.160; jests, amusement 31.237
geddryng *vbl.n.* gathering, assemblage 2.64
gedy *adv.* rashly, precipitately 26.105
gedir *see* gadir; **gedlyng** *see* gadlyng; **geffe, geffyn** *see* **giue**
generacio(u)n *n.* breeding, lineage 30.28, 45.15, 132

genolagye, genolgie *n.* genealogy 25.242; pedigree, descent 30.29
gente, jente *adj.* gracious, worthy 28.161, 36.261, 46.74
gentries, gentrys *n.* noble family 30.29; noble qualities 31.16
ge(e)re *n.* clothes, apparel 13.300, 31.283; things, provisions 8.140, 10.149; equipment, tools, tackle 34.42, 35.29, 38.179; affairs, matters 24.2
ges(se) *v.* plan, intend for 2.93, 168
gest(e) *n.* guest, stranger 40.155, 47.295; wicked man 30.520, 36.339
get(t)(e), gytt *v.* get, have 17.364, 25.193; suffer, have (need) 3.74; reach, come to 45.95; **geten, getyn** *p.p.* 19.255; won 37.11
geue, geve *see* **giue**
gy *v.* guide 14.45
gydis *n.pl.* guides 45.95, 312
gif(f)(e), gyf(f)(e) *conj. see* if; **gyf, giffe, gyffyne** *see* **giue**
giffer *n.* giver 44.64
gyle *n.* guile 6.49
gilery *n.* treachery 37.160
gilte *n.* fault 6.138
gynn(e) *n.* device, contrivance 35.197; tool for fastening joints 8.101
girde *v. p.p.* clothed 31.344
gyrnes *v. 3sg.pr.* grimaces 33.23; **gyrnande** *pres.p.* snarling 1.103
gyrse *see* gres; **gyrth** *n. see* grith
gyrth *v.* protect, defend 1.133
gytt *see* get(t)(e)
giue, gyf, giffe, geffe, geue *v.* give 1.147, 7.61, 70, 37.114; **geve** *3sg.pr.* 25.406; **gaffe** *pa.t.* 7.61, 37.163, 42.39; **gyffyne, geffyn** *p.p.* 3.56, 7.108; **gaffe . . . noght** did not scruple 6.14, 47.7; **giffe þe noght ill** do not be concerned 42.216; **gyvis tale** thinks worthwhile 28.292; **giffe . . . wiste** make aware 44.57
glade *v. pa.t. see* **glyde**
gladde *adv.* cheerfully 6.85, 161
gladly *adv.* easily 16.328
gle(e) *n.* radiance, brightness 1.82; pleasure, joy 6.7, 17.318, 25.477; **gladdere þanne þe glee** overjoyed 39.135
gleme *n.* gleam, ray of light 16.328, 32.21
glent *n.* subterfuge 22.38
gleteryng *vbl.n.* glittering, sparkling 1.82
glyde, glide *v.* glide, move smoothly 17.120, 32.339; **glydis** *3sg.pr.* 30.76; **glydand** *pres.p.* 45.118, **glade** *pa.t.* 16.328
glyfftyng *vbl.n.* glaring 26.158
glitterand *ppl.adj.* glittering 30.76
glorand *v. pres.p.* glowering 26.157
glorious *adj. as n.* glorious one 45.262
glotonye *n.* gluttony 22.47

goo *v.* go; fare, prosper 38.323; **gone** *inf.*
occupy, amuse (oneself) 35.200; **goos,
gose** *ipv.pl.* 2.57, 9.49; **gone in grete eelde**
very aged 10.32; **gose þe by** (of sound of
voices) drowns you 25.331

God *n. gen.sg.* God's 12.180, 16.222, 23.38

go(o)de, gud *n.* goods, possessions 7.41,
25.449; good things, victuals 40.155

Godhead, -hede *n.* divinity, God 2.7, 5.3,
16.327

gollyng *vbl.n.* shouting, outcry 30.235

gome *n.* man 26.52; child 19.255; **gomes** *pl.*
people, persons 30.229, 33.219

gome *n.* game *see* **game**

gone *v.* stand open-mouthed 15.59

gone *v. inf., p.p. see* **goo; gon(e)** *v. auxil. see*
gan(e)

goodely *adj. as n.* worthy person 45.262

good(e)ly *adv.* in a becoming fashion
28.283, 31.381

goos, gose *v. ipv.pl., 3sg.pr. see* **goo**

gost(e)ly *adj.* spiritual 22.77, 27.158

gouernaunce *n.* behaviour 33.181

gowlande *v. pres.p.* howling, wailing 1.103

grace *n.* favour 23.80; miracle 23.40; **saue
thy grace** may it not displease you 21.109

gracious *adj. as n.* gracious person 30.116

grayth, grath *v.* make, cause to be 12.19;
provide instruction 45.312; **grayd(e)** *pa.t.*
arrayed, framed 23.171; gave, bestowed
upon 12.141; **grayd(e), -ied, -yed,
grathid(e)** *p.p.* prepared, made ready
12.190, 225, 35.39; put in hand 24.2;
given a greeting 28.250; built, made
10.159, 186; created 36.98; **grath hym . . .
gate** make ready to go 32.16; **grath(ed) in
graue** bury, buried 24.161, 36.340

gramercy(e), -marcy, graunte mercy *interj.*
many thanks 13.92, 20.281, 30.106

granyng *vbl.n.* lamentation 40.59

grath *n.* ? *for* **garth** enclosure, *sc.* grave
(prob. error for **graue***)* 31.221

grath *adj.* wise 45.312

grath, grathide *v. see* **grayth**

grathe *adv.* diligently 16.251

grathely, grathly, gratthely *adv.* directly,
forthwith 24.126, 37.92; plainly, truly
8.85, 36.98; properly, suitably, worthily
2.114, 10.144, 12.225

graue *n.* grave, sepulchre 24.140

graue *v.* bury 36.338, 390; dig the earth
9.23; put to death 26.105; **graued** *pa.t.*
45.259; **graued, grauen** *p.p.* 24.140, 38.203

graunte *v.* agree (to) 22.158, 25.266; admit
(to) 29.252, 30.475; **grauntest** *2sg.pr.*
29.147; **graunte, graunted** *pa.t.* allowed
30.448; claimed to be 30.221, 33.294;
graunte, graunted 4.2, 44.33; **permitted**
30.23; **graunte . . . till** agree with 25.254

graunte mercy *see* **gramercy(e)**

grec *n.* seemly manner 36.338

greeffe *v. see* **greue**

greffe, griffe *n.* trouble, affliction, temptation 22.206, 26.106, 36.397; grievance
26.201

gres, gyrse *n.* grass 2.91, 3.9

grete, grette *n.¹* weeping 18.192, 29.79

grete *n.²* earth 38.203, 284

grete, grette *adj.* great 32.214, 42.184;
gretteste *spv., as n.* most important persons 30.510

grete *v.¹* greet 24.58; **grete, grette** *pa.t.*
25.191, 30.341, 33.55

grete, grette *v.²* weep 39.116, 40.59

gretyng *vbl.n.¹* salutation 46.116

gretyng *vbl.n.²* weeping 34.200

grette *n., adj., v. see* **grete** *n.¹, adj., v.²;*
gretteste *see* **grete** *adj.*

greuaunce, grevance *n.* offence 7.104; affliction, distress 11.314, 17.364

greue, greve, greeffe *v.* harass, oppress
11.279, 24.42; injure, (do) harm 11.131,
22.190; anger 6.53, 16.185; feel anguish
10.177; grieve for 27.72; **greues** *3sg.pr.*
26.13; **greved** *p.p.* 7.104, 9.275

greuous *adj.* angry 33.181

grewe *v.* live, dwell 45.112; **grewes** *3pl.pr.*
16.220

griffe *n. see* **greffe** *n.*

gryll, grill *adj.* furious 33.181; bold 33.219

grymly *adj.* angry 26.158

grise *v.* shudder with horror 32.214

grissely *adj.* bitter 40.59

grissely *adv.* sorrowfully 39.116

grith, gyrth *n.* safety, protection 9.154,
16.206; favour 17.396

groche *see* **grouche**

grome *n.* servant, underling 32.29

grone *n.* groan (of disapprobation); **for a
grone** with a groan 26.13

grope, groppe *v.* enquire (of), (into), seek
23.194, 29.204, 45.259; **gropes** *ipv.pl.*
touch 41.51

grouche, groche, grucche, grughe *v.* be-
grudge, refuse 7.70, 30.475; complain,
demur 10.177, 19.28, 36.117; **grucchis**
3sg.pr. 32.245; **grucchand** *pres.p.* 22.206

grounde, grunde *n.* world 11.85; earth,
horizon 30.76, 77; basis, foundation (of a
principle) 10.51; reason, evidence 26.106;
source 1.74; place indicated 36.299

grounded *v. p.p.* confirmed, established
45.196

growe *v.* (of the heart) swell with indignation 26.158

grubbe *v.* dig, delve 9.23

grucche, grucchand, grughe *see* **grouche;
grunde** *see* **grounde; gud** *n. see* **go(o)de**

gud(d)(e) *adj.* good; *as n.* good person 16.327

gudly *adv.* in a seemly manner 30.99, 116

gudnes *n.* goodness, benevolence 42.13

gulles *n.* gules, red tincture 16.19

gun(e) *see* **gan(e)**; **gwisse** *see* **iwys(se)**

ȝa(a), ȝae *see* yaa; ȝappely *see* yappely; ȝare *see* yhare; ȝate *see* yate; ȝe, ȝhe *see* ye; ȝede *see* yo(o)de; ȝeff *conj. see* if; ȝelde ȝelde *see* yeelde; ȝeme *n. see* yeme

ȝem(e) *v.* take care of, look to, pay heed to 3.18, 27.66, 31.418; **ȝemed** *p.p.* 43.128

ȝemyng *vbl.n.* care, keeping 42.46

ȝenge *see* yhing; ȝer(e) *see* yhere; ȝerned *see* yarne; ȝet, ȝhit, ȝitt *see* yhitt; ȝing, ȝynge *see* yhing

ȝister-even *n.* yesterday night 34.107

ȝhit, ȝitt *see* yhitt; ȝo *see* ȝou; ȝo(o)ne *see* yon(e); ȝonge *see* yhing; ȝoode *see* yo(o)de

ȝou, ȝo, ȝow *pron.* you

ȝour(e), ȝour *pron.* your

ȝouþe *n.* youth 27.66

haale *v.* pull, haul 35.116; **haylle** *ipv.* 35.140; **hales** *3sg.pr.* pours 33.399

had, haffe *see* **haue**

haftis *n.pl.* matters, business 20.76

haylle *v. see* **haale**; **haylsing** *see* **halsyng**

hayre *n.* heir 11.7

halde *n., v. see* **holde** *n., v.*

hale *adj. see* **hole** *adj.*; **hales** *v. 3sg.pr. see* **haale**

halfe *n.* behalf 25.192

halfe *v. see* **haue**; **haly** *adv. see* **holy**

hall, all *n.* residence, place 31.57, 32.108

halow *v.*[1] shout 30.368

halowe *v.*[2] respect 20.172, 29.259; bless 42.73

halse *n.* neck 26.104, 36.24

halse *v.* embrace 17.382, 36.381; **halsed** *pa.t.* 37.64

halsyng, haylsing *n.* greeting 12.149, 213

halte *adj.* lame 30.441

hande, honde *n.*[1] hand; **on all hande** on every side 1.95; **comen on hande** drawing to an end 29.65; **haue . . . on honde** have in hand 29.194; **takis . . . on hand** indulge in 43.162

hande *n.*[2] breath; **drawe thyn hande** be quiet 13.223

handeled *v. p.p.* dealt with 26.27

hane *n.* enclosure; *in phatic phr.* **hyde and . . . hane** 28.289

happ(e) *n.* fortune, luck 13.271, 16.67; **ille happe** bad luck, a curse 29.305; **þi happe is hentte** your luck has changed 18.39

happe *v.*[1] wrap 14.120, 18.195; cover 30.154

happe *v.*[2] fare 33.305; **happed** *p.p.* befallen 33.149; **hopp illa hayle** a curse (on you) 11.245

happenyng *vbl.n.* luck 29.39

happing *vbl.n.* covers, bedclothes 29.82

harde, herde *adj.* violent, severe 32.286; **harde lande** dry land 9.77

harde *adv.* quickly 5.15; tightly, closely 37.151

harde *v. pa.t. see* **here** *v.*[1]

hardely, hardly *adv.* forthwith 33.251; boldly, fiercely 11.150, 29.137; confidently, indeed 11.286, 44.59; not easily, scarcely 20.42

hardy *adj.* bold 34.13

hardinesse *n.* presumptuous behaviour 43.162

hardly *see* **hardely**

hare, hore *n.* hair 32.22, 33.242

harȝé *see* **harrowe** *v.*

harkens *v. ipv.pl.* listen 37.37

harle *v.* drag 34.226, 345; **harlid** *p.p.* 30.291

harling *vbl.n.* buffeting 45.5

harlot(t)(e) *n.* rascal, scoundrel 19.130, 26.174, 37.185

harnes, harnays, -eys *n.* harness (for horses) 11.389; ornament 15.102; baggage 18.161; brains 33.399

harneysed *ppl.adj.* in armour 28.196

harre *see* **herre** *n.*[1]

harrowe *n.* commotion, uproar 31.81, 37.98

harrowe, harro *v.* rob, plunder 17.119; **harȝé** *ipv.* attack (him), beat (him) 33.352; **heryed** *pa.t.* 47.33; **harrowe of** drag away 33.161

harrowe, herrowe *interj., cry for help, vengeance etc.* 1.97, 9.99, 38.292

harste, harstow *see* **here** *v.*[1]

harte-bloode *n.* life-blood 47.31, 259

hartefully *adv.* warmly, sincerely 47.294

hartely *adj.* heartfelt, earnest 28.140, 37.245

hartely *adv.* earnestly, sincerely 8.69, 10.229

hartyng, hertyng *vbl.n.* encouragement 16.112, 171

hase in *see* **haue**

hast *n.* swift process 33.455

hastely *adv.* quickly, soon 40.34

hastis *v. 3pl.pr.* hasten, act precipitately 37.307

hate *adj.* hot, intense 32.81

hate *adv.* severely 26.27

hatell, -yll *n.* man, person 18.223, 33.293

hatereden *n.* malice 32.57

haterell *n.* garment 31.355

hatir *n.* garment, ? hood 29.357

hatte *v.* hate, despise 25.403; **hatted** *p.p.* 42.69

haue, haffe, halfe *v.* have 34.51, 40.3; **havand** *pres.p.* 17.276; **had** *pa.t.* learned 23.39 **hadde** *p.p.* taken 38.26; **haue, haues done** cease, say (do) no more 11.370, 13.86, *as expr. of impatience* 17.153, 30.95; **hase in** go away 30.63; **haue mynde on** remember 18.15

haugh *n.* vale, river valley 4.35

hauk *obscure; ?* hawk *n., as term of contempt, or* **auk** *adj. as n.* miscreant, wrongdoer 28.302

haunch *n.* posteriors 33.368

haunted *v. pa.t.* sought 30.222; engaged in, practised 33.292

hauttande *(B copy* **haunttande***) adj.* haughty, presumptuous 3.27

hawberke *n.* coat of mail 39.101

he *adj. see* **high** *adj.*

hedesman *n.* leader 45.5

hedir *see* **hether**

hedirward *adv.* in this direction 28.261

hedis *see* **heed(e); hedouse** *see* **hydous**

heed(e) *n.* head 35.87, 40.35; leader 45.55; **youre hedis** you, you yourselves 45.261

heele *see* **hele** *n.*; **heete** *see* **hight(e)** *v.*; **hefe, heffe** *see* **heue; heght(e)** *see* **hight(e)** *n.*; **heyld, heild** *see* **helde** *v.*; **heyll** *see* **hele; heynde** *see* **hyne** *n.*; **heyne** *see* **henne** *adv.*; **heyned** *see* **hone** *v.*

helde *n.* favour 19.18

helde, heyld *v.* fall, descend 33.207; stoop 30.136; incline 17.306, 45.138; yield 22.147; **heldis** *3sg.pr.* 30.75; **heledande, heldand** *pres.p.* 1.95; pouring forth 1.6; **heild, hilded** *pa.t.* 7.21; bowed down 33.187; **heldes/-is out(e) of herre/harre** behaves in a disorderly fashion 30.380, 33.135

hele, heele, heyll *n.* health, well being 8.56, 20.187; comfort, consolation 10.140, 17.373; salvation 12.240, 37.38

helesome *adj.* wholesome 45.138

helme *n.* helmet 39.104

helples *adj.* (I am) helpless, doomed 1.97

helte-full *adj.* full to the hilt, possessed 26.198

hem *see* **tham; hemselue** *see* **þam(e)self(e)**

hende *n.¹* an end 9.39

hende *n.² pl.* hands 22.105, 25.464, 37.400

hende *adj.* worthy, gracious, polite 7.44, 11.123, 22.148; **hendest** *spv.* 45.134; *as n.* worthy person 41.101, 116

hendfull *adj. as n.* worthy man 25.508

hend(e)ly *adv.* lovingly, graciously 23.77, 24.176; in a seemly manner 29.82, 30.88

heneusly *adv.* cruelly 28.298

henne, heyne, hyne *adv.* hence 20.228, 30.133, 32.290, 36.272

henne-harte *n.* chicken-heart, coward 33.197

hent(e) *v.* seize, take hold of 11.150; hold, embrace 17.392; remove 23.77; receive 17.314; experience, know, suffer 2.94, 16.375; **hente** *pa.t.* 44.43; **hent(e)** *p.p.* 35.189; conceived 33.122; taken up 43.3

hepe, heppe *n.* crowd; **al þe heppe** the lot of you 19.132; **walke a wilde hepe** come in a great crowd 26.260

herand *n.* errand, message 20.233

herber *v.* (*tr. and intr.*) lodge, shelter 45.15; **herber(e)d** *pa.t.* 47.294; *p.p.* 8.137, 14.11, 29.181

herberles *adj.* homeless 47.352

herber, herberow(e), herborowe *n.* lodging 14.6, 23.162, 37.136, 47.343

herde *n.* shepherd 27.144; **herdes, herdesmen** *pl.* shepherds, herdsmen 11.58, 15.51, 90

herde *adj. see* **harde** *adj.*

here *v.¹* hear 29.32; *(ipv.)* listen 23.176; **harde** *pa.t.* 19.49, 36.227; **harste þou, harstow** do you hear 26.208, 33.184

here *v.²* bestow, wish upon 32.286

herely *adv.* early 47.205

heretill *adv.* to this end 10.298

heryed *see* **harrowe** *v.*

herre, harre *n.¹* important matter 31.142; orderly state, **heldes/-is out(e) of herre/ harre** behaves in a disorderly fashion 30.380, 33.135

herre, nere *n.²* ear 29.142, 31.286; **he turnes his herre** he ignores me 25.325; **neres** *pl.* 12.214

herrowe *see* **harrowe** *interj.*

hertyng *see* **hartyng**

heste *n.* east 15.46

hete *see* **hight(e)** *v.*

hether, hedir, hyder, -der, -ir, yther *etc. adv.* hither

hethyng, -ing *n.* scorn, mockery 29.325, 34.73; **till hethyng ... dryff** hold up to scorn 13.151; **halfe for hethyng** partly for amusement 29.33

hetyng, hettyng *vbl.n.* promise, words of promise 9.22, 28.140, 42.21

hetis, hette *see* **hight(e)** *v.*; **hettyng** *see* **hetyng**

heue, hefe, heffe *v.* lift, raise 11.401, 17.376, 31.94; **heued, -yd** *p.p.* 35.215; exalted (himself), put (himself) forward 32.11

heven *n. gen.sg. see* **hewuen**

heuenyng *vbl.n.* vengeance 32.286

heuen-ryke *n.* the kingdom of heaven 12.101

heuys *v. 3sg.pr.* fills 32.81

heuys *v. 3sg.pr.* grieves *see* **hewe** *v.*

hewe *n.* colour 12.91, 14.106, 45.168; **hyde and hewe, hewe and hyde** bodily, entirely 8.22, 17.96

hewe *v.* cut 8.73; shape 8.97; **heuys** *3sg.pr.* grieves 32.65; **hewed** *p.p.* grieved 30.208

hewuen, -yn *n.* heaven 1.88, 2.35; **heven** *gen.sg.* 17.358

hy *see* **hye** *v.*; **hydder** *see* **hether**

hyde, hide *n.¹* skin 40.34, 47.247; **hyde and hewe, hewe and hyde** bodily, entirely 8.22, 17.96

hyde *n.²* land; *in phatic phr.* **in hyde and in hane** 28.289

hyde, hide *v.* hide 5.135; blindfold 29.357; protect, shield 35.187, 43.49; **hydande** *pres.p.* 1.6; **hidde** *pa.t.* concealed, secreted (myself) 37.249; **hydde, hidde** *p.p.* covered 5.130, 40.34; **noght to hyde** there, evident, plain to see 8.3, 28.15; 38.229

hydid *adj.* of skin; **tendirly hydid** tender-skinned 31.49

hyder, -ir *see* **hether**

hydous, hedouse *adj.* terrifying 47.115; odious, repellent 32.72; loud, noisy 45.46

hydously *adv.* terribly 37.138; frighteningly 23.206

hye *n.* haste; **in hye** swiftly 7.122, 8.46, 37.367

hye *n.* eye *see* **eyne**; **hye** *adj.* see **high** *adj.*

hye, hy *v.* go quickly, hasten *(often refl.)* 5.15, 9.61, 28.198; strive 30.542; **high** *ipv.* 22.3; **hyed, hied** *pa.t.* 40.123, 45.55

high, hye, he *adj.* high, tall 22.178, 25.417, 28.115; proud 27.78; **hye wordis** angry speech 16.194

high *v. ipv. see* **hye**

highly *adv.* intensely 23.62; up high 40.43

highnes *n.* exalted position 30.222

hight(e), heght(e) *n.* height 30.75; **on hight(e), heght(e)** on high 1.88, 37.88; without delay 24.51

hight(e), hyght(e) *v. (pass.)* was, is called, named 4.7, 10.27, 37.231; **hytist** *2sg.pr.* 26.225; **hete, heete, hette** *(act.)* promise, assure 22.114, 26.223, 31.121. 35.121; threaten 11.286, 18.136; **hetis** *3sg.pr.* 23.161; **hight(e), hyght** *pa.t.* 1.112, 10.168, 16.140; *p.p.* 12.12, 37.351, 396

hylde *see* **holde; hilded** *see* **helde** *v.*; **hill** *adj. see* **ill(e)** *adj.*

hille *v.* spread over, cover 29.82; **hillis** *3sg.pr.* 32.22

hymself(f)(e), hymselue *pron.* he himself, him 25.132, 29.299, 44.11

hyndir *v.* injure, slander 29.313

hyne, heynde *n.* person, man 26.198, 31.94, 38.197

hyne *adv. see* **henne** *adv.*

hyng(e) *v.* hang 2.71, 5.28; be fixed 20.149; **hyngis** *3sg.pr.* 10.140, 20.160; **hyngand** *pres.p.* 40.176

hir(e) *pron.* her; herself 46.15

hir, hyr, *adv.* here 16.346, 40.121

hire, hyre *n.* reward, recompense 10.167, 35.47, 37.167

hirselff *pron.* she, she herself 24.32

his, is *pron.* his, its 1.125, 13.131, 16.231G

his *v. 3sg.pr. see* **be** *v.*

hit(t) *pron.* it 20.31, 43.117

hythyn *adv.* hence 10.89

hytist *see* **hight(e)** *v.*

hoy *n.* loud cry 30.368

hoyly *see* **holy** *adv.*

holde, halde *n.* captivity 37.151; support, comfort 38.197, 47.343

holde, halde *v.* hold; remain, stay in one place 2.43, 22.172 *(refl.)*; keep (a promise) 19.248, 23.55; **haldis** *3sg.pr.* 42.183; observes (holy days) 26.103; **hylde, holden** *p.p.* 17.89, 29.381, 43.113; **holde in** be quiet, restrain yourself 26.104; **halde on, furth** continue (like this) 15.63, 32.53; **holdis of** believes in 19.277; **halde vppe youre heede** be of good cheer 36.267; **halde vs payde** are content 25.287

hole, hale *adj.* whole, healthy, healed 11.155, 29.143, 28.291; flourishing 2.108

hole *adv.* together 29.235

hole-hede *n.* unanimous voice 38.20

holy, haly, hoyly, holly(e) *adv.* wholly, completely 8.22, 11.4, 14.147, 28.16, 34.14

homely *adv.* affectionately 37.64

honde *see* **hande** *n.¹*

hone, hune *n.* delay 25.198, 272

hone *v.* delay, hesitate 11.352; tarry, linger 35.13; **honed** *p.p.* 30.35; **heyned** *p.p. (? error, for ho-)* waited 30.310

honours *n.pl.* gifts 2.109

hoo *n.* hill 4.36

hoo *adv.¹ (interrog.)* how 13.160

hoo *adv.²* continually, always 30.509

hope *v.* think, believe, expect 10.117, 16.87, 19.46; **hopes, hoppis** *2sg.pr.* 19.93, 31.83

hopp *v.* befall, *prob. error for* **happe** *v.², q.v.*

hoppis *v. 3sg.pr.* throbs 31.163

hoppis *v. 2sg.pr. see* **hope; hore** *see* **hare**

horne spone *n.* spoon made of horn 15.124

horosonne *n. (quasi-adj.)* son of a whore 30.60

hote *n.* heat 1.97

houe *v.* remain suspended 2.43; **houes** *3sg.pr.* waits 26.197; **houe** *3pl.pr.* wait 31.70

hover *v.* wait, hesitate 11.352; **houerand** *pres.p.* 9.252

howe *interj.*; *call to attract attention* 15.37, 34.33, 37.213

howe-gates *adv. (interrog.)* how 26.227

hower *n.* time, period; **tender hower** ? mating season 4.23

hune *see* **hone** *n.*

hungris *v. 3sg.pr., impers.* **hym hungris** he suffers hunger 22.46; **me hungris** I hunger 22.80

hurle *v.* drag or push violently 28.298; **hurled** *pa.t.* 29.137; *p.p.* 30.222

hurlyng *vbl.n.* violence, rough treatment 45.5; **hurlyng in hande** violence taking place 40.76

hurth *n.* injury 40.34

ych *see* **ilke** *adj.²*

yendles *adj.* eternal 37.124

if, yf, gif(f)(e), 3eff *etc., conj.* if 6.107, 10.48, 375, 13.58, 29.373; even though, even if 29.328, 30.124; **giffe for** seeing that, because 6.69; **if all** even though, for all that 20.122, 25.415, 26.20

ile *n.* island; detached part of the universe 1.26

ilkan(e) *see* **ilkon(e)**

ilke *pron.* þis **ilke** this same, this person 9.31

ilke, ilke a, ilka *adj.¹ (after* the, this, that*)* very, same

ilke, ych a, ilke a, ilka *adj.²* each, every

ilkon(e), ilkan(e) *pron.* each one, every one

ill(e), yll *n.* evil 3.75, 4.56, 25.160

ill(e), hill *adj.* wicked, harmful; severe 8.147; **ill happe** misfortune 33.199

ill(e) *adv.* badly, evilly; through evil 25.7; only with difficulty 18.205; to a great degree, excessively 22.46, 80, 41.13; **likid ill** been worried 20.254

ille haile, illa hayle *n. and interj.* misfortune 34.199; a curse (on you) 11.245, 35.116; curses, damn it 28.291

ymagyn *v.* plot, contrive 26.92

inbrace, inbrased *see* **enbrace**

insens *n.* incense 16.331

indowre *v.* continue 46.132

ingendis *n.pl.* weapons of war 31.14

inlike *adv.* alike, equally 8.99; unchangingly 11.102

in-mange *prep. see* **emang(e)(s)**

inowe *n.* enough, a sufficiency 6.44, 25.135

inowe, anowe *adv.* very; **newe inowe** very suddenly 15.54; **wele anowe** perfectly well 31.354

insaumpillis *see* **ensampelys**

instore *v.* reinvigorate 28.45

intente *see* **entent(e)**; **intere** *see* **enteere**; **interly** *see* **enterly**

intill *prep* into 42.129

inwardly *adv.* intensely, earnestly 7.92, 16.381, 24.75

ire *n.* wrath 26.198, 47.242; sinful turmoil 8.57

irke *adj.* weary 38.113; remiss 43.30

is *pron. see* **his**; **yther** *see* **hether**

iwys(se), ewys(se), gwisse *etc., adv.* to be sure, for certain, indeed 1.81, 17.219, 30.68, 398, 31.116

jangelyng *vbl.n.* noise, prating 29.1

jangillande *ppl.adj.* jabbering, prating 7.47

jangle, jangill *v.* talk 40.19; prate, chatter 30.59, 32.15; **jangelis** *3sg.pr.* 35.265; **jangelid** *pa.t.* 36.57

jape *n.* evil deed 22.6; **japes** *pl.* 30.389; jests 29.382; 'tricks of the trade' 34.54

jape *v.* play; *refl.* **jape þe** (go and) play the fool 7.47, 32.239; **jappis** *3pl.pr.* 30.235

japer *n.* deceiver 32.44

javell *n.* rascal, scoundrel 30.59

jeauntis *n.pl.* giants 31.14

jente *see* **gente**

jocounde *adj.* joyful 26.280; fortunate 30.28

joined *see* **june**

jolynes *n.* joy 31.16

jolle *v.* jostle 32.15

joppon *n.* tunic 31.357

journay, jornay *n.* task, undertaking 28.217, 42.153; **jorneys** *pl.* 28.49

juger *n.* judge 30.58

juggemen *n.pl.* judges 40.25

june *v.* join 8.101, 28.161; **joined** *p.p.* gone to battle 31.14

justice, -ise *n.* judge 30.58, 42.109

justifie *v.* bring to justice 30.24; **justified** *p.p.* 26.226

kacched, -id *see* **catche**

kaydyfnes *n.* misery 47.237

kayssaris *n.pl.* lords 16.15

kaitiffe *n. see* **caytiff(e)**

kaytiffe *adj.* wretched 38.271

kan(n)(e) *see* **con**; **kantely** *see* **cantely**; **kare** *v. see* **care** *v.¹, v.²*

kares *n.pl.* tribulations 45.70

karle, karll *see* **carl(e)**; **karpe** *see* **carpe**; **kast(e)** *v. see* **cast(e)**; **kautelles** *see* **cautellis**

kele *v.* relieve, comfort, assuage 9.198, 29.223, 31.232

kempis *n.pl.* knights 30.523

ken(n)(e) *v.* make known, teach, show 11.196, 28.34; direct 34.349; look for, seek 11.25; know, understand, perceive 9.8, 11.49, 19.184; **kens** *ipv.pl.* 23.236; **kens** *3sg.pr.* 20.90; **kende** *pa.t.* 6.154, 12.14, 37.50; *p.p.* 10.120, 11.260, 31.59

ke(e)ne, kyne *adj.* sharp, intense 6.46, 9.7, 14.103; (of knights) ready for action 19.150; (of words) provocative 22.115; (of face) malicious 26.200

kenely *adv.* vigourously, sharply 24.64

kepe *n.* care, heed 13.246, 26.257, 39.73

ke(e)pe *v.* look after, care for, tend (animals) 3.21, 4.91, 11.93; hold to, comply with 10.120; **keppes** *ipv.pl.* 9.173; **kepis** *3sg.pr.* cares, wishes 45.227; **kepid** *p.p.* 15.52

kest(e) *see* **cast(e)**

keuellis *n.pl.* big men 33.218

kid, kyd, kidde *v. pa.t., p.p. see* **kythe** *v.*

kydde *v. ipv.* behave; **kydde þe** behave yourself 30.63

kynd(e) *n.* nature 1.99, 12.21, 21.84; species, race 4.65, 9.213; offspring, son 25.122; **kyndis** *pl.* tribes 27.163; **by cours of kynde** by nature 10.209; in due course 42.105; **take kynde** assume the nature 5.4, 12.21; **aungell kynde** of angelic nature 5.7

kynde *adj.* natural 1.155

kyndely *adv.* naturally, in accordance with nature or custom 2.118, 10.120, 30.200

kynd(e)ly *adj.* innate, natural 38.391; **kyndly witte** natural reason 21.87

kyndynes, -ynesse *n.* good will 16.15, 40.149; natural affection 36.189

kyne *see* **ke(e)ne** *adj.*

kynne *n.* race, people 11.195; ancestry 37.232; kind of, sort of 32.101

kynrede(n) *n.* forefathers 16.60, 26.60

kyrcheffe *n.* piece of cloth 10.288

kirke *n.* temple 38.111; **haly kirke** the true (Christian) Church 43.28

kirtill *n.* garment 35.290

kyth, kith, kytht *n.* kindred, people 7.123, 16.316; native land 16.202, 18.91, 31.231; country, place 29.157

kythe, kith(e) *v.* make known, show, reveal 16.48, 19.69; **kythes** *3pl.pr.* 16.15; **kyd** *pa.t.* 7.25; **kid(de), kydde** *p.p.* 16.298, 37.251; known 22.49, 32.30

knave, knafe *n.* low-born person, underling 15.100, 29.52, 37.244

knave-childer *n.* male children 18.56, 116

knawyng *see* **knowyng** *vbl.n.*

knew, knwe *v. pa.t.* knew 9.270; showed 38.89

knyth *v. 3sg.pr.* afflicts, crushes; *(impers.)* **me knyth it sore** I regret it deeply 6.135

knytt(e) *v.* join, make fast, bind 33.350, 35.133; **knytte** *p.p.* 21.85; closed, shut up 9.190; enclosed 12.107, 17.130; nailed 36.26; **knotte knytte** sealed bargain 26.152; **knott for to knytt** conclude a deal 26.233

knott(e) *n.* deal, bargain 26.152, 233 *(see prec.)*

knowyng, knawyng *vbl.n.* knowledge 4.86, 5.72, 24.181

knwe *see* **knewe; kon(n)(e)** *see* **con; konnand** *see* **connyng** *ppl.adj.*; **kouthe** *see* **con**

laby *n.* burden 26.62

lach(e) *v.* catch, capture 26.253, 32.107; **laght, laught(e)** *p.p.* 30.254; brought 33.285; taken hold of, afflicted 30.283

ladde *n.¹* low-born person, insignificant person 11.217, 16.167, 37.243

ladde *n.²* thong, strap 34.224

lade *n.* burden 34.300

laght *see* **lach(e); lay** *v. pa.t. see* **ligge**

laie, lay(e) *n.* law 10.346, 16.203, 17.42; manner of living 30.423, 424; country 15.18, 32.41; obedience to law 34.119; **layse** *pl.* 11.44, 20.193

lay(e) *v.* wager 16.275, 30.131, 41.149; **layes** *3sg.pr.* specifies 33.102; **laide, layde** *p.p.* laid to rest 30.131; (of law) laid down established 37.329; stored up 12.188, 231; **lay fro þe** let go 19.198; **laye on** *(ipv.)* beat, smite 35.245, 37.143

layke, lake *n.* sport, game 29.190, 377, 33.373; way of proceeding 33.227

layke *v.* play; play the fool 30.453 *(refl.)*; **laykis** *3sg.pr.* sports, makes light 26.238

layne *n. see* **lane**

layne *v.* hide, conceal, remain silent (about something) 18.95, 23.233, 29.279; **noght (for) to layne** not to be concealed, should be mentioned *(often phatic)* 9.88, 14.132, 32.93

laynyng *vbl.n.* concealment 25.101

layre *n.* earth, the ground 31.218

layre *n.* lore *see* **lare** *n.*; **layse** *n.pl. see* **laie** *n.*

layte, late *v.* seek 16.167, 20.192, 38.233

laith, laytheste *adj. see* **lothe** *adj.*

lak *n.* defect, doubt; **withoutyn lak** assuredly 11.109

lak(ke) *v.* find fault with 13.297; want 38.102; **lakke, lakkid** *pa.t.* was found wanting 31.273, 34.119

lake *n.* stream 34.64; dungeon 34.214

lake *n.* game *see* **layke** *n.*; **lakke** *v. see* **lak** *v.*

lame *n.¹* lamb 17.40

lame *n.²* earth, the ground 39.5

lane, layne *n.* gift 10.60, 23.48, 44.27

lang(g)age *n.* faculty of speech 29.278, 31.190; words, talk 30.495; florid speech 33.53; **oppen langage** careless talk 26.202

lang-are *adv.* some time ago 13.299

lange, langar *adj. see* **longe** *adj.¹*

lange *adv.* a long time 9.225, 10.142; **lange or** it will be a long time before 33.396; **to**

lange and late at last, in the end 47.25
lange, langis *v. see* **longis** *v.'*
langly *adv.* for a long time 31.280
langour, langure *n.* illness 30.283, 45.142
lapp(e) *v.* cover (with bedclothes) 30.136; embrace 17.180; perceive 33.310; **lapped** *p.p.* enclosed 33.13; **lappid** kissed, caressed 30.51; **lowe . . . lapped** brought low, degraded 45.3
lare, layre, lore *n.* knowledge, information, teachings, doctrine 9.105, 20.140, 24.76; ? skill, facility 11.181, 30.498; counsel, advice 5.124, 8.145; conduct 13.98
large *adj.* (of language) unrestrained, extravagant 33.131
largely *adv.* unrestrainedly 30.495
lassched *v. p.p.* scourged 33.153
lasshe *n.* stroke, blow 33.199; **lasschis** *pl.* 31.11
last(e) *v. intr.* continue, remain 11.35, 102, 304; *tr.* sustain 8.141; **lastande furth** flourishing 2.76
lastand(e) *ppl.adj.* (ever)lasting, sustained 1.57, 3.54, 23.72 (*see prec.*)
lastandly *adv.* lastingly, eternally 23.61, 44.18; for any length of time 42.10
laste day *n.* Day of Judgement 30.225
lat(e) *v.* let *see* **let(t)(e)** *v.'*
late *n.* appearance, aspect 44.175; noise, fuss 44.106
late, latte *adv.* recently, lately; **nowe late, of latte** just recently 25.400, 37.162, 329; **lattar** *cpv.* at a later time 45.244
late *v.* seek *see* **layte; lath(e)** *adj. see* **lothe** *adj.*
lathe *v.* loathe, hate 32.210; *impers.* **me lathis, -es, vs lothis** (it) is hateful to me, us 13.149, 32.301, 41.8
latt *n. see* **lette** *n.*
lattar *adj.* latter, which follows 38.140
lattar *adv. see* **late** *adv.*; **latte, latten** *v. see* **let(t)(e)** *v.'*; **latte** *adv. see* **late** *adv.*
laude *n.* praise 46A.5
laude *v.* praise; **laude . . . of** praise for 37.384
laue *n.* law 10.4
laugher *see* **lawe** *adj.*; **laught(e)** *see* **lach(e)**
launce *v.* hasten 30.178
launces *n.pl.* spears 33.182
lawe *adj.* low 1.122; base 33.178; small of stature 25.417; **laugher** *cpv.* a lower place 30.276
lawe *v.* overthrow, abase 30.225
lawmere *n.* fool, blockhead 31.181
leche *n.* healer, saviour 20.102, 21.136, 38.262
leche *v.* save, redeem 15.10, 16.212, 45.293; **lechis to liffe** resurrects 29.264

ledar *see* **leder**
lede, leede, leyd *n.'* man, human being 7.32, 17.82, 20.55; country, place, inhabitants of a country 44.97, 45.293; *in phatic phr.* **in lede, ilke a lede** 2.76, 10.132, 39.11
lede, leede *n.²* lead 20.207, 28.21, 36.262; **caste leede** take a sounding 9.199
lede, leede *v.* lead; **at lede** to lead 11.282; carry 35.175; expound, teach 29.8, 32.61; uphold, keep up (laws) 16.120, 20.64; detain 31.339
leder, -ar *n.* leader 1.111; **leder of lawe, lawis** one who expounds the law(s) 29.111, 30.55
ledgyd *see* **legge; ledir** *see* **lithre**
lee *n.* peace, tranquility 30.248
leede *n. see* **lede** *n.', n.²*; **leede** *v. see* **lede** *v.*
leefe *n.* leaf 45.174
leeffe *adv. see* **lefe** *adj. and adv.*; **leeffull** *see* **leffull; leelly** *see* **lel(l)y** *adv.*; **leere** *see* **lere; leerid** *see* **lered** *ppl.adj.*; **lees** *n. see* **lese** *n.*
leese *v.* destroy 36.29; **lorne** *p.p.* 11.72; lost 1.108, 11.253, 22.17
lefe *n.* sir 13.248
lefe, leeffe, leffe, leue *adj., adv.* dear, beloved 5.121, 13.101, 18.86, 40.12; (+ *forms of 'to be'*) **was leeffe** was willing, chose 40.8; **had, were, wolde leuer(e)** would rather, would prefer to 10.142, 241, 27.138, 31.252
lef(f)e *v. see* **leue** *v.'*; **leffis** *v. 3sg.pr. see* **liue** *v.*; **leffand** *see* **liffand**
leffull, leeffull *adj.* lawful, legitimate 30.83, 425; rightful, fitting 30.276, 300
lefte *v. pa.t. see* **leue** *v.'*
legge *v.* make allegations 26.45, 30.471; appeal to (for evidence) 30.457; **leggis** *3sg.pr.* expounds 31.168; affirms 33.102; **ledgyd** *p.p.* affirmed 17.205; **legge agayne** speak against 16.203
leggyng, legyng *vbl.n.* making of accusations 26.107; expounding 33.119; declaration, affirmation 45.42
legh *n.* lie 31.157
leyd *n. see* **lede** *n.'*; **leyf** *v. see* **leue** *v.'*; **leyffe** *n. see* **liff(e)** *n.*; **leym** *see* **le(e)me; leythly** *see* **lightly; lekyng** *see* **likyng**
lele *adj.* faithful, truthful, true 12.238, 20.185, 34.77
lele *adv.* truly 7.1
lel(l)y *n. see* **lilly**
lel(l)y, leely, lelye *adv.* loyally, truly 1.77, 20.64, 30.192, 36.31
leman *n.* lover 24.8
lemand *ppl.adj.* shining 40.116
le(e)me, leym, lymme *n.* brightness 16.26, 28.258, 31.218; beam of light 17.114; source (of light) 17.329

lemed *v. pa.t.* shone 28.267, 44.96; **lemyd**
p.p. ? caused to glow, illumined 25.519
lemer *n.* that which glows; **lemer of light**
radiant one 14.111
lemyd *see* **lemed**
lende *v.* dwell, remain, be 1.52, 8.124,
10.116; descend, light upon 37.47, 54;
pass, occupy (time) 47.368; **lende** *3sg.pr.*
9.226; **lendande** *pres.p.* 45.150; **lente** *p.p.*
44.73
lende *v.* bestow *see next*
lene, lende, lenne *v.* grant, bestow, allow
28.178, 33.414; lend 32.353; **len** *ipv.*
17.151; **lens, lenys, lennes** *3sg.pr.* 9.219,
10.4, 16.153; **lent** *pa.t.* 17.390; *p.p.* 6.5;
þat **liffe has lente** who lives 7.32, 20.55;
þat **lennes vs lyffe** who gives us life 9.219
lenge, lenghe *v. tr.* prolong 11.110, 36.289;
intr. dwell, remain 33.420, 36.398, 42.212;
lenghis *3sg.pr.* 42.10; **lengand** *pres.p.*
42.226
lenghyng *vbl.n.* preservation 27.175
lenghis *see* **lenge** *v.*
lenght, lenghe, lenthe *n.* length 34.77,
36.379; space, area 33.13
length *v.* prolong 17.146
lenne *see* **lene**
lente *v. p.p.* laid 38.300
lent(e), *pa.t., p.p.* bestowed *see* **lene** *v.,*
dwelling *see* **lende** *v.*
lepe, leppe *v.* leap, move hastily 19.134,
26.203, 33.147; escape 32.377; **lepe ouere
lande** travel about 16.167G
lepfull *n.pl.* basketsfull 31.211
leping *vbl.n.* escaping 26.291
leppe *see* **lepe**
lepre *n. gen.sg.* (as a) lepper's 11.154
lere, leere *v. tr.* instruct, teach, guide 2.34,
11.181, 37.330; disclose 23.234; *intr.* learn
20.81, 26.22, 37.313; **lereth** *1pl.pr.* tell
31.157; **lered, -yd** *pa.t.* 11.226, 12.16; *p.p.*
10.267, 30.503
lered, leerid *ppl.adj.* learned 38.68, 47.67
(see prec.)
lerne *v.* teach 3.76, 29.8, 349; **lernes** *3sg.pr.*
20.185; **lernynde** *pa.t.* 10.20; **lerned** *p.p.*
35.19; **lerne at** learn from 8.123
lese, lees, lesse *n.* falsehood, lie 11.331,
25.225, 33.310; **withouten lees** truly
37.127
lese *v. see* **leese** *v.*
lesyng(e) *n.* lie, falsehood 5.24, 21.2
lesse *n.* lie *see* **lese** *n.*
leste *adj.* smallest 35.228, 47.363
leste *v. see* **liste** *v.¹*
let(t)(e), lat(t)(e) *v.¹* let, permit, allow 2.14,
4.88, 13.98, 37.65, 194; **lete (at)** *pa.t.*
believed, took notice (of) 5.124, 30.225;
latten, leteyn *p.p.* 9.113, 38.366; **lat(t)e be**

cease, leave off 9.271, 19.99; **lat(e) loke**
see here 1.120; let us see 22.89; **let/lat see**
let us see 15.63, 20.143; *as expr. of eager-
ness, impatience etc.* 17.153, 19.167, 20.67
lett(e) *v.² tr.* obstruct, hinder 18.12, 30.91;
disrupt, put an end to 5.21, 26.204; *intr.*
refrain (from), forbear 3.83, 4.25, 20.117,
25.61; **lettis** *3sg.pr.* 31.256; **lette noght** do
not fail 5.95
lette, latt *n.* delay 25.248, 32.344
lettir *n.* preventer 45.142
leuand *see* **liffand** *ppl.adj., liue v.*
leue, leve *n.* permission 16.125, 187, 25.58;
leave 31.389
leue *adj. see* **lefe** *adj.*
leue, lef(f)e, leyf *v.¹* leave, abandon 9.77,
13.261, 17.415, 39.149; spare, allow to
survive 8.29, 26.46, 30.535; remain 20.20;
leue(s), leves, -is *ipv.sg., pl.* cease, put an
end to 31.292, 37.284, 42.99; stand back
29.272; **lefte** *pa.t.* 31.211; **leued** *p.p.* 43.5
leue, leve *v.²* believe 22.192, 30.471,
31.256; **leuys** *ipv.pl.* 43.67; **leued** *pa.t.*
45.76; **leue on** believe in 34.3
leue, leues, -ys, leued, -yd *v.* live *etc. see* **liue**
v.
levene, leuyn *n.* lighting 2.33, 44.175
lever, leuer(e) *see* **lefe** *adj., adv.*
leverie *n.* ? authorising document 25.65
leuyn *see* **levene**
levyng, lewyn *vbl.n.* life 15.129, 21.36; way
of life 9.273
lewde *adj.* uneducated 47.67
lewdenes *n.* misconduct 30.147
lewyn *vbl.n. see* **levyng**
lewté, lewty *n.* loyalty, truth 26.266,
28.178, 29.350,
liaunce *n.* allegiance 33.1
liberall *adj. as n.* generous one 33.51
license *n.* permission 36.354
liddir *see* **lithre**
lidrone, lidderon *n.* knave, scoundrel
31.168, 190
lye *v.* deceive, lie 26.266; **lise** *2sg.pr.*
33.184
lyf-days *n.pl.* life, term of existence 17.155
liff(e), leyffe, lyue *n.* life 3.76, 36.140;
haue, had liff(e) live(d) 20.275, 25.358;
liffe has lente lives 7.32; **oure liffe** *epithet
for Christ* 28.25
liffand, leffand, leuand *ppl.adj.* living
23.234, 42.128, 131 *(see* **liue** *v.)*
liffand, liffeand *v. pres.p. see* **liue** *v.;* **liffe,
liffis** *see* **liue** *v.*
liffelod *n.* livelihood 26.175
liffely *adv.* quickly 36.392
lyft(e) *adj.* left 3.38, 47.78
ligge, lygge *v.* lay, lie 8.98, 34.331, 46.115;
put, deposit 31.214; **lay** *pa.t.* lived 31.217

lyghame *n.* body 5.110
lyghte *n.* guiding spirit, inspiration 1.111
light(e) *adj.*[1] bright, radiant 1.100, 30.80
light, lyght *adj.*[2] happy, carefree, 13.285, 23.11; unsteadfast, fickle 6.133; feeble 35.166; weightless 23.198
light *adv.*[1] brightly 28.267
light *adv.*[2] easily 32.377
light(e) *v.* descend, alight 7.93, 12.177, 21.18; **lighted** *p.p.* 1.122
lightfull *adj.* brightly shining 15.16
lightly, leythly *adv.* effortlessly 2.143; quickly 29.278, 40.122; unnecessarily, thoughtlessly 9.175, 28.68
lyk *n.* pleasure, will 2.14
likand, lykand *ppl.adj.* pleasant, lovely 23.150, 42.8, 45.106
like, lyke *adj., adv.* likely
likes, lykes, -ys *v.* *3sg.pr., impers.* pleases 1.159, 2.124, 3.88, 30.495; **likid ill** been worried 20.254
likyng, lykyng, lekyng *vbl.n.* bliss, felicity 3.95, 11.304, 32.377; behest, pleasure 16.6, 32.353
likyng land *n.* the Promised Land 11.282; **lande of lykyng** 11.362
lylly, lel(l)y *n.* lily 12.91, 16.228, 25.519
lyme *n.* limb 25.385, 30.82; **lymmys** *pl.* 31.11; **lyme and litht** the entire body, everything 16.204; **lyme and lande** life and livelihood 19.2
lymett *v. p.p.* bound (in loyalty) 33.1
lymme *n.* light *see* le(e)me; **lymmys** *n.pl. see* **lyme**
lynage *n.* nation, people 11.130
lyne *n.*[1] linen; **leues vndir lyne** live 9.53
lyne *n.*[2] measuring line 8.98; straight line 33.244; **lynes** *pl.* principles, indications 26.164
lyolty *n.* truth 28.25
lyre *n.*[1] flesh, body; **liffe and lyre** life and limb 11.20
lyre, lire *n.*[2] face, appearance 28.200, 31.53, 45.197
lirte *n.* trick, deception 26.254
lise *v. 2sg.pr. see* **lye**
liste *n.* will, desire, liking 10.345, 25.37, 30.535
liste, leste *v.*[1] *impers.* **me, þe, hym liste** (it) pleases me, you, him; I, you, he desire(s) *etc.* 7.48, 11.259, 12.34, 20.81; *interrog.* **leste 3e** are you, do you mean to be 29.191
liste, lyste *v.*[2] pay attention, take heed (to) 22.97, 25.189; **listes** *3sg.pr.* 16.6
listyn *v.* listen, take heed 16.46, 33.438
lite *n.* short time 31.339
lith(t) *n.* limb, part of body 35.228; **lyme and litht** the entire body 16.204
lith(e), lythe *v.* pay attention (to) 33.240

(ipv.); hear 30.371, 495; **lithes** *3pl.pr.* 16.16
lithirnesse *n.* wickedness 47.44
lithre, ledir, liddir *adj.* wicked 30.147, 254, 33.119
litht *see* **lith(t)** *n.*; **lyue** *n. see* **liff(e)**
liue, liffe, lyf(fe), leue *v.* live 6.38, 17.138, 37.68, 322; **leves, leffis, liffis** *3sg.pr.* 9.1, 43.77; *3pl.pr.* 37.70; **liffand, lyvand, leu-and** *pres.p.* 17.305, 29.291, 37.55; **leued, -yd** *pa.t.* 25.142; *p.p.* 37.243, 353; **leuys with** lives by means of 37.160
lodsterne *n.* guiding light 16.24
loffe *n. see* **luffe; loffely** *see* **luffely; lofsom(e)** *see* **lufsome**
loghte *v.* seize 19.181
loyse *see* **lose; lokand** *see* **luke**
loke *n.* arm-lock (as in wrestling) 28.296
loken, -yn *v. p.p.* locked, shut in 12.10; buried 31.218, 39.5
longe, lange *adj.*[1] (of time) long 24.124; (of size, extent) large 3.48; tall 33.220; **langar** *cpv.* 23.223; **þis longe daye** throughout this day 39.26
longe *adj.*[2] dependent (on), owing (to); **wheron is it longe** what is the reason for it 5.140
longis, -es, langis *v.*[1] *3sg.pr.* belongs, is fitting, is appropriate 28.154, 30.435, 32.110; pertains 25.154, 30.425; **longes, lange** *3pl.pr.* 5.48, 25.441
longis *v.*[2] *3sg.pr., impers.* **me, vs longis** I, we long 38.218, 42.24
looffis *n.pl. see* **loves**
loppis *n.pl.* flies 11.293
lordan, lordayne *see* **lurdan(e)**
lordynges, -is *n.pl.* rulers, potentates, 30.225, 31.405; people 30.247
lords(c)hipp(e) *n.* district, province 31.128; realm, kingdom 11.36, 33.397; magnates, men of rank 11.6; authority, power 26.274
lore *see* **lare**
lorell *n.* scoundrel, rascal 29.111, 30.254
lornc *see* **lecse**
lose, loyse, louse *v.* destroy, ruin 11.20, 16.272, 30.423; **loses, -is** *3sg.pr.* 11.272, 19.174; **lost** *pa.t.* 1.115
losed *v. p.p. see* **lowse**
losell *n.* wretch, knave 16.132, 26.238
lothe, lath(e), laith, lotht *adj.* hateful, opprobrious 13.51, 26.39, 128; burdensome to 9.147; in aversion, displeasure 40.132; **laytheste** *spv.* most loathsome 1.100; **me were ... lotht, is vs ... lothe** I would not wish, we do not wish 5.63, 19.218
lothly *adj.* horrible, ghastly 19.210
lott(e) *n.* power, prerogative 26.68, 33.182; **loke þe lotte** draw lots 35.291
lotterell(e) *n.* scoundrel, knave 30.381, 32.261, 382

loue *v.¹* love; **louys** *ipv.pl.* 3.67; **luffes** *3sg.pr.* 37.403; **luffed** *pa.t.* 42.16

loue, louffe, love, lowe *v.²* (*sometimes hard to disting. from v.¹*) praise, worship, give thanks 3.78, 4.50, 8.41, 9.2; **louys** *ipv.pl.* 3.67; **loued, -yd, -id** *p.p.* 1.43, 121, 3.52

louely *adj. as n.* dear one 20.20

loves, looffis *n.pl.* loaves 25.134, 31.202

louffe *v. see* **loue** *v.²*

louyng(e), loving *vbl.n.* (*see* **loue** *v.²*) praise 1.24, 14.48, 20.116

lourdayne *see* **lurdan(e); louse** *v.* loose *see* **lowse; louse** *v.* destroy *see* **lose; loute** *see* **lowte**

lowde *adj.* (of lies) flagrant, bold 5.24, 29.271; *in phatic phr.* **lowde and still** 8.41, 145

lowe *adv.* to a poor state; **lowe … lapped** brought low, degraded 45.3

lowe *v. see* **loue** *v.²*; **lowys** *see* **lowse**

lowly *adv.* humbly 26.22, 30.178

lowse, louse *v.* loose, untie 29.272, 33.384; **lowys** *3pl.pr.* 41.95; **losed** *p.p.* 41.95

lowte, loute *v.* reverence, pay homage 1.46, 16.56, 29.351, 31.320; **at lowte** to worship 1.24

luf *n.¹* praise 1.46

luffand *ppl.adj.* loving 41.67 (*see* **loue** *v.¹*)

luffe, loffe *n.²* love 3.20, 45.106; loved one, beloved 30.25, 45.3; **with luffe** in peace 26.46

luffed *see* **loue** *v.¹*

luffely, loffely *adv.* in a seemly manner, courteously 16.16, 30.131; beautifully 30.51

luffer *n.* lover 46A.10

luffes *v. see* **loue** *v.¹*

luffull *adj.* loving 30.248

lufly, luffely *adj.* dear, beloved 1.43; *as n.* dear one 38.233

lufsome, lofsom(e) *adj.* lovely, beneficial 25.519, 28.200, 45.286; *as n.* fair one 39.11

lugge *v.* pull, haul 35.137

luke *v.* look; **lokand** *pres.p.* 42.218; **luke howe** however 6.58; **luke vnto** take care of 28.154

luprus *adj.* leprous; **Symond luprus** Simon the leper 26.130

lurdan(e), lordayne, lordan, lourdayne, lurdayne *n.* wretch, scoundrel 1.108, 115, 11.226, 229, 28.275, 301

lurkand *ppl.adj.* skulking 29.105

lurkis *v. 3sg.pr.* skulks about 31.301

lusshe *n.* blow 28.275

lusshe *v.* beat 31.11; **lusshed** *pa.t.* 45.37; **lusschyd** *p.p.* 33.153

luste *n.* pleasure 47.58

lusty *adj.* strong, flourishing 45.106; *as n.* strong man 33.51

ma *adj. see* **mo(o); ma** *v. see* **make** *v.¹*

mached *v. pa.t.* attacked, set upon 30.198

madde *v.* behave madly 26.216; **maddes** *2sg.pr.* 15.38; **maddis** *3pl.pr.* 43.74

may(e) *n.* maiden 15.20, 16.326, 45.209

maiden *n. gen.sg.* maiden's 44.193

mayne *n.* strength, power, prowess 1.93, 9.181, 19.62; **with mayne and myght, myght and mayne** determinedly, earnestly 3.84, 20.162; **with, in mayne and mo(o)de** with supernatural power 38.331, 43.153; **with a good will** 7.69; **in health and strength** 22.75

mayne *n.* moan *see* **mone** *n.¹*

mayntayne *v.* uphold, support 38.11, 71

maistir *n.* master; **maistir** *gen.sg.* master's 25.192, 29.97; **maistir(i)s** *pl.* learned men 20.119, 24.21

maistir *n.* need *see* **myster** *n.*

maistry, -ie *n.* mastery, great deed(s) 6.137; **make maistrie** exercise mastery 5.58; **make, made, maistries; mustirs … maistris** perform(s), performed high-handed deeds 11.30, 37.202, 217

make *n.* spouse; wife 5.14; husband 5.144

make, ma *v.¹* make 6.29; give, impart 25.505; cause to flourish, prosper 11.115, 12.72; **mase** *3sg.pr.* 11.194; does, performs 37.116; **make ende** determine (a case in court) 38.36; **make, made in mynde** remember(ed) 16.313, 35.50

make *v.²* mate 2.132

makeles *adj.* without equal, peerless 16.326; *as n.* innocent person 26.92

makyng *vbl.n.* creation, act of creating 3.30, 68

malyngne *v.* accuse falsely 30.508

malis, malles *n.* malice 17.121, 45.29

malysoune, malyson, malisonne *n.* curse, malediction 5.153, 7.91, 108

man *?v.* moan, complain 28.137

man(e) *n.* man 3.87; **man** *gen.sg.* (a) man's 16.230, 25.463, 30.163

maner(e) *n.* a certain type 11.29; a certain respect, one particular 8.122; **as þe manere is** according to custom 29.86

mang *see* **meng**

mangery *n.* meal 31.213

manhed *n.* human form, flesh 21.132, 28.4

manyfolde *adj.* numerous, diverse 6.47

manyfolde *adv.* in large numbers 10.47; in many forms 47.345

mankynde *n.* male 11.71; the nature and appearance of man 21.92

mankynne *n.* mankind 39.111

manly *adv.* in a proper manner, courteously 31.89

mantell *n.* garment 35.298

mar(r)(e), merr *v.* prevent, obstruct 9.60,

12.39, 16.234; destroy, put an end to
11.356, 17.100, 39.4; harm, injure
11.224, 26.172, 27.119; defile 13.182;
become fuddled 43.166; **marres, -is**
3sg.pr. impairs 23.87; subverts 32.45;
troubles 22.43; **marrande** *pres.p.* weaken-
ing, falling away 1.93; **marre . . . To** prevent from 37.173

marc *v. see* **mark(e)** *v.*

marchaundyse *n.* deal, bargain 26.215

mark(e), merke *n.* object (of attention)
25.498; knowledge, understanding 8.68;
(astrol.) mark of a dominant planet
26.163; **markis** *pl.* measurements (in
woodworking) 8.64; **tane oure merke**
have aimed (at a target) 38.397

mark(e), marc, merk- *v.* show 32.307; undertake 30.405; select, designate 16.313,
325, 30.521; ordain, allot 31.199; **merkis**
ipv.pl. take note of ·40.185; **marked, -id**
pa.t. created 1.58, 130; **marked, -id(e),
merked** *p.p.* 1.49, 7.35; observed 36.312;
afflicted 11.162; **marke in . . . mynde**
remember 36.365; **marked in . . . mynde**
intended, undertaken 26.172

martiris *n.pl.* martyrs 46.143

mase *v. 3sg.pr. see* **make** *v.*[1]

mased *ppl.adj.* distraught, bewildered 6.82,
28.91, 41.98

mast *adj. see* **moste**

mate *adj.* distracted 45.4

mater(c) *n.* matter, business; tale, story
5.43; substance from which a thing grows
2.76; **materis** *pl.* compositions 2.131

me, my *pron.*[1] *(indef.)* individuals, people
10.280; somebody, a person, **meves me** is
spoken 12.73

me *pron.*[2] *(refl.)* myself

mede *n.*[1] reward, profit, benefit 10.335,
16.325, 21.128; deserving 32.307

mede *n.*[2] mead (the drink) 39.89

medecyne, medicyne *n.* remedy 38.195;
salvation 25.498

medill *v. see* **mell(e)** *v.*[1]; **medil(l)erth(e)** *see*
middilerth; meen *n. see* **mene** *n.*

meene *adj.* (of persons) low, paltry 26.32

meese *v.* assuage 42.236; *refl.* **vs meese**
restrain ourselves 26.62

meete *n., adj. see* **mete** *n., adj.*; **mefid, mefte**
v. p.p. see **meve**

meyné, mené, menȝe, menȝhe, menyhe *n.*
company, group, people 11.277, 20.74,
42.148; household 27.12, 31.23

meyne *v. see* **mene** *v.*[1]

meke *n.* friend, companion 12.103

meke *adj.* obedient, submissive 37.1

meke *v.* subdue, chastise 26.32; **mekis**
2sg.pr. humble 37.350; *refl.* **mekis hym** de-
fers 31.179; **meke yowe** pay attention to

30.239; **meke ȝou** agree, condescend
26.122

mekely *adv.* obediently 1.15

mekill *adj.* great 1.41, 10.335, 11.97

mekill, mykill *adv.* greatly 5.2, 9.22

mele *n.* time, occasion; **at ilk a mele**
continually 43.62

mell(e), medill *v.*[1] mix, mingle 20.229,
37.302; breed 2.132; **melles** *3sg.pr.* in-
fuses 17.393; solicits 26.91; **melle (of),
medill** *(often refl.)* meddle, interfere (with)
7.55, 27.279; be concerned with 26.112,
31.314, 35.90; **melle hym, vs** concern
himself, ourselves (with) 31.64, 34.326,
40.140

mell(e) *v.*[2] speak, refer to 17.116, 26.182,
30.369; **melle of** speak to 7.56

membres *n.pl.* limbs 27.49

mendar *n.* one who makes amends 28.57

mende *v.* amend, reform, free from fault
6.156, 12.18, 20.214, 37.359; improve
upon, augment 2.149, 17.4, 37.79; cheer
19.39; **mendand, mending** *pres.p.* 44.193;
feeling better 44.152; **mended** *pa.t.* benef-
itted 34.156; **mende** *p.p.* 8.22; restored
27.151; redressed 28.120; **mende of** recover from 11.283; **mende you** compose
yourself 30.64

mende *v. p.p. see prec.,* **mene** *v.*[1]

mene, meen *n.* intermediate area 2.42;
intermediary 46A.42

mené *see* **meyné**

mene, meyne *v.*[1] intend 2.42, 10.286,
11.287; mention, speak of 7.2, 11.98;
menys, mennes *3sg.pr.* says 31.199; pre-
sages 37.46; **mente** *pa.t.* 1.139; **mende,
ment(e)** *p.p.* 7.10, 11.121, 23.194; *(impers.)*
me menys it occurs to me, I recall 29.53;
vs mene call to mind 20.1; **in mynde gon
mene** recorded, made note of 14.137

mene *v.*[2] doubt 45.81

meng *v.* mate, couple 2.147; **mengis** *3sg.pr.*
disturbs 13.4, 45.123; **mang** *2pl.pr.* are
confused 41.132; **menged** *p.p.* mixed, mingled 36.245

menȝe, menȝhe, menyhe *see* **meyné**

menyng *vbl.n.*[1] purpose, stated intention
16.197, 25.97, 31.88; deeds, doings
19.107; mention 37.103

menyng *vbl.n.*[2] lamentation 47.139

mennes *see* **mene** *v.*[1]

menske *n.* honour, credit 30.325

mensk(e) *v.* worship, honour 14.107, 31.97,
44.19; imbue 28.47, 57, 30.545; **mensked,
-id** *pa.t.* 25.536, 40.44; **menske in mynde**
pay attention to 31.33

menskfull *adj.* worthy, exalted 25.501

menskfully *adv.* in a fitting manner 40.185
mente *see* **mene** *v.*[1]; **merke** *n. see* **mark(e)** *n.*;

merkis, -ed *see* **mark(e)** *v.*; **merknes** *see* **myrknes; merour** *see* **myrroure; merr** *see* **mar(r)(e)**

meruayle, meruell *n.* wonder, extraordinary or unnatural occurrence 12.1; feeling of surprise 44.67

meruellis *v. 3sg.pr., impers.* **me meruellis, -ailes** it amazes me 30.508, 45.230

message *n.* messenger 11.121; errand 46.2; **in message** with a message 21.15

mesellis *n.pl.* lepers 11.317

messe *n.* visitation (of suffering) 11.162

mesure, mesore *n.* an indication 9.136; moderation 37.302; **mesures** *pl.* measurements 8.64, 86

mete, meete, mette *n.* food, sustenance 5.99, 32.306, 41.64

mete, meete, mette *adj.* equal 16.337, 23.116; ready 27.49; fitting, appropriate 35.257

mete, melte *v.*[1] meet, encounter with 11.288, 27.158; **mette** *p.p.* had sexual intercourse 13.166; found, taken 18.113

mett *v.*[2] *pa.t.* arranged 16.325

mette *n., adj., v. see* **mete** *n., adj., v.*

meve, meffe, meyve, moue, moffe, moyfe *v.* move, go, travel 2.41, 16.104, 108; live 11.277; speak (of), refer to, say 10.124, 29.276; indicate 16.63, 17.233; **moffes, moues, movis** *3sg.pr.* disturbs 5.2, 23.189; occurs to 24.54; **meving** *pres.p.* 30.405; **moved, moued** *pa.t.* 5.44, 12.39; **mefid, mefte** *p.p.* tried 31.303 *(refl.)*; happened 43.152

my *pron. (indef.) see* **me** *pron.*[1]

middilerth, medil(l)erth(e) *n.* the earth, all worldly things 8.8, 28, 9.158, 10.269; part of the earth outside Paradise 5.167

myddyng *n.* dungheap 11.296

mydes, -is *n.* middle 2.159; **in mydis** in the middle 2.40

mydwayes *n.pl.* midwives (? *mis-spelling*) 11.69

might(e) *n.* power; **mightes, -is** *pl.* powerful deeds 23.148, 37.174; orders of angels 1.33

might(e)full, myghfull *adj.* imbued with power, almighty 1.58, 18.15, 44.1; loud 25.263

myghtyng *see* **mytyng; mykill** *adv. see* **mekill** *adv.*

myldely *adv.* meekly, obediently 21.55, 44.159; prudently 26.122

myn(e) *adj.* less, smaller; **more and myne** *phatic phr.* 2.131, 4.6, 10.261; **more or myne** in effect 21.82

mynde *n.* recollection 13.207; thought, intention 32.159, 16.197; sobriety of thought 20.85; **haue mynde (on) (of)** remember 18.15, 28.107, 36.207; decide 26.122; **haue in mynde** remind 3.29; **es in mynde** are intended 2.77; **makis . . . mynde** makes particular mention 43.188

myne *adj. see* **myn(e)**

myne *v.* ponder 11.193

mynysters *n.pl.* deputies, agents 1.29

mirakills *n.pl.* magical tricks 36.93

mire *n.* swamp, *sc.* desperate plight 37.256

myre *v.* ensnare 26.92

mirke *n.* darkness, the dark 37.53

mirke, myrke *adj.* dark 11.344, 14.41, 38.10; obscure, mysterious 43.32

myrknes, merk(e)nes *n.* darkness 1.149, 14.63, 28.300; **myrknes emel** in the midst of darkness 1.146

myron *n.* minion, lackey 30.138, 146; idler, good-for-nothing 33.61

mirre *n.* myrrh 16.342

myrroure, merour *n.* mirror, reflection 1.34; model, example 21.93, 22.195

myrth(e), mirth(e) *n.* pleasure, delight 1.49, 11.188; joys of heaven, eternal bliss 1.48, 44.164; joyful throng 25.361; **mirthis, myrþes** *pl.* 11.194, 20.1

mirthe *v.* comfort 28.30

mys(se), misse *n.* sin, evil, wickedness 2.17, 12.2, 13.132; harm, injury 10.303; mistake 29.122; **misseis** *pl.* 16.314; **misse of** sin on the part of 40.44; *in phatic phr.* **withouten mys** 23.30

mys(se) *v.* fail (to succeed, prevail), do badly 1.83, 8.86; **myssand(e), myssyng** *pres. p.* lacking 1.149; failing (to act) 10.293; failing (to have) 30.195; **myste, miste** *p.p.* lost 11.116; gone astray 16.284; seen to be absent 38.55; gone missing 38.404; **me bus þe mys** I must lose you 10.231

misbeleue *n.* doubt, lack of faith 42.99

myscarie *n.* go to waste 10.268

myschance *n.* misfortune 17.359

myscheue *n.* harm, misfortune 35.258, 38.195; miscreant, evil-doer 26.31

myscheue *v.* injure, harm 26.148, 45.29

misdo *v.* do wrong, offend 30.413; **mysdone** *p.p.* 10.256

myself(f)e, miselue, myselue *pron.* I myself 21.92, 44.53, 47.180

myses *n.pl.* midges, gnats 11.273

mysese *n.* distress 20.213

misfare, mysfare *n.* misfortune 7.116, 25.324

misgone *v. p.p.* erred, mistaken 41.151

myslykyng, mysselykyng *n.* tribulation, sorrow 27.149, 42.17

mismarkid *v. p.p.* mistaken 29.121

myspaye *v.* displease 5.64

misplese *v.* displease; **misplese noȝt youre persone** do not be displeased 30.459

myssande, myssyng *v. pres. p. see* mys(se) *v.*

missing, myssyng *vbl. n.* lack, absence 1.48, 42.9, 44.164

miste, myste *v. p.p. see* mys(se) *v.*

myster, -ir, maistir *n.* need, requirement 8.52, 30.195, 369; **as mystir wore** such being the need 34.90

misty *adj.* portentous, significant 38.43

mystir *v. (impers.)* need; **vs mystir** we need 26.194; **what mystris þe** what need is there for you 7.54

mistrowand *ppl.adj.* lacking in faith 41.179, 42.135

myte *n.* jot, bit 31.335

mytyng, myghtyng *vbl. n.* infant 18.113; nonentity, insignificant person 22.26, 31.107; *as adj.* small, scant 32.307

mo(o), ma *adj.* more in number 2.53, 37.358; in addition 6.73, 22.60; others 39.4; **no moo** nobody else 23.4; **withowten moo** alone 8.134

mob(b)ardis *n.pl.* fools 28.137, 43.74

mode *see* moone

modir *n.* mother 44.151; **modir** *gen.sg.* mother's 25.241

modirhed *n.* motherly affection 42.201

moffe, moyfe *see* meve

moght, mowght *v.* might 10.7, 175, 47.379

molde *see* moulde; **momeland** *see* mummeland

momelyng *vbl.n.* mumbling 31.195

momellis *v. 3pl.pr.* mutter 27.106

mon(e) *v. (aux.)* must, shall

mone, mayne, mane, moone *n.'* complaint, lamentation 10.199, 13.190, 36.395; **hade mayne** complained 1.130

mone *n.²* moon 2.113, 10.258, 16.14

moneth *n.* month 12.183

moode, mode *n.* mind, disposition, frame of mind 17.28, 25.515, 35.65; strength of will 28.47; bearing, conduct 40.44; **with, in mayne and moode** *see* mayne *n.*

moolde *see* moulde; **moone** *see* mone *n.'*

moote *v.* argue 35.159; **motes** *2sg.pr.* lead astray (through agrument) 37.256

mop *n.* fool 31.199

more *n.* moor 11.296

mornand *ppl.adj. see* mournand

morne *n.* morning 25.512, 34.112, 38.126

morne, murne *v.* grieve 25.470, 26.78

morne-slepe *n.* morning sleep, 'lie-in' 30.195

mornyng *vbl.n.* sorrow, grief 9.210, 13.1, 36.273

mornys *n.pl.* lamentations 10.199

mort *v.* put to death 26.77

mortaise, mortas, mortcyse *n.* mortice 35.161, 220, 230, 40.95

morteysed *v. p.p.* fixed 26.163

moste, mast *adj.* great, greatest 20.140, 33.457, 36.251

mosteres *see* muster

mot(t)(e) *v.* may, must

motes *v. see* moote; **move** *see* meve

mouyng *vbl.n.* incitement, subversion 26.77

moulde, molde, moolde *n.* earth, dust 1.141; the earth, world, *in phatic phr.* **on (þis) mo(o)lde** 7.35, 17.381, 26.147

mounte *n.* hill 28.84

mournand, mornand *ppl. adj.* weeping, grieving 38.235, 40.4

mourthered *v. pa.t.* murdered 40.90

mowe *v.* pull faces 36.78

mowes *n.pl.* grimaces; **make mowes on** pull faces at 35.286

mowght *see* moght

multyplyeand *ppl.adj.* prolific 11.115

mum *v.* whisper 11.175

mummeland, momeland *ppl.adj.* mumbling 31.318, 32.242

murne *see* morne

mused *ppl.adj.* conscious, aware 42.247

muste *n.* new wine 43.164

muster, -yr, -ir *v.* show, manifest, display 1.145, 37.174; **mustirs, musteris, mosteres** *3sg.pr.* 11.30, 16.14, 43.130; **musteres** *3pl.pr.* 37.104; **mustered** *pa.t.* 37.86; *p.p.* 22.9, 23.84; **vs musters** shows (itself) to us 26.32

mutyng *vbl.n.* disputing 31.335

na *conj.* nor 11.352

name *n. in phr.* **by name** particularly 37.190

namely *adv.* particularly 30.172

names *v. 3pl. pr.* set forth, tell 23.222

nan(e) *see* non(e) *pron., adv.*

nape *n.* ape 29.105

nappe *v.* sleep 29.353; **napped** *pa.t.* 30.186

napping *vbl. n.* sleep 29.84

nare *adv.* near *see* nere *adj. etc.*

narre, nare, nerre *adv.* nearer 9.62, 100; **neuere þe nerre** no nearer (the purpose) 31.334

narmes *n.pl.* arms 17.376

natheles *adv.* nevertheless 40.31

nawe *adj. see* awne

ne *adv. (neg. particle)* **ne were** were not 3.17; **ne myght** might not 5.113

ne *conj.* nor 42.14

nede *n.* necessary 20.62, 38.321; **with nede** of necessity 30.172

nede *adv.* of necessity 34.309

nedfull *adj. as n.* needy people 47.358

ned(e)lyng(is) *adv.* of necessity 9.109, 31.178, 33.476

neffes *n.pl.* fists 29.367

negh(e), neyghe *v.* come near to, approach 4.68, 5.33, 16.121; **neghes, negheth** *3sg.pr.* 29.366, 30.183; **neghand** *pres. p.* 28.3, 30.139; **neghed** *pa.t.* 6.65

neghbour *n.* friend 28.169

neȝe *adv.* nigh 25.415

neyd *v.* need 37.242

neyne *adj.* nine 7.16

neyre *see* **nere** *adj. etc.*

neme, nemen, nemyn(e) *v.* mention, refer to, speak of 6.144, 24.37, 29.193, 31.286; **nemys** *ipv.pl.* 31.96; **nemed** *p.p.* 20.278

nemely *adv.* swiftly 29.217, 35.120

nenys *see* **neuen; nere(s)** *n. (pl.) see* **herre** *n.²*

nere *adv.¹* never 16.186M

nere, neyre, nare *adj., adv.,² prep.* near 4.92, 13.34, 22.52, 37.224; **comes nere** come back again 9.49

nerhand *adv.* nearly, almost 9.85, 16.121

nerre *adv. see* **narre**

nerthrist *adj.* lowest 33.265

nese *n.* nose 33.196, 42.238

neuen, neven, -yn *v.* name, mention, utter, tell 1.25, 12.13, 31.32; call (as a name) 12.64; **neuenes, nevynnes** *ipv. pl.* 38.442, 44.21; **nenys** *2sg. pr.* 32.187; **likes to neven** it is suitable to mention 9.15

neuenly *adv.* ? namely, *sc.* plainly 36.6

ncvill *adj.* cvil; **a nevill happe** a curse on you 29.365

new(e), nowe *adv.* newly, lately, recently 16.164G, 165G, 37.314; anew 42.11; **of new(e)** immediately 31.82; peremptorily 11.141; just recently 19.41, 111; **newe inowe** very suddenly 15.54

newe *n. see* **noy** *n.¹*; **newe** *v.* annoy *see* **noy(e)** *v.*

newes *v. 3sg.pr.* arises, springs up 16.214; renews (itself), continues 25.530

newly *adv.* soon 28.3; until recently 31.228

newsome *adj.* troublesome 30.182; **noysomemare** *cpv.* 32.100

nexile *n.* wing (as of a building) 1.25 (= **ile** 1.26)

nexte *adv.* next in rank; **moste nexte after** immediately subordinate 1.33

nygard *n.* worthless individual 33.364

nyse *adj.* foolish 29.284; **leste ȝe be nyse?** are you fools? 29.191

no *adv.* not 4.73

noble *adj.* fine 8.107

nociens *n.pl.* notions; **be my nociens** according to my inclinations 32.293

noddil *v.* strike (on the head) 29.367

nodir *see* **othir** *adj.*

noght(e), noȝt *pron.* none, nothing 1.10, 5.29, 36.195; **righte noghte** nothing at all 1.44

noght(e) *adj.* worthless, evil 1.31; futile 19.231

noght(e), nough *adv.* not 2.41; **righte noghte** not at all 1.71

noy(e), newe *n.¹* annoyance, vexation, trouble 1.85, 27.105, 44.144; **noyes, newis, -ys** *pl.* 11.386, 31.228, 46.105

noy *n.²* cry of 'oyes' 30.367

noy(e), newe *v.* annoy, vex, concern 1.71, 10.125 *(refl.);* torment 40.94; be troubled 30.130; **noyed** *p.p.* 19.41, 31.391; *pa.t.* oppressed 23.205

noynte *v.* annoint 38.215

noysed *v. p.p.* spoken of, put about 32.100

noysomemare *see* **newsome**

nokyn(s), no-kyn(nes) *adj.* no kind of 5.76, 18.152, 38.162, 208

nolde *v. pa.t.* would not 38.405

non(e), nan *pron.* none, nobody, no one 2.19, 3.51, 31.210; nothing 38.329

non(e), noon *adj.* no, not any 4.77, 29.194, 36.205

none, ? nowe *n.* noon, midday 6.91, 33.476, 34.45; midnight 31.46; **nowe of the nyght, nowe in þe nyght** ? noon of the night, midnight 29.177, 346

none, nane *adv.* not, not at all 3.17, 4.68, 21.79, 42.31

nonys *n.* nonce, purpose; *in phatic phr.* **for þe nonys** 29.284, 31.333, 35.219

note, noote, nott *n.¹* matter, business, news 11.141, 16.131, 34.306; use 36.383; **notes** *pl.* evidence 29.298

note *n.²* song 15.65

nother, nowder, -ir, nowþere, nowthir *adj., adv.* neither

nothyng *adv.* not, in no way 11.323, 38.281, 39.123

nott *see* **note** *n.¹*

novellis *n.pl.* extraordinary things 20.106

novelté *n.* a new and unusual thing 15.127; news 25.118

nough *see* **noght(e)** *adv.;* **nowder, -ir** *see* **nother; nowe** *n. see* **none** *n.*

now(e) *adj.* new 16.131M, 20.106

nowe *adv. see* **newe** *adv.*

nowele *n.* owl 29.117

nowys *n.pl.* news, information 28.43

nowþere, nowthir *see* **nother**

obeyesaunce *n.* obedience, homage 45.143

obitte *adj.* dead 37.269

ob(b)lissh(e) *v.* dedicate, pledge 14.146, 35.53, 47.207

of *adv.* sometimes written for **off**, *e.g.* 33.161, 251

of, off *prep.* of 3.50, 25.128; above 18.216; by 33.291; for, on account of 1.43; on 9.291; out of 26.254; over 5.59, 42.38; some of 30.521

off *conj. see* þof

offende *v.* violate 38.34; *? error for* **defend** 46A.38; **offende** *pa.t.* offended, caused offence 18.66

offerand(e) *n.* offering, sacrifice 10.99, 138, 17.41

ofte-sithes, -is *adv.* frequently 40.109, 47.315

ofte-tymes *adv.* frequently 30.197

of-turned *v. p.p.* reversed, overturned 45.236

oght *n., adv. see* **ought** *adv.*, **ought(e)** *n.*; **oght** *v. p.p. see* **awe** *v.*

oyes, oȝes, oyas *interj.* hear ye 30.370, 31.333, 33.264

olde *see* **elde**; **omange** *prep. see* **emang(e)(s)** *prep.*; **omys** *see* **amys(se)**

one *prep.* on 4.36

one *adj.* singly 12.107; alone 33.465

ones *see* **anes**

ongayne *adj.* troublesome 30.513

ongaynely *adv.* with trouble, uneasily 6.99

ongentill *see* **vngentill**; **ongladde** *see* **vngladde**; **ongodly** *see* **vngoodly**

on-hanged *ppl.adj.* not yet hanged (but ought to be) 26.174, 32.188

onys *see* **anes**

on lif, on lyffe, on lyue *adv.* alive, living 9.87, 11.254, 19.13

on-thinke *v. (refl.)* consider, reflect 42.242

ontill *see* **vntill**

oon *adv.* on 29.148

oondis *v. 3pl.pr.* breathe 14.132

ooste *n.* host, army 11.366

oppen *adj.* careless 26.202

or *conj., prep.* ere, before

or *adv.* now 17.248, 31.192

ordayne, ordan *v.* plan, arrange, set up 10.8, 164; **ordayned, ordand(e)** *pa.t.* 12.18, 37.25; *p.p.* 2.29, 8.128; prescribed 6.106; intended 11.261

ordinate *v. p.p.* ordained 46A.30

os *conj.* as 8.66, 140

ospring *n.* descendants 47.23

othir, oþir, nodir *adj., n.* other(s) 6.73, 25.167, 34.306; another, the other 27.68

othir *adv.* otherwise 23.164, 27.110

ouer-cruell *adj.* vindictive 26.95

ouereall *adv.* everywhere 41.194

ouere-brathely *adv.* too violently 33.17

ouere-fast *adv.* too quickly 20.19

ouere-ȝonge *adj.* too young 20.91

ouere-hande *n.* mastery 10.344

ouere-lange *adv.* too long (time) 9.148

ouere-large *adv.* too boldly 20.118

ouere-lat(t)e *adv.* too late 11.226, 19.70, 20.35

ouere-paste *see* **ouerpasse**

ouere-skantely *adv.* inadequately (as to distance), in the wrong place 35.111

ouere-wyde *adj.* too wide 35.231

ouere-wyn *v.* conquer 32.105

over-farre *adv.* too far 11.307

ouer-ga *v.* pass by 13.66; **ouere-gone** *p.p.* 26.277

over-grete *adj.* excessive 23.219

ouerhyld *v. p.p.* decked, adorned 2.121

ouerpasse *v.* avoid 28.58; **ouer(e)-past(e)** *p.p.* ended 11.306, 44.115

ouersprede *v.* diffuse, put about 32.70

ouer-thyn *adj.* too thin 8.76

ovir-nere *adj.* too close at hand 40.146

ovir-poure *adj.* too poor 15.110

ought, aught, oght, ouȝte *adv.* at all, to any extent 5.33, 10.177, 43.168, 45.260; **is oght** exists 47.3

ought(e), oght, aught *n.* something, anything 3.18, 10.256, 11.322, 37.100

ought *? prep.* before 27.110

our *adv.* over, above 10.70

oure, owre *n.* hour, time 10.278, 28.74; **þis owre** immediately 25.119

oure *pron. (pers.)* of us; **oure vnwittyng** unbeknown to us 33.188; **oure awe** (his) fear of us 38.361

oure-fone *adj.* too few 34.41

oureself(f)(e), oureselue *pron.* ourselves 14.5, 20.168, 38.322

oute-caste *v.* expel 42.140

oute-tane, outtane, owtane *prep.* except for, but for 6.9, 10.224, 24.147

outhir *see* **owther**

outrayes *v. 3sg.pr.* goes beyond the limit 33.99

owe *interj. expr. of* consternation, affirmation *etc.* 1.81, 11.347, 37.149

owre *n. see* **oure** *n.*; **owtane** *see* **oute-tane**

owte, owte on *interj. expr. of* lamentation, abhorrence, reproach *etc.* 1.97, 108, 9.99, 37.185

owte *adv.* out, extinguished 17.162

owt(e)-tayke *v.* reserve, make an exception of 4.67, 90, 94

owther, -ir, ather, awdir, outhir *adv.* either 8.16, 9.216, 13.9, 44.71; *pron.* each one 1.155

Paas, Pase *n.* Easter 27.4, 29

page *n.* knave, rascal 28.182, 29.378, 37.125; **page** *gen.sg.* boy's 18.101

pay(e), paie *n.* satisfaction, liking 2.49, 16.207, 21.75; money 32.192

paye *v.* please, satisfy 47.118; *impers.* **me paies** I am pleased 37.82; **paied, payed, payde, paide** *p.p., adj.* pleased, content 10.192, 11.359, 12.186, 16.247

payere *n.* ? one who pays (i.e. deals out punishment) 33.374 *(but ? error for* **playere***)*

payn(e), peyne *n.* suffering, distress; penalty 17.17; **putte to peyne** plunged into distress 9.180; **of a payne** under threat of punishment 30.402; **peyne of lyme** upon pain of limb 19.2

payre, paire *v., intr.* deteriorate 1.54; *tr.* impair, lessen, damage 26.114, 34.255

pakald *n.* bundle 18.169

pakke *n.* various things 18.166

palle *n.* fine robe 32.26

palmeres *n.pl.* pilgrims 32.334

panyer *n.* basket 17.252

pappe *n.* breast 40.103

parceyue *v. ipv.* take heed 36.274; **parsayued** *pa.t.* saw 5.4

pardé *interj.* by God, indeed 15.45

parellis *see* **perellis**

parfite, perfyth *adj.* perfect 3.17, 21.34, 46A.2

parfitely *adv.* perfectly 22.91

parformed *v. p.p.* perfected 20.116

parlament *n.* conference 32.34

parred *v. p.p.* flayed 33.33

parsayued *see* **parceyue**

parte *n.* portion 26.145; cause, part (in a question), **þare parte** concern for them 26.144

parte *v. p.p.* divided 34.324

party, partie *n.* part 27.26; number (of persons) 47.224

pase *n.* pace, course (of action), **his pase pursue** follow in his footsteps 43.103

Pase *see* **Paas**

passe *v.* avoid 32.147; **passis** *3sg.pr.* surpasses 39.140; **passande** *pres.p.* surpassing 1.56, 134

passhed *v. pa.t.* crushed, smashed 45.38

paste *ppl.adj.* dead 36.181

passioun *n.* painful course 28.104

patris *v. 3sg.pr.* patters, prattles 35.266

paunch(e) *n.* belly 33.371

peere *n. see* **pere**

peere *v.* appear 26.16

pees, pese, pesse *n.* peace; silence 40.84

pees *adj.* quiet 36.162

peyne *n. see* **payn(e)**

peyne *v. refl.* **me peyne** exert myself 18.185

peyre *n.* pair 9.140

peysed *v. pa.t.* forced 40.96

pele *n.* formal accusation in court 26.110

peny *n.* penny 26.272; **penys, pens** *pl.* pence, money 26.136, 152

pere *n.* peer, equal 5.70, 30.38, 46.126; **peere of** equal in 42.13

perellis, parellis *n.pl.* dangers 11.306, 45.188

perelous, perillus *adj.* greatly to be feared 26.16; dangerous 31.126

per(e)les *adj.* matchless, unequalled 10.239, 24.120; *as n.* peerless one 44.78

perfyth *see* **parfite; perillus** *see* **perelous**

periurye *n.* breach of oath 26.75

perloyned *v. pa.t.* put aside 30.31

persed *v. pa.t.* pierced 45.61

perte *adj.* open (of speaking) 31.259; clever, sharp 33.109

pert(e)ly *adv.* openly 29.134; boldly 30.166, 449; over-boldly 30.32

pese *n.pl.* peas 15.125

pese, pesse *n.sg. see* **pees** *n.*

pestelence *n.* fatal disease, plague 11.345

pety, petie *see* **pité**

py *n.* magpie 35.266

pight *v. p.p.* situated 14.4; adorned 16.12

pike *v.* steal 5.18; **pikis** *3pl.pr.* choose 16.11

pilche *n.* garment 33.374

pynakill *n.* pinnacle 22.91

pyne *n.* pain, suffering, punishment 9.54, 11.214, 13.56

pyne *v. tr.* torment, inflict suffering upon 37.219; *intr.* **at pyne** to suffer, to undergo torment 1.32; **pynande** *pres.p.* 1.72; **pynd** *pa.t.* made great efforts 33.278; **pynde, pyned, pyn(n)yd** *p.p.* made to suffer, languish 9.217, 16.350, 22.12, 43.184

pynyng *ppl.adj.* tormenting 33.33

pynne *v.* nail 40.96

pitaunce *n.* portion of food and drink 40.156

pité, pety, petie *n.* pity 26.143, 33.371, 372

pytefull *adj. as n.* one filled with pity 25.526

pitously *adv.* grievously 36.32

playe *n.* mirth, joy 27.100, 37.392; **plaies** *pl.* plays, pageants 40.192

playne *n.* flat open space 31.5

playne *adj.¹* unobstructed 11.358; palpable, outright 24.31; honest, straightforward 26.143; **plener** *cpv.* unconfined 11.200

playne, pleyne *adj.²* full, plenary 20.103, 42.37, 43.199

playn(e), pleyne *adv.¹* plainly, openly 11.242, 17.205, 23.83; (of speaking) clearly, unambiguously 20.127

playne *adv.²* fully, completely 9.179, 16.248; **playnere** *cpv.* more fully 20.127

plasmator *n.* creator 46A.2

plates *n.pl.* pieces of plate armour 39.102

plat(e)ly *adv.* directly 33.243; in an orderly manner 30.3

platte *v.* fall down, kneel 31.5

pleasaunce *n.* good will, indulgence 36.105; joy 45.139

pleyne *adj. see* **playne** *adj.*²; **pleyne** *adv. see* **playn(e)** *adv.*¹

pleyne *v.* complain, grumble 18.170; **pleyned** *pa.t.* lamented 47.296

pleyntes *n.pl.* grievances 29.386, 30.3

plenall *adj.* full 46A.46

plener *see* **playne** *adj.*¹

plenté *n.* (in) abundance 2.122, 6.89, 28.281

plesyng *n.* pleasure, liking 1.12

plete *adv.*, *in phr.* **and plete** fully, all told 26.229

plete *v.* argue 25.176

plextis *v. ipv.pl.* plead, wrangle 31.5 (*? for* **pletis**, *see prec.*)

ply(e) *v., intr.* comply, submit 26.76; *tr.* **at ply** to mould 1.12

plight, plyght *n.*¹ danger 32.164; sin 35.52; guilt 42.44

plight *n.*² manner, bearing 30.13; **in plight** in a state of urgency 40.192

plight *v.*¹ *p.p.* promised 17.330

plight *v.*² embrace 17.81

poynte *n.* matter, question 16.102, 37.105; detail 1.54; indication 22.99; **no poynte** not in the least 29.315

pontificall *adj.* high (priestly) 30.206

poors *see* **poure** *n.*; **poostee** *see* **pousté**

popse *n. ?pl.* blows, slaps 29.355 (*? name of a buffeting game*)

porte *n.* gate 26.155

post(é) *see* **pousté**

postelis *n.pl.* apostles 42.81, 47.185

poudre *n.* dust, ash 11.315

pouerté *n.* poverty 47.296

poure *n.* power, authority, strength 11.242, 16.188, 37.219; **poors** *pl.* 17.122

poure, power, powre *adj.* poor 17.49, 19.1, 40.156

pousté, post, po(o)sté, poostee *n.* power, might 2.47, 10,181, 26.88, 114, 38.248; **of posté** powerful 44.78

power *adj. see* **poure** *adj.*

powll *v.* pull 33.471

powre *see* **poure** *adj.*

pray(e) *n.* prey 5.18, 29.118, 37.175

praty *adj.* clever, intelligent 20.276

preceptis *n.pl.* commands 30.31

preces, -is *see* **presse** *v.*

preche *v.* preach (to) 45.304; **prechand** *pres.p.* 44.66

prees *see* **presse** *n.*; **preffe** *see* **preue**

preysyng *vbl.n.* suit, appeal 40.26

prente *v.* inscribe, *in phr.* **prente vndir penne** commit to writing 26.75; **prente, prentyd** *p.p.* stained, permeated 36.111; imprinted 7.133

presande *n.* a present 15.110

prese *n., v. see* **presse** *n., v.*

presence, presens *n.* presence, *in phr.* **latt your presence** may you 33.134; **in presens** here 42.191

present *n.* presence 20.137; assembly, company 20.51, 25.345; **in present** numerous 29.314

present *v. p.p.* presented 17.193, 302

presiously *adv.* dearly, with great cost 45.79

presse, prees, prese *n.* crowd, assembly 14.12, 29.135, 34.12; commotion, uproar 37.125; adversity 47.289; **putte...in presse** strive, endeavour 11.15; push forward 15.122; make the attempt 30.166

presse, prese *v.* press, act firmly 26.114; desire urgently 40.145; quell, repress 30.20; advance boldly 30.207; **preces** *3sg.pr.* solicits 26.230; **precis in plight** presses urgently behind, queues up 40.192

preste *adj.* swift, hasty 26.271, 30.115, 47.339; close at hand, pressing 29.135

preste *adv.* quickly, readily 30.376, 518

prestis *n.pl.* priests 26.150, 27.109

prest(e)ly *adv.* quickly 28.11, 33.27, 40.186

preualy *see* **pryuely**

preue, preve, preffe, proue *v.* prove, establish, show 20.153, 25.60, 29.134; enquire into 16.102; make trial of, encounter 26.16; **preuys, proues** *3pl.pr.* 43.17; experience 26.113; **preued** *pa.t.* 15.7; **preued, -yd, prouyde** *p.p.* 29.15, 30.18, 34.22; **proue till** grow up to be 20.276

preued, proved *ppl.adj.* proven, acknowledged 25.489; trustworthy 16.225 (*see prec.*)

preuely(e), prevely *see* **pryuely**

price, pris(e) *n.* worth, value 5.98, 22.127, 29.15

prike *v.* fasten 13.302; **priked** *pa.t.* induced, incited (the conscience) 26.144

prime *n.* the first hour (of the day) 6.90

principall, -epall *n.* leader, chief 27.75, 37.111

principall *adv.* principally, in the first place 7.68, 36.62

pris(e) *n.* value *see* **price**

prise *n.* prize 30.37

pryuely, preualy, preuely(e), prevely *adv.* secretly, without attracting attention 10.35, 24.62, 29.118, 47.131; stealthily 30.92

priuité, pryuyté *n.* divine mystery 23.76;
in priuité in privacy, privately 13.197,
29.315

prisounes *n.pl.* prisoners 37.220

processe, prossesse *n.* legal proceedings
33.123; procession 40.192; **fayre processe** due course 2.170

prokering *vbl.n.* contriving, plotting 40.82

propheres *v. 3sg.pr.* offers up 33.372

prophetable *adj.* good 33.37

prophicy *n. gen.sg.* prophicy's 25.24

prophyte, -ite, -ete *n.* benefit, good 21.155,
38.402, 42.253

prophite *v.* advance, bring forward (a
charge in court) 26.110; **prophitis** *3sg.pr.*
is profitable 30.70

propir *adj.* own 26.15

propirly, -yrly *adv.* in person 8.44, 33.206,
346

prossesse *see* **processe**

proue *adj.* proof, firm, fixed 5.17

proue *v. see* **preue; proved** *adj. see* **preued**

prowde *adj. as n.* proud person 30.14

prowe *n.* good, benefit 9.241, 26.156,
29.355; **for thy prowe** to your credit
23.37

publysch *v.* show, display 2.30; **puplisshid**
p.p. 37.59

puplicans *n.pl.* tax-collectors 25.413

purchace *n.* advantage, grace 17.47

purgens 28.285 *meaning unkn.*; *? scribal error*

purpose *n.* plan 38.415

purpose *v.* intend 32.330; **purposed** *pa.t.,
refl.* strove 45.28

purpure *n.* purple attire, royal garment
33.390

purser *n.* purse-bearer, treasurer 26.136

pursue, pursewe *v.* follow, abide by 37.316;
go, pursue (a way) 27.109; **þe soþe to
pursewe** truly to tell *(phatic phr.)* 26.129

purvey(e), puruay, purvaye *v.* provide,
prepare, arrange 12.122, 26.272, 38.158,
42.151; **purueyed** *p.p.* 37.69; **purueyse
none** are unprovided for 27.24

putte *v. pa.t.* thrust, pushed 40.96;
putte ... by set aside, thwart 5.17; **putte
to peyne** plunged into distress 9.180;
putte ... to pees forced to be silent 40.84

putry *n.* sexual misconduct 24.31

quarte, qwarte *n.* health, physical fitness
17.159; **oute of qwarte** unfit, infirm 8.50;
in quarte alive 29.167

quelle, qwelle *v.* destroy, subvert 11.61,
19.209, 32.49

quenys, -es *n.pl.* shrewish women 19.209,
34.191, 210

quyk, quike *adj.* alive 20.211, 23.118; *as n.*
living 25.539, 43.16

quyte *v.* recompense, reward (for) 42.272;
quytes *3sg.pr., refl.* behaves 33.255; **quitte**
p.p. 31.395; repaid 47.46

quytte *adj.* even 19.203

quoke *v. pa.t.* quaked 38.390

qwantise *n.* cunning 11.61

qwarte *see* **quarte**

qwat(e), qwhat *pron., adj.* what

qwell *n.* death, execution 33.66

qwelle *v. see* **quelle**

qwen *adv.* when

qwy *n.* man 31.39

qwhat *see* **qwat(e)**

qwilke *pron.* which

qwitte *adj.* free, *in phr.* **go qwitte** get away
with it 9.119

rable *n.* crowd 33.108

race, rase *n.* course of events 35.283;
course of action, behaviour 30.214

racleyme *n.* the action of being called
again; **comys to racleyme** returns when
called 32.79

radde *adj.* frightened 21.59, 38.377

radly *adv.* soon, quickly 11.390, 30.177

raffe *v. inf., 1sg.pr. see* **raue** *v.¹*; **raffe** *v., pa.t.
see* **ryue** *v.*; **rafte** *see* **reue**

ragged *v. p.p.* torn to shreds 36.120, 253

ray *v.* set forth, expound, arrange 26.38,
246; **rayed** *p.p.* dressed 30.42, 31.359

rayke *v.* go, proceed 30.150, 33.224; **raykes**
3sg.pr. happens 30.438; **raykand** *pres.p.*
running, rushing on 16.3, 26.93

rayse *v. intr.* ascend 30.233; rise, get out of
bed 30.263; *tr.* **rayses** *3sg.pr.* raises, resurrects 30.446; **raysed** *pa.t.* roused (from
bed) 24.6; **raysede** *p.p.* arisen 26.34

rayst *v. p.p.* see **rased**

rayued *v. p.p.* split, torn open 14.18

rakand *vbl.n.* hurrying 31.219

rake *v.* go 36.293; **rakis** *3sg.pr.* 30.125;
rakid *p.p.* been gone, been away 45.237

rakke *n.* rack, mass of clouds 16.7

ranke *adj.* rebellious 26.33

ranne *see* **run**

ransake *v.* make a thorough search 45.215

rapes *see* **roppe**

rappe *v.* smite, beat 26.285; push sharply
30.233; **rapped** *p.p.* 33.154

rappely *adv.* quickly 16.7

rappes *n.pl.* blows 28.112, 33.362

rare *v. see* **rore**

raryng *vbl.n.* wailing, lamentation 31.220

rase *n. see* **race**

rase *v.⁽¹⁾ pa.t.* rose 33.290

rased, -id, rayst *v.*⁽²⁾ *p.p.* wounded 39.66, 45.60; marked with wounds 41.85
rasely *adv.* cruelly 45.60
ratheley *adv.* quickly, promptly 28.6, 29.269, 31.390
raþere *adv.* sooner 33.314
raue, raffe *v.*¹ talk wildly 13.146, 23,164; cry out in pain 26.286, 34.53; writhe in agony 35.248
raue *v.*² wander disconsolately 24.159
raught *v.* give 33.403
ravisshed *v. p.p.* carried away 42.179
rawe *see* **rowe** *n.*
rawnsom *n.* ransom, redemption 25.9
rawnsoner *n.* redeemer 25.525
rawsoune *v.* redeem 40.111
read *n. see* **rede** *n.*¹
reame, reme *n.* realm, kingdom 16.72, 26.34; **remys** *pl.* 30.22, 164
reasoune, resoune *n.* saying, statement, speech 29.307, 30.62, 37.337; reasoning, argument 37.255; (good) sense, what is reasonable 10.119, 16.126, 37.263; **as resoune will** as is reasonable 25.100; **be gode resoune** according to what is reasonable 25.75; **by þat resoune** with that intent 37.248
rebalde, ribald *n.* knave, rascal 29.269, 30.145, 33.277
reche *v.* get hold of, seize 26.285; come to an understanding of 20.98; *ipv.* give 29.307; **rechid** *pa.t.* was, went 45.281
recorde *v.* take note of 19.5; perceive 33.314
recover *n.* recovery, redemption 17.439
recoueraunce *n.* recovery 26.101
recours *n.* source of help 27.141
recrayed *ppl.adj.* recreant, cowardly 38.364
recreacioun *n.* consolation 45.20
rede, read, reed(e) *n.*¹ understand, wits 13.146, 36.265; advice, counsel 17.240, 18.103, 21.40; scheme, plan 4.44; **wille of rede** at a loss 39.91; **toke to rede** took counsel 34.112
rede *n.*² reed, stick 33.403
rede, reede *adj.* red, bloody 32.24, 33.355
rede *v.*¹ believe 20.145, 29.157; expound, tell of 11.64, 20.144; read, understand 22.164, 30.16; *ipv.* prophesy 29.373; **rede ... on rawe, redde by rawes** expounded in due order 20.50, 86; **rede by rawe** rightly understand 23.122, rightly understood 37.317; **red be reasoune** understood through reason 12.102
rede *v.*² adviser, counsel 11.17, 13.109, 16.277; **reedis** *3sg.pr.* 23.164; **red** *pa.t.* 6.35; **redde** *p.p.* 30.89
redely *adv.* wilfully 30.145

redolent *adj.* fragrant 45.108
redresse *v.* reform, correct 30.22
redused *v. pa.t.* disabused 45.82
reed(e) *n. see* **rede** *n.*¹; **reede** *adj. see* **rede** *adj.*; **reedis** *see* **rede** *v.*²; **refe** *see* **reue**; **reffuse** *see* **refuse**
reflars *v. 3sg.pr.* rises up 17.367
refte *see* **reue**
refuse, reffuse *v.* release, dismiss 33.314; condemn 32.77
regally *n.* kingdom 44.190
regent *n.* deputy, governor 26.2
regentte *n.* regency 44.190; ? *error for* **regentcé** *or* **regentré**
regnys *see* **rengne**
rehers(e) *v.* recite 29.308; report 45.25; **rehersed** *p.p.* 35.283
rehete *v.* assail 33.362, 363; rebuke 29.285
reynand, reyned *see* **rengne**
reke *n.* commotion 26.34
reken(ne) *v.* enumerate, summon up 33.108; presume to advise 26.246; agree, conform 30.355; **rekens** *2sg.pr.* judge 30.492
rekenyng *vbl. n.* account 47.95
rekkles, rekles *adj.* heedless 13.146; *as n.* reckless person, fool 26.285
reles(se) *n.* discharge, release 17.149, 37.288
releue *n. (coll. sg.)* leftovers 31.212
releue *v. 2pl. subj.* be of assistance 33.132
reme *see* **reame**
remelaunt *n.* remainder 27.23
remened *v. p.p.* compared 12.50
remewe *v., tr.* lead away 11.310; *intr.* go, depart 33.334; **remoues** *3sg.pr.* is going 27.112
remys *see* **reame**
remytte *v. pa.t.* sent, directed 30.22
remoues *see* **remewe**; **renand** *see next*
rengne *v.* reign 28.122; **regnys** *3pl.pr.* are 32.5; **renyng, reynand, renand** *pres.p.* flourishing 8.14, 17.457, 91.18; **reyned** *pa.t.* prevailed, was 45.34
renke *n.*¹ man 16.54, 45.31; **renk(k)is, -es** *pl.* people 30.16, 22, 31.18
renke *n.*² sovereignty (over) 29.18; ? *error for* **renge** reign
renne *see* **run**
rennyng *vbl.n.* running (? to escape pursuit, ? as letting of blood) 26.286
rennoune, -owne *n.* renown 36.380, 38.182
rente *n.* revenue; **of rente** having revenue 26.1
rente *v.*⁽¹⁾ tear, cut 30.36, 33.356
rente *v.*⁽²⁾ *p.p.* torn asunder 28.112, 36.120, 40.168
repaire *v.* return 31.382

repleye *v.* ? *for* **repleve** bail out, redeem 37.380

repreue *n. see* **reproffe** *n.*

repreue *v.* disapprove of, challenge 31.17; **reproues** *3sg.pr.* convicts 32.243; **reproued** *pa.t.* rebuked 45.28; *p.p.* rebuked 42.85; ? redressed 26.245

reproffe, repreue *n.* disgrace 13.45, 56, 30.92

reproued, reproues *see* **repreue** *v.*; **resayue, resave** *see* **ressayue**

resen, resynne *v. p.p.* risen 38.245, 408

resoune *see* **reasoune**

respete *n.* delay 10.285

respouns *n.pl.* answers 32.291

ressayue, resayue, resave *v.* receive 1.90, 26.245, 41.90; greet 25.207; *ipv.* take heed 33.86

rest(e), ryste *n.* peace 26.2, 28.122, 45.170; **be rest** peaceably 16.32; **in ryste** unchecked, unmolested 11.43

reste, ryst *v.* rest 3.86; placate 45.31; **reste** *pa.t.* hung 47.29; **reste of** cease from 30.62

restreyne *v. refl., ipv.* **restreyne you for** cease, desist from 30.2

reue, refe *v.* deprive of, rob 30.164, 519, 42.22; **reves** *3sg.pr.* 16.54; **refte, rafte** *p.p.* taken away (from), removed 13.146, 25.477, 30.174, 300

reuerand *adj.* respectful 31.18

reuerant *n.* reverence 31.239

reuerent *adj.* holy 45.170; *as n.* one worthy of reverence, holy one 36.380, 45.82, 281

revers *v.* resist 45.24

revette *n.* rivet 8.109

reuyn *see* **ryue; reuthe** *see* **ruth(e)**

rewarde *n.* regard; **take rewarde** pay heed 20.235

rewarde *v. p.p.* rewarded 28.236

rewe *n.* rove; burr or plate over which a nail is clenched in shipbuilding 8.109

rewe *v.* pity, take compassion 7.116, 13.204, 32.235; **þou rewis** you will regret it 30.62; *impers.* **me rewes, rewes me, þam rewe** *etc.* I, they regret, repent of 6.151, 8.15, 9.39, 13.36

rewfull *adj.* distraught 31.219; pitiful 39.121

rewfully, ruffully *adv.* pitifully, by grievous means 36.265, 39.119, 40.42

rewl(l)e *n. see* **rule**

rewle *v. refl.* conduct, behave; **rewle vs, you, rewles þame** behave our-, your-, themselves 26.94, 34.16, 36.15; dress me 16.147M

rewly *adj.* calm 26.38

rewþe *see* **ruth(e)**

riall, ryall *adj.* royal 16.32, 17.370, 45.62;

ryallest, ryolest *spv.* 17.457, 26.1; *as n.* royal one, one of royal blood 17.412, 44.2; ? realm, kingdom 29.18 (*but text corrupt*)

ryally *adv.* royally 19.88

rialté, ryalté *n.* kingdom 16.3, 28.122; dignity 30.111

ribald *see* **rebalde**

richesse *n.* wealth 30.42, 174

rid *see* **ridde**

rydand *v. pres.p.* riding 19.88, 25.27

ridde, rid *v.* clear 16.7; set free 30.519; **rid(de) vs** relieve ourselves of, escape from 45.228; help us 45.237

ryf(f)e, riffe, ryve *adj.* abundant, generously bestowed 9.3, 10.22, 17.412; deeply ingrained 21.48

ryfe, ryue *adv.* abundantly, everywhere 8.14, 25.136, 371

ryff, riffe *v. see* **ryue**

rigge *n.* back 34.72

right *adj.* straight, most direct 20.40; true 37.255

right(e), ryght(e), righit *adv.* (*usu. intensive*) very 2.50; indeed, certainly, truly 9.292, 22.4; accordingly 15.95; correctly 20.144; **ryght vprise** rise upright 37.31

right *v.* impute 21.151

rightwis(s)(e), rightis *adj.* righteous, proper 21.116, 24.46, 32.161, 38.23

rightwysnes, rightwissenesse *n.* righteousness 1.124, 21.118

ryolest *see* **riall**

rising *vbl.n.* resurrection 41.191

risse *n.* branch 46.41

ryst *v. see* **reste** *v.*; **ryste** *n. see* **rest(e)** *n.*; **ryve** *adj. see* **ryf(f)e** *adj.*; **ryue** *adv. see* **ryfe** *adv.*

ryue, ryve, ryff, riffe *v. tr.* rive, split or tear asunder 30.36, 391, 41.140; *intr.* split 35.248; **raffe** *pa. t.* tore 38.111, 40.42; **reuyn** *p.p.* wounded, gashed 41.85; **to-ryff** break down completely 13.153

robard *n.* vagabond, felon 7.47

rode *see* **roode; roght** *see* **rought**

roy *n.¹* ? fellow 26.286 (*or perh. ironic use of next in light of 26.115*)

roy(e) *n.²* king 26.1, 31.359, 33.408

royis, royse *v. 2sg.pr.* talk nonsense 15.69, 37.99

rolyng ? *n.* ? *term of contempt or personal abuse; see OED s. vv. 'riveling' and 'rilling'*

rollis *n.pl.* documents; **rollis of recorde** rolls of parchment recording the laws 31.401

romour *n.* report; what is said (of a person) 26.34

ronne *see* **run**

roo, rowe, *n.*' peace, tranquillity 4.38, 6.76; pause, leisure 30.177; **als haue I roo** as I hope to have peace 14.19

roo *n.*² roe, deer 30.263

roode, rode *n.* cross 28.112, 36.120, 253

roppe *n.* rope 22.4; **rapes** *pl.* 40.42

rore, rare *v.* shout, create a disturbance 30.145, 33.162; **raris** *ipv.pl.* 31.310

rote *n.* root 45.170

roþe *v.* talk nonsense 16.178G *(M version* **roye;** *cp.* **royis)**

rought *v. pa.t.* cared (about) 30.125, 47.149; **roght** *subj.* should fear 5.137

rouk *v.* talk privately 7.48

roune *see* rowne

rowe, rawe *n.* row, orderly sequence; **on (a) rowe, on rowes** in due order, accordingly, duly 1.124, 20.141, 25.149; all together 16.3; **rede by rawe** rightly understand 23.122; rightly understood 37.317; **reherse by rawe** recite in order 24.23

rowe *n.* peace *see* roo *n.*'

rowne, roune *v.* mutter, whisper 7.48, 31.310; **rownand** *pres.p.* speaking 16.35, 45.289

rowses *v.* *3sg.pr.*, *refl.* **rowses hym** boasts, vaunts 29.269

rowte *n.*' crowd, assembly 19.149, 32.5

rowtes *n.*² *pl.* blows 33.355, 363

rowted *v. p.p.* severely thrashed 33.154

ruddy *adj.* red 17.370, 25.504

rude *(for* **royde)** *adj.* great 30.174

rudely *adv.* discourteously 23.164; suddenly 33.277

ruffe *n.* roof 14.18

ruffully *see* rewfully

rug(ge) *v.* pull violently 30.214, 391, 34.53; **rugged** *pa.t.* 45.60

rule, rewl(l)e *n.* conduct, behaviour 19.46, 26.33, 246

run, renne *v.* run, go 33.223, 45.215; pierce 34.148; **ranne** *pa.t.* 40.52; **ronne** *p.p.* 29.28, 195; **furthe are . . . run** have prospered 11.43

russhed *v. p.p.* dragged violently 33.154

ruth(e), reuthe, rewth, rewþe *n.* pity 25.324, 30.306; shame, remorse 13.24, 153; grief, affliction 24.159, 33.162, 45.228

saande *see* **sand(e)**

sab(b)ott *adj.* sabbath 26.99, 29.45

sad(de) *adj.* grave, sober 8.33; serious 33.44; grievous 39.53; **sette hym sadde** give him grief 37.204

sadly, saddely *adv.* firmly 8.102; earnestly, diligently 9.242, 16.195, 30.98; seriously,

soberly 28.165, 31.172, 32.63; perceptibly 33.247

sadnesse *n.* solemn manner 31.26

safe *v. see* **saue** *v.*; **saff(e), saffyd** *see* **saue** *v.*

saffe, saue *adj.* sound, whole 26.99; **saue thy grace** may it not displease you 21.109

saffyng *vbl.n.* salvation 14.102

sagates *adv.* in this way 10.30

saggard *n. term of abuse*; ? one who sags 36.82

saie, say(e), sege *v.*' say, tell, talk 23.140, 25.296, 31.102, 33.18; **segges** *3sg.pr.* 33.97; **seggid** *p.p.* 32.17; **say þe** say of you 24.39; **at saye** to say 18.89

saie *v.*² taste 30.98

sayff *v. see* **saue** *v.*

sayne *v.* bless, make sign of cross 28.127, 287

sak *n.* charge 12.195

sakles *adj.* innocent, in a state of innocence 13.180, 26.288, 32.141

sal(l), sill *v.* shall 28.92; **sulde, sculde** *pa.t.* 1.116

sale, sall *n.* place, room 26.294, 33.86

salue *n.* remedy 18.114, 42.192, 44.4

salue *v.* heal, remedy 20.136, 21.170, 47.28; **salued** *pa.t.* 29.261; *p.p.* 20.266

saluer *n.* healer 25.328, 45.278

saluyng *vbl.n.* healing 10.334

salus *v.* *3sg.pr.* assails 22.194

sam(e), samme *adv.* together 3.73, 8.126, 26.126

samen, -yn *adv.* together, mutually 10.235, 34.128, 46.135

samme *adv. see* **sam(e)**

samme *v.* assemble 43.87; **sammed** *p.p.* 34.43

sample *n.* example 17.221

sand(e), saande, seand, sonde *n.* message, command 10.244, 12.220, 13.234, 23.165; (act of) sending 30.294; messenger 18.64, 43.30

sand *v.* send 10.108 (*? error; see textual note*)

sange *n.* song, theme 11.128, 408

sare *n. see* **sore** *n.*; **sare, sararre** *adv. see* **so(o)re** *adv.*

sarye *adj.* sorry 13.189

sarteyne *see* **certayne**

sattles *v.* *3sg.pr.* sinks 33.247; **sattillis** *3pl.pr.* (of emotions) sink deeply into the mind 28.69

saue *adj. see* **saffe**

saue, saff(e), safe, sayff, sauffe *v.* save, preserve, bring to salvation 8.36, 13.273, 31.54, 37.108; look after, protect 4.24, 35.294; keep, hold 37.109; observe (a holy day) 29.45; store, lay up 4.12; **saffyd** *p.p.* 9.142

sauely *adv.* safely 28.127; certainly 38.307

sauerly *adv.* with relish 29.80

sauffe *see* **saue**; **saugh(e)** *see* **se(e)** *v.*

saule *n.* soul 10.178, 37.376

saunteryng, -ing *vbl.n.* ? trifling, idle behaviour; ? babbling 35.70, 150

sauterell, sawntrelle, sawterell *n. term of contempt*; ? saintling, pretender to holiness 28.191, 31.323, 32.92, 276

sawe *n.* saying, word(s), speech 11.79, 17.199, 37.397; **sawes** *pl.* proverbs 37.281; talking 11.17

sawen *v. p.p.* sown, cast abroad 26.189

sawntrelle, sawterell *see* **sauterell**

sawter *n.* psalter 37.187

scape *see* **skape**; **scathe** *see* **skath(e)**; **scatheles** *see* **skatheles**; **sch-** *see* **sh-**; **schath** *see* **skath(e)**; **sclake** *see* **slake**

sclaunderes *v. 3sg.pr.* slanders 29.302

sclyk *see* **swilke**

score, skore *n.* score, group of twenty 19.278; **oute of score** outrageously 26.81

scored *v. p.p.* drilled 35.111

scourges *n.pl.* whips 33.337, 40.32

sculd *see* **sal(l)**

se(e) *n.* sea 2.63, 127; *in phatic phr.* **by se and sande**

se(e) *v.* see; *with* **(vn)to** *or* **(vn)till**, look after 15.26, 16.332, 18.202; **se(e), sees, ses(s)e** *ipv.* take heed, pay attention, listen 11.18, 15.109, 27.117, 29.2, 36.1; make sure 29.235; **saugh(e)** *pa.t.*; **sene, seyn** *p.p.* attended to 8.77; visited (upon) 38.17

seall *see* **sele**; **seand** *see* **sand(e)** *n.*

secomoure *n.* sycamore tree 25.426

secrete *adv.* secretly, in mysterious ways 25.228

se(e)de, seyd *n.* seed, offspring 7.74, 9.312, 10.361; matters, business 16.189

seece *see* **ses(s)e** *v.²*; **seen** *n. and v. see* **se(e)** *n. and v.*

seede ? *v. pa.t.* ? was born 37.58

seeg(e) *n.* man *see* **sege** *n.²*; **seeges** *n.* seats *see* **sege** *n.¹*; **seele, seell** *n. see* **sele**

seele *v.* certify 26.109

seer(e) *adj., adv. see* **sere** *adj., adv.*; **sees** *v. ind. see* **ses(s)e** *v.²*; *ipv. see* **se(e)** *v.*; **seete** *n.* seat *see* **sete**

seett *n.* sect, party 33.193

sege *n.¹* seat, throne 12.67, 40.154, 45.137; **seeges** *pl.* 27.159

sege, seeg(e), segge *n.²* man 14.59, 26.190, 29.33, 30.280

sege, segges, seggid *v. see* **saie** *v.¹*

segger *n.* braggart 28.202

seggyng *vbl.n.* speaking, talk 30.361, 486, 33.433; **sigging** 43.133 (? *error for* **singing**); **seggynges** *pl.* 33.91

seyd *n. see* **se(e)de** *n.*; **seill, -yll** *see* **sele**; **seyn** *v. p.p. see* **se(e)** *v.*; **seyniour** *see* **seniour**;

seys *n.* ending 8.19

seys *v. see* **ses(s)e** *v.²*

seke *n.* sick (people) 25.130, 26.99

seke *adj.* sick 24.104, 29.35, 44.167

sekeness *n.* sickness 24.107

sekirly(e), -ie *adv.* surely, for certain 13.63, 38.303, 47.47

selcouth *n.* remarkable thing 31.140

selcouth(e), selcowthe *adj.* amazing, wondrous 9.159, 15.53, 16.74; various 3.57; *as n.* various people 16.106

sele, cele, seall, seele, seell, seill, -yll *n.* prosperity, well-being 2.25, 7.137, 9.129, 17.334, 391, 19.37; *in phatic phr.* **with seele** 30.338

selffe, selue *adj.* same, selfsame, the very 30.292, 31.115, 47.364

sely *adj.* poor, helpless 44.171

selle *n.* prison-cell 37.342

selue *see* **selffe**

semand *v. pres.p.* psalming, singing praises to 30.342

semand(e) *ppl.adj.* seemly, fitting 16.331, 42.205, 45.111

semand(e) *v. pres.p. see* **seme**

sembland *n.* outward aspect 16.149, 29.93

sembled *see* **semlys**

seme *v.* befit, appear seemly 25.540, 31.266, 42.122; appear, be seen 3.20; think fit 30.450; **semes** *3sg.pr.* 27.6; **semande** *pres.p.* 2.82; *impers.* **me semys** it is seemly for me 29.7; it appears to me 30.65, 482; **how semes you?** what do you think? 30.352

semely *adj.* beautiful, handsome 1.51, 19.195, 20.15; **semelieste** *spv.* 30.280; *as n.* lovely creature 30.96, 121; worthy person 30.339, 33.397

semelid *see* **semlys**

semelyté *n.* seemliness 25.116

semes *n.pl.* seams, spaces between planks in a ship's hull 8.77

semlys *v. 1pl.pr.* assemble 31.25; **sembled, semelid** *p.p.* 13.27, 44.74

sen(e) *adv.* then, next, afterwards; *conj.* since, seeing that

sende *v. p.p.* sent 6.166, 10.118, 37.398

sene *v. p.p.* see **se(e)** *v.*; **senge** *n. see* **syne** *n.¹*

seniour, -your, seyniour *n.* elder, lord 17.78, 30.400; *as epithet* 30.73

senous *see* **synnous**

sente *v.* assent 9.124, 32.146; **sente** *p.p.* 32.168, 197

septoure, -ture *n.* sceptre 31.258, 33.405

ser *see* **sire**

serche, sers *v.* question 29.273, 32.121, 277; **serchid** *p.p.* examined closely 30.354

sere, seer(e) *adj.* special, particular 9.248, 17.33, 37.41; various, diverse 2.80, 3.59, 37.122

sere, seere *adv.* separately, apart 2.40, 117; variously, diversely 2.54, 16.106

serely, serly *adv.* separately 2.46; variously 43.24

sermones *v. ipv.pl.* speak 30.303

sers *v. see* **serche; sertayne** *see* **certayne; sertis** *see* **certes**

seruand *n.* servant 14.3

serue *v.*[1] deal with, treat 37.206; **serues** *3sg.pr.* signifies, is of use 32.272; **serued** *p.p.* complied with 30.215; supplied 32.368

serued, -id *v.*[2] *p.p.* deserved 2.16, 47.323

seruise *n.* food 27.6

sese *v.*[1] seize, hold in custody 38.35; **sesid** *p.p.* 33.193

ses(s)e, seece, sees, seys *v.*[2] *intr.* cease, come to an end, stop 9.234, 11.17, 16.73; *tr.* stop, put an end to 9.248, 14.59, 18.38; kill 16.41; **sessid** *pa.t.* 47.377; *p.p.* 38.374

ses(s)e (to) *v. see see* **se(e)** *v.*; **sesid** *see* **sese** *v.*[1]

ses(s)oune *n.* time 38.101; **(in) þis ses(s)oune** at this time 10.117, 26.42

sethen, -yn *see* **sithen**

set(t)(e), sitte *v. (many transf. and fig. senses)* sit, remain, be 25.332, 30.363; make, cause to be 16.28, 30.204, 37.204; express (sentiments) 31.26, 173; secure, make fast 8.102; found, establish 43.28; plant 4.24; set down, write 36.110; accompany 29.112; **sette** *pa.t.* directed 23.14; *p.p.* put, placed 37.387, 47.141; spent 5.19; **sette noght, sette nothyng** set no store 38.105, 117

sete, seete *n.* seat, resting place 29.7, 45.137; **seetis** *pl.* thrones 47.189

seueynt *adj.* seventh 3.90

sewe *v.*[1] sew, join the seams between the planks of a vessel *(see* **semes** *n.pl.)* 8.105

sew(e), suye *v.*[2] follow as an example 7.33; take as leader 29.112; proceed, advance 29.210, 36.281, 342; harass, afflict 11.160; pursue 11.392; **sewes** *3sg.pr.* 11.270, 33.436; bids, asks for (admittance) 26.190; **sewe for** bring a legal action against 30.400

sexte *adj.* sixth 12.183

schaftes *n.pl.* spears 33.168

schake *v.* flee 28.141; **schakis** *3sg.pr.* quavers 33.245; **schuke** *pa.t.* trembled, became agitated 33.168

schalke *n.* man 30.296; *pl.* 33.2

shame *v. intr.* feel shame 6.63; **schamed** *p.p. tr.* disgraced, condemned 29.299, 32.209; *impers.* **shames me, þam schamys** I am ashamed, they are ashamed 6.62, 19.57; **me shames with** I am ashamed of 5.110

shamely *adv.* shamefully, unjustly 30.296

schames *n.pl.* great dishonour 33.245

shamously *adv.* shamefully 32.145

s(c)happe *n.* appearance, likeness 3.23, 36; body, physical aspect 5.129, 26.287, 45.59

s(c)hap(p)e *v.* create, fashion, make; make provision 36.28; **schappe** *3sg.pr.* is likely to 26.50; *refl.* **schappe hym, shappis hym, schapes þem** he intend(s), they design 11.365, 37.155, 43.172; **schapist þiselffe** store up for yourself 32.179; **schappe 3ou** address yourselves (to), take hold (of) 33.241; **s(c)hop(p)e** *pa.t.* 7.3, 25.114, 39.18

schappely *adj.* fine, handsome 33.2

scharid *see* **schere**

scharpely *adv.* maliciously 43.172

schath *see* **skath(e)**

shaves *n.pl.* sheaves 7.73

schawe *n.* appearance, spectacle 30.56

schawe *v.* be seen, appear 33.2; **schewys** *3sg.pr.* 30.27

schemerande *ppl.adj.* shimmering 1.69

s(c)hende *v.* destroy, kill, injure 11.365, 18.72, 26.287; **shendes** *3sg.pr.* is guilty of 33.245; **schente** *pa.t.* 32.145; **s(c)hent(e)** *p.p.* 6.79, 8.21, 17.23; condemned 24.67; exhausted 35.191

s(c)hene *adj.* radiant 46.1; fair 33.2, 46.154; good, suitable 29.361; *as adv.* brightly 16.78

schenely *adv.* brightly 33.241

s(c)hepe *n.* sheep 10.304, 312

schere *v.* cut 41.161; **sheris** *3sg.pr.* 29.169; **scharid, schorne** *p.p.* sheared 28.141; cut off 29.282

schewys *see* **schawe** *v.*

schewyng *vbl.n.* outward appearance 1.69

shylle *adj.* resonant, well-sounding 18.43

s(c)hynand(e) *v. pres.p., ppl.adj.* shining 1.69, 23.202, 25.531, 39.19, 41.22

shippe-craft *n.* the trade of shipbuilding 8.67

schire *adv.* brightly 45.202

s(c)ho(o) *pron.* she

schoffe *v.* thrust 36.297

schogged *v. pa.t.* shook 40.100

s(c)hon(e) *v.* shrink back in fear 10.244; hesitate, hold back 33.105; **schonnys** *2sg.pr.* refrain, avoid 32.246; **schonte** *pa.t.* 45.59

s(c)hop(p)e *see* **s(c)hap(p)e** *v.*; **schorne** *see* **schere**

schortely *adv.* quickly, briefly 26.50, 30.17
schorwe *see* **shrewe** *n.*
schotte *v. pa.t.* jerked violently 40.100
schoures *n.pl.* afflictions 44.146
schoutis *n.pl.* cries of pain 45.59
shrewe, schorwe *n.* shrew, evil person 19.169, 29.361
schrew(e) *v.* curse 28.180, 188
shrewdnesse *n.* wicked behaviour 33.158
shrowde *n.* garment 29.361
schuke *see* **schake**
sybe *n.* kinsperson 3.40
side, syde *n.* side; **sidis** *pl.* sides (of the body) 13.102; **ilke a syde, sides seere** everywhere 3.46, 35.224; **on side** aside 17.122, 24.173; **alle sidis** everybody's interests 35.294
sier *see* **sir(e)**; **sigging** *see* **seggying**
sight(e), syght(e), seyghte, si3tte *n.* sight 1.89, 45.185; **sitis** *pl.* 45.122; **to sight** to behold 37.90; **in syghte** very clearly 1.127
sight(e), si3te *n.* sorrow *see* **syte**
signifie, syngnyfie *v.* presage, betoken 15.15, 16.74; **signified** *p.p.* made in reference to 12.119
siker, -ir *adj.* certain, effective, true 29.35, 30.297, 40.178
syle *v.* slip down 18.196
sylypp *n.* syllable 10.26
sill *v. see* **sal(l)**
symonde *n.* cement 8.102
symple, sympill, simpyll *adj.* lowly, humble 3.30, 14.64, 15.100; *as n.* innocent man 30.289; **symplest** *spv.* 3.25
symmplenes *n.* lowly condition 18.16
syne, senge, syngne *n.*[1] sign 3.81, 9.290, 296, 11.100, 12.58
syne *n.*[2] sin; **thynke no syne** consider it a trifle 41.167 *(Sy reading)*; **synes** *pl.* 17.34
syn(e), synne *adv.* then, next, afterwards; later 30.137, 32.125; *conj.* since, seeing that
synfull *adj. as n.* sinful person 47.236; **synnefull** *pl.* 44.4
syng(e), syngne *n. see* **syne** *n.*[1]; **syngnyfie** *see* **signifie**
synke *v.* sink, vanish into the ground or water (under the weight of sorrow or sin) 5.113, 6.61, 9.36; **sownkyn** *p.p.* sunk (to hell) 47.36; drowned 8.30, 59
synne *adv. see* **syn(e)** *adv.*; **synnefull** *see* **synfull**
synnous, senous *n.pl.* sinews 35.103, 132
sir(e), ser, sier, syre *n.* lord, master; father 15.21, 30.10
syte, cytte, sight(e), si3te *n.* sorrow 6.16, 16.273, 19.136, 22.67, 36.157
sytfull, sithfull *adj.* grievous, sorrowful 6.129, 34.150

sithen, sethen, -yn, sythen, syþn *adv.* then, next, afterwards; *conj.* since, seeing that
sithis *n.pl. (with number)* times 7.131, 16.18
sitis *see* **sight(e)** *n.*
sittand *ppl.adj.* becoming, proper 30.65; 544; **wele sittande** (of a garment) neat, tidy 31.74
sittand(e) *pres.p. see next*
sitte *v.* sit in judgement 30.83; stay, remain, live 24.148, 37.272, 342; **sittand(e)** *pres.p.* sitting 26.53, 45.185; *impers.* **vs sittis, it sittis vs, itt sittis you** it behoves us, you 26.288, 30.422, 31.26; **3ou satt** you allowed yourselves 33.202; **sitte you, vs full sore** be the worse for you, us 26.168, 30.525; **sytt hym full sore** will make it the worse for him 33.25; **sittis me full sare** afflicts me grievously 44.92; **satte me** afflicted me 35.207
sitte *v.* set *see* **set(t)(e)** *v.*
skale *n. coll.sg.* (fish) scales 2.130
skape, scape *v.* escape 9.141, 19.224, 30.143; avoid 36.47
skath(e), scathe, schath *n.* injury, harm, malefaction 9.141, 26.41, 130, 33.34
skatheles, scatheles *adv.* without harm or injury 29.280, 30.143, 33.369
skaunce *n.* joke 30.292
skell *n. coll.sg.* shells 2.130
skelpe *v.* beat 33.337; **skelpte** *pa.t.* 26.81
skelpys, -is *n.pl.* blows 33.34, 41.110
skemeryng *see* **skymeryng**
skiffte *n.* plot, stratagem 26.130
skyfte *v.* escape 26.41
skylfull *adj.* rational 3.22
skyll(e), skill(e) *n.* reason (faculty of) 3.15; cause, reason (for doing something) 3.26, 5.46, 9.46; what is reasonable, rightness 10.323, 16.126; **by skyll** for this reason, accordingly 25.48; **oute of skill** unreasonably 22.72
skymeryng *vbl.n.* glittering 16.179G, M **skemeryng;** agitation, commotion 34.191
skippes *v. 3sg.pr.* escapes 33.369; **skippid** *pa.t.* ? caused to skip or leap (by whipping) 45.41
skore *see* **score**
skorne *n.* harm, injury, affront 29.103, 280, 30.143
skorne *v.* behave negligently 34.29
skwyn *in adv. phr.* **of skwyn** obliquely, on a slant 8.74
sla, slee, slo(o) *v.* slay, put to death 6.164, 7.127, 10.92, 33.325; **slees** *3sg.pr.* 7.130; **slone** *p.p.* 11.391, 24.153, 30.162
slake, sclake *v. intr.* diminish, end 2.26, 18.174, 39.45; subside 9.41; *tr.* put an end to, mitigate 22.67; assuage 47.286; **slakis** *3pl.pr.* extricate 30.8

slang *v. pa.t.* threw away 32.323
slee *see* **sla**
sleghte *n.* trick, contrivance 22.88; **sle(y)ghtis** *pl.* 30.8, 31.161
slely(e) *adv.* cunningly, surreptitiously 30.8, 137
slepe *v. pa.t.* slept 47.152
slyk(e), slike *see* **swilke**
slippe *v.* sink gradually into; **slippe on slepe** faint 44.105
slo(o), slone *see* **sla**
sloppe *n.* gown 31.74
small *adj. (absol.)* little 38.367
smerte *adj.* sharp, acute 8.54
smerte *adv.* severely 47.134
smert(e)ly *adv.* quickly, sharply 24.2, 34.5, 40.32; keenly, painfully 25.467
smyte *v.* smite, beat; **smote** *pa.t.* 40.32; **smetyn, smytte** *p.p.* 37.338; burnt 47.134
smore *v.* suffocate 1.117
smote *see* **smyte**
snell *adj.* wise 17.111
snelly *adv.* swiftly 35.118
so *adv.* as 2.33
sobir *v.* allay, moderate 28.116
socery *see* **sorssery**
soc(c)our(e) *n.* help 16.230, 17.125, 20.216
socoure *v.* help 44.145
sodayne *adj.* mysterious, unexpected 16.98, 38.100
soferans *n.pl.* rulers, men of importance 32.341
sofferayne *adj. see* **souereyne**
softe *adv.* comfortably 25.195; **softe sir** take care, do not be hasty 26.58
soght(e) *see* **sought**
soile *v.* release 32.361
soiourne *v.* dwell, stay, remain 24.115; **soiorned, soionerd** *p.p.* 11.53, 37.221
solace, solayce, solas, solys *n.* bliss, joy 4.34, 25.508; good news 10.118
solace *v.* comfort 30.335
solde *v. p.p.* paid for; **sore solde** dearly paid for 29.330
solempne *adj.* awesome 23.78, 37.355; impressive 20.3
solempnité, -yté *n.* ceremony 30.315; feast 36.281; majesty 46A.13
solys *see* **solace** *n.*
som, someuere *adv. (with* **what***)* soever 20.46, 28.179
somkyn *adj.* some kind of 13.137
somwhat, sumwhat *n.* a certain amount 7.26; something 9.84
son(e), sonne *n.*[1] son 7.111, 37.81, 237; **sone** *gen.sg.* son's 42.204
son, sonne *n.*[2] sun 2.103, 37.90
sonde *n.* safe-keeping 30.163

sonde *n.* message *see* **sand(e)** *n.*; **sondered** *see* **sundir**
sondre, soundre *adj.* sunder; **in so(u)ndre** asunder, in discord 33.91; apart 35.194; out of joint 35.190
sone *n. see* **son(e)** *n.*[1]
sone, sonne *adv.* soon 2.92, 5.22, 45.160; immediately, at once 23.159, 37.22; easily 37.205; **so sone** as soon as 45.87
soone *n. see* **son(e)** *n.*[1] *or* **son** *n.*[2]
sonner *adv.* within a short time 11.46
sore, sare *n.* suffering, affliction, injury 10.334, 21.170, 39.52
so(o)r(e) *adj.* in pain, afflicted 9.303, 37.204; dire 12.7
so(o)re, sare *adv.* deeply, intensely 6.62, 151; bitterly 9.279; urgently 30.305; **sar-rare** *cpv.* 11.160
sori(e) *adj.* distressed 29.35; **sorie of** upset by 29.41; **soriest** *spv.* 47.333
sorowe *n.* humble circumstances 37.244; a curse 32.362; ? *as adj.* full of grief, sorry 39.61
sorssery, socery *n.* witchcraft 29.97, 38.104
sotell *see* **subtill**; **sotelly** *see* **suttilly**; **sotelté** *see* **suttelté**
soth(e) *n., adj.* true, the truth
sothely, sothly, sothtly, suth(e)ly *adv.* truly 2.98, 120, 3.91, 27.17
sothfastnesse, suthfastnes *n.* truth, faith 14.70, 17.456, 42.72
sotill(e) *see* **subtill**; **sotilly** *see* **suttilly**
sott(e) *n.* blockhead, fool 16.28, 26.288, 29.260
souerand *see* **souereyne**
soueranly, soueraynely, souerandly *adv.* above all, surpassingly 12.155, 20.136, 35.55
souereyne, sofferayne, souerand, sufferayne, suffraynd *adj.* sovereign, principal 9.295, 10.163, 11.18, 14.59, 40.194
sought, soght(e) *v. pa.t.* persecuted 47.112; *p.p.* gone, resorted 9.128, 41.25; visited (upon) 6.16; pursued (to death) 19.272; applied to, asked 23.139
sounde, sownde *adj.* safe, unharmed 26.292, 45.96
soundely *adv.* safely 32.358
sounderes *see* **sundir**; **soundre** *see* **sondre**; **sounkyn** *see* **synke**
sowme *n.* total 26.142
sownde *see* **sounde**; **sownkyn** *see* **synke**
space *n.* place, area 37.110; (of time) period 3.4, 12.9, 14.97; **gode space** a long way, far 25.376; **þe space** for a while 9.199; **in space** shortly 36.66
spare *v.* forbear, refrain from 6.139, 10.180, 20.202; be sparing 36.241
specifie *v.* speak fully of 15.2

speche *n.* special pleading 19.188
speciall *adv.* in particular 44.148
spedar *n.* one who aids 1.110
spede *n.* good fortune, success, benefit 10.330, 27.97
spe(e)de, speyd *v. intr.* fare, prosper, progress 37.139, 39.15; *tr.* help, assist 7.77, 8.55, 10.130; hasten the time 36.39; expedite matters 36.241; **speydes** *2sg.pr.* 4.58; **spedis** *3sg.pr.* hastens 36.66; **speyd** *2pl.pr.* 4.89; **sped(d)e** *p.p.* 10.357, 29.185; gone on your way 34.240
spell *n.* speech 26.193; discourse 43.187; **spellis** *pl.* idle talk 29.238, 275
spell *v.* speak of, relate, say 30.246, 33.63
spence, spens *n.* expense 36.241; money 32.136
spende *v.* dispense, disburse 37.28; use 10.369; pass (time) 30.470; discharge 25.466; **spende** *p.p.* 3.4, 9.18, 34.78; dispensed with 27.29
spens *see* **spence**
spere *n.* spear 36.292, 40.52
spere *v.¹ ipv.sg.* close, fasten 37.139; **spers** *ipv. pl.* 9.161; **sperde** *p.p.* imprisoned 37.110
spere, spir(r)(e) *v.²* ask, enquire 14.82, 16.163, 19.172, 20.41; **speres, -is** *ipv. pl.* 16.195, 251
sperit(e), sprete *n.* spirit 1.18; ghost, evil spirit 41.35, 149; **the sperite** the Holy Ghost 46A.6
spetyffull *adj.* cruel 40.52
spie, spye *v.* search 20.41; see 25.327; discover 26.222; **spied** *pa.t.* sought to discover 21.23
spill(e), spyll *v. tr.* bring to ruin, destroy, put an end to 1.110, 4.58, 11.24; *intr.* come to grief, die 9.50, 10.180, 19.230; **spilte** *p.p.* 6.140, 38.273
spir(r)(e) *see* **spere** *v.²*
spirringes *vbl.n. pl.* questionings 33.63
spites *n.pl.* insults 30.327
spitous *adj.* cruel 42.48
spitously *adv.* maliciously 36.39, 306, 47.261
spitte *v. pa.t.* spat 40.29, 47.261
spoile *v.* strip 40.30
sporne *v.* stumble 39.15
sporte *n.* pleasurable activities 29.275; good idea, promising course of action 26.222
sprede *v.* increase, multiply 12.44; **spredde** *p.p.* 10.361
sprete *see* **sperit(e)**
springe *v. intr.* multiply 10.47, 361; rise up 16.215; *tr.* bring forth 12.44; **springe on** hasten 30.538

stabely, -ily *adv.* firmly, fixedly 16.62, 196, 35.247, 43.2
stabill *adj.* fixed, steady 8.34, 9.19, 29.108; **stabill in thoght** obedient, loyal 1.30, 62
stabill *v.* hold 33.186, 194
stadde *see* **sted(d)(e)** *v.*
stages, -is *n.pl.* compartments 8.127, 130
stakir *v.* stagger, trip 30.85
stale *v. pa.t.* stole 26.138
stales *see* **stalle**
stalke *v.* walk stealthily 29.176; **stalkis** *ipv. pl.* 31.62
stalkyng *vbl. n.* stealthy movement 30.156; walking about 33.14
stalland *v. pres.p.* coming to a standstill 33.14
stalle *n.* place, position; place of standing, rostrum 33.261; **stawllys** *pl.* compartments 8.129; **stales of astate** court 31.72; *in phatic phr.* **in stede and stalle, in stall and strete** 8.34, 45.94
stalworthe *adj.* strong 34.90
stalworthely *adv.* firmly 30.85
stande, stonde *v.* stay, remain, be still 11.8, 37.193; **stande, standith** *3sg.pr.* (of a place) is 18.177, 180; **stande styll** remain obedient 1.75; **stande . . . in stede** provide for 22.59
standerdes *n.pl.* banners 33.194
standyng *vbl. n.* place of standing (in court) 30.383
stark(e) *adj.* prostrated, rigid 38.395; thoroughgoing, absolute 26.166
starne *see* **sterne**
state *n.* estate, place in the order of things 5.61; fortune, livelihood, condition 34.255, 38.431; exalted position, splendour 26.33, 33.330; **states** *pl.* magnates 30.262; **in ilke a state** of every degree 25.107
stately *adj.* bold, fierce 33.229
stately *adv.* in a proper manner, legitimately 26.82
stature *n.* size 4.28
stawllys *see* **stalle**
sted(d)(e) *v. intr.* tarry, stop 36.294, 45.94; *tr.* settle, steady 36.170; **stedde** *pa.t.* placed, set 16.84; **sted(d)(e), stadde** *p.p.* placed, set, fixed 14.22, 15.88, 28.73, 33.50, 148; situated, dwelling 10.363; settled, brought to an end 30.516; beset, afflicted 44.137, 47.289; **harde stedde, straytely sted(de)** hard pressed 13.37, 22.187, 31.277
stede *n.¹* horse 33.50
sted(d)e, steede *n.²* place 10.74, 15.88; **steedis** *pl.* 30.439; **stande . . . in stede** provide for 22.59; *in phatic phr.* **in stede and stalle** 8.34

steeles *n.pl.* rungs 34.90
steere, stere *v.* control 33.214, 34.192, 36.170
stele *v.* steal, move stealthily 24.14
steme *v.* cease 45.98; **stemmys** *3sg.pr.* checks, diminishes 30.74
stente *see* **stynte**
steppe *v.* advance (himself) 33.330
sterand *ppl. adj.* active, keen 28.175
stere *v.* control *see* **steere; stere** *v.* stir *see* **stirre**
sterne, starne *n.* star 14.97, 16.84, 30.230
stertis *v. 3sg.pr.* moves quickly 29.356
steuen(e), -yn, stevyn *n.¹* voice 1.75, 9.19, 31.251; speech, speaking 12.15, 29.49; word 2.31 *(but cf. next)*
steuen, -ven *n.²* bidding, command 9.6, 12.118
steuen *v.* command 31.28; **steuened** *p.p.* appointed 23.64
steuenyng *vbl. n.* clamour 32.6
stye *n.*⁽¹⁾ path 28.233
stied *see* **stigh**
sties *n.*⁽²⁾ *pl.* ladders 34.52
stiffe *adj.* strong, solid 29.266
stiffely *adv.* stoutly, resolutely 22.207, 30.165, 33.261; dangerously, in jeopardy 44.137
stigh *v.* ascend 39.85; **stied** *pa.t.* 46.121
stighill *v.* intervene, become involved 31.72
still(e) *adv.* always, all the time 5.145, 26.138; secretly 24.14
stille *adj.* (of a voice) quiet 28.45
stilly *adv.* quietly 47.263
stynkand *ppl. adj.* stinking, polluted 24.13
stynte *v. tr.* put an end to, cut short 9.222, 10.61; *intr.* come to an end 44.52; desist, forbear 30.374; **stente** *ipv. pl.* 19.3
stynter *n.* one who puts an end to things *(see prec.)* 10.24, 17.413
stirre, -yrre, stere *v. intr.* move, go 11.8, 33.335, 34.2; *tr.* appeal to, entreat 31.278; rouse, agitate 33.376; **stered** *p.p.* moved 38.95
stodmere *n.* mare kept for breeding 24.13
stok(ke) *n.* tree-stump 29.117, 31.278, 45.171
stoken, -yn *v. p.p.* closed, shut in 37.193, 43.60
stole *n.* stool 29.356
stond *ppl. adj.* stunned, in confusion 30.262
stonde *v. see* **stande**
stonyed *ppl. adj.* stunned 38.379
stonyes *v. 3sg.pr.* is stupified; **he stonyes for vs** he is stupified (by fright) because of us 30.223
store *n.* goods, merchandise 26.82
store *adj.* loud 31.251

stormed *v. p.p.* exposed to the elements 14.16
stounde *n.* while, short time 28.8, 36.295, 45.113
stoure *n.* battle 37.130; struggle 28.73
stoute, -wte *adj.* (of voices, noise) loud 19.3, 32.6
stoutely *adv.* peremptorily 33.330
stoutnes *n.* persistent movement 33.14
straytely *adv.* oppressively; **straytely sted(de)** hard pressed, sorely tried 13.37, 22.187
strake *v. pa.t.* struck 47.263
strakis *n.pl.* blows 30.2
strandes *n.pl.* shores 17.380
strang(e) *adj.* strong, extreme 6.100, 22.180, 41.7; flagrant, bold 19.125, 26.49, 166; **strangest** *spv.* 33.214; *as n.* strong man 33.415
strase *n.pl.* straws 13.13
straue *v. pa.t.* argued amongst (themselves etc.) 42.91, 205
streyned *v. p.p.* assailed 33.229
stremys *n.pl.* beams of light 30.74
strengh, strenkyth *n.* strength 2.31, 30.2
strenghe *v.* fortify, strengthen 28.45, 30.422
strenkyth *see* **strengh** *n.*
stresse *n.* force 20.188
stressed *v. p.p.* disturbed 30.156
stretis *n.pl.* streets 31.62
strewed *v. p.p.* scattered 10.17
striff, -yffe, stryve *n.* tribulation, difficulty, doubt 9.222, 10.24, 25.360; commotion 30.156; efforts 30.173
stryve *n. see prec.*
stryuyng *vbl. n.* wrangling, causing commotion 30.2, 374
stroye *n.*, *prob. error for* **strye** hag 24.3
stroye *v.* destroy 8.28; **stroyed** *p.p.* 30.173
stubbe *n.* short thick nail 35.102
stuffe *n.* material (for making a garment) 39.98
sturdely *adv.* fixedly 15.50
suapped *see* **swapped**
subgett, sugett *n.* subject, subordinate 14.64, 16.5, 21.139; **suggettes** *pl.* 4.16
subgett(e) *adj.* obedient 21.73, 22.123
subtill, sotell, -ill(e), sutyll *adj.* clever, ingenious, cunning 2.53, 11.79, 246, 16.261, 20.195
sudary(e) *n.* shroud 36.387, 38.243
sufferayne *n.* sovereign, ruler 14.46
sufferayne, suffraynd *adj. see* **souereyne**
sufferand *ppl. adj.* patient 30.238
suffir, suffre *v.* permit, allow 11.119, 157, 21.128; be allowed 23.228
suffirrantly *adv.* patiently 22.204

suffre *see* **suffir**
sug(g)ett- *see* **subgett; suye** *see* **sew(e)** *v.*²;
suld(e) *see* **sal(l)**
sumdele *adv.* somwhat 10.82
summe *pron. (indef.)* some; **all and summe**
everything 43.151
sumwhat *see* **somwhat**
sundir *v.* part, separate 37.240; **sondered**
p.p. 45.89; **sounderes** *ipv. pl.* 47.73
suppowle *v.* aid 34.11
sure *v.* assure; **me sure** assure myself (of
the truth) 5.101
sureté *n.* bond, legal engagement 34.253
surffette *n.* transgression 28.93
suth(e)ly *see* **soth(e)ly**
suthfast *adj.* true 20.126
suthfastnes *see* **sothfastnesse**
sutyll *see* **subtill**
suttelté, sotelté *n.* cunning, ingenuity
30.505, 33.193; **soteltes** *pl.* cunning
schemes 34.113
suttilly, -elly, sotilly, -elly *adv.* skilfully,
cleverly 8.77, 105, 16.5, 34.149
swa(a) *adv., conj.* so
swage *v.* make an end (of) 30.373, 33.126
swayne *n.* man, fellow 11.246, 20.276,
22.19; boy 15.128, 16.265, 18.159
swang *see* **swyng**
swappes *n.pl.* blows 33.361
swapped *v. pa.t.* smote, struck 29.142,
30.188; **suapped** *p.p.* slaughtered 31.15
swarand *see* **warrand(e)**
sware *n.* square; *in adv. phr.* **be sware**
squarely 8.74
sware *v. pa.t.* swore 38.22
sweght *n.* force 33.361
sweying *vbl. n.* noise 30.373
swelte *n.* deadly sickness 45.189
sweltes *v. 3sg.pr.* is overcome (with pain)
33.383; **sweltid** *pa.t.* died 40.56
swemyd *v. p.p.* overcome, rendered uncon-
scious 40.40
swete, swelte *adj. as n.* dear one 38.282,
40.57, 41.110
swete *v.* sweat 33.360, 45.189; **swete** *pa.t.*
40.41
swetyng *vbl. n.* toil, exertion 40.40
swetnes *n.* pleasure 31.15
swette *n.* sweat 40.41
swette *n.* sweet *see* **swete** *adj. as n.*
swettyng *n.* beloved creature 40.40
sweuene *n.* dream 30.188
swilke, -ylke, sclyk, slike, -yke *adj.* such
swyng *v.* aim blows 33.360 *(ipv.)*; **swang**
pa.t. whipped 40.41; **swongen** *p.p.* 41.110
swyngis *n.pl.* blows 40.41
swynke *n.* toil, labour 5.161, 45.189
swyre *n.* neck 33.360

swithe *adv.* quickly, immediately 11.393,
30.373, 40.57
swongen *see* **swyng**
swonyng *vbl. n.* swooning 40.57
swoune *n.* swoon, faintness 45.189
swounes, *v. 3sg.pr.* faints 33.383

ta *see* **take**
tabyls *n.pl.* (writing) tablets 17.10
taburnakill *n.* tent 23.153
tacche *v.* fasten 35.119
tadys *n.pl.* toads 11.271
tag *n.* smallest piece 45.44
taile, -yle *n.* bottom, foot 31.196; **toppe to
taile** throughout, in every detail 37.159;
toppe and taile head and feet 35.114
taynte *n.* one who is attainted, traitor
26.279
taynte *v.* attaint, convict 26.6; **teynted** *p.p.*
35.77
taynted *ppl. adj.* suspect, inclined to falsehood 33.234
take, ta *v.* take; give, do 3.24; put 8.109;
endure 22.71; **take** *3pl.pr.* accept, approve
37.331; **takys** *ipv. pl.* receive 3.41; **takande**
pres.p. 29.371; **toke, tuke** *pa.t.* gave 17.11,
32.269, 42.46; **taken, tane, tone** *p.p.*
24.162, 26.279, 27.166, 43.11; given, entrusted 6.77, 37.172; received 2.115,
6.119; **take (en)tent, take kepe, take reward** pay attention, take heed 19.244,
20.235; **tayke ... thought** worry 4.39;
tane myght might have taken 5.10; **outt ...
tane** made an exception 5.32;
tane with apprehended (in) 24.31
taken, -yn *n.* token, sign 11.143, 230,
13.277
takyng *vbl. n.* (fear of) capture 40.88
takkid *v. pa.t.* nailed 40.92
talde *see* **telle**
tale *n.* word(s), what has been spoken,
information 37.149, 273; command 6.77;
tales, -z *pl.* 10.128, 11.182, 23.24; matters,
questions 20.79; **geue ... neuer tale** do
not care 29.233; **gyvis tale** considers it
worth while 28.292
talent(e) *n.* inclination 42.215; ? power,
force 21.69; **talente will take** inclination
will lead 1.144
talking *vbl. n.* discourse 40.138
tall *adj.* seemly 45.272
tane *see* **take**
tarand *n.* abusive epithet; ? *for* **tarandre,** a
creature supposed to have chameleon-like
power of changing colour 33.380; *see*
OED, s.v.
tarie *v. intr.* wait, loiter, hesitate 10.272,
25.16, 33.96; *tr.* delay, hinder 26.159,

28.81; **taried** *pa.t.* 30.258; **terryed** *p.p.*
17.63

tarying *vbl. n.* loitering 43.207

tase *see* **tose**

taste *v.* touch 27.42, 28.203; experience,
undergo 9.317, 37.358; put to the test, try
33.96, 379; **taste** *pa.t.* 33.81

tastyng *vbl. n.* handling 30.134

taught(e) *see* **teche**

te *prep.* to 21.91, 26.194, 36.184

teche, teeche *v.* show, direct 26.255,
34.101; inform, teach 16.47, 37.364;
taught(e) *pa.t.* 6.10, 29.226; **taught,
teched** *p.p.* 30.197; delivered, entrusted
26.135; exposed 30.302

techyng *vbl. n.* instigation 5.105

teene, teyn *see* **tene** *n.*; **teynd(e)** *see* **tente** *n.²*,
adj.; **teynted** *see* **taynte** *v.*

telde *n.* cover (of earth) 24.162

telde *v. p.p.* lodged 10.14

telle *v.* count, enumerate, 26.72, 35.227,
43.65; believe 38.293; **telles** *3sg.pr.* expounds 25.150; **talde** *pa.t.* showed 11.230;
talde *p.p.* numbered at 11.51; accounted,
considered 12.184

tempre *v.* moderate 33.400

tendand *ppl. adj.* complimentary 30.66

tendande *v. pres.p.* ministering 45.148

tendyr *adj.* young; **tendyr 3ere** infancy
25.298

tene, teene, teyn, tyne *n.* trouble, affliction,
grief 8.39, 25.386, 36.30; **in a tene** in a fit
of rage 40.92; **fedd/Be tyne** deceived
12.26

tene *v.* harm 30.134; **me tened** *pa.t., impers.*
I was aggrieved 26.145; **tened, -yd** *p.p.*
16.370; enraged 29.324, 45.27

tenefull *adj.* grievous, troublesome 32.154

tenyd *ppl. adj.* inaccurate 33.234

tente *n.¹* heed, attention 2.23, 6.1, 142; **take
tent(e)** pay attention, take heed; care,
responsibility for 26.5

tente, teynd(e) *n.², adj.* tenth, a tithe 7.19,
40, 58, 26.138

tente *v.* have charge of, attend to, look after
5.86, 20.79, 37.172; **tentis** *ipv. pl.* 31.68;
tent *p.p.* protected 22.37

tentyng *vbl. n.* temptation 28.81

tere *v.* tire 29.255, 33.378

termyne *v.* declare, state 32.60

terryed *see* **tarie**

texte *n.* very word 25.534; truth 32.59

þa *pron. 2sg. see* **þou; tha, þai, þay** *pron. 3pl.*
see **þei; thaymself** *see* **þamself; þaire** *poss.*
adj. see **thar(e)** *poss. adj.*

tham(e), þaime(e), þam(e), hem *etc. pron.*
them 25.22

þamself, thaymself, þameselffe, -selue,

<hr/>

hemselue *pron.* themselves, they themselves 6.4, 24.82, 86, 27.147, 37.307,
42.237

þan(n)(e) *adv.* then

thar(r)(e) *v., impers.*; need, be under a
necessity; **thar(r) vs, ye** need we, you, **þam
thare** they need 1.64, 4.10, 23.159; **thurte**
pa.t. 47.316

þar *dem. adj. see* **þir(e)**

thar(e), þaire, þar(e), þer(e), ther(e) *etc. poss.*
adj. their

þarby, þorbe *adv.* thereby, because of (it)
9.188, 24.44

þare, þore *adv.* there

thare *v. see* **thar(r)(e)** *v.*

þareinne *adv.* in there 47.34

þareowte *see* **þeroute**

tharne *v.* lose 18.137, 42.15

tharnyng *vbl. n.* want, lack 42.12

þaron *adv.* thereon, on it 2.69

tharr *see* **thar(r)(e)** *v.*; **þas** *dem. adj. see*
þois

þat *rel. pron.* those whom 37.8

þe, the *pron.¹* thee

þe *pron.² (unstressed)* thou 9.89

the *v.* thrive 20.61, 31.361

þedir, -yre, thedir *adv.* thither, there
24.145, 25.41, 27.80

theffe *n.* scoundrel, villain 26.166, 28.298

þei, tha, þai, þay, thy *etc. pron.* they 10.117,
12.30

þens *adv.* thence, from there 30.539,
37.161; that time 25.258

þer, ther *adv.* where 1.60, 21.141, 39.15

þer(e), ther(e) *poss. adj. see* **thar(e)** *poss. adj.*;
þer(e), ther(e) *dem. pron., adj. see* **þire**

þeraftir *adv.* after that matter 34.79; in
accordance with which 47.110

þeragayne, thereagayne *adv.* against that,
it, this 10.191, 19.28, 26.11, 36.117

þeretyll, theretyll, þertille, thertill *adv.*
thereto, to it 4.15, 5.147, 6.142, 35.12

þeron *adv.* on it 34.100

þeroute, þareowte *adv.* outside, out there
9.185, 47.328

þi, þy *poss. adj.* thy

thy *pron. 3pl. see* **þei; thiding** *see* **tydingis**

þikk *adj.* bulky 33.398

thyng *n.* anything 38.231, 405

thynke *v.* wonder 6.105

þir(e), þar, ther(e), þer(e) *dem. pron., adj.*
these 2.5, 85, 8.92, 11.284, 306, 12.53,
42.137

thyrll, thirle *v.* pierce 27.441, 39.100

this *dem. pron. (sg.)* here, this place 10.253;
now, this time 29.63

this, þis *dem. pron., adj (pl.)* these 1.28,
8.118, 10.197, 33.129

þiselue, theyselfe, thyselue *pron.* you, you yourself 22.59, 64, 37.299, 44.5

thithynges *see* **tydingis**

þo, tho *dem. pron., adj.* those

þof(f), off, þow *conj.* though 18.70, 19.164, 25.12, 30.45; **þof all** even though 15.101, 121

thoght(e), þought, þouʒt *n.* intention, purpose 1.19, 25.273; mind, attention 42.63; concern, perplexity 29.72, 41.2; **haue no þought** do not worry 8.69, 29.102; **where is his þought?** what is he thinking of? 25.325

þois, þas *dem. pron., adj.* those 16.51, 42.63

thole *v.* suffer, endure 22.182, 47.48; **tholed(e)** *pa.t.* 38.283, 41.140; **tholed, -id** *p.p.* 37.3, 47.57

thondour-slayne *v.* destroyed by 'thunder' (*sc.* lightning) 11.320

thondres *n.pl.* thunderbolts 16.8

þore *see* **þare** *adv.*; **þorbe** *see* **þarby**

þorne *n.* crown of thorns 33.398

thorowe *see* **thurgh**

þou, þa, þow(e), thu *pron.* thou 31.238

þought, þouʒt *see* **thoght(e)**

þow *conj. see* **þof(f); þow(e)** *pron. see* **þou**

thraldome *n.* captivity 42.134

thraly, thrally(e) *adv.* earnestly, sincerely 10.3, 33.60; violently, fiercely 16.8, 33.398, 45.35; completely 28.150

thrall *n.* slave 21.115, 22.130

thrall *adj.* captive, in subjection 4.64, 21.173, 37.134, 47.111; recaptured 11.376

thrally(e) *see* **thraly**

þrang, thrang *n.* crowd 25.445, 26.256; crowding, commotion 22.2

thrange *v. pa.t.* pressed 45.43

thraste *see* **threste**

thrawe *n.¹* crowd of people 29.113

thrawe *n.²* while, time 16.365

thre *adj.* three, *used indef., sc.* a few 10.252

threpe *n.* dispute 26.256

threpe *v.* chide 1.114

threpyng *vbl. n.* disputation 40.105

threste *v.* thrust, push into (a crowd) 29.113; **thraste, thristed** *pa.t.* thrust 40.35, 45.43; pierced 40.104; **threst** *p.p.* crushed, beaten down 11.320

threte *v.* behave offensively 25.178; **thrette** *p.p.* threatened 47.254

thries, -yes *adv.* thrice 28.150, 29.161

thryng *v.* thrust 33.398; press (together) 35.246; **thryngand** *pres.p.* being pressed (in a crowd) 26.256

thryffe *see* **þryve**

thryst *n.* thirst 7.80

thristed *see* **threste**

thristis *v. 3sg.pr., impers.* **me thristis** I thirst 36.221

thrivandly *adv.* skilfully 8.76

þryve, thryffe, -iffe *v.* thrive, prosper 3.12, 33.419, 40.117

throsten *v. p.p.* pierced 47.257

thu *see* **þou**

thurgh, thorowe, thur *prep.* through, because of, by means of 1.84, 90, 12.194

thurghoute *prep.* through, by means of 6.49

thurte *see* **thar(r)(e)** *v.*

thus-gate(s), þus-gates, -is *adv.* in this way 12.212, 13.11, 26.153

tydandis, -es *see* **tydyngis**

tyde *n.* time 17.60, 27.81; **þis tyde** now 7.7, 37.184; **þat tyde** then 7.16

tydes, -is *v., impers.* **tydis vs** we will receive 19.92, **ʒou tydes** you will receive 33.43

tydyngis, thiding, thithynges, tydand(is), (-es), tythande(s), (-is), tythynge(s) *n. sg./pl.* tidings, news, happenings 7.105, 9.224, 246, 10.43, 49, 11.206, 13.161, 15.72, 16.160, 38.28, 29

tyght *adj. as n.* **þe tyght** those in captivity 25.516

till(e), tyll(e) *prep.* to, towards; for the sake of 38.182

tille, tyll *v.* labour for 6.59; cultivate 7.109

tyme *n., in phr.* **in tyme** opportunely 37.149

tymely *adv.* early 30.180

tyne *n. see* **tene**

tyne *v. tr.* lose 7.27, 13.58, 32.363; waste 35.300, 42.52; *intr.* be lost, die 36.271

tyraunte, tiraunte *n.* villain, malefactor 6.48, 32.229; **tirauntes, tirrauntis,** *pl.* princes 45.27; outlaws, ruffians 36.30

tyte *adj.* quick, sharp 26.236

tyte, tite, tytte *adv.* quickly, readily 5.167, 26.279, 45.247; **tyter, -ar** *cpv.* 11.280, 25.60; **as, als tyte** forthwith 21.45, 28.129, 34.132

tythandis, -e(s), tythynge(s) *see* **tydyngis**

title, tytill, titill *n.* claim, legal right 32.38, 347, 45.57

tytt *v.* snatched, pulled 33.349

tytte *adv. see* **tyte**

tyxste *v. pa.t.* taxed, accused 32.289

to *conj.* till, until 8.30, 9.52, 11.306

to *adj. see* **twa**

to *adv.* too 6.103

to-balk *v.* shirk; **not to-balk** not to shirk in the least 29.29

to-bring *v.* heap upon 31.182

todir *see* **tothir; toke** *see* **take**

tokenyng *vbl. n.* sign 9.245, 12.152

tole *v.* haul 9.281; **toled** *pa.t.* 45.58

toles, -is *see* **tooles**

tome *n.* leisure, time 32.345, 33.359, 40.18

tome *adj.* empty 29.247, 40.127
tomorne *adv.* tomorrow 11.356, 29.389, 30.146
tone *pron.* one 23.138
tone *v. see* **take**
tongis *n.pl.* languages 42.141
tonne *n.* barrell 29.247, 40.127
tooles, toles, -is, tulles *n.pl.* tools, equipment 34.297; weapons 37.179; domestic utensils 9.110, 18.172
top(pe) *n.* top; **toppe and taile** head and feet 35.114; **toppe to taile** throughout, in every detail 37.159
torfoyr *n.* misfortune, disaster 40.160, 174
to-ryff *see* **ryue** *v.*
torne *n.* action, trick 32.302
torne *v. see* **turne**
tose, tase *n.pl.* toes 22.108, 35.180
tothir, todir *pron., adj.* other 13.51, 23.101, 138
touche *v.* come into contact with (involuntarily) 28.293; pertain, concern 13.183; **touches** *3sg.pr.* 36.60; **touched** *pa.t.* 36.54
touchyng *prep.* concerning 31.410, 32.319
toure *n.* tower, dwelling place 26.86, 46.44; *in phatic phr.* **toure and toune, towne and toure** 16.226, 22.146
toure *adj.* excessive, violent; **on toure deraye** in utter confusion 9.78
tourne *see* **turne; tow** *see* **twa**
toward *adj.* co-operative 26.159; sympathetic to (what) 26.224
to-whils, to-whyls *conj. adv.* whilst 1.30, 62
towre-begon *adj.* turreted, adorned with towers 26.5
to-yere *adv.* this year 35.164
trace, trayse *n.* way, course (of action), progress 16.262, 26.159, 33.378; **teche þem a trace** teach them a lesson 16.47; **turne on no trayse** do not deviate 30.117
trace *v.* seek out 36.55
tray(e) *n.¹* affliction, suffering 18.227, 22.29, 30.286
traye *n.²* trick, stratagem 29.61
traied *v. p.p.* betrayed 42.114
traylle *v.* drag 33.482
trayne *n.* deceit, guile 26.267, 37.9; stratagem, trick 16.261, 22.23; **withouten trayne** without doubt 10.102, 22.121
trayse *see* **trace** *n.*
trayste, trast(e) *v.* trust, have confidence in 5.78, 11.139, 26.252; be assured 16.241; **trastis** *3pl.pr.* 24.192
traitourfull *adj.* traitorous 32.302
traitoury *n.* treachery 32.229
traytourly *adv.* traitorously 32.139
trante *n.* trick, act of deceit 29.232, 32.254; **trantis** *pl.* 36.73, 37.159

trapped *v.¹ p.p.* ensnared 30.187, 286
trapped, -id *v.² p.p.* loaded 26.267, 33.15
trased *v. p.p.* ? checked, restrained *(as OED* trash *v.¹)* 31.2
trasshes *n.pl.* rags 33.349
trast(e) *adj.* trusty 25.440; sure, assured 29.121, 32.378, 38.382
trast(e), trastis *v. see* **trayste**
trastyng *vbl.n.* trustworthiness 40.45
trauaile, -yle, travaylle, trauell *n.* efforts, toil, labour 5.19, 6.70, 9.317, 43.52; (evil) works 28.293
trauayl(l)e *v.* work, labour 5.162, 6.78; **traueylis** *ipv. pl.* 31.8
trauell *see* **trauaile** *n.*
traueses *v.* 3sg.pr. thwarts, crosses 37.150
tree *n.* cross 33.481, 34.246; spade *(? sc. its wooden shaft, resembling the cross)* 6.113, 165
trespas(s)e *n.* offence, sin 28.52, 32.213, 36.124
trespassed *v. p.p.* transgressed 10.256, 34.115
treste *n.* trust 36.191
treste *v.* trust in 45.172
tresurry *n.* treasure 16.302
trete *v.* negotiate 30.541; discourse 33.22
tretyng *vbl. n.* speaking 31.3
trew *adv.* faithfully 7.29
trewe *adj.* truthful 29.215; *as n.* true man, steadfast one 32.313, 38.276
trewys *n.* truce, good faith 30.9
trye *v.* sort 26.72; **tried** *p.p.* separated, picked out 7.19
tryfils, triffillis *see* **trufuls**
trymble *v.* tremble 21.141
trymbelyng *vbl. n.* trembling 47.242
trine, tryne *v.* step, walk, move 2.10, 13.13, 33.225
trippe *n.* short journey 18.133
triste *n.* hope 18.13, 36.176
tryste, trist *adj.* certain, sure 30.539; honest 33.125
trist(e) *v.* trust, put faith in 6.150, 10.349, 25.84; **tristis** *3pl.pr.* 31.8; **triste** *pa.t.* 32.289
trystefull *adj.* trustworthy 25.513
tristely *adv.* faithfully 46.111
tristy *adj.* trustworthy 32.313, 45.172
trone, troone *n.* throne 2.10, 25.165, 46A.35
troned *v. p.p.* enthroned, given sovereignty 30.34; *adj.* enthroned 26.86
troone *see* **trone** *n.*
trowe *v.* believe, think 9.226, 13.99, 25.258; **trowes** *2sg.pr.* 5.75; **trowed, -yd** *pa.t.* 5.125, 6.36
trowed *ppl.adj.* (well) reputed 32.137 *(see prec.)*

trufuls, tryfils, trifullis, truffillis, trufullis
etc. n.pl. lies, idle tales 5.125, 26.108, 31.3,
32.112, 43.76; little things 31.313

trusse, trus *v.* carry, heave things about
9.281; pack (for a journey) 9.110; go,
move, depart 9.81, 23.151, 32.378; **trusse
of towne, trusse . . . a towne** go into the
country 7.46, 10.115

tugged *v. p.p.* ? nailed, roughly attached
36.138

tuke *see* **take**

tule *v.* harass, assail 41.168; **tulyd** *p.p.*
28.118

tulles *see* **tooles**

turmentis *n.pl.* torments 28.118

turne, torne, tourne *v.* change, be transformed 11.152; pervert 37.332; **torned**
p.p. gone 28.90; **tourne vp** ascend, get up
9.78; *refl.* **torne me** go 45.288

turnement *n.* tournament, *here fig.* trial
28.90

turtill *n.* turtle-dove 45.32; **tyrtles** *pl.*
17.247

turtour *n.* turtle-dove 45.110

tussch *interj. exclamation of disdain* 33.120

twa, to, tow *adj.* two 2.44, 5.171, 6.20

twelmoth *n.* twelvemonth, year 9.251

twyes *adv.* twice 29.159, 193

twynne, twyn(e) *v.* part, divide, go asunder
1.153, 4.10, 8.78, 100, 36.151; **twynnes**
3sg.pr. 42.4; **twynnand** *pres.p.* 44.182

twyne *v.* ? warp, twist 8.100

twyne *v.* part *see* **twynne**

twynnyng *vbl.n.* parting 42.182

vayle *n.¹* benefit; *in phr.* **at vayle** healed
28.290

vaile *n.²* veil 38.111

vayle *v.* be of service to 28.143

vayne *adj.* empty 1.146; **in wane** in vain
9.300

vayne-glorie *n.* inordinate pride 22.93

vaynes *n.pl.* veins 28.290

vanyté *n.* illusion 41.29

vath *interj. exclamation of contempt* 35.273

ve *pron.* we 11.277, 26.292

velany(e) *n.* evil, wrongdoing 22.70, 31.106

vengeaunce *n. in phr.* **in þe wilde vengeaunce** *expr. of malevolent encouragement*
with a vengeance 30.547

venym *n.* poison 42.143

veray *see* **verray(e)**

verament *adv.* truly 46A.4

verely, verilye *adv.* truly 17.315, 42.77

vernand *adj.* blooming 25.497

verray(e), veray, verrey, werray(e) *adj.*
true, the true 12.219, 19.35, 21.136,
36.323, 44.125, 46A.41

vertue *n.* operative power 21.101

vgly, vggely *adj.* horrible 11.265, 37.101

vilaunce *adj.* wicked 24.15

vill *see* **will(e)** *v.*

visit(t)e *v. pa.t.* visited 47.306, 334

vyssyon, vysioune, visioun *n.* vision 10.71,
86, 23.233

vmbelappid *v. pa.t.* surrounded 44.66

vmbycast *n.* confine, tie up 33.467

vmsitte *v.* surround 44.186

vnarayed *adj.* naked 24.6

vnbaynly *adj.* cruel 40.37

vnbaptymde *adj.* unbaptised 21.90

vnbende *v.* untie 33.444

vnboune *ppl.adj.* released 33.386

vnbraced *ppl.adj.* untied 33.386

vnbraste *v. p.p.* let loose 9.320

vnbrente *ppl.adj.* unburnt 29.318

vnbuxumnes *n.* disobedience 1.123

vnclene *adj.* sinful 47.238

vncleth *v.* strip 33.142

vncomely *adj.* repugnant 26.200

vncon(n)and *adj.* foolish 30.240, 32.49,
33.413

vncouth *adj.* unusual, strange 10.116, 31.77

vndewe *adj.* illegal 30.379, 33.82

vndewly *adj.* unlawful 30.199

vndewly *adv.* unjustly 45.35

vndirstand *v.* comprehend, take in (facts)
11.145, 177, 13.79; signify 25.306; *1sg.pr.*
am minded, have decided 10.97

vndyrtake *v.* understand 23.23; **vndirtane**
p.p. undertaken, agreed 38.302

vndo(o) *v.* destroy 30.189, 288

vndughty *adj.* feeble 33.410

vnendande *adv.* endlessly 1.8

vnethis *adv.* scarcely 47.59

vnfyld(e), vnfiled *ppl.adj.¹* pure, not polluted 17.308, 357, 45.116

vnfylyd *ppl.adj.²* (in an) unpolished, rude
(manner) 17.360

vngayne *v.* harm 33.38

vngentill, ongentill *adj.* base, unmannerly
30.389; violent 31.14

vngladde, onglad *adv.* in a sorrowful manner 39.6, 41.99

vngo(o)dly *adj.* wicked 31.393, 32.375

vnhappe *n.* misfortune 18.152, 33.47;
holde it vnhappe think it a pity 36.33

vnhende *adj.* unworthy 26.174, 45.157

vnhendly *adv.* evilly 33.305

vnhonest *adj.* objectionable 11.76

vnysoune *n. meaning unkn.*; *? error for*
vrysoune orison *(so OED)* 25.262

vnjent *adv.* unjustly 36.353

vnkyndynes(se) *n.* injustice, wrong 40.64,
45.235

vnknowen *v. p.p.* rejected 32.228

vnlappe *v.* arise (from bed) 30.256; unfold, display 36.31

vnlase *v.* loosen (clothes) 31.43

vnlele *adj.* untrustworthy 30.332

vnlely *adv.* disloyally 31.404

vnlokynne *v. p.p.* opened up 37.197

vnmeete *adj.* wrong, out of place 35.127

vnmyghty *adj.* (too) weak 33.411

vnrewly *adv.* discontentedly 16.35

vnride *adj.* harsh, cruel 39.67

vnright *adv.* wrongly 30.492, 36.15

vnseele *n.* trouble, misfortune 32.179

unsitting *ppl.adj.* unbecoming 33.191

vnsoftely *adv.* loudly 33.18

vnsoght, onso(u)ght *adj.* not sought for, unexpected 2.16, 13.44, 32.287

vnspende *ppl.adj.* unspent, in store 25.449

unte *prep.* + *pron.* to you 29.86

vnterly *? error for* **enterly** 40.159

vnthrifty *adj.* unprofitable 35.90

vnthryuandely *adv.* unprofitably 1.114

vntill(e), ontill, vntyll(e) *prep.* to 42.106

vnto *prep.* until 25.433, 41.17; over 19.56

vntrewly *adv.* falsely, dishonestly 30.197, 32.364

vntrewþe *n.* falsehood 30.302

vnwarly *adv.* unexpectedly 30.273

vnwelde *adj.* feeble 8.93, 10.221, 14.74; impotent 13.6

vnwittely *adv.* foolishly 6.52

vnwitty *adj.* unwise 16.166, 40.66

vnwittyng *ppl.adj.* unbeknown; **oure unwittyng** unbeknown to us 33.188

voice, voyce *n.* sound 7.102; noise 25.331; duty 16.10

voyde *adj.* empty 1.146

voydes *v. 3sg.pr.* renders (something) ineffectual 28.285

vowchesaffe, voutsaue, wochesaff *v.* condescend, deign, be willing 3.62, 14.65, 17.257; **fouchest saffe** *2sg.pr.* 23.147; **fouchesaffe** *3sg.pr. subj.* 23.160; may grant (knowledge) 23.57; **vowchesaffe, vouchydsaue** *pa.t.* 9.27, 10.202

vphalde *v.* maintain, contend 33.149

vpholde *n.* support 26.282

vpperight *adv.* straight up 2.86, 37.394; **vpperightis** upright 40.93

vppe-tane *v. p.p.* taken up 42.220

vpryse *n.* resurrection 42.90

vprise *v.* rise up; **ryght vprise** rise upright 37.31

vprysing, vpperysing *vbl.n.* resurrection 42.91, 98

vpsoght, vppe-sought *v. pa.t.* sought out, thought up 34.113, 35.68

vpstritt *v. pa.t.* sprang up 33.274

vse *v.* pursue, put into effect 24.92; **vses**

3pl.pr. hold customary 27.30; **vsed** *pa.t.* observed (laws) 25.144; *refl.* **vse hym** accustom himself 30.232

vttir *v.* express 26.204

vttiremest *adj.* furthest 37.232

wa(a) *see* **woo**

waferyng *v. pres.p.* wandering 7.112

waffe *v. tr.* put aside (with a wave of the hand) 31.257; *intr.* blow (away) 12.54

wage *v.* bribe 33.121; reward 31.419

way(e) *n.* way, course; **wayes, wais, weyes** *pl.* 37.74; means 5.76; course of events 40.181; **in waye** along the way 30.342

wayke, weyke *adj.* weak, feeble 8.93, 14.25, 23.90

wais *see* **way(e)** *n.*

wayte *v.*[1] look out for, keep watch 29.25, 27; seek 32.332; lie in wait (with malevolent intent) 16.243, 29.118, 43.91; **waitis** *3sg.pr.* 29.249; **waites, wayte** *ipv.pl.* look, pay attention 33.254, 43.169; make sure 29.352

waite *n.*[2] wrong, shame 13.115

wayteskathe *n. (nickname)* mischief-maker, nuisance 34.59

wakand *vbl.n. see* **wakyng**

wakand(e) *ppl.adj.* watchful 28.10, 78; awake 29.352, 369

wake *v.* watch, be vigilant 2.24, 47.196; keep watch over 28.144

waken *v.* incite; **waken of** incite to 30.511

wakyng, wakand *vbl.n.* vigil 38.357; rousing 30.273

walaway *see* **welaway(e); walde** *n. see* **welde** *n.*

wale *v.* choose 2.110

walke *v.* toss restlessly 39.10; **walke** *3pl.pr.* are abroad, are happening 29.27; **walkand** *pres.p.* 39.2; walking 27.93, 37.53

walked *ppl.adj.* weary with walking 13.249 (*see prec.*)

walowe *v.* move awkwardly 39.10

wan *v. pa.t. see* **wyn(n)(e)**

wan(n)(e) *n.* evil 7.38, 13.164; dark, gloomy 8.2, 9.156, 36.314; cruel 41.108; pale 36.278

wande *n.* rod, stick 11.147, 13.28; young shoot 12.76; **wandes** *pl.* battens, long and narrow strips of timber 8.75

wande *v.* hesitate 34.139

wanderede *ppl.adj.* exhausted with wandering 28.5

wandyng(e) *vbl.n.* state of uncertainty 28.9, 77

wane *adj. see* **vayne**

wane *v.* subside 9.186; **wanand** *pres.p.* 9.204

wane *n.* thought *see* **wone** *n.²*; **wanes** *n.pl.* habits *see* **wonne** *n.*

wanes, -ys *n.pl.* walls 9.240, 13.123

wangges, wonges *n.pl.* cheeks 10.275, 13.41

wanhope *n.* despair 41.75

wanyand, waneand *vbl.n.* waning (of the moon), i.e. an evil hour; *used by bad characters in expressions of anger, impatience etc.* 7.45, 16.37, 32.389, 33.485; **wanyng** subsiding (of the flood) 9.188

wanne *adj. see* **wan(n)(e)**; **wanne** *v. pa.t. see* **wyn(n)(e)**

wanne-trowyng *vbl.n.* state of weak faith 42.83

wappe *v.¹* tear, pluck 33.342; **wapped** *p.p.* (*fig., of emotions*) plunged (into), consumed (by) 31.13, 45.1

wappe *v.²* wrap, encircle 45.275

war(r)(e), werre *adv.* worse 1.113, 9.64, 65, 17.98, 37.154

warand(e), warrand(e), swarand *v.* warrant, affirm 8.111, 11.54, 221, 24.5; **I (s)warand** I'll be bound 1.96, 33.383; **noght to warande** not to be believed 43.8

warande *n.* authority 16.123

warde *n.* custody, keeping 26.43, 37.222

ware, warre *adj.* aware, vigilant 24.81, 30.167, 33.136

ware *adv. see* **war(r)(e)** *adv.*

ware *v.* were

warely *adv.* vigilantly 28.77

wary, wery *v.* speak against, curse 32.109, 33.95, 430; **waried, weried** *p.p.* 30.259, 31.234

warisoune *n.* reward 36.89

warke *see* **werke** *n.*

warly, werly *adv.* circumspectly 9.215, 43.91, 47.222

warlowe *n.* scoundrel, rascal, traitor 22.115, 29.185, 30.140, 259; sorcerer 11.219; **warlous** *pl.* 36.278

warne *v.* tell, instruct 13.71; **warned** *pa.t.* 8.121; *p.p.* 31.55, 350

warrand(e) *see* **warand(e)** *v.*

warre *n.* war; **in warre** in confusion 30.401

warr(e) *adv. see* **war(r)(e)** *adv.*; **warre** *adj. see* **ware** *adj.*

warred *adj.* (of wood) knotted; **wele warred** very knotty, i.e. strong 34.76

warrok *v.* bind 30.528

wassaile, -ylle *interj. salutation usu. used in drinking;* good health 29.369

wast(e) *adj.* futile 7.60, 16.244; impure 12.196; *quasi-adv.* **(in) waste** to no effect 33.98, 41.87

wast(e) *v. tr.* destroy 9.288, 22.186; dispel 2.104; *intr.* decay 25.146; **waste(d), wastyd** *p.p.* 9.12, 43, 39.9

waste *v. + pron.* was it 47.305

wat(t)(e) *see* **wit**

watches *n.pl.* watchmen 37.140

wathe *n.* peril, a danger 5.65, 22.109; **wathes, wothis** *pl.* 11.138, 27.165; **it will be wathe, it is in wathe** there is danger 19.173, 34.57

wathe *adj.* dangerous 9.145

wave *v.⁽¹⁾* move to and fro 35.232

wauyd *v.⁽²⁾ p.p.* thrown, waived 32.320

wax(e), wex *v.* grow, flourish 2.68, 8.11; become 23.90, 37.344; emerge 11.65; **wexe** *pa.t.* 26.134; **waxen** *p.p.* 9.192, 13.95

we, weme, whe *interj. expr. of amazement, indignation, consternation, grief etc.* 1.115, 7.45, 30.380, 34.308

wedde *v.* pledge, wager 29.187, 31.206

wedde-sette *v.* mortgage 32.346, 351

wede *n.¹* herb or small plant; **wedis** *pl.* 2.92; **worthe to wede** ripen, be fruitful 2.68

wede *n.²* (*often coll. sg.*) clothing, garments 12.30, 13.301, 14.67; *in phatic phr.* **in wede** 20.242, 30.113, 537

wede *v.* run mad 39.23

wedir, weedir *n.* weather 14.71, 36.314; **wedris** *gen.sg.* 2.83

weelde *n. see* **welde** *n.*; **weendande** *see* **wende** *v.¹*

wegge *n.* wedge 35.242; **wegges** *pl.* 35.235

weyes *n. see* **way(e)** *n.*; **weyes** *v. see* **whe** *v.*; **weyke** *see* **wayke**; **weyll** *n. see* **wele** *n.*; **weill** *adv. see* **wele** *adj., adv.*; **weyn** *see* **wene** *n.*; **weke** *n.pl. see* **woke**

welaway(e), walaway *interj. cry of lamentation* woe, alas 1.104, 5.148, 6.92

welde, walde, weelde, wolde *n.* power, possession, keeping 1.67, 86, 6.50, 32.275; **wrapped in wolde** placed under arrest 30.358

welde, wolde *v.* wield 32.66; know, have, enjoy 1.28, 10.36, 32.275; cause, put 16.37; look after, protect 10.57, 17.438; **weledande** *pres.p.* 1.86; **at welde** to enjoy 42.146

welding, weledyng *vbl.n.* command 44.166; possession 1.139

wele, weyll, well *n.* prosperity, (the) good 17.352, 369, 443, 45.206; health 42.146

wele *n.* source *see* **well** *n.*;

wele, weill *adj., adv.* well; **wele þe be** good health to you; **weill mette** greetings 36.352

weledyng *see* **welding**; **well** *v.* (*aux. fut.*) *see* **will(e)** *v.*

well *v.* boil, i.e. suffer in hell 1.104, 131, 42.127

well, wele, welle *n.* source, spring 17.76, 23.73; **welle of witte** source of wisdom

16.391; **welle of welthe** source of felicity 19.22, 25.505

well *n.* prosperity *see* **wele** *n.*

welland *ppl.adj.* raging, raving 11.334

welth(e) *n.* happiness, felicity 1.28, 37.324

welth-wynnyng *n.* attainment of salvation, bliss 1.3

weme *see* **we**

wenche *n.* maid, girl 13.12, 101

wende *v.*[1] *intr.* go, depart; *tr.* remove, dispel 2.84; **wendes** *ipv.pl.* 9.161; **wendand, weendande** *pres.p.* 1.96, 42.129; **went(e)** *p.p.* 8.94, 11.329; used, adopted 33.201; consigned 6.3

wende *v.*[2] think 13.3

wende *v. pa.t. and p.p. see* **wene**

wending, -yng *vbl.n.* departure 13.71; journey 16.276; death 44.36

wene, weyn, wyne *n.* doubt; **withowten wene** without doubt, certainly 2.50, 8.35, 11.104, 38.15

wene, wyne *v.* think, believe 20.5, 23.90, 36.373; **wenys** *2sg.pr.* 9.119; **wenes** *3sg.pr.* 20.90; **wende** *pa.t.* 6.26, 20.29; *p.p.* 36.187

wenyng *vbl.n.* intention 31.84

went(e) *see* **wende** *v.*[1]

wepand *v. pres.p.* weeping 20.256

were *n.*[1] danger 26.213, 33.213; misery 6.57; suspicious behaviour 31.386; state of confusion, perplexity 5.1, 28.5, 40.83; *in phatic phr.* **withouten were** 8.133, 9.146, 15.3

were *?n.*[2] guard, defender 28.82 *(but perh. as prec.)*

were *v.*[1] wear 13.301, 45.277

were *v.*[2] guard, defend 7.38, 11.138, 28.77

were *v.*[3] instruct, warn 45.292

wery *adj.* troubled 13.204

wery *v.*, **weried** *p.p. see* **wary**

weried, weryed, wer(r)yd *ppl.adj.* accursed, refractory 11.27, 22.73, 32.236, 257 *(see* **wary***)*

werkar *n.* worker (of miracles) 36.313

werke, warke *n.* deed(s), action(s) 1.125, 37.17; piece of work 1.15; matter, business 23.102

werke, wirke, wyrke *v.* perform, act, do 1.138, 35.97, 37.334; make 8.35; shape 8.110; *impers.* **me wyrkis** cause me 13.41; **wroght(e)** *pa.t.* 1.63, 134; **wroght(e), wrothe** *p.p.* 1.116, 2.160; come about 16.276

werkemen *n.pl.* workers 37.17

werly *see* **warly**; **werray(e)** *see* **verray(e)**; **werre** *see* **war(r)(e)** *adv.*; **wetand** *see* **wittande**

wete *n.* rain, dampness 2.83

wete *adj.* wet with blood, bloody 38.200, 283, 41.51

wete *v.* moisten 10.275; **wette** *p.p.* refreshed 30.93, 135

wete(n) *v.* know *see* **wit(t)(e)**; **wette** *v. p.p. see* **wete** *v.*

wetterly *see* **wittirly**; **wex(e)** *see* **wax(e)**

wha *pron.* who 5.25, 18.104

whallis *n.pl.* whales 2.128

whame *pron.* whom 5.121, 42.43

whapp *n.* sudden blow 33.198

whare *see* **wher**

whar(e)so, wherso, whoreso *adv.* wherever 2.144, 10.156, 20.171, 41.120

whare-som *adv.* wherever 6.168

wharto *adv.* why 36.216

what *interj. expr. of surprise and indignation* 24.40

what *adv. used for emphasis:* how ...; to what an extent... 1.65, 6.133, 14.71

whateuer *pron. (interrog.)* what, whatever can 18.41, 23.85

what-kynne *adj.* of what kind, what kind of 5.52, 6.22

whatso *pron.* whatever 41.144

whe *interj. see* **we**

whe *v.* weigh 30.135; **weyes** *3sg.pr.* 35.213

whedir *conj.* whether 20.211, 25.424, 29.147

whedir, whethir *pron.* whichever 13.53, 25.359

whedir *adv.* whither 16.95, 18.175, 19.97

when *adv.* whence, from where 11.219, 16.180

whens-euere *adv.* from what place 20.105, 131

wher, whare *adv., conj.* wherever 20.271, 23.144, 38.409; **whare ... become** what has become of 1.99

wherso *see* **whar(e)so**

whereto *adv.* why, to what end 20.257, 31.276

whethir *pron. see* **whedir** *pron.*

whesid *v. pa.t.* wheezed 33.198

whikly *adv.* vigorously 2.128

whilke, wilke *adj., pron.* which

whil(l)e, whyle *n.* time 6.52; *in expr. of lamentation* **wa worthe þe whyle** 6.51, **allas the whille** 6.104, 20.32

whillis, whils *conj.* whilst 29.165, 44.51, 45.301

whilom *adv.* formerly 11.126

whoreso *see* **whar(e)so**

wicchis *n.pl.* witches 19.221

wide, wyde *adj.* vast 2.5; spacious 9.240

wyelly *adj.* happy 17.333

wight(e), wiȝt, wyte *n.* person, individual 18.208, 29.10, 34, 45.56; child 18.54; **wightis** *pl.* men, people 16.30, 20.256

wight(e) *adj.* robust, bold 9.212, 18.219;

angry 24.63; **wighter** *cpv.* 35.201; **wyght-est** *spv.* 33.213

wyght *adv. see next*

wight(e)ly, wyghtly, wyght, wight *adv.* briskly, quickly 2.12, 84, 18.92, 22.160, 34.110

wightnes *n.* strength 10.58

wik *adj.* deadly 42.143

wilde *adj.* mad 13.212; impure 12.175; **wilde of thoght** headstrong 10.222; *as intensive epithet with sinister implications, with* **wanyand** *and* **vengeaunce** 7.45, 30.547, 33.485

wile, wyle *n.* trick, deceitful act 6.102, 30.159, 293

wyle *v. (aux. fut.) see* **will(e)** *v.*

wyle *v.* slip (away), wander off 20.30

wilke *see* **whilke**

will(e) *n.* will; consent 37.297; **willis, -es** *gen.sg., in phr.* **and youre willis were, yf thy willes be** if it should be your will 28.36, 110

will(e), wylle *adj.* wild, perplexed, distraught 18.208, 40.69, 47.293; at a loss (in) 35.205; **wille of wone (wane)** *see* **wone** *n.²*; **wille of rede** *see* **rede** *n.¹*

will *adv.* well 2.50, 3.88, 25.226

will(e), well, wyle, woll(e), vill *v.* intend, wish, desire *and aux. fut.* 2.30, 66, 25.106, 29.244, 37.21, 240; **willid** *p.p.* gone 28.17

willy *adj.* willing 42.79

willis, -es *see* **will(e)** *n.*

wilsom(e) *adj.* lonely, desolate 16.299, 18.188, 45.100; bewildered 27.92, 40.86; erring 12.127

wynd *v., refl.* **þe wynd** make your way 9.215

wyn(n)(e), wonne *(pres.) v.* win; rescue, redeem 9.167, 11.199, 37.266; obtain, acquire, get 5.56, 104, 9.318; go, make one's way 8.32, 9.267; **wan(ne)** *pa.t.* 37.9, 171; escaped 11.91; **wonne** *p.p.* brought 23.102, 37.406; **wonne in . . . witte** grasp (mentally), understand 30.167

wynde *n.* breath 29.119, 35.204

wyne *n., v. see* **wene** *n., v.*

wynes *n.pl.* vines 11.319

wynke *v.* (go to) sleep 29.76, 31.41

wynly *adv.* pleasantly, worthily 2.24, 29.295, 47.196; excessively 44.103

wynne, wyne *n.* profit, advantage 2.125, 9.30, 30.94; felicity 16.306; **with wynne** to good effect 30.93, 45.277

wynnynge *vbl.n.* advantage, profit 5.68

wirke, wyrke *see* **werke** *v.*

wirkyng *vbl.n.* action(s), deeds 20.112, 42.6; behaviour 29.375

wyrschip, wirshippe *n. see* **worshippe** *n.*

wyrschippe *v.* reverence, honour 1.137; **wirshipped** *p.p.* 5.55

wys, wys(s)he, wisse *v.* guide, direct, teach 6.107, 8.70, 88, 13.238; **wyssande, wysshyng** *pres.p.* 1.152, 157

wyscus *adj. meaning unkn.; perh. a scribal error* 26.14

wys(s)he *v.,* **wysshyng** *pres.p. see* **wys**

wysse *adj. as n.* wise men, sages 20.242

wissyng *vbl.n.* knowledge 16.68

wiste *n.* knowledge 44.57

wiste, wyste *v. pa.t. see next*

wit(t)(e), wyt(t)(e), wat(t)(e), wot(t)(e) *v.* know, learn, be aware; inform 33.313; **wete** *subj., pl.pr.* 16.151, 26.25; **weten** *inf.* 38.47; **wote, wotith** *3sg.pr.* 5.54, 10.2; **wyste, wiste** *pa.t.* 1.116, 10.351, 23.35; **weten, witte, wyttyne** *p.p.* 9.123, 47.19, 130; **done . . . to witte** given to understand 5.91; **witte þe for to saie** inform you 18.62; **witt of well** *? error for* **well of witt** 2.136 (cf. 16.391)

wyte *n. see* **wight(e)** *n.*

wite, wyte *v.¹* blame 5.120, 6.146, 19.123

wite *v.²* commend, give into the keeping of 10.291

with *prep.* by means of 37.160; by 18.112, 42.70, 46.143

withall(e), wythall *adv.* therewith 6.59, 8.36, 13.158

withdrawe *v.* hold back 27.128

within *adv.* in, inside 2.127

witnes *v.* admit 33.185

witnesse *n.pl.* witnesses 33.121

wytt(e), witte *n.* knowledge, wisdom 1.67, 16.391; mind 5.1; **witte is in warre** mind is confused 30.401

wittande, wetand *vbl.n.* knowledge, understanding; **at my wittande** knowingly 31.76; **be my wetand** to the best of my knowledge 44.72

wittandly *adv.* knowingly, wilfully 26.249

wittely *see* **wittirly**

wittering *n.* cognisance 18.124

witty *adj.* intelligent 3.69, 15.18, 16.22, 22.55

wittyne *see* **wit(t)(e)** *v.*

wittirly, wetterly, wittely *adv.* surely, truly, wisely 4.21, 8.88, 23.157, 44.138

wo *adj.* woeful, distressed 24.150

wochesaff *see* **vowchesaffe**

wode *n.* wood, faggots 10.110, 151

wode *adj. see* **woode** *adj.*

woke *n.* week 42.199; **weke** *pl.* 9.251

wolde *n. see* **welde** *n.;* **wolde** *v. see* **welde** *v.;* **woll(e)** *v. see* **will(e)** *v.*

woman *n. gen.sg.* woman's 6.150

wombe *n.* belly 5.155

won(n)(e) *v.* dwell, remain 1.28, 3.73, 4.47; **wonnys** *3sg.pr.* 37.235; **wons** *3pl.pr.* 17.451; **wonnande** *pres.p.* 16.33; **wonne, wonnyd, wonte** *p.p.* 6.26; accustomed, wont 16.350, 29.249, 39.15

wonder(e)s, wounderes *n.pl.* miracles 25.129; extraordinary occurrences 29.27; clever tricks 29.96

wondering *vbl.n.* marvel, object of wonder 29.38

wonderus *adv.* very, extraordinarily 41.109

wondir *n.pl.* wonders, strange things 30.299

wondir *adj.* extraordinary 38.123

wondir, -yr, woundir *adv.* very, most 5.135, 26.134, 35.207

wondirfull *adj.* clever 29.110

wondirly *adv.* perfectly 32.177; strangely, in a sinister fashion 34.111

wondir-thyng *n.* marvel 16.173

wondir-werke *n.* miraculous occurrence 23.135

wone *n.¹* place, dwelling 1.59, 30.81; *in phatic phr.* **in wone, in þis wonys** 28.106, 31.331

wone, wane *n.²* thought, belief; **wille of wone (wane)** distraught, at a loss 6.121, 18.144, 19.217; abundance, *in phr.* **grete wone** in large numbers 29.270

wonges *see* **wangges; wonys** *n.pl. see* **wone** *n.¹*

wonne *n.* custom, habitual behaviour 29.250; **wanes** *pl.* habits, types of conduct 33.106

wonne *v. pres.* win, *p.p.* won *see* **wyn(n)(e); wonnande** *v. pres.p.*, **wonne** *v. p.p.* wont *see* **won(n)(e)**

wonnyng *vbl.n.* dwelling 4.3, 47.376; **wonnyng-steed** dwelling-place 21.42

wonnys, -yd, wons, wonte *see* **won(n)(e)** *v.*

woo, wa(a) *n.* woe, state of misery 6.4, 13.97, 37.406; evil behaviour 30.511

woode, wode *adj.* mad, furious 1.105, 9.91; **welland woode** raving mad 11.334

worde *see* **world(e); wordely** *see* **worldly** *adj.*

world(e), worde *n.* world 18.208; **worldys** *pl.* universe 2.5

worldly, wordely *adj.* of this world (i.e. not supernatural) 11.103; earthly 27.128, 47.375

worldly *adv.* in a worldly manner 23.26

worme *n.* serpent 5.91, 147; **worme** *gen.sg.* serpent's 5.23; **wormis** *pl.* reptiles 2.155; **wilde wormes** locusts 11.339

worshippe, wyrschip, wirshippe *n.* honour, esteem 1.81, 5.56, 68

worth *adj.* worthy of, deserving; **we are worth** we deserve 17.242

worth(e), worþe *v.* become, pass away 2.68, 9.156, 302; happen 7.94, 16.317; prove to be 23.89; **worthed** *p.p.* come 38.358; **worþe on** happen to 38.270; **worþe . . . in** tend towards 31.386; **woo worthe the, wa worthe 3ou** a curse upon you 5.107, 13.97

worthely, -yly *adj.* worthy, valued 1.17, 30.26, 36.333

worth(e)ly, worþely *adv.* worthily, in a seemly manner 1.42, 28.94, 44.14

worthy *adj. as n.* worthy person 44.56

wot(t)(e) *see* **wit(t)(e); wothis** *see* **wathe** *n.*; **wounderes** *see* **wonder(e)s; woundir** *see* **wondyr**

wrayste, wraste *v.* twist (the hands, in grief) 19.240; twist (the body, in order to afflict) 33.338; drag away 30.528; seek to influence, turn aside 11.137; **wraiste, wrasted** *p.p.* turned 33.269; forced out 31.272; **wrang wrayste** twisted (mentally) 29.248

wrake *n.* retribution, vengeance 11.252, 26.120; pain, suffering 40.66, 47.200

wrake *v.* free (from) 39.49

wrang(e) *adv. see* **wronge**

wrange *n.* error 16.276

wranges *v. 3sg.pr.* contravenes 30.427

wrapped *v. p.p. in phr.* **wrapped in wolde** placed under arrest 30.358

wraste *n. see* **wrest; wraste** *v. see* **wrayste**

wrathenesse *n.* violent anger 31.13

wreye *v.* betray 47.129; **wreyes** *2sg.pr.* denounce 29.322; **wreyes** *3sg.pr.* proclaims 19.122; **wreyede** *pa.t.* declared 21.25

wreke *n.* vengeance 8.58, 37.191; **wrekis** *pl.* punishments 30.7; afflictions, calamities 9.267

wreke *v.* avenge 26.154, 30.494; **wroken** *p.p.* 37.199

wrekyng *vbl.n.* punishment 29.321

wrenchis *n.pl.* cunning tricks 30.484

wrest, wraste *n.* evil trick 16.243, 26.248

wreth(e), wretthe *n.* wrath, malevolent feelings 1.136, 26.119, 30.494

wrethfull *adj.* full of anger 40.172

wretyn *see* **write** *v.*

wretthid *v. p.p.* vexed 26.214

wriche *n.* wretch 31.375; **wrytches** *pl.* 17.443

wrye, wrie *v.* avoid 30.7; go 35.182

wrighte, write *n.* carpenter 29.55, 30.504, 37.230

wryng(e), wring *v.* wring (the hands, in grief) 19.240; wring, twist (the body, in order to afflict) 33.338, 36.76; slip away, escape 26.119; **wryngis** *3sg.pr.* deviates (with a twisting motion) 33.249

wrynkis *n.pl.* tricks 30.67

wrytches *see* **wriche; write** *n. see* **wrighte**

write *v.* inscribe, make record of 39.94; **wretyn** *p.p.* written 22.103

wrythe *v.* writhe; *in phr.* **wrythe hym away** destroy him 30.484

wroght(e) *v. see* **werke** *v.*

wroghte *n.* desert, what has been deserved 1.125

wroken *see* **wreke** *v.*

wronge, wrang(e) *adv.* wrongly; askew 35.182; in a sinful manner, through sin 6.3; **bowrde al wrange** play idle games 9.66

wrothe *adj.* angry 5.87, 19.223

wrothe *v. p.p. see* **werke** *v.*

yaa, ye(i), yha, yhe, ȝa(a), ȝae *adv.* yea, yes

yappely, ȝappely *adv.* promptly, readily 30.231, 43.127

yarne *v.* long for 21.113; **ȝerned** *p.p.* 23.10

yarnyng *vbl.n.* longing 16.88

yate, ȝate *n.* gate 30.231, 32.15, 47.326

ye, yhe, ȝe, ȝhe *pron.* you

yeelde, ȝelde *v.* render up (as sacrifice) 10.227; give thanks (to) 10.53, 43.127; be fruitful 10.30

ye(i) *adv. see* **yaa**

yeme, eme, ȝeme *n.* heed, care 27.160, 42.128; **all þat eme is oght** all that needs to be done 2.158

yha *see* **yaa**

yhare, ȝare *adv.* quickly, readily 5.138, 25.404

yhe *see* **yaa**

yhere, ȝer(e) *n. (usu. coll. sg.)* year(s) 9.308, 23.123, 43.128

yhing, ȝenge, ȝing, ȝynge, ȝonge *adj.* young 9.139, 12.92, 14.96, 27.86, 47.89

yhitt, ȝet, ȝhit, ȝitt *adv., conj.* yet, still

yo(o)de, ȝede, ȝoode *v. pa.t.* went 9.151, 11.336, 19.219, 34.80

yoman *n.* yeoman, underling 31.418

yon(e), ȝo(o)ne *dem. adj.* yonder, that (over there) 17.350, 23.8, 33.45; that 19.208

yore *adj.* ready 7.30

yore *adv.* long since 9.307

youreself(f)(e) *pron.* you, yourselves 4.89, 20.156, 25.230

Glossary of Proper Names

Where a character is one of the *dramatis personae* of a play, the number of the play is given in roman numerals, and in such cases the use of the name in the dialogue is ignored. References to the name elsewhere in the dialogue are recorded in arabic numerals.

Abell Abel VII; 37.306
Abacuc Habbakuk 14.137
Abiron Abiram 37.309
Abraham, Abram Abraham X; 12.34
Achaia Achaia (part of mod. Greece) 45.293
Adam(e) Adam III, IV, V, VI, XXXVII; 23.123, 126; **Adam** gen. Adam's 35.52; **Adam-kynde** Adam's offspring 35.62
Adonay *sacred name, often applied to second person of Trinity* 38.37
Amys *a Jew, a false witness* 33.115
Anaball *a devil* 37.113
Andreas, Andrewe Andrew XXVII, XLII
Anna, Annay Annas XXVI, XXVIII, XXIX, XXX, XXXII, XXXIII, XXXVI, XXXVIII
Anna Prophetissa Anna the prophetess XVII
Anne Anne, mother of BVM 46.37
Antecrist Antichrist 23.119
Arabie Arabia 16.72
Archedeclyne Architriclin *(master of ceremonies at Marriage of Cana, John ii.8)* XXIIA
Archedefell Achitophel 37.308
Assia Asia 45.298
Astrotte Astoreth 37.113
Atus *supposed maternal grandfather of Pontius Pilate* 30.13–18

Balam, Balaham Balaam 14.99, 105, 15.14, 16.215
Barabas Barabas XXXIII
Barsabé Beer-sheba 10.378
Batwell Bethuel 10.367
Bedlem(e), -eem, Bedleham, -em Bethlehem 13.279, 16.115, 19.168, 267, 25.510
Bele-Berit Baal-Berith 37.115
Belial, Belliall Belial XXXVII; **Beliall** gen. Belial's 29.286, 31.329, 32.114
Belsabub Beelzebub XXXVII
Bephagé Bethpage 25.88

Bethany, Betannye Bethany 24.102, 37.162
Brewbarret 'Troublemaker' VII

Caym(e), Came Cain VII; 37.306; **Kaymes** gen. 47.317
Caiphas, Cayphas, Kayphas Caiaphas XXVI, XXVIII, XXIX, XXX, XXXII, XXXIII, XXXVI, XXXVIII
Caluary, -arie, -ery(e) Calvary 32.350, 33.451, 34.37, 349
Cesar, Sesar Caesar 30.10, 21, 33.97
Cherabyn, Cherubyn Cherubim *(as name of a specific angel)* I, V; (5.166)
Cleophas Cleophas XL
Colle *dim. of* Colin XV (15.39, 54)

Danyell Daniel 17.108
Datan[1] Dathan *(Num. xvi)* 37.309
Datan[2] Dathan, *a Jew, a false witness* 33.113
Dauid, Davyt David XXXVII; 17.108, 20.113, 25.162ff., 30.343; **Dauid** gen. David's 12.67, 163

Ebrewes, -owes Hebrews 11.70, 387, 16.218
Egipte, Egippe Egypt 11.9, 222, 263, 18.61, 79
Elias, Ely, He(e)ly Elijah XXIII; 36.227
Elyzabeth Elizabeth XII
Ely *see* **Elias**
Emanuell Imanuel, 'God with us' 12.64, 16.221, 17.185, 25.155
Emax Emmaus 40.14
Ennok Enoch 23.112
Esmaell Ishmael 10.39
Eua, Eue, Eve Eve III, IV, V, VI, XXXVII

Gabriel(l) Gabriel XII, XIII, XLIV
Galylee, -alé, -ely, -ylé, -ilé Galilee 12.137, 21.53, 23.16, 30.509, 31.127, 38.249
Gamaliell Gamaliel, *a Jew, a false witness* 33.113

Moyses Moses XI, XXIII, XXXVII; 17.11, 25, 194, 20.82, 140, 146, 25.148, 234, 27.8

Nazareth Nazareth 12.138, 25.81, 39.7 etc.; **Nazarene** of Nazareth 40.79
Neptalym¹ Naphtali *(the place, Isa. ix.1)* 37.51
Neptalim² Naphtali, *a Jew, a false witness* 33.114
Nichodemus Nicodemus XXXVI
Noe, Nooe, Noye Noah VIII, IX

Osee, Osye Hosea 15.6, 16.225

Percula Procula XXX
Petir, Petrus Peter XXIII, XXV, XXVII–XXIX, XLI–XLIII; 34.109
Pharao, Phar(r)o Pharaoh XI
Phebus Phoebus *(epithet for God the Father)* 46A.1
Philippus, Phelippus Philip XXV
Pila *supposed mother of Pontius Pilate* 30.13–18
Pounce Pontus 30.20, 253, 407, 32.9
Pounce Pilatt, Pilate, Pilatus Pontius Pilate XXVI, XXX, XXXII, XXXIII, XXXVI, XXXVIII; 28.201, 31.95ff.

Rabek Rebekah (Rebecca) 10.365
Rabony Rabbi ('my master') 39.70

Rede See Red Sea 11.375
Rebald *name of I Diabolus in XXXVII; see glossary s.v.* **rebalde**
Romans Romans 45.289

Salamon Solomon 25.240, 37.281
Samaritanus the Samaritans 45.291
Sara, Sarae Sarah 10.27–9
Satan, Satanas, Sathanas, Sattan Satan V, XXII, XXXVII; 31.52; cf. 30.157aff.
Saturne Saturn 16.5
Seraphyn Seraphim I
Sesar *see* **Cesar**
Symeon Simeon *(N.T., Lk. ii.25)* XVII, XXXVII; 34.147
Symon¹ Simon *(of Cyrene)* XXXIV
Simon² Simon, *a Jew, a false witness* 33.112
Symond luprus Simon the Leper 26.130
Synay, -ey Mount Sinai 11.94, 17.9
Syon Zion (= *Jerusalem*) 25.26

Thomas Thomas XXVII, XLI, XLV

Wymond Wymond 34.46, 59, 60

ʒarus Jairus, *a Jew, a false witness* 33.112

Zabulon Zebulun 37.52
Zaché Zacheus XXV